The Last Prodigy

A BIOGRAPHY OF
Erich Wolfgang Korngold

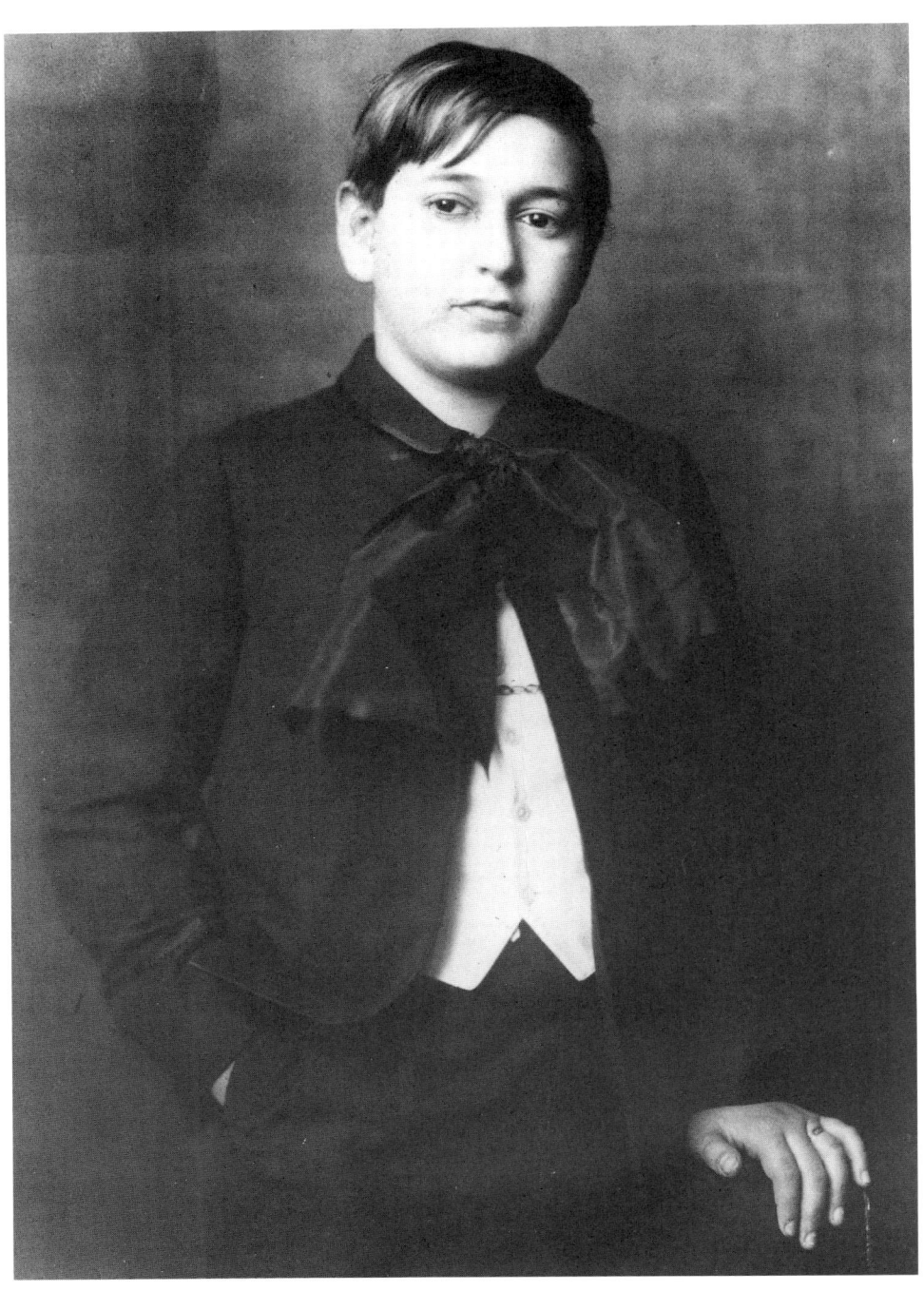

Korngold at age twelve, around the time of the *Der Schneemann* premiere (Korngold estate).

The Last Prodigy

A BIOGRAPHY OF

Erich Wolfgang Korngold

BRENDAN G. CARROLL

Reinhard G. Pauly, General Editor

AMADEUS PRESS
Portland, Oregon

ISBN 1-57467-029-8

Printed in Hong Kong

AMADEUS PRESS
The Haseltine Building
133 S.W. Second Avenue, Suite 450
Portland, Oregon 97204, U.S.A.

Library of Congress Cataloguing-in-Publication Data

Carroll, Brendan G.
The last prodigy: a biography of Erich Wolfgang Korngold /
by Brendan Carroll
p.   cm.
Discography
Includes bibliographical references (p.   ) and index.
ISBN 1-57467-029-8
1. Korngold, Erich Wolfgang, 1897–1957.
2. Composers–Austria–Biography. I. Title
ML410.K7356C37 1997
780'.92–dc21
[B]   97-4963
                                                                 CIP
                                                                 MN

This book is dedicated to the two people without whom it could never have been written—my wonderful parents. For my late father, Michael, who taught me the beauty of the written word, and for my beloved mother, Valentine, who has given me the joy of music and a love for the golden age of Hollywood. To them this book is respectfully and lovingly dedicated.

Contents

Foreword, *by Ernst W. Korngold* 9

Acknowledgments 11

Introduction 15

The Early Years: 1897–1913

ONE. "A Genius!"—*Gustav Mahler* 21

TWO. The Prodigy Reveals Himself 35

THREE. Fame and Honors 48

FOUR. The Prodigy Goes on Tour 62

FIVE. "We Will Have to Burn Our Books on Harmony"
  —*Edward Dent* 76

A Born Opera Composer: 1913–1918

SIX. "He Is a Young Eagle"—*Jean Sibelius* 97

SEVEN. Operatic Triumphs 109

EIGHT. The Prodigy Falls in Love 117

The "New Music" and the Aftermath of War: 1919–1923

NINE. "One of the Most Important and Successful Composers of Our Time"—*Max Kalbeck* 129

TEN. "He Is the Greatest Hope of German Music"—*Giacomo Puccini* 143

ELEVEN. A New Order in Music—Schoenberg and Serialism 156

The New Dark Age—Hitler's Rise to Power: 1924–1933

TWELVE. "Mama, We Are Playing at Being Married, a Whole Life Long!" 171

THIRTEEN. Korngold versus Křenek 186

FOURTEEN. The Youngest Music Professor in the World 201

FIFTEEN. The Search for a New Opera 216

From Vienna to Hollywood: 1934–1944

SIXTEEN. Lights! Action! Korngold! 231

SEVENTEEN. Operas Without Singing 245

EIGHTEEN. Escape from Hitler—Exile in Hollywood 262

NINETEEN. The Golden Age of Film Music 280

TWENTY. New Triumphs—Hollywood and Broadway 300

The Return to Absolute Music: 1944–1955

TWENTY-ONE. Farewell to Films 317

TWENTY-TWO. Return to Europe 333

TWENTY-THREE. Faith in Music 351

TWENTY-FOUR. Afterword—The Korngold Renaissance 367

Notes to Chapters One Through Twenty-three 373
The Complete Works of Erich Wolfgang Korngold 396
Selected Bibliography 407
Discography: 1914–1996 415
Index 437

Foreword

*H*ow could a young man, resident of Liverpool, the nest of the Beatles, possibly know more about a Viennese composer, whose career ended in apparently dismal failure, than the composer's son? Should I give him access to the composer's correspondence, even though most of it was in German and the young man had no knowledge of German? Should I perhaps try to narrate the story to him as I saw it? Surely my version of the fate of this unusual musician would then be tinged by my own unavoidable prejudices and rejected by its readers with a shrug. That anyone would attempt to write a biography was remarkable, which would have to be a tale of Horatio Alger in reverse, with a brilliant beginning and an unsatisfying ending, of a composer whose works were wrested from him by all the distinguished artists of the era and performed all over the world, a world that first sent him accolades of praise and appreciation and then promptly forgot him.

I eventually decided that my best course would be to stay out of the young man's way entirely and simply await results. These results—the story that Brendan Carroll has chosen to tell—-is an amazing chronicle of a genial young man, handicapped by a willful father and the forces of the Third Reich, told without undue sentimentality and with a sense of humor, which Brendan undoubtedly shares with my father It captures with astonishing accuracy the events leading to a prestigious, soaring career in serious music, to a digression in which Korngold revealed a fluent facility for adapting the works of Johann Strauss II and others, which was criticized by his fellow musicians as a waste of time. This portion of his career was very much enjoyed by my father. He did his adaptations because he knew how. Many of his contemporaries, including Puccini, tried to do what Korngold did in that respect, but failed.

Mr. Carroll's book captures with great accuracy Korngold's career as a Hollywood musician, where, first of all, he established the form of film music that became the mainstay of cinematic art and yet remained true to himself, writing the kind of romantic, voluptuous, thematic music that was in accord with the picture, yet, as numerous recordings prove, was listenable on its own. Finally, the book chronicles his decision to give up film music and return to serious concert music. I am perhaps most impressed by Mr. Carroll's description of the last two stages, because I was a witness to them.

I am impressed by the wealth of materials synthesized by Mr. Carroll, to whom I shall always be grateful. I believe that the reader will be similarly fascinated by the tale of a man, true to himself, who is only now, forty years after his death, beginning to be acknowledged as one of the true artists of the twentieth century.

Ernst W. Korngold
1925–1996

Acknowledgments

This book could not have been completed without a tremendous amount of work by many people who have given their time generously during the past twenty-five years. Chief among these are Erich Wolfgang Korngold's two sons. It was my great privilege to know them both: George, who died in 1987, and Ernst, who died in November 1996 just as this book was being placed into production. Both gentlemen, together with Ernst's widow Helen, brought me close to this great composer by sharing unique reminiscences and by accepting me into the family. They allowed me unlimited access to the Korngold estate and loaned many private photographs and other material, much of it reproduced here for the first time. Ernst Korngold, in particular, was tremendously supportive during the last eight years of this project, and it is of great personal regret that he did not live to share in the celebrations of his father's centenary or to see this book in its final published form.

Apart from the Korngold family, one man has been an indispensable help to me: Bernd Rachold, director of the European office of the Korngold Society. He labored seven years to prepare a catalog of Korngold's private correspondence, a task that required deciphering the almost cryptic handwriting of the composer and his father. For providing information, new sources, and rare photographs, for reading the entire manuscript of this book and correcting my errors, and for providing help in innumerable ways, I am eternally grateful.

Konrad Hopkins, with whom I founded the Korngold Society in 1983, has also been supportive. He published my short monograph on Korngold in the early 1980s when no other publisher would even consider a text on the composer. It subsequently went to four editions. Many of the professional translations used in the present book were commissioned and paid for by him. His encouragement, often when I felt this work would never be finished, has been inspiring. He also read the entire manuscript and made many helpful suggestions.

Apart from the great musicians, conductors, composers, actors, directors, writers, designers, and other wonderful people who worked with and knew Erich Wolfgang Korngold and shared their memories and private correspondence with me, certain other key individuals have helped me beyond the call of duty. Deserving of special mention are Tony Thomas, who first introduced me to what was left of the "old Hollywood" in the 1970s before it disappeared forever; Rudy Behlmer, the noted film historian, whose knowledge of Warner Brothers and the Korngold films is without equal; and the late musicologist Harold Truscott, whose understanding of Korngold's music and incomparable musicianship was indispensable and inspiring.

In the course of researching this book, I have interviewed and corresponded with a great many people who knew and worked with Korngold, many of whom are now deceased. Their memories are preserved in these pages, and this book would be the poorer without them.

I am grateful to the following individuals who graciously gave their time in assisting in my research; shared memories, correspondence, and photographs; and helped in countless other ways: Gusti Adler, Rosette Anday, George Berris, Rudolf Bing, Henry Blanke, Magda Breisach, Ronald Button, Shura Cherkassky, Marc Connelly, Lady Diana Cooper, Aaron Copland, Bette Davis, Olivia de Havilland, Tilly De Garmo, Anton Dermota, Elisabeth Duschnitz, Marta Eggerth, Paul Elbogen, Dr. Edwin Eisler, Dr. Guido "Poldi" Engelmann, Nanette Fabray, Rudi Fehr, Fritz Feld, Marta Feuchtwanger, Hal Findlay, Joan Fontaine, David Forrest, Dr. Hans Gál, Dr. Egon Gartenberg, Albert Glasser, Prof. Berthold Goldschmidt, Art Grier, Desi Halban, Paul Henreid, Prof. Wolfram Humperdinck, Brian Desmond Hurst, Elisabeth Kallina, Charles Kalman, Bronislaw Kaper, Louis Kaufmann, Annette Kaufmann, Dr. Ludwig Kaufmann, Leonid Kinskey, Lotte Klemperer, Olda Kokoschka, Ted Krise, Meta Krogel, Max Lanner-Lamm, Evelyn Laye, Lotte Lehmann, Mervyn LeRoy, Edwin Lester, Dr. Herman Lewandowsky, Herman Lowin, Gertrud Löwy, Anna Mahler, George Marischka, Dione Neutra, Jarmila Novotná, Eugene Ormandy, Karl Pollak, Vincent Price, LeRoy Prinz, Irving Rapper, Ronald Reagan, Ellen Reichert, Maria Reining, Bert Reisfeld, Dame Flora Robson, David Rubin, Winthrop Sargent, Margit Schenker-Angerer, Fritzi Schlesinger-Czaptka, Prof. Wolfgang Schneiderhan, Prof. Max Schönherr,

Prof. Rudolf Schwarz, Dr. Willi Schuh, Lea Seidl, Eleanor Aller Slatkin, Nicolas Slonimsky, Dr. Franz and Frau Alice Strauss, Hans Sommers (von Sonnenthal), Diana Napier Tauber, Prof. Vilem Tausky, Hal Wallis, Harry Warren, Carol Weiskopf, Eva Maria Wiesner, Prof. Hilde Zadek, Louise Zemlinsky, and Dr. Fritz Zweig.

I would like particularly to thank the music departments of Christ's College, Liverpool and the University of Liverpool, which helped me so much in the early stage of this book.

The major academic institutions, libraries, and archives that have provided unlimited help to me over the years include Österreichische Nationalbibliothek, the Musik-, Druck- und Handschriftensammlungen der Wiener Stadt- und Landesbibliothek, Österreichisches Staatsarchiv-Kriegsarchiv, Staatliche Akademie für Musik und darstellende Kunst in Vienna, Theatermuseum der Universität zu Köln, The British Library, The British Film Institute, The National Film Archive, London, The Academy of Motion Picture Arts and Sciences, The American Film Institute, The University of Southern California—Special Collections (Doheny Library), The Chicago Historical Society, Schott Musik International GmbH & Co., Mainz, Universal Edition, Vienna and London, Josef Weinberger Ltd., London, The New York Public Library, The Moldenhauer Archive, The Moravian Museum, Brno, Staatsbibliothek, Berlin, Stadttheater Saarbrücken, Bühnen der Hansestadt Lübeck, Library of the Sibelius Academy, Helsinki, BBC Written Archives, Caversham, England, The Library of Congress, Washington D. C., Gesellschaft der Musikfreunde, Vienna, Gemeente Archief, The Hague, Bayerische Staatsbibliothek, Munich, Stadt-und Universitätsbibliothek Frankfurt, Hessische Landesbibliothek–Hessisches Staatstheater, Wiesbaden, EMI Records Ltd., Österreichischer Rundfunk (ORF), The Boston Public Library, The Royal Academy of Music, London, The Royal College of Music, London, The Alma Mahler Collection–State University of New York at Binghampton, The Max Reinhardt Archive– State University of New York at Binghampton, The Musical Museum, Middlesex, England, Warner Brothers Studios Music Department (Daniel Franklin), Hollywood, California, Paramount Pictures Corporation Music Department (Elridge Walker), Hollywood, California, and the archives of the following musical institutions: Deutsche Oper, Berlin, Staatsoper unter den Linden, Berlin, Vienna State Opera, Theater an der Wien, Wiener Volksoper, Hamburg State Opera, Berlin Philharmonic Orchestra, Leipzig Gewandhaus Orchestra, Vienna Symphony Orchestra, Vienna Philharmonic Orchestra, Los Angeles Philharmonic Orchestra, Chicago Symphony Orchestra, New York Philharmonic Orchestra, Royal Opera House, Stockholm, Brno State Theater Opera, Mozarteum, Salzburg, The Salzburg Festival Archives, Národní Muzeum, Prague, St. Louis Symphony Orchestra, Pittsburgh Symphony Orchestra, and Stadttheater Bern.

This book has been in gestation for so long that many of the archivists I originally dealt with have either retired or gone to a better place. To all the many wonderful people from these institutions who have endured the barrage of questions and requests for information and material from me and my colleagues during the past quarter century, a very sincere and heartfelt thank you.

I would like to offer my special thanks to Lawrence J. Burton and Rudy Behlmer for permission to reproduce unique material from their correspondence with the late Hugo Friedhofer, and to Charles Gerhardt for many valuable insights and advice about Korngold's compositions and methods. I also thank the film historian Jack Docherty, who read the chapters on Korngold's career in Hollywood and made many useful suggestions.

In addition, many translators have contributed to the preparation of the manuscript, including Professor L. A. Aina (Liverpool University), Ernst Korngold, George Korngold, Liselotte Leschke, Andrew Long, Ernst Pories, Monika Simpson, Laurie Thompson, Graham Watson, Damian Whiteley, and Michael Young.

For special photographic restoration and production prior to publication, I thank John Taggart and John Duncan, together with Roger Quayle and Leslie Forbes, who worked on material earlier in the project.

In addition, I thank my secretary Lyn McGowan for retyping the manuscript and the following individuals who helped in various ways: Colin Oxenforth, Ken Grundy, Dr. Thomas Gayda, Olaf Kiener, Ray van Orden, Christian Heindl, Prof. Fred Flindell, Dr. Alfred Clayton, Josef Adler, Brian Rust, Steve Orfanos, Gary Graffmann, Clifford McCarty, Prof. Leonard Fiedler, Steven Atack, Dr. Russell Lloyd, Brian Harvey, Mark Armstrong, Carmen Ottner, David Beams, Jack Kohl, John Kobal, David Kram, Vivian Liff, Norman Lebrecht, Mary Peltz, Philip Maxwell, Donald Ross, John Allan, Roger Wilmut, Prof. Josef Albrecht, John Gregson, Lennox Berkeley, Ida Cook, Alexander Leonov, Dr. Rudolf Fiedler, Leslie Halliwell, Prof. Fritz Neumeyer, Ulric De Vaere, Dr. Jan Kralik, Harold Rosenthal, Erika Redlich, Lilly Segall, Dr. Pavel Eckstein, Henry P. Adams, Geoffrey Smith, Dr. Dr. Peter Aistleitner, Hans W. Schmitz, Marjan Kiepura, Philip Mosely, Christopher Hailey, Miles Kreuger, Jim Silke, Irene Atkins, and Caspar Wintermans.

Finally, a sincere and heartfelt thank you to Reinhard Pauly, Eve Goodman, Suzanne Copenhagen, and the staff of Amadeus Press for being so patient with me and for helping to realize the completion of this project.

If I have failed to mention anyone who has contributed to my work during the past twenty-five years, be assured that this is an oversight and please accept my warmest thanks for your help.

To everyone—thank you. Without you all, this book would never have been.

Introduction

Almost twenty-five years ago—a period that represents virtually my entire adult life—I began the task of creating the first, full-length biography of the composer Erich Wolfgang Korngold. Had I known how long this huge undertaking would take, I might not have started at all. How it came to be written and the many adventures I have had along the way makes an interesting tale in its own right.

In 1971, when I was still a teenager, I noticed a new long playing recording (imported from America) entitled *The Sea Hawk: The Classic Film Scores of Erich Wolfgang Korngold* in the window of the local record shop. The cover showed a beautiful black and white photograph of two sixteenth-century galleons engaged in battle, which was a still from the classic 1940 swashbuckler starring Errol Flynn, one of my favorite films as a child to watch whenever it was shown on television. It was a favorite largely because of its superb music, and here was an opportunity to own a stereo recording of it. I was so fond of the score that I had already made a tape recording of the film soundtrack by fastening a microphone to the TV speaker, a method that was unpopular in the Carroll household because everyone had to remain silent during the recording!

The name of Erich Wolfgang Korngold was little known to me then, or indeed to most people, as I subsequently was to discover. As I read a brief outline of his life included with the LP, I was intrigued to learn that he was not just a movie composer but that his career had also embraced opera and symphonic and chamber music, and that he had been a celebrated child prodigy and a victim of the Nazis. My two great passions in life had always been classical music and the golden age of the movies (the 1930s and 1940s), and here these passions appeared to converge in the career of one man. I resolved to find out more.

I wrote a letter to RCA, the company that produced the LP, to ask for more information on future recordings, which resulted months later in a most unexpected and providential reply from Korngold's younger son George from his office in New York, inviting me to visit him in London. This was the beginning of a long journey. I was still a music student and had initially decided to write my dissertation on Korngold, but as my knowledge and enthusiasm grew and I realized how little published information in English there was, and particularly as I heard more of his music, I determined to write his biography. George Korngold and his elder brother Ernst opened up for me the fascinating story of their father's extraordinary life and career. They also became cherished friends and encouraged me at every step of the way, even when it looked as though my task would never be completed.

A quarter of a century is a long but not surprising length of time, given the task I had set for myself. I have had to become something of a detective in piecing together this remarkable story. So much material was lost, destroyed, or scattered to the four corners of the globe during the upheavals of World War II. I began a slow but thorough trawl of libraries and archives throughout Europe and America not only to collate whatever material and information had survived, but also to corroborate the known facts of Korngold's life.

Korngold's first biography was written in 1922 when he was just 25 years old by Dr. Rudolf Stefan Hofmann, a prominent music critic in Vienna who had also written an early biography of Franz Schreker. This book contained a good deal of important information and clues as to Korngold's early career, and it was written in close collaboration with its subject, but it contained many errors, as did his widow Luzi Korngold's otherwise charming and personal account published in 1967. Nevertheless, these were my primary sources from which it was possible to build a framework for detailed research. Dr. Hoffmann and Luzi Korngold had the considerable advantage of knowing their subject and his milieu extraordinarily well, whereas I had to start almost from scratch. With only a limited knowledge of German (in which most documentary evidence was written), I found the research a formidable task.

In 1983, Konrad Hopkins and I formed the Korngold Society to provide a meeting point for the many enthusiasts of Korngold's music and a repository for archival material. With the formation of the Society, my work became somewhat easier, as with Konrad Hopkins's help and that of our European director Bernd Rachold in Hamburg, material could be acquired more quickly.

The added focus provided by the Society was not enough to produce this book, however. A good biography relies on personal remembrance and private correspondence to bring its subject alive. Consequently, in 1975 I embarked on a long series of interviews in Europe and America with musicians, actors, directors, writers, relatives, and friends. They ranged from his governess, who had taught him French and English as a ten- and eleven-year-old (discovered accidentally, when I asked the Arts Council of Great Britain for a grant; though they refused, the man who read my letter just happened to be this lady's son—I interviewed her when she was 97 and again when she was 105!) to a long-lost cousin who lived just four streets away from me in Liverpool, and included legendary singers and musicians and some of the great stars from Hollywood's golden age. The result was over 300 taped hours of a unique oral history now distilled in these pages.

Correspondence proved difficult to obtain in the early part of my research. Much of it was missing, presumed destroyed. Gradually, however, this presumption has proved untrue. Korngold and his famous father, like most professional men of their time, were prolific correspondents and many thousands of letters have survived—far too many to be incorporated into a book of this size. A general knowledge of the contents of this huge archive has considerably enriched the text, however. Just as I was completing the manuscript, a new collection of some 2000 letters—the correspondence library from Korngold's home in Vienna, previously thought lost— turned up in Vienna. Material and information from this treasure trove are still being gathered and classified by my colleague in Hamburg, Bernd Rachold. I am afraid that discussion of it will have to wait for a later edition.

My primary aim in this book is to provide a comprehensive and definitive biography of Korngold for the widest possible readership and to aid future scholarship. No future biographer should have to repeat the lengthy research I have done. Therefore, this book contains a comprehensive bibliography providing all major published and unpublished sources. Archival material on Korngold is now classified and preserved in four main locations: the Library of Congress, which holds most of his original musical manuscripts, the Korngold Society Archives in Hamburg and Scotland, and my own collection in Liverpool, which holds copies of correspondence, reviews, articles, photographs, most of the published scores, an extensive sound archive, copies of all the motion pictures on videotape, and other ephemera.

This book is by no means the final word on Korngold. There is much still to be done, and much still to be found. For example, I had hoped until the last moment that the only known photograph of Korngold with his teacher Alexander von Zemlinsky, taken on stage in Prague in 1922 and given to an American university by his widow (she could not recall which, alas!), would turn up. Regrettably, it remains lost. If members of the institution in question should happen to read this, I hope they will contact me.

Also, the recently discovered correspondence library in Vienna contains nothing from Mahler, Zemlinsky, and other major figures. Only one letter from Richard Strauss and just two small postcards from Puccini have ever been found, yet contact between Korngold and these eminent musicians was known to be frequent. Clearly, the choicest items, having been sold at the time of Germany's annexation of Austria in 1938, remain in private hands.

The published scores of Korngold's major works are badly in need of revision, and the film music remains largely unpublished, save for some short suites. Yet this music is among the most popular on gramophone records and should be readily accessible in the concert hall. I hope that these outstanding issues will be resolved following Korngold's centenary.

Opinion has changed during the twenty-five years since I first began this labor of love. In the early 1970s, Korngold was a forgotten man, or if he was remembered at all, it was more often with a sneer than a salute. Now, he has emerged as one of the most gifted prodigies in history, a major operatic and symphonic composer, a seminal figure in the tumultuous period of artistic revolution in the inter-war period, and the leading pioneer in symphonic film composition. Major recordings of his work continue to be made, while the films for which he composed such marvelous music (and for which he used to be condemned) ironically have led to a reawakening of interest in his concert works and are shown so frequently on television that he is now arguably among the most listened to, and popular, of all twentieth-century composers.

Korngold's remarkable story provides a mirror for the musical life of this century. In his relatively short life, he was extremely active and was well acquainted with most of the major figures in music, theater, and film. He deserves, in his centenary year, to take his place finally among the last of the great romantic composers, as a true heir to Brahms, Mahler, Strauss, and Puccini, yet with his own distinctly original and personal voice.

I have delayed you long enough with my preamble. Now read on, the full and engrossing story of one of the most remarkable figures of recent musical history.

The Early Years:
1897–1913

CHAPTER ONE

"A Genius!"

—Gustav Mahler

*E*rich Wolfgang Korngold (1897–1957) was that rarest of beings: a composing child prodigy—a child so gifted that even before his teens he was producing mature works of genuine worth that the greatest musicians of his time clamored to perform. His early music was not the juvenilia of an apprentice but was extremely sophisticated, structurally complex, and marked by an original, individual style from the very first opus. A melodic sweetness revealing a strong lyrical gift, together with an extraordinary personal sense of harmony and rhythm, have ensured that these early works have survived in the repertory. A new generation of artists has discovered them since the 1980s.

The title of this book may seem provocative. Why is Korngold the last prodigy? Child prodigies in the history of music are a ubiquitous species even now, yet among musicians this phenomenon is mostly confined to performers. Child composers, on the other hand, and especially those of worth, are extremely rare, perhaps amounting to less than twenty over the past 300 years. The most famous examples of composing prodigies are well documented: Handel, Mozart, Schubert, Mendelssohn, Glazunov, and Liszt. Exhaustive modern research has revealed others: Juan Arriaga, Georges Enescu,[1] Georges Bizet, Max Bruch, and Niels W. Gade, for example.[2]

Thereafter, the number of boy composing prodigies almost dries up; among girls the phenomenon is virtually unknown. Korngold was the last true example, and in many ways one of the most fascinating: a child genius worthy of comparison with his most illustrious forebears and embraced by the aristocracy of *fin de siècle* Vienna and its musical cognoscenti, just as Mozart had been before him.

Korngold's later career is equally fascinating. Although he did not develop into the musical prophet of the twentieth century as was first predicted, he nevertheless deserves recognition and study, for he was a unique musician. To understand and evaluate his achievements and milieu, however, we must begin with his status as a *Wunderkind*.

In the latter half of the twentieth century, child composers of genius have all but vanished, presumably a result of the emergence of mathematical and atonal methods in composition. Precocious children perhaps do not so easily lean toward such abstract musical construction. Clearly, one may infer that the spontaneous creative child needs to be nurtured in a "tonal environment."

In surveying the prodigies who did produce substantial musical works, another factor emerges. Youthful compositions that actually endure and exhibit artistic merit are practically unknown. Even Mozart's juvenilia, though precocious and technically proficient, have yet to exhibit the true personality of the composer or be worthy of regular performance. The music of the early opera *La Finta Giardiniera*, delightful though it is, gives no real indication of the composer of *Don Giovanni*. Korngold was unique in this respect. He produced music in his extreme youth that practically has no parallel. Yet comparing Korngold's music with the early music of Mozart, Schubert, and others is made futile by the disparity of their times. Korngold was composing in an altogether more complex age, circa 1910, in which the prevailing musical idiom was already at the very extremes of tonality.

The luxuriant, contrasting styles of Richard Strauss and Gustav Mahler, Claude Debussy and Igor Stravinsky, all of whom influenced Korngold, dominated the years of his childhood. He embraced their highly sophisticated language wholeheartedly, and from it forged a style of his own without intellectualizing the process. His astonishingly early maturity was entirely natural, and seemed a miracle to his contemporaries. His story is not just that of a forgotten child genius but is a strand of musical history that has, until recently, been overlooked.

The age of Romanticism, eclipsed by Arnold Schoenberg and his pupils, lived on far longer than might be supposed; some believe that it never actually ended, as the current reevaluation of Korngold and his contemporaries suggests. In Austria and Germany, the music of Franz Schreker, Alexander von Zemlinsky, Hans Gál, Berthold Goldschmidt, Wilhelm Grosz, Max von Schillings, and many others continued the heady, post-Wagnerian trend toward musical expressionism right up until 1933, when the rise of the Nazis snuffed it out along with the work of the radicals who opposed it.

The Nazis called it *Entartete Musik* or degenerate music, a label they also attached to Schoenberg and his followers.

Although serialism and atonality, repressed in totalitarian Europe for fifteen years, reemerged as the dominant force there after the Second World War and was acclaimed as the music of the future, the music of what might be termed the "opposition," that of Korngold, Schreker, and even Gustav Mahler, continued to be suppressed, ridiculed, forgotten, and unperformed. Not until the 1960s were Mahler's symphonies performed regularly. Korngold and his colleagues therefore suffered in two suppressive environments—in the 1930s and in the 1950s.

Erich Wolfgang Korngold was a pivotal figure in the early 1920s, when his reputation and his creative output seemed to promise that he would be a major voice for the future. He was proclaimed by some to be the avatar of modern music, by others to be a conservative reactionary. By 1938, he was identified exclusively with the traditional nineteenth-century ideal, and his music, whether admired or despised, proclaimed itself synonymous with melody and an epic romanticism quite at odds with the revolutionary ideas of serialism, constructivism, atonalism, and the countless other "isms" that flourished and faded during that era. His extraordinarily rich musical language, at its most passionate and complex in his operatic masterpiece *Das Wunder der Heliane*, is considered excessive by some, yet its powerful emotional appeal immediately establishes his individuality among other composers of the period.

He did not, could not, abandon tonality entirely, although his language could be astonishingly ambiguous. The harmony is completely original, while his rhythms give the essential impetus to his music—elastic, restless, dependent on free rubato and that inherent Viennese lilt so beloved of Johann Strauss. Above all, he had a highly personal melodic gift, and he strove to create memorable and unusual themes, which were always the result of spontaneous inspiration.

His all-powerful father, the critic Dr. Julius Korngold, was a profound influence on his life. The critic undertook almost single-handedly to rebuff the modern trends that offended his sensibilities. He was a conservative, and made no secret of it. It is with Julius Korngold that this story really begins, and his relationship with his son is crucial. As Eduard Hanslick's successor as chief music critic at the *Neue Freie Presse*, his power was extraordinary. An opinionated, domineering man, his professional activities frequently encroached on his son's career.   To understand the child, one must know the father, and so I begin this book by introducing this formidable man, giving a brief account of his career up to the birth of his famous offspring.

Julius Korngold was born in Brünn (now Brno) on 24 December 1860. Brünn was then part of Moravia in the Austro-Hungarian Empire (today it is in the Czech Republic), and it was an important industrial town, having earned the nickname "the Austrian Manchester" from its preponderance of chimneys and factories that sprang up in the nineteenth century. Despite its industrial roots, it had a small but thriving opera house and a busy, enthusiastic musical life.

Julius Korngold came from a lower middle-class Jewish family with aspirations for a better life. Although Julius displayed innate musical talent as a young man (he was a competent pianist, possessed a fine tenor voice, and had inherited a love of music from his mother), he was destined for law school, a highly desirable career for a young man from a good Jewish family at that time. His father, Simon Korngold, managed his own liquor store in Brünn (coincidentally, his future wife's father, Hermann Witrofsky was in a similar business, as a distiller). Music was in the family genes. On his mother's side was the minor composer Max Mareczek,[3] who in 1840 had written an opera, *Hamlet*.

Music was not encouraged as a profession by young Julius's father, and he was especially determined that Julius not follow in the footsteps of his elder half-brother Eduard, who had become an actor,[4] a profession considered even more disreputable. The brother further angered the family by marrying Hansi Fuehrer, an actress who enjoyed great favor at the time, chiefly because of her considerable feminine "endowments." But that, as they say, is another story.

Julius qualified as a lawyer in 1885 and joined the firm of Josef Weingarten, whose son Paul became a noted pianist and later gave the first performance of young Erich's Piano Sonata No. 3 in C Major. Although Julius had fulfilled his promise to become a lawyer (and a well-qualified one—he was now rejoicing under the title of *Dr. Korngold*), he had maintained his studies in music, and while at the University of Vienna and the Vienna Conservatory he frequented the classes of Eduard Hanslick and Anton Bruckner far more than those on jurisprudence.

Julius's era at the university was especially fruitful: other students included Franz Schalk, and among the teachers were Robert Fuchs and Franz Krenn. Julius's career in law did not prevent his continuing a passionate interest in music, and initially he had enough spare time to accept an offer from Heinrich Penn, editor of the *Brünner Morgenpost*, to review concerts. Thus his career as a critic began, although his tenure on the *Morgenpost* did not last long; the owner of a local printing company persuaded Julius Korngold to become editor of a new Monday paper, and after some hesitation, the *Brünner Montags-Zeitung* was born. The young lawyer wrote reviews, feuilletons, lead stories on major events, and even rhyming epigrams. Among the contributors was the young playwright (and later librettist of Erich's operas) Hans Müller.

A significant turning point was reached when Julius wrote a defensive and critical feuilleton against the leading critic on the main newspaper following publication of a disparaging article against Brahms's Fourth Symphony. Julius's article was read by Eduard Hanslick (Brahms's champion and friend), and he immediately wrote the following letter of commendation to the paper (not knowing the author's name):

Dear Sir,

Even though I did not have the honor of knowing you or even your name I am taking the liberty of writing to you, since you may be pleased to learn how Johannes Brahms has received your essay about his fourth symphony. . . . Brahms today made a point of bringing me the paper with the expression of sincerest joy about your critique. Since Brahms pays very little attention to the reviews of his works, and never talks even about the best ones, the exception he made for your critique might give you pleasure. Considering this degree of recognition, it may not mean very much that I, too, find your essay excellent. At any rate, I would be pleased to learn on occasion, the name of my esteemed colleague and musical friend in Brünn.

Sincerely yours,
Your devoted
Professor Eduard Hanslick[5]

Brahms also wrote a letter of thanks to Julius, in his curt, polite style. Seizing the opportunity, Julius immediately wrote a letter to Hanslick introducing himself, and later visited him in Vienna. Shortly after that, he left the *Montags-Zeitung*, having been offered a position with Brünn's leading newspaper, the *Tagesbote*, an offer he later learned was due to Hanslick's intercession. Hanslick liked the young lawyer, admired his honesty and candor, and was obviously glad that his views on music were mostly in accord with his own.

Through Hanslick, Julius met Brahms (surely his goal in developing the relationship), and he frequently spent an afternoon in deep discussion with the great composer. Julius must have impressed him, for it was rare for Brahms to be convivial or familiar with young men, especially if they were critics by profession.

On 27 September 1891, Julius Korngold married the daughter of one of his father's business associates, Josephine Witrofsky, a young woman of "musical talent and searing temper," as he later described her. She came from a good family that was slightly higher up the social ladder than the Korngolds, and she was renowned for her sparkling wit, a quality she passed on to Erich in abundance. In many ways, she was the ideal wife for Julius Korngold, quite the antithesis of the brooding pessimist. Ever at his side, she was the perfect hostess whenever he had official duties to perform, and later she ran the large household when his tenure as Vienna's leading critic at the *Neue Freie Presse* began. Though she submerged her own personality and ambition, forfeiting her aspirations to those of her husband and, later, to those of their brilliant son, she was a strong-willed, talented woman, accomplished and intelligent. She was also a highly competent pianist and amateur singer, and in old age could sing practically the whole opera repertory from memory, having attended the opera almost every night for fifty years.

With the achievement of a successful marriage, and with an ambitious and determined wife at his side, the lawyer inevitably soon gravitated toward better things. He also had a powerful ally in Hanslick, who regarded him as highly promising. Hanslick was already considering who was to succeed him at the *Neue Freie Presse*. The next time Julius visited Vienna, Hanslick decided that it was time he was introduced to Moritz Benedikt, the editor and publisher of the *Presse*, then at the zenith of its prestige and influence as Vienna's leading newspaper. This interview led to commissions to write reviews of provincial concerts for the paper and later to submit reports from further afield.

A trip to Paris in 1900 allowed Julius Korngold to be the first to write about Claude Debussy in a German newspaper. His pungent, shrewdly observed, succinctly witty invective against the Impressionists, and his caustic appraisal of Charpentier's *Louise* were not wasted on either Hanslick or Benedikt. Nor for that matter did his talents go unnoticed in Brünn or Vienna. His reputation was growing far beyond the scope of provincial Brünn. In November 1901 Julius Korngold moved to Vienna, and left behind his inauspicious origins forever.

From now on, he would inhabit a completely different world: the rich, cosmopolitan, cultural "melting pot" that was Imperial Vienna in the fabulous decade just before the First World War. It was the Vienna of Sigmund Freud, Arthur Schnitzler, Gustav Klimt, Egon Schiele, and, above all, of Gustav Mahler. The intoxicating world of *fin de siècle* Vienna has been described as the "crucible of contemporary culture,"[6] a fertile breeding ground for innovation, style, and revolution. It provided the fascinating backdrop for the most exciting and intellectually dynamic years of the twentieth century until the "new dark age," as Winston Churchill called it, arrived in 1933.

In 1901, Vienna was the center of the art world. Initially, Julius Korngold went to Vienna as a lawyer, not as a critic, but events at the *Neue Freie Presse* soon changed the course of his life. Hanslick's official "number two" on the paper was composer Richard Heuberger, renowned for his operetta *Der Opernball*, but he was no friend of Hanslick's, and soon it became apparent that Hanslick favored "the young gate- crasher from the provinces" over Heuberger as his eventual successor. In August 1902, Moritz Benedikt engaged Julius Korngold and effectively displaced Heuberger.

From the beginning, the new critic on the *Presse* was at the center of controversy. Mahler was already effecting major changes at the Vienna Court Opera, and most established critics were against him, including Heuberger. Julius Korngold persuaded Moritz Benedikt to run a lead article supporting Mahler, which caused a sensation. This was a clever move, for it ensured that Julius Korngold's name would be immediately in the forefront of the public eye, where it would remain for the next thirty years. In 1904 Hanslick died, and his young protégé succeeded him as the leading music critic in the German-speaking press.

This was the environment that nurtured the child who would become the realization of Julius Korngold's dreams and ambitions. In his memoirs, Julius freely admitted that he had really wanted to become a musician. A conductor, a composer, a singer—all were careers he considered, but he was honest enough to admit that he did not have the requisite talent. This accusation could never be leveled at his youngest son. Erich was endowed with musical gifts far above any that Julius Korngold could ever have hoped to realize.

The Early Years of Erich Wolfgang Korngold

Julius Korngold had two sons, both of whom he named after a favorite composer. The eldest, Hanns Robert (after Schumann), was born 25 July 1892; the youngest, Erich Wolfgang (his middle name in homage to Mozart), on 29 May 1897. (As a further connection with the earlier prodigy, Julius bore as his middle name the name of Mozart's father, Leopold.) Erich was born at the family home in Brünn, 1 Franzensglacis, which still stands today.[7] In the memoirs of Julius Korngold, Erich dominates the text, whereas his brother is mentioned only once—to state, tersely, that he was born. This deliberate omission reflects Hanns Korngold's position as the black sheep of the family who lived forever in the shadow of his famous brother, yet nonetheless revered and almost venerated him. A boyhood friend of Korngold's, Paul Elbogen, was one of the few who recalled this brother well:

> Hanns—as he preferred to be called—was devilishly good looking, married three times, was always in debt and frequently expected his brother to pay off his debts, which were usually due to gambling; he was an unequivocal scoundrel and good-for-nothing who in later years blackmailed his brother and his wife.[8] He never wanted to work and was almost a character out of an opera libretto, and his problems were clearly a result of parental indifference, which was a natural by-product of Erich's arrival. The older boy was practically ignored, superseded by his talented younger brother. . . . Yet, the most amazing thing was that, instead of hating his gifted brother . . . he absolutely adored him, and was present at every performance of new works.[9]

Significantly, the manifestation of Erich's extraordinary talents coincided with the emergence of Hanns into adolescence. The elder boy's existence was a tragic one and became increasingly so as his fabulously gifted younger brother grew up and eclipsed him. Later, Hanns would become a constant source of stress and embarrassment.

Erich Wolfgang Korngold and his
brother Hanns Robert, circa 1902
(Korngold estate).

The prodigiousness of Erich Wolfgang Korngold's talent is singular. His near contemporary, Erwin Nyiregyhazy,[10] who exhibited many of the accomplishments of a child genius, produced numerous compositions between the ages of seven and twelve, but they are childish, imitative, clumsy, and totally uninteresting. The early music of Erich Wolfgang Korngold, however, is strikingly original, mature, and innovative. Korngold's astonishing creativity separates him from other gifted children and places him on par with the great musical prodigies of history.

The young Korngold's achievements are significant for another reason. The musical style of most prodigious composers (and, in fact, composers of any age) usually takes the preceding generation as its first point of reference. The most obvious example is the early music of the young Beethoven, which despite its rugged individuality and original thinking is couched in the idiom of the eighteenth century—all Mozartian grace and elegance. There are rare exceptions, however, in which a composer begins writing in a contemporary, even futuristic, style. For a child to do this is rarer still. Mozart as a twelve-year-old was already writing in the style of the (then) new Mannheim school. Mendelssohn, at the age of seventeen, with his incidental score to Shakespeare's *A Midsummer Night's Dream*, was considered a major composer of contemporary music.

Korngold, whose early works were written in a style that in its harmonic and melodic sophistication was beyond even Richard Strauss in certain respects, is another rare exception, and he is arguably the most remarkable prodigy in history because of his extraordinary grasp of a language so complex at such a tender age. Moreover, he produced music of genuine mastery well before the age of sixteen.

He began to exhibit this precocity at the age of three. His parents were amused when he beat perfect time with a cooking spoon. At five, he was playing themes from *Don Giovanni* by ear on the piano, and other operas he heard his father play. One day Eduard Hanslick called at the Korngold household. Told of the little boy's ability, he immediately asked for a private performance. Julius Korngold regarded this performance as no more than a party piece, and so he sat his little boy on the stool and together they gave a brief recital. Hanslick took a pinch of snuff and good humoredly remarked, "The little Mozart."

Still, his father attached little significance to his child's obvious abilities. He did, however, give him some elementary instruction in chord formation at the piano. At the age of five, Korngold could assemble chords of three, four, and five tones in all keys and on each note of every scale, and while out walking with his father could name them by heart in all combinations and inversions. This achievement prompted Julius Korngold to send the boy to a piano teacher. Seemingly unaware of his son's potential, instead of engaging a professional teacher, he sent the boy to a needy relative, one Emil Lamm.

The lessons began uneventfully, but soon the teacher began to write letters expressing his amazement at the six-year-old's competence, his rapid strides in theory, and the extraordinary aptitude he displayed in harmonizing at the keyboard and in forming chordal progressions. His musicianship outstripped his teacher's wildest expectations. Later, it was discovered that Korngold possessed absolute pitch, and his faultless ear enabled him to play and improvise with tremendous facility, even from an early age.

Korngold was not taught by any of the great piano teachers then residing in Vienna, yet he became, by the age of eleven, an exceptional pianist with his own unique style—a style that was fashioned by his powerful hands that even as a boy gave him tremendous resource in tone and touch, a completely natural and idiosyncratic technique (his fingering was highly unorthodox), and a phenomenal musical ear. Later, when conducting, he could detect precisely even the most minute error, no matter how complicated the orchestration. He also possessed an extraordinary musical memory. For him to forget a piece of music once he had heard it, read it, or played it through was virtually impossible, as he demonstrated with often startling results throughout his life.

The dramatic development during his early period of tuition crystallized when, a few months after his first proper lessons, the boy armed himself with music paper and began to scribble assiduously, seriously, the notes of his first little compositions. He had just commenced school near his home in the Paniglgasse, and the year was 1904.

What was he like, the young Korngold? Were there any distinguishing traits that would betray the existence of innate genius? Outwardly, he was a very normal little boy, apparently very lovable, with big brown eyes and flaxen hair. Chubby as a child, he never lost his plump, jovial appearance, even as an adult. His weight and his devotion to rich food —especially chocolate—would ultimately cost him his health.

Around this time Dr. Korngold finally began to take notice of his son's remarkable potential. By now, the critic was an exceedingly important figure in Vienna. His reviews and feuilletons, with their biting wit that deflated many a pompous talent and their subtle, caustic asides that effectively diminished the reputation of many a virtuoso, were usually the main talking point of the cafe circles. He had ghost-written several of Hanslick's last articles, so trusted he was by the ailing critic. Once he succeeded Hanslick in 1904, his power was absolute. To consolidate his position, he ensured that several former colleagues joined the staff of contributors to the *Presse*, among them Hans Müller and his brother, the poet Ernst Lothar. Following Hanslick's death in August 1904, Julius Korngold wrote the great critic's obituary for the *Presse*, became heir to his notes and indexes, and was thus privy to his methods.

Although Julius Korngold followed in Hanslick's footsteps, he advocated, in contrast to his predecessor, the music of Wagner and Bruckner, thereby revolutionizing the musical outlook of the rather conservative *Neue Freie Presse*. Almost immediately, he became the target of jealous rivals in the world of music criticism. Among them was Robert Hirschfeld of the *Neues Wiener Tagblatt*, who envied Korngold's position, realizing he would never join the *Presse*, first because of Hanslick and second because Korngold was Hanslick's successor. Even more opposed to the new critic was Max Graf.[11] In the eyes of Julius Korngold, this noted writer was a mortal enemy. In his memoirs, he refrains from even naming him, preferring instead to give him the nickname of "Iago" because, when he was once asked by a colleague what he had done to Max Graf to stimulate such vicious dislike, he replied, "What had Othello done to Iago?"

I mention these adversaries at this early stage of Erich Korngold's story because the constant quarrels of the elder Korngold were to have a profound effect on the career of his son. This is not to say that the father's many friends did not have a favorable influence, for Julius Korngold had as many friends as he had enemies. For instance, once he became the chief critic in Vienna, a change in circumstance was called for. The family moved to a larger apartment in the Theobaldgasse, and the musical and intellectual cognoscenti of that remarkable period flocked to it.

A byproduct of Dr. Korngold's new post was that he could now move in the finest artistic circles with ease. He became friends with musicians and composers, singers and pianists, writers and artists. He was frequently a guest at the salon of Adele Strauss, the widow of "the Waltz King," who introduced him to many of the leading figures of the time, notably

Hermann Bahr, Karl Goldmark, Max Reger, and Guido Adler. Frau Strauss became so fond of Julius Korngold that she asked him to write her late husband's biography, but he declined and recommended Dr. Ernst Decsey instead.[12]

At about this time, Erich Korngold's creative genius began undeniably to manifest itself. The early scribblings had grown into little compositions, which by the age of seven filled his music notebooks. As Julius Korngold recalled:

> These were preferably waltzes. Once, traveling from Karlsbad to Karersee I met my family at a small railway station and my wife hastened to tell about a curious incident. During my absence Erich had contracted chicken pox. He had insisted that the piano be pushed to his bedside and he then launched into strange improvisations. In our hotel, I convinced myself of this new inclination, which he practiced with zeal.[13]

These jottings were strong enough to find their way into Korngold's mature works. On this particular holiday, which must have been in 1904, the young prodigy played and improvised in public for the first time when, in their hotel, the Prince of Schaumburg-Lippe and his wife begged Dr. Korngold to allow them to listen to his son's improvisations.

The childhood sketches of Erich Wolfgang Korngold have survived to the present day, almost in their entirety. In 1980, I was allowed to examine and photograph the faded sketchbooks and sheaves of pencil manuscript, partly in preparation for this biography and partly to assist the Korngold family, who were about to donate the composer's entire memorabilia to the Library of Congress in Washington. At first sight, it was clearly obvious to me that Korngold's earliest attempts at composition contained all the idiosyncrasies of his later music, no matter how embryonic in form in these sketches. The earliest dated pieces are from 1905: Melodie Opus 1 (sic) and Melodie Opus 2 (sic) in childish handwriting. They are quite simple, yet already an occasional dissonance creeps in that is foreign to the otherwise diatonic harmony, which, if one did not know the composer's later music, might be dismissed as a mistake.

Some of the early attempts at song writing include lyrics written in the hand of his father. Dr. Korngold had begun to date his son's compositions (rather like Leopold Mozart had done), and although he claims that he was unaware of his son's abilities at this age, this judicious practice would only seem necessary if he attached some importance to these juvenile pieces. Luise von Sonnenthal, later the wife of Erich Wolfgang, wrote perceptively in her memoirs:

> Dr. Korngold tried hard to convince himself that his son was making astonishing progress, but Erich, who was such an affectionate and

sensitive child, as time went on, developed a strong resentment against his father, complaining that he had been deprived of the freedom due to the young. He whose brain overflowed with musical ideas, repeatedly said, "I did not really want to compose. I did it only for my father's sake." This should not be taken seriously; he just *had* to compose music. What he did not like was that his father was ceaselessly urging him to do better and better. It was like having the sword of Damocles hanging over his head.[14]

This description was further qualified by an anecdote related by the great conductor Karl Böhm:

Personally, I knew the family Korngold well, having spent many a holiday together in Velden am Wörthersee. I remember that young Korngold's father, Dr. Julius Korngold, constantly encouraged his son to compose—so much so that on one occasion, when we all went to bathe in the lake, he shouted after him: "Erich! Don't bathe—compose!"[15]

At Easter 1906, Julius Korngold went for a brief vacation in Abbazia in Yugoslavia, and while there he called on an old friend, the singer Karoline von Komperz-Bettelheim. While playing four-handed piano with her, he was interrupted by the arrival of a parcel. As he recalled:

It contained a composition by Erich. We were lost in amazement. The boy had composed a cantata for solo singers, chorus, and piano entitled *Gold*. An older schoolmate had provided the verses which, understandably awkward and confused, dealt with the power of gold and undoubtedly had been stimulated by *Das Rheingold*. The opening measures of the music showed the influence of d'Albert's opera *Tiefland*, which Erich, not yet an opera-goer, had heard me play on the piano. The melodic character of the composition was completely different, however. It barely pointed to d'Albert but had a peculiarly chromatic streak, and was saturated with dissonances, departing from all norm. I had the choice of either applying to it Tchaikowsky's description of Mussorgsky's harmonies as "filth" or of considering this an inexplicable product . . . of emerging modernity.[16]

Regrettably, this cantata no longer exists except in a fragmentary sketch that gives no indication of its character or format. The events of 1938 and the confiscation of the Korngolds' property clearly took *Gold* as one of its first victims. *Gold* was not the only attempt at serious structured composition that year, however. A schoolfriend librettist, Wilhelm Fabri, had also supplied a story called *Die Nixe*, and there were innumerable waltzes and little dances, some of which found their way into Erich's ballet score, *Der Schneemann*, which he completed in 1909 at the age of eleven.

As a result of *Gold*, and realizing at last that his son was unusually gifted, Dr. Korngold decided that his son needed expert instruction and sent him to Robert Fuchs, whose former pupils included Franz Schreker, Hugo Wolf, Alexander von Zemlinsky, Franz Schmidt, and even Gustav Mahler. Fuchs reluctantly accepted the boy as a pupil after much persuasion and great misgivings. He did not believe it worthwhile to instruct a child of nine in counterpoint and harmony. Within a week or two, however, he changed his mind. Writing to Dr. Korngold, he expressed amazement at the acuity of the boy, which, he said, would put to shame a pupil of twenty years of age, let alone one of nine and a half.

These lessons had a decisive impact on Korngold's compositions. Their length and complexity increased. The notebooks from this time contain various little works entitled "Moderne Sonate," Andantino (a delightful movement in A major, already Korngoldian, harmonically), a sketch for a "Rondando," and various Scherzandos, Waltzes, and Sonatinas. An effective "Theme and Three Variations" points to Korngold's facility for thematic development, while a very Viennese "Valse Charmante" shows that the influence of his adopted city was already strong. There are also some very early songs, including a short, plaintive setting for soprano and piano entitled "Kleiner Wunsch" (A Little Wish) from November 1907.[17]

His father, meanwhile, was worried, justifiably, that he might have overreacted to his son's talent with the zealous love of a proud father. Yet if his son really did have promise as a composer, was the aged Robert Fuchs the right teacher to bring out this talent? Fuchs was very much of the old school, a gentle, erudite musician who had composed some charming serenades that had been popular in the 1880s. Dr. Korngold had not dared to allow his son to play some of his more modern compositions for fear of offending the venerable professor. Clearly, the professional advice of a creative musician was needed, and without any hesitation, Julius Korngold turned to the one man whom he regarded as a true genius and a great composer. That man was Gustav Mahler.

Gustav Mahler was then coming to the end of a stormy and controversial tenure as director of the Vienna Court Opera. Throughout his career there, he had received staunch support from Julius Korngold, often in the face of unanimous disapproval from rival critics on other papers. A grateful Mahler had bestowed the rare honor of regularly sending scores to the critic for study prior to performance. He was a frequent guest of the Korngold family at their summer residence at Landro, just as they were his at Toblach.

In May 1907 Mahler confided to Julius Korngold that he was about to resign from the Vienna Court Opera. Devastated by this news, Dr. Korngold wrote an impassioned article accusing the Viennese public of driving a genius away, prophetically predicting that one day they would look back on the Mahler years as a "Golden Age." The article caused a sensation when it appeared in the *Presse* and precipitated a stream of letters of support. Nevertheless, Mahler had made up his mind. In October, after he had conducted a final, brilliant performance of *Fidelio* to a half-empty house, he left for good. Julius Korngold, as outspoken as ever, shouted at the top of his voice outside the Cafe Museum, so that his critic-adversaries should hear, "Whoever succeeds him had better watch out!"[18]

His support for the beleaguered composer had become all the more intense since he had taken his precocious son to play for him the previous year. He recalled the occasion with particular warmth in his memoirs:

> And so it was on a beautiful June day in 1906, I took my little composer, who virtually disappeared under his large sailor's hat, on a pilgrimage to Mahler's apartment in the Auenbruggergasse. Erich played his cantata by heart, as he invariably did from now on, no matter how complicated the score. Mahler, leaning against the piano, read from the manuscript in his hand. But he did not remain still for long. Instead, he began to pace hastily to and fro in the curious limping rhythm peculiar to him when he was excited. He kept exclaiming "A genius! A genius!" in ever more strident tones. The melodic structure, formative power, and revolutionary sense of harmony had strongly impressed him. "Send the boy to Zemlinsky," he advised me with mounting urgency. "No conservatory! No drill! He will learn everything he needs to know from Zemlinsky during the free give and take of creative instruction."[19]

Mahler was the first public figure to recognize the extraordinary gifts of young Korngold. In the coming years, nearly every great musician of this era would come to agree with him. Korngold was indeed a genius, and would confound the finest musical minds with his compositions. His early works are just as remarkable to today's audiences as when Mahler and his contemporaries heard them. Mahler set Korngold on the path that would bring him world fame and take him from the leading concert halls and opera stages in Europe to the film studios of Hollywood.

CHAPTER TWO

The Prodigy Reveals Himself

*T*he support of Mahler was crucial. Not usually given to compliments, his advocacy of the young Korngold, even when controversy and gossip began to accompany his development, was all the more inexplicable to enemies of both Mahler and the elder Korngold. The later accusation that praise was accorded the prodigy to win the favor of his all-powerful father could not be leveled justifiably at Gustav Mahler, who was never party to such political machinations and never courted the favor of critics. His opinion was unbiased and genuine, and the choice of Zemlinsky as tutor was inspired.

This ugly little man was a brilliant musician who enjoyed an enviable reputation as a teacher, conductor, and composer in Vienna. His opera *Es war einmal* (Once Upon A Time) was performed by Mahler with great success at the Vienna Court Opera in 1900. Prior to 1900 he had been Schoenberg's only teacher. (His sister Mathilde became Schoenberg's first wife.) Among his other pupils had been Alma Schindler, Mahler's wife, who described him in her memoirs: "He was a horrid little gnome, chinless, toothless, always stank of coffee houses, unwashed, and yet, through his mental perception and power he was utterly fascinating."[1]

Zemlinsky was admired by Mahler, who engaged him as a conductor at the Vienna Court Opera. Although Julius Korngold did not rate Zemlinsky highly as a composer, he agreed with Mahler about his gifts as a teacher.[2] Initially, however, Korngold's father proceeded cautiously, despite Mahler's urgent advice, and was reluctant to interrupt the instruction with Fuchs. Before exposing young Erich to the volatile, creative influence of Zemlinsky, he wanted his son to acquire traditional roots in all of the basic musical disciplines. By 1908, however, the child was developing so quickly that the father hesitated no longer, and the lessons with Zemlinsky began.

The effect on the boy's development was immediate and dramatic. His father recalled:

> This tuition was not methodical in style, diction, and form, but highly fruitful as to musical spirit and substance. Sparks flew between teacher and pupil. Erich developed deep affection for this man, who fully opened up to him the wonderland of music that he had as yet sensed but instinctively. When Zemlinsky wanted him to add, in counterpoint, an appropriate melody to a Bach prelude, the boy delivered the goods.[3]

Judging from the little compositions in the sketch books from 1908 onward, Zemlinsky had a profound effect on how the child set down his ideas. From this year on, his compositions took on real substance and form, and he began to write cohesive works worthy of performance.

He had begun to read Cervantes's *Don Quixote*. Encouraged by his father, he devised a musical accompaniment to the story. Eventually, he decided to arrange his material into a piano suite of six character studies, which became *Don Quixote: Six Characteristic Pieces*. For one of the movements he included a cantata that he had written in 1907 with his friend Wilhelm Fabri, entitled *Der Tod*. This now became the highly dramatic first piece in the suite, "Don Quixote's Dreams of Heroic Deeds." These miniatures are still impressive today for their remarkably idiosyncratic harmony. Here, in these first real works, Korngold's musical thinking is completely formed and sounds like that of the mature composer. Although there are obvious influences, the profile is nevertheless an individual and personal one.

Another remarkable feature of his music of this period is the effortless and highly effective character delineation. The humor, capriciousness, and charm of the second piece, "Sancho Panza and His Gray Donkey," which even includes an imitation of the braying of the donkey, are quite infectious and endearing. This ability to depict character and image points ahead to Korngold's development as a major operatic composer.

A third remarkable feature of this early work is its pianistic brilliance. Of course, what Korngold wrote he could also play. By the age of ten he had already developed a strong and highly individual style of playing that characterized him all his life. A conversation with anyone who knew him always comes around to his piano playing. One of his close friends in America, the Russian actor Leonid Kinskey, explained: "When Erich played, it was difficult to know where his body ended and the piano began! Such was the total effect you felt that he and the piano became one."[4]

Manuscript of *Der Tod*, composed 1907, with lyrics (written in the hand of Julius Korngold) by school friend Wilhelm Fabri (Korngold estate/Library of Congress).

Korngold's style of playing, although extremely unorthodox, was admirably suited to his own music, for although he played an extensive repertoire (and from memory; for instance, he thought nothing of playing Richard Strauss's *Elektra* without a score), he was renowned for playing his own music, and played it as no one else could. He often remarked, "I play two instruments, the piano and the orchestra—the orchestra is such a nice instrument on which to play." When Korngold played the piano, it sounded as though he did play an orchestra, such was the overwhelming effect. The regrettably few recordings he made often give the definite impression of more than one player.

Like those of many great pianists, his transcriptions were always favorite encores. Especially famous was his version of the waltz sequence from *Der Rosenkavalier*. Once, on the radio, after Korngold had played this exuberantly, the announcer made a memorable but highly apt slip of the tongue:

> You have just heard a Bösendorfer piano *wounded* in the paraphrase of Richard Strauss's *Rosenkavalier* Waltz by Erich W. Korngold. (". . . *verwundet wurde ein Bösendorfer Flügel*": *verwundet* = "wounded" instead of *verwendet* = "played").[5]

When he wrote *Don Quixote*, young Korngold's playing had not yet assumed its full orchestral character, and these pieces and the Piano Sonata No. 1 in D Minor, both completed in 1909, are the most traditionally pianistic works he ever composed. Especially striking is the third study, "Don Quixote Goes Forth," which is a fiery, scherzo-like explosion replete with the octave-doubling typical of his later piano music, and "Dulcinea von Toboso," a Schumannesque andante that nevertheless contains many subtle and unexpected harmonic turns. The remaining two studies are descriptive, evocative "musical incidents"—"Adventure" and "Don Quixote's Conversion and Death"—both remarkably assured, harmonically daring, truly dramatic, and highly innovative for the year in which they were composed. The sketches for these pieces, which have survived, show clearly that they were the products of spontaneous inspiration, for little, if any, revision can be detected.

If Zemlinsky's influence had a maturing effect on Korngold's musical personality, his emotional development was accelerated by an incident that occurred at school around this time (1908). In a game, he had wounded a friend with a paper knife so near the jugular vein that for a time the boy's life was in danger. During the crisis, Korngold was disconsolate: he did not want to live if his friend would die. Fortunately, the friend recovered, but the whole episode profoundly disturbed the child, and he gave vent to his feelings in the only way he knew—through his music.

He composed the first two movements of the Piano Sonata No. 1 in D Minor and a mournful, quite extraordinary Adagio in C Minor, which formed the basis for the slow movement of the later Piano Sonata No. 2 in E Major, completed at the age of thirteen. This first sonata was a remarkable work for a boy of eleven to write. Its harsh, severe character, rent with jagged chromatic harmony, was as audacious harmonically as Alban Berg's Piano Sonata written that same year (though Berg's work was not published until the 1920s).

Korngold played the first two movements of the sonata to Mahler, who was very impressed. He recommended that Korngold add as the finale a passacaglia on a theme by Zemlinsky that he had written earlier. This passacaglia was the first demonstration of Korngold's enormous skill for variation, which was to become a hallmark of his music.

Zemlinsky, excited by his pupil's progress, encouraged him ever onward. He gradually introduced him to complex contrapuntal studies, thematic and harmonic analysis, and, most important of all, orchestration. Later, Zemlinsky provided these insights into their unique relationship:

> He began his tuition with me by practicing scales, and after one year he was already playing his first Beethoven sonata. Almost at the same time, he mastered harmony, and soon after this I began an analysis of form with him. He grasped all these things with uncanny speed, and in the second year we were analyzing Bach motets and such, and I was able to communicate with him as with a musician who had already learned all these things but in fact much better, since an intuitive grasp is something quite different from theoretical knowledge. He was then eleven years old, child-like, warm-hearted, and enthusiastic. At that time, he had a great passion for Puccini—a passion which I believe has since changed very much. I also did orchestration with him by letting him watch me orchestrate his ballet *Der Schneemann* after first discussing the piece with him. Also under my direction, he then orchestrated three of his fairy-tales for piano, which he had composed at about that time. He showed a very unusual gift for this also.[6]

The ballet-pantomime *Der Schneemann* (The Snowman) was, in fact, Korngold's next complete work and his most significant composition to date. His skill at illustrating characters, incidents, and scenes in musical terms was always being put to the test at home as a sort of party game, and it was from one of these improvisation sessions that *Der Schneemann* took shape.

Relatives and friends made suggestions. A picture postcard showing the whiteness and blackness of a snowman and chimney sweep contributed to the plot, but the principal influence was his father who drew his attention to the characters of the commedia dell'arte and the ancient idea of inanimate characters coming to life. Work on the score began in earnest at Christmas 1908. Young Korngold drew on earlier sketches he had made for some of the ideas, but in general the music was almost entirely new and freshly imagined. The work was complete by Easter of the following year.

Though 1908 had been a signal year for his development, he was as yet an unknown. His sonata had shown the severe, modernistic side to his personality; later, when it was published, it would contribute to the perception that Korngold was "the voice of the future." Yet in September 1908, Arnold Schoenberg, Zemlinsky's other famous pupil, was the *enfant terrible* in waiting. Schoenberg completed his String Quartet No. 2 in F-sharp Minor, which audaciously introduced a soprano voice in the last movement and dispensed with a key signature. The opening words of Stefan George's text were particularly appropriate: *"Ich fühle Luft von anderen Planeten"* (I breathe the air of other planets).

Der Schneemann

Der Schneemann marked a turning point for Erich Wolfgang Korngold. It was to become one of his most famous compositions, and it prepared him for the world of opera, which would soon dominate his creative life. This charming, two-act ballet pantomime contains the core of the composer's method and approach. It is intrinsically Viennese in character, with some passages reminiscent of Puccini, but the confidence of its tight construction, the development and interplay of the main themes, the use of *leitmotivs* for the principal characters, the correlation of text and music, and, above all, the original harmonic thinking and the aptness of the music to the individual characters—all these traits point to a born dramatist.

The simple yet effective plot was coauthored by Julius Korngold, and takes place at dusk in a small town. The first act is set in the square. To the left of the stage is Pantalon's home, so devised that the first-floor bay window is visible and the figure of Columbine can be seen through it.

Amid the usual market bustle with merchants and urchins, the musician Pierrot appears in the square. Pantalon, Columbine's uncle, is trying to keep Pierrot away from her, as he himself is seeking her favors. Pantalon pursues Pierrot, then turns to the nearby market stalls to buy something amusing for his little Columbine. He chooses a life-sized Father Christmas, which he tries to have carefully carried into the house by the servants, but children get in the way and dance round him throwing snowballs. Afterward, they build a snowman under Columbine's window with his arms outstretched.

Darkness falls. Pierrot approaches the window, gazes at Columbine, and plays a little serenade of love on his violin. Then he has an idea: he carries the snowman offstage and dons a costume he has been making for the carnival—a snowman's costume. He takes the snowman's place outside the window and can now gaze up at his beloved to his heart's content without any worry about Pantalon.

It is a dark, winter evening. Lights flicker, bells ring, and a light snow begins to fall. After an entr'acte, the second act opens in a room at Pantalon's house. Columbine gazes down at the snowman. Pantalon enters and becomes angry that she seems more interested in the snowman than in him. He jokingly summons the snowman up the stairs. To his amazement and fear, the snowman obliges. Pantalon rings for the servants, who appear, terrified; then he summons a chimney sweep for help, but with one wave of the snowman's arms the chimney sweep staggers back. The two perform a grotesque dance, while Pantalon fortifies his courage with a bottle of wine.

Pantalon's senses become clouded, and he imagines he sees two, three, four, and eventually countless snowmen. He falls asleep. Pierrot and Columbine escape after a tender declaration of their undying love. Pantalon awakes, and the servants tell him what has happened. He storms around in a rage and then chases after the two lovers as the scene changes. Once again the real snowman is back in his place. In the distance, the post horn sounds as the stagecoach carries the lovers away.

Pantalon appears, realizes the situation, and listens, paralyzed by the post horn, whose notes sound distorted. The love melody then plays from a distance as Pantalon wrings his hands in despair. At last he rushes up to the snowman, beats him into pieces, and then stands with raised arms, unconsciously like the snowman. From both sides, the children tip-toe in and surround him, pointing with their fingers. This is the final tableau as the curtain falls.

The scenario provided excellent opportunities for imaginative musical treatment, and Korngold's score—an articulate, enchanting complement to the story—is packed with incident. Julius Korngold regarded the completed work with concern and anxiety. For the first time, it occurred to him that he really had no right to deny the public any knowledge of the precocious genius under his roof.

Foreign trips permitting, Mahler had continued his interest in the boy. After Mahler left the Vienna Opera, Julius Korngold tried to persuade him to write an article for the *Neue Freie Presse* but he declined in a very touching letter. In conclusion, he wrote: "And now our warmest regards to you and your wife, and don't forget your little boy, whom we cannot get out of our minds and who astounds us more every day."[7]

Despite the opinions of Mahler, Zemlinsky, and Károly Goldmark, who had been given a performance of *Der Schneemann* while visiting the Korngold household, Julius Korngold still held back from revealing his talented son to the world. As a prominent critic, he had learned that his many adversaries would probably find a way to take advantage of the situation if it became known that his son was a budding, composing *Wunderkind*. As future events would prove, his doubts and fears were well founded. He continued to exercise caution and shielded his son from the public until December 1909. To ensure proof for posterity of his son's precocious talent, he had the Piano Sonata No. 1, the *Don Quixote: Six Characteristic Pieces,* and *Der Schneemann* printed privately and prefaced with the following statement:

These compositions are printed with the explicit stipulation that they are not to be brought before the public; they are sent privately in numbered copies to musicians and musical experts for the exclusive purpose of stating the fact that these compositions were written by a boy of ten, eleven, or twelve [respectively].[8]

He dispatched about forty copies of these privately printed works to musicians and experts who lived outside of Vienna. The letters he received in return were unanimous in their praise and excitement.

Hermann Kretzschmar,[9] Joachim's successor at the Berlin Hochschule and Germany's foremost musicologist at that time, wrote:

> Even among the most extraordinary examples of musical precocity, your son's must be rated phenomenal. As to modernity and virility of style, the only analogy that springs to my mind is that of the young Handel.

Arthur Nikisch,[10] the great conductor, wrote in a similar vein:

> This is totally phenomenal. I am really excited about these pieces— that is, about the pieces themselves, without the restrictive consideration that an eleven-year-old boy has written them. What luxuriant invention, what imagination . . . honestly, one does not know what to admire most! My God, to think of all the treasures that this genius will give to the world. . . . May the Almighty grant good health to this blessed human being. One need not worry about anything else.

Engelbert Humperdinck,[11] the composer of *Hänsel and Gretel*, commented on the "almost frightening precocity" and the "extraordinary inventiveness" of the fabulous prodigy but expressed reservations about the Don Quixote pieces because of their "modernity."

Dr. Arthur Seidl[12] of the Leipzig Conservatory used the compositions as material for his seminars. The minutes from these seminars, entitled "The Impressions and Opinions of the Concert and Discussion of the Compositions of Erich Wolfgang Korngold,"[13] concluded, as did other experts, that young Korngold's accomplishments were miraculous.

Among the other notable figures who wrote letters of extravagant praise and encouragement were the composer Max von Schillings,[14] the critic Otto Lessmann,[15] the musicologist Hugo Leichtentritt,[16] the music critic Ferdinand Pfohl,[17] the Budapest Professor of Music Viktor von Herzfeld,[18] the theorists Karl Stumpf and Erich von Hornbostel[19] (the latter conducted scientific studies on young Korngold later that year), and the composer Károly Goldmark,[20] who expressed a wish to see the works in Vienna and wrote a letter that, in spite of his reservations, summed up the feelings of all the others:

> I must confess that I was struck by all this as if confronted by something inexplicable: a miracle to be marvelled at, but which one

cannot comprehend. Who would expect an eleven-year-old boy capable of this almost mature virility, harmonic assurance, formal perfection, thematic invention (and inventiveness), and logical development? It remains a miracle. And yet I have one reservation. I mean his tendencies. Not that I would want to clip the wings of such a rich talent at this early stage. Besides, it would seem precarious for an eighty-year-old to judge an eleven-year-old. Experience and development lie too far apart. It is a daily occurrence that youth seizes upon the new. Yet the newest is not new enough. Youth, so insatiable for novelty, for innovation, tries to reach even farther. This has been demonstrated and proven by the development of young Haydn. But, we have reached a point where the question "Where to next?" seems justified. Consider that just as Beethoven left behind Mozart's and Haydn's formal structures, Erich Wolfgang Korngold might leave behind Richard Strauss, Debussy, and others in the course of his development. Then it might well be justified to ask: "Where to?" Probably my worries are unfounded because I am addressing a careful father whose rich, mature, and artistically clarified judgment will be on guard lest this glorious blossom might come to harm. For it is a blossom of the noblest kind, and may a benevolent fate reserve its undefiled bloom so that it may become a blessing for art. Strindberg was right: "The only way to become a genius is to be born one." It is a miracle and will make me believe in the miracles of the Bible from now on.[21]

By far the most important letter (portions of which have been widely quoted ever since) came from Richard Strauss, who wrote from Schierke im Oberharz. Here is the full text:

Today I received your son's compositions and have read them with the greatest astonishment. This case hardly calls for mere congratulations: the first feeling one has when one realizes that this was written by an 11-year-old boy is that of awe and concern that so precocious a genius should be able to follow its normal development, which one would wish him so sincerely. This assurance of style, this mastery of form, this characteristic expressiveness in the sonata, this bold harmony, are truly astonishing. How happy you must feel! But now take this young genius away from his desk and his music; send him to the countryside for tobogganing, skiing . . . lest his young brain becomes prematurely tired and worn out before it reaches its full productivity. I am looking forward to making the personal acquaintance of this arch-musician. My best wishes accompany him on his future paths. With best regards and thanks again for the most interesting dispatch.[22]

High praise, indeed. Strauss could hardly have failed to notice that this prodigy had already absorbed some of the modern harmonic techniques that he himself had introduced. His concerns perhaps reflected memories of his own childhood and the burden of having exceptional talent, although Strauss's early works hardly point to the great composer he grew up to be.

Strauss met the "arch-musician" for the first time in Munich during the festival where Mahler's Eighth Symphony received its world premiere. The encounter may have taken place at a soiree at the home of the music publisher Thomas Knorr, a famous meeting place for the musical and literary celebrities of the time. Korngold remained a devoted admirer of Richard Strauss and his works all his life.

The views expressed to Julius Korngold in response to the private edition of his son's early works represent those of the leaders of conservative musical opinion in Austria and other German-speaking nations. The only exception is Zemlinsky, who enjoyed the favor of both the radicals and the conservatives. The scores were not sent to Schoenberg for an opinion, as he was then still a minority figure.

Goldmark's comments on the protective, guiding hand of the prodigy's father are significant. Throughout his son's life Julius Korngold attempted to influence the development of his son's musical taste and ideas, but he was largely unsuccessful. Submissive and obedient as a child, exhibiting deep filial love for his father in all other things, Korngold protested violently if his father tried to interfere or infiltrate his own tastes into his son's musical thinking.[23]

If the father could not achieve his aims directly, his influence nonetheless prevailed indirectly in many instances. Some parents try to live their own lives through their children, and it cannot be denied that subconsciously, imperceptibly, young Korngold had absorbed a great deal of his father's musical leanings even before the boy's first creative effort. The influence of Wagner's *Das Rheingold* and d'Albert's opera *Tiefland* on the cantata *Gold* is a case in point.

Julius Korngold regarded himself as the defender of tradition and the self-appointed opponent of what later became known as the New Viennese School. Stubborn in his views, his stance certainly contributed to the general antipathy accorded to his son by Webern, Eisler, Hindemith, Bartók, Křenek, and others. Schoenberg kept his distance, only later becoming friendly when both lived in Hollywood during the Second World War.

Alban Berg was highly impressed by the young Korngold (and said so, on occasion, in correspondence with his wife) and would have liked to have developed an artistic relationship with him. Edwin Eisler, dramaturg of the opera house in Graz in the 1920s, recalled:

> Berg really admired Korngold, especially for his fabulous technical mastery. I think he admired *Die tote Stadt*[24] for its all-pervading feeling of "Weltschmerz" and its remarkable orchestration. But his attempts to form an artistic friendship, to take the young composer

under his "wing" as it were, were completely thwarted by Korngold's father, who I think was horrified at the thought that his son (who was around twenty at the time) would become infected in some way by Berg's ideas. Also, there was an unfounded rumor doing the rounds then that Berg was a homosexual; I think Britten was forbidden to study with him for the same reason. Anyway, Julius Korngold got his way, as always, and what would certainly have been an interesting situation, never developed.[25]

Even earlier than this, young Korngold experienced a form of musical censorship from his father. At the Vienna premiere of Stravinsky's ballet *Petrushka* given by the visiting company of Sergei Diaghilev in 1912, young Erich was greatly enthused by the coruscating rhythms of the score and applauded wildly at the end, only to be admonished and physically restrained by his father, who sat next to him.[26]

Despite this and similar attempts at restraint, Erich Wolfgang Korngold retained his independence. His musical convictions, like those of his mentor Richard Strauss, simply did not extend into the realm of serialism. Although he fully comprehended the philosophies of his more notorious contemporaries, he chose not to follow their example. His style, no matter how extravagant or dissonant his harmonic language became, was firmly founded on diatonic melody and traditional form. In his early years, however, he was considered modern, daring, almost a musical rebel. Of particular importance is an article written by Paul Bekker, then Germany's leading critic, who was later to become the staunchest advocate of Schoenberg and his pupils. He, too, had been sent the private edition of the early works, and in an article titled, "Sounds of the Future," wrote:

> One looks in vain for the traces of youthful uncertainty, for exaggeration and clumsiness. Here there are no rough edges, no loss of control, nothing borrowed, nothing imitated. This music looks at the world with a new face, a face that shows fresh, innocent features but of a totally original coinage. . . . I would like to touch on one point on which these pieces throw no direct light; namely the boy's sense of color. An attentive study of *Der Schneemann* soon shows that the piece is not only incidentally suited to an orchestra but has been directly rooted in the whole gamut of orchestral colors.[27]

Later, in the 1920s, Bekker (who was subsequently director of the Opera at Kassel) would present Korngold's first opera *Der Ring des Polykrates* but later still would become one of Korngold's most venomous opponents. These remarks, written in 1910, indicate what a stir Korngold's early works must have caused, and the reference to the orchestral character of the music leads us directly to the next phase of Korngold's career: his emergence into the public gaze and the start of his meteoric rise to fame.

That these "private" editions of the early works would not remain private for long was predictable. The noted Budapest music critic Dr. August Beer wrote an article in the journal *Pester Lloyd*[28] proclaiming the arrival of the new *Wunderkind*, and soon similar articles appeared in other major newspapers. Clearly, the child prodigy could not be hidden from the public in Vienna any longer.

Moritz Benedikt, the editor of the *Neue Freie Presse,* insisted that such a phenomenon could not be ignored by Vienna's leading paper. Realizing that it would be improper for Julius Korngold to write about his own son, he commissioned Dr. Ernst Decsey in Graz to write an article.

Events reached a climax when Dr. Ludwig Winter, the director of the Court Theater Administration, who had heard the ballet score played in the Korngold home, promised Baroness von Bienerth, the wife of the prime minister, that she could give a performance of the work in the ministerial palace. The baroness was hosting a soiree at the ministerial palace and wanted a novelty to amuse the distinguished guests. Under the circumstances, Dr. Korngold could hardly refuse permission. At the same time, he was approached by Universal Edition, the renowned Viennese music publishers, for the rights to publish the ballet and the sonata, and the offer was accepted with the strict proviso that the ballet could not be released to any theater without the permission of Dr. Korngold.

This public performance, the very first anywhere of a work by Korngold, took place on 14 April 1910. The thirteen-year-old Korngold was joined by the noted accompanist Richard Pahlen at the piano in a hastily arranged four-hand version of the ballet, with Fritz Brunner playing the violin solos. The dancers of the Imperial Ballet, Wopalensky, von Hamme, and Godlewsky, took the main roles.

Archduchess Blanca was the principal guest, and the cream of the Austrian aristocracy attended. Other guests included the famous pianist Alfred Grünfeld and Dr. Ludwig Winter. The auspicious event was so successful that a second performance was hastily arranged for 26 April to aid the Emperor Franz Josef's Home for Widows and Orphans. Though the price of a ticket was an exhorbitant one hundred crowns, the performance quickly sold out. Julius Korngold recalled:

> Gaily the youngster bowed before the aristocratic society and high-court dignitaries, went unconcernedly from one to the other, then talked just as naturally with the Archduchess Blanca, who was holding court. The father, waiting outside in the dark, anxiously glanced at the festively lit windows of the ministerial palace: an ordeal similar to many others in store for him during his son's future premieres.[29]

In fact, according to the press report in the *Neue Freie Presse*, both "Herr and Frau Dr. Korngold" were received at the soiree by Archduchess Blanca—as one might expect the proud parents to be present at their son's debut. Dr. Korngold, relying on memory, obviously recalled the later, second performance. A little further on in his memoirs he states that he feared that his presence would arouse hostile reactions, aware that his many enemies, both in the world of journalism and among musicians, would use his gifted child as a weapon of recrimination and reprisal. This was to be an understatement.

From this first public performance on, the career of Erich Wolfgang Korngold would be beset by intrigue, scandal, and smear campaigns, brought about indirectly by his father's activities as Vienna's leading critic. Although many considered Korngold extremely fortunate to have the most powerful critic of the time for his father, he could never fully escape the burden of being the son of Julius Korngold. The successes he enjoyed were always clouded by rumor and insinuation. The coffee houses were full of tales about *alte Korngold* or *kleine Korngold*. When his ballet was announced by imperial command for performance at none other than the Vienna Court Opera on the Emperor Franz Josef's name day, 4 October 1910, the drone of gossip rose to a roar.

CHAPTER THREE

Fame and Honors

The premiere of *Der Schneemann* on the hallowed stage of the Vienna Court Opera was the first major public event in young Korngold's life. The relatively short period of formal instruction was now coming to an end. Zemlinsky had been appointed principal conductor of the German Landestheater in Prague (where he would remain until 1927) and had other commitments in Germany. He was due to leave Vienna at the end of the summer. Yet Zemlinsky would always remain faithful to his pupil, regularly presenting his music, including the first orchestral works and three of his operas.

Zemlinsky had a profound influence on Korngold.[1] Just how influential teacher and pupil were each to the other can be judged by remarks made by Korngold in 1921 for the Prague journal *Auftakt*. In an article entitled "The Exemplar of My Youth," Korngold describes their unique relationship with disarming candor and affection:

It was Gustav Mahler who advised my father to engage Alexander von Zemlinsky for my further musical education. I was then eleven years old, and had been studying counterpoint for over two years with Professor Robert Fuchs. Next to this contrapuntal instruction, that of Zemlinsky's came freely and unceremoniously in matters of structure, form, and voice-leading, and especially in piano playing, which up until that time I had neglected. It was stimulating instruction, free of all fuss, in which Zemlinsky seemed to be trying to test, as it were, how much he would demand of me, how far he could eliminate all the usual and normal progression from the simple to the complicated.

My young imagination was deeply impressed by this fascinating teacher with fabulous musicianship, who radiated unconditional authority with the originality of his opinions and convictions and expressed himself with gentle irony in instruction and conversation. I was completely devoted to him from the beginning.

When I began my studies, I had already composed *Der Schneemann* for piano, among other works. Zemlinsky never asked me about my compositions, and I did not show them to him. When I included a composition assignment in my first piano sonata— passacaglia-like variations on a chordal theme which Zemlinsky had given me—I did so at the suggestion of Gustav Mahler (who in 1909 had asked me to play the first two movements of the sonata and the variations for him.)

On the other hand, Zemlinsky would show me nothing of what he had in progress, plead as I might. "You're a scoffer," he would say, jokingly. Zemlinsky's rigorous logic in harmony—together with his freedom and daring in chord structure, his search for the distant relationships and connections of sounds, and his own technique of "delayed resolution"—became decisive factors in my entire musical development and my outlook in regard to that which is called "modern," toward which I instinctively leaned from the beginning.

One voice moving naturally and consistently allows freedom for the others—this was Zemlinsky's basic principle; he was particularly emphatic about the logical structure of bass lines—that they should lead and give direction. Thus I owe everything to Zemlinsky in matters of modern voice-leading and harmony, especially the avoidance of anything arbitrary.

For Zemlinsky himself, who at the time (as I later recognized) was going through a kind of crisis of artistic self-assertion against the new and seductive radical theories of his brother-in-law, Arnold Schoenberg (whom he respected), it was fundamentally impossible to abandon or suppress his powerful sense of tonality. A chord "pulled him" as he liked to say, logically from one tonality to its precisely defined successor.

At that time, in 1910, he was working on *Kleider machen Leute* (Clothes Make the Man), a spirited, greatly under-valued opera of enchantingly original harmony and melody, which already showed a predilection for the Schoenberg fourths, as well as recent French elements. I felt at once a deep fondness for this work as soon as I studied the score.

I could not have been more overjoyed when I heard recently from Zemlinsky that he intends to revise the opera to improve its stage-worthiness. I am convinced that this work—which in its inventiveness, originality, and subtle, ingenious technique stands far above what is presently being produced—can look forward to the greatest success.

After about a year and a half, Zemlinsky began to instruct me in orchestration. He spent only a short time on a general introduction to the nature and character of the instruments, and made me plunge "in at the deep end," as it were, in that he assigned to me the instrumentation of Schubert lieder and movements from Beethoven piano sonatas. By coincidence, my *Schneemann* had been given, contrary to the publishing agreement, by the publisher (Universal Edition) to the Vienna Court Opera for a performance on October 4th, 1910 (the Emperor's name day) because of a remark made by the old Kaiser that he wished to hear it.[2] At the wish of Universal Edition, Zemlinsky undertook the orchestration, which he had already partly accomplished during our lessons, so I now had a fine opportunity to watch him at work. An orchestration of my *Sieben Märchenbilder* (Seven Fairy-Tale Pictures) composed originally for piano, marked the end of my instruction in orchestration,[3] for Zemlinsky left Vienna at the end of summer 1910 to follow a call to Prague, where he was to be so influential on the city's musical life. Thus, barely 13 years old, I lost my honored and beloved teacher all too early.

How often have I lamented, and lament it still today, that Zemlinsky, through his departure for Prague, was snatched from me after such a short term of study. I had lost a most idealistic teacher, a most fascinating musical "stimulator," the model and inspiration of my youth. Vienna, too, had lost one of its greatest and most powerful musicians.

Those of ill will have attempted to spoil my relationship with Zemlinsky; but despite experiences of such kind, I remain unshake-able in my grateful veneration of Zemlinsky—teacher, conductor, and creative genius.[4]

In this article Korngold provides the clues to the dominant influences that helped make him a fully rounded composer. His description of Zemlinsky's theories of harmonic relation reflect Korngold's own markedly personal harmonic profile. The sense of tonality and key relationships is never com-pletely absent from Korngold's music, no matter how exotic his harmonic pallette became or how ambiguous the chordal progressions. Even in his fourth opera, *Das Wunder der Heliane*—the final frontier of tonality as far as Korngold is concerned—this tonal certainty is ever present, acting as a guide for the ear no matter how convoluted the language becomes.

Korngold's reference to Zemlinksy, "one voice moving naturally and consistently allows freedom for the others," that is, a single melodic voice leading a complex harmony, aptly describes Korngolc's own procedures. Likewise, Korngold was extremely fond of "delayed resolution," which he also seems to have inherited from his teacher. Numerous examples spring to mind: the final chord of the song "Mond so gehst Du wieder auf" (Opus 14), and the questioning, altered ninth chord that dominates the opera *Violanta* (Opus 8), to name but two.

Korngold's mention of Zemlinsky's opera *Kleider machen Leute* is significant. The rising fourths that characterize the musical structure of this work undoubtedly influenced Korngold, who also employed rising fourths in his thematic writing. The reference to recent French elements in this opera undoubtedly alludes to Paul Dukas, in particular his opera *Ariane et Barbe-Bleue*, which remained a great favorite of Korngold's throughout his life and which he repeatedly held to be of decisive importance in his development.

From all these observations, we can appreciate the impact that Zemlinsky had. Sadly, his own fate was not to match that of his pupil, who in terms of success was to eclipse him entirely. Though esteemed by Mahler, Schoenberg (who made the prophetic statement "Zemlinsky can wait"), Berg, and even Stravinsky (who, after hearing him conduct *The Marriage of Figaro,* said it was one of the most satisfying experiences of his life), Zemlinsky suffered years of obscurity and ended his days in poverty in New York in 1942. Like Korngold and the other members of the Vienna *Jugendstil,* Zemlinsky became a victim of the tremendous upheaval resulting from the artistic revolution of the early twentieth century that rendered his style, even the musical language he used, obsolete.

Zemlinsky left Prague in 1927 to join Fritz Zweig and Otto Klemperer as conductor at the Berlin Kroll Oper. Political events forced him to return to Vienna in 1933 and then to flee Vienna for America in 1938. Korngold dedicated his Piano Sonata No. 2 in E Major to him, and always expressed his debt of gratitude in the most glowing terms.

In the second year under his guidance, young Korngold worked diligently on counterpoint, orchestration, and reharmonizing the music of Bach and Schumann, while also completing his own Piano Trio in D Major, the first work he felt good enough to be given an opus number. He had begun composing it in December 1909 and completed it just before his thirteenth birthday in May 1910.

This was the last Korngold composition to be published by Universal Edition. The relationship between his father and the historic publishing house had become strained. Dr. Korngold claimed a breach of contract on the part of Universal Edition in allowing *Der Schneemann* to be offered to the Vienna Court Opera. Also underlying Dr. Korngold's displeasure was his view that Universal Edition represented the radical branch of modern music. He was grateful, therefore, when Ludwig Strecker, the son of the senior partner of B. Schott's Söhne, the music publishers in Mainz, offered him an attractive contract to publish all of his son's works from then on. It was to prove a happy association, and Schott remained Erich Korngold's principal publisher for the rest of his life. The Strecker family became close personal friends for over forty years. In 1959, Strecker wrote a memoir for Luzi Korngold's biography of her husband, which amusingly relates how this contract was concluded:

> It must have been 1910 that I first read of the phenomenon of Erich Wolfgang Korngold in the press. At that point I had been active in my father's publishing house for a year. . . . here there appeared to me my first opportunity to gather laurels for Schott. It began with a correspondence with Korngold's father and an agreement to meet and, if warranted, to negotiate [a contract] on the occasion of a public performance in Berlin. . . . The performance was a matinee "audition" during which Erich was to play not only his Trio but also movements of the new E Major Piano Sonata and some excerpts from the *Märchenbilder*. . . . The concert was public—in Bechstein Hall— but without admission tickets. It was primarily intended for the press. About 150 people attended.
>
> It was a great moment for me, the young publisher, to make a decision here in the presence of the entire professional community and my far more experienced colleagues, and I felt many an observant eye upon me. Young Erich went to the piano, a boy, not only in years but in appearance and demeanor. As soon as his hands touched the keys, however, he could not be distinguished from an adult virtuoso in any way. Becoming one with the instrument, he performed miracles. Even then, he played the piano as I have never heard it again by anyone else, as if he were an orchestra, as if he had twenty fingers.
>
> First and foremost, he and his performance created such a singular impression that the compositions were easily appraised. . . . under ordinary conditions, a decision [to negotiate a contract] would have been no problem at all. The conditions were, however, decidedly unusual.
>
> The entire effort implicit in the presentation, the heated atmosphere created by the paternal impresario, the general expectation that we were apparently dealing in high stakes, awoke the feeling in me that I was on the verge of courting an Indian princess and had to tender a whole train of elephants laden with gifts for that purpose. . . .
>
> Whatever the state of things, I did not permit myself to be either encouraged or frightened away and offered my services to Father

Korngold for the purpose of negotiations. He imparted his thoughts to me, or rather, his demands, formulated quite obviously long before.

The demand was for ten thousand Marks[5] as an advance tribute for the piano sonata and the *Märchenbilder*. This maneuver characterizes better than anything else the expectations that the father had for his son's future worth and the acknowledgment of which [expectation] he demanded of the future publisher. The price was indeed unheard of and—calculatedly—could not be justified in terms of these compositions. I considered it, however, to return to the above metaphor, as the bridal gift for the intended marriage.

In this sense I successfully represented these demands at home to my alarmed father and colleagues. On this basis came the consummation of a contract that bears the signature of the father as representative of his son, who was still a minor. The publisher never regretted the marriage begun by this contract and—if I may surmise—neither did Erich. In any case, soon after, personal bonds developed out of the business relationship, bonds which in time also encompassed family members on both sides. . . . One can truly characterize our relationship as a lifelong friendship. The boy Erich, whose dearest wish we fulfilled for Christmas 1911 with an electric train, grew under our eyes into a youth and celebrated artist. . . .

As the last survivor of both of our generations, I preserve my memories of that dear, wonderful human being, Erich, to whom my family and I were bound by a friendship that endured through all vicissitudes. How we laughed, hoped, and planned together, how much beauty created by him went out into the world, how much did a cruel destiny hinder or destroy! With how much dignity he took it all as it came! And with what modesty toward himself he could revere the greatness of others. Thus he will live on for us, unforgotten as a human being and as an artist.[6]

After lessons with Zemlinsky ceased, Korngold continued to consult noted pedagogues in Vienna on an informal basis up until his fifteenth year. These discussions were not typical of master and pupil but were more the deliberations of equal minds. How, then, did Korngold rapidly become such a master of orchestration, considering the brevity of his instruction? His intuitive grasp was such that six months after the premiere of *Der Schneemann*, he was able to try his hand at orchestration of his Opus 4, the *Schauspiel Ouvertüre*, without help. Rumors that Zemlinsky had actually composed *Der Schneemann* were now replaced by rumors that he was the real orchestrator, if not the composer, of *Schauspiel Ouvertüre*. Nonetheless, when Zemlinsky scheduled the work in Prague, his first question when its composer arrived at the rehearsal was: "Now tell me Erich, did you really do it all by yourself?" As Korngold remarked later, this acknowledgment was an honor for the pupil, but an even greater honor for his teacher.

In the following year Korngold had some informal lessons from Hermann Grädener in choral composition. Professor Grädener succeeded Anton Bruckner as lecturer in harmony and counterpoint at Vienna University, and he also composed music, although nothing by him has lived on in the repertory.[7] From 1911 to 1912, Erich Korngold's composition notebooks contain a great many fugues and psalm-settings for choir and orchestra, including a highly effective Fugue for String Quartet dated Friday 20 December 1912, Vienna.

Shortly after these lessons with Grädener began, Zemlinsky, with his customary insight, sent Korngold a postcard from Prague: "I hear that you are studying with Grädener now. Is he making any progress?"

Apart from these informal sessions with Grädener, Korngold had discussions with four other eminent musicians during the course of 1912. He discussed musical analysis with the composer Karl Weigl, who incidentally was also a pupil of Zemlinsky; he had been the *répétiteur* at the Vienna Opera and was a prolific composer of Lieder, a Piano Concerto in E-flat Major for the Left Hand, and other works. (He also settled in America in 1938.) With consultations with the conductor and pupil of Bruckner, Ferdinand Löwe, and composer/conductor Oskar Nedbal, the boy filled out his knowledge of repertoire and musical form—in fact, the whole gamut of musically related subjects. Finally, he had further seminars on instrumentation with the conductor Franz Schalk.

By his sixteenth birthday, his musical education came to an end. These later informal lessons were not overly important, however. Korngold was his own master when Zemlinsky left him in September 1910, and a glance at his work from that year shows him to be in total command of a very great talent.

During the busy summer of 1910, young Korngold's fame spread before him as he and his father traveled to the Salzburg Festival. The patron of the music festival, the Archduke Eugen, had heard of the charity performance of *Der Schneemann* and asked to meet "the little wonder." A recital was arranged in the room of the aged virtuoso Theodor Leschetizky at the Hotel Österreichischer Hof on 3 August. Several notable foreign musicians were also staying at the hotel and naturally asked permission to attend; among the dozen illustrious and discerning people crowded into the room were Paul Dukas, Jules Écorcheville (secretary of the Société Française des Amis de la Musique), and the critic and biographer of Jules Massenet, Louis Schneider. A cushion had to be placed on the piano stool, which was too low for the little composer. His recital included the Passacaglia from the Piano Sonata No. 1 in D Minor, parts of *Der Schneemann*, his *Don Quixote: Six Characteristic Pieces*, and even a movement from the newly completed Piano Trio in D Major. His bravura performance and his music aroused astonishment, incredulity, and great enthusiasm.

Dukas remarked on the subtle usage of the whole tone scale in the music. Écorcheville asked permission to publish the *Don Quixote* pieces in his magazine as a demonstration of how modern harmonic thinking and inventiveness had penetrated the musical imagination of a child. He later had to be dissuaded from mounting *Der Schneemann* as a silhouette show in Paris, on the grounds that a work conceived entirely in white could hardly be transformed into something completely black.

The following day, the Korngolds attended a festival matinee at the University of Salzburg. The Archduke Eugen entered with his retinue and walked down the center aisle amid the audience, which had respectfully risen. He stopped when he reached the Korngolds and thanked them for the piano score of *Der Schneemann,* which he had requested, promising to study it diligently. The interruption of the Archduke's procession caused a considerable stir and was duly reported. Later, Erich dedicated his *Sieben Märchenbilder* for piano, Opus 3, to the Archduke in gratitude for his patronage.

From Salzburg, the Korngolds proceeded to Munich to attend the premiere of Mahler's Symphony No. 8 in E-flat, the "Symphony of a Thousand," which was scheduled for 12 September and also to attend another festival of French music dedicated to further rapprochement between the two nations. Mahler was to conduct the work, and he invited Erich and his father to rehearsals. Julius Korngold recalled:

> We followed the rehearsals of the colossal symphony with great suspense. Erich was strangely excited. In the semi-darkness of the huge exhibition hall, way up on the podium, thickly crowded with singers and instrumentalists, he saw Mahler swing his magic wand. Erich felt timid veneration for him. Mahler's personality was deeply imprinted on his mind. (He had once been taken to a *Figaro* rehearsal directed by Mahler and could remember every detail for decades afterwards.) Here, as we watched, the slight man with the gestures of a ghost out of E. T. A. Hoffmann looked even more ghost-like when he raised his baton to conjure the spirits. He seemed to draw odd signs in the air, to bless and to execrate, and to toss flowers and firebrands into the auditorium. Significantly, whenever he was asked in future what he wanted to become, Erich invariably replied "Director Mahler."[8]

The premiere of Mahler's monumental Symphony No. 8 in the Neue Musikfesthalle, a concert hall built especially to coincide with this first performance, has passed into legend. It attracted the leaders of European cultural life and many great musicians, among them Arnold Schoenberg, Anton Webern, Alfred Casella, Richard Strauss, Bruno Walter, Arnold Rosé, Otto Klemperer, Oskar Fried, and Leopold Stokowski. The writers Stefan Zweig and Thomas Mann were also present, as was Siegfried

Wagner, the son of Richard Wagner. To complete the experience, young Korngold made the acquaintance of the rising genius of the theater, Max Reinhardt, who would later have a profound effect on his life and career.

A few days later, the festival of French music began, and Munich was invaded by a host of famous French musicians, among them Saint-Saëns, Widor, D'Indy, and Leon Sachs. Sachs, a member of the festival committee, insisted that the prodigy from Vienna give a performance as part of the program. This took place at a glittering soiree held at the old Hotel Regina before the many distinguished guests, including Prince Ludwig of Bavaria. As the boy exuberantly performed his Piano Sonata No. 2 in E Major, storming across the keyboard in his chord-studded and inimitable style, the seventy-five-year-old Saint Saëns advanced toward the piano. He mumbled some words of praise, staring in disbelief at the young performer, almost as if he could scarcely believe such music could have been written by him. Then he took the boy's hand and held it for a long time.[9]

Erich Korngold was the object of much interest and discussion among the distinguished gathering in Munich. The press interviewed him, some benevolently and some with barely concealed hostility. Not surprisingly, his reputation had grown apace by the time he returned to Vienna for the October 1910 premiere of *Der Schneemann*. He could hardly have predicted that his success would be tempered by envy and gossip, or the machinations that lay ahead.

When Gustav Mahler resigned from the Vienna Opera in March 1907, he was succeeded by Felix von Weingartner, remembered today as a great interpreter of Beethoven and of Liszt, who had been one of his teachers. Weingartner's tenure at the Vienna Court Opera was a controversial one, for although his conducting was justly renowned, he was criticized for his tendency apparently to ignore whatever happened on stage and concentrate entirely on the orchestra. He had vast experience in opera, however, and conducted many notable performances in Hamburg, Berlin, and Munich. Like many conductors of the period, he was a prolific composer (seven operas, six symphonies, symphonic poems, and much chamber music) and was also a highly respected writer of treatises on conducting and related subjects. His five marriages and numerous affairs (especially with the rising star of the Vienna opera of that time, Lucille Marcel, later his wife) ensured that he was the source of continuous gossip. By far the biggest thorn in his side was Julius Korngold, who was so loyal to Mahler's memory that his antipathy toward his successor, whose achievements paled by comparison, was inevitable. Even the anti-Mahler faction led by critic Robert Hirschfeld, a sworn enemy of Korngold's, waned in their support of Weingartner as a result of Dr. Korngold's criticism. It was all the more surprising then, that Weingartner should insist on premiering the new ballet by Korngold's son.

How *Der Schneemann* came to be staged in such prestigious surroundings can be traced back to the first performances at the ministerial palace, where one of the guests had been Prince Montenuovo (the Court

Chamberlain from 1909 to 1917, one of the most senior and influential members of the Austrian court), whose many responsibilities included the administration of the Vienna Court Opera. Impressed, he had immediately brought the work to the attention of the Emperor Franz Josef. Each year it was customary to present a novelty for the Emperor's name day (4 October), and *Der Schneemann* seemed the ideal choice. Almost at once, Alfred Hertzka, the director of Universal Edition, offered it to Weingartner, who accepted it immediately.

The Vienna premiere of *Der Schneemann*, 4 October 1910. From left: the ballerina Louise Wopalensky (Columbine) with Karl Godlewsky (Pierrot), who also designed and choreographed the production (Korngold estate).

All of this happened without the slightest acknowledgment of the composer's father, who had, after all, stipulated that no performances should take place without his permission. Dr. Korngold was horrified. First, the performance was to take place in Vienna, which was the very center of his activities as a critic. Second, the work was being presented by a man who would clearly have every reason to jeopardize it. Third, his young son's first public performance would take place under the prejudicial scrutiny of Dr. Korngold's many adversaries in the press and in artistic circles. Finally, that it was almost an imperial command performance meant that it would have to go ahead, even though Dr. Korngold still attempted to change Weingartner's mind.

Weingartner genuinely admired young Korngold's gifts but, more importantly, did not want the Vienna Court Opera to miss the opportunity to present the first staging of what undoubtedly would be a much discussed work. He must have been mindful, too, of the gossip that would surround his decision. Indeed, the coffee houses resounded with the question: Why had Weingartner agreed to present the work?

Looking back, it is easy to see why. If the evening were a fiasco, it would be a wonderful reprisal against Julius Korngold. If, in the more likely event, it went well (and Weingartner had seen the score), it would be a feather in the director's cap and his enemy would have to come crawling in gratitude—or so he supposed. The ballet was a tremendous success, but its success did not affect Julius Korngold's peppery reviews of Weingartner's subsequent productions, much to the conductor's dismay.

A prerequisite of the work's performance at the Vienna Court Opera was that it be orchestrated. Preternaturally talented though young Korngold was, he had only just commenced his orchestral studies with Zemlinsky, so he was not yet fully up to the task (though he was able to complete his first orchestral work, the *Schauspiel Ouvertüre,* Opus 4, just six months later). Initially, Alfred Hertzka suggested Franz Schreker for the task. Schreker was a respected composer and teacher who had founded the Philharmonic Chorus. Julius Korngold did not care for his music, however, and had expressed his disdain on numerous occasions in his reviews, so the task was assigned to Zemlinsky, who could orchestrate the score with the boy at his side. Young Korngold attended the rehearsals and, despite his extreme youth, more or less took over. He changed much of the stage action and took over the piano part from the *répétiteur,* who found it too difficult. It must have been quite a scene with the already chubby twelve-year-old Korngold seated at the piano, beating time while accompanying the dancers and gradually bringing the whole performance together as he would do on so many occasions in future productions of his works.

Although *Der Schneemann* was the highlight of the program, the evening was long. The ballet was preceded by Max Kalbeck's German translation of Wolf-Ferrari's one-act opera *Susanna's Secret* with Marie Gutheil-Schoder in the title role. The evening concluded with Richard Goldberger's now-forgotten ballet *Mondweibchen,* but it was *Der Schneemann* that stole the honors. Conducted by Franz Schalk, with Arnold Rosé (the leader of the Vienna Philharmonic and the famous Rosé Quartet, and brother-in-law of Gustav Mahler) playing the violin solos and Godlewsky and Wopalenska again dancing the principal roles, it charmed and enchanted the distinguished audience. They gave the work and its composer a rousing ovation. Dr. Rudolf Stefan Hoffmann, who later wrote the first biography of Korngold, declared:

> I first wrote about this score in the *Vienna Monday Review* and there is nothing to add to my former judgment . . . the delightful Intermezzo which has been added can be compared with the very best ballet

music . . . after a brilliant performance which brought the house down for the young arch-musician as Richard Strauss called him, I would like to express the wish that this blessed fruit be allowed to ripen in peace.[10]

The thirteen-year-old Korngold's letter of thanks to Johann Strauss's widow Adele for a gift of chocolates that were a "sweet surprise"; written on the day of the *Schneemann* premiere, for which Frau Strauss presumably sent them as a congratulatory gift.

Clearly, the editors of the *Neue Freie Presse* could not ignore the premiere, but equally clearly they could not assign the review to the composer's father. So they called on another distinguished critic, Richard Specht, to cover the event.[11] He wrote of *Der Schneeman*:

[This work] . . . can be compared with every kind of genre of pantomime, and yet its delicate grace, surprising rhythmic charm, and bold assurance in creating a character in a laconic couple of bars is truly amazing and even rather frightening when one considers the tender age of its creator. The ovation grew to noisy proportions when, after numerous curtain calls from the principal, the young composer of the little work appeared on the stage. He took his bow before the great curtain as clumsily as a little bear, and the public clamored to see him return again and again. It must be the first time since the beginning of opera that such a young composer was able to acknowledge the applause for his work, having had it performed in such a place as this.[12]

After the performance that night, it was said that the little boy seemed more impressed with the big white snowman on the stage than with the tremendous success of his work. His typical child-like behavior gives an indication of how unaffected by success and fame Korngold was at this age, and how normal he remained as a child. He remained so as a man, and retained a child-like quality even in maturity.

Caricature from the time of *Der Schneemann*, 1910, showing a large statue of Korngold as the Snowman that dwarfs the Vienna Opera House (Korngold estate).

Der Komponist des „Schneemann" erhält ein Standbild vor dem Hofoperntheater.

The aftermath of this spectacular success was predictable and justified Julius Korngold's forebodings. He had missed the performance, remaining at home playing Beethoven sonatas, but he knew that his enemies would use the event, whether it was a success or a failure, as a weapon. Immediately, gossip began to spread that just as Zemlinsky had orchestrated *Der Schneemann*, he must indeed be the real composer. It was even suggested that Julius Korngold himself was the real composer, a claim that he indignantly dismissed with the repost: "If I had such creative talents as a composer, I would not have devoted my life to being a mere critic."

Max Graf wrote a typically scurrilous article that appeared in both the Berlin and Vienna papers in which he "revealed" that the elder Korngold had forced Weingartner to stage the ballet. Dr. Korngold protested in a circular letter to all Vienna papers, but the letter was ignored. Shortly after the premiere of *Der Schneemann*, the smear campaign began in earnest.

CHAPTER FOUR

The Prodigy Goes on Tour

*F*ollowing on the extraordinary acclaim for the pantomime *Der Scheemann*, Korngold's Piano Trio in D Major, Opus 1 received its world premiere exactly one month later, on 4 November in Munich, safely removed from Vienna. The performers were Heinrich Schwartz and his trio, and the reviews were, as usual, incredulous.

Only a week later, Korngold's music reached the United States for the first time. The Margulies Trio performed the work in New York on 11 November,[1] before the work was performed in Vienna. The American critics were as astonished as their German colleagues. W. J. Henderson, writing in *The New York Sun*, commented:

> Maybe his papa is trying to bring him up to be a real modern composer, but if he is not, then something ought to be done. If we had a little boy of twelve who preferred writing this sort of music to hearing a good folk tune or going out and playing in the park, we should consult a specialist![2]

This assured composition soon begged for attention in Austria's capital. The respected musical magazine *Der Merker*, which had arranged a celebrity concert in Vienna for its subscribers, immediately made plans to include the Piano Trio in D Major on the program. Although the editors, Richard

Specht and Richard Batka, had intended the concert to be a private one, a great deal of publicity was naturally focused on the event because Bruno Walter, Friedrich Buxbaum, and Arnold Rosé were to perform.

These three great musicians were to remain Korngold's devoted friends and admirers, and they frequently performed his subsequent works. Previous to this performance, Bruno Walter had known of the boy's precocious gifts, not only through Gustav Mahler but also from having heard the child improvising for hours at a time from his flat above the Korngold family when they first moved to Vienna. Buxbaum, a lively, genial man and a brilliant cellist, became an especially close personal friend.[3] Arnold Rosé, who also knew of Korngold through Mahler, eventually gave possibly more Korngold premieres than any other musician.

The concert was to take place on 11 December 1910, and young Korngold, together with his father and mother, was invited to the rehearsal. A much-told anecdote from this occasion sums up the relationship of the child to his domineering parents. Korngold sat down with his parents on either side of him. As soon as Bruno Walter began to play, Julius muttered, "Too fast," whereas his wife muttered, "Too slow." Indignantly, Julius Korngold repeated, "I say it is too fast," while his wife countered with, "No, Julius it is too slow." Their little son, who was, after all, the composer of the piece and presently sat squashed between them, interrupted, "I think the tempo is just right," whereupon both parents turned on him and shouted in unison, "*You* shut up!" Whatever the disputes about the tempi, the performance was a great success.[4]

The Piano Trio in D Major was a major advance in Korngold's musical development. Even today it is a remarkable work. In writing a piano trio he was following in the tradition of his great forebears—Haydn, Beethoven, Schubert, Mendelssohn, and Brahms. He could hardly have chosen a more difficult chamber grouping for a first attempt, yet he accomplished an effective piece with ease. Despite its opulent harmony and highly modernistic rhythms, its mood clearly emanates from the world of Brahms and the Vienna of the late nineteenth century. Its lyrical themes have a warm autumnal glow, and it breathes with life effortlessly and spontaneously. The ambitious four-movement scheme is given added unity by the ingenious cyclical cross-referencing between the movements, a trait of many future works.

It opens with a bold, commanding theme that dominates the expansive sonata structure of the first movement. This theme, so confident and expressive, reveals Korngold as more than merely a clever child. In the very first bars of his Opus 1 is the unique voice of the mature composer. The Scherzo is almost improvisatory; its playfulness and angular contours are typical of his highly personal approach to the scherzo form. A beguiling trio (in a slow 2/4 in F) is based on a beautiful phrase characterized by rising and falling sevenths, which Korngold would later reuse in his first opera, *Der Ring des Polykrates*, composed at the age of sixteen.

BÖSENDORFER-SAAL.

Sonntag, den 11. Dezember 1910, abends ¹/₂8 Uhr:

II. Konzert der Zeitschrift

„DER MERKER"

Ausführende:

Theo Drill-Orridge, Mitglied der Volksoper, Emmy Heim, Konzertsängerin, Prof. Friedrich Buxbaum, (Cello), Paul Graener, Robert Konta, Prof. Arnold Rosé, k. k. Kammervirtuose, Bruno Walter, k. k. Hofopernkapellmeister, Kapellmeister Alexander von Zemlinsky und Dr. Karl Weigl.

PROGRAMM:

1. Paul Graener	Regenlied.
	Der toten Mutter.
	Vom jüngsten Tage.
Robert Konta	Drei Gesänge nach Dichtungen von Friedrich Nietzsche.
	Der Wanderer.
	Venedig.
	Vereinsamt.
	Die Monduhr. (Reinick.) **Emmy Heim.**
	Am Klavier: **Die Komponisten.**
2. Alexander von Zemlinsky . . .	Vier Lieder nach Dichtungen von Maurice Maeterlinck.(Manuskript, Uraufführung.)
	Theo Drill-Orridge.
	Am Klavier: **Der Komponist.**
3. Erich Wolfgang Korngold . . .	Trio D-dur für Klavier, Violine und Cello.
	(Erste Aufführung in Wien.)
	Allegro non troppo con espressione.
	Scherzo.
	Larghetto.
	Finale.
	Bruno Walter, Arnold Rosé und . **Friedrich Buxbaum.**
4. Alma Maria Mahler	Die stille Stadt.
	In meines Vaters Garten.
	Laue Sommernacht.
	Bei dir ist es traut.
	(Manuskript, Uraufführung.)
	Theo Drill-Orridge.
	Am Klavier: **Alexander von Zemlinsky.**
5. Karl Weigl	Bilder und Geschichten. (Uraufführung.)
	Es war einmal.
	Schneewittchen.
	Storch, Storch, Steiner.
	Schlaf, Kindlein, schlaf.
	Dornröschens Grab.
	Im Mondenschein.
	Am Klavier: **Dr. Karl Weigl.**

Preis 20 Heller.

Concert bill for the first Vienna performance of the Piano Trio in D Major, Opus 1, in 1910, organized by the magazine *Der Merker*. The twelve-year-old Korngold was in good company.

A particularly fine slow movement begins with the cello alone, sounding a deeply felt melody that appears to be atonal until the piano joins it. There are some wonderful harmonic flights of fancy in this movement. Unity is everything, as the joyous last movement begins with this same cello theme, now transformed into rapid quarter-notes. A charming idea in triplets gives way to a rondo of two themes: the first has rapidly changing time signatures, the second is *amabile e giocoso* in Brahmsian sixths, and is linked with the opening theme of the work.

Korngold turns this rondo into a roundelay wherein all the themes of the preceding movements are made to dance a waltz. It is finely crafted with many witty and original touches; one can scarcely believe that a boy in short trousers actually composed it. The coda, in which the principal themes of the previous three movements are ingeniously subsumed in the appoggiatura of the final chords, is a master stroke. The most important feature of this early work is its supreme confidence, revealing how completely formed the musical personality was, even to the extent that certain thematic ideas turn up, transformed, in the later operas and orchestral works. This is not clever juvenilia, demonstrating skill and technique, but music of real genius, mature and inspired. It is no wonder, then, that when the Piano Trio in D Major reached London in February 1911, the critic of the *Daily News* headed his review with the famous words "Hats Off! A Genius!" recalling Schumann's salute to Chopin. Today, this piano trio has become enormously popular once again, with no fewer than five recordings and many performances.

Like many composers, Korngold never wasted a good idea, and he liked to use his musical ideas in a number of works. Haydn was the foremost practitioner of this, although Korngold's boyhood idol, Gustav Mahler, was perhaps Korngold's most relevant and influential model. The way Korngold's music assumes the character of a sort of personal currency is especially unusual. Themes and harmonic progressions, which appear unexpectedly in works almost thirty years apart, seem to circulate in his musical thinking in a wholly unconscious way and give his music an individuality, especially harmonically, that is immediately recognizable for anyone acquainted with his work.

The success of the Piano Trio in D Major aroused the envy of Julius Korngold's enemies, who seized on the fact that the premiere concert was in aid of a prominent journal. The subsequent reviews prompted Dr. Korngold to resign from the Association of Vienna Music Critics, which he had joined on the proviso that personal attacks among colleagues would cease. Robert Hirschfeld then arranged a "trial" *in absentia* during a meeting of the association. Eight of the twenty-six members of the association who attended sent a letter accusing Julius Korngold of collaborating with editor Richard Specht of *Der Merker* and using his influence to procure performances for his son. This letter, on official notepaper and signed by eight leading critics, was a very weighty document intended to arouse Julius Korngold's anger and provoke a public argument. According to his memoirs, however, he was advised not to open it by a colleague who had left the meeting in disgust. Instead, he filed it away unopened for future reference. Apparently, Max Graf photographed the letter, a copy of which was in the files of the association, and distributed it for years afterwards, especially to anyone who received a caustic review from "old Korngold," even though the letter was formally revoked several months later by a full meeting of the Association.

A lawsuit resulted from an unfortunate scene that followed on the evening of the meeting revoking this letter. Dr. Korngold and his wife, who had been attending a concert, had news of the outcome of the meeting brought to them by a friend. As they walked home, Max Graf walked past them and Frau Korngold, noted for her volatile temper, hurled insults at him. Graf took the Korngolds to court as a result, and the Korngolds filed counter charges. Graf appealed to Moritz Benedikt to intervene, and after gentle persuasion to both sides, an out-of-court settlement was reached. Nonetheless, the ensuing publicity and gossip that young Korngold's career was furthered by his father's influence and under-handed methods rather than by his own considerable talent were far more harmful than any libel suit, and were the source of much future gossip and several more unsavory legal wrangles.

Caricature by Rudolf Herrmann, circa 1910, depicting the prodigy as the musical "messiah" in the "temple" of the critics. Korngold's father is swinging the censer at front, while Richard Specht is gesticulating front left.

That musicians often testified that young Korngold's individual musical merits stood on their own seemed to matter little. His greatest handicap was having the most influential critic of the period as a father. Erich bore the brunt of every public row. Looking back at these hysterical "dramas," which would be inconceivable today, the truth is easy to discern: Julius Korngold overstepped the mark in his professional and personal attitude to those he perceived as enemies of his son's music. Because of this failing, he became a constant thorn in Erich Wolfgang's side throughout his early career. By far the most perceptive indictment came not from a rival critic but from one of the most respected teachers and pianists of the time, Richard Robert, who wrote in the *Wiener Sonn- und Montags Zeitung*:

> Dr. Julius Korngold is the music critic of a prominent newspaper and as such has the greatest influence. Dr. Korngold, however, is not only a critic but also the father of a young composer. And that is his misfortune: he judges all events of the musical life *only* from that view point. He does not ask: "How does this or that artist conduct, compose, play, or sing?" but rather, "What is his or her attitude to Erich Wolfgang?" Composers, interpreters, even modern music literature are being judged from that point of view. . . . Dr. Korngold divides the whole world of artists into two camps: those who perform Erich Wolfgang and critics who unreservedly praise his works—and those who do not.
>
> I respect Dr. Korngold's factual knowledge, his conscientious preparation, his undeniable critical faculty—but since his son entered public life, he has lost all sense of responsibility, even common sense. And this vitiates all his advantages. An inner shift of roles has occurred: the critic has become weaker, the father stronger. This is quite a touching trait: the father likes only those who like his son.
>
> There remains the concrete question as to whether the whole musical world is obliged to regulate its relationship to art in accordance with the views of Dr. Korngold. Of course, there are still artists who are not so afraid and so obstinate . . . but they have to pay the price: the boycott is their fate.
>
> How many musicians have fallen by the wayside, since Erich Wolfgang's star has been in the ascendant? As for me, I do not deserve anything better. True, I have always recognized his extraordinary talent which is so great that not even his father can harm it; but I have never sunk on my knees before him, and that is *lèse majesté*.[5]

Strong words from one of Vienna's most erudite musicians, who had felt the wrath of the critic against several of his pupils. The key phrase is his declaration that Korngold's musical gift was so remarkable that not even his father could harm it. The opposite was also true: neither did Erich's musical gift require his father's "help," as was evidenced by the comprehensive popularity of his compositions far outside the sphere of his father's influence. By 1915, Korngold's music was performed all over the western world, including most European countries, Russia (*Der Schneemann* was performed in Moscow in 1912), England (Sir Henry Wood presented his works regularly), and the United States. Clearly, its reach was not due to the influence of his father.

Korngold with his parents Julius and Josefine Korngold in the garden of his home in Vienna, circa 1911 (Korngold estate).

Also significant was the loyalty of Felix von Weingartner, who despite constant criticism from the elder Korngold, chiefly of his directorship of the Vienna Court Opera, continued to champion the works of Erich Korngold without hesitation. In an article in *The Almanac for the Musical World 1914–1915,* he emphasized that his interest in young Korngold's work was prompted solely by the mastery of the little boy's music, without any persuasion by the father, and maintained that Julius Korngold indeed had tried to prevent him from presenting *Der Schneemann* at the Vienna Court Opera. About the Piano Trio in D Major, he wrote a letter of extravagant praise to Julius Korngold, saying in part:

> This is stupendous. It seems as if Nature has gathered together all the accomplishments of modern musical language for which others have

to struggle step by step and placed them in the cradle of this extraordinary child. There is no bar which does not offer a surprise. . . . What sense of form! How strangely the three instruments go together. I am curious about the tonal effect of certain passages, for instance the ending of the third movement, which must sound full and very beautiful. I keep asking myself; when is the boy going to make a blunder? But though I searched diligently, I could find no blunders. All the passages—even the extravagant ones, and there are many of these—are developed logically. This child is truly a phenomenon.[6]

Weingartner remained steady and impartial in his support, and he conducted Korngold's first orchestral works in 1912 and 1913.

In December 1910, Korngold completed his Piano Sonata Number 2 in E Major, Opus 2, and also his *Sieben Märchenbilder* (Seven Fairy Tale Pictures), Opus 3, seven delightful pieces for piano set to a text by Hans Müller. The Piano Sonata No. 2 shows a tremendous advance over the first and betrays an already blossoming orchestral imagination. Tuneful and beautifully written for piano, the *Sieben Märchenbilder* is a twentieth-century work comparable to Schumann's *Kinderszenen*.

Up until now, Korngold had been a Viennese phenomenon, but by Christmas (and the family's celebration of Julius Korngold's fiftieth birthday), he was receiving invitations from far and wide—like the young Mozart of the 1760s. Little Erich's career as a traveling *Wunderkind* was about to commence. Now that he was a celebrity, it was only natural that invitations would be forthcoming from the great centers of German musical life and those anxious to witness his talent at first hand. Although his father had initially cautiously refused, then had only reluctantly presented him to the public (unlike Leopold Mozart, who had paraded his two prodigious offspring), fearing the detrimental effect of a premature public career, now it seemed sensible to allow his son to take his place in the world of music.

In 1911, this world of music was dominated by Richard Strauss. The master of the symphonic poem had already scandalized and shocked musical society with his operas *Salome* and *Elektra*, and with this latter opera had pushed tonality to its furthermost boundaries. Yet Strauss then withdrew from the radical sound world he had created and, together with librettist Hugo von Hofmannsthal, composed what he hoped would be a twentieth-century *Marriage of Figaro*. This opera was *Der Rosenkavalier*.

As the New Year began, all of Austria was talking about Strauss's new creation. Julius Korngold was among the prominent figures who assembled in Dresden in January for the world premiere. His less than enthusiastic review of the work in the *Neue Freie Presse* probably stemmed from his rigorous loyalty to the other Strauss, Johann II, the "Waltz King," whom, he assumed, Richard Strauss was trying to eclipse.

This was not the first time that Dr. Korngold had criticized Richard Strauss's works. That Strauss would continue to advocate young Korngold's music was all the more surprising then, especially when later, during Strauss's tenure as director of the Vienna State Opera in the 1920s, the pithy remarks of the critic became openly hostile. For now, however, relations remained more or less cordial, probably because of a clever tactical maneuver by Dr. Korngold in 1909.

Although he wrote a critical review of *Elektra*, which had not met with his approval because of its savage harmonic language, he had nonetheless supported its continued place in the repertoire and had publicly campaigned for the work to be brought to Vienna. Such advocacy of a work that he clearly disliked is so out of character for Dr. Korngold that one suspects other motives for appeasing Strauss. Whatever the reasons for this uncharacteristic action, Strauss deeply appreciated the support and said so in a letter:

> You have pleaded for performances of my *Elektra* in Vienna and in such kind fashion that I wish to thank you from the bottom of my heart, also on behalf of Hofmannsthal. Since I know that you personally do not even care for *Elektra*, I was doubly pleased with your equitable objectivity in supporting my interests. The author, even if his work is successful, has no way of enforcing its fair treatment on the part of the directors.[7]

For the moment, then, Strauss remained a benevolent, amicable friend.

Young Erich, meanwhile, continued to make progress by leaps and bounds, and in 1911, his fourteenth year, he began his first orchestral composition. He chose to devise an overture and deliberately entitled it *Schauspiel Ouvertüre* (Overture to a Play). Over the years, confusion has arisen as to the specific source of inspiration for this work. Some attributed Shakespeare's *The Tempest*, possibly because Korngold later composed a setting of Heine's poem *Der Sturm* for male chorus and orchestra in December 1913 (which, for reasons unknown, was neither published nor performed). Later on, Shakespeare's *A Winter's Tale*[8] was said to be the inspiration for the *Schauspiel Ouvertüre*, but probably the overture had no clear antecedent (at least none that was revealed by the composer), even though the young Korngold already had a passion for Shakespeare's works, which would last his lifetime.

He began to compose the music in the spring of 1911 and completed the instrumentation (without any preliminary sketch) during the summer holidays at Landro. Meanwhile, he was enjoying a busy, itinerant life as a traveling prodigy.

In March 1911 his father took him to Berlin for a performance of the Piano Trio in D Major, a performance instigated by the conductor of the Royal Opera, Leo Blech, who had heard the work at the Vienna premiere.

Through him, young Erich was introduced to Louise Wolff, the director of the foremost concert agency in Germany at that time, founded by her late husband, who in the 1890s had been von Bülow's agent.

A highly influential woman, Louise Wolff held a celebrated salon. The intellectual cognoscenti of Europe met in her home and attended her lavish dinner parties. At these soirees, musicians were promoted and allowed to perform before what was probably the most discriminating audience of the time. Large, corpulent, and blessed with a wicked sense of humor, she resembled Lillian Bayliss, the founder of Sadlers Wells, in more ways than one, especially in her energetic travels throughout Europe, tirelessly arranging and attending performances.

Acting on Blech's recommendation, Louise Wolff arranged for the Piano Trio in D Major to be played, as in Vienna, by Rosé, Buxbaum, and Bruno Walter on 9 March 1911, and to be preceded by a special matinee for invited guests given by young Korngold himself in a recital of his most significant works to date, which he played from memory. Bruno Walter became indisposed and was unable to perform, however, so Korngold took the piano part in the performance of the Piano Trio. These two concerts were a tremendous success. Many notable celebrities were in the audience, among them Engelbert Humperdinck, Leo Blech, the noted choral conductor Siegfried Ochs, the musicologist Max Friedländer, the writer Oscar Bie, and, most important of all, the conductor Arthur Nikisch.

Louise Wolff adored Nikisch, indeed the two were soulmates and practically inseparable. The conductor Egon Pollak liked to describe how these two unlikely friends would sit beside each other at dinner, hand in hand, and indulge in the most inconsequential conversation, but enjoying it nonetheless with beaming smiles, each fearful of offending the other. As Pollak remarked drily, "No discussion of music was ever allowed to interrupt the banality."[9]

Nikisch was the foremost conductor of his time. This internationally renowned musician had been deeply impressed by the young Korngold's first works, and he made Julius Korngold promise to dispatch the *Schauspiel Ouvertüre* to him in Leipzig for consideration as soon as it was complete. Nikisch was the deciding factor in the acceptance of the young Korngold by the rest of the critical fraternity in Germany, his father notwithstanding, particularly in Berlin, for although he enjoyed success and notoriety, Korngold had remained a novelty in many people's eyes.

The issue of Korngold's religion is never discussed in either his father's memoirs or his wife's biography. He had already suffered anti-Semitic demonstrations, especially in Graz in February 1911 at a performance of his Piano Trio in D Major—an ominous portent of later events. By all accounts, he was not a religious Jew, nor does it appear that he had a bar mitzvah. Certainly, he did not attend synagogue, and the Korngold household was not kosher. Nonetheless, according to his first biographer, Hoffmann, he regularly suffered from the kind of racial prejudice that afflicted other prominent Jewish artists at the time, especially Mahler. Indeed, it may have been a contributing factor to the critical bias against his works, never admitted by his father but implied.

Unlike Mahler, Korngold's "Jewishness" does not appear to have influenced his artistic or spiritual development as a composer. If anything, he showed a greater preference for Catholic ritual and mysticism. Given his apparently nominal religious feelings, he probably felt especially aggrieved by the racial purge of the 1930s. Interestingly, many of Korngold's most fervent supporters during his early period were also Jews: Bruno Walter, Richard Specht, Zemlinsky, Louise Wolff, Arnold Rosé, Rudolf Kolisch, and of course Mahler. The exception was Richard Strauss.

Korngold was endorsed wholeheartedly by those who really mattered. Humperdinck called him "this wonder-child from fairy land," an apt remark from the foremost composer of fairy-tale operas. Leo Blech studied the scores of Korngold's works assiduously and became a staunch ally (although his enthusiasm cooled later when Blech embraced the music of Schoenberg et alia and waned further while Blech enjoyed the protection of the Nazis as late as 1937, in spite of being Jewish). The great Karl Muck similarly expressed interest in him and became an enthusiastic interpreter, especially of his second orchestral work, the Sinfonietta in B Major, Opus 5.

The summer vacation of 1911 was especially fruitful. Young Erich worked diligently on his overture. He attended the first performance of the orchestral version of his *Sieben Märchenbilder* in a private rehearsal in Karlsbad arranged especially for him on 27 June by the *Kurkapelle* and conducted by Robert Manzer. (Sadly, this version was never published, although the manuscripts survive.) He also played before other distinguished artists, among them Max Reinhardt, who coincidentally was preparing his first production of Offenbach's *La Belle Hélène*.

Reinhardt invited Erich to the rehearsals, where the legendary Maria Jeritza, the star of the production, met the boy-composer for the first time. The extraordinary artistic triumvirate of Korngold, Reinhardt, and Jeritza would collaborate on some remarkable productions over the coming two decades. Eventually, Korngold would devise his own adaptation of *La Belle Hélène* for Reinhardt in the 1930s.

From Karlsbad—at the suggestion of the composer Oskar Nedbal, the viola player of the Bohemian String Quartet, who had settled in Vienna—the Korngolds proceeded on to Prague, then second only to Vienna as a musical capital, and a reunion with Zemlinsky. The National Theater of Prague was staging *Der Schneemann*. Meanwhile, Nedbal, a devoted supporter, announced the Hungarian premiere of the *Schauspiel Ouvertüre* in Budapest in January of the following year. When later he turned to composing operettas, Nedbal would frequently play his ideas to Korngold, who would offer "improvements."

After attending *Der Schneemann*, the Korngolds' next stop was Salzburg, where they encountered Artur Schnabel. Korngold played his

Piano Sonata in E Major for the great virtuoso, who decided immediately to incorporate the work into his repertoire. In his biography of Schnabel, Cesar Saerchinger described this historic meeting:

> There is no doubt that Korngold, at thirteen, was not only a phenomenally gifted composer, but that the sonata in question was a remarkable work well worth performing. Speaking about it nearly forty years later, Schnabel called it "still a most amazing piece." Never afraid of doing the unusual, he decided to play the work in public. . . . Aside from the objective estimate of its merit (which it got), one would have expected only favorable comment on Schnabel's gesture in the press. There appeared, however, several malicious innuendoes regarding his motives—in view of the fact that Korngold senior was at that time the most influential critic in Austria. The gossip that went around is best summarized by the imaginary conversation in which a colleague asks Schnabel whether Korngold's sonata is rewarding to which he replied, "No—but his father is!" Schnabel paid no attention to the rumors and not only continued to play the work, but he and Carl Flesch also played young Korngold's Violin and Piano Sonata [Sonata in G Major, Opus 6] (composed in 1912) at their regular recitals in Berlin.[10]

The background to these innuendoes centered on a bitter quarrel between Julius Korngold and the celebrated concert pianist Moriz Rosenthal, noted for his feuds with a variety of notable people, and not just music critics. Rosenthal was twenty years older than Schnabel but considered him to be his most serious rival. In 1909, the two great pianists gave recitals in Vienna, and both were reviewed by Julius Korngold. Rosenthal sought to win over the critic to his interpretation and might have elicited a good review had he not broken a hammer in the Bösendorfer piano in trying to exceed the sheer volume that Schnabel had been able to command. Rosenthal promptly claimed that the accident had been caused by a piece of his watch chain that had found its way into the piano.

Ludwig Bösendorfer was incensed by this and insisted that his instruments were so soundly constructed that such a thing could never have happened; the only explanation for the breakage was the excessive banging of the keys. In his review, Julius Korngold compared Rosenthal's excessive dynamics to the earthquake of Messina in 1908, and concluded by saying, "No doubt he will play beautifully next time."

Rosenthal was furious that his own story had not been accepted. From that moment on, he turned on Julius Korngold and his son. To condense what became a rather protracted affair, matters came to a head when Rosenthal suddenly declared his intention of playing Erich Korngold's new piano sonata in Vienna. The elder Korngold, worried that perhaps Rosenthal would extract the maximum damage that he could from this

piece of political chicanery, and adhering to his principle of avoiding premieres of his son's compositions in Vienna whenever possible, telephoned
Rosenthal and, thanking him politely, advised the pianist that the premiere
had been set for Berlin and had been offered to Schnabel.

To exacerbate the situation, it so happened that Schnabel gave a recital
in Vienna a few days later at which he played no fewer than five Beethoven
sonatas. Consequently, Julius Korngold accorded him a lengthier review
than his next review for Rosenthal's recital. The temperamental pianist considered this an affront and conclusive proof that he was being victimized.

Enter Max Graf, alias Iago, into the fray. He had the ideal weapon to bestow on Rosenthal: the illegal copy of that condemnatory letter from the Association of Vienna Music Critics mentioned above. First, Rosenthal regis-
tered a complaint about the biased views of Dr. Korngold (reinforced with
the signatures of three other pianists) to Moritz Benedikt at the *Neue Freie
Presse*. Although Benedikt dismissed it, the matter did not end there.
Rosenthal still had the letter provided by Graf, and apparently he used it un-
scrupulously for ten years, thereby ensuring that rumor and counter-rumor
flourished whenever an artist was criticized by his enemy at the *Presse*.

The whole episode reached a climax in 1922 during the most fractious
period of public arguments between Dr. Korngold and Richard Strauss
while Strauss was co-director of the Vienna State Opera. By then, singers
and conductors alike had refused to appear in productions of Erich
Wolfgang Korngold's operas because of the vicious reviews some of them
had received by the composer's father. Several times Korngold had to conduct his own operas without a fee, on short notice, because a conductor had
been offended by some snide comment by his father. The situation became
such a public scandal that it even reached the British musical press.[11]

Rosenthal, still bearing a grudge, made an unprovoked attack and published a sworn affidavit in the *Sonn- und Montagszeitung* quoting from
the reviews of Dr. Korngold, which he maintained were praiseworthy up
to the day of the conflict over his son's sonata. He ensured that his letter
(co-signed by Leopold Godowsky, Leschetizky, and others) was printed,
and concluded:

> My firm belief is that Dr. Korngold's practices are such as to tend
> seriously to injure the reputation of both the musical public and
> critical fraternity of Vienna.

By this time, Moritz Benedikt had died, and his son Ernst was now editor of the *Neue Freie Presse*, and he allowed Julius Korngold to defend himself. The next headline was even juicier than usual and ensured excellent
business at the coffee-houses: Rosenthal had imprudently decided to sue the
Presse! Although a trial date was definitely set, Rosenthal withdrew and
settled out of court.

During the settlement proceedings, Julius Korngold produced over half a dozen critics with whom Rosenthal had fought over the years. Nonetheless, the damage was done. This was but one of many unfortunate incidents fought by Korngold's father in the public arena, with attendant publicity, over the next two decades, and these events often attracted greater attention than his son's compositions. In 1911, however, the media battle had only just begun.

CHAPTER FIVE

"We Will Have to Burn Our Books on Harmony"

—Edward Dent

*A*rtur Schnabel premiered Korngold's Piano Sonata No. 2 in E Major in Berlin on 13 October 1911, and it was quickly established as a major new work. In its ambitious four movements, it encompasses the gamut of emotions and displays the burgeoning orchestral thinking soon to be exhibited in the *Schauspiel Ouvertüre*, together with flashes of Lisztian keyboard diablerie and some extraordinary percussive effects.

Harmonically, the style is even more assured, and the use of free variation extends even to the harmonic scheme with profligate use of the whole tone scale—yet another of Korngold's trait deployed with remarkable skill. The fiendishly difficult Scherzo is an ingenious and technically extremely demanding set-piece. Cascading octaves and glittering runs embellish the structure, and there is a melting, bittersweet, almost parodistic Trio section (characteristically, a waltz). Schnabel enjoyed such success with the piece that he repeated his performance in November and December in Vienna; the latter performance took place during the annual Music Week.

Korngold's Piano Sonata No. 2 was to become a Schnabel speciality. When Korngold was invited to give a concert the following year in Frankfurt by the Society for Esthetic Culture, Artur Schnabel shared the bill with him. Schnabel performed the second sonata, and Erich the first. Completing the bill, the Piano Trio in D Major was performed by the composer and members of the Adolf Rebner Quartet.

At the invitation of the Philipps-Duca company, Korngold also made his very first piano rolls: the complete *Sieben Märchenbilder*, Opus 3, which had yet to receive a first performance. Schnabel had recorded rolls of the entire Piano Sonata in E Major the previous month. These early rolls would be fascinating to trace, particularly since they would provide unique evidence of Schnabel's interpretation and, perhaps more interestingly, of how Korngold played his works while still a child.

In the years that followed, the Piano Sonata in E Major was performed frequently by other prominent pianists of the time, especially Richard Buhlig (who gave the British premiere), Georg Zscherneck, Leo Sirota, Marta Malatesta, and Richard Springer. Rudolph Ganz gave the first performance in the United States.

On 14 December 1911, Arthur Nikisch gave the world premiere of the *Schauspiel Ouvertüre* with the Gewandhaus Orchestra in Leipzig, a city that had enjoyed many performances of Korngold's works already that year, including a gala production of *Der Schneemann* in March under the direction of Egon Pollak, later to become one of Korngold's foremost interpreters and closest friends. The *Wunderkind* traveled to Leipzig with his father and stayed with Nikisch, getting to know his family, especially his son Micha, who was a fine pianist.

The preceding day, the directors of the Gewandhaus had arranged an invitation recital with Korngold as soloist. The perceptive reviewer was astounded by his musicianship and skill as an interpreter of his own works:

> Korngold played the first movement of his Piano Trio in D major, the whole of the Piano Sonata No. 2 in E Major, and four pieces from his *Sieben Märchenbilder*, all from memory and with great vividness of inimitable expression.
>
> One fact became definitely obvious: Korngold creates the way he must. The understanding of the printed score is made more difficult by the fact that he very often does not write note values as he intends and plays. His great predilection for altered diminished seventh chords has the effect of feeling completely spontaneous, as is everything he does. The last two sonata movements, performed with stormy, passionate technique and unbelievable rhythmic freedom (not caprice), . . . were astounding feats of composition as well as of piano-playing, in which the composer's age is not to be taken into consideration. Without doubt, he is already a complete adult.[1]

This trait of almost improvising and embellishing his works at the piano had clearly already manifested itself and remained a feature of his performances all his life. It is especially notable in his few recordings. The first rehearsal of the overture was a revelation to Julius Korngold:

> I shall never forget the astounding effect of the rehearsal. The tempi, accents, expression—all constituted a surprise growing almost into

bewilderment. Nikisch virtually conducted the work *against* the composer. But what marvellous results came out *for* the composer. Nikisch, the most ingenious modifier of tempi, understood balance; everywhere the sound was deepened, and invisible scenes were conjured up in the music.[2]

The review by Richard Specht confirmed the success of the actual performance:

The work was a complete and outstanding success. Invention, evocative expression, and rich instrumentation aroused the greatest admiration. . . . Nikisch performed the work with obvious affection and a wonderful sense of plasticity and delicacy. The young composer—one so young can never have appeared at a Gewandhaus concert before—was repeatedly hailed with great enthusiasm.[3]

Julius Korngold was not present to see his son's triumph. He had nervously left his seat before the performance began after hearing two members of the audience express the wish that the work be a failure. He spent the entire evening tramping up and down the street outside, awaiting the outcome. Backstage afterward, he found his son with Nikisch in his dressing room. Nikisch cried enthusiastically, "After this success, the piece will go out into the world!"

The *Schauspiel Ouvertüre* deserved its enthusiastic reception. Remarkably assured, its orchestration is highly sophisticated, its ideas strong and characteristic. Few could doubt that the *Wunderkind* had indeed made the successful transition to *"Wunderadolescent."* The evolution of Korngold's orchestral style from this first work onward is fascinating to observe. Already adept at writing effectively and brilliantly for brass, he showed an immediate preference for multi-divided strings after the manner of Richard Strauss. The orchestra in the overture really sings, and the choice of instruments for solo coloring is striking. Although the orchestra is smaller than that used in later works, it is no less effective. As for his acute sense of the dramatic, Rudolf Stefan Hoffmann, Korngold's first biographer, stated: "Korngold's early orchestral works dream of opera; logically, with an eye to the theater, the first work was an overture to a play!"[4]

Other features so typical of Korngold are also present: the preference for brilliant, chromatic keys (the overture is in B major and consequently is frequently in F-sharp major and related keys), the use of bombastic timpani, and the support of the orchestral fabric with the harp. Every aspect of his style was already present in this early work. Korngold dedicated the work to Nikisch. From the premiere until the great conductor's premature death in 1921, Korngold and Nikisch remained close friends.

Life in Vienna: Salons and Personalities

Korngold was not only a celebrity in the concert halls, he was a pampered favorite with the art-loving Viennese beau monde. As his fame grew, he invariably accompanied his parents socially as regular guests of the most fashionable salons of that time. Adele Strauss's was the most fashionable salon of all. The widow of Johann Strauss, whose home was open for visiting artists, always enjoyed Erich's brilliant renditions of her late husband's music. Here Erich met the celebrated Austrian pianist Alfred Grünfeld, who thus became acquainted with the *Sieben Märchenbilder* just completed and in turn became the first to make a commercial recording of any music by Korngold. He recorded "Die Wichtelmännchen" (The Goblins) from *Sieben Märchenbilder* for the Gramophone Company in Vienna in 1914.

Another lively salon was held by the vivacious Jenny Mautner, wife of the noted industrialist, whose circle included Richard Strauss, the famous Burgtheater actor Josef Kainz, and Max Reinhardt. Korngold first met and played for the conductor Fritz Steinbach at this salon. After hearing the boy play his *Schauspiel Ouvertüre*, Steinbach immediately secured the rights, performed it in Cologne, and inaugurated what amounted to a "Korngold Week" in Cologne in January 1913, with performances of the *Schauspiel Ouvertüre*, the Piano Trio in D Major, *Der Schneemann* (at the opera house), and the newly completed Sinfonietta in B Major.

By far the most important salon in Vienna, however, was that of Dr. Hugo Ganz and his wife. Dr. Ganz was the political and foreign correspondent of the *Frankfurter Allgemeine Zeitung* and occasionally wrote for the *Neue Freie Presse*. His wife held a soiree each Sunday, and the Korngolds attended nearly every week.

In the course of researching this book, I met possibly the last surviving witness of this stimulating early period of Korngold's life, a woman who also attended the Ganz Salon: Gertrud Löwy. By the time I interviewed her, she was ninety-five years of age and living in a nursing home in Scotland, having married a Scot and emigrated there in 1919. A teacher, she was engaged by Dr. Korngold to give private instruction to his son in 1911 in French and English. Living as she did in the most fashionable part of Vienna, she was an excellent source for this book. Like many people who live to a great age, her powers of recall were especially strong concerning her youth. Her vivid description of the people and the times is unique:

From my childhood, I was devoted to music, as was my whole family. As a young girl I was an eager guest at my cousins Hugo and Ida Conrat, who were close friends of Johannes Brahms, who frequently dined there accompanied by a grubby little boy who was nonetheless a brilliant pianist. He grew up to be Artur Schnabel. Hugo wrote the text for Brahms' *Zigeunerlieder* (Gypsy Songs), and he had a beautiful villa in the Walfischgasse, which on Sunday was open house to musicians. Later, his daughter, a talented sculptress, designed the Brahms memorial in the Centralfriedhof.

In 1907 I moved to the Döbling district, which was where the Ganz family lived, and my neighbor was Marie Gutheil-Schoder, Mahler's favorite at the Opera, and she took me to the Ganz's salon, which is where I first met Erich and his formidable parents.

I remember the wicked stories that always circulated about Gutheil-Schoder. My friend Retty (who was an actress) used to say, "All her furniture can be made into beds!" (You know how you can pull out things.) Well, at the time she was expecting a child and she said, "How convenient that Gustav Schoder and Gustav Mahler have the same name," when it turned out to be a boy!

Well, the Ganz salon was a treat, believe me. Every Sunday, upwards of twenty-five people gathered, including visiting musicians who were playing that week in Vienna, and other celebrities who happened to be in town. The emphasis was always on good conversation, good music, and wonderful food. There were certain regulars too: the Korngolds of course, and Friedrich Buxbaum, the cellist.

Then there was the sculptor Gustinus Ambrosi whom I particularly liked; very Italian looking, very handsome, and *very* vain. He was a devil with women. I recommended him to the Taussigs, where he got some good commissions but nearly wrecked the not too solid marriage. I remember, too, the novelist Rudolf Bartsch would come, Alma Mahler, and of course Oskar Kokoschka. It was around the time he was having an affair with her, but they were careful to arrive and leave separately, although everyone knew what was going on.

The evening was given over to chamber music, and sometimes Erich played the piano. Occasionally, a singer of note would perform: I remember Alfred Piccaver did so on one evening.

Erich was still only a young boy of about fourteen then, but he was always the life and soul of the party. He was round and chubby, *not* good looking, and never looked straight: he had almost a squint! But above all he had a *wicked* sense of humor, and I recall that he always arrived with an enormous score under his arm, which I later saw him working on, in the dining room, while the adults talked in the drawing room after lunch. Frequently, he was wont to slip away quietly with Dr. Ganz's pretty daughter Margit (nicknamed Manzi), who I think was his first sweetheart.

I remember, too, the striking contrast between Erich and his father, Julius Korngold, who was of course the all-powerful critic. I have to say that I never saw Dr. Korngold smile, and it seemed to me that he only showed an interest in you if you *were* somebody; I, of course, was an insignificant little teacher, so he had no time for *me*.

Later I was engaged for a short time to teach Erich. I saw only his mother (who incidentally was a delightful person, and from whom I am sure Erich inherited his wit). Erich was an obedient pupil but was not really interested in learning French. His mind was always on music, and he was often given to dreaming, as if he were in another world. I got the impression that he was only taking instruction to please his father, who had both Erich and his mother very much under the thumb, it seemed to me.

I married a young Scottish diplomat in 1916, and my teaching career came to an end, and in 1919 I left Vienna for good and never saw the Korngolds again.[5]

Manzi Ganz had not been the only girl to have awakened Korngold's romantic soul. Earlier, he had lost his heart to Mitzi Kolisch, daughter of Dr. Rudolf Kolisch, whose son Rudolf formed the famous Kolisch Quartet and whose other daughter Trudi became Arnold Schoenberg's second wife in 1924. Mitzi had not evinced much interest in the young composer, however. Margit Ganz was to be his soulmate for four years (she eventually married the actor Jacob Feldhammer, while coincidentally, an earlier fiancee of hers, Hans Jellinek, married the sister of Luise von Sonnenthal, or Luzi as she was called, Korngold's future wife). These boyhood romances never amounted to anything, largely because young Korngold was so strictly chaperoned. In her own memoirs, Luise von Sonnenthal recalled:

Dr. Julius Korngold viewed Erich's little romances with suspicion and distrust. He regarded the girls as cunning and leading his son astray. He clouded these innocent friendships with pessimistic warnings that they would harm his work. Erich was angry at this and tension ensued; this was the first manifestation of Erich Korngold's independent will.[6]

Distracting or not, these "cunning" girls did inspire music in Korngold. Among his manuscripts is a set of four waltzes, each named after a different girl. Mitzi Kolisch and Manzi Ganz are both represented, and he later gave the manuscript of the exquisite song "Liebesbriefchen" (A Little Love Letter, part of *Sechs Einfache Lieder*, Opus 9) to Mitzi Kolisch.

Around 1912, Erich was sent to the clinic of Dr. Guido Engelmann, a noted orthopedic surgeon, in an attempt to correct a round-shouldered stoop. The treatment was not very successful (throughout his life, his mother continually entreated him to throw his shoulders back and "sit up straight!"), but it did afford an opportunity for the young Luise von Sonnenthal, also a patient of Dr. Engelmann, to see the *Wunderkind* for the first time, even if he did not see her. She recalled:

He was standing by some apparatus, which required him to pull out two handles that were weighted, and this he did, but very disinterestedly and absent-mindedly. He seemed as if he were in a trance, and sang to himself, sometimes quite loudly, and did not pay any attention to anyone around him. He was completely lost in his own world of music.[7]

The Engelmann family became close friends of the Korngolds, and Korngold struck up a lifelong friendship with Dr. Engelmann's son "Poldi," who was a talented pianist, although he became an orthopedic surgeon like his father. Poldi's uncle, Rudi Duschnitz, and his wife Lilly became perhaps Korngold's closest friends and certainly his friends of longest standing. Their home was to be a frequent refuge for him when he found it difficult to work at home if, as so often happened, relations with his parents became strained.

The Engelmanns also held a regular salon. In these formative years of Korngold's life, his social circle grew ever wider. Here, at the Engelmanns', as in the Ganz household, the emphasis was always on music and the arts, but the Engelmanns' salon was not just a Sunday occurrence but was held practically every night of the week. The guest list included many famous personalities: Hugo von Hofmannsthal and his sister Mimi Schlesinger (who was a cousin of Mrs. Engelmann), the painter Nicholas Schattenstein, Otto Klemperer, the celebrated architect Richard Neutra, the English pianist Fanny Davies (a pupil of Clara Schumann), and the extraordinary painter Tamara di Lempicka, who was also a relative of the Engelmanns.

One of the most extraordinary personalities whom Korngold met in these last days of Imperial Vienna was the sculptor Gustinus Ambrosi,[8] who, as Frau Löwy recalled, was a frequent guest at the Ganz Salon. After a serious illness at the age of fifteen left him temporarily blind and permanently deaf, thus ruining a promising musical career, he turned to sculpture. At age 16, he caused a stir with one of his first works, *Der Mann mit dem gebrochenen Genick* (The Man with the Broken Neck), and in 1913, though only twenty years old, was awarded the State Prize in Vienna for his works. Thereafter, he began a successful career as a maker of portrait busts. His catalog of work lists most of the great figures of his day, including Gerhart Hauptmann, Richard Strauss, Stefan Zweig, Siegfried Trebitsch, Romain Rolland, August Strindberg, Mussolini, Clemenceau, and Peter Altenberg, as well as Manzi Ganz. A full-length portrait-bust of Erich Korngold that he created in 1912 was destroyed by the Nazis when they broke into Korngold's home in Vienna in 1938.

On 18 May 1911, Gustav Mahler died from heart disease. An extraordinary outpouring of grief by the hypocritical Viennese was accompanied by sensationalized articles in the leading newspapers. Julius Korngold wrote an obituary in the *Neue Freie Presse* in which he compared Mahler to the conductor Hans von Bülow "with a creative gift," a statement that almost trivialized his compositions. It was indeed a curious phrase from one supposedly loyal to the memory of the man whom he considered the greatest composer of the age. His article, though glowing with praise, carefully avoids an assessment of Mahler the symphonist:

> Gustav Mahler was one of the last great idealists of our time . . . who in his art reached for the unattainable, who on his way to the impossible, attempted to conquer the possible. Once under his spell, the public remained faithful to him . . . . He played the orchestra like a virtuoso . . . . What a splendid leader . . . unbending in his art, bestowed with such rare magic . . . . This star is now extinguished. If Vienna only knew what it had lost, how much poorer the city has become through the death of this master whose last breath belonged to Vienna.[9]

For Erich Korngold, the loss was catastrophic. Until the end of his life, he spoke reverently of Mahler—the first important creative musician he had known and who had expressed admiration for his own gifts.

Bust of Korngold by Gustinus Ambrosi, completed 1912, presumed destroyed following the Nazi invasion of Austria in 1938 (courtesy of Ambrosi Museum, Vienna).

Two months earlier, Felix von Weingartner, Mahler's successor at the Vienna Court Opera, had tendered his resignation after three stormy years. In his memoirs he blamed Dr. Korngold for his failure,[10] but whether or not he felt bitterness toward Julius Korngold, his loyalty and enthusiasm for Erich Korngold continued unabated. Although he departed for a conductorship at the Hamburg Opera, he retained his connection with Vienna as director of the Philharmonic until 1927. Consequently, upon hearing of the success of the *Schauspiel Ouvertüre*, he successfully sidestepped objections from the father and conducted a brilliant performance of it in November 1912. Korngold later expressed his gratitude for Weingartner's support by dedicating his next work to him, the Sinfonietta in B Major. Weingartner later conducted its world premiere on 30 November 1913 in Vienna (a rare first performance for Korngold in the Austrian capital), again in spite of parental objections.

By Christmas 1911 there were some new compositions: Erich presented a set of twelve Lieder, composed at various times during the year, all to texts by Eichendorff, as a birthday gift to his father (born 24 December). On the original manuscript, he designated them as his Opus 5, but he changed his mind when he began composing the Sinfonietta in B Major in the spring of 1912. Only three of these songs were ever published ("Schneeglöckchen," "Nachtwanderer," and "Das Ständchen" as part of the *Sechs Einfache Lieder* Opus 9, published in 1916). In addition to these twelve, there are numerous other songs from this time, all of which were rejected by the composer. As Luzi Korngold states in her memoirs:

> At 15, he had become sharply self-critical, which kept him from just scribbling. He worked for twelve hours each day, and in the evenings would improvise until late at night. He was more of a child than his contemporaries; conversely, he was mature as an artist.[11]

The orchestra continued to dominate young Erich's thoughts. Fresh from the success of the *Schauspiel Ouvertüre*, he began to think of writing a full-length work. In the year 1912, he began the Sinfonietta in B Major. Even more complex, and more ambitiously scored than the overture, it is probably the least aptly named composition in the Korngold canon, for it is really a fully fledged symphony. The music is full of youthful optimism, exuberance, and playful humor—hence the light-hearted title. The orchestra, on the other hand, is very large. Besides a full complement of strings (including eight double-basses, four of which have a C string), there are a piccolo, two flutes, two oboes, a cor anglais, two clarinets, a bass clarinet, two bassoons, a double bassoon, four horns, three trumpets, three trombones, a tuba, two harps, a celeste, and a battery of percussion (including deep bells).

For the first time, Korngold includes the piano with his orchestra. With the exception of the *Schauspiel Ouvertüre*, his opera *Der Ring des Polykrates*, the Violin Concerto in D Major, and the *Symphonic Serenade* in B-flat major for string orchestra, the piano would always play an essential part in his orchestral thinking. He uses it at key moments as an unexpected color, and couples it with other keyboard instruments in his scores as a means of harmonic support. Occasionally, he also uses it as a percussion instrument, spiking the music with staccato octaves or emphasizing cadences. Just as in his own piano playing, he uses the piano to double the effect of the harp glissandi, which makes the typical and irresistible Korngold "sweep." Few composers have utilized the piano so effectively in the orchestra, and it says a great deal for Korngold's ingenuity that he recognized its potential so early in his work.

In the *Dictionary of Twentieth Century Music* (ed. John Vinton, 1974, London: Thames & Hudson), over thirty-five composers are listed as having written a work entitled "Sinfonietta," among them Janáček, Britten, Eugene Goossens, Poulenc, and Zemlinsky. None of them wrote a work so polyphonically complex or so richly orchestrated as the one by the fifteen-year-old Korngold, in which unity is the preeminent concern.

Korngold's Sinfonietta in B Major develops from a motto theme, "Motiv des fröhlichen Herzens" (Motto of the Cheerful Heart).[12] This joyous melody, characteristically built on rising fourths, is of great importance in Korngold's entire musical output, appearing in many guises in the chamber works, operas, and even the film scores.

The Sinfonietta is a radiant work. The opening of the first movement, a rapturous, seemingly endless statement of the main theme, grips the attention—a feature of his style even from the beginning. In all of his works, the opening bars are striking, arresting, and firmly stamped with the composer's signature.

Each movement is dominated by the motto theme. In the Scherzo (a triumphal and heroic "explosion" scored brilliantly for timpani and brass), the motto theme decorates the music as a piccolo obbligato and then, completely varied, moves to the fore again in the melting Trio in F-sharp Major, a favorite key of Korngold's. In the dreamy Andante, it is hidden in the pizzicato bass of the strings, and it forms the second subject in yet another variation before providing the reflective, mysterious conclusion. In the final bars, the five notes are sounded by the harp, glockenspiel, and woodwind—harmonized with Korngold's favorite augmented triads. In the Finale, the motto theme (in a strident statement in the minor key) leads to a fugal treatment of what becomes the first subject. In this movement, Korngold demonstrates his formal mastery as the music undergoes every conceivable rhythmic and harmonic variation. The exquisite second subject is a development of the first theme and, significantly, is treated almost operatically. Melodically and structurally, it is a close relative of the aria "Reine Liebe" from his second opera *Violanta* (composed in 1914–1915).

After the development section, where the motto theme weaves in and out, even becoming an ostinato bass at one point, the recapitulation leads to the triumphant conclusion, which the critic Richard Specht described as "a symphonic Song of Songs!" This exultant work marks the culmination of Korngold's years as a prodigy and looks ahead to the beginning of his

Sinfonietta

I

"Motiv des fröhichen Herzens" (Motto of the Cheerful Heart), the first five bars from Sinfonietta in B Major, Opus 5. (Reproduced by permission of the publishers Schott Musik International, Mainz, Germany.)

operatic career. Having served his apprenticeship in composing for the orchestra (although neither Opus 4 nor 5 is in any way experimental or hesitant), Korngold was ready to move on to the next phase of his extraordinary development.

The *Schauspiel Ouvertüre* and excerpts from *Der Schneemann* were presented by Sir Henry Wood at the London Promenade Concerts in 1912. Ernest Newman,[13] one of the most distinguished musicologists of the day, wrote an extended eulogy about the boy prodigy in *The Nation* magazine, which apart from a small excerpt, has never been reprinted. It is a valuable example of just how highly Korngold was regarded by the world of music, far beyond his native Vienna—and far from his father's influence:

> Erich Wolfgang Korngold . . . is the most amazing phenomenon in present-day music. Of the boy himself I know nothing more than is told in his published scores. . . . No one who has not seen these works can form any idea of the uncanny maturity of genius that they exhibit. We have had plenty of youthful composers before, but I can recall the name of none other who at the age of eleven or twelve was already a master of the most subtle musical idiom of his day, and had at his command a fund of ideas that the best of living composers would not disdain to possess.
>
> The strange thing about Korngold is that mentally he never seems to have had a childhood. Promising musical children generally write like promising children; one approaches their work with a certain tolerance. Practically all the great men have begun with work that was palpably immature. It took Bach and Beethoven and Wagner many years to find a style of their own; and their earliest compositions are plainly very boyish affairs.
>
> One can hardly repress a smile now as one reads through the amusingly cocky little "Festmarsch" that is Richard Strauss's Opus 1; it irresistibly reminds us of a very healthy but self-assertive gamin showing off a little before the grown-ups. Mozart, when a child, wrote like a child. Mendelssohn turned out the beautiful "Midsummer Night's Dream" overture when he was seventeen or so, and Schubert and Hugo Wolf had both written remarkable songs at that age; while Wolf's string quartet, written at the age of nineteen, is still a marvel for the closeness of its texture and the audacity of its thinking.
>
> But there is a wide gulf between seventeen or nineteen, and eleven or twelve; and Korngold's case, I think, is quite without parallel. Anyone who picked up his scores at haphazard, and played them through without any knowledge of the composer's age, would take him to be a man of between thirty and forty. who by incessant practice of his art had attained a fine distinction of style and an

imposing weight of idea. The wholly delightful *Schneemann* music is the sort that an adult writes for children or for those who would love to become children again. Humperdinck himself could not have done it with a surer hand or an imagination more rightly tuned to the key of the thing.

Humor, irony, tenderness—these are not the qualities one expects from a boy of eleven. The invention is endlessly fertile and curiously distinguished; the delicious little entr'acte waltz in D major, for example, is a wittier and more winsome thing than any of the waltzes in *Der Rosenkavalier*. Here, as in his later works, Korngold's imagination is always taking the most enchantingly unexpected turns. Of the commonplaces, the sentimentalities, the laborious insistence upon the obvious, that most young composers only get rid of after years of cubbish or calf-like outpouring of themselves, there is here—or indeed anywhere else in Korngold's music—not the shadow of a trace.

His mind, with its freshness, its boldness, its freedom from anything like vapors, seems to have had the superfluous emotional fat trained out of it as superfluous physical fat is trained out of the body of an athlete. It is refreshing, indeed, to see this vigorous young spirit beating its way through tracts of thought far remote from those of all but a few of the most original composers of today—the thinking tense, alert, and sanely passionate, the style both amazingly subtle and amazingly free.

His disdain of easy courses may be seen in the slow movement of the second (piano) sonata, where he gives what appears to be shaping for a common arpeggio figure the most unexpected of turns, and proceeds to evoke from this unconventional phrase, a long largo full of elevated and impassioned melancholy.

His harmonic writing is astoundingly complex, but perfectly logical and free from all obscurity or experimentation. Harmonic oddity is, of course, within the reach of anyone who chooses to force various tones to go together whether they will or no; but the result is no more complex, in the psychological sense of the term, than spilled milk or a badly cracked window-pane. . . .

Amateurs persist in believing that some of us hold back from certain pages in the later Strauss because our conservative minds cannot follow his original harmonic thinking. The truth is that when Strauss is talking harmonic sense, and not merely flinging a handful of notes at the score and trusting to some of them sticking, his harmonic writing, even at its most daring, is not nearly so subtle as that of a composer like Arnold Schoenberg, for example, in comparison with whom Strauss is a mere classic.

Korngold's complexity is that of the better, not the worse, Strauss. His imagination often takes the most unexpected harmonic flights, but I cannot recall more than one or two passages in his work that are not coherently related to their context. If ever a composer had the logic of subtle harmonic thinking in him, it is he. He is always master of himself and his material; always comes out easily from what looks like a tangle, and so proves it to be no tangle at all.

You may incidentally see his mastery of every sort of harmonic combination and transition in graceful trifles like "Die Prinzessin auf der Erbse" and the "Rübezahl" from the *Märchenbilder* where he plays laughingly with one or two of the devices by which Debussy sets such store, and then throws them aside as toys that a man ought not to take too seriously. In the two Sonatas and the Trio the harmonic idiom is generally as subtle as anything Strauss can give us, and far more subtle than most other contemporary composers. And that the boy is no mere technician, that he has abundant and excellent ideas, is clear from every one of the works he has published. The only question is will the brain last out to ripe manhood!

No one of course dares prophesy: but if Korngold's development is not arrested, there is no saying to what amazing heights he may reach. Can the scientists give any explanation of this phenomenon? I take it that no one will seek to account for it by direct hereditary transmission. Too many of the great composers have come from parents of little or no musical gifts for us to need to posit even latent musical genius anywhere in Korngold's musical ancestry.

The truth probably is that musical or any other genius is simply a particular direction given, by the presence of some tiny factor, to a brain of unusual energy and scope; that is to say, a brain like Korngold's represents no flowering of long dormant musical faculties in his ancestors, but merely a flowering and concentration of general nervous and intellectual aptitudes that, by something we can only call chance, happen to have taken a musical rather than any other direction.

But how are we to account for the *stage* at which Korngold commences his thinking, except on the supposition that the general mental requirements of one generation are stored and may be available for drawing upon by the next! To put it concretely: Mozart and Korngold are two geniuses who begin to write music in their earliest childhood. Why does Mozart spontaneously lisp music in the simple idiom of his own day, while Korngold lisps in the complex idiom of his? It may be replied that the difference is due to Korngold having been brought up on a more advanced kind of music than Mozart. That, however, is no explanation.

If the child's brain at birth is not—to put it crudely—the product of
something that is in the air at the time, and therefore a more complex
thing in a complex epoch than it is in a simple epoch; if the complex
brain is only a lucky throw of Nature's, why could she not throw a
Korngold in the seventeenth or the eighteenth century? Korngold can
hardly have derived his harmonic system from the study of other
composers, for in what composer's work could he have found it? It is
the spontaneous product of the most subtly organized brain, that at
the first span embraces practically all we know and feel today in the
way of harmonic relation.[14]

A rare snapshot of Korngold with his young friends, probably Rudolf and Mitzi
Kolisch and Manzi Ganz (on Korngold's immediate left) and an unidentified girl,
in the Austrian countryside, circa 1913 (Korngold estate).

Newman's astute reflections give an indication of how shocking the early
works of Korngold were to the ears of the great music theorists and
thinkers of the time. Edward Dent, later the leading figure in the
International Society for New Music, which did so much to promote
Schoenberg and his pupils in the 1920s, wrote a salute to Korngold proclaiming him to be the prophet of the century:

Korngold's is literally the freshest imagination in Europe. To pretend he is as learned as Reger or Strauss is unnecessary. But in the matter of sheer invention, he is already their equal. His precocity is marvellous. Individuality from the first has always been in evidence. Korngold—if one may look ahead—will be the founder of a new order of music. The whole-tone system will scarcely hold its own against him. We shall have to burn our books on harmony and counterpoint . . . . and start anew with a fecund, fertile, imaginative method which admits nature and the whole jarring universe of sounds as the material upon which to draw.[15]

There were literally dozens of laudatory reviews in the newspapers and magazines of the time in almost every European country and in the United States. All concurred on three key elements: the amazing precocity, the extraordinary individuality, and the completely radical nature of Korngold's music. But as Oscar Wilde once cautioned: "Nothing is so dangerous as being too modern; one is apt to grow old-fashioned quite suddenly." Within fifteen years of the publication of Newman and Dent's articles, Korngold was no longer seen as a prophet but as a conservative reactionary in light of some of the more extreme compositions of the *Neue Wiener Schule*. For the present, however, he remained the boy wonder, although the enemies of his father remained sceptical.

After the Sinfonietta in B Major, Korngold turned to chamber music again. This habit of retreat into the smaller, purer confines of chamber music after the composition of an opera or major orchestral work continued throughout his life. Korngold seemed to desire a cleansing of his imagination by means of a string quartet or a set of songs. Following the completion of the iridescent, vibrant Sinfonietta, Korngold began to compose the Sonata in G Major for violin and piano, Opus 6, which may have been suggested to him by Artur Schnabel. Schnabel at that time gave many joint recitals with the celebrated violinist Carl Flesch, and the idea of a work for them both obviously appealed to Korngold. In any case, he dedicated the piece to them and the finished work is undoubtedly written with virtuoso performers in mind.

The Sonata in G Major is unusually long and somewhat introspective. In many ways it is one of the most unusual (and unlikely) works that Korngold composed. Without giving a lengthy analysis, it is worth considering the most interesting features of this beautifully crafted (and unjustly neglected) sonata.

The piano part is unusually dominant. The abundant keyboard style of the Piano Sonata in E Major is further developed here, and the interplay between the two instruments at times turns them into musical protagonists. The music clearly reveals the dramatic inclinations of the composer, even more than his previous works. The ideas are very "Korngoldian," especially the opening theme of the first movement—a sweeping arc of two rising sixths—that seems to point to the opening of his Violin Concerto in D Major, composed many years later (1937–1939, revised 1945).

Like many of Korngold's principal subjects, that of the Sonata in G Major for violin and piano is unusually long and begins to develop almost immediately. Besides the familiar trait of organic unity (evident especially in the main themes of the first, third, and fourth movements, which are of markedly similar contours), the richness of the harmonic language is surprising, given that only two instruments are playing.

The typically boisterous Scherzo contains many bitonal passages and a particularly striking *misterioso* in which a series of ninths leads the ear on a journey into very unfamiliar territory within the context of the piece. The Andante is an elegiac rhapsody—the form is difficult to grasp, so wayward is the music. Here Korngold's ability to write eloquent slow movements, already in evidence in his earlier compositions, is even more significant. The music assumes the character of a recitative, and the delicate effects and subtle harmonic changes reveal his growing maturity. The Finale is a set of free variations on "Schneeglöckchen" (composed in 1911 and published in 1916 as one of the *Sechs Einfache Lieder*, Opus 9).

Once again, a Korngoldian trait is established: the practice of using a song as the basis for a chamber movement. Perhaps he was influenced by Mahler in this, whose Lieder were of such overall importance in his symphonies. (In Korngold's works, the best example is in his Piano Quintet in E Major, Opus 15). Into the variations of this Finale Korngold introduces a humorous fugato, which depends on a highly individual use of the trill for its effect.

The Sonata in G Major ends uncharacteristically in a restrained, expansive manner without the usual Korngoldian joie de vivre. In all, it is one of the most satisfying of Korngold's chamber works. The premiere, given by Schnabel and Flesch, took place in Berlin on 21 October 1913. As usual, the redoubtable Richard Specht wrote the most pertinent, knowledgable review, saying in part:

> One can sense in this new sonata how much more freely, more relaxed, and more compatibly the interplay of forces now proceeds. Young Korngold's ability to forge everything into a whole, to develop one theme out of another, to make one theme dependent on the other, and to make the one heighten the effect of the other, has increased to an almost uncanny degree; . . . the encircling power that makes everything into an organic whole, does not tolerate accidental or spontaneous improvisation, . . . is wrought by a truly creative talent that is subject to an inner authority.[16]

In November 1913, Schnabel and Flesch repeated their success in Vienna, and played the Sonata in G Major many times over the ensuing years. Later, in May 1914, Korngold himself gave a performance of the sonata with the violinist Adolf Busch at the music festival in Bonn.

The premiere and success of his Sinfonietta in B Major prior to this effectively overshadowed the impact of the Sonata in G Major, however. His thoughts had already turned to his next major project. Ever since *Der Schneemann* he had dreamed of composing for the stage. From now on, he would concentrate his talents on what was to become the real vocation of his life—dramatic music!

A Born Composer: 1913–1918

CHAPTER SIX

"He Is a Young Eagle"
—Jean Sibelius

On 13 November 1913, Felix Weingartner conducted the world premiere of the Sinfonietta in B Major in Vienna. The concert was given by the Vienna Philharmonic Orchestra[1] for the *Gesellschaft der Musikfreunde*, and it created an enormous stir. Throughout the next two years, the work made a triumphant progress around the world and was accompanied everywhere by incredulous reviews.

Arthur Nikisch immediately took it up and by all accounts gave a tremendous performance in Berlin on 9 February 1914. At this performance, the young Korngold shared his box with Richard Strauss. Strauss's admiration for the young composer had grown. He now clearly regarded Korngold as his protégé, and was undoubtedly pleased that a composer critically acclaimed to be the hope of the future should be so adept at using the tools of musical construction beloved by Strauss himself—even more adept, it was said—and so gifted in manipulating an orchestra the size of that used for *Elektra*.

Unknown to Korngold and Strauss, another great composer was present in Berlin: Jean Sibelius. In his diary, he noted: "At the morning concert I heard the Philharmonic in Mahler's *Kindertotenlieder* and Korngold's Sinfonietta; *he is a young eagle*."[2]

A year later, in the Royal Opera House, Berlin, Richard Strauss himself conducted the Sinfonietta—the greatest accolade the great composer could give his younger colleague.[3] In the meantime, the work had been performed by Fritz Busch in Aachen, Fritz Lederer in Mannheim, Ferdinand Löwe in Munich, Hugo Grüters in Bonn, Josef Stransky in New York, Hermann Kutzschbach in Dresden, Karl Muck in Boston, and Fritz Steinbach in Cologne, and was subsequently performed by Nikisch around Germany, beginning with Hamburg. The *London Daily Telegraph*, reporting on the Cologne performance, said:

> That wonderful boy, Erich Korngold, has been astonishing the Cologne public and rousing the critics there from their usual lethargy. The last work of his heard in London was the Violin Sonata performed by Messrs. Nandor Zsolt and Richard Epstein at the Aeolian Hall a month or two ago. "His powers are uncanny," wrote one of the critics: a statement that those who have heard examples of the boy's preternatural gifts in London are not likely to deem an exaggeration.[4]

The work was especially well received in the United States, where it was performed not only in New York, but also Chicago, Pittsburgh, and Philadelphia. *The Musical Courier*, reviewing the New York performances of 10 and 11 December 1914 at Carnegie Hall by the New York Philharmonic under Josef Stransky (Mahler's successor as director of the orchestra), said:

> There is no living composer who might not be proud to have penned this work, . . . his radicalism has every evidence of being inborn. His music flows easily and naturally in spite of the fact that he adheres to no fixed tonality or traditional form . . . this composition is extraordinary for a boy . . . . and would be indeed extraordinary for a composer of any age.[5]

Meanwhile, Korngold was putting the finishing touches to an even more ambitious project: his first opera. Since the success of *Der Schneemann*, he had been striving toward the creation of an opera. His early works reveal his dramatic inclinations, and he had slowly built up a small library of books and plays as possible subjects for an opera libretto. A voracious reader, his knowledge of literature was almost as great as that of music.

At the age of only ten, he had read a charming comedy by Heinrich Teweles, the Director of the German Theater in Prague, entitled *Der Ring des Polykrates*. He put it aside, only to come across it again in the summer of 1913. Once again, it impressed his imagination, and the seeds of his first opera were sown. Julius Korngold relates the events of that summer vividly in his memoirs:

> In 1913, the last year of peace, we undertook an enjoyable Rhine journey and then went for a seaside holiday to Westend. Erich's dramatic inclinations had been rumbling again for some time. In the

books which he had accumulated, he had been looking for a plot for a comic opera, in one act as I advised from the beginning.

One evening, he jumped out of bed and rushed into my bedroom, brandishing a booklet containing a comedy: *Der Ring des Polykrates* by Heinrich Teweles . . . . Erich was attracted by the amusing twists of the story . . . . and let his imagination roam. . . . He quickly decided to go to Prague to call on the author. Teweles looked at us wide-eyed when we presented our idea, but he was pleased to see his long-forgotten little comedy revived, and agreed to the changes necessary for the musical setting.

We invented a second couple for the sake of musical contrasts and ensemble numbers, turned the husband into a musician and the husband's friend into an unlucky and envious fellow, and elaborated on the basic motive of marital happiness.

But whom could we engage to give the whole thing a dramatic shape? Our choice was the Viennese writer Leo Feld,[6] who had frequently suggested operatic subjects to Erich. He had the appealing idea of moving the plot into the later eighteenth century . . . however, his draft was awkward in verse and scenario, not well suited for musical treatment. So I wrote a revised version in Ostend, thus turning librettist—unofficially, of course; the text would be credited to Feld.[7] Erich immediately started to compose with zest at the home of a local embroiderer, who let him use her piano for a small fee.

In Ostend we received an interesting visitor. A renowned pianist and piano teacher from Manchester in England introduced himself as an admirer of Erich and said that he was promoting his compositions in England with the conviction of an apostle.[8] Later he sent us a collection of essays written by his young female pupils attempting to describe their impressions of the *Märchenbilder*. From Westend we went on to Ostend, where Erich played his Sinfonietta for Arthur Nikisch.

An incident became significant because this placid summer was followed by the ominous year of 1914. In the popular Cafe Rumpelmayer [in Berlin], the heir to the Austro-Hungarian throne, Archduke Franz Ferdinand, and his family sat down at a table adjoining ours. Their visit did not go unnoticed; the orchestra intoned the Austrian national anthem. At the first measures, the Archduke and his family rose and, of course, so did we, the only Austrians in the large room.

This attracted the Archduke's attention; he probed us intently and had his aide inquire as to who we were. I could observe to my heart's content the tall, stately man with the somber face, which lit up only when he addressed his wife and children. A year later, he and his wife had been shot and killed, and the world trembled in momentous horror of war as an aftermath of their tragic deaths.[9]

During this vacation, the first opera began to take shape, and by Christmas 1913, Korngold had entirely completed the piano score. The plot, which derives from Schiller's ballad, is fairly typical of the contrived pastiche of the late 1880s:

It is the end of the eighteenth century. Wilhelm Arndt, newly appointed court conductor, lives in marital bliss with his charming wife Laura. They have everything they could possibly wish for: a beautiful baby, a lovely home, an assured income. Wilhelm can boast of a loyal servant Florian, who is also his music copyist, and Laura's maid Liesel sees to her mistress's every need. Florian not only copies his master's music but would like to emulate him in every way, including achieving a happy marriage by marrying Liesel, whom he loves.

The only black cloud in this domestic heaven is that Wilhelm has not seen his best friend Peter Vogel (who should be called "Pechvogel," i.e. "unlucky fellow," such is his existence) for years. Vogel, once a secret admirer of Laura, lives in circumstances quite different from those of the happy Arndt family. Unmarried, he is bitter, unsuccessful, and plagued by bad luck.

Florian brings the news that Vogel has just arrived and is waiting at the coach station; someone has stolen his purse and he has no money. Wilhelm is delighted at the prospect of seeing him and asks Florian to bring him to their home immediately. Laura, in the aria "Kann's heut nicht fassen," reads from her old diary and remembers how the awkward Peter once tried to court her. Her true and only love, however, has always been Wilhelm.

Vogel arrives. Jealous of his friend's happiness, he shows him Schiller's ballad about the King Polykrates whose constant good luck has made the gods jealous, and who is thus advised to make a sacrifice of something dear to him, namely his finest gold ring, which he flings into the sea. With characteristic good fortune, however, he receives it back in the fish served to him next day.

"You, too, must sacrifice something dear to you," Vogel admonishes Wilhelm. He insists that Wilhelm ask Laura if she has ever loved anyone else. Hoping that this will cause a rift between them and thus constitute the "sacrifice," Vogel leaves. Wilhelm finds the whole idea ridiculous but, unable to resist temptation, tries to provoke Laura, who only finds him even more manly and lovable. Finally, he admits that he planned to ask her the fateful question about her fidelity. Now Laura does become angry. Florian, who has overheard Peter's talk with Wilhelm, wishes to ask Liesel the same question. She merely slaps his face. In an effort to explain himself to Liesel, Florian picks up what he thinks is the ballad, but instead finds himself reading from Laura's diary. There is great confusion, but in the end the two couples are happily reunited.

Liesel, wishing to show Florian just how much she loves him, takes her ring, the gift of a former suitor, and flings it away. Peter, returning from the station, catches it and triumphantly brings it inside. "The Ring of Polykrates!" he proclaims. "Now a sacrifice truly must be made!" It is decided to sacrifice the "friend" who has caused all the trouble and strife by throwing *him* out!

This slight framework is dressed in a most delightful score, which is a model of concision at just short of an hour in length. As a first attempt at opera, the overall result is even more remarkable. After the richness of the Sinfonietta in B Major, the orchestra for *Der Ring des Polykrates* is of chamber proportions but is nonetheless effective. It comprises a string quintet and a woodwind section whose players are merely doubled: two flutes and piccolo, two oboes (the second player also plays the cor anglais), two clarinets, two bassoons (and a contrabassoon), and only three horns, two trumpets, and one trombone. The percussion, on the other hand, calls for four players and is particularly rich, often achieving original, witty, and unusual effects. It includes a glockenspiel, xylophone, snare and bass drums, tambourine, rattle, two kettle-drums, triangle, cymbals, and tam-tam. The entire ensemble appears almost to create a small orchestra of its own, capable of providing the merriest of commentaries on the actions of the characters on stage. A harp and a celeste characteristically complete the orchestra.

Portrait of Korngold circa 1915, at the time he was composing *Violanta* (Korngold estate).

Harmonically, this score is one of Korngold's simplest, and he has clearly set out to provide music that is uncluttered by anything too complex yet that retains a distinct twentieth-century pulse in its rhythmic concept. It is his solution to the problem of mirroring an eighteenth century story (the opera takes place in 1797) in an idiom that a modern audience will accept. He does not resort to archaism or try to emulate the style of the classicists, but occasionally recalls the period in parody, especially in the use of the celeste in the "Diary Song" (in the manner of a harpsichord accompanying a recitative). He further recalls the Mozartean era in the way the opera is constructed by ample usage of vocal ensemble and by clearly marking all the principal arias.

Melodically, this work again contains the motto theme (almost the first sounds we hear are a bubbling variation of it), but the score is replete with melodic invention, not only of variants of this all-important motif but also some of Korngold's most engaging melodies. The score fairly overflows with good humor.

The orchestration of *Der Ring des Polykrates* was complete by the spring of 1914. Meanwhile, the composer's father speculated on how his gifted son would treat a tragic subject. Up to now, his works had been characterized by playful, carefree subject matter, but the slow movements of his principal compositions had indicated that he might be capable of more profound work. Dr. Korngold also realized that *Polykrates* alone was insufficient to sustain a whole evening performance, so he approached Hans Müller, his former colleague in Brünn who now contributed regularly to the *Neue Freie Presse*, and asked him for a libretto.

Müller was by now an experienced and well-known playwright and novelist. He was one of the "personalities" in Vienna, as famous for his eccentricities (he was a confirmed hypochondriac) as for his great talent as a raconteur.[10] Müller admired the young Korngold and had provided a short text for his *Sieben Märchenbilder*. He clearly understood what type of opera libretto might suit the needs of such an extravagant imagination, and he offered two stories. The first, a treatment of the life of Girolamo Savonarola, the fifteenth-century reformer, was rejected (the reason is unclear). The second, however, appealed immediately and, with some dramatic changes to Müller's outline made by Korngold himself, was given the melodious title of *Violanta* after the name of its principal character. It was a renaissance tragedy set in Venice, and its plot was redolent of many similar plays and operas popular during the years up to and during the First World War, including Franz Schreker's *Die Gezeichneten* (The Branded) and his unproduced play *Der rote Tod* (The Red Death), Max von Schillings's *Mona Lisa*, and Alexander von Zemlinsky's *Eine Florentinische Tragödie* (A Florentine Tragedy), and the plays *Mona Vanna* by Maurice Maeterlinck and *Beatrice's Veil* by Arthur Schnitzler, all of which were written around this time. Though the melodramatic plot of *Violanta* owes something to all of these works, it is enhanced considerably by the music, which elevates its occasionally contrived situations into a potent theatrical experience. The story is as follows:

Violanta, a grande-dame of fifteenth-century Venice, has vowed to avenge the suicide of her sister, the abandoned lover of the handsome Alfonso, Prince of Naples. During the carnival, she finds Alfonso and lures him to her house, where, at a pre-arranged signal (Violanta will sing the blasphemous carnival song) her husband Simone will kill him, and thus avenge her sister's death. After initial hostility, however, she falls in love with the prince herself. After a rapturous duet ("Reine Liebe," Everlasting Love) she sings the carnival song. When her husband appears from behind an arras, dagger drawn, she throws herself between the two men and dies, thereby expiating her adultery.

Korngold's response to this tale is one of the most remarkable scores he ever produced. I consider it to be the most significant of his early works. He seemed to leap with one bound across the void spanning the *"Wunderadolescent"* to the fully mature adult (although there was nothing immature about his early music). It is the *character* of his music that suddenly changed. The charm, humor, and endearing boyishness pervading his early music is swept aside and replaced by an intense erotic fantasy, which even now packs an enormous punch.

The challenges of setting this highly charged story to music to make it dramatically plausible are met superbly. In the vocal writing, Korngold shows himself to be a master of unrelentingly high tessitura, which makes his operas so difficult to cast. Korngold's vocal line lies almost invariably in the *passaggio* of the voice, and this, coupled with his emancipated rhythms that throw an unexpected extra pulse or bar of unusual meter into the melodic line, makes the major Korngold roles devilishly difficult to sing. The exciting rubato of these waywardly impish rhythmic inspirations creates the impression of music in a constant state of ferment and adds to the overall tension.

The orchestra is large, with a full complement of strings, three flutes and a piccolo, two oboes, an English horn, three clarinets, a bass clarinet, two bassoons, contra-bassoon, four horns, three trumpets, three trombones, bass tuba, two harps, celeste, piano, kettle drum, cymbals, triangle, glockenspiel, xylophone, tambourine, snare and bass drums, deep bells, and tam-tam. There is a full operatic chorus.

Considerable progress is evident since the Sinfonietta in B Major. Once again sonority is all-important, and the instrumentation is translucent, shimmering, and pointillistic. The keyboards and harps, which supported the harmony in his previous works, assume even greater importance here, particularly in the luscious rising arpeggio figure from the Vorspiel (Prelude).

Harmonically, this opera is a completely new departure for Korngold. He seems to have consciously decided to reflect physically (in a way that would be felt by his audience) the immensely pent-up sexual frustration and passion felt by the characters on stage by drenching the score in the densest chromaticism. The unsettling atmosphere is created immediately with the very first sounds we hear—the "Violanta chord," spaced across the whole orchestra, arching four and a half octaves. This peculiar, altered ninth chord, comprising a deep E pedal (on a low tubular bell) with a central augmented triad in the horns and an inverted C-sharp pedal point, could have been written by no other composer.[11] The spacing of chords in this manner is entirely Korngold's. This opening poses a sinister musical question mark, which is only answered in the second half of the opera.

The score abounds with masterly effects. Korngold's use of the chorus is truly virtuosic, as in the opening scene, where three separate choral groups sing in conjunction with each other, one on stage and the other two off stage, with a superbly handled climax. Aside from the main roles, there is a glittering scherzo written for a minor character, Bracca, a foppish painter who is infatuated with Violanta. As Violanta enters for the first time, Korngold deftly segues Bracca's exultant music into her theme by means of an ingenious bridge passage. More impressive than all of this, however, is Korngold's treatment of the second half of the opera: the confrontation of Violanta and Alfonso.

Once the plan to kill Alfonso has been agreed, Violanta sits down to have her hair dressed by her elderly maid Barbara. This scene, recalling that in *Othello* in which Desdemona prepares for bed, was added by Korngold as a means of releasing the tension before building it up again. In the same vein, as a twentieth-century equivalent to Verdi's "Willow Song," the old maid sings a lullaby from Violanta's childhood. The music tries to stay in the diatonic confines of D major but is persistently and disturbingly penetrated by shrill harmonies that bitonally color it with stark minor chords, filling the scene with foreboding. These inflections represent the disturbances in the mind of Violanta, as she contemplates the murderous act to come. They are extremely effective.

The major melodic highlights are Alfonso's serenade, his long aria, and the beautiful duet "Reine Liebe," which are linked by heroic passages of impetuous declamatory singing. When the duet does come, it has the effect of a soothing balm, even to the extent that the musical language is purified, "dipped" as Richard Specht described it, in the warm key of B major.

The plot here is somewhat far-fetched and improbable. After all, the writer has to convince us that Violanta can change from hating Alfonso so much that she has planned to kill him, to falling under his spell, and then deciding that he is the man of her dreams.

Alfonso, too, has to undergo a veritable metamorphosis: first he learns that the woman he expects to be a willing lover is bent on killing him; then, after her change of heart, he realizes that she is the one true love he has been searching for all his life and that, having found her, he no longer fears death. It sounds implausible (what opera libretto does not?)—that it becomes convincing on stage is a tribute to the power of the music.

VIOLANTA

Violanta, Opus 8, the first eight bars. (Reproduced by permission of the publishers Schott Musik International, Mainz, Germany.)

As a radical work, *Violanta* must have made a striking comparison to contemporary operas at the time. One has only to listen to, say, *Mona Lisa*—a solid but highly conservative score by von Schillings—to understand how original Korngold's harmonic thinking was and how bold and individual his concepts were. As an example of precocity, this score is still without equal for a composer so young.

The composition of *Violanta* occupied most of 1914, especially during the summer vacation, when the Korngold family took a small villa in Alt-Aussee in the Austrian Salzkammergut. Julius Korngold recalled:

> We no longer went to the Dolomites . . . and I remained faithful to Alt-Aussee for several years, but eventually I renounced its charm. The reason was the invasion by intellectuals, writers, and musicians. Once I counted thirty pianists, violinists, and composers. Wherever one went, pianos were pounded, fiddles were played, or someone sang; you virtually were afraid of stepping into a sonata. The regular summer guests who owned large, comfortable villas outdid each other in opulent musical soirees and vied for the presence of celebrities. In this manner a mini–summer season developed, which was more than uncomfortable for someone saturated with music during the winter.
>
> In 1914 this music-making stopped abruptly. War had broken out. The first sign was the requisitioning of horses in the entire district. A sad pair of oxen slowly dragged us and our belongings to the station. Erich's luggage contained the *Violanta* sketches and the beginnings of his Sextet for Strings in D Major. It was a miserable trip, a miserable arrival. The sky seemed flooded with red light, like a threat of blood. In Vienna we were greeted by the calls of paper boys announcing disaster—"World Conflagration!" In my wild imaginings I saw my young opera composer, so ill-suited for the trade of war, swept along by the storm. The endangered boy, however, was little concerned about the events around him. Work on both operas progressed and the anxieties of wartime coincided with Erich's artistic advancement.[12]

These remarks were amply supported by the memories of the poet and writer Paul Elbogen, Erich's boyhood friend, who later recalled meeting Julius Korngold in the street sometime in 1914 while Elbogen was on his way to join up: "With tears running down his cheeks, he took hold of me and cried, 'It's all right for you my friend, you have nothing to risk but, remember, I have to protect a treasure for the world!'"[13]

Although the early war news did tend to upstage the latest events at the opera house, attentions were refocused after a while. War or no war, life in Vienna went on much as before. Around this time, Julius Korngold became a close friend of the Russian privy counselor Alfred von Fraenkel, who with his wife Luise von Fraenkel-Ehrenstein (a former star of the Vienna Court Opera) kept one of the liveliest musical salons of the time. Julius Korngold remarked:

> With sparkling eyes, dimpled cheeks, and enormous charm which never stiffened into empty dignity, Luise Ehrenstein was not only gracious herself, but she managed to make the people around her become gracious. This was the secret of her salon, which may have been the last of its kind.[14]

Young Erich was feted in these surroundings and was frequently called upon to play his works, or occasionally Frau Ehrenstein and her pupils would perform his music for his approval. He dedicated his *Sechs Einfache Lieder,* Opus 9, (composed 1911–1916) to her in gratitude for her interest and support.

The *Sechs Einfache Lieder* are the first songs Korngold published, although he had been composing songs since the age of seven. In his childhood composition notebooks are well over two dozen unpublished songs composed between the ages of eleven and fourteen, which presumably he did not feel were good enough. The Opus 9 set, however, certainly is good enough. Based on texts by Eichendorff and some lesser poets, the songs are filled with a nostalgic melodic sweetness that is most affecting. The first, "Schneeglöckchen" (Snowdrops) to a text by Eichendorff, was written in 1911. Its radiant melody had already been used again for the Finale of the Sonata in G Major for violin and piano, published later. It is full of unexpected harmonic turns. In spite of his youth, Korngold had already mastered the art of matching words to a pointed harmonic inflection by constantly phrasing the text and bringing it alive.

All of the songs are masterpieces in miniature. The fourth, "Liebesbriefchen" (A Little Love Letter), is perhaps the most famous. Its ravishing melody, in spite of its simple ABA structure, is quite complex in detail. "Das Heldengrab am Pruth" (The Hero's Grave at Pruth) opens with a strange, bitonal introductory figure in which the right hand plays an eerie triplet motif centered on the key of C (both major and minor), set against a left hand accompaniment in C-sharp minor that reflects the text, a poem despairing of a lost love. "Nachtwanderer" (Night Wanderer) is a heart-rending hymn of despair in D minor, with its somber accompaniment of bare open fifths like a mournful bell tolling. The harmonic scheme is extremely advanced and subtle, revealing Korngold's extraordinary skill. He modulates from B-flat major to C-sharp major within just two bars by judicious use of an enharmonic pivot note (F natural/E-sharp). At the final bars, the accompaniment combines B minor and B major to mimic the call of a rooster mentioned in the text. This song could be described as Korngold's "Erlkönig."

"Ständchen" (Serenade), in contrast, is a radiant, playful, and thoroughly extrovert piece. Once again, in spite of the nominal C major tonality, the harmonic language is remarkably sophisticated. "Sommer" (Summer), the last song, is perhaps the most exquisite, with its apt recollection of the Adagietto from Mahler's Symphony No. 5 in its opening bars before the broad, heartfelt melody accompanied by one of Korngold's richest piano settings begins. In these early songs, Korngold proved himself a master composer of Lieder and a worthy descendant of Schubert, Wolf, Mahler, and Richard Strauss. The songs were probably first performed at one of the Ehrenstein soirees before the great singers of the period took them up, including Elisabeth Schumann, Lotte Lehmann, and Selma Kurz.

Meanwhile, the two operas awaited a first performance. At the Ehrenstein salon, a distinguished and influential man heard the young Korngold play his newly completed operas for the assembled guests. This man was none other than Hans Gregor, Weingartner's successor as director of the Vienna Court Opera.

CHAPTER SEVEN

Operatic Triumphs

*W*ith Hans Gregor, another door opened for the young Korngold.[1] The business-minded director of the Vienna Court Opera appreciated the dramatic qualities of the two operas, especially when they were played by the composer himself in his inimitable, tempestuous style. During the summer of 1915 following that all-important performance at the Ehrenstein salon, Gregor requested the rights to perform both operas. Julius Korngold, who until now habitually opposed the premieres of his son's works in Vienna, this time agreed wholeheartedly. He had good reason, as he recalled later:

> In those days, musicians, writers, and artists of rank were exempted from military duty, and a government assignment would all but guarantee release for Erich. . . . With the approval of the Lord Chamberlain's office, the Court Opera requested two one-act operas from him, which of course were identical to those already started. In the Ministry of Education, which administered the Court Theaters, the matter was supported by Dr. Carl Ritter von Wiener, an artistically minded official who had succeeded in having the Conservatory nationalized just before the war. Later, he was reappointed to his old position as president of the Staatsakademie, and he remained Erich's loyal admirer. One of his first actions in his reorganization was the appointment of the young artist as an

instructor of operatic dramaturgy and instrumental performance. In gratitude, Erich dedicated his Sextet for Strings in D Major to him.[2]

Although it had been explained to Gregor that the contract was purely a formality to safeguard the composer from the dangers of war and to keep him in Vienna, Gregor tried to enforce the terms of the contract and actually to present the world premiere in Vienna.

Julius Korngold did not hold Gregor in high esteem, and his relations with Gregor were as cool and strained as they had been with Gregor's predecessor, Weingartner. As the critic wrote caustically in his memoirs:

> The choice of Gregor . . . for the Opera . . . was a strange one, not only because he was . . . completely unmusical, but primarily because he had been imported from Germany to improve the Opera's finances after having failed in this very area at the Komische Oper in Berlin.

Later on, he remarked: "When he heard excerpts from Erich's operas at the von Fraenkel-Ehrenstein salon he sensed if not their *musical* then at least their dramatic qualities."[3]

The matter of the premiere was unresolved as the Korngold family left for their annual summer holiday, once again in Alt-Aussee, preceded by a trip through Germany. In Frankfurt, they met again with Egon Pollak, who had followed the career of the prodigy ever since he had conducted *Der Schneemann* in Leipzig in March 1911. He was entranced by the two one-act operas, and later conducted them in Hamburg.

The Korngolds traveled on to Garmisch in Bavaria to visit Richard Strauss. Julius Korngold recalled the memorable visit in his memoirs:

> To arrive at Strauss's grand-seigneurial summer residence, one had to evade dangerous watchdogs. The master had entrenched himself thoroughly against unwelcome visitors; only barbed wire was missing. A sign at the garden gate instructed Tamino, who wanted to enter the Temple, that he had to announce himself through a megaphone and wait to see if a resounding *Zurück* would not make him turn on his heels. Then, as you set foot on the manicured paths, you had to overcome the fear of coming into conflict with Frau Pauline's housewifely fanaticism.
>
> With the diligence which the gods have placed before the fruits of genius, Strauss was deeply involved with a new opera *Die Frau ohne Schatten*. He worked in a loggia with the most beautiful shadows imaginable, and the first pages of the score were lying in the front of him.
>
> Strauss seemed to have taken over Wagner's pedantry in the external aspects of his working method, in the appearance of the score, in the minutely ruled and measured bar lines, page after page, in the neatness of his manuscript. I admired the delicate small notes resembling little pigeons fluttering over white space. Of the new

opera, only the first act was ready, but a new symphonic poem—*Eine Alpensinfonie*—was finished.

The master was kind enough to play it for us in its entirety. He felt that it was not revolutionary at all but rather reactionary, and he commented candidly that sometimes one also had to have the courage of banality.

One episode he played twice, with a twinkle at the young admirer seated next to him: the tourist climbs through a narrow canyon and the listener also has to surmount towering peaks of sharp chords. This was something for Erich, he said. One thing became clear to me during this performance spiced by running commentary: Strauss really needed the stimulant of external associations, or he had at least become used to focusing his inspiration on them.

The outbreak of the war had interrupted the performances of his ballet *Die Josephslegende* in Paris, and the diabolical dance of hand grenades could not replace for him the saintly leaps and pirouettes of his shepherd. Richard Strauss could be very amiable and also appealingly Bavarian, candid to the point of roughness.

In those days, when he still promoted young talents, he was unusually open-hearted toward Erich and me. We departed, our mutual sympathy in full bloom. Erich was devoted to Strauss from the moment of their first contact and remained so throughout his life, later frictions notwithstanding.[4]

Following the visit to Garmisch, the Korngolds finally arrived at Alt-Aussee. Their cottage naturally was equipped with a piano, and the sound of Korngold playing excerpts from *Violanta* and *Polykrates* soon attracted nearby residents. Among these was Baron Clemens von Franckenstein, the intendant of the Munich Court Opera, a fine musician and composer in his own right and one-time fellow student with Percy Grainger and the noted pianist Cyril Scott at Frankfurt. Greatly impressed with the two operas, he asked Julius Korngold for the rights to give the first performances. Dr. Korngold saw at once a solution to his problem in Vienna. Other musicians vacationing in the area encouraged him to agree to the Munich premiere, among them Bruno Walter (who, according to Julius, compared Erich to Verdi) and Anton Fuchs, the noted stage director. Fuchs and Walter were both attached to the Munich Court Opera. Julius Korngold agreed to the baron's request, and Walter conducted the two operas in Munich in the staging by Fuchs.

A possible confrontation in Vienna over the contract was avoided. In his memoirs, Julius Korngold states that Gregor threatened legal action and finally went to see Moritz Benedikt at the *Neue Freie Presse* and demanded that he intervene. Benedikt supposedly "ordered" Gregor to renounce his rights, saying that the operas should first prove their merit in another major theater. According to archived correspondence, however, what actually happened was that Julius Korngold loftily advised Gregor that his son would attend the Munich rehearsals and premiere. As Gregor did not want to risk a premiere in Vienna without the composer present, he postponed his production until April.

Even then, problems beset the production. Korngold was taken ill with an inflammation of the middle ear but nevertheless supervised everything from his bed—the correction of the score, the copying of the parts, the production of the piano score. This material had to be sent to Munich piecemeal. He was only sufficiently recovered in time for the dress rehearsal. His father attended the dress rehearsal (accompanied by the writer Hermann Bahr, who praised the works vociferously), but as usual declined to attend the first night, having been warned by a colleague of a possible hostile reaction from his enemies.

The premiere took place on 28 March 1916. Bruno Walter's "discovery," Maria Ivogün, sang the part of Laura opposite Karl Erb in *Der Ring des Polykrates*. In *Violanta*, the *Heldentenor* was replaced by an operetta tenor at the last minute,[5] but the house soprano Emmy Krüger apparently gave a good account of the title role. The whole evening was an unqualified success. Despite Dr. Korngold's anxieties, the operas met with critical approval in the German press. Richard Specht was ecstatic in his praise:

> Both these works belong—I say this with deliberation and emphasis and without a liking for superlatives—to the most profoundly rich dramatic music with which, along with the works of Richard Strauss, we are blessed today. . . . here speaks one of the greatest hopes of our music, perhaps the greatest. Not only is it what he is capable of, but what he is in possession of, that settles the matter. New sources can be heard murmuring in his music.[6]

Leopold Schmidt noted Korngold's instinct for stagecraft:

> The important thing is . . . that in both works, the demands of the stage have been instinctively recognized and so assuredly met that there can no longer be any doubt about Korngold's dramatic gifts, and it is perhaps precisely in this area that we may expect his future to lie.[7]

Bruno Walter was singled out for special praise, particularly as he had not really distinguished himself before as an opera conductor. Years later in a memoir he fondly recalled:

> The experience of hearing the young Korngold play and sing for me the two operas which I was going to perform, I shall never forget. One might have compared his interpretation of his own works on the piano to the eruption of a musico-dramatic volcano, were it not that the lyrical episodes and graceful moments also found their insinuating expression in his playing.[8]

The premiere was crowned with a lavish party given by Prince Leopold of Prussia (who had already given a reception before the performance at which excerpts were performed). Korngold was feted by prominent members of Munich society and the artistic elite, an experience to which he was thoroughly accustomed by now.

The following month, the operas reached Vienna, where Gregor, determined to outdo his colleagues in Munich, had spared no expense or effort in making the production a gala affair. The cast was star-studded: the main roles of *Der Ring des Polykrates* were sung by Alfred Piccaver and Selma Kurz, while Maria Jeritza, the legendary diva who positively exuded glamor and sex appeal, took the title role in *Violanta*. Hermine Kittel brought distinction to the small but important role of Barbara the nurse. Both productions were designed by Wilhelm von Wymetal[9] and both were conducted by Leopold Reichwein. The performance on 10 April 1916 was a triumph. It marked a turning point in the career of Jeritza and established her as a great singing actress. It also began an artistic collaboration and a warm friendship with the young composer. "Eritschko," as she called him, later conceived his opera *Die tote Stadt* with her in mind. She sang the part of Violanta on many occasions throughout her spectacular career and brought her unique portrayal of this part to the United States after the First World War.[10]

The success in Vienna started these operas on a triumphant journey around Germany. Between April and December 1916, they were performed in Breslau, Chemnitz, Düsseldorf, Dortmund, Halle, Frankfurt, Bremen, Nürnberg, Hannover, and Dresden. One of the most enthusiastic interpreters was Otto Klemperer, who conducted the operas in Strasbourg in November 1916.

In Hamburg, the new intendant Dr. Hans Loewenfeld, who had been a Korngold supporter ever since the days of *Der Schneemann* when Engelbert Humperdinck had recommended the ballet to him, naturally secured the rights to the operas. Here, Vera Schwarz sang the title role in *Violanta*, while Klemperer's "obsession," Elisabeth Schumann, sang Laura in *Der Ring des Polykrates*.[11] This auspicious performance took place in February 1917, and it began the special relationship Korngold was to enjoy with the musical city of Hamburg—the "Korngold City," as he always called it.

In Prague, Alexander von Zemlinsky enthusiastically scheduled the two operas for the Neues Deutsche Theater, and the premiere took place on 16 November 1917 with Zemlinsky himself as conductor. Later that year, Wilhelm Furtwängler conducted the operas at Mannheim. But the real baptism of fire, as always, was Berlin.

The intendant, von Hülsen, had acquired the rights immediately after the Munich premiere but understandably waited until Vienna had presented the operas. The musical director in Berlin was Leo Blech, the noted conductor and composer and one-time pupil of Humperdinck, who had been an enthusiastic supporter of the young Korngold since he had heard him play his early works at the salon of Louise Wolff. Since then, he had been somewhat envious of Erich Korngold's meteoric rise to fame as an opera composer. Whatever the reasons, he was intractable in his decisions concerning the production of the two operas. When Korngold offered to play the operas on the piano for him, he declined; he refused permission for Korngold to be allowed to coach the singers. On the question of casting, he insisted on Lilly Hafgren as Violanta, despite being advised against her. Inexplicably, he only called a dress rehearsal for *Der Ring des Polykrates*. *Violanta* faced the critics without adequate preparation. As the curtain rose, on 2 November 1917, the problems did not end, as Julius Korngold recalled wittily:

> From the prima donna's behavior, the press might have deduced that the heroine had fortified herself during Carnival night with an overdose of Chianti in a Venetian *osteria*. But while the prima donna tottered, the success did not.

Indeed, Korngold's first operas remained in the repertoire until political events in the 1930s forced them from the stage. They were given in Switzerland, Hungary, Finland, Czechoslovakia, and Sweden. Few German or Austrian stages neglected them.

In spite of his initial great success with these two significant works, Korngold could not escape the Great War. The earlier exemption from military service was called into question, particularly as the conflict became more terrible and more prolonged. Intrigues behind the scenes eventually brought matters to a head: Korngold would be made an example to show that favoritism did not exist in Austria.

Apparently, the defense minister became enamored with the thought of turning the prodigy into a war hero. When he was eventually summoned for a medical, the fates dealt Korngold an unexpected card: the doctor who was conducting the examination had been the resident physician and throat specialist to the singers at the Vienna Court Opera. Spotting Korngold in the waiting room, he asked him whether he had yet acquired his B classification (that is, exemption from active military service). Korngold ruefully replied that he had not. The doctor reassured him that all would be well, and, as it turned out, he was exempted from going to the front. Instead, he was made musical director of his regiment and consequently confined to Vienna.[12]

Private Korngold was in charge of the archives and the acquisition of music for the library, as well as conducting the regimental band. He composed several marches, one of which was published by Schott and was the source of a famous story. After conducting a preview performance for his commanding officer, the response was less than enthusiastic. The general was clearly perplexed: "Isn't it a little fast, Korngold?" he asked. "The men can't march to that." To which Erich replied, "Ah yes, well, you see Sir, this was composed for the retreat!"

KONZERTDIREKTION GUTMANN

WIEN, I.   (HUGO KNEPLER)   SCHELLINGGASSE 3

**Freitag, den 12. Oktober 1917, abends 7 Uhr
im Großen Musikvereins-Saale**

Orchesterkonzert

mit Werken von

Erich Wolfgang Korngold

Ausführende: Kammersängerin **Selma v. Halban-Kurz**,
Hofopernsänger **Hans Duhan**,
der **Philharmonische Chor** und
das **Wiener Tonkünstlerorchester.**
Dirigent: **Der Komponist.**

PROGRAMM:

1. Vorspiel und Karneval aus „Violanta".
2. Lieder mit Klavierbegleitung:
   Nachtwanderer (neu).
   Schneeglöckchen.
   Das Heldengrab am Pruth (neu).
   Österreichischer Soldatenabschied (neu).
                                    Hans Duhan.
                        Am Klavier: Der Komponist.
3. Tagebuchszene aus „Der Ring des Polykrates".
   Lieder mit Orchester: Sommer (neu).
   Liebesbriefchen (neu).
   Das Ständchen.   Selma v. Halban-Kurz.
4. Kaiserin Zita-Hymne für großes Orchester, Orgel, Baritonsolo, gemischten
   und Kinderchor. (Erste Aufführung.)
                        Solo: Hans Duhan.
                        Orgel: Prof. Georg Valker.
                        Chor: Der Philharmonische Chor und der Knaben-
                            chor des kath. Jünglingsvereines „Maria Hilf"
                            (Dirigent: Direktor D. J. Peterini).
                        ===== PAUSE =====
5. Sinfonietta H-dur, op. 5 für großes Orchester.
   Fließend, mit heiterem Schwunge.
   Scherzo (rasch und feurig).
   Molto andante (träumerisch).
   Finale (Patetico—Allegro giocoso).

Klavier: **Bösendorfer.**

**Das Reinerträgnis fließt der Weihnachtsbescherung für Waisenkinder
nach Gefallenen des k. k. Schützenregiments Nr. 1 zu.**

STERN & STEINER G. M. B. H., WIEN

Preis 20 Heller.

Gala charity concert in Vienna featuring an entire evening of Korngold's works,
conducted by him on 12 October 1917, and including the first performance of his
Kaiserin-Zita Hymne in its grandiose orchestral version (Korngold estate).

He also raised money for the orphans of war victims by conducting and giving recitals. In 1916, he had composed an epic *Kaiserin Zita-Hymne* for solo voice, choir, and piano (later for full orchestra, organ, soloists, and children's chorus), which was written and dedicated to the young Empress Zita, the last Habsburg monarch in Austria. Korngold conducted a special performance of it at the Schloss Schönbrunn in her presence.[13]

CHAPTER EIGHT

The Prodigy Falls in Love

The little Korngold had given way to the young Korngold. Now at the age of nineteen, he was fast becoming Korngold the man, yet he was a complete innocent where sexual matters were concerned. He had passed through the turbulence of adolescence relatively unscathed. His friendships with girls were innocuous, merely a series of schoolboy crushes. In contrast, his intellectual development was immense. Korngold had already absorbed a vast literature, and his knowledge of the music of the past and present was comprehensive. His abilities were not confined to music: he was a mathematical genius as well, which probably explains why he was capable of writing such complex rhythmic structures with ease.

How these opposites of naiveté and intellectual brilliance can be reconciled remains unanswered. The child in him thrived until the end, possibly because his parents constantly screened his friends and chaperoned him until he was nearly twenty. Young Korngold was cocooned from the pressures of life, yet with his vivid imagination he was able to inform his music with the gamut of emotions. There is nothing bland about the music of Korngold: it breathes and lives and is fired by a vital energy.

What was Korngold like at this age? Commentaries by two contemporary witnesses can tell us something. One was a local critic and friend; one was to become of unique importance in his life. The critic Julian Sternberg wrote for two newspapers in Vienna at the time, but eventually joined the

Neue Freie Presse. He observed Korngold in Vienna during the rehearsals for the one-act operas and wrote his impressions in the *Fremdenblatt* published in Vienna in March 1916:

> I recently saw him one evening stepping from the director's door out into the Kärntnerstrasse. He had quite clearly been present at the rehearsal. Lost in a dream and as though in a trance, he walked along, seeing everybody and recognizing no one, his coat wide open, his collar turned up, his hat on the back of his head so that the evening breeze might cool his brow. And then, walking faster all the time, he went along the Ringstrasse and past all the world.
>
> Involuntarily, I gazed after the youth. Something unusual struck me, but I did not know immediately what it was. At last I hit upon it: this was the first time I had seen him out without the accompaniment of his parents! Just think: a young man, eighteen years of age, recognized and acknowledged by the whole musical world, the hope of all, the fulfilment of many, a youth who as a sixteen-year-old before the war already came to stand second only to Richard Strauss in the number of performances of his works in Germany, Russia, England, and America—an artist of such standing may still in fact feel like a child.
>
> It must have been about eight years ago when Erich Korngold was still a schoolboy and not yet recognized as a wonder-child, that I met with Bruno Walter . . .and Maestro Rosé. The gentlemen were discussing the boy Korngold. Or rather, Walter was complaining about him. Walter had recently moved into a house on the Theobaldgasse. Above his lodgings are those of the critic, Dr. Korngold, whose son Erich fantasizes a great deal on the piano. He, Walter, is disturbed in his work by it because he involuntarily listens to everything he does and is thus forced to eavesdrop and listen on because the boy is a genius. It is incomprehensible what goes on in this child's brain, the way fantasy and precision wrestle with each other without one overcoming the other. The boldest flights of imagination are still kept within the confines of contrapuntal laws that the child must obey intuitively. . . .
>
> If we study a page of his score for *Violanta*—recently, one written in his own hand was to be seen in one of the rehearsal rooms at the Court Theater—we are amazed at its extraordinary yet ordered diversity. Just imagine: the page of such a score often contains thirty parts and therefore thousands of notes . . . and yet there are scarcely any corrections or rubbings out to be found. Everything that the finely pointed pencil of the young composer has written down seems to be permanent and as though for all eternity, and yet much is written straight into the score without any preparatory sketch! Erich

Korngold goes for a walk, composes and works out the instrumental parts as he does so, and then when he returns home he sits down and "copies it all down from [his] head" as he describes it himself. And what he has once heard and written down he never forgets! Or rather, he is incapable of forgetting it. In this sense we are also confronted by a phenomenon. Korngold is capable of playing with one finger on the piano or of simply singing the part of every instrument in the score of *Violanta*, of *Der Schneemann*, of the Sinfonietta all by itself (e.g. the viola part or the horn) from beginning to end *from memory*. Even the layman will grasp what that means; the miraculous nature of such proceedings, when one considers that Richard Strauss or Weingartner, for example, are incapable of playing their own works without a score, even when they have but recently completed it.[1]

Korngold at the piano at his parents' home, circa 1917. Note the Ambrosi bust in the background (Korngold estate).

It was apparent to all just how protective Korngold's parents were. In 1917, a young girl came into his life—the second important witness —who was eventually to break their suffocating dominance forever. Her name was Luise von Sonnenthal. Luzi, as Erich Korngold called her, was born in 1900, the granddaughter of Adolf Ritter von Sonnenthal, the great actor and matinee idol of the Burgtheater. She was one of three sisters, all renowned for their beauty. Helene became an actress and worked with Max Reinhardt for a time. Susanne was a painter and married Paul Jellinek, an import-export agent. Luzi was by far the most talented of them. She painted, played the piano, sang very well, and also acted. She even appeared in a few Austrian silent films directed by the legendary Michael Curtiz,[2] who later directed some of the classic films that Korngold would score in Hollywood. She idolized Mozart and was an avid reader. The Sonnenthal sisters had a brother Paul, who married Ilse Dehmel, the daughter of the poet Richard Dehmel. The household was brimming with culture. Close friends of the Sonnenthal children included the musical son of the writer Arthur Schnitzler. Like most good middle-class Jewish families, the Sonnenthals loved to entertain.

Significantly, a distant relative of theirs was Rudi Duschnitz, a very close friend of Korngold. Quite by chance, one evening in the spring of 1917, Luzi von Sonnenthal found herself at the same dinner table as Erich Korngold, having been invited by Otto Seligmann, a former admirer of hers and by now married to Mitzi Kolisch. Also present were Rudi Duschnitz and Trudi Kolisch (not yet married to Schoenberg). Luzi described her first impression of Korngold thus:

> He was not yet 20 years old and still in uniform. Above this towered the unconforming head of an artist. He had dark and already thinning hair, which stood up unevenly around his high forehead. His nose was broad and slightly bent and his mouth was soft and beautifully carved. His dark brown eyes were unusually large and shadowed by long and strangely obstinate lashes. His face was very pale . . . . After the black coffee, Erich was asked to play the piano. He reflected for a moment then said: "I will play you the entrance of Marietta." I sat among his disciples and did not know that in a few moments I was to become one of them.
>
> I heard him play for the first time—and it was the starting point for the respect I felt for the artist Korngold all my life. I don't know why I felt such strange "empathy" between him and myself that evening, I didn't meet him again for months . . . and then only by chance.[3]

Nevertheless, that first meeting was the beginning of the great love of Korngold's life. Luzi was the ideal partner for him and she in turn worshipped him, completely subordinating her own life to his according to the custom of the time, much as Korngold's mother had done in marrying Julius. Luzi von Sonnenthal was extremely talented in her own right. Her musical ability was a great bonus in her relationship with her husband. He would often ask her to play the piano for him. Their devotion was touching: "From the moment my friendship with Erich Korngold began, to the last when I lost this friend for good, I may say that my life has been one long and happy love story."

The "entrance of Marietta" referred to on that evening was from the opera *Die tote Stadt,* after Rodenbach's novel *Bruges la Morte,* which

Korngold had begun to compose in 1916. It was to become his most famous work.

Written in 1892, Georges Rodenbach's *Bruges la Morte* is one of the most significant works of the symbolist movement and is Rodenbach's most famous work, despite its brevity (it is barely 100 pages long). The story is set in Bruges, and concerns a man, Hugues, who mourns his dead wife. A miracle occurs: he meets a woman in the street who could pass for his dead wife's double. Impulsively he invites her home, seduces her, provides her with a house, and then, tormented with guilt, strangles her with the braid of his dead wife's hair, which she has sacrilegiously removed from its case (where he keeps it as a relic) and profaned. The story is filled with symbolic references as well as an intense undertone of Roman Catholicism.

Rodenbach adapted the novel into a four-act play entitled *Le Mirage*. Although it was accepted by the Comédie-Française in Rodenbach's life-time, it was never actually produced there or, in fact, anywhere else. It was translated into German (in 1902) by the Viennese playwright Siegfried Trebitsch as *Die stille Stadt* (The Silent City) and produced at the Lessing Theater, Berlin in September 1903.[4] In 1913, Trebitsch republished this version of Rodenbach's play as *Das Trugbild* (The Mirage) together with his translation of another play, *La Voile* (Der Schleier).

Trebitsch was a good friend of Julius Korngold's, and one day in 1916, the two met in the street. The conversation turned by chance to *Das Trugbild* and then to the possibility of turning it into an opera libretto. In an unpublished memoir, Trebitsch relates how he subsequently "met the young master Erich Wolfgang Korngold in search of a scenario or, even better, a mood or operatic background that could be dramatically elaborated. I urged him to take up *Das Trugbild*."[5] Julius Korngold recalled:

> As soon as Erich read the play, he drafted a scenario for a one-acter, but Hans Müller urged him to get away from one-act operas and he sketched the first of three acts in prose. However, his work on two of his own plays prevented him from getting much further, and since his prose was wordy and unsingable anyway, we gladly excused him from the task.[6]

The Korngolds decided to write the libretto themselves. They quickly realized that a pseudonym would have to be used, since Julius Korngold could not be publicly involved as he was both the composer's father and a leading critic. As had often occurred in the past, rumors were bound to spread that he had secretly authored the music as well, or used his influence to secure performances. The libretto was attributed to one "Paul Schott," which was an amalgam of the name of the principal tenor role in the opera and that of the composer's publisher Schott, to whose senior partner, Dr. Ludwig Strecker, the work is dedicated.[7] In his memoirs, Julius Korngold gives some indication of their joint work:

It was not difficult to find another writer inasmuch as Erich participated in the construction of the plot. The transformation of the action into a dream was my idea. I suggested it to soften the impact of the strangling of a woman, to create a conciliatory, elegiac ending.[8]

Korngold began to compose the music in 1916. One of his very first ideas was the famous "Lautenlied," also known as Marietta's "Lute Song," which became perhaps his most renowned melodic inspiration, described by some critics as "the last hit tune in German opera." An exquisite melody, it is deceptively simple in construction and is supported by unusually straight-forward harmony (for Korngold) to sound like an old-fashioned song from Paul's youth.

Military service caused him to put the opera aside for almost a year. When he found his way back to his inspiration, the particular part that had given him so much trouble—the entrance of Marietta—became one of the highlights of the score. His father recalled that in 1919 Korngold began to approach the problems of orchestration in a new way. He felt that up to then the sound of his orchestration had been too consistently rich. Now he aimed for what he called "Wagner's ingenious moderation in adhering whenever possible to the middle registers."[9]

Korngold confessed that he was deeply attracted to Rodenbach's novel because of its atmosphere—"characteristic of Bruges, melancholy, low keyed; the spiritual conflict between the two protagonists; the erotic force and drive of the living woman contending with the powerful sway still exerted by the dead one; the more fundamental concept of the struggle between death and life, and particularly the question of how the claims of life must cause us to moderate our grief at the departing of loved ones."[10]

The novel underwent a considerable transformation before it emerged as *Die tote Stadt* (The Dead City). The decision to make most of the drama into an extended dream afforded Korngold greater opportunities to create a colorful phantasmagoria of sound and image. The names of the chief char-acters were changed and Germanized: Hugues, the man obsessed with the memory of his dead wife, became Paul; and Jane Scott, the dancer he encounters who looks so like his dead wife, became Marietta. These changes were made presumably for musical reasons: Paul and Marietta are far easier names to sing than Jane and Hugues. Korngold also gave the dead wife a name—Marie, a nobler form of Marietta—to highlight the difference between the two women. The roles of Marie and Marietta are sung by the same singer. Also, the servant Barbe became Brigitta, and a new set of char-acters was added—Marietta's troupe of players—to allow for an exquisite harlequinade in Act II. During this scene, directly from *Bruges la Morte* in which Jane performs as a dancer in an opera, Marietta and her troupe dance a parody from Meyerbeer's 1831 opera *Robert le Diable* (in particu-lar, the graveyard resurrection scene).

Paul's house is still a reliquary to his dead wife, and prominently dis-played is a long braid of her hair (as in the novel). There is also a portrait of

Marie, which at the end of Act I in the original stage directions, comes to life. Marie steps out of the frame to warn Paul about his involvement with the young singer.

The shifting of the main action of the story into an hallucination considerably softened the mood of Rodenbach's book. If *Die tote Stadt* had been composed by, say, Franz Schreker or even Arnold Schoenberg, the approach would have been to emphasize the elements of violence and horror in the story and to underline the more lurid aspects. In particular, the necrophilous tendencies of the main character's obsession would undoubtedly have been highlighted. This approach was quite out of character for an optimistic composer like Korngold, however.[11] The opera as a whole, while containing morbid and fantastic elements, is more like an epic, heroic tone poem for voices and orchestra set to a passionate, romantic theme. If anything, it is a celebration of life rather than a reflection of death.

The musical language of *Die tote Stadt* is even more extravagant than that in *Violanta*, although the sense of being at the limits of tonality is not as strong. Each of Korngold's operas has its own definite world of sound reflected in the harmony and the orchestration. *Die tote Stadt* has a heroic quality in much of the music that is quite absent in *Violanta*. The orchestra is larger still—the largest Korngold ever used: triple woodwind, four horns, three trumpets, the rarely used bass trumpet, three trombones, tuba, timpani, and a full complement of strings. In addition there are five percussion with an extra five at the end of Act I, two harps, and of course the all-important keyboards: piano, celeste, and the additional effect of a full church organ and a harmonium, which is used to give some eerie effects. There are also a wind machine, a mandolin, two sets of bells (both tuned and untuned), a stage band of four trumpets and three trombones, another stage band of two trumpets and two E-flat clarinets, as well as a large chorus, a separate children's chorus, a chamber choir of 16 voices, and (for the "Pierrotlied") eight additional sopranos offstage.

All of this is handled with enormous skill, and one is frequently staggered by the sheer richness and kaleidoscopic brilliance of the sound. Particularly effective is the Zwischenspiel (Interlude) to Act II, which conjures up, in almost impressionistic fashion, the atmosphere and vista of Bruges, its bells, organ, and the rushing wind through its dank alleyways—even though Korngold never actually visited it until after the Second World War.[12]

Like Mahler, Richard Strauss, and Franz Schreker, Korngold strove to make the orchestra (especially the strings) sound like a single, intensely resonant instrument. He wanted to give the timbre and texture of the orchestral sound a cohesion that would be recognizably "his" sound. In *Die tote Stadt* and, more importantly, in *Das Wunder der Heliane*, his greatest work, he achieved this aim with consummate mastery. Korngold was one of the greatest orchestrators of this century, quite apart from his other achievements. This "sound," which certain critics claim to be derived from Strauss, is unmistakably personal to Korngold.

Die tote Stadt occupied Korngold for four years (1916–1920), yet astonishingly during that time he managed to complete his military service and begin yet another career: that of conductor. On 2 May 1917, the Rosé Quartet with Franz Jellinek (viola) and Franz Klein (violoncello) gave the first performance (from the manuscript) of the Sextet for Strings in D Major, Opus 10, which Korngold had begun simultaneously with *Violanta* and completed in 1916.

This is unquestionably his finest chamber work, and within its four-movement scheme it encompasses an astonishing range of moods. The delightful Intermezzo with its free variation of the "Motiv des fröhlichen Herzens" (Motto of the Cheerful Heart), from the Sinfonietta in B Major, is perhaps the most endearing music Korngold ever wrote. After the premiere, Josef Reitler wrote:

> From the *very first bar*, Erich Wolfgang Korngold's signature is unmistakable. Of the composers alive today, apart from Richard Strauss, there can be none who writes as personally and as individually as he; he represents the greatest musical talent in Austria.[13]

Later that month, on 26 May 1916, three days before his twentieth birthday, Korngold made his debut as conductor at the Vienna Court Opera on the occasion of the twentieth performance of his one-act operas. The occasion was a triumph, even though both father and son had had misgivings about the venture. About his conducting, his father had the following to say:

> His technique combined the sign language of great conductors, yet it also had a personal touch. Erich had thoughts of his own about the breathing, so to speak, of a musical work, when tone colors change and modulation takes place; about the preparation for a change of key toward which everything must pull; he also had his own ideas about the significance of the upbeat.
>
> Arnold Rosé told me with amazement how refreshing it had been to play under this young man. The daring deed found Erich calm and self-disciplined. When shortly before the curtain time the librarian rushed into Erich's dressing room and reported with extreme excitement that the conductor's score was nowhere to be found, Erich's instant reaction was that he would conduct from memory, in spite of the fact that over four hundred impractical time changes make *Violanta* a dreaded piece among modern works.
>
> Maria Jeritza later told us that after a phrase she had sung to his particular satisfaction, he had clapped his hands, applauding while beating time; she had been dumbfounded by such confidence.[14]

Meanwhile his works continued to make their mark. In January 1917, *Der Schneemann*, now in a fully revised orchestration by Korngold,[15] was performed for the first time in Berlin. *Violanta* and *Der Ring des Polykrates* continued on their triumphal progress. Korngold himself conducted them for the first time in Berlin early in 1918, when Leo Blech was called away. In November 1917, he took part in another special charity concert, this time for the widows and orphans of the war. On the program were three of his *Sieben Märchenbilder,* which he played himself; and Karl Godlewsky, who had danced the first *Der Schneemann,* danced it again with other members of the Imperial Ballet.

That autumn, Luzi von Sonnenthal commenced singing lessons with Professor Eduard Gartner. One evening, she attended a concert organized by Dr. Hertzka, who was the director of the Vienna Sanatorium for Merchants. As she recalled:

> . . . when I entered the room, I recognized Erich Korngold among the guests. He immediately came toward me and greeted me. When the performance started, we sat down together in one corner of the room. We had little opportunity to talk then—so we started a game: Erich passed me a piece of paper with humorous critical remarks on it, and I hurriedly scribbled some answers on the back. After the concert Erich offered to take me home. The strange feeling of intimate understanding was even stronger than at our first meeting.
>
> Then one day, I got an invitation from the Duschnitz family and when I arrived, Erich was there, and by the conspiratorial wink with which he greeted me, I was in no doubt as to who had arranged the invitation.
>
> From them on, I got to know Erich—both as an artist and as a human being. And that invitation wasn't the last: I was invited repeatedly to the Duschnitz home, obviously at Erich's request.[16]

Korngold was by now deeply in love with Luzi von Sonnenthal. Aided and abetted by his friends, he contrived to see her at every opportunity. He little realized how opposed their respective parents would be to the relationship: hers because they keenly observed the rigid rules of etiquette and were highly protective of their daughter, and his because of their over-protective concern and obsession that the "right girl" would have to be found for their son.

In the meantime, Erich received a commission to write some incidental music to Shakespeare's play *Much Ado About Nothing*. It was to become one of his most popular and widely loved scores. Its radiant music speaks clearly of his state of mind at that time—that of a young man who was deeply in love.

The "New Music" and the Aftermath of War: 1919–1923

CHAPTER NINE

"One of the Most Important and Successful Composers of Our Time"
—Max Kalbeck

Toward the end of the First World War, the demands on Korngold's time from his military commanders increased considerably. Morale was low and the need for entertainment grew. Music became more important than ever. Even though he remained in Vienna and never experienced the horrors of the trenches, he found it difficult to focus his thoughts on the new opera or indeed on creative work of any kind.

During 1918, up until the Armistice in November, little of any significance came from his pen, and work on *Die tote Stadt* (which at this stage had the working title *Der Triumph des Lebens*, The Triumph of Life) ceased altogether. He had, however, written a patriotic "Austrian Soldier's Song of Farewell," which he completely revised in 1920 for inclusion in his *Vier Lieder des Abschieds* (Four Songs of Farewell), Opus 14.[1] If work on the opera had reached an impasse, Korngold welcomed the commission from Messrs. Rundt and Ziegler, directors of the Vienna Volksbühne, to compose incidental music for Shakespeare's comedy *Much Ado About Nothing*, and he set to work immediately.

Realizing the limitations imposed on the forthcoming production by the effects of the war, including that only a small orchestra could be mustered for the premiere, Korngold ingeniously scored the music for just nineteen performers. This chamber orchestra comprised one flute/piccolo, one oboe,

The only photograph taken of Private Korngold in uniform, circa 1918, in the garden of his home (Korngold estate).

one B-flat clarinet, one bassoon, two horns in F, one trumpet in C, one trombone, a small string ensemble, and an unusually large percussion section augmented by harmonium, harp, piano, and timpani. Resourceful use of the piano and harmonium enriched the sound considerably.

The music (in fourteen sections) was complete by the end of 1918 and orchestrated the following summer. For reasons that have proved impossible to determine, the production scheduled by the Volksbühne was cancelled. Fortuitously, the Burgtheater offered to mount a production of the play to take advantage of the newly completed score. The director of the Burgtheater scheduled the premiere to take place at the delightful little baroque theater in the Schönbrunn Palace.[2]

Meanwhile, in January 1918, Korngold had once again appeared as conductor in a concert devoted entirely to his own works, with the Vienna Symphony Orchestra. This time, in addition to presenting his *Schauspiel Ouvertüre* and the "Vorspiel und Karneval" from *Violanta*, he was joined by Lotte Lehmann, who sang the "Diary Song" from *Der Ring des Polykrates* and two of the *Sechs Einfache Lieder,* Opus 9, which Korngold had recently orchestrated: "Sommer" and "Liebesbriefchen." This was the first time they were given in their orchestral version.[3]

As the year 1918 drew to a close, work on *Die tote Stadt* commenced again in earnest, and the three acts were completely drafted by the summer of the following year, when the long process of orchestration was to begin. Korngold was probably inspired as much by the war's end as by his blossoming relationship with Luzi von Sonnenthal. Throughout 1917 and for much of 1918 they had been meeting as guests at the home of the Duschnitz family. Luzi later provided a fascinating glimpse of these intimate soirees:

> The evening program was always the same. After dinner, Erich went to the piano and played his own works for hours. I learned a great deal then. Guests made requests for *Violanta*, the Largo from the Piano Sonata No. 2, or some new music from *Die tote Stadt* on which Erich had been working for a year then. Later in the evening, waltzes by Johann Strauss were often requested. One evening, Rudi Duschnitz put *Elektra* by Richard Strauss on the piano—but Erich didn't need the score . . . . no bar or note was strange to him.[4]

In the aftermath of the war, poverty, deprivation, and inflation were as much a part of life in Austria as in Germany. Yet despite the restrictions these conditions placed on musical life, Korngold's career continued to flourish. With the coming of peace, he began a new career as an itinerant conductor of his own works, and he made visits to Hamburg, Berlin, Frankfurt, Budapest, and even his home town of Brünn.

Korngold at the piano in his study, circa 1918 (Korngold estate).

On 4 December 1918, almost as a celebration of the cessation of hostilities, a "Korngold Evening" was held in Vienna with the faithful Rosé Quartet and Korngold himself in a program comprising the Piano Trio in D Major, the Piano Sonata No. 2 in E Major, and the Sextet for Strings in D Major.

In 1919, Hans Gregor was succeeded by Richard Strauss and Franz Schalk as co-directors of the Vienna State Opera. The unsatisfactory decision to split the responsibility of running the great opera house between these two noted musicians was weakened further in that it was unfairly loaded in Strauss's favor. Julius Korngold was highly sceptical about the arrangement, but for the moment he contented himself with quoting Homer's remark, "One shall be Master," and as it turned out, he was correct. The fiftieth anniversary of the Vienna Opera was celebrated that spring, and in May the new duumvirate invited Korngold to be guest conductor for a gala performance of his one-act operas during the special anniversary festival.[5]

The cast was star studded: the part of Laura in *Der Ring des Polykrates* was given to Lotte Lehmann, with Alfred Piccaver and Rose Ader supporting; while Maria Jeritza repeated her triumphant portrayal in *Violanta*, co-starring with Leo Slezak as Alfonso.

The performance of the operas was predictably a triumph, not only for Korngold the composer but for Korngold the conductor. Franz Schalk, in a letter to the composer, declared the performance the "high spot of the Festival," while the acclaim in the press was unanimous. The faithful Richard Specht noted that "Korngold conducted *Violanta* as in a sleep-walking hypnosis." Max Kalbeck remarked: "Erich Wolfgang Korngold has rendered all discussions about his amazing talent to nothing. He is one of the most important and successful composers of our time."[6] But the most telling appraisal was written by the composer and musicologist Egon Wellesz, who said in part:

> In these works of a sixteen-year-old, the problem of the personal experience seems to have become non-existent if one considers that an adolescent purely by intuition could have reproduced so uncannily the emotions and passions he cannot have yet experienced. In both of the operas all phases of love are described, ranging from delicate flirtation to the most sensual eroticism, and nothing can erase the impression that the presentation is important in its own way and shows an amazingly sure instinct for the scenic requirements of drama.

Much has been written already about these works: time and again, however, the naive gaiety of *Der Ring des Polykrates* enchants while the powerful sensuality of *Violanta* fascinates with its magical orchestral sounds. Korngold was acclaimed after both operas with extraordinary fervor. Of those composers who conduct their own works, one must particularly think of Erich Wolfgang Korngold's magnificent interpretation. We can expect some outstanding things from him in his field of creation.[7]

Korngold was proud to conduct the operas for the festival, especially as he had had to withdraw them from production the previous year because of the insinuation that they were being mounted at the opera house to curry favor with the *Neue Freie Presse*, an accusation that would acquire a familiar ring in the coming years.

Strauss was sufficiently impressed with Korngold's conducting to offer him a permanent engagement as conductor at the Vienna State Opera and to share the repertoire with Schalk and himself. Julius Korngold protested, however, that if his son were so engaged he would have to resign as a critic. The offer was therefore politely refused but, typically, news of it leaked out. Dr. Korngold's enemy Max Graf made a considerable issue of it when another aspiring conductor was denied the post. Graf claimed it was through fear of Julius Korngold that the young man was turned down. Strauss was angry at the innuendo that he was a puppet of the *Neue Freie Presse* and published an emphatic denial. This was the first of many occasions in which Strauss would be implicated in Korngold's affairs.

Just prior to his appearance at the Vienna festival, Korngold had enjoyed a wonderful meal at the home of Rudi Duschnitz, which was quite a rare occasion in the time of austerity following the war. The first course had been a magnificent gooseliver paté, and Korngold (who loved food) was stimulated to write a waltz-song to his own humorous text, which he presented to his hosts a short while later. This piece *Die Gansleber im Hause Duschnitz* (The Gooseliver in the Duschnitz House) was never published, but the manuscript survives and it is one of his most charming occasional pieces.

Major composition also preoccupied him once more, and he sought out a country retreat in Gmunden on the Traunsee so that he might work undisturbed. Luzi was on holiday with her family at Strobl on the Wolfgangsee. Each day after working on the orchestration of the new opera, which had now been definitely titled *Die tote Stadt*, he journeyed to see Luzi in the evenings.

Korngold also began a new orchestral piece: his Opus 13, *Sursum Corda*, a grandiose symphonic overture for large orchestra. The title, taken from the Latin invocation from the Roman Catholic Mass (Lift Up Your Hearts), indicates the nature of this work, which is a direct successor to the Sinfonietta in B Major and is filled with optimism and hope. Perhaps Korngold wanted to create a work that would reaffirm life and the hope of his countrymen after the horror of war. Certainly it is an exuberant creation. Significantly, he dedicated it to Richard Strauss; indeed, the character of the work is closely aligned with the symphonic poems of Strauss, although without a specific program.

The principal motif for solo trumpet is a heroic, rhythmically complex inspiration that has much in common with the earlier "Motto of the Cheerful Heart" in Opus 5, although it could not be described as a variation on it.[8] Whereas in the Sinfonietta in B Major, a childlike innocence and joy colors the music, here the emotion and mood reflect Korngold's maturity. The music is vigorous and complex in its rhythmic demands, and although the form of the work is structured around a ternary plan, Korngold adopts a very free approach within that framework. Roaming counterpoint, iridescent coloristic effects, ever-changing meter, and constant interplay between the motifs make the piece a challenge for conductors.

Korngold delighted in throwing the most unexpected rhythmic changes into the melodic line, which contribute to the sense of restlessness in his music. There are also frequent glimpses of *Die tote Stadt* in this score, which was being orchestrated at the same time. *Sursum Corda* was completed by Christmas 1919 and received its premiere in Vienna by the Vienna Symphony Orchestra conducted by Korngold himself on 24 January 1920. The program also included the Vorspiel und Karneval from Korngold's *Violanta*, three pieces from the newly completed score for Korngold's *Much Ado About Nothing*, Beethoven's "Egmont" Overture, a symphony by Leopold Mozart, and Mahler's *Kindertotenlieder* sung by Hans Duhan.[9] While the music to *Much Ado About Nothing* had to be encored, *Sursum Corda* was, in Luzi's words "the first noisy flop for Erich."

The audience hissed and booed the work, for the music was difficult to grasp on first hearing—though this seems incredible today, when one considers the subsequent development of modern music. According to Luzi, Korngold was not depressed by the failure but astonished, rather like a child who thinks himself unfairly punished.[10]

The premiere of *Much Ado About Nothing* on 6 May 1920 dispelled memories of the failure of *Sursum Corda*, however. Korngold himself conducted in Schönbrunn Castle, and he had the bonus of having members of the Vienna Philharmonic Orchestra for the performance. Luzi was present, naturally, and considered the work to be a little masterpiece. Korngold laughed at being told this and quipped: "Eine kleine Bühnenmusik!"[11]

Clearly no one realized that the production with Korngold's delicate and witty score would be so popular. When the Philharmonic musicians departed to fulfil other previously booked engagements in the autumn, Korngold was faced with a dilemma. Ever resourceful, he quickly made an arrangement of the score for violin and piano to be played by himself and his friends Paul Breisach and Rudolf Kolisch.[12] He even persuaded the principal horn player of the Vienna Philharmonic, Karl Anton Stiegler, to come on his night off to join them in the brilliant Hornpipe (with the bribe of a good cigar). The production even outstayed its welcome at Schönbrunn.

Much Ado About Nothing finally transferred to the Burgtheater in October 1920. Meanwhile, the music was so popular that Korngold arranged a five-movement suite for orchestra that was played all over the world, while the arrangement for violin and piano was taken up by many prominent violinists, including Mischa Elman, Fritz Kreisler, Jascha Heifetz, and Toscha Seidel. Along with the "Lute Song" from *Die tote Stadt*, the music to *Much Ado About Nothing* became one of Korngold's most famous and most recorded works.

Korngold in 1919, at the time he was working on *Die tote Stadt* (courtesy of Bernd O. Rachold).

The full score of *Die tote Stadt* was completed on 15 August 1920, a little before nine o'clock in the evening. This was deliberate, for Korngold liked to set deadlines for himself, meet them pedantically, and then celebrate with his family and friends. The following day, he set off for a short vacation in the Salzkammergut. Meanwhile, he had already played the score for his publishers in Mainz, and, as was the custom, the contract was sealed with a wine-tasting spree in the famed wine cellars there.

The news of the new opera by Korngold precipitated vigorous campaigning by many of the leading opera houses. Franz Schalk was anxious to secure the rights for the world premiere for Vienna. As always, the delicate situation in Vienna due to the position of Korngold's father made this problematical. Julius demanded that the opera be given to a theater outside the radius of his influence. In Hamburg, the brilliant intendant Dr. Hans Loewenfeld,[13] who respected and admired Korngold, insisted that the rights be assigned to him. Korngold trusted Loewenfeld and readily agreed, especially when he learned that one of his closest friends and finest inter-preters, Egon Pollak, was to conduct.[14] Meanwhile, Cologne Opera had also requested the work. Here, the production was designed by the inten-dant, Hofrat Fritz Rémond,[15] and was to be conducted by the young Otto Klemperer (already much admired), with his wife Johanna in the lead opposite Karl Schröder, and Karl Renner doubling the roles of Frank, the hero's friend, and Fritz, the Pierrot.

As it turned out, Hamburg and Cologne gave simultaneous world pre-mieres of *Die tote Stadt* on 4 December 1920. At one point, there was almost a triple premiere, as Schalk tried to move the Vienna date forward—an indication of the high regard in which Korngold's new work was held.

Korngold preferred to be in Hamburg, however, which he had more and more come to regard as "his" city. Even though he was preoccupied with rehearsals in Vienna that had already started for the eventual production in January of the following year, he maintained a close eye on the progress of the Hamburg rehearsals, and was in constant touch with Pollak.

Loewenfeld had designed a striking and imaginative production that influenced many subsequent productions elsewhere, especially in the way the dead Marie stepped out of her portrait, which was illuminated from behind. In October, when casting problems arose, Korngold wrote anxious-ly to Pollak:

> My dear Herr Kapellmeister!
>
> I am really quite astonished not to have heard from you *at all!* How goes *Die tote Stadt* in Hamburg? I once did a little work with Mr. Schubert[16] in Vienna and I must say I was . . . impressed by him even then. It's the rest of the cast that causes me some concern. Am I right in thinking that—contrary to our agreement—Münchow and Degler,[17] and not Wedekind and Grönen, will sing the roles of Marietta and Frank? Do you think the woman playing the Artist [i.e. Marietta] is right for the part? Doesn't the role call at least for a performer who is popular and who is already . . . relatively well-respected by the public—that is, a performer whom one might expect could play certain roles (Salome, Violanta, Mona Lisa, and so forth)?
>
> And the orchestra?
>
> In Vienna we are in the middle of correction rehearsals for the first scene, and we've already had a full orchestra rehearsal of the first half of Act I. We shall have a good twenty-five to thirty orchestra rehearsals. Everybody says it's so incredibly difficult; for myself, I must say I consider it quite simply "only beautiful music!!!"
>
> My dear Herr Kapellmeister, I would be very grateful if I might hear something from you *before* I leave. I plan to come around the twentieth.

In Vienna, a great deal of energy (and money) is to be lavished on costumes and staging. Is it the same in Hamburg? I am frankly amazed that I have not been asked for my views on a single aspect of the direction; in Vienna I am faced with formidable problems, the solutions to which are becoming increasingly difficult (Entrance of the Procession in Act III, how to make the portrait come alive in Scene 1, the beginning of Act II, and a good deal more besides). I sincerely hope the reason I am not being kept informed is that no such problems have occurred in Hamburg and thus that no extraordinary "solutions" are even necessary. If I were to discover any other reason than this, I confess I would be rather disappointed.

My very best wishes and . . . above all thank you for everything that you are doing for my new work which, with you at the helm, I know to be in the best of hands![18]

If he was concerned about preparations in Hamburg, he had no such worries at the rehearsals in Vienna, which he attended daily. Julius Korngold recalled:

Erich came home happy and excited. Everything sounded as he had imagined it; every bar had character, color, and originality. But of course sometimes he had worked on one page for a whole day! "In the last five years, Korngold has enriched the orchestra, alongside Strauss and Pfitzner," said Franz Schalk. Erich told us that the stage director Wilhelm von Wymetal demonstrated every detail to Jeritza and that she, as though in a trance, absorbed every word, every gesture with wide-open eyes, while enhancing them and filling them with life.[19]

Before leaving for Hamburg in November, the atmosphere was soured by yet another "incident" in the press. The Munich critic Wilhelm Mauke accused Korngold of plagiarism from a book given to him called *The Triumph of Life* by Beatrice Dovsky. Subsequently, the case was brought before the court of arbitration of the Society of Dramatic Authors, which decided in Korngold's favor. Mauke resigned his post in Munich shortly afterward. Probably this affair convinced Korngold to change the title of the work. Once this affair was over, Korngold went to Hamburg with his mother. Julius Korngold remained at home, as was customary. Erich and his mother stayed with Dr. Loewenfeld.

Dr. Loewenfeld's daughter Eva Maria Wiesner recalled the weeks leading up to the production vividly. In a conversation lasting some three hours, she, more than any other eye-witness I encountered while researching this book, gave the most detailed description of the extraordinary musician that Korngold was and the fabulous milieu in which he thrived. She began by describing her own background and what it was like to grow up in the house of one of the most respected opera producers of that time:

> We had a very big house in Hamburg, in the Hochallee: it was our family house. My father bought it from my grandparents because one of his obligations was to entertain, quite naturally, visiting musicians, singers, and the like. The house was enormous, quite above our simple requirements. The music room, for instance, could easily seat two hundred people and had the very large Steinway concert grand at one end.
>
> Many great musicians stayed with us, and most of them played that piano. Strauss, I remember was a frequent guest, and Eugen d'Albert also. . . . I heard Erich Wolfgang Korngold play the piano for the first time when he had come to stay with us for the final rehearsals leading up to the world premiere of *Die tote Stadt* in December 1920. I was a child then and had the habit of grabbing a cushion from the sofa to lie under the Steinway in order to read and listen to any playing that was going on.
>
> Korngold had gone into the room to play for himself, I suppose. He had not noticed the little girl lying quietly under the piano. I was quite overwhelmed. Even then at that early age, I recognized the power and brilliance of his playing. He could conjure up the effect of a whole orchestra, painting the colors of the various instruments. He played mostly his own works, and frequently gave vent to torrid, impassioned improvisation.
>
> I recall so many great artists who visited our home in those days. . . . My two favorites, as a child, however, were Klemperer and Nikisch. Klemperer I loved because he was so immensely tall that when he lifted me onto his shoulders, I could reach the ceiling, so this became a ritual which had to be observed whenever he came. Nikisch I loved above all, though. I practically grew up with him and his family. To my father, he was the greatest. "The symphonies of Beethoven are forever marked by Nikisch's interpretation," my father was fond of saying. After my father's premature death, Nikisch wanted to adopt me, but then, sadly, he died himself within a few months. . . .
>
> Then there were the Pollaks, Egon (the conductor) and his wife Annie. Pollak was an immensely witty man, never lost for a pun or a mischievous aside. When he died, his wife and I remained great friends. Once, I recall, she took me to visit Alma Mahler and her daughter Manon (by Walter Gropius, her second husband), and Alban and Helene Berg were also there.
>
> Well, as you see, it was a rich period in my life, but you must realize that at the time, I was not struck by the importance of these acquaintances. People say to me, "Oh, how marvellous that you met

Strauss and Korngold and Nikisch," but really, at the time, it was just an everyday occurrence. These were just people one knew. . . .

My father came to become an opera producer by accident. He was a thorough musician and had worked with Mahler. He had stepped in and assumed the role of producer when someone had walked out, while he was working as a musician in Stuttgart. From there he went to Leipzig, where he had distinguished himself (1908–1912) and where Engelbert Humperdinck had drawn his attention to the fabulous new *Wunderkind*—Erich Wolfgang Korngold.

He became the intendant at Hamburg in 1912, and one of his first productions was *Der Schneemann*. As it happened, my mother was related to Luzi Sonnenthal's mother.[20] Well, he remained loyal to Korngold and naturally wanted to secure the rights for the world premiere of *Die tote Stadt*, and succeeded in doing so.

He frequently called production conferences in our house. So when I saw the door open to the living room [where the meeting took place], I crept onto the stairs in my nightgown to listen—something I frequently did as a child, especially when there was a chamber music evening or a recital. Egon Pollak, who was to conduct the opera, Korngold, my father, and the designers of the scenery and costumes were in animated discussion. I heard my father explaining how he wished the apparition of the dead wife, Marie, to be: "The stage is completely dark. The painting of Marie over the mantelpiece is beginning to glow with an inner light, like a glass window in a cathedral through which the sun shines. Out of the frame steps Marie."

I was tremendously excited and longed to see and hear such a miracle. My wish was granted. I was taken to the premiere. The opera was, needless to say, a triumphant success.[21]

The premiere in Hamburg created a furor, and this was reflected in the press. Before 1933, *Die tote Stadt* became one of the most popular operas in the Hamburg repertory, with well over fifty performances. Loewenfeld, barely remembered today, was a brilliant producer and highly effective administrator. He realized Korngold's gifts as a conductor and, moreover, he and Korngold shared musical tastes.

Before Korngold left Hamburg for the Christmas 1920 holiday, he had agreed to sign a contract with the Hamburg Opera as conductor and artistic adviser, in which capacity he would be able to conduct his own works, advise on the other repertoire, direct orchestral concerts, and collaborate with Pollak and Loewenfeld, while at the same time be free to pursue his composing and his other activities in Vienna.

Meanwhile, the news from Cologne was equally encouraging. Klemperer, one of the most brilliant opera conductors of the twentieth century, had only recently arrived in Cologne but he was already familiar with

Korngold's work, having earlier conducted the one-act operas in Strasbourg. He must also have certainly heard *Der Schneemann* in Hamburg while he was conductor there. After the Cologne premiere, Arthur Regeniter wrote in *Signale*:

> It must be said, however, that the orchestra which mastered the difficulties in virtuoso fashion had in Klemperer a most reliable leader, whose feeling for modern music caused him to be lovingly engrossed in the work of the young master, leaving nothing unexplored and achieving the utmost delicacy of shading imaginable.[22]

One of the most informed reviews came in the *Kölnische Zeitung,* which said in part:

> Korngold constantly unleashes the full riches of the orchestra (both its possibilities and colors) and the most modern harmony . . . his instrumentation employs the piano most subtly . . . . a masterly piece of tone painting is in the scene where Paul describes his first meeting with the dancer. The opera was performed without interruption of the first two acts, which helped the understanding of the dream sequence . . . whose unreality was stressed by having the action performed behind a gauze curtain.[23]

After this joint success, Korngold hoped for a triumphant production in Vienna. Christmastime 1920 was more than the usual celebration, for it also marked the sixtieth birthday of Julius Korngold. As usual, Erich presented his father with some new compositions, this time a set of songs: four songs of farewell on which he had been working for much of the year. These *Vier Lieder des Abschieds* were published as his Opus 14 and are perhaps his finest essays in the genre. Each of them is unusually intense and deeply felt, although the last song, "Gefasster Abschied" (Serene Farewell), an expanded version of the "Austrian Soldier's Song of Farewell," is in a much more nostalgic mood. It is one of Korngold's loveliest melodies. Throughout the cycle, the writing for piano is incredibly rich, with a great emphasis on sonority, and it is not surprising that Korngold later orchestrated the songs. For now, however, they remained within the bosom of his family as a private gift.

Perhaps the first time he performed some of them was at a private party in the spring of 1920. Among the guests was the noted architect Richard Neutra, who would later come to know Korngold well in Hollywood. He wrote a letter to his mother dated 20 March 1920 in which he described the experience of hearing Korngold play at this gathering:

> I had the great joy of hearing Erich Korngold. I understand perfectly well all the objections one could voice against him. *Die Neue Freie*

Presse is indeed his paternal home. His exuberance, his wit, which he richly mixes with pathos, originate from the same source. But he is a human being. I am happy to have had a chance not only to hear him but to see him, and there was a lot for me to observe, from his divergent starry eyes to his pale corpulent body, which penetrates the instrument by fits and starts, to dissolve again into a languid loosening up of tension. Roaring with agitation, he produces a thin thread of spittle dropping from his wide open mouth. This is not beautiful but strangely does not seem abhorrent to the beholder.

At first he played wonderfully from Mahler's *Das Lied von der Erde*, and I was perhaps more enthralled than anyone else because I had never heard anything quite like it, and I quite forgot that he played on an ordinary piano. I am sure you will deride me if I confess that I finally even fell in love with his voice, which he mistreats so outrageously. At once harsh and puffed up, then strident and overturning into a pitiful falsetto, while singing a nonsensical galamathias "papa-tapa" text. . . .

He then rushed through *Trovatore* . . . at whose highlights he often acclaimed wildly. "Marvellous!" he frequently added to the words. The pearls in this opera he sang with melting sweetness, weaving them into the text in a simply fabulous way.

Then Countess Spiegelfeld sang in a powerful voice some of his own Lieder. "Sommer" (from Opus 9) was quite the most beautiful, and "Sterbelied," simply ravishing. (He is best described as being nearest to Gustav Mahler). After that he launched into *Aida* and we listened breathlessly to the finale.[24]

This is an important letter because it is one of the earliest contemporary (and highly graphic) descriptions of how Korngold performed at the keyboard and the extent of his repertoire. This party was given by Korngold's friends, the Duschnitzes, at whose home Neutra was a frequent guest.

The Opus 14 songs were not the only compositions on Korngold's desk at this time. Among his sketches are three almost indecipherable pages of music written out without revision. Across the top is scrawled "Streichquartett A dur—Hauptthema" (String Quartet in A major, Main Theme), and it is dated Christmas 1920. This would eventually become the String Quartet No. 1 in A Major, Opus 16, completed in the spring of 1923.

Life was not all joy and contentment, however. The strain concerning his relationship with Luzi was beginning to show. Before the Hamburg premiere, Luzi's mother had issued an ultimatum: "Either finish it, or get engaged." A separation was imposed on them, but just before they parted, Erich gave Luzi a copy of the new Lieder. As Luzi recalled:

At the end of one of the songs, there was a phrase which only he and I understood. Erich simulated my voice when I used to say "Wenn ich's erlaub" (If I consent). From that moment on, he used to work this little motiv into his concerts somehow, when he was improvising, as a signal or greeting to me: a little message that found its way to me when no one suspected anything.[25]

The new decade would bring even greater success and acclaim: the triumphant progress of *Die tote Stadt*, a growing reputation as a conductor, the composition of his greatest work, a happy marriage, and children. It would also find Korngold increasingly in the middle of his father's ongoing crusade against the radical trends in art and music, which was about to receive a new impetus with far-reaching consequences. By the end of the 1920s, however, far from being regarded as a modern composer, Korngold would be labeled as a conservative, and would feel increasingly marginalized and completely out of step with the "new music."

Luise "Luzi" von Sonnenthal circa 1920, one of Vienna's great beauties (Korngold estate).

CHAPTER TEN

"He Is the Greatest Hope of German Music"

—Giacomo Puccini

With the appointment of Franz Schalk and Richard Strauss as co-directors, the Vienna Opera entered one of its most glamorous yet one of its most controversial eras. The main problem lay in the unfair advantages accorded Strauss in his contract. Furthermore, it was only natural that a composer and personality of the rank of Strauss would overshadow Schalk, worthy musician though he was, and the situation was further exacerbated by the immense popularity Strauss enjoyed with the Viennese public, which gave him virtual carte blanche to do as he pleased.

The new regime had begun cordially enough with the world premiere of Strauss's new opera *Die Frau ohne Schatten* in October 1919, conducted by Schalk with a star-studded cast headed by Maria Jeritza and Karl Aargard-Oestvig. Dr. Korngold was not impressed with Strauss's latest opera, however, and wrote a fairly dismissive review. This marked the beginning of the end of the composer's friendship with his son.

During Gregor's and Weingartner's terms as director, Dr. Korngold's critical barbs had had little effect on the career of his son. But by 1920, with three successful operas to his credit, the problems arising from his father's vigorous campaign against the new administration were to sour an otherwise happy and successful period in his life. Dr. Korngold's main line of attack concerned the way the Vienna Opera House was transformed into what amounted to a Richard Strauss Theater. The roster of singers at the

Vienna State Opera was unrivaled at that time, and naturally Strauss took full advantage of this wealth of talent to mount his works in ever more glamorous stagings. Yet he was a great supporter of other contemporary talents.

One of the first productions in 1920 was Schreker's erotic masterpiece *Die Gezeichneten* (The Branded). It received a gala production following its successful premiere in Frankfurt, and, of course, with both Strauss and Schalk as allies of young Korngold, the impending premiere of *Die tote Stadt* was also accorded special care and attention. For the time being, Julius Korngold reserved his remarks, although he was far from impressed with Schreker's opera, and said so in an especially damaging review.

Rehearsals for *Die tote Stadt* proceeded with few problems—few, that is, until the dress rehearsal. Luzi recalled these events vividly in her memoirs.

> Erich took me to the dress rehearsal. I went in great anticipation and was bitterly disappointed. When Erich sat at the piano playing his opera, he was more Jeritza than Jeritza herself up there on the stage— or was a more poetical dreamer than the dreamy and poetic tenor Oestwig. I heard a more intoxicating orchestral sound in his piano playing than in this rehearsal of the Vienna Philharmonic. I was shocked—the more so when I saw Erich's disconcerted, anxious face.[1]

Korngold in 1920, just after he completed *Die tote Stadt* (Korngold estate).

But all was different on opening night. The old superstition that the dress rehearsal must be a failure for the production to be a success certainly proved correct in the case of *Die tote Stadt:*

> When the curtain arose at the first performance, I immediately felt the tension that I had felt to be missing during the dress rehearsal. When Oestwig entered the room of his unforgettable departed loved one, he was nervous, overstrained, and lonely. He *was* Paul, the man who still lives in the domain of the dead and still searches for life.
>
> The tension before the entrance of Marietta was almost unbearable. And it was not only myself who felt this tension. With every nerve in my body, I could feel how fascinated the audience really was. . . . Again and again, the singers were called out in front of the curtain to acknowledge applause. Erich had already appeared after the first act with Jeritza and Oestwig. Richard Strauss had sent a note from his box telling Erich not to be "naughty" but to acknowledge the applause of his audience.[2]

The "Mariettalied" brought a storm of applause, and in the second act, Richard Mayr literally stopped the show with his "Pierrotlied."

A glance at the cast reveals how wonderfully sung that performance must have been. In the small but telling role of Brigitta. Paul's housekeeper, Hermine Kittel scored a personal success. In Marietta's troupe of dancers, Maria Hussa, who would later sing the title role in Korngold's fourth opera *Das Wunder der Heliane* at its world premiere in Hamburg in 1927, was here serving her apprenticeship. Also cast were Maria Rajdl, Georg Maikl, and the great Hermann Wiedemann, who sang the role of Paul's friend Frank. The production, designed by Wilhelm von Wymetal, was painstaking and (judging from contemporary descriptions) owed much to Loewenfeld's innovative staging in Hamburg.

In all, the evening was a major triumph, and the reviews following the first night bear this out. All of the critics from the leading Vienna papers put aside their differences with Korngold's father and praised the opera and the performance. Dr. Elsa Bienenfeld wrote in the *Neues Wiener Journal*:

> What was in *Violanta* still a fortunate experiment is here assured mastery . . . . Since music was first written for the theater there has never been a composer who has achieved so much, so young . . . . A youthful tempest is bursting over us. . . . Who can tell whither this demon will lead, this young and glorious artist, this original musician![3]

These sentiments were echoed by Heinrich Kralik, Richard Specht (of course), Max Springer, Josef Reitler, Ferdinand Pfohl, and Leopold Schmidt. Among the leading critics, only Paul Bekker from Berlin sounded a sour note. The public heartily endorsed the new work, and the house was sold out five times in nine days.

Regrettably, the principals had several leaves of absence, which interrupted the run, but even so, *Die tote Stadt* was the most successful and most performed new opera that season in Vienna. It remained a prominent feature in the repertory in the coming years, to say nothing of its triumphal progress around the world. By the mid-1920s, it ensured Korngold a unique position as the most performed Germanic composer in Austria and Germany after Richard Strauss.[4]

The following month, Korngold left Vienna for Hamburg, at the invitation of Dr. Loewenfeld, to commence his obligations at the opera, and it was there that he conducted his new opera for the first time, on 21 February 1921. While preparing for this performance, he received an invitation from Wiesbaden to attend the first night of the production there (10 April 1921). He later conducted the opera there on 30 April, but not before he had directed a performance of his new work in Vienna for the first time on the 29 March. Meanwhile, *Die tote Stadt* was beginning its journey around the leading stages. There was hardly an opera house in Austria and Germany that did not present this extraordinary product of late German romanticism.

In the season of 1921–1922, *Die tote Stadt* achieved notable success in Chemnitz, Karlsruhe, Königsberg, Breslau, Bremen, Stettin, Nürnberg, and Halle. In Frankfurt, the leading expressionist designer Ludwig Sievert staged the opera in one of his most stylized and nightmarish visualizations, with false perspectives, reeling, chaotic, and "Caligarian" room settings for the dream sequences, and dark menacing shadows dominating the procession, and indeed nearly everything else. It is a pity no photographs survive of this production, save for some charcoal sketches by Sievert that show how powerfully the stage imagery matched and enhanced the score.[5]

Korngold's career as guest conductor at the Hamburg Opera had begun promisingly. His first task, apart from preparing to conduct *Die tote Stadt*, was to direct a chamber concert of his own works on 13 March and to follow this on the next evening with a performance of his one-act operas. He returned from Wiesbaden at the beginning of May to take part as pianist in another chamber evening performance of *Much Ado About Nothing* in Hamburg.

Meanwhile, *Die tote Stadt* had been so successful in Wiesbaden that it was announced as one of the Wiesbaden Festival operas for that coming summer, along with Schreker's *Der Schatzgräber*, Pfitzner's *Christelflein*, and Strauss's *Der Rosenkavalier*. Korngold and Schreker were both invited to conduct their respective operas along with Pfitzner, just as they were at the music festivals held in Bremen and Karlsruhe.

Nikisch gave the first performance of *Sursum Corda* in Berlin that summer of 1921, but in spite of the brilliant performance the audience was once again divided in its opinion. Nikisch, one of Korngold's most enthusiastic and committed champions, then journeyed to Vienna to assist in the unveiling of the Johann Strauss monument in the Stadtpark by leading the Philharmonic in the "Blue Danube" waltz. Naturally, the Korngolds were present, and invited him to a performance of *Die tote Stadt* at the Vienna

State Opera the following night. The great conductor embraced the young composer after the performance with emotion and great warmth, almost as if for the last time, which, sadly, it proved to be. He left shortly afterward for a conducting tour in the United States, and Korngold never saw him again: he died of a heart attack the following winter, aged only 66.

Sketch for the opening main theme (Hauptthema) of the String Quartet No. 1 in A Major, Opus 16 (dated Christmas 1920 on the reverse). Written in extreme haste, it nevertheless corresponds almost exactly to the published score, with some interesting variations, thus indicating how immediate Korngold's inspirations were. Even the inner parts were "heard" when he got an idea (Korngold estate/Library of Congress).

Die tote Stadt was admired by many eminent musicians and critics, but by far its most significant advocate was Giacomo Puccini. Puccini had known Korngold since his *Wunderkind* days and was always a welcome guest in Vienna. He seemed oblivious to the somewhat dismissive critiques of *Tosca* written by Julius Korngold (who had felt its libretto to be vulgar and contrived). With Erich, in whom he felt a kindred spirit, he was a close friend. Julius Korngold recalled a special encounter around the time of the premiere of *Die tote Stadt* in his memoirs:

> I remember a stimulating afternoon when he and his taciturn wife came to tea. They brought the musical globe trotter Schnabel-Rossi, who was also a friend of Toscanini and Carlo Clausetti, director of the noted Italian publishing house, Ricordi. Erich played from *Violanta*. Immediately, our guests' Italian joy in melody and their Italian temperament responded. Puccini followed the score. "Bello! Bello!" he exclaimed repeatedly; during the B major melody in the final duet ["Reine Liebe"], he let the score drop on his lap and listened with rapt attention. He also wanted to hear excerpts from *Die tote Stadt*, which Schalk had described to him as being so difficult. During the "Lautenlied" he sat closely at Erich's side while the others grouped themselves around the two composers and listened with bated breath. "Miracolo!" exclaimed the grateful chorus of listeners. Tactfully, Erich tried to divert the attention from himself by improvising a sort of Puccini fantasy. He played it so much in the spirit of Puccini that the Maestro later asked him repeatedly to help him salvage his *La Rondine* [The Swallow], which the Volksoper had mistreated. Due to the composer's premature death, this little swallow fluttered away from the planned revision. An emotional farewell kiss from Puccini made Erich blush with joy. And to me went Puccini's congratulations on having such a son. "A compensation for much grief in this life," he remarked. He must have realized what pains were taken to punish the father for having this son.
>
> Puccini proved to be a true friend. After the war, a letter to him was sufficient to make him intervene for the release of my stepbrother, who was a prisoner of war in Italy. An interview he gave in Munich caused a sensation; he called Erich the strongest hope for new German music. And his letters—he never failed to encourage Erich to pursue his melodic style and the simplicity and naturalness of his dramatic music.[6]

That Puccini admired Korngold, and most especially *Die tote Stadt,* is not entirely surprising. On more than one occasion Korngold was described by critics as the "Viennese Puccini." The nickname arose specifically because of Korngold's predilection for doubling the melody line in his orchestration with the divided strings—an effect that was particularly beloved by the Italian school and especially by Puccini. In an early autobiography, published in 1924, Maria Jeritza wrote of Korngold:

> Practically all his vocal parts are melodious along the Italian line of beautiful, warm melody . . . . *The Dead City* [contains] in some ways one of the most difficult roles [Marie-Marietta] a singer could undertake because of the dual part the artist has to play and the rapidity—she dare not lose a moment—with which she must pass from one part to the other. Its music is theatrically vivid in the highest degree and fairly inspires the singer in the outstanding dramatic moments.[7]

I mention the correlation between Korngold and Puccini in their respective styles, and it must also be stated that while Puccini certainly inspired the young Korngold, the reverse was equally true. Anyone listening to the climactic duet of Act II of *Die tote Stadt* must surely be struck by the resemblance to the love duet from *Turandot* written some years after.[8]

The ingredients that make *Die tote Stadt* so potent a force on the stage are easily discernible: a strong and fascinating libretto ideally suited to musical treatment, vivid characterization, and the hallucinatory element that allowed Korngold to infuse the "dream" portion of the story with religious mysticism. But more important is the sound Korngold created for this work—a sound world quite unlike any other and certainly different from anything he composed afterward, although traces of it can be found in his later work, such was the strength of the original conception. The orchestration has a sheen that leaves the audience breathless (particularly in Act I).

It is an exultant score, brimming with youthful ardor. Although most would consider Marietta to be the leading role, probably because of Jeritza's indelible impression, this opera really belongs to the principal tenor role—that of Paul, who after his entrance in Act I, ten minutes after the curtain rises, is never offstage until the curtain falls in Act III.

Die tote Stadt marked the turning point in Korngold's fortunes. Never again would he achieve a success on this scale, even though some of his subsequent works were in many respects of greater importance. The musical climate was changing. After the Great War, a developing artistic freedom made the 1920s perhaps the most exciting and fruitful decade of the century for music and the arts in general. Not only were the activities of Arnold Schoenberg and his supporters coming into prominence, which up until now had been regarded as an interesting experiment, but the face of modern music was undergoing radical change. In many ways *Die tote Stadt* marked the end of an epoch. German romantic opera was about to be replaced with a desire for realism on stage, a craving for objectivity. This age of *Neue Sachlichkeit* (New Realism), in which sport and technology mixed with dance-music and jazz, was to have profound effects on the course of art and music and, inevitably, on the future operatic career of Korngold.

"Vienna is always Vienna—that is the greatest curse I know." The oft-quoted remark by satirist Karl Kraus seems worthy of repetition here, for despite the success of *Die tote Stadt* and *Much Ado About Nothing* and the continued popularity of Korngold's earlier works, intrigue and gossip continued to fester in the press and elsewhere.

It was around this time that the scandal with Moriz Rosenthal, who had obtained an illegal copy of the later rescinded letter from the Association of Vienna Music Critics condemning Julius Korngold, erupted into the public gaze. Furthermore, insinuations that Korngold's opera was being staged so often to curry favor with the *Neue Freie Presse* had begun to circulate. The gossip gathered momentum until eventually Korngold wrote indignantly to Karl Lion (the administrator of the Vienna State Opera) to remove all of his operas from the program. Lion wrote the following reply:

> In answer to your letter, which has just been received, the undersigned administration regrets that for reasons of principle and artistic considerations with regard to the public it cannot comply with your wish to cancel performances of your work in the State Opera.[9]

The background to this was the unfortunate clash between Julius Korngold and Richard Strauss. The elder Korngold, although he was an admirer of Strauss's music, lost no opportunity to criticize Strauss for his running of the Vienna State Opera. The implication that the younger Korngold enjoyed favors that he did not deserve was explicitly stated when an advertisement appeared in most newspapers after the premiere of *Die tote Stadt*, which said: "The performance of Korngold's opera *Die tote Stadt* last evening could not be avoided for technical reasons."

Julius Korngold smoldered not only over this, but at the way his beloved Vienna Opera was being subjected to the whims of Strauss. When Strauss decided to absent himself (taking the Vienna Philharmonic with him) to South America and later New York, it was greeted with a tirade of objections, principally because of the huge salary Strauss commanded as co-director. The immediate post-War period depleted the income and reserves of many artists, however, who readily accepted offers to conduct and perform in the United States to reap hard currencies (Nikisch and Furtwängler also made American tours at this time).

The acrimonious situation never really healed. Following the refusal to withdraw his operas from the repertoire, Erich Korngold wrote the following letter to Franz Schalk, which gives some indication of the status quo:

> Highly honored Herr Direktor!
>
> Allow me to thank you for conducting my opera yourself, today. . . . . Unfortunately, I cannot be present at today's performance; when Dr. Strauss explains that it is incompatible with his dignity to regard as the guest of the Opera House "the son of a critic" who is, in his opinion, hostile to him, I must maintain that it is incompatible with

my own dignity to intrude into this house as a guest. (The premiere of *Josephslegende* at which I *was* present is an exception. I'm still a Straussonian!) It is amusing that *Die tote Stadt,* which had its last performance on one of the worst days of the year in the theater—one day before Christmas Eve —is being given, by chance, on another wretched occasion: when demonstrations have been announced.

This situation eventually led to the formation of two camps—those for young Korngold and those for Strauss. This was a ludicrous turn of events, for although Strauss and Korngold's father had distanced themselves from each other, Strauss always maintained a benevolent attitude toward his young disciple. Korngold was merely caught in between.

The worsening situation at the Vienna State Opera did not completely cloud the early 1920s, however. Apart from the failure of *Sursum Corda,* Korngold's career continued to blossom. In December of 1921, he traveled to Dresden to see the production of *Die tote Stadt* mounted by the intendant there, Georg Hartmann. Luzi recalled:

> He returned in an elevated mood. Never before had he experienced a production such as the one in Dresden. Hartmann . . . had worked with projections which represented the ghostly scenery of the second act and had also projected the whole of the procession during the third act onto the stage. Erich had been particularly impressed by the singer who took the part of Paul, a relatively unknown artist named Richard Tauber. He told me that Tauber's incredible musicianship had had a profound effect on him, saying: "It was as if I myself had been standing up on stage singing every phrase, every note, exactly as I had composed it." Erich later said that because of his devilish musicality [Tauber] was able to use his otherwise not sensational voice to bring out every nuance; indeed he imparted an interpretation to every role in a very personal way.[10]

Richard Tauber was to become one of Korngold's closest friends, and the composer later gave the tenor an autographed photograph inscribed, "To Richard Tauber—My ideal 'Paul'."

On 19 May 1921, Dr. Loewenfeld had died suddenly in Hamburg. This was a great blow, and immediately the future of Korngold's association with the Stadttheater there looked precarious. Loewenfeld's death and the events that followed it pose something of a mystery. A man of some means, Loewenfeld was actually the lessee of the Hamburg Stadttheater, and his resources supported the entire venture. On 6 May Korngold had signed a new contract with the Opera, but following Loewenfeld's death, the Hamburg Senate announced that it would take over the running of the theater and that Wilhelm von Wymetal would come from Vienna to assume the post of intendant. Wymetal did come that autumn, but after a couple of months, he wrote to the Hamburg Senate to try to cancel his contract because of the "unfortunate mood here and unbridgeable difficulties."[11]

Not surprisingly, the Hamburg Senate refused and insisted that he work according to his contract; finding a replacement would take time. The frustrated Wymetal took the extreme step of staging an accident in the Opera house itself when, in an act of self-mutilation he jumped down some stairs and broke his leg. He immediately returned to Vienna, taking Korngold with him. Just prior to this, in late November, an announcement appeared in the newspapers of "Korngold's Farewell Concert Before Leaving to Go to New York—US Premiere of *Die tote Stadt*." In fact, Korngold canceled his trip, for unknown reasons, a few days before sailing.

The files of the Hamburg State Opera were destroyed when the Opera house was bombed during the Second World War, so it will never be known what really happened. Korngold conducted *Die tote Stadt* for the last time in Hamburg on 2 November 1921 (the thirtieth performance). On 31 January 1922, Leopold Sachse (another friend) was appointed as the new intendant of the Hamburg State Opera, a position he retained until 1933. Both Korngold and his father later explained the decision to leave Hamburg as being entirely due to Loewenfeld's premature death, but clearly the reasons are more complex than that.

It may be that Korngold enjoyed a favored position in Hamburg entirely due to Loewenfeld, and that the Senate objected to Korngold, his star-status, and his artistic plans, which included many performances of his own works. Also, the Hamburg Senate was not over-generous in this time of high inflation and was anxious to make every possible economy. The position of Korngold's father and his indirect influence through his son, which would not have been tolerated, may have been another issue.

Korngold also had a personal reason to leave: Luzi von Sonnenthal. The prospect of spending a considerable amount of time away from Vienna and his beloved Luzi was not attractive, particularly as the Opera would not pay for a hotel (these were still hard times after World War I) and he had to lodge with friends (the singer Rose Ader, in particular). Then there were the considerable administrative burdens of a permanent conducting post, which would not have appealed to him. When the atmosphere in Hamburg cooled toward him, he probably seized his chance to end the appointment, using the death of his friend Loewenfeld as the excuse.

During the summer, Korngold began work in earnest on the String Quartet No. 1 in A Major, which he had sketched the previous Christmas, and he simultaneously began to write the Piano Quintet in E Major. For the quintet he wrote an ingenious set of nine free variations on the newly completed *Vier Lieder des Abschieds*, principally the third song, "Mond so gehst du wieder auf" (Moon, you rise again). The Piano Quintet in E Major was completed the following year, while the String Quartet No. 1 in A Major was not finished until the spring of 1923.

Meanwhile, toward the end of 1921, Korngold saw the premiere of two more of his compositions thousands of miles apart: the American premiere of *Die tote Stadt* took place in New York on 19 November 1921; and on 5 November 1921 the world premiere of the *Vier Lieder des Abschieds* was given in Vienna by Maria Olczewska (who had created the part of Brigitta in *Die tote Stadt* in Hamburg the previous December). Korngold himself accompanied, as part of a concert given by Egon Pollak. The *Vier Lieder des Abschieds* are the composer's finest songs, all deeply felt and filled with surprising harmonic development. By now, his song style had developed into a quasi-operatic form. Though reminiscent of Strauss and Mahler, harmonically and melodically these songs could have only been written by Korngold.

He had become meticulous and almost over-cautious in his use of performance directions, almost as though he did not trust musicians to interpret his work. Out of some 200 bars that make up this cycle, only two do not contain some instruction or marking. These instructions, together with the frequent tempo modifications and changes in meter, demand the utmost free rubato in performance and make the songs among the most difficult to interpret.

There are melodic connections between the songs, especially between the first and third. The arching seventh that opens the cycle, "Sterbelied" (Requiem), sets the mood, as the voice enters on E natural, a note completely foreign to the harmony, thus making the tension of the exposed interval even greater. The second song, "Dies eine kann mein Sehnen nimmer fassen" (The one thing my longing can never grasp) is perhaps the most operatic—a restless, angular melody introduced by a dramatic appoggiatura, reminiscent of the opening of the Adagio in the Sextet for Strings in D Major or the apparition of Marie in *Die tote Stadt* The vocal line contains some punishing leaps (ninths, elevenths, and thirteenths are common) reflecting the anguish of the despairing words of Edith Ronsperger's poetry. The third song, "Mond, so gehst du wieder auf" (Moon, you rise again), is a tone poem in miniature. Extraordinarily voluptuous, with its downward leaps and original harmony, it creates a strange mood, unexpected in Korngold. "Gefasster Abschied" (Serene Farewell) is a completely revised version of the earlier "Austrian Soldier's Song of Farewell." Here, the opening A flat is sharpened to A natural to create an effect similar to the opening bars of the first song. It is a lovely melody, clearly a homage to Mahler's Symphony No. 4 in G Major, and quite expansive in structure.

The cycle, dedicated to Franz Schalk, was a considerable success and was given numerous subsequent performances, especially by Rosette Anday and later by Maria Nemeth. Korngold orchestrated the songs in 1923 and recorded them in their original version with Anday in Berlin the following year.

In New York, *Die tote Stadt* conquered the American audience. The performance was in the hands of an Austrian colleague of Korngold's—the conductor Artur Bodanzky, who since 1915 had been resident in New York and who gave a number of notable first performances, including Mahler's *Das Lied von der Erde* (The Song of the Earth) and, later, Korngold's *Violanta*. A distinguished visitor attended the premiere—Richard Strauss en route to South America, where he was to tour with the Vienna Philharmonic. Despite the brickbats he had suffered at the hands of Korngold's father, Strauss still sent him a postcard to report on how successful the performance had been.

Not everything went as smoothly with the production as could be wished, however. Several critics remarked on the faux pas at the crucial point in Act I when Jeritza, as Marietta singing the "Lute Song," picked up a *guitar* to accompany herself, but as she herself explained later:

> At the dress rehearsals, I clamored for a lute and a search was instituted for one. New York seemed to be luteless, however, though I know every effort was made to procure one, and on the night of the premiere I had to make the best of the available guitar. . . . It is not that the use of the guitar is an anachronism; yet the lute is . . . the one instrument Marietta must play . . . . . At the time I felt so strongly about it that when they handed me the guitar, I felt I might just as well have been given a hand organ.[12]

Jeritza's co-star was Orville Harrold, whose energetic singing of the role of Paul, with apparent disregard of its exceptional vocal demands, is commonly held to have impaired his voice permanently.

By Christmas 1921 *Die tote Stadt* had been performed thirty times in Hamburg and almost as many times in Vienna, while numerous theaters in Europe were preparing their own productions for the New Year. It overtook both Schreker's *Der Schatzgräber* (premiered in the same year) and Strauss's *Die Frau ohne Schatten* in popularity, and the orchestral suite from *Much Ado About Nothing* was scoring a similar success. One of the first new productions was to be in Chemnitz, which had negotiated the services of Richard Tauber for the role of Paul. On New Year's Day 1922, Korngold wrote to the dramaturg Hans Zesewitz, delighted with the news, adding that "Tauber is my *ideal* Paul."[13]

It seemed as though nothing could halt the career or the spectacular success of Erich Wolfgang Korngold, no matter what his adversaries might say. He was so highly regarded that in 1922, the writer and critic Dr. Rudolf Stefan Hoffmann published the first biography of Korngold—a considerable accolade for a twenty-five-year-old composer. Hoffmann's book presents Korngold as the leading composer of Austria's younger generation. In particular, he devotes considerable space to Korngold's revolutionary harmony as the direction that modern music must undoubtedly take.

However, as Hoffmann's book was published, Arnold Schoenberg was planning a revolution of a more radical nature—a revolution in which Korngold would not participate and that would completely polarize musical opinion in the coming decade.

A slightly disheveled Maria Jeritza as Marietta (with the offending guitar standing in for a lute) and Orville Harrold (Paul) during the dress rehearsal of *Die tote Stadt*, New York, 4 November 1921 (courtesy of the Metropolitan Opera Archives).

CHAPTER ELEVEN

A New Order in Music —
Schoenberg and Serialism

*I*n 1921 Arnold Schoenberg announced to his pupil Josef Rufer that he had "discovered something that will assure the supremacy of German music for the next hundred years." Later, in 1923, he was to write to composer Josef Hauer, "After a fifteen year search, I have discovered a method of composition that allows me to compose with a freedom and fantasy such as I knew only in my youth."[1]

This "discovery" was, of course, serialism. Since Schoenberg's *Pierrot Lunaire* in 1911, what Julius Korngold described as "the atonal roar" had been gathering momentum. To Schoenberg, however, the mere suspension of tonality was an unsatisfactory solution to the problems that he believed arose from the excesses of the post-Wagnerian idiom of the early twentieth century. He was disturbed by the lack of system, and serialism offered him a new means of achieving order.

The use of the series—the twelve notes of the chromatic scale arranged in a fixed order that remains binding for a whole work and provides the strict basis for melody and harmony, thereby placing the creative element of composition on an abstract, almost mathematical plane without the necessity of chance inspiration—appealed to Schoenberg's methodical temperament. To his many critics, however, he often retorted: "My works are twelve-note *compositions*, not *twelve-note* compositions."

Schoenberg introduced his new method with three works: the Serenade, Opus 24, the *Five Little Piano Pieces*, Opus 23, and the Piano Suite, Opus 25, all written between 1920 and 1923. Almost simultaneously, his pupil Alban Berg was completing his revolutionary opera *Wozzeck*. Also around this time, Schoenberg's supporters and pupils, under the aegis of the noted English writer and musicologist Edward Dent (Korngold's early champion), began to explore the possibility of forming an international association for promoting modern music. The result was the Internationale Gesellschaft für Neue Musik (International Society for New Music), which was to dominate the 1923 Salzburg Festival. These developments were to have a profound effect on music in this century and on Korngold's subsequent career.

Julius Korngold, dismayed by the growing stronghold gained by the radicals, appointed himself the official spokesman against all the new trends espoused by Schoenberg and his followers. Edward Dent once referred to him as the "most dangerous adversary of the movement," although paradoxically he remained on cordial personal terms with the critic and his son.[2]

Almost immediately, the International Society for New Music made overtures to Erich Korngold, possibly in the hope that if he consented to join them, his father and like-minded colleagues would relent in their merciless attacks through their columns. It was a vain hope: young Korngold was not to be persuaded. Like Richard Strauss, Gustav Mahler, and to a certain extent Alexander von Zemlinsky, he could not embrace complete atonality or serialism. All of his works sprang from uninhibited inspiration and were based on a strict adherence to traditional musical forms, although within this framework Korngold experimented with innovative extensions of them. He regarded an abrogation of *melody*, in a strictly tonal sense, as wholly unacceptable. Consequently, as the years passed, he was frequently branded as a "backward" composer. The modern, futuristic prodigy of 1910 of whom the same Edward Dent had said, memorably, "We shall have to burn our books on harmony," was now accused of stunted growth.

Korngold was not the only composer in the Vienna of the 1920s who felt unhappy at the new developments. Hans Gál was equally disenchanted. At the age of ninety-five, he was one of the last survivors of that period when I interviewed him in 1985. I asked him about the prevailing mood in the early 1920s, especially toward Schoenberg. His comments are revealing:

> It is now forgotten that the so-called "New Music" was accorded a rather lukewarm reception. We regarded these experiments as simply that: experiments. Schoenberg, I may say, was a monomaniac, completely obsessed with his ideas. He broke with the past because, in my opinion, he could not achieve an original voice within its tradition. He was so heavily influenced by Wagner and couldn't shake it off. So, he invented his own system. Korngold, on the other hand, whom I very much admired—his father, less so [laughs]—had established his own voice and was, like myself, completely unable to

embrace this new procedure. This "revolution" disturbed the natural growth from what had gone before into fresh development. We, my colleagues and I, felt very strongly that a statement had to be made.[3]

The "statement" was a special, separate Austrian section to the 1923 Salzburg Festival, under the artistic leadership of Joseph Marx and Erich Korngold. This special section took place between 8 and 11 August, after the main festival had finished. Works by Franz Schreker (his chamber symphony), Richard Strauss (excerpts from *Le Bourgeois Gentilhomme*), Zemlinsky (his String Quartet No. 1), and Hans Gál (his fine incidental music to Levetzhof's *Ruth*), and songs by Paumgartner and Julius Bittner were performed. Works by Eduard Kornauth, Joseph Marx, Karl Weigl, Wilhelm Kienzl, and some early songs by Schoenberg (with the deliberate inference that his more recent works were not acceptable) completed the program. Korngold was represented by his newly completed Piano Quintet in E Major[4] and the Suite for violin and piano from *Much Ado About Nothing*.

Korngold and composer Wilhelm Grosz (who had been his friend since childhood) acted as pianists and accompanists throughout, with the assistance of singers Hans Duhan, Gertrude Geyersbach (who had sung Marietta and also the *Vier Lieder des Abschieds* in Wiesbaden), Emilie Bittner (wife of the composer), violinist and close friend Robert Pollak, and the conductors Rudolf Nilius and Bernhard Paumgartner. To the chagrin of his opponents, Korngold's "alternative" festival was a considerable success. It resulted in more attacks against him in the press, however, for it provided a completely fresh "angle" of criticism. Unfortunately, it also provided Julius Korngold with fodder for a brand new campaign. Far from receding, the regular battles in the press were to gain fresh currency.

Political considerations aside, Korngold's own career at home and abroad continued vigorously on its successful path. He was especially proud to receive the approbation of Puccini in a much-quoted interview in the *Neue Freie Presse*:

> With regards to modern German music, my biggest hope lies with Erich Wolfgang Korngold. He is exceptionally talented, has a formidable technical knowledge and, most important of all, superb musical ideas. . . . he has so much talent that he could give half of it away and still have enough left for himself.[5]

Puccini had been friendly with Julius Korngold ever since he had visited Vienna for the premiere of *Madam Butterfly* at the Vienna Court Opera in 1907. A mutual friend, the journalist Angelo Eisner-Eisenhof, had introduced them. Puccini did not actually meet Erich Korngold until October 1913, when he was again in Vienna for the Austrian premiere of *Fanciulla del West*. Korngold was a great admirer of Puccini and emulated the Italian master. Puccini, in turn, had enthusiastically recommended that his own publisher, Ricordi, produce an Italian translation of *Die tote Stadt*.

In 1922, *Sursum Corda* reached the United States, where it was performed by Josef Stransky and the New York Philharmonic. Perhaps mindful of the problems encountered by the work in previous performances, Korngold took the rare step of providing an introductory note:

I have meant to suggest by the subtitle of the piece—*Sursum Corda*! (Lift Up Your Hearts)—merely the general character of the work: a mood of struggle and aspiration, a joyous deliverance out of storm and stress. The work (beginning "stormily" C major 3/2) has two main themes: the first, a fanfare-like subject for the trumpet in C, continued by the first violins of which the closing phrase—a downward leap of an octave—has significance in the development. The second theme is a broad, heroic theme in G major. A lyrical passage follows, employing material derived from the two chief themes. The development section is in two parts, the first beginning in F major (4/4) broadly and songfully, the second beginning in the tempo of the first theme. There is a brief reprise; violins and two trumpets in unison declaim the chief theme, followed by a fermata; then a stormy climax and a diminuendo to *ppp*. A portion of the second subject returns, with a melodious counter-theme for solo violin. Then begins *(sehr ruhig, geheimnisvoll 4/4)*, with solemn harmonies, the two-part coda, the first part ending with the ardent A-major song of the full orchestra, which leads to a triumphant proclamation, in abbreviated form, of the chief theme in C major and a joyfully tumultuous close.[6]

This concise analysis shows how carefully Korngold structured his works. In spite of the clarity of his introduction to *Sursum Corda*, however, the work met with only a limited success in the United States, whereas the orchestral suite from *Much Ado About Nothing* triumphed, as elsewhere, and was widely played by many American orchestras.

Korngold traveled to London, where he made several piano rolls and may have had discussions about *Die tote Stadt*, and to Brussels. Upon his return on 29 May 1922, his twenty-fifth birthday was celebrated by a gala performance in Vienna of his Sextet for Strings in D Major by the Rosé Quartet. Luzi, by now a pupil at the Vienna State Academy and engaged to Erich, was able to organize her own celebration for his birthday:

My connection with the music academy allowed me to celebrate Erich's birthday in a special way. . . . I arranged a private performance of *Much Ado About Nothing* under my leadership. The evening was a success and not only Erich and his friends were invited but also his *parents*. The surprise was complete when I appeared in full evening dress to conduct.[7]

By now Luzi was also an actress in silent films in her spare time,[8] an avocation not calculated to endear her to Erich's parents. Both the Sonnenthals and the Korngolds were opposed to the relationship, but the young couple would not be swayed. With the enormous rise in inflation, Korngold had lost his savings and to a very large extent he relied on his parents for financial support, especially as his father continued to control and negotiate his royalty commissions. Since he would not ask his father for help in any way, marriage for the time being was out of the question.

An indication of why Korngold's parents were so entrenched in their desire to prevent their son from marrying can be gleaned from the following rather touching excerpt from Julius Korngold's memoirs:

My strongest reminiscences are those concerning emotions. How could I resist the temptation of dwelling on those unforgettable days of affectionate family life, which left fame at our doorstep as an unessential ornament. My wife and I could bestow our care on an exceptional son and enjoy his days with him. Already his awakening in the morning was accompanied by a joke. Immediately after breakfast he went into the music room, to a small table near the piano and from time to time one heard him play occasional chords as he was orchestrating. In between were digressions of the fingers in improvised chord progressions; then the music might break off and he would appear in the kitchen to extol his mother's virtues as a cook with all kinds of jokes. In the evening we sat on the sofa and talked about music. We tested each other's knowledge of the dates of birth and death of the great composers; we discussed the productivity of Mozart and Schubert, which in our own day would have been impossible, what with the purely manual chores imposed by the complicated technique of composing and orchestrating.[9]

One can easily understand the possessiveness that denied acceptance of Luise von Sonnenthal, even after she and Erich were married. While Erich traveled with his father to performances of his works, Luzi had to make do with written reports, and for these Korngold devised a code based on musical notation. Each note of the scale stood for a letter, and to further complicate matters, different clefs placed before the notes ensured greater secrecy. The domestic tension notwithstanding, Korngold's fame continued to separate them.

One of Korngold's most important trips was to hear Alexander von Zemlinsky conduct *Die tote Stadt* in Prague. The premiere was scheduled for 4 February 1922. The teacher and his former pupil exchanged a friendly correspondence, which provides some insights not only into Korngold's own movements during this period but also the degree of equanimity and respect they must have enjoyed despite their difference in age. Judging from a letter dated 29 January 1921, Zemlinsky had apparently sent Korngold a telegram of congratulations following the Vienna premiere of *Tote Stadt*. Korngold replied:

> Thank you for your kind telegram which gave me great pleasure. It does seem to be a great dramatic success. Five perfcrmances in Vienna fully sold out—in Hamburg, already more than ten performances fully booked. Have you already got the score? Yesterday I played through *Kleider machen Leute* with a view to a possible performance in Hamburg—I take up my post there on February 1. Did you carry out your projected revision? I think a few (sizeable) cuts, particularly in the first act, would suffice to give the work its stage life, which is long overdue. Please send me a few lines c/o the Hamburg Stadttheater.

Korngold did not conduct Zemlinsky's opera at Hamburg, as his tenure there was so short-lived. Zemlinsky admired his pupil's opera and presumably wanted to present it in Prague in the autumn of 1921, judging from Korngold's next letter dated 9 October that year:

> My journey to America has not taken place this year for a number of reasons. I remain therefore in Europe and shall try to come to Prague for the premiere of *Die tote Stadt*.

The projected trip to the United States, which is not mentioned in the memoirs of either Julius or Luzi Korngold, was to coincide with several performances of his works, especially *Die tote Stadt* at the Metropolitan Opera in New York, scheduled for November 1921. Korngold goes on:

> In the next few days I am leaving for Dresden—Berlin—Hamburg and could be in Prague on November 2nd for a rehearsal (or at least some sort of discussion with you and the producer). The premiere is not likely to take place in October? . . . I am looking forward to meeting you again and to get to know your new operas at last!
>
> Of your tenth Jubilee in Prague I have read everywhere—as a Viennese, who through your departure for Prague has lost his respected teacher and master, I could not congratulate you personally. . . . I hope, however, that my modest contribution to your Festschrift (without too many distortions and misprints!) will have given you proof of my feelings of admiration and affection.[13]

The first performance did not take place until February, however. Korngold attended and posed for a photograph with his teacher, which unfortunately is now lost, on the stage of the theater during the dress rehearsal. Regrettably, neither Zemlinsky's letters to Korngold nor evidence of any subsequent contact between them has survived, and the occasion of the first Prague performance of *Die tote Stadt* may have been their last meeting.

Korngold's marriage to Luzi was finally made possible by a lucrative offer from Hubert Marischka,[11] the great operetta idol and director of the Theater an der Wien, to adapt and conduct a new performance of *Eine Nacht in Venedig* by Johann Strauss II. The contract also provided for the possibility of further adaptations. Korngold was a great admirer of the music of Strauss, a passion he had inherited from his father. Quite apart from the financial reward, he was genuinely interested in the prospect of conducting the work. It had never been a success with the public (it suffered from a particularly weak libretto), but the music was a delight. Korngold the dramatist set to work. He tightened the weaker scenes and rearranged others, and he reorchestrated some sections while preserving the spirit of the original.

The operetta also definitely lacked "star" numbers. As this particular production was to be led by the great Richard Tauber, Korngold found two "Tauberlieder" in other Strauss works, and interpolated them along with some other little pieces. Thus, a new version of *Eine Nacht in Venedig* was born.[12]

The premiere on 25 October 1923 was an unprecedented success. Tauber was supported by a strong cast that included Betty Fischer, Otto Langer, and Fritz Imhoff, and the production was so successful that it traveled throughout Austria and Germany almost as widely as Korngold's operas. After important stagings at Darmstadt and Frankfurt, a completely new version was mounted at the Vienna State Opera as a vehicle for Maria Jeritza. Korngold revised his original "new version" and conducted the first four performances. Jeritza was supported by an even finer cast, which included Alfred Jerger, Adele Kern, Koloman von Pataky, and, of course, Hubert Marischka.

That Korngold had total sympathy with the music of Strauss was shown by a strange incident after the premiere in 1923. In the second act, the original version had a certain duet that was usually cut, but Korngold had reinstated it and conducted it each evening with special care. After the first performance, he was visited backstage by Strauss's widow Adele, whom he had known since childhood as a frequent guest at his parents' home. She asked him why he had revived this particular duet. Korngold replied that the explanation was easy: it happened to be his favorite piece. "Remarkable!" answered Frau Adele thoughtfully, "It had been his favorite, too." Luzi recalled, "Each time he reached that point in the operetta, he would look up to me, in my box."

Success in the world of operetta with this new adaptation of *Eine Nacht in Venedig* had several repercussions. Young Korngold came to be recognized as a Strauss expert, and this inevitably led to a spate of revivals and a reawakening of interest in Johann Strauss II, who until this time had only really been represented in the repertory by *Die Fledermaus* and *Der Zigeunerbaron*. In effect, Korngold began what amounted to a second career arranging and conducting his new stage adaptations; the implications of this success, however rewarding and enjoyable as it undoubtedly was, gave cause for concern to his father, who rightly felt that this time-consuming work inevitably distracted him from his serious composition.

A glance at his worklist prior to 1923, and for the period from 1923 until his death shows a tremendous difference in the sheer weight of his output. The majority of his major works comes from this early period, when he lived at home with his parents and was able to devote himself exclusively to composing. After his marriage, his entire routine altered. On the back of a recently discovered letter from this period, Korngold had outlined a list of compositions that he was planning, including four symphonies, but this grandiose artistic plan never materialized.

With the exception of the Piano Sonata No. 3 in C Major, Lieder, the Suite for Two Violins, Cello, and Piano for the left hand, the *Baby Serenade* for salon orchestra, and *Geschichten von Strauss* (Tales from Strauss), a piano fantasy on the music of Johann Strauss I and II, the period from 1926 to 1933 is dominated by his work in adapting operettas. Once he began his career in films in 1934, he spent even less time composing, and with the outbreak of World War II in 1939, his creative activity, except for composing film scores, all but ceased until the end of the war.

For now, though, he managed deftly to combine his activities. In early 1923, he embarked on what was to become the most significant creative enterprise of his entire career: the composition of his fourth opera, *Das Wunder der Heliane*—arguably his greatest work. Luzi recalled how it came about:

> One day he asked me to meet him in a small cafe in the Wiedner Hauptstrasse because he had to tell me something important. As soon as we sat down at one of the small marble tables, Erich took a manuscript out of his pocket. He gave it to me with the words: "Will you read this?" "Now? Here?" I replied, in amazement. "Yes," he said. "I must hear what you think about it." I looked at the manuscript and read the title—"Die Heilige" (The Saint) by Hans Kaltneker. I was soon absorbed in the story. When I had finished, he remarked: "Well, shall I do it?" I knew that he didn't need my approval any more—he had decided already to compose "The Saint" and had, in fact, already started.[13]

Korngold realized that the poetic and somewhat diffuse mystery play by Kaltneker would have to be refashioned into an opera libretto. Though Kaltneker and Korngold never met (Kaltneker died at age twenty-four of tuberculosis in 1919), there was a peculiar affinity between them. Korngold felt drawn to Kaltneker's poetry. He later confirmed in a newspaper interview (*Neues Wiener Tagblatt*, 23 October, 1927) that Kaltneker's publisher Zsolnay had sent him the text. Only later, after he had composed the score, did he learn that Kaltneker had actually intended for him to write an opera based on the strange story, and had, in fact, written it for him.

Kaltneker, a shadowy but fascinating figure from an era that seemed to abound in them, was Rumanian but grew up and lived in Austria. He was heavily influenced by Wagner, and his works are steeped in mysticism. His best-known work was a trilogy of plays, best described as an expressionistic redemption cycle: *Bergwerk* (The Mines), which like *Heliane* had a central theme of love as the only means of salvation; *Die Opferung* (The Sacrifice) about sin as the route to faith, and *Die Schwester* (The Sister), an early treatment of homosexuality in which a lesbian is redeemed after a life of unbridled lust. These remarkable works, unknown today, are pervaded by an exaggerated and somewhat extreme atmosphere. We can only surmise that this was probably also true of *Die Heilige*, as unfortunately the manuscript is lost.

The only evidence we have of the original story is a 1931 dissertation on Kaltneker by Emmy Wohanka, who had access to Kaltneker's manuscripts and provides some insights into the poet and his strange, mystical play.[14] Wohanka, who must have seen the opera, claimed that Korngold's *Das Wunder der Heliane* bore little resemblance to the original play, but from her dissertation it would appear to differ only in a few elements. Briefly, the young prisoner (called the Stranger in the opera) is not strangled to death as in the play, but commits suicide by stabbing himself with the King's dagger while embracing the Queen (Heliane). The Queen is asked to raise the Stranger, not an unknown plague victim as in the play, to life. After she successfully brings him back to life, she is then murdered by her jealous husband and in turn is raised from death by the power of love. In the final scenes, she and the Stranger are seen to walk in paradise.

Korngold turned again to Hans Müller for help in writing the libretto and fashioning a drama from the dream-like mystery play. Müller must have regretted withdrawing from *Die tote Stadt* after witnessing its tremendous success. In 1921 he had approached Korngold to write music for his new play *Der Vampyr* (a gothic tragedy). Perhaps to compensate Müller for the work he had done on *Die tote Stadt*, Korngold did compose a considerable amount of highly atmospheric music for small chamber ensemble for this play, which was performed at the premiere at the Deutsches Volkstheater on 3 February 1923, although Korngold did not conduct it.[15]

No record remains as to when Müller worked on the draft of the libretto based on *Die Heilige*, how many revisions there may have been, or how much input Erich Korngold had in the final libretto. Later correspondence between Korngold and his father reveals that Julius Korngold contributed a good deal to the text. What stands out very clearly, however, is that *Das Wunder der Heliane* gripped Korngold's imagination as no other project in his life, as it is written with an intensity and passion that leaps off the page. Kaltneker's original story must have been a potent stimulus.

Some of this intensity found its way into one of Korngold's rare commissions, which came from the celebrated one-armed pianist Paul Wittgenstein[16] to write a piano concerto. Korngold eagerly accepted: the problem of writing for the left hand alone while achieving the effect of two hands appealed to him. He decided to cast the work in a single movement within which would be four discernible, contrasting sections, and to score the work for a large and (particularly in the percussion section) diverse orchestra. The music of the Piano Concerto in C-sharp is clearly influenced by the new opera. It occupies a similarly erotic, harmonically bizarre sound world. He began to write the work in early 1923 as soon as he had finished the String Quartet No. 1 in A Major, but its composition was frequently interrupted by other commitments.[17] That Korngold was able to combine his work composing his opera and this concerto, conducting and performing his earlier works, and adapting *Eine Nacht in Venedig* all at the same time is remarkable. The score for the opera was completed during his summer holidays. The manuscript is inscribed "Finished Alt-Aussee, September 21, 1923."

The Piano Concerto in C-sharp for left hand is one of the most uncharacteristic and original of all Korngold's compositions. The piano is more than matched by the extravagant orchestration. Indeed, the work is really a large symphony for piano and orchestra in which the piano becomes part of the orchestral fabric as well as developing its solo position. An air of tragic gloom is sustained by unusually stark and dissonant language. Even for Korngold, this score is exceptionally chromatic.

He chose deliberately to be nonspecific about its key: the work was entitled Piano Concerto in C-sharp without major or minor specified, although the written key signature is actually C-sharp minor. The ambiguous nature of its tonality is heightened further by the opening statement. The piano begins alone, and its first three notes are in C major. Only on the fourth note (A-sharp), followed by a thunderous C-sharp major chord, do we settle into a recognizable tonality. Almost immediately, however, the brightness of this major key harmony is contradicted by a swing into C-sharp minor in the second bar. The late Harold Truscott described this four-note motif as a kind of emphatic acciaccatura. Josef Reitler, in reviewing the first performance the following year, remarked on its peculiarly Korngoldian "physiognomy."

The intervals and the rhythm of this main theme are so typical—a perfect fifth followed by a perfect fourth—and the rhythm is identical to the opening theme of his equally tragic score for the film *The Sea Wolf* (1941). From this arresting and highly original beginning, Korngold demonstrates his virtuosity in extracting new sounds and harmonies from basically tonal music. He had no need for complete atonality, as he found the possibilities of the existing language of music illimitable.

This concerto is remarkable for many other reasons. First, it inhabits a unique sound world: nowhere else did Korngold orchestrate in quite the same way. Its structure is highly innovative. Although it is set out in a broad sonata form, it is extraordinarily complex. If one charts the interplay among the main themes and the links between each section, Korngold's conscious striving for thematic unity in this work quickly becomes apparent.

Second, his solution for writing for one hand alone set the modern blueprint for creating the illusion of two hands playing. (That Korngold completed his work long before Ravel, Prokofiev, and Strauss is often forgotten.) By judicious use of the pedal and crucial use of the thumb as a pivot, he was able to make the piano sound as though two hands were playing. This effect was enhanced by the nature of the piano part as written, with its multiple glissandi, powerful octaves, a spread of the hand across four octaves, and an octave bass held by the pedal as support. These devices were actually fundamental features of Korngold's own piano style.

Sixty years later, Gary Graffman rediscovered the concerto when he injured his right hand, and he promptly declared it to be a lost masterpiece. As one of the few contemporary pianists to have studied the work, his opinions are instructive:

> To begin with, I find the concerto marvelously pianistic. It explores so many possibilities of the instrument—those of achieving different types of sonorities—and is wonderfully constructed, formally. I find his bittersweet harmonies hauntingly expressive. He achieves not just the effect of two hands, but sometimes three or four! I agree with Harold Truscott in his description of this work as a large symphony for piano and orchestra. In fact, I'd go even further and say that the concerto is almost operatic.
>
> As I have said, it is the *only* left-hand concerto that gives back to me the feeling of playing the great romantic concertos for two hands, of Tchaikovsky, Rachmaninov, and Liszt. It is not easy to perform, which may account for its neglect. In a work such as this, with its . . . rhythmic complexity and varied sonorities—sufficient and detailed rehearsal is absolutely essential for a coherent performance. But it is worth it to be given the chance to play a keyboard *Salome*.[18]

In addition to composing, Korngold's commitments as a conductor of his own works made increasingly severe demands on his time. Even when not conducting, he would often spend time preparing artists who were to interpret his music. On 14 January 1923 the premiere of the orchestral version of his *Vier Lieder des Abschieds* was given by the Chamber Orchestra of the Vienna State Opera with Rosette Anday as the soloist. Just before her death in 1978, this great singer wrote a letter of personal reminiscence to me:

> We met shortly after my engagement at the Vienna State Opera. Like him, I was a *"Wunderkind,"* starting as a violinist at the age of seven,

before becoming a singer later on. Music was the element I grew up in; enthusiasm, devotion to art, and the joy of making music were the basis of a spontaneous understanding and harmony between us. Korngold asked me to sing his *Lieder des Abschieds* at a concert. These songs, which are certain to achieve a comeback in the repertoire of our great singers, were at the time "modern" in the best sense of the word, unusual, original, and quite personal in melody and harmony. He wrote a personal dedication to me, humorous and quite typical, which is, alas, untranslatable as it involves German word-play: "Der (unberufen) berufensten Interpretin dieser Lieder" (The [knock on wood] best interpreter of these songs).

At first sight, Erich Korngold was a rather shortish, fat man and certainly did not look as one would imagine a musical genius to look. At closer acquaintance, a sparkling wit and winning charm would begin to show. But then, he sat down at the piano, and suddenly a volcano broke loose. Fire, temperament, and extraordinary power characterized his performance. His hands hit the keys like animal pranks and made the instrument give forth almost orchestral tones. We invented a game: we did not speak to each other with words like ordinary people, but he played virtual cascades of notes and I, singing, improvised an appropriate text. In this manner we conversed for hours . . . . what a pity we had no tape recordings in those days.[19]

On 16 February 1923, the world premiere of the Piano Quintet in E Major took place in Hamburg, followed by its first performance in Vienna a few days later. It was a tremendous success. Korngold took the piano part on both occasions, and his impassioned performance no doubt contributed to the work's impact.

In March 1923, he was called to Berlin for his debut as conductor with the Berlin Philharmonic Orchestra, and he took Rosette Anday with him, who again sang the *Vier Lieder des Abschieds*. Korngold conducted his Sinfonietta in B Major and the Suite from *Much Ado About Nothing*. Despite some inevitable critical barbs, the concert was a success. The Suite meanwhile had also enjoyed triumphant performances in Rio de Janeiro and Buenos Aires, where the Vienna Philharmonic was once again on tour with Richard Strauss as conductor. (Strauss's absence from the Vienna State Opera for another long period, with flagrant disregard for the bad feeling this would cause at home, was yet another excuse for the anti-Strauss feeling in the local press, especially the *Neue Freie Presse*).

Korngold was in demand not just in Austria and Germany. After directing the "supplementary" Austrian section of the Salzburg Festival, mentioned above, Korngold received an invitation from Bernardino Molinari, the noted Italian conductor, to come to Rome. He was to conduct a concert made up entirely of his own works at the famed Augusteo. At the end of October, Korngold traveled to Italy with his father for the concert, which was scheduled for 2 December 1923. For his program, Korngold chose a cross section of his most important works to date: the "Vorspiel und Karneval" from *Violanta*, the Sinfonietta in B Major, *Sursum Corda*, "Marietta's Dance" and the Epilog from *Die tote Stadt*, and finally the Suite from *Much Ado About Nothing*

The audience, predictably by now, disliked *Sursum Corda* and greeted it with their traditional call of "Basta!" (Enough!), but after the Suite from *Much Ado About Nothing*, the requests for a repeat were so vociferous and the disagreement over which movement was to be repeated so pronounced that Korngold was left standing on the rostrum for several minutes until the question was resolved.

Julius Korngold sat in the audience with the composers Alfredo Casella, Ottorino Respighi, and, of course, Puccini, who had traveled to Rome to take part in the selection of the new director of the conservatory. He showed the greatest interest in the concert, and loyally attended all nine of the rehearsals.

Shortly before their departure from Rome, the Korngolds dined with Casella in the local artists' restaurant, where Erich was asked to sign the guest book. He wrote the main theme from *Sursum Corda* and a theme from *Much Ado About Nothing*; next to the first he wrote "Hissed," and next to the second, "Applauded," and continued underneath, "In a hundred years, may be the other way around."

The New Dark Age —
Hitler's Rise to Power:
1924–1933

Chapter Twelve

"Mama, We Are Playing at Being Married, a Whole Life Long!"

The year 1924 began promisingly with another world premiere: the String Quartet in A major, Opus 16, was performed on 8 January by the faithful Rosé Quartet, to whom Korngold dedicated the score. The new work was hailed by audience and critics alike, and its four movements afforded every opportunity for the Rosé Quartet to demonstrate the virtuosity that had made it one of the most renowned of pre-war ensembles.

The work was a worthy counterpart to the earlier Sextet for Strings in D Major. The agitated first subject of the opening movement, with its serenely beautiful counter-melody, is one of Korngold's finest inspirations. Double and triple stopping add a richness to the music and give the impression that far more than four instruments are playing. (For this reason Korngold was often criticized for not writing true chamber music. He deliberately tried to achieve greater sonority and more varied textures.) Well received in Vienna and elsewhere, it even moved the normally sour Paul Bechert to write the following in *The Musical Times*:

> The Quartet abounds in persistent sevenths which are distinctly the composer's own and in the second and best movement, in some original chromatics. The third movement which treats the theme in the manner of a fugato accompanied by many pizzicato effects is of a rugged and unique humor heretofore unknown in this composer.[1]

Mr. Bechert did not care for the Finale, however, which was another hymn to nature, reminiscent of the Intermezzo from the Sextet for Strings in D Major, and bears a quotation from Shakespeare's *As You Like It:* "When birds do sing hey ding a ding ding: Sweet lovers love the spring." The principal theme is an elaborate variation on the Motto of the Cheerful Heart from the Sinfonietta in B Major.[2]

This premiere was followed by another triumph on 7 February 1924. Wilhelm Furtwängler gave an acclaimed performance of the Suite from *Much Ado About Nothing* with the Leipzig Gewandhaus Orchestra, thereby continuing Korngold's association with that great orchestra in spite of the death of Arthur Nikisch. In March, Korngold conducted the first complete performance of the orchestral version of his *Sechs Einfache Lieder,* Opus 9, with the Vienna Symphony and Ella Flesch (from the Vienna State Opera) as soloist.[3]

Korngold was also working to complete the orchestration of the Piano Concerto in C-sharp for Wittgenstein and was making some headway with *Das Wunder der Heliane*, but foremost in his mind was his approaching marriage to Luzi, which thanks to Marischka could now go ahead. Luzi recalled with particular warmth the events leading up to their wedding:

One day, in October 1923, Erich asked me if he could come and visit my mother and me, after the performance of *A Night in Venice*. I agreed and promised him a late-night snack. He appeared at about eleven o'clock at night, just as he had left the performance—in his tail coat. When he entered he immediately walked towards my mother and asked her to follow him into the adjoining room. I waited in consternation and excitement until the two emerged after a lengthy conversation.

When Erich dared to kiss me in the presence of my mother I was in no doubt about the reason for which he had abducted her to the other room. "You see," he beamed, "I always told you I would ask for your hand dressed in tail coat and white waist coat." For the time being, our engagement was supposed to be secret, so secret that even Erich's parents didn't take any notice of it, in spite of having been informed about it by their son. I often met them at the opera or at a concert. We greeted each other ceremoniously and the only sign that the parents knew about the engagement, was an expression of indescribable sadness in the eyes of Dr. Korngold.[4]

A few weeks before the wedding on 30 April 1924, the happy couple went to Berlin, chaperoned by Robert Pollak, to attend a performance of *Die tote Stadt*.[5] As they boarded the train, Dr. Korngold, in deep melancholy, took Pollak to one side and whispered "Don't let the children be alone together," and Pollak followed this instruction almost to the letter.

Korngold and his
bride, Luise von
Sonnenthal, taken
on their wedding
day, 30 April 1924
(Korngold estate).

Die tote Stadt reached Berlin after a comparatively long delay due to
another "incident" directly involving Korngold's father. In 1923 the legendary conductor Erich Kleiber had been appointed general music director
of the Berlin State Opera following the resignations of Wilhelm
Furtwängler (from the post of conductor of the Staatskapelle) and Leo
Blech (as principal conductor of the Opera). The new title combined both
positions in one. Kleiber accepted the post after a period of fruitless negoti-
ation during which the intendant of the Opera, composer Max von
Schillings, attempted to secure the services of a string of distinguished conductors, including Alexander von Zemlinsky and Bruno Walter. When Otto
Klemperer was offered the job, he imposed such extravagant conditions of
acceptance that negotiations inevitably foundered. Kleiber, at the age of 34,
had enjoyed a fairly pedestrian career as conductor of provincial orchestras
in Darmstadt, Düsseldorf, and elsewhere, so it came as something of a surprise when he was offered this major position.

Although Max von Schillings, a curious and contradictory figure, admired Korngold's gifts, he was an acknowledged anti-Semite and was seldom complimentary about other composers. During his troubled tenure as intendant in Berlin, he overhauled the entire repertoire, improved the staging, and mounted several interesting productions of works by Schreker, Pfitzner, and Busoni. He had met the Korngolds (father and son) in 1920 after a performance of the ballet *Die Josephslegende* by Richard Strauss, and had expressed the wish to perform *Die tote Stadt* even then, before the simultaneous world premieres had taken place.

Kleiber was assigned the task of conducting the new production, to be staged by Franz Ludwig Hörth[6] with striking sets designed by Emil Pirchan.[7] Kleiber wrote a warm letter expressing his dedication to his forthcoming task and flattering the young composer on his work. Before the production took place, however, Kleiber's concert debut in Vienna failed to impress Julius Korngold, who felt unable to flatter the conductor in a similar vein. Kleiber subsequently walked out of the assignment, and von Schillings, keen to remain on at least cordial terms with his new musical director, allowed it.

Nonetheless, the production, which had been an expensive undertaking, had to proceed, especially since the two stars, Richard Tauber and Lotte Lehmann, had been imported from Vienna for the occasion. It was premiered on 12 April 1924 and was a triumph. Its two stars recorded the famous Act I duet in what is now considered an ideal interpretation that has never been out of the catalog in seventy years. The guest conductor for the production was the young Georg Szell, who was the same age as Korngold and had also been a child prodigy in Vienna as a piano virtuoso.

Erich and Luzi enjoyed a hectic few days in Berlin, hectic largely because Szell and Tauber had just discovered the joys of racing cars. Daily they sped around the local autobahn at speeds in excess of 100 miles per hour, with the betrothed as trembling passengers.

Several other distinguished musicians were in Berlin then, including Leo Blech (who remained as a conductor despite resigning from the Opera) and Artur Schnabel, who spent much of his time trying to win Erich Korngold over to the merits of the *Neue Musik*, to no avail.

On their return, Korngold decided that he would have to begin introducing Luzi to everyone he knew in Vienna. Until now, the two had met and socialized mostly with the Duschnitzes and with friends and relatives of Luzi's, especially her many aunts, all of whom were noted hostesses of the period. Apart from relatives and close friends, Erich had a wide circle of acquaintances, and it was to these that he now presented his bride-to-be. Emmerich Kálmán, the famed operetta composer, and his beautiful wife Vera were close friends and remained so even during the later separation imposed by the Second World War. The composer Julius Bittner and his wife Emilie, owing to their considerable age difference, were to become almost second parents to the newlyweds, an ideal role for this kindly couple. Korngold later remarked that all of his friends seemed to be fifteen to twenty years older than he, commenting, "That is so, because I am in truth, already fifteen to twenty years older—I began too young."[8] Less enjoyable by far was Luzi's official visit to her prospective parents-in-law:

> Dr. Korngold expressed all of his melancholy and the mother avoided a kiss when Erich, embracing us both, tried to bring us together. I had dark forebodings. In spite of my youth I understood the feelings of the old man. I felt compassionate and didn't get angry about his openly demonstrated regrets.[9]

The happy day arrived, 30 April 1924. Erich collected Luzi in a taxi. On the way to the town hall, where they were to be married,[10] he realized that he had forgotten the bridal bouquet. They stopped at the famous flower shop on the Schauflergasse, where he bought an enormous bunch of flowers and pressed them into her hands. It was a quiet wedding, with only the immediate family and a few friends present. They lunched at the town hall, then went on to a reception at Luzi's mother's. Finally, at six o'clock, they boarded a train for Salzburg for a few days' holiday. Next morning, Korngold gave Luzi another wedding present. From under his pillow, he took a copy of *Contes Drolatiques,* the somewhat salacious collection of stories by Balzac, with the words: "Thank God, you are finally allowed to read this, now you are married!"[11] From Salzburg, Korngold sent a postcard to Luzi's mother:

Dear Mama,

We are playing at being married—a glorious game! Luzi is winning almost every time. Yes, we are playing at being married a whole life long.[12]

Returning to Vienna, Korngold acted as accompanist at an evening of his Lieder given by Bella Paalen and Beate Roos-Reuter, and then the two newlyweds could finally begin their proper honeymoon in Paris, London, Hamburg, and Berlin. The trip was partly private and partly professional, and again they were accompanied most of the time by the violinist Robert Pollak.

In Paris, their host was Paul Géraldy[13] and his wife, the Polish singer Germaine Lubin.[14] At the home of Paul and Sophie Clemenceau[15] they met other noted personalities, including the composer Maurice Ravel and, more importantly, Berta Szeps-Zuckerkandl,[16] Sophie Clemenceau's sister and a close friend of Alma Mahler. A noted patron of the arts, she arranged for Korngold to give three concerts during his visit, including his very first broadcast on the new invention—radio. Mme. Zuckerkandl also arranged an evening with the son of Georges Rodenbach, Constantine, who had already met Korngold several times.

It was during this sojourn in Paris that Luzi discovered a peculiarity of her husband's that gave her much pause for thought and presented a marked contrast to his otherwise very normal disposition. They were invited to an elaborate dinner party by the Géraldys, and already she noticed Korngold becoming more and more agitated as the hour approached. Upon arrival and the sight of the several sets of cutlery indicating the many different courses, he quickly excused himself, complaining of a headache, and spent the duration of the meal lying on a divan in the adjoining salon. When his concerned hosts enquired about his well-being, he rejoined the party, apparently completely cured—but after the meal was over. Luzi realized that Erich Korngold was not as uncomplicated and "normal" as his cheerful, out-going personality might lead one to believe. Indeed, his great wit and *joie de vivre* very often camouflaged his true feelings and personality.

A slightly less serious characteristic, but unusual all the same, was the intense sensitivity of Korngold's hands—so much so that he would sit with his hands facing outward to avoid them coming into contact with fabric. In the family limousine, he always rested his hands on a special cushion made of a material that did not irritate them. This was not an affectation but was absolutely necessary for his comfort. In addition, he never learned to drive because of his concern that he might easily mistake the accelerator pedal for the *sostenuto* pedal of the piano whenever his mind was distracted by musical inspiration. He once remarked that there was never a moment when music was not passing through his mind, and, realizing the danger, he never learned to drive a car.

Luzi remembered that a dreamy expression would often come into his eyes when he was out driving or walking, and he would become very flushed in the face. When this happened, she knew that he was inspired with a musical idea. If she urged him to write it down later, he would shrug it off, maintaining that if it was important it would come back to him when he needed it. (This phenomenon is similar to one observed in Franz Schubert.)

Her realization that Korngold was not the simple, uncomplicated human being he appeared, reminded Luzi of a remark he had once made that "one can't ever presume to truly know anybody with any thoroughness." In spite of their seven-year friendship, even Luzi had only a slight inkling of "the true rhythms of his soul," as she put it. Despite his friendly nature, Erich Korngold was a very reserved person who did not easily confide in anybody. Luzi von Sonnenthal probably knew him better than anyone ever did, including his parents.

From Paris, they went on to London, where Robert Pollak made several recordings with Korngold for the old Homochord company. From London, the happy couple took a small steamer from Southampton to Hamburg, leaving the loyal Pollak behind. In Hamburg, Korngold introduced Luzi to his close friend Egon Pollak, to whom he often referred as "my dear and esteemed First Performer," because Pollak had given so many premieres of Korngold's works.

Erich and Luzi Korngold on their honeymoon, Alt-Aussee, in the summer of 1924 (Korngold estate).

Finally, the Korngolds journeyed to Alt Aussee for their summer holiday, arriving on 18 June 1924 to find two letters from Paul Wittgenstein awaiting them. Korngold had already dispatched the Piano Concerto in C-sharp to Wittgenstein in the spring, and the premiere was scheduled to take place in Vienna at the Municipal Music and Theater Festival later that year. On 19 June 1924 Korngold wrote, in part:

I am so terribly sorry that we could not take you up on your welcome invitation and that you had to wait for an answer. About your plan of playing my (rather "your") piano concerto for this distinguished conductor, I hail it wholeheartedly. It also pleases me that you obviously like the work and that you wish to play it. Playing it in front of someone I take as superfluous. For, apart from the fact that any conductor in Germany performs any new piece of mine automatically, they also know who you are and what you are capable of.

There is one thing I want to insist on: come to Aussee in the next few days. We could talk about it all so splendidly, and it wouldn't be useless to go through the piece again for tempos and nuances.

(I trust you agree to the first performance at the Wienermusikfest at the beginning of October?)

If you could come the 25th or 26th of June you will find my wife and me by ourselves; my parents are not due until the 29th . . . and you'll find a charming room in the Park Hotel. Please wire your acceptance and day of arrival, and accept cordial greetings as well as compliments from myself and my wife—also to your revered mother.[17]

Whether Wittgenstein ever visited them is unknown, but the concerto did receive its world premiere, with Korngold conducting, not in October, but on 22 September 1924. Judging from contemporary reports, Wittgenstein gave a superb account of the difficult solo part.

The festival was the second of its kind, the first having been mounted in 1920 on a much more modest scale owing to post-war economic difficulties. The official opening was spectacular: 30,000 people assembled to hear the opening speech made by Mayor Seitz from the steps of the city hall, which was followed by a specially composed *Fanfare* by Richard Strauss, who was adept at providing such musical flourishes, performed from the tower of the city hall.

This festival coincided with several anniversaries, including Schoenberg's fiftieth birthday and the centenary of Bruckner's birth. Schoenberg was honored officially by the Austrian government for the first time and had several works premiered during the festival, including *Die glückliche Hand*. Two of Richard Strauss's works were premiered: the new reworked version of *Le Bourgeois Gentilhomme* and a new ballet entitled *The Ruins of Athens* (based on music by Beethoven, to a book by Hofmannsthal).[18] Strauss conducted these works and, in spite of continued stormy relations with Julius Korngold, mounted a special festival production of *Die tote Stadt*.

Prior to these festivities, the newlyweds had enjoyed a pleasant summer. The arrival of the Korngold parents on 29 June signaled the end of the idyllic holiday for them, however, and Luzi was saddened that in spite of her valiant efforts, relations remained cool. Julius was almost won over in the first few weeks, and Erich happily informed his wife that "he's almost in love with you himself," but this was short-lived, and in fact Luzi was never accepted by Erich's father. As Luzi explained:

He didn't only view my dark origins with suspicion (as a Viennese girl from a family of actors, who had also been a film actress)—but he also noticed with growing displeasure that I let myself go freely with other young people who were jolly and happy; the first quarrel came when I was so "sinful" as to dance repeatedly with a few young people, among them the baritone Hans Duhan, at the home of Friedrich Buxbaum, the cellist of the Rosé Quartet. Father Korngold immediately left the house and disappeared into the pitch-black night, alone and disgruntled, making his long way back to our farmhouse.

Meanwhile, mother Korngold took the running of the household completely out of my hands, thereby spoiling my beautiful game of playing "Hausfrau." So we lived like children would in the house of their parents. The daily routine was planned by them; our friends had to be their friends, even if they didn't interest us very much, and almost daily there was some open or implied criticism about me— which often led to scenes, with Erich courageously and tactfully taking my part. . . . In spite of this, I felt much more for Erich than myself. The parents' judgment of my character and behavior seemed to me to be slightly comical. I felt something like compassion for these stubborn, blind people who couldn't give up their lifelong struggle for their son against me.[19]

Korngold tried to make progress on *Das Wunder der Heliane*, and had also to prepare the proofs of the Piano Quintet in E Major, about to be published that autumn. At the same time, he had been asked by Schott to join the panel of judges for a special competition that Schott announced in June of that year. The contest was designed to encourage young composers, who were asked to submit works in *Kammerstil* (the style of chamber music) for either a single instrument or ensemble. The other judges were Paul Hindemith, Joseph Haas,[20] Lothar Windsperger,[21] and Dr. Ludwig Strecker, the head of the publishing house. The winners were chosen from the many entries by the end of the following summer, when a special concert of the three winning compositions was given. These were works by Ernst Toch, Alexander Tcherepnin, and Hermann Munsch. This was the only occasion that such a competition was held by Schott, and it reveals which of their composers were held in highest esteem. Equally fascinating is that composers as diverse as Hindemith and Korngold were able to agree on the winners.

The concept of helping young talent must have appealed to Korngold, especially as it did not attach labels to the music to be submitted. The influence of the International Society for New Music was not prevalent here, and the cliquish, unhealthy cultivation of the "new" at any price, which only served to isolate new music and young composers, was not part of Korngold's outlook.

In this rare involvement with composers of a more radical persuasion, Korngold kept his distance. He did not participate in the famous annual Donaueschingen Festivals, for instance, where Schoenberg, Webern, Berg, Bartók, Křenek, and others received such important first performances. He was probably not invited, since the directors of this event included Franz Schreker, no friend of Korngold's father, given the scathing reviews meted out to his operas by the critic. This alienation from the mainstream activity of contemporary music began to have a drastic effect on Korngold's career. Performances of his work became more sporadic, and to support himself and his wife, he became increasingly reliant on journeyman conducting chores in Vienna's various theaters and on adapting operettas.

Domestically, a kind of truce with his parents was reached that first summer. Relieved of running the house, Luzi became Erich's assistant and proof-read and helped to correct music, a task she would perform many times in years to come. On their return to Vienna, they had to remain with the Korngold parents because of a general shortage of living accommodation. The mayor of Vienna, Karl Seitz, rescued them and gave them a flat after they had visited him personally. Even though the flat was hardly habitable, the Korngolds preferred it to the parental home, from which they departed quietly at night, after the usual unpleasant scenes.

If Korngold avoided contemporary musical circles in Germany, he could hardly do so in Austria. The activities of the International Society for New Music at their 1924 festival held in Vienna were no less controversial than they had been in Salzburg in 1923, and this being Vienna, Julius Korngold was right at the center of events. The city of Vienna was chosen as the venue because, in the words of Edward J. Dent (the president), "they wished to express the gratitude felt by the celebrating society, toward the country of its origin."

Representatives from some three hundred newspapers turned up, and Vienna, already crowded with visitors for all the other cultural events that summer, had to play host to an even larger influx of international guests. Julius Korngold, Joseph Marx, Josef Reitler, Hans Liebstöckl, and Richard Specht represented the critical bulwark against what Julius Korngold later described as the "atonal twilight of the false gods."[22]

Dent and his colleagues nevertheless extended the olive branch by inviting the younger Korngold, Wilhelm Kienzl, and Franz Schmidt to be on the festival committee, but inevitably the two camps remained entrenched. The supporters of New Music in Our Time, as it was now called, declared that Julius Korngold and his colleagues were unfairly biased against the radical composers because of Dr. Korngold's all-pervasive influence and his unfair concern about promoting his son. The critic Willi Reich, who despised Julius Korngold and his son, wrote a long article that did not mince words:

> One might believe that Julius Korngold's summary dismissal was based on some method—painted enthusiastically by Ernst Decsey in the following manner: "Korngold becomes, every time, a dedicated

student of the composer he must examine and the work he has to judge. He studies the score, its history, and pre-history for weeks on end, in monastic isolation." Since when was the "Cafe Museum" a monastery?[23]

Reich went on to make such outlandish claims against his rival critic that the result was yet another libel suit, which was settled out of court, as usual.

The ramifications of all this squabbling were not the only talking point that summer. A series of events that directly involved the elder Korngold with far more serious implications for the younger Korngold were taking place at the Vienna State Opera. The increasingly stormy relations between Richard Strauss and Julius Korngold presented an incredible state of affairs judging from the extant correspondence and press coverage. Although Julius was initially disposed to a detached acceptance of Strauss as co-director, by 1921 the situation in the venerable institution had deteriorated sufficiently that Julius Korngold repeatedly declared himself in opposition to the regime. Strauss's practice of "borrowing" the leading singers of the opera for performances elsewhere of his own works, or consenting to their requests for leave to fulfill engagements in other cities to sing his music, inevitably gave Julius Korngold ammunition that he used unsparingly. No matter what he thought of Strauss the composer, the Vienna State Opera was sacred to him (and to all of Vienna for that matter), and no one, not even Richard Strauss, had the right to jeopardize its reputation or its traditions. To add fuel to the flames, Schalk, who was disgruntled by the unfair treatment of having to run the Vienna State Opera single-handedly during Strauss's long absences, began to intrigue against Strauss.

The first serious exchange of fire had taken place in 1922, when Julius Korngold attributed the failure of a performance of Meyerbeer's *The Huguenots* to the lack of a strong cast owing to the absence of too many regular, contracted artists whose places were filled by unsuitable guest singers. He added a postscript which read:

> The critic cannot and must not suppress such complaints . . . ;
> however, management is entitled to refer to the current handicaps and
> difficulties under which it is working.[24]

This was clearly meant to sugar the pill, but it proved ineffective. Erich Korngold was summoned into Strauss's presence and not for the first time had to listen to a critical tirade about his father. He returned home so distressed that Julius Korngold (who rarely responded to any retort to his writings) wrote the following letter to Strauss:

> According to my son, you have remarked, in the presence of Director
> Schalk, about an alleged connection between the performances of my
> son's opera *Die tote Stadt* and the opera reviews in the *Neue Freie Presse*, such remarks undoubtedly being intended to reach me and my
> newspaper. You have declared:

1. That the matter of the opera *Die tote Stadt* cannot be separated from the reviews of the *Neue Freie Presse*, that is, that those reviews are influenced by whether or not this opera is scheduled for performance.

2. That the singers of the *Staatsoper* (and even those of other opera houses) sing the roles of *Die tote Stadt* only out of fear of the *Neue Freie Presse* and that singers who volunteer to perform in this opera (like Mme. Lotte Lehmann the other day) do so only for fear of the *Presse*.

3. That I wanted a Jew[25] to be given your post at the *Staatsoper* and that as a composer's father I am automatically prejudiced against you.

4. That, considering my attitude towards the Opera House, as some of its members also agree, it had become incompatible with your and the *Staatsoper's* dignity that my son continues to appear there as a guest conductor of his operas.

I have to refute these statements as entirely unfounded, inadmissible, and improper. I emphatically protest the efforts to exert pressure on the musical criticism of the *Neue Freie Presse* which cannot let itself be limited in its freedom and independence in appraising the questions of opera management, which are vital to the well-being of the Opera House. Having repeatedly and unequivocally proven my esteem of your person and creativity, I deeply regret that a man of your standing is surrendering to intrigues and overwrought nerves to think of allegations of this kind and even to raise them with the son against the father, bringing in the issue of religion and attacking a critic who can look back on forty years of activity, the nature of which has not remained unknown to you.[26]

Julius Korngold submitted the letter to Ernst Benedikt,[27] editor-in-chief of the *Neue Freie Presse*, before mailing it, leaving a copy on file. In support of his father, Erich Korngold then wrote to Karl Lion requesting the removal of his operas from the schedule, but they nevertheless remained in the repertory that season. Relations had remained cool for most of 1923.

In 1924, the whole matter came to a boil once again on the occasion of a gala performance of *Die Fledermaus* that summer, scheduled to coincide with the Municipal Music and Theater Festival. Elisabeth Schumann, who had joined the Vienna Opera in 1919, had risen to become one of its brightest stars and was a particular favorite of Richard Strauss, so much so that when she joined the company, she was able to stipulate that one of the conditions of her coming to Vienna was that her husband Carl Alwin[28] be engaged as conductor at the opera as well.

Her interpretation of Adele in *Die Fledermaus* was legendary, ever since her introduction of an imitation of a canary's trill into the third act in a 1922 production—a vocal trick she had learned in childhood.[29] Naturally it was expected that Elisabeth Schumann would repeat her performance for such a special staging of the operetta. Although she sang the first performance, she failed to appear for the rest; Lotte Schöne[30] substituted for her while she and Alwin went on tour.

Julius Korngold, who had viewed the disintegration of the repertory that season with growing dismay, wrote one of his most effective articles and it stirred up fresh rancor:

> Two nights ago, my professional duty, combined with private inclination, took me to a performance of *Fledermaus*. Can it be said that the cast remains at the level we have been encouraged to expect?—until the day before yesterday, yes, in spite of Frau Schumann's absence after the first performance. Guest engagements seem to constitute the chief clause in the contract concluded with this bird of passage.
>
> Frau Schöne as Adele had the fuller voice; a pretty face, gay natural acting, and—not least—the necessary Viennese dialect are valuable adjuncts. Frau Schöne was warmly applauded. Frau Olzcewska, too, has surrendered Prince Orlowsky to Fräulein Anday, who speaks her lines with a comic gravity and sings as prettily as ever. Fräulein Vera Schwarz and Messrs. Richard Tauber, Hans Duhan, and Karl Renner retain their old parts and contribute to a gay and vocally strong ensemble. Herr Oestvig was also in the cast, his last appearance. The Opera House, showing exemplary consideration to questions of leave, even put the hour of the performance forward to 6:30 (many of us arrived late)—in order that Herr Oestwig might catch his train. Evidently leave of absence is again being freely granted, despite the contrary assurances of the management.
>
> Frau Lehmann is spending a lengthy "intermezzo"[31] in Dresden, and even the corps-de-ballet has had to supply twelve dancers to Breslau so that Viennese *"Schlagobers"*[32] [whipped cream] might the more easily be turned into German *Sahne* [cream].
>
> The old mischief is beginning again and threatens the repertory, which hitherto has been kept at the same high standard as the performances. The difficulty of filling the house in these hard times— apart from a few evenings like *Fledermaus*—should serve as a warning. The management, however, obviously believes that what cannot be cured must be endured. But there is a cure, and it should be applied.[33]

Shortly after this article appeared, Strauss requested one year's leave of absence to fulfill various conducting engagements, and requested that his close friend and ally Josef Turnau[34] replace him as chief producer. Schalk was exasperated that he should be expected to run the opera with one of his rival's cronies in joint command. The leave of absence was not granted, and to no one's surprise, Strauss cabled from Dresden his immediate resignation.

As soon as Strauss resigned, Schalk, in a rare moment of tactlessness, published an article condemning Strauss, thereby (in Julius Korngold's words) "slamming the door behind his partner with a loud bang."[35]

Even more inappropriately, on 14 February 1925, Dr. Karl Lion engaged Korngold to conduct *Violanta* as the first production following Strauss's departure. Because Strauss's supporters held Julius Korngold to be solely responsible for his departure, this event was like a red rag to a bull. A demonstration was organized to hiss Korngold off the podium.

As soon as Korngold entered the pit, an almighty uproar broke out. Whistling, hissing, and stamping of feet and cries of "Hoch Strauss! Pfui Korngold!" filled the air, with the fourth gallery (where most of Korngold's supporters were seated) shouting "Hoch Korngold!" in reply. The police were summoned and the five ringleaders ejected. Still, the booing continued. As Luzi recalled, there was then a slight respite during which the tiny voice of a woman rang out across the auditorium—with a rather unlady-like word—"Kusch!" (a slang expression, like "shut the hell up!" with which in Vienna one would command a dog to go sit in a corner). The effect of this was startling—uproarious laughter throughout the house—until even the hostile group joined in the hysteria. Then, suddenly, there was silence, and at last the performance could begin. At the end of the opera, the young Korngold (naturally) received a standing ovation as though nothing had happened. Afterwards, he told Luzi, "I am proud of one thing: during all those demonstrations I kept the baton up high and very steadily, without even a hint of trembling."[36]

Richard Specht wrote later that the demonstration was really against Julius, not his son. Erich Korngold believed that Carl Alwin, the conductor and close friend of Strauss and husband of Elisabeth Schumann, was the real ringleader behind the affair, and he said so in public later that evening, as did his father.

On 2 March 1924, the *Deutsche Zeitung, Berlin* announced the sensational news that Alwin had filed a lawsuit for slander against both Erich and Julius Korngold. Alwin also tried to get the theater administration to reprimand Korngold, but this was deferred until the outcome of the court proceedings. The affair was settled out of court, as usual. The whole episode of Strauss leaving eventually fizzled out. It was typical of Vienna that a witty *bon mot* helped to defuse the situation:

> If it must be Richard, then Wagner, and if it must be Strauss, then Johann; if there must be an Intermezzo, then the one from *Cavalleria Rusticana* and if there must be "Schlagobers" . . . then at Demels.[37]

Yet, as though nothing had happened, Schalk mounted a new and lavish production of *Die Frau ohne Schatten* the following year, and Strauss agreed to be a freelance guest conductor at both the Vienna State Opera and the Vienna Philharmonic. The Viennese could not turn their backs on the box office, after all.

Meanwhile, one of the most significant productions of *Die tote Stadt* had taken place in Munich in 1922 under the baton of Hans Knappertsbusch,[38] but that particular occasion was also the scene of an unpleasant episode, one that served as a portent of things to come. A large delegation of the National Socialist Party, carrying torches and swastikas, made a strong presence at the premiere. The hostile clique tried unsuccessfully to disrupt this performance, not because of anything to do with Strauss, but on racial grounds. At the end, Knappertsbusch bravely stood behind young Korngold on the stage, and the public doubled its applause to drown the hissing and booing of the Nazi demonstrators.

Furious at this, the Hitler group entered an interpellation in the Bavarian diet against the performance of "this non-Aryan opera of Viennese derivation." The work had to be removed from the schedule after seven sold-out performances. The Nazi movement—still regarded as a fanatical minority— would eventually remove not only Korngold's work from the repertoire but also that of his rivals in the International Society for New Music.

CHAPTER THIRTEEN

Korngold versus Křenek

Christmas 1924 was marked by a more enjoyable occasion. Korngold was invited by Rudolf Nilius, the director of the Vienna Symphony Orchestra, to share the podium for the final concert before Christmas on Sunday, 24 December, arranged by the Wiener Konzert-Verein in the Grosser Konzerthaus-Saal. Korngold chose his *Vier Lieder des Abschieds* and once again invited Rosette Anday to sing them.

The holiday season, the first shared by Korngold and his young bride, passed quietly. Significantly, Korngold had no new compositions for his father's birthday. Already, the demands made on Korngold's time by his increased conducting activity were beginning to tell on his creative work. This must have been hard to bear for his father, who saw less and less of his famous son.

Early in 1925, Korngold received a number of invitations from abroad to conduct and perform, which he readily accepted. His income was largely dependent on the fees he commanded as a musician rather than as a composer. By now Luzi was expecting their first child, and it was clear that the small apartment provided by Mayor Seitz was inadequate for their needs. They began to look for a house, but a house for a man of Korngold's eminence would prove to be expensive. Any significant offers that came his way to conduct, arrange, or perform would be accepted from now on. For the time being, however, the tiny flat would have to suffice. Not until 1928 would a handsome property in the fashionable Sternwartestrasse become available.

On 9 March 1925 their first child, a boy, was born, and the couple decided to call him Ernst Werner in order to preserve, as Luzi said, "the initials E. W. K. in the laundry." Even this happy event was preceded by a cynical barb in the press: one paper noted that Korngold's first son would be christened Johann Sebastian. Little did the joker realize that Ernst Werner Korngold's arrival had been forecast for 21 March, Johann Sebastian Bach's birthday. "He screams—but screams tonally," the proud father quipped after the birth.

In spite of the difficulties of the previous year, Korngold's star continued to shine brightly at home and around the world. In January, Korngold visited Schott to discuss the final title for the new opera. Dr. Strecker preferred *Das Wunder der Heliane* to the tentative *Das dunkle Reich* (The Dark Kingdom). The title *The Miracle* was ruled out because a famous play of that title by Karl Vollmoeller already existed, so *Das Wunder der Heliane* (The Miracle of Heliane) was the final choice.

Back in Vienna, Korngold was still contracted to the Theater an der Wien to conduct not only his own adaptation of *Eine Nacht in Venedig* but also Offenbach's *La Belle Hélène* and Johann Strauss's *Wiener Blut*.

The summer of 1925 was unusually busy and saw the family separated, as Korngold was engaged in numerous conducting engagements. After a brief sojourn to Aigen-Vogelhub (near Salzburg), where his parents were staying, he left for Berlin to be guest conductor for a new production of *Eine Nacht in Venedig* starring Richard Tauber at the Berliner Theater, in his revised version. Luzi remained in Vienna, but joined him in Berlin in September. The premiere of this new successful production took place on 22 September. In the meantime, the Frankfurt Opera also announced a lavish production of his adaptation of *Eine Nacht in Venedig* for the following month, stunningly designed by Ludwig Sievert, with a cast that included Viorica Ursuleac, Adele Kern, Richard von Schenck, Hermann Schramm, and Elizabeth Friedrich, and conducted by Clemens Krauss. It was nothing short of sensational. The critics bestowed lavish praise on Korngold "the great arranger," as they were now fond of calling him.

While in Berlin he was invited to dinner by the publisher Fürstner (who was Richard Strauss's principal publisher), who offered Korngold a huge sum, much higher than his fees from Schott, for the rights to *Das Wunder der Heliane*. Korngold, flattered as he was by the offer, responded with a loyalty typical of him, declining the generous offer and explaining that he had been with Schott since his childhood and could not think of changing publishers now. Fürstner persisted, even telephoning him the next morning at his hotel, but Korngold was not to be persuaded.

In the summer of 1925, Korngold received two invitations, one from the Concertgebouw in Amsterdam to conduct his own works and the other from the Scala Theater in Copenhagen to conduct a new production of *Die*

Fledermaus. The performances were scheduled for November, and Korngold accepted.

Meanwhile, he had the great personal satisfaction that his String Quartet No. 1 in A Major had been a major highlight of the festival held by the Incorporated Society of Contemporary Music in Venice, where the Kolisch Quartet gave a spirited reading. The concert, on 5 September 1925, had included chamber works by Jacques Ibert, Honegger, Ravel, and Albert Roussel, among others, but Korngold's quartet had taken the honors and the notices were glowing, a result that must have irritated Edward Dent and his colleagues.

The Danish production of *Die Fledermaus* was a tremendous success, despite some casting problems. The role of Rosalinde was sung by Amelie Kierkegaard-Rothe, who was well past her prime and could only softly breathe her top notes. Adele was sung by the actress Liva Weel, who was not really a singer at all, so that her rendition of "Mein Herr Marquis" sounded more like a parody than the virtuoso set piece it is supposed to be. Nevertheless, Korngold allowed for all these shortcomings, and the performance was a triumph. He had stipulated as part of his contract that he must have the freedom to leave for Amsterdam to conduct a concert of his own works, and consequently on 24 November 1925 he and Luzi set off. For some reason, Korngold had imagined that reaching Amsterdam would be easier from Copenhagen than from Vienna. Although they had quite a strenuous train journey, they arrived on time.

Korngold was to share the podium with the great conductor Pierre Monteux,[1] who was to conduct the first half of the concert, a Haydn Symphony and the new *Parergon zur Sinfonia Domestica* by Richard Strauss, written for Paul Wittgenstein, the soloist at the concert. After the interval, Korngold would conduct a program made up entirely of his own work, beginning with the *Schauspiel Ouvertüre*, followed by the Suite from *Much Ado About Nothing,* and concluding with the "Vorspiel und Karneval" from *Violanta*. After rehearsals, however, Korngold was worried, for although the Concertgebouw was of an extremely high standard, its members were rather cold and indifferent to this young guest conductor. As he told Luzi: "That is typical of a great orchestra: they show you their proficiency and their superiority, and that makes it more difficult to work with them more thoroughly afterwards."[2]

He need not have worried. His superior musical knowledge, ability to detect wrong notes in the densest orchestral textures, and his tremendous charm soon won the respect of the orchestra, which showed him full co-operation. The concert was a great success with the public, and on the following evening, Korngold acted as soloist in a program of his chamber music: the Piano Sonata No. 2 in E Major, the *Vier Lieder des Abschieds* (with soloist Mia Peltenburg), and the Piano Quintet in E Major. Then it was back to Denmark to complete the run of *Die Fledermaus* before returning home for Christmas.

He signed a new contract with Schott to publish his new opera, which by now was beginning to take shape in piano score, but the increased conducting activities and the resulting itinerant lifestyle prevented Korngold from beginning work on the orchestration, which was now postponed until the following summer.

In the meantime he had written three new songs (Opus 18)[3] based on poetry by Kaltneker, which he intended, in his words, as "character studies for my new opera." With *Das Wunder der Heliane*, these remarkable songs share a more advanced harmonic language and give a clear indication of the new course of his musical thinking.

As the year 1925 closed, however, it was becoming increasingly obvious that Korngold was becoming more renowned for his work in the field of operetta than for his serious compositions. Perhaps Korngold saw the dangers arising from his second career, perhaps not. He certainly placed his heart and soul into his new opera; which he felt sure would redress the balance in favor of Korngold "the creative musician."

Nevertheless, early in 1926, he accepted yet another operetta commission. The Wiener Bürgertheater (Theater of Vienna's Citizens), aware of the success of *Eine Nacht in Venedig*, approached him with the offer of a collaboration with Dr. Ludwig Herzer to revitalize another forgotten Johann Strauss II operetta, *Cagliostro in Wien*. Once again, the result was a box office success, due in no small part to Korngold's own conducting, as the *Neues Wiener Journal* was quick to point out:

> The main attraction of the performance is Erich Wolfgang Korngold's participation at the podium. Korngold is a consummate conductor . . . and interprets the score with a truly infectious gusto.[4]

The cast was led by Jacob Feldhammer opposite Ida Russka, and the adaptation fully occupied Korngold for much of 1926. Around this time, he was contacted by the great Max Reinhardt, whom he had known since the days of *Der Schneemann*. This contact was to be pivotal for the future.

Reinhardt was planning a spectacular production of Volmoeller's adaptation of *Turandot* at Salzburg during the festival that summer, and he asked Korngold to compose a score of incidental music for it. He was highly persuasive: the sets were being designed by Oskar Strnad,[5] one of the leading designers of the time, and there would be an all-star cast, including Helene Thimig (later Reinhardt's wife), Lilli Darvas, Max Pallenberg, Luise Rainer, Oskar Homolka, and Hans Moser. It was a tremendously exciting project, and Korngold would be able to conduct his score with the famed orchestra of the Mozarteum.

Yet Korngold turned it down. Puccini's last unfinished opera based on the same play by Carlo Gozzi and completed by his pupil Alfano after his death, had already received its first performance in Milan, conducted by Toscanini. It was shortly to receive its first performance in

Vienna, and Korngold wanted neither to detract from his late friend's work nor invite comparison with it. Still Reinhardt persisted. Korngold even refused to give Reinhardt his decision personally, declaring "I don't want to be talked into it!"

Although Max Reinhardt was indeed a very persuasive man, he finally conceded defeat and commissioned the score from Bernhard Paumgartner, and it has not been performed since.[6] Regarding what Korngold might have produced if he had gone ahead we can only speculate.

On his wedding anniversary, Korngold received a new honor, along with his colleagues Hans Gál and Franz Salmhofer: the *Kunstpreis der Stadt Wien* (Arts Prize of the City of Vienna). This was given to him for his achievements as a pianist, conductor, and composer. From Willy Strecker at Schott, Korngold also received a commission to write some new piano music for a modern anthology of keyboard works that Schott was planning.

The *Vier kleine Karikaturen für Kinder* (Four Little Caricatures for Children), Opus 19, is an ingenious set of miniatures, but with a sting in the tail. Each piece satirizes the styles of four leading modern composers— Arnold Schoenberg, Igor Stravinsky, Bela Bartók, and Paul Hindemith—yet each of them is Korngoldian. Each little piece gives just the vaguest impression of the composer it mimics; the melodic and rhythmic impetus are synonymous with Korngold alone. As for the title, "for children," clearly Korngold regarded some of the efforts of his more notorious contemporaries to be child's play.

The gentle satire proved too much for Willy Strecker (after all, Hindemith was also published by Schott). He eventually omitted them from the publication, fearful of offending the eminent composers they satirized, and they remained in manuscript form except for a limited publication in a musical journal in 1931.[7]

With the coming of the summer holidays, Korngold could again work on *Das Wunder der Heliane*. He was under some pressure from Franz Schalk in Vienna, who wanted to give the world premiere of the new work and with whom negotiations were already in progress. Once again, however, the first performance was to be in Hamburg, particularly as Korngold's father did not want any of his political machinations to mar the event (with good reason). Korngold was confident that the Hamburg Stadttheater would produce the work splendidly, and as the musical direction was in the hands of his friend Egon Pollak, he could be sure of a faithful interpretation.

In June, he rented a house in Klamm am Semmering for himself, Luzi, and little Ernst. Apart from occasional engagements to conduct his operas in Vienna, he worked diligently on Heliane from the early morning, devoting the afternoons to long walks in the spectacular countryside around that area.

Toward the end of the summer, the Korngolds went on a short business trip, first to Salzburg, where Luzi was introduced to Bruno Walter for the first time. Bruno Walter was recovering from a bout of pneumonia and was shortly to celebrate his fiftieth birthday, for which Korngold wanted to congratulate him in person. They discussed the new opera, and Korngold expressed the wish that Walter might perform it in Berlin, where he was now the general music director of the State Opera House. Bruno Walter agreed without hesitation, and Luzi recalled that later, in 1926, he conducted the Prelude to Act III from *Das Wunder der Heliane* at a rehearsal especially for Korngold.

From Salzburg they traveled to Nürnberg, where Korngold met with the director of the opera there. It so happened that the National Socialist Party was holding a congress at the same time. In the evening while Korngold was discussing the possibility of *Heliane* being staged in Nürnberg, Luzi had to remain in the hotel alone. She recalled the experience with particular vividness:

> With fearful forebodings, I watched the Nazis stamping past my window in their torchlit demonstrations and listened to their pounding marches. As I heard the dull drumbeat mixed with the high-pitched sound of the piccolo, an inexplicable fear gripped me concerning Erich. This nightmare weakened during the sunny daylight hours. But there always surfaced a sudden and incomprehensible dread from the subconscious, which would persist. Only the happy and heart-warming meeting with our friends, the Streckers in Mainz, let me forget the frightening impressions that Nürnberg had given me.[8]

Back in Austria, he resumed work on the orchestration of the long and complicated score, while still composing music for the third act, which would not be completed until May 1927. From his country retreat, he wrote warmly to Egon Pollak:

> This summer . . . I'm working on the instrumentation of the second half of the second act of *Heliane*. With Intendant Sachse, I am busy exchanging letters; however, whether I shall be able to manage to come for a meeting to Hamburg in the near future (as he would like me to do) remains doubtful, although I am greatly tempted to be present for the opening of the Opera House. I do hope that not too much of a good thing has been done, that the level of the orchestra pit is not too high. I would not have the sound of my *Heliane* undergo a reduction.
>
> You know how much I loved the "play" sound of the *Die tote Stadt* under your direction.[9] The libretto of the opera I take it is already in your hands, and it has since undergone two important changes. The alto part has become of a different character and the ending of the work has become more human and more comprehensible. Thank God! I have the feeling that the new ending is particularly successful in terms of composition. The symphonic

interlude before the third act (composed separately) you are unacquainted with as yet, or did I show it to you at the time in Vienna? I guess not.[10]

Korngold's orchestration for the new opera was indeed grandiose, and he was particularly anxious that its effect not be minimized by any technical expedience—hence his reference to the possibility of a reduction in forces because of the alterations to the pit in Hamburg.

Korngold composed *Das Wunder der Heliane* especially for Maria Jeritza in the leading role, and his hopes were centered on her being able to sing the first performance in Vienna, just as she had done for *Die tote Stadt*. Since 1921, however, Mme. Jeritza had become an international celebrity, and had begun to divide her time between Europe and America. Her debut in New York as Marietta had been so successful that she was now under contract there. The Metropolitan Opera was keen to sign her again for the 1927–1928 season, which commenced somewhat later than in Vienna. If *Heliane* could be given in Vienna in September 1926 or earlier (Schalk was hoping to produce it in August), she would be available to sing it. To Korngold, her participation was absolutely crucial. Jeritza was a magnetic performer, and with her exceptional stage presence and glamorous appearance, she was ideal for the main role. Irrespective of her vocal shortcomings (she frequently sang "under the note" and often missed top notes altogether), the public flocked to her every performance.

Korngold returned to Vienna after the summer for further negotiations with Schalk and also with Leopold Sachse in Hamburg. Having assigned the world premiere to Hamburg, Korngold had to accommodate the needs of the Hamburg calendar before a date could be fixed for Vienna. Schott was unable to guarantee that all the orchestral material would be ready in time for the provisional dates, and the whole situation began to look extremely tenuous. Finally, Sachse agreed on a date in September 1927, and Korngold wrote anxiously to Pollak on 13 November 1926:

So it will have to be September, although I cannot conceal that, owing to this, the Vienna performance with Jeritza may become questionable. If I will have to spend half of September in Hamburg, I fear that the last ten days up to September 25th (which would have to be the latest date for the Jeritza premiere, so that she could sing at least the first six performances) will hardly be enough to change and improve all the bad things which will have happened in Vienna during my absence, be it decor, orchestra, production (and correction rehearsals without me!!!). . . . I shall advise my publishers today of our decision (they have not yet been able to give the necessary time and attention to me, due to the impending Hindemith premiere).[11]

The orchestra material can now be produced without haste under my control. . . . The most important point will be that you write to me as to when in June you will hold the correction rehearsals in Hamburg, because there will also have to be such rehearsals in Vienna before the summer, and it looks as if there will be only one hand-written score, as only after the correction rehearsals can the score be photographed.

The final version cannot be used for conducting (though all changes will have to be entered). Still, it will be quite some time until then. At the end of January you will, in any case, receive the piano score for the first two acts to enable the singers to study it (1 1/2 acts are already engraved).

By January 1927, Korngold was beginning to get anxious for a response from Jeritza. On 20 February 1927, he wrote a long letter to her in New York,[12] in which he described how the vocal line of the role had been created with her voice in mind, even with her special high notes as a feature, particularly the very last phrase. Jeritza's reply, if there ever was one, has not survived.

The final pages of this mammoth score were not actually composed until a few days before Korngold's thirtieth birthday in May 1927. Julius Korngold recalled the scene thus:

The final duet was invented and written down in an inspired hour. I shall never forget how Erich, entranced with blazing eyes and breathing heavily, played and sang it for us as it had just occurred to him. He felt that nothing had to be changed any more. This happened a few days before his thirtieth birthday and was like a preliminary celebration. . . . He said that this music should disarm all enemies; he had the feeling of having created a great work.[13]

Given the imminent premiere, it is remarkable that the orchestration was only finally completed on 9 August 1927 "in the morning," according to the manuscript. This may account for the unusually large number of errors still extant in the original printed parts.

Das Wunder der Heliane provides us with the most complete example of Korngold's art and a true synthesis of his style. From Opus 17 onward, he had become less and less compromising in his approach. His musical language was moving away from the early lyrical vein that had blossomed so fully in *Die tote Stadt*. In a rare interview given to the *Neues Wiener Tagblatt*, he described what he had tried to achieve in his new work:

As in my previous operas, I use closed forms in *Das Wunder der Heliane*. Harmonically speaking, *Heliane* is more radical than *Violanta* and *Die tote Stadt*. By no means do I isolate myself against the harmonic enrichments which we owe to say, Schoenberg. But I will not give up claim to the eminent possibilities offered by "old music." In my Kaltneker songs, there are places that one might designate as truly atonal. I do not subscribe to any one doctrine. My musical creed may be called the inspired idea. With what displeasure one hears this concept nowadays! And nevertheless, how could the artificial construction, the most exact musical mathematics triumph over the moving principle of the inspired idea![14]

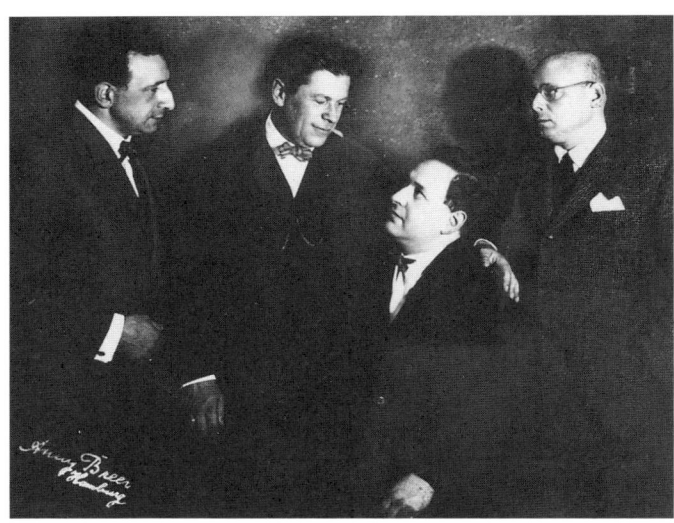

After the dress rehearsal of *Das Wunder der Heliane* in Hamburg, 5 October 1927. From left to right: Leopold Sachse, intendant, the conductor Egon Pollak, Korngold (seated) and librettist Hans Müller (Korngold estate).

Das Wunder der Heliane is superbly written. The orchestration is incredibly detailed and the overall effect of the work intoxicating. Korngold creates some ravishing sounds; for example, at certain times, the string section is so divided into parts that it occupies almost three quarters of a page. Even more than previously, Korngold demands the utmost precision and plasticity, a constantly fluid rubato. He changes meter not just from bar to bar but even in mid-bar, thus creating a mood of constant excitement and tension, as well as problems for the conductor.

Each act contains a love duet, and the vocal demands on the singers, especially the chorus, are exceptional. The orchestra is also severely tested. Every part is written as if for a virtuoso. The score is overflowing with instructions to performers and conductor—Korngold took no chances. Often, so many notes are written that playing them accurately at speed is impossible. Perhaps Korngold was composing for an orchestra that only existed in his imagination. Even today, with vastly improved standards of musicianship and performance, this music is fiendishly difficult to play.

The opening of Act I is one of the most magical. A broad chordal theme for full orchestra with harmonium sweeps up through a series of bitonal progressions, which on the page look impossibly dissonant but in orchestration merely dissolve into diffuse harmony. This theme, a chain of diminished seventh chords, is pivotal to the entire score. Its melody notes are also those of a diminished seventh chord, while the very first phrase becomes significant on its own, reappearing throughout the opera in ever more exotic harmony.

The major highlight of the score is Heliane's aria in Act II, "Ich ging zu ihm," so carefully constructed for Jeritza's vocal range. Loosely based on a center of D major, it is the most sophisticated harmonically of all Korngold's arias. In it, Heliane proclaims her innocence, denying her love for the Stranger, but in music so ardent that the audience and the Judges are left in no doubt of her true feelings.

It is constructed in two parts: the first is a long, arched arioso that describes what happened in the cell. Here, the music reprises the Act I duet. Then, after a magical modulation to F-sharp major (Korngold's favorite key and the characteristic tonality of the whole opera) at the words "Doch schön war der Knabe" (But the youth was beautiful), the aria proper travels ever upward by means of a chromatically ascending melody, becoming increasingly intense. Korngold's delay of the climax by dropping an entire octave at the crucial phrase, then continuing on to the inevitable high A-sharp, is a masterstroke. This is a testing piece for soprano and, like *Tristan*, it attempts a musical expression of the sexual act. The aria is written in 5/4, and this is emphasized by Korngold in the placing of small lines under the notes to avoid the temptation of conducting it in implied three quarter time.

In the final act, the chorus becomes a key protagonist in the action, in passages that have no parallel anywhere else in Korngold. This music would have delighted Janáček in its barbaric rhythms.

The "miracle," when Heliane raises the Stranger to life, is accompanied by a huge blanket of voluptuous sounds underpinned by massive harp and piano arpeggios. The final pages are truly inspired. Here, the chordal theme becomes a flowing diatonic melody in the rapturous conclusion. No other opera composed during this period (or since) has the hypnotic and overwhelming effect of *Das Wunder der Heliane*. It still awaits an effective modern stage presentation. Perhaps, because of its difficulties, it will never receive one, but remain realizable only in concert performance, as given by the Concertgebouw, Amsterdam, in 1995.

With the opera completed, pre-production could now begin. Korngold knew how much was riding on a success. Everything that had gone before, the whole of his twenty-five years of creative work, was but a prelude to this work. His reputation would stand or fall by the result. He could not foretell that his hopes of triumph would be dashed, thanks to the machinations of his own father.

If the activities of his father had merely caused embarrassment in the past, they now seriously affected the birth of his new work. Old Korngold loved campaigns. Through his influential column, he had contributed most to the end of Richard Strauss's tenure at the Vienna State Opera, and he had maintained a vendetta against all composers who had followed

Schoenberg's lead. These campaigns were minor, however, compared to that mounted against Křenek and his opera *Jonny spielt auf*.

Korngold meanwhile somewhat naively threw himself into the preparations for his own work. The final details concerning the premiere of *Das Wunder der Heliane* were now settled, and it was agreed that the world premiere would take place in Hamburg on 7 October 1927, with Vienna following three weeks later. Franz Schalk had decided that there would be two gala premieres on successive evenings with separate star casts.

A rare candid shot on stage at the dress rehearsal of *Das Wunder der Heliane* in Vienna, 28 October 1927: Lotte Lehmann and Jan Kiepura with producer Lothar Wallerstein behind (courtesy of Marjan Kiepura).

By this time, Jeritza had declined the role and returned to America (where perhaps as a consolation to Korngold, she sang the American premiere of *Violanta*), and Schalk suggested that Vienna's other star *prima donna*, Lotte Lehmann (justly admired as Marietta in *Die tote Stadt*) might consider the role of Heliane. Initially, she refused. Everyone knew that Jeritza had been the favorite for the role. She was not going to accept as second best. The Korngolds invited her to dinner. After dinner, Korngold sat down at the piano and played and sang the entire opera for her in his unique manner. Not surprisingly, her original misgivings were swept aside under the mesmeric spell of his performance, and she agreed to sing the part. Decades later, she recalled :

> I had a letter from Erich after I had sung in *Tote Stadt*—a much too flattering letter. In it, he expressed his gratitude for my performance in the role, which actually is an absolute Jeritza role. Nobody could be better in that part than she was. I also think that Heliane should have been given to the very young and lovely Margit Angerer. I have never ceased to be objective with myself—and now in retrospect, I cannot understand that I accepted parts that were really not right for me.[15]

In spite of Frau Lehmann's characteristically modest dismissal of her own interpretation, she was to enjoy great success with the role, and her recording of the principal aria from the opera, "Ich ging zu ihm," is one of her best.

Her co-star, Jan Kiepura,[16] playing the handsome young Stranger condemned to death for spreading love and happiness in the mythical kingdom of the story, was perfect for the role. He was then a newcomer to the operatic stage and had taken the world by storm when he had sung Calaf in the first Vienna performance of *Turandot* in October 1926.

By the mid-1920s, opera had, like every other mode of musical expression, undergone some radical changes, primarily as a result of the tumultuous changes wrought by Schoenberg and those composers directly or indirectly influenced by his work. A glance at the repertoire of the major opera houses in Germany and Austria from that period reveals it as a richly varied, highly productive era in the sheer diversity of the new works offered. Consider the following list of operas receiving their first performance from 1924 to 1928: Franz Schmidt's *Fredigundis*, Bittner's *Das Rosengärtlein*, Schreker's *Irrelohe*, Hindemith's *Cardillac*, Berg's *Wozzeck*, Gál's *Das Lied der Nacht*, Richard Strauss's *Intermezzo* and *Die ägyptische Helena*, and Křenek 's *Jonny spielt auf.*

Julius Korngold had greeted all of these with disdain, but it was the last of them, *Jonny spielt auf,* that caused the most controversy at the time and that provided him with the ammunition to mount an unprecedented offensive against what he believed was the corruption of modern opera. It also made for a highly unsavory backdrop to the premiere of Korngold's *Das Wunder der Heliane.*

Křenek's opera was the novelty of the day. Hailed as a jazz opera, it contained all manner of controversial effects and curious props such as a radio, an automobile, and a locomotive, none of which had ever made an appearance in an opera before. After a triumphant premiere in Leipzig (10 February 1927), it was quickly translated into no fewer than eighteen languages and announced by theaters everywhere. The leading stages, eager to capitalize on its popularity (especially in those days of high inflation, when having a box office success was even more important), began to prepare their own productions. Understandably, Julius Korngold and many of his older, more conservative colleagues regarded this irreverent work with contempt. In his memoirs, he wrote:

> this opera [had] . . . a text which could have been written by a high school pupil. A bustle of jazz and sundry props foreign to opera were meant to stun the public. After efforts to gain a foothold in Germany, [Křenek] befriended Vienna—because of the good wine, so he proclaimed publicly—and declared himself for Schubert, confirming this bold endorsement by active imitation. It is not surprising that this flexible schemer, who might turn a chorale into jazz or a Beethoven scherzo into operetta, engaged in pranks against insubordinate critics.[17]

The stage was set for yet another battle in the press, and Julius Korngold led the attack. Initially, Franz Schalk supported his old friend and had refused to produce *Jonny spielt auf* at the Vienna State Opera, but the new general administrator of the Austrian State Theaters, Franz Schneiderhan, with his eye firmly on the box office, intervened. Incensed at the prospect of losing what appeared to be a solid gold hit that was badly needed by the financially ailing institution (the Volksoper went into receivership in 1925 and the State Opera, in the aftermath of Strauss's departure, which was due largely to Korngold Sr.'s campaign, was also in a precarious position), he insisted that the opera be staged as soon as possible.

Immediately, Julius Korngold leapt to Schalk's defense, demanding that the autonomy of the director of the Vienna State Opera be respected in artistic matters at least. He was certainly no friend of Schneiderhan, whom he regarded as a meddling bureaucrat. For weeks before the premiere (scheduled for New Year's Eve 1927), attack and counter attack dominated the newspaper columns of Vienna.

All of this was to have a serious effect on the forthcoming production of *Das Wunder der Heliane*. Schalk was powerless to prevent Křenek's opera from being produced, and meeting his superior's demands, he assigned designer Oscar Strnad and producer Lothar Wallerstein to the production. Robert Heger was to conduct, with a star cast including Vera Schwarz, Elisabeth Schumann, Alfred Jerger, and Koloman von Pataky. In desperation, Schalk rashly turned to his old German Nationalist friends—some of whom were already allied to the National Socialist Party. The Nazi propaganda machine swung into action, and in the months that followed, the bewildered Viennese could read anti-Křenek articles in both the *Neue Freie Presse* and the Nazi propaganda papers. The Nazi paper *Deutsch-österreichische Tageszeitung* known as *Dötz*, published a front-page appeal to the Viennese not to support what they described as "this Jewish desecration of the State Opera by a work containing jazz tunes and a pornographic plot."

By this time, public opinion had become divided into two camps. The Austrian Tobacco Company contributed to the general uproar by announcing its intention to produce two new cigarettes called "Jonny" and "Heliane." The two operas thus also became opponents in this unseemly fray (it could only happen in Vienna!). The cigarettes indicated a certain point of view, however. The brand named "Heliane" was an expensive, exotic, delicately perfumed creation with a mouthpiece shaped like a rose petal, and was very popular with the more bohemian operagoer. The brand named "Jonny," however, was a cheap smoke, at the bottom end of the market, a market position that delighted Korngold.

While his father fought the battle against Křenek's opera, aided and abetted by Nazi propaganda (which must have looked very curious at the time and, given subsequent events, looks even more curious today), Korngold went to Hamburg for the world premiere of his *Heliane*. The cast was finally settled. Maria Hussa, the principal high dramatic soprano in the Hamburg company of that time, was to sing Heliane, with Rudolf Bockelmann as her husband, the Ruler. The lyric tenor Carl Günther sang the role of the Stranger, and Sabine Kalter, who had succeeded the legendary Ottilie Metzger-Lattermann as principal mezzo soprano, sang the difficult part of the Messenger. The production was designed by Heinz Daniel, personally produced by the intendant Leopold Sachse, and conducted by Egon Pollak.

Uncharacteristically, Julius Korngold acceded to his son's wish and traveled to Hamburg for the performance, where he was reunited with his old colleague Ferdinand Pfohl, with whom he stayed. He attended the dress rehearsal but not the first performance. Mindful of his position, he stayed away and spent the evening in a cinema watching newsreels of the First World War.

The performance was a genuine success, apart from a slight technical mishap in the third act. A gala reception was held afterward at the palatial home of Dr. Ludwig Seligmann (Hamburg's leading gynecologist). The Seligmanns were noted patrons of the opera and promoted many young singers. Their parties were legendary in pre-war Hamburg. The following day, the reviews were fairly indicative of the prevailing social mood. In Hamburg, the critics greeted the new work with praise and commendation; in Berlin, it was dismissed as backward and conservative. Ferdinand Pfohl, the most eminent critic in Germany, was undeterred by his colleagues' disapproval, however. He wrote a long, insightful essay on the opera that expertly summed up the feelings of most of the audience after that first performance.

Erich Wolfgang Korngold has remained true to himself and to music, both in his new opera and in the new period of development and maturity that followed *Die tote Stadt*, the mighty creative effort of his youth. He, who belongs to no partisan trend . . . trusts in his own talent which has no equal among contemporary musicians. . . . And was the work a success? It was really extraordinary, rising from act to act, ending in a storm of applause for artist, conductor, and above all, the composer himself, who took repeated curtain calls.[18]

Hamburg remained true to *Das Wunder der Heliane* and to Korngold. Earlier, on 11 February 1927 the State Theater had given the fiftieth performance of *Die tote Stadt*. *Das Wunder der Heliane* achieved eighteen performances there. Yet despite this initial success in Hamburg, the fate of this opera was a curious one. It received its baptism by fire in Vienna, where the intrigues were gathering momentum, and from there it went on to stormy critical weather in Berlin. After Berlin, it achieved little success before it disappeared, with little chance of revival once Hitler became chancellor.

It was in America that Korngold's future lay. As he read the reviews of the world premiere in Hamburg, his eye might have been caught by an item in the foreign news column describing a premiere of a different sort, which had taken place thousands of miles away on the previous evening. It was that other premiere, and not the first performance of his greatest opera, that was to have a decisive influence on his future and that would eventually save his life. That "other premiere" was of the world's first talking picture, *The Jazz Singer*, starring Al Jolson. It changed the face of the motion picture industry and elevated Warner Brothers into a major studio. Within seven years Korngold, too, would be working with Warner Brothers.

CHAPTER FOURTEEN

The Youngest Music Professor in the World

*V*ienna awaited the coming of *Das Wunder der Heliane* with an excited expectancy that presaged a momentous event. The prolonged and vituperative press coverage that had been accorded the anti-Křenek battles of Korngold's father and the laudatory articles by the staunch pro-Korngold faction led by Richard Specht had ensured an almost artificial atmosphere for the premiere.

Perhaps it was impossible to live up to these expectations. No Korngold opera had yet emerged in the wake of *Die tote Stadt*, which was still enjoying considerable success.[1] Many were of the opinion that *Die tote Stadt* would be a hard act to follow, while others viewed the optimistic reviews from Hamburg with scepticism. There were many (especially those loyal to Richard Strauss and, still more, those allied with the International Society for New Music) who fervently wished the young Korngold to fail.

Nevertheless, the house was sold out for the opening night on 29 October 1927, and Lotte Lehmann overcame her physical inadequacy to portray the lissome, beautiful Heliane by using her thrilling and wholly individual voice to the greatest effect in the soaring vocal lines of the major scenes. Jan Kiepura was perfectly cast as the handsome young Stranger, and the Vienna Philharmonic Orchestra played the taxing score with consummate skill under the baton of Franz Schalk. The entire performance was relayed live on radio, the first Korngold opera premiere to be broadcast.

201

The reviews, while good, focused on the opera's shortcomings. That Korngold had produced a remarkable musical work was clear, but it was poorly served by the somewhat abstruse libretto, based on material not ideally suited to the operatic conventions of the time, which left the audience and the critics cold. The unrealistic stage directions hardly helped. In Act I, when Heliane is asked by the young Stranger to show her nakedness so that he may carry the memory of her great beauty with him to his death, Wallerstein was faced with a dilemma. Today, this would present no problem for an opera producer: in 1927, nudity on stage was out of the question. A compromise was reached when Lotte Lehmann "revealed" herself in a flowing white nightgown.

The critics wrote at length of the opera's textual problems while praising the remarkable scoring. Hans Liebstöckl wrote in the *Neues Wiener Tagblatt*:

> Right into the middle of the turbulent ravings of today's modern musical impotents now falls the glowing light of Korngold's new opera, which while experimenting freely with new tonal and expressive possibilities faithfully preserves the pure substance and essence of post-Wagnerian musical drama. . . . In the text, many things appear contrived and coldly constructed; Korngold's music ennobles them. . . . the opera is cast in one mould . . . from the infant prodigy, Korngold has emerged as a great master.[2]

Richard Specht, Ferdinand Pfohl, Josef Reitler, Heinrich Kralik, and the others all wrote in similar vein.

The ambitious plan of two premieres with two star casts on consecutive nights did not materialize. Piccaver was simply unable to learn the difficult role of the Stranger, possibly because the vocal demands of the role were simply too much for him. Following several quarrels with the tenor, Schalk decided to substitute *Die tote Stadt* instead. As is typical in Vienna, the rumor sprang up that the second performance had been canceled because the opera was a failure. This interpretation has persisted to this day, but *Heliane*, while not enjoying the runaway success of Korngold's earlier works, went on to conquer a dozen stages.

The only sour note was sounded in Berlin, where the production was in the capable hands of Bruno Walter and the cast was impressive. Grete Stückgold[3] was to sing Heliane, and several guest artists were engaged for the other roles, including Emil Schipper[4] as the Ruler and Hans Fidesser[5] as the Stranger. The Blind Judge was sung by the great bass Alexander Kipnis,[6] and the production was designed by the legendary Oscar Strnad. The premiere was scheduled for 5 April 1928. A good reception in Berlin was critical for the opera's ongoing success, but as Luzi Korngold recalled:

> At the dress rehearsal, Fidesser insisted on "saving" his voice, only singing the last act in full voice, and then only after repeated and

friendly encouragement from Bruno Walter. To my amazement, Fidesser remarked later: "I will show him! At the premiere, I won't open my mouth!" and he carried the ridiculous threat through.[7]

Hans Fidesser's were not the only prima-donna antics to jeopardize the production. Shortly after the first few performances, Bruno Walter left for a vacation, and several other cast members were suddenly "unavailable." The critical reaction in Berlin was particularly savage.

Křenek, of course, had many friends in Berlin, almost as many friends as Julius Korngold had enemies. Following the Viennese premiere of *Das Wunder der Heliane* the previous October, Křenek's opera *Jonny spielt auf* had finally been given its premiere on New Year's Eve to a tumultuous reception that quite overshadowed Korngold's opera. Franz Schalk, who hated this new operatic sensation, made a droll remark that became famous: "The box office takings exceeded my direst expectations. We have a success without an opera."[8]

At the rehearsals for *Das Wunder der Heliane* in Berlin, 26 April 1928. A worried Korngold (the production was not a happy one) with his close friend Bruno Walter, who conducted the opera (Korngold estate).

The premiere had been attended by violent Nazi demonstrations, which, though they did not prevent the performance, doubtless added a sense of excitement to the proceedings. Notoriety is almost a guarantee of success. Julius Korngold was not ready to throw in the towel, however. He wrote a scathing twelve-column article with a vehement plea to the Viennese not to see the opera. Of course, the article simply had the opposite effect: the public could not be kept away.

Julius Korngold then pompously sent copies of his article to all theaters that had not yet accepted Křenek's opera and to all music critics who had not yet heard it. The "enemy camp" had responded in like manner: Universal Edition (Křenek's publishers) printed leaflets quoting what leading critics had said about the opera in one column and excerpts from Dr. Korngold's article in a facing column. They also prepared an advertisement detailing the success of the opera and placed it in all the local papers. They even sent it to the offices of the *Neue Freie Presse*, where it was accepted and a proof actually forwarded to Universal Edition for correction. When enquiries were made after it mysteriously failed to appear, the reply was, "At the last moment, fortunately, the advertisement was seen and stopped. What would have happened if it had slipped through, we dare not imagine."

The innocent source of this information seemed unaware that Julius Korngold had always claimed his complete impartiality in all musical matters. Now that his all-pervading influence had been exposed as even extending to the classified columns of his paper, the chorus of protest against him became a roar, and the *Neue Freie Presse* devoted its front page—normally reserved for major political stories—to a lead article entitled "The End of the Opera Rumpus" in a vain attempt to defuse the situation. The Korngold–Křenek wrangle almost paralleled the historic battle between the partisans of Gluck and Piccini in eighteenth-century Paris.[9]

This was to be the last embarrassing public scandal to be led by Korngold's father. He was due to retire in 1932, and although he continued to fire the occasional broadside against his musical enemies, he clearly was awakening to the reality that his protestations may well have seriously damaged the success of his son's greatest work. Certainly, the reaction in Berlin was fueled by his campaigns. In his memoirs, Julius Korngold wrote the following:

> The Berlin experience had a disastrous psychological effect on Erich. Being wronged, persecuted by an active musical party, boycotted in its German sphere of influence, he awakened from the naive dream of creation and lost his joy of it. These were hard times for me also, since I had to admit to myself that my convictions as a critic had contributed to reprisals against my son.[10]

Despite the failure in Berlin, *Heliane* did enjoy success elsewhere. Munich, Nürnberg, Chemnitz, Lübeck, and Breslau all presented it, and it continued to be popular in spite of everything in Hamburg and Vienna. Korngold was able to conduct the twenty-fifth performance in Vienna, and the aria "Ich ging zu ihm" became a popular concert item. Even so, whether the mixed reaction and political intrigues were responsible or not, Korngold seemed to withdraw from major composition for several years.

True, his earlier works continued to be widely performed: his Piano Concerto in C-sharp was especially successful in several brilliant performances by Paul Wittgenstein in Salzburg (just prior to the Vienna premiere of *Heliane*), followed by an acclaimed Swiss premiere at Basel under Felix von Weingartner in November.[11] Meanwhile, his early success, *Violanta*, had reached the United States with Maria Jeritza,[12] and it was revived by Karl Böhm in Darmstadt.[13]

Korngold's reputation was such that he had been overwhelmed with professional offers from the establishment in Vienna. Almost simultaneously, he was asked to become a Professor at the State Academy, the principal conductor of the Vienna Philharmonic Chorus, and director of the Volksoper. He was awarded the title of *Professor Honoris Causa* by the Austrian president in July 1927 (the press declared him to be the youngest music professor in the world), and subsequently he accepted the post at the State Academy, then under the direction of Franz Schmidt, but his career as a teacher was to be short-lived. Korngold's perfectionism would not tolerate the rich, indolent pupils with no talent who were attending the Academy at that time mostly for social reasons, and he later resigned in disgust after a particularly embarrassing orchestra rehearsal of d'Albert's opera *Tiefland* in 1931.

Korngold's compositions of this period were small in number and scale. As was his custom, he retreated into the softer realm of chamber music after writing a major work. Coincidentally, Paul Wittgenstein commissioned a second, smaller work from him in 1928. The result was the Suite for Two Violins, Cello, and Piano for the left hand alone, Opus 23, one of Korngold's most unusual works.

The scoring is economical and sparse, yet it never lacks substance at climactic moments. The five contrasting movements allow for the maximum pianistic display, and the melodic charm of the finale is highly effective following the somewhat caustic tones of the opening Prelude and Fugue. The slow movement is a variation of one of the songs from the Opus 22 cycle, which he completed just prior to this work.[14] It is one of his loveliest melodies and in the characteristic key of F-sharp major. (The songs of Opus 22 stand in stark contrast to those of Opus 18, almost as though the composer was making a determined statement of return to his former, more lyrical style. To call this a musical regression would be mistaken, for the results are too precious.)

In the spring of 1928, Luzi announced that they were expecting another child. This inspired Korngold to write another charming work that showed the lighter side of his musical personality. The five-movement *Baby Serenade* was completed in time for the birth of their second son Georg (nicknamed Schurli) on 17 December 1928, although it would not receive its premiere until four years later.

Around the same time, another operetta adaptation, *Rosen aus Florida* (Roses from Florida), to music by Leo Fall, was begun, again at the behest of Hubert Marischka for a production at the Theater an der Wien. It was created from sketches in Leo Fall's estate given to Korngold by his widow. The material was insufficient to complete the operetta, so the resourceful Korngold set about composing most of the second act himself in a style as close to Fall's own as he could adopt.

The most beautiful melody in the score, "Irina's Song," is entirely Korngold's own work. For a cue entitled "Miss Austria," Korngold composed a melody that would later become one of his most famous themes: the "March of the Merry Men" for the 1938 film *The Adventures of Robin Hood*, for which he would win an Academy Award. *Rosen aus Florida* was another huge success. It opened on 22 February 1929 with a star-cast including Rita Georg, Fritz Imhoff, Otto Langer, Hans Moser, and of course, Marischka himself. It ran for much of the year, often with Korngold conducting. The critics were unimpressed, however, and complained that there was too much Korngold and not enough Leo Fall in the score.

At the Vienna State Opera, Lothar Wallerstein had meanwhile devised a new production of *Der Ring des Polykrates*, which was first given on 14 March 1929 under the direction of Robert Heger. Korngold later conducted the new production as a guest, as well as *Violanta* and *Die tote Stadt*. *Die tote Stadt* achieved its fiftieth performance on 30 May in Vienna, with Korngold conducting.

Die tote Stadt at the Hague 24 January 1929: the Hamburg company in jolly mood with their Dutch colleagues after the dress rehearsal. Pictured left to right: intendant J. Meihuizen, chorus director Henk van den Berg, a Miss van den Laan, Gertrude Geyersbach (Marietta) Korngold, and Leopold Sachse (intendant, Hamburg) (courtesy of Gemeentarchief, The Hague).

In addition, the Vienna State Opera mounted its own version of the famous Korngold-Marischka adaptation of *Eine Nacht in Venedig*, which opened on 23 June 1929 and settled into a long run with a stellar cast that included Maria Jeritza, Hans Duhan, Alfred Jerger, and Adele Kern. Once again, Korngold was engaged to conduct many of the performances, including the premiere. In fact, Korngold was conducting one or another of his works or adaptations on most evenings, or he was doing much the same out of town. Sometimes these engagements were prestigious: on 26 January 1929, for example, he had been invited to conduct a gala presentation of *Die tote Stadt* at The Hague (the Hamburg production, especially imported), but such occasions were the exception.

Julius Korngold was increasingly anxious about the continual distractions in his son's life. He felt, perhaps rightly, that most of these activities were not fitting for a composer of his son's stature, and the regular arguments between father and son became ever more bitter. Soon, however, an even greater distraction was about to make his entrance.

Early in 1929, Max Reinhardt contacted Korngold with another offer of collaboration, this time for *La Vie parisienne* by Offenbach. He wished Korngold to adapt, re-orchestrate, and conduct the work at the Deutsches Theater in Berlin, but Korngold was very reluctant to accept the commission. He regarded *La Vie parisienne* as weak and uninspired and not a particularly worthy subject for treatment. More important, he knew the compellingly persuasive charm of Reinhardt, how easy it was to become sucked into his magnetic, theatrical field of influence, and the many months of time and effort that this might require. He was wary of the deal, with good reason, but he did not wish to seem discourteous. He assured Luzi that he would be firm but polite, and arranged to meet Reinhardt in the Theater in der Josefstadt, but as Luzi recalled:

> He returned to me with an amused and slightly apologetic smile . . . and a signed contract! He had expressed his doubts to Reinhardt about the project and had thought the discussion was finished. But Reinhardt quietly remarked, "Now, what other work would you recommend?" Erich answered spontaneously, "Why don't you do *Die Fledermaus* by Johann Strauss?" He explained that with three first-rate singers for Rosalinde, Adele, and Alfred, he could arrange the rest of the music to suit the actors of the theater.
>
> He recommended Maria Rajdl as Rosalinde, who, from the point of view of voice, acting talent, and appearance was an impressive young singer at the Vienna Opera. Reinhardt called his secretary and, as if it was merely a matter of course that *Die Fledermaus* was going to be produced, gave orders that Frau Rajdl be engaged for the part of Rosalinde. Already in the first half-hour Reinhardt and Korngold had discussed the main issues of the production. For the first time, the

question emerged as to whether the part of Orlofsky, traditionally played by a woman, should be played by a man. Strangely enough, Reinhardt—who was normally an enthusiastic innovator—was reluctant to alter this part. But Erich convinced him that musically there would be no difference whether the couplet *Chacun à son gout* was sung by an alto voice or a baritone. So the change was made.[15]

Neither Reinhardt nor Korngold realized how much of an impact their new version of *Die Fledermaus* would make. Although many purists complained, this completely re-interpreted version was to revitalize and revive interest in what was and remains the greatest operetta ever written.

The opening night on 8 June 1929 at the Deutsches Theater in Berlin was a landmark in the history of that theater. A packed house witnessed a *Fledermaus* like none ever seen before. Reinhardt opened the show with the overture played against a scene in a wine garden, in which Dr. Falke sits alone, smoking a cigarette in a holder. Near the end of the scene, he rises from his seat, pays the bill, and then dances to the final waltz strains of the overture—his cape becoming the wings of a bat, thus establishing the motif of the work from the start in a most memorable way.

For the party in Act II, Reinhardt employed a revolving stage. The guests arrived one by one in a vestibule and then were admitted into a grand Biedermeier ballroom that literally spun into view. It was probably the most memorable staging that *Die Fledermaus* has ever received. Ellen Reichert, the widow of Heinz Reichert, who was a frequent collaborator with Korngold in various operetta adaptations, recalled the opening night:

> You cannot imagine the tremendous feeling of expectancy in the theater, or the shock of the production which was outlandish and at the same time intoxicatingly pleasurable. Reinhardt had the brilliant conception, it is true—although I know that Erich contributed many ideas of his own. Reinhardt respected Erich's dramatic judgment greatly, which was a tremendous compliment to Erich.
>
> I really believe the success of that production was heavily dependent on Erich's conducting of the performance. Later, when other, less capable musicians took over, it lacked the sparkle and the dynamism which he brought to it. It was as if he was in control of the orchestra, the singers, and the audience—all of us at once. I will never forget it.[16]

The conductor Fritz Zweig recalled attending the twenty-fifth jubilee of the theater, when this production was chosen:

> Korngold was simply magnificent on the podium. When it came to this operetta, I don't think I ever heard a greater performance than that one. He simply excelled in this type of music—it was in his

blood. I am quite sure that a very large percentage of the success of Reinhardt's operetta adaptations was due to Erich.[17]

The superb cast included Hermann Thimig as Eisenstein, Maria Rajdl as Rosalinde, Adele Kern as Adele, Hans Moser as Frosch, and Oskar Karlweis as Orlofsky. The production ran for 136 performances. During its run, Reinhardt mounted another production simultaneously at the Theater am Nollendorfplatz with Maria Schreker (wife of the composer Franz Schreker) as Rosalinde and Anni Frind as Adele that ran for 81 performances.

In spite of the innovations on stage, the score of the operetta remained untouched. Any additions (mainly small scenes, all in 3/4 time, and all to music by Strauss) were accompanied and conducted by Korngold at the piano on a dais in front of the orchestra. This touch delighted the audience, and it was Korngold's way of showing which pieces he had interpolated and of taking full responsibility.

Reinhardt was inexhaustible when it came to verse, which was inserted sometimes as recitative, sometimes as songs. Somehow, Korngold always found a suitable waltz by Strauss to fit the words, even if sometimes only a few bars. As Luzi recalled:

> Who could resist any spoken or unspoken wish by Reinhardt? . . . Whenever Reinhardt turned away his gray eyes in disappointment or resignation one felt guilty . . . as if one had hidden away a child's favorite toy.[18]

The success of this adaptation depended on another facet of Korngold's musical personality—his uncanny musical kinship with the music of Johann Strauss II, and his playing of this music on the piano was, by all accounts, an unforgettable experience. Despite his youth, he was a very close friend of Strauss's widow Adele, who heartily approved of the new version of her husband's greatest work. For Korngold, there were no academic explanations to be made—no false ritardandi or accelerandi. He would adhere to his tempi with rhythmic stringency. The lyrical points blossomed without being sentimental but were delicately phrased; each part of a waltz grew logically and naturally out of the part that came before.

The tremendous success of *Die Fledermaus*, together with the ongoing triumph of the Korngold-Marischka version of *Eine Nacht in Venedig* in the new production at the Vienna State Opera and *Rosen aus Florida* at the Theater an der Wien, made Korngold a "hot property" as a conductor and an arranger. In Berlin, the operetta *Im weissen Rössl*, which became *White Horse Inn*, had made the prospect of a similar box-office success irresistible to Hubert and Ernst Marischka. They began to plan a new production that would rival the success of all other operettas. Ernst Marischka and Heinz Reichert collaborated on a book, originally entitled *Strauss—Father and Son*, and showed it to Korngold. He liked the treatment, seeing the immediate potential for utilizing a great deal of the very finest music in the Strauss canon. This became *Walzer aus Wien* (Waltzes from Vienna), one of Korngold's greatest stage successes.

It also highlighted the generous side of Korngold's nature in a touching gesture that was typical of him. He decided to ask his old friend Julius Bittner to collaborate with him on the adaptation. Luzi recalled:

> He displayed that sly shyness of his which he used when he feared that people might fathom his real emotions. By then our friend Julius Bittner had been gravely ill for some time, but was suffering his illness with heroic optimism. We knew that he didn't feel well and Erich tried to cheer him up as much as he could. When conducting concerts, he often included a piece by Bittner on the program.[19]

In asking Bittner to assist him, Korngold knew that his friend would be able to do very little of the massive job of arranging and orchestrating, but by placing his name on the score he ensured that Bittner and wife Emilie (who were living in modest circumstances) would be sure of a portion of the royalties. These proved to be so considerable that they relieved Bittner of financial worries up to his death in 1939.

The creators of one of the most successful Johann Strauss II productions ever staged, *Walzer aus Wien* (which became *The Great Waltz)*, Vienna, after the premiere on 30 October 1930. From left: Ernst Marischka, Erich Wolfgang Korngold, Julius Bittner, and Heinz Reichert. Korngold looks unhappy, yet this production was his greatest success in operetta (Korngold estate).

Cleverly utilizing the biographical elements that had made *Drei Mäderlhaus*[20] such an enormous success, *Walzer aus Wien* was perhaps the most successful of all the Johann Strauss II pasticcios. It opened to general acclaim on 30 October 1930 at the Municipal Theater. The cast, headed by Hubert Marischka as Johann Strauss II, also included Betty Fischer, Paula Brosig, Willy Thaller, Fritz Imhoff, and Mizzi Zwerenz.

The show was presented in London the following year by Oswald Stoll as *Waltzes from Vienna* with additional arrangements by G. H. Clutsam and Herbert Griffiths (Clutsam had made *Lilac Time*, the English version of the Schubert biography, a success in 1928), and was again a sensation. It ran at the Alhambra Theater for 607 performances with the American stars Robert Halliday and Evelyn Herbert. Simultaneously, a French version entitled *Valse de Vienne* played in Paris. In 1933, it was filmed in Britain with Jessie Mathews, although most of the Korngold score was discarded because the studio (Gaumont-British) could not afford the rights, and new arrangements were undertaken by Hubert Bath. The director was, improbably, Alfred Hitchcock, who in later years refused to talk about the film, disowning his contribution. It reached New York's Broadway as *The Great Waltz* in 1934, and went on to innumerable other manifestations, many by Korngold.

In January 1930, Julius Korngold's half brother, the famous comedian and actor Eduard Kornau, celebrated forty years on the stage, and this was the occasion of a rare family collaboration. A special late-night concert (to enable artists performing at other theaters to participate), organized under the auspices of Max Reinhardt, took place at the Theater in der Josefstadt and included Erich Wolfgang and his brother Hanns appearing on the same bill for the first and only time. Hanns was now leading his own jazz band, and his ensemble opened the evening. Helene von Sonnenthal (Luzi's sister), Maria Nemeth, Koloman von Pataky, Rita Georg, Betty Fischer, and Hans Duhan all took part. Korngold conducted from the piano a short work by Leo Fall, *Brüderlein Fein*.[21]

Somehow, in the midst of all these labors, Korngold found time for his own creative work, albeit not very much. He completed the Suite for Two Violins, Cello, and Piano for the left hand, Opus 23, in the Spring of 1930. Paul Wittgenstein and the members of the Rosé Quartet gave the world premiere on 21 October 1930 in Vienna. The work was extremely well received. Its performance coincided with the infamous newspaper poll that linked Korngold with Arnold Schoenberg. This poll was undertaken by the *Neues Wiener Tagblatt* to establish the most highly regarded Austrians among its readers. Among those in the arts section, Korngold was seventh and Schoenberg twelfth. Afterward, this result was rather exaggerated as asserting that both composers were regarded as the "greatest composers" of the time, but in fact the highest poll went to Richard Strauss, who did not even qualify, as he was Bavarian, but at least Korngold was in good company.[22]

By Christmas 1930, Max Reinhardt was already working on a new project, not a work by Strauss but *La Belle Hélène* by Offenbach. It was one of his personal favorites, and he wanted Korngold and none other to prepare the adaptation, *Die schöne Helena*. Korngold consented; he had little option, for Reinhardt invited him to collaborate over dinner on the occasion of his first invitation to the Korngold's new home in the Sternwartestrasse. Reinhardt engaged Egon Friedell and Hanns Sassmann to work on the book.

Friedell was also to act in the production. Korngold became very fond of him, especially because of his tremendous sense of humor. He lived close to the Korngolds in the Gentzgasse. Tragically, he committed suicide in 1938, anticipating his fate after the annexation of Austria by Hitler. He threw himself from his apartment window, having first thoughtfully warned the innocent passers-by down below, for he was a heavily built man.

The new adaptation of *La Belle Hélène* was much more innovative musically than was *Die Fledermaus*. A witty, vivacious, and lively treatment with a major contribution from Korngold uplifted the original. The score was preserved, but a great deal of other music by Offenbach was incorporated. The newly created scenes, for example the Bacchanale at the beginning of Act II, not only required adaptation but the talent of a real composer. As usual, time was against him, and Korngold, unable to find a suitable piece by Offenbach, composed his own music for the instrumental background without signing his name to the score.

Caricature of Korngold, circa 1931–1932, in mock-Greek costume, possibly in reference to his new version of *La Belle Hélène* with Max Reinhardt in Berlin (Korngold estate).

Reinhardt chose his cast with meticulous care. Jarmila Novotná, one of the most beautiful singers of that time, portrayed Helena, Friedel Schuster was Orestes, and Hans Moser was Menelaus. Venus was portrayed by the beautiful dancer La Jana. Normally, Venus would not have appeared at all, but Reinhardt wanted this tableau. He also put a Greek chorus on either side of the stage, which interacted with the main story line in rhythmic chants. The entire production was exquisite, and it opened in Berlin at the Theater am Kurfürstendamm on 14 June 1931. Korngold conducted, as usual.

Luzi went on to Aschau near Ischl with the children for the summer holiday, and he was to join them later. Just before she left Berlin, Luzi had been warned by a family friend that the Darmstädter Bank was about to collapse and that on no account should her husband deposit money there. She recalled: "I tried to convey this message to Erich, but he only looked at me and remarked 'ridiculous' and that was the end of the matter."[23]

Just prior to his departure for Dresden, he had gone directly to the Darmstädter Bank to deposit his entire savings. He arrived late, finding it closed. On looking through the window, he discovered a lone clerk working, whom he persuaded to open the door. He then insisted that he accept his money, in spite of the clerk's strenuous protests. Korngold never saw a penny of his savings again: the bank's doors remained closed. It was a typical example of Korngold's stubborn determination to demonstrate his confidence and faith in something he believed in and to stand by his convictions. His sense of humor prevented him from becoming bitter or resentful over his loss.

During the summer holiday of 1931, he was able to return to his own music. He composed his Piano Sonata No. 3 in C Major, Opus 25. It was a more restrained work than his previous two excursions in this particular genre. The four movements provide yet another example of Korngold's constant search to find new avenues and to explore new possibilities within existing forms. The introspective and economical Adagio is the most surprising movement; its spare textures, limpid harmonies, and quiet restraint create a special mood. The engaging Intermezzo that follows was written for his baby son Georg; it has an infectiously loveable quality about it. The Finale is reminiscent of the Hornpipe from *Much Ado About Nothing*.

Meanwhile *Die schöne Helena* had notched up 144 performances. It was such a success that Charles B. Cochran, the famed English impresario, asked Reinhardt to bring it to London as soon as the Berlin run ended in November 1931. He had commissioned an English translation from A. P. Herbert, and was already assembling a formidable creative team. Leonide Massine was to choreograph the new production, and the costumes were to be specially created by Oliver Messel, who gave the entire production a

Baroque style. The show was to be called *Helen,* and Cochran had cast the legendary English actress Evelyn Laye in the leading role. The rest of the cast was to be equally impressive, led by George Robey, who was a hysterically funny Menelaus, W. H. Berry as Calchas, and Hay Petrie as Mercury. Cochran acceded to Reinhardt's insistence that Korngold be engaged to conduct the first performances, so Reinhardt cabled Korngold. Refusing Reinhardt's call was difficult, and the Korngolds prepared to depart for London in January 1932, leaving the children with the elder Korngolds.

Before he went to England, however, Korngold completed yet another operetta adaptation: *Das Lied der Liebe* in collaboration with the writer Ludwig Herzer. It was designed to showcase the considerable talents of Korngold's old friend Richard Tauber, who by now was the uncrowned king of operetta in Europe, especially those by Franz Lehár. This production was another "utility job," in which the scores of the Strauss family were lovingly mined and re-orchestrated. The core of the work was a revision of Strauss's neglected operetta *Das Spitzentuch der Königin* (The Queen's Lace Handkerchief), which Korngold had been considering adapting as early as 1926.

It was essential that there be at least one Tauberlied. Korngold obliged by creating two: "Du bist mein Traum" (You Are My Dream) and "Die eine Frau" (The Only Woman) were based on two fragments by Johann Strauss but for the most part were original compositions by Korngold.

The show opened with Tauber and Anny Ahlers in a production staged by Alfred Rotter at the Berlin Metropol Theater on 23 December 1931; Korngold on the podium led a bravura performance. The rare gramophone recording he made of the Overture is the only commercial disc of him conducting the music of Strauss, and it is a fascinating snapshot of his seductive style in this music. One can actually hear him urging the orchestra on. I am 99 percent certain that it is Korngold playing the piano solo in "Du bist mein Traum"—just as he would have done in the theater. He also recorded both Tauberlieder with the great tenor, and they are among Tauber's finest recordings.

On the evening (Christmas Eve) following Korngold's conducting the premiere of *Das Lied der Liebe, Helen* had its regional preview in Manchester, England with Reinhardt in attendance. The official premiere in London was not due to take place until 30 January 1932, when Korngold would conduct it. Before he left for London, however, there were still important commitments to be fulfilled. The most important of these came with an invitation from Bruno Walter.

On 3 July 1931, the Berlin Kroll Oper had closed its doors for the last time after a precarious and difficult period. Walter had decided to mount a special benefit at the theater for the poor of Berlin, who were facing the winter months with little or no prospect of finding work or food. The Great Depression was already beginning to bite, especially in Germany.

The concert was arranged for 2 January 1932, and the program was conducted jointly by Korngold and Bruno Walter, with guest artists Gitta Alpar, Richard Tauber, Lotte Schöne, Willi Domgraf-Fassbaender, Max Hansen, Max Pallenberg, Grete Mosheim, Bronislaw Huberman, and many others in music by Mozart, Korngold, Millöcker, Verdi, and Johann Strauss II. The Berlin Philharmonic Orchestra gave their services for free, and the remarkable concert was broadcast throughout Europe.

The London premiere of *Helen* was equally remarkable, and the opening night boasted a society audience of unusual splendor. Sitting in the best seats were Herbert Marshall and Edna Best, Lady Diana Cooper, Lily Elsie, J. B. Priestley, Adolphe Menjou, Charles and Elsie Mendel, Ina Claire, Ivor Novello, Ellaline Terriss, Princess Alice of Athlone, Noël Coward, Vivien Leigh, Prince Obolensky, Tallulah Bankhead, Laurence Olivier, Irene Vanbrugh, Gertrude Lawrence, Lewis Casson, Sybil Thorndyke, Max Reinhardt, and Helene Thimig. The gala first-night supper at Claridges was one of the grand social events of the 1930s, and the evening was crowned by the early morning reviews that were enthusiastically positive. James Agate wrote in the *Daily Telegraph*:

> Professor Korngold . . . has done for Offenbach what Mozart did for Handel; [he was] compelled to augment the score to the size of the Adelphi Theatre and the scale of Reinhardt's production has given volume to delicacy without encroaching on it.[24]

Korngold remained in England until the beginning of March. Even while *Helen* was breaking box-office records at the Adelphi, Reinhardt was planning another presentation of it at the Grosses Schauspielhaus in Berlin and yet another at the Volksoper in Vienna. He wanted the productions to run simultaneously, and he wanted Korngold to divide his time between the productions. Korngold expressed his doubts at being so heavily committed, and finally the two productions were scheduled consecutively: the Berlin premiere was scheduled for 19 April and that in Vienna for 6 June 1932.

Reinhardt then began to prepare a French version of *Die Fledermaus* with Jarmila Novotná. His energy was inexhaustible and his demands on Korngold inexorable. Korngold, meanwhile, was desperately seeking to return to his own work and in particular to find the subject for a new opera.

CHAPTER FIFTEEN

The Search for a New Opera

While Korngold was almost exclusively preoccupied with operetta commitments, events at the Vienna State Opera took a dramatic turn. In the spring of 1929, fueled by the intrigues surrounding *Das Wunder der Heliane* and the unholy alliance between Julius Korngold and Franz Schalk in the matter of Křenek's *Jonny spielt auf*, machinations to unseat Schalk as director of the Vienna State Opera got underway. The general intendant's office had brought out a new set of instructions the previous year granting Franz Schneiderhan special powers that allowed him to supersede Schalk in most of his decisions and duties. From now on, Schneiderhan would select premieres, choose the casting of the major productions, and decide which guest artists would be engaged.

The inference was obvious: never again would the administration face the wrangle over a major premiere like that which almost prevented Křenek's opera from being given. It might be construed also that the operas of Erich Wolfgang Korngold, which had always enjoyed an almost privileged position in the repertoire of the Vienna State Opera, would henceforth not be accorded quite the same importance.

Naturally, Schalk did all he could to oppose this move, but to no avail. By the summer of 1929 he was already a sick man. Schneiderhan was intractable, and there was nothing else for Schalk to do but resign. This he did, on 31 August of that year. He retained a position as guest conductor

216

with the opera, but after a final performance of *Tristan* in June 1931, he retired. The following August, he died.

It was assumed that his successor would be Wilhelm Furtwängler, who had already scored a major triumph with the Vienna Philharmonic and conducted a stunning performance of Wagner's *Das Rheingold* in October 1928. Furtwängler decided to sign with the Berlin Philharmonic Orchestra instead, however, by which time Schalk had already resigned (he had certainly learned of the intrigues with Furtwängler, and possibly resigned because of them). The Vienna State Opera was once again without a director, and a crisis seemed imminent.

The newspapers were full of the story. Predictably, Julius Korngold led the attack on the authorities that had brought these circumstances to bear: "An authoritative, working conductor is what is needed to help out the present director," he said repeatedly. Cynics suggested that this was another attempt to position his son, a claim that he vehemently denied.

After weeks of speculation, it was announced that Clemens Krauss was to be the new director, having signed a five-year contract effective from 1 September 1929. Krauss, a native of Vienna, had been intendant of the opera in Frankfurt am Main and had built a steadily growing reputation in Vienna as a guest conductor of the various orchestras. Immediately upon his appointment, he was nicknamed "Frankfurtwängler" by the Viennese.

Julius Korngold apparently approved of the new appointment. In his memoirs, he devotes only two pages to the Krauss regime, but typically his remarks on the strengths and weaknesses of Krauss as director have the acuity for which he was famous. "Krauss," he wrote, "had remarkably good judgment, particularly about voices—not always the forte of a talented conductor . . . . However, he soon revealed his weakness of surrounding himself with a guard of devoted favorites, while the others, disregarded or completely ignored, had to stay in the background. He had another weakness: he could not tolerate criticism of himself or of his protégés."

The favorites, of course, included his wife Viorica Ursuleac; the "others" were singers of the Strauss-Schalk era such as Elisabeth Schumann and Lotte Lehmann, both of whom eventually left for greener pastures. Krauss controlled the Opera House totally. He hated cast changes and conducted virtually every performance himself, with Carl Alwin and Robert Heger as his occasional assistants. Richard Strauss, who was largely responsible for his appointment, was a notable exception. Strauss was now living in Vienna for much of the time and naturally wanted an ally as director of the Opera to ensure that his works would continue to receive prominence in the repertoire.

For Erich Korngold, however, Krauss's appointment was to mean the end of his career as guest conductor at the Opera. Krauss did not want to be seen as the puppet of Julius Korngold, or be accused of favoring his son. Krauss did value Korngold's work, however, and a new production of *Violanta* was mounted in 1931, to be followed by a revival of *Der*

Schneemann in 1933, again in a new staging. Korngold revised the scores of both works.

In addition to operetta, a new distraction had entered Korngold's life. By 1931, the German film industry had converted totally to sound film production. As in the United States, this development created an entirely new genre—the screen musical. Whereas in Hollywood the early musicals were based on Broadway originals (*Rio Rita, The Desert Song, Show Boat*), in Germany the new medium focused on screen operettas, either newly composed or filmed versions of existing scores. Between 1931 and 1935, major screen adaptations of the works of Lehár, Kálmán, Robert Stolz, and Oscar Straus were made, often in several languages, with the composers fully involved and even conducting their scores.

Through Hans Müller (by this time, one of the chief writers at the leading German film studio, UFA), Korngold received his first invitation to work in films. In the spring of 1930, Erich Pommer asked him to compose an original score for *Der Kongress tanzt* (The Congress Dances), which became one of the most famous of the early German sound films. Korngold declined (though the reasons are unstated, he was already fully committed with operetta work at this time) and the score was eventually composed by Werner Heymann. The film was an international success and made its star, Lilian Harvey, a household name. The following year, Korngold was approached again with a film project while in Berlin for discussions with Reinhardt. Surprisingly, his father, who was never happy about Reinhardt's influence and later opposed his son's film work in the United States, wrote to him in May, saying: "I can imagine the torture of making this decision. If it was not for the Reinhardt project, I would without hesitation advise you to do the film."[1] The "Reinhardt project" was the adaptation of Offenbach's *La Belle Hélène*, which Korngold had decided to accept in June. What this second film was to have been is not known.[2]

In spite of these distractions, Korngold had also begun to search for a new opera libretto. By now resigned that *Das Wunder der Heliane* was out of fashion with the times, Korngold sought a lighter subject, perhaps even a comedy. He had considered a one-act play, *The Chinese Hat* by Franc Nohain (a pseudonym for Maurice Legrand), the author of Ravel's *L'heure espagnole*, as early as 1926. This was a short Chinese fairytale that the Frenchman had adapted quite charmingly. According to Luzi, Korngold composed the whole manuscript in a matter of days, although this was probably just a sketch. It was not to be, however. The *Société des auteurs* requested such exorbitant fees for the rights to the book that the entire project had to be abandoned.

In November 1931, while again in Berlin with Reinhardt to discuss preparations for the London production of *Die schöne Helena*, he saw a film at the cinema called *Ariane*, a story by Claude Anet starring Elisabeth Bergner and directed by her husband Paul Czinner, which he was much taken with, and he wrote of his enthusiasm to Schott. The reply encouraged him to press ahead with this theme.[3] Yet *Ariane* was temporarily shelved when his interest was awakened by another story in June 1932. The writer Heinrich Eduard Jacob[4] sent him his novel *The Maid from Aachen* about a German servant girl and a soldier of the French occupying forces in Germany. The theme was the rapprochement of the German and the French nations through two brave lovers. Korngold became interested in the material. His father advised him to have it dramatized by Dr. Ernst Decsey,[5] a music critic colleague who was also an author. Decsey commenced work immediately, while Korngold, as always whenever he started a creative period, walked around with a dreamy expression.

According to Luzi, as soon as the decision was taken to compose the new opera, he met with his publisher Willy Strecker, by now senior partner at Schott, to tell him the plot of the new work. Strecker was decidedly lacking in enthusiasm. He explained to Korngold that in Germany, a story that showed fraternization with France would be impossible to stage. Korngold was speechless. His little folk-tale a political embarrassment? "You do not understand what is going on in Germany, Erich," replied Strecker. For the second time, Korngold put away a manuscript after much preliminary work. He had, as Luzi noted, "lost interest for the present."

Korngold again took up *Ariane*, this time in a new version prepared by Descey with his own libretto. It was a historical romance entitled *Sissys Brautfahrt* (Sissy's Bridal Journey) about the young Emperor Franz Josef and his love for the sister of his betrothed, the Princess Elisabeth of Bavaria. Korngold declined it after more reservations from Schott, and this play was entirely reworked by the Marischka brothers to a score by Fritz Kreisler.[6]

Still, the search continued. Next, he was struck with the idea of setting the novel *Little Dorrit* by Charles Dickens, only to discover that Eduard Künneke had just composed an opera on that subject that was to be premiered in Stettin in October 1933. To make matters worse, a film of the novel had also just been made with a score by Leo Leux. Korngold wrote of his disappointment to Willy Strecker at Schott on 19 July 1933, and that idea was dropped as well.

Still dreaming of the earlier story, Korngold asked his colleague from *Das Lied der Liebe*, Dr. Ludwig Herzer, to prepare a new treatment with Descey of *The Maid of Aachen*, this time combining it with plot elements of *Ariane*. The new story was called *The Wedding of Ariane*. In October, he wrote to Clemens Krauss at the Vienna Opera:

I should have liked to discuss something with you, but since we could not meet, I shall choose the written way and summarize briefly. I am leaving for Paris on Saturday for six weeks (Fledermaus, Reinhardt). Meanwhile two gentlemen are supposed to be working out an operatic text for me which today is ready in a poetically unrefined [but in its essentials completely finished] scenario.

I need not dwell on current German publishing and performing possibilities, nor on the fact that it would be an almost hopeless, unprofitable virtually purely "idealistic" enterprise to spend 1 or 2 years on the music for an opera! Despite this, I would like to write this opera but not without previous knowledge that the acceptance of this work by the Vienna Opera would at least not be hindered because of the book.

I have now the following request; I would like to read this scenario to you, Prof. Wallerstein, and Mr. Peruter.[7] It would take about twenty minutes. Could you arrange this joint meeting (the Opera House would be the best venue)? . . . I would be much obliged to you if you can phone me at home . . . . I shall gladly give you further details over the telephone about the book, which has four marvelous roles and has in my opinion great chances for success.[8]

Whether this meeting took place is not known, but in any case, the new libretto was also rejected by Schott on the same grounds as before, at which point Julius Korngold stepped in and advised his son to reopen discussions with Ernst Decsey, which he agreed to do.

Meanwhile there had been little to cheer him elsewhere. His Piano Sonata No. 3 in C Major had been given its first performance in March 1932 by Paul Weingarten in Vienna without too much of a stir. The critics had commented only briefly, and there had been only a few subsequent performances by other pianists. The *Baby Serenade*, which Korngold hoped would become as popular as his Suite to *Much Ado About Nothing*, still languished without a performance. Finally, it was given in a celebrity concert conducted by Korngold and Oswald Kabasta on 5 December 1932 with the legendary tenor Joseph Schmidt, who was friendly with Korngold.

Schmidt, who possessed a magnificent voice, was known as the "pocket tenor" because of his diminutive size. As part of this concert he sang the "Mariettalied" as a tenor solo and made a popular and very beautiful recording of it shortly afterward.[9] The concert, in which the composer Otto Schulhof also performed his *Paraphrase on Themes by Josef Strauss* for piano and orchestra for the first time, was broadcast live and was repeated some days later, so great was the success, again live.

The *Baby Serenade* is a delightful and, for this composer, rare excursion into program music, a kind of Korngoldian "sinfonia domestica" that also provides the first example of the influence of jazz in his style. In five movements, it is scored for fourteen wind instruments (including jazz trumpet and three saxophones), banjo, piano, harp, percussion, and strings. Each movement bears a title depicting a whole day in the life of the baby:

1. Overture. Baby tritt in die Welt (Baby Makes His Entrance in the World)
2. Lied. Es ist ein braves Baby (It is a Good Baby)
3. Scherzino. Es hat auch die schönsten Spielsachen (It Has Really Beautiful Toys)
4. Jazz. Baby erzählt eine Geschichte (Baby Tells a Story)
5. Epilog. Und nun singt es sich in den Schlaf (And Now He Sings Himself to Sleep)

Korngold, during an interview some years later,[10] related that he had written the touching melody for the second movement at the age of seven. He also described how he had tried to provide a "concerto grosso" effect in his use of the various instrumental groups. He used a variation on the *Radetzky March* in the third movement (while baby plays, appropriately, with his toy soldiers) and traditional children's songs such as "Kommt ein Vogel geflogen," "Tannenbaum," "Ach, Du lieber Augustin," and "Hänslein klein." Korngold said that because this is a modern baby, the tunes are treated accordingly, as a modern baby might hum them. Because few babies can hum real melodies, one must assume that only the baby of a child prodigy might be able to do this!

The fourth movement is a *perpetuum mobile* to create the effect of a little boy talking endlessly, repeating himself over and over, as children do. Korngold apparently liked the final movement best. Its ending is delightful: the little one has crooned himself to sleep; his eyelids grow heavy, and he falls asleep. After the baby's final sigh of contentment, we hear from afar a heavy stroke of the church bell.

The score is full of novel and witty effects. This is a choice example of Korngold's unique ability to adapt himself to light music. He would exploit the experiment with a trio of saxophones again in his last opera *Die Kathrin*, which also reuses the second subject of the Overture. Like so much of Korngold's music, the *Baby Serenade* deserves wider currency.

Korngold's first house, 35 Sternwartestrasse, Vienna, circa 1933, taken from the garden. The exterior has scarcely changed in sixty years (Korngold estate).

In the autumn of 1932, Korngold undertook what would prove to be his final and most troublesome operetta adaptation, *Die geschiedene Frau* (The Divorced Woman) by Leo Fall, which was produced in Berlin in February 1933 with a star cast led by Lucie Mannheim, Maria Rajdl, and Anton Walbrook, and including the unknown Harold von Oppenheim. Korngold conducted his revised score. This project came about when Dr. Miksa Preger, the director of the Theater am Nollendorfplatz, suggested a new adaptation of this work, which was one of Fall's greatest successes.

Victor Leon collaborated with Heinz Reichert (who had co-written the libretto for Puccini's *La Rondine* and *Das Dreimäderlhaus* and worked on *Walzer aus Wien*) and lyricist Max Colpet (who provided witty rhyming couplets) for a revised version of the original book, and Korngold once again combed the surviving manuscripts in the Fall estate to enhance the score and probably added some music of his own. I say "probably" because the entire musical score and parts for this adaptation were never published but in fact were lost. This was February 1933—the elections that swept Hitler to power interrupted the run.[11]

Die geschiedene Frau was the most unhappy stage production of Korngold's career. Surviving photographs of the rehearsals show Korngold, looking tired and vexed, his normal good humor on the podium completely absent. From the beginning, there were severe financial problems, and on 31 January 1933, just one day before the premiere and one day after Hitler became chancellor, the production was almost canceled. The tenor, Harold von Oppenheim, whose one and only leading role this was to be, rescued the situation by approaching his father, a famous Cologne banker, who immediately advanced 30,000 marks to enable his son to make his debut.[12] The intendant of the theater, Heinz Saltenburg, had to repay this from the box office receipts, with the result that no salaries were paid to the cast and no payments to Korngold. The ensuing arguments cut short Korngold's engagement, and he placed the manuscript of his score in his lawyer's office. Arthur Guttmann, the UFA conductor, took over, but without Korngold the production closed on 3 March 1933. The Reichstag had been destroyed by fire only five days earlier.

Korngold had already left in a great hurry, on the 17 February. He wrote a postcard to Schott from a railway station, in which he described the production as "a disaster." Even so, he did manage to record some very rare 78s of the score for Electrola before he departed, although the fourth side is conducted by Guttman, indicating the speed of his decision to leave. The disks were available for only a few weeks before being withdrawn. This was to be Korngold's last visit to Germany until 1949.

Around this time, the Korngolds began to look for a country residence. It had long been Korngold's custom to devote the summer months to composition and (lately) operetta adaptation, and the family would usually decamp to Alt-Aussee or some equally beautiful place outside of Vienna. With his children growing up, Korngold wanted a place in the country where they could be free to enjoy themselves and he could have privacy and solitude to work. After much searching, Luzi learned that a castle near Gmunden (another famed Austrian beauty spot) was for sale. In the middle of winter, with deep snow everywhere, they went to view Schloss Höselberg. Luzi described their first sight of the place:

> It was late afternoon and already dark when we undertook the climb which led through a little wood. When we stepped out into a clearing we could see the building up on the hill in front of us. It wasn't a castle at all but a beautiful, large old farmhouse. A former owner, Count Sulkowski, had added one floor at one side with beautiful little turrets. We worked our way up through the high glittering snow. In front of the house was the inevitable lime tree, and the courtyard was lined with heavy old fir trees. As if we had been there before, we entered "our" house. We stood in front of the heavy oak door above which was carved *1767* and then entered the ante-room with the low ceiling and gothic arches; we felt at home immediately. . . . Before we had even inspected the whole building with its 18 rooms or discussed the selling price, I whispered to Erich, "This belongs to us," and he nodded in agreement, [as] charmed as I was.
>
> A chicken farm with 2000 white hens belonged to the estate. The old stables stood empty and the neighbors brought groceries—milk, butter, bacon, and dark farmhouse bread. When Erich returned from Berlin after finishing *Das Lied der Liebe* we began hunting for furniture . . . we even managed to renew an old billiard table, for Erich was an enthusiastic billiard player![13] The low ceiling of the dining room had four strange emblems on it: an eye, an ear, an axe, and a fist, meaning "God sees, God hears, God takes revenge, God punishes." Every time my eyes fell on the hundred-year-old ornament I was overcome with superstition and foreboding.[14]

In spite of the omen, the Korngolds moved into Schloss Höselberg in March 1933, as soon as *Die geschiedene Frau* was over. It was to bring them much happiness in the few years that remained before they were to become exiles in Hollywood along with so many of their friends.

Shortly before this, the Austrian Composers' Society held an interesting chamber concert in the Kleiner Musikvereinssaal, Vienna, in which six leading composers were invited to perform recent works. Julius Bittner, Karl Weigl, Josef Hauer, Wilhelm Grosz, and Egon Kornauth joined Korngold for the evening. He selected his most recent Lieder, Opus 22, and accompanied Clarissa Stukart at the piano.

Released from operetta chores, he spent the summer of 1933 contemplating a new opera and working steadily on a new song cycle called *Unvergänglichkeit* (The Eternal) based on poetry by Eleanore van der Straten.[15] The music of these songs continues the rich, lyrical style of his

Opus 22 Lieder, and as in the *Vier Lieder des Abschieds*, there is a strong and consistent uniformity that even extends to a deliberate repetition of the first song, "Release," at the end of the cycle.

In the autumn, Reinhardt cabled again about staging a new production of the Korngold-Reinhardt version of *Die Fledermaus* in Paris and asked for a meeting. Korngold went, naturally, as by now he found that he could not refuse Reinhardt. He left for Paris alone to begin preparation. By the time he arrived in Paris, he was faced with more than the usual distractions and problems, and for the first time he came into conflict with Reinhardt.

Korngold had begun auditioning women for the chorus and had chosen them for their musical ability. When Reinhardt saw the "Korngold selection," some of whom were frankly rather stout and dumpy, he was appalled. "I can't understand Korngold's taste," he exclaimed in despair. "He has engaged a whole lot of tree trunks!" Korngold had to let the "tree trunks" go and begin the auditions all over again to find more beautiful singers to please Reinhardt. Luzi remembered, with some amusement:

> He then told me that in his despair, he started asking pretty girls in the streets, in the bistro, and on buses—"Pardon, mademoiselle, but can you sing?" which must have startled quite a few Parisians.[16]

The cast was an exceptionally good one, however. The beautiful Jarmila Novotná, who had been Helen in the Berlin production of *Die schöne Helena*, was to sing Rosalinde; her understudy was Maria Rajdl from Vienna (who was also no stranger to Korngold productions). Adele was sung by Lotte Schöne, a gifted singer with a superb, feather-light coloratura. Her "top" was like spun silver, and she had recently sung the part of Lieserl in *Der Ring des Polykrates* in its revival at the Vienna State Opera. She had also been in the 1931 Berlin production of Korngold's version of *Eine Nacht in Venedig* with Helge Roswaenge and Tilly de Garmo, conducted by Erich Kleiber. A marvelous recording made during the production that year reveals the remarkable quality she brought to the part of Annina.

The curtain went up on *Die Fledermaus*, now called *La Chauve-souris*, at the Théâtre Pigalle on 28 November 1933, with Korngold conducting. Predictably, it was a resounding success. Korngold conducted all subsequent performances and spent Christmas in Paris with Luzi, renewing old friendships. The star Jarmila Novotná remembered the production with particular affection. She recalled in a letter to me in 1978:

> Korngold was very thoughtful to me, and a great conductor. I first met him in Berlin in May of 1931 before the rehearsals for Offenbach's *Die schöne Helena* began. He was always full of helpful and innovative ideas and was, for Reinhardt, indispensable. Later, I was called to Paris by Reinhardt to sing Rosalinde in *Fledermaus* and

again Korngold was the conductor. It was a great success and was due in no small part to the correct idiomatic interpretation by Korngold.[17]

No sooner had they settled into the Paris run than Reinhardt announced that an offer had come from Italy to stage the production there, first at San Remo, later at Milan. In the middle of January 1934, they set off by car. The winter weather was atrocious, and many times they were held up in the snow. When they arrived at San Remo, the weather was mildly spring-like, but their troubles were far from over, as Luzi recalled:

> We were shocked, when on arrival, we learned that the premiere had been already scheduled for ten days hence, at the Casino Theater, and we did not even have a répétiteur. Erich quickly decided that I should help out. Being familiar with the music and Erich's every idea I was able to assume responsibility for the coaching of the singers and of stage management too—because there was no stage manager either!
>
> The dress rehearsal was a success but Reinhardt was disconcerted. He did not like the choreography by the Italian ballet mistress and he disliked the singer who was playing Rosalinde. With three days to the premiere, a hectic search was under way for a replacement. We eventually found a pretty, musical girl with a good voice. She had to start rehearsals immediately. Erich and I did our best and the first two acts went reasonably well.
>
> But when we arrived in Milan we had another unpleasant surprise. The orchestra pit in the theater was too narrow and hardly had enough room for the musicians. In addition, the theater was so badly built that the conductor was compelled to stand up in order to give a sign to the singers on stage—but then could not be seen by the orchestra. We arrived in the evening, and the following morning went to the station to meet the celebrated ballet mistress Grete Wiesenthal . . . (hastily called in by Reinhardt).
>
> The premiere was scheduled for the next day. There was no piano or enough space for dance rehearsals so Mme. Wiesenthal was forced to rehearse in the foyer while rehearsals proceeded on stage. I tried to compensate for the missing piano by singing the music at the top of my voice.[18]

Korngold became increasingly worried and implored Reinhardt to postpone or even cancel the entire production. Reinhardt, however, never changed his mind once it was made up. On top of an under-rehearsed ballet, a new and not quite ready Rosalinde, and an unrehearsed orchestra, the last straw came when Reinhardt brought in a new Orlofsky, Memo Bernassi, who apparently used to be a classical actor. In spite of much coaching, his mannered performance was the last nail in the coffin. He remained completely out of step with the rest of the production and with the spirit of *Die Fledermaus*. The production in San Remo, which opened on the 10 February 1934, was truly a fiasco and perhaps the most resounding failure ever suffered by Reinhardt. The production simply could not overcome such conditions.

An hour before curtain time, Korngold lay in bed with a fever, shaking with nervous anticipation. The audience booed and stomped, but somehow the company managed to reach the end of the show. Afterward, the manager staged a supper party. The meal started with a beautiful liver pate, then to Korngold's surprise ice-cream was served. By this time, he had regained his sense of humor. He declared that the manager had obviously had time to read the early reviews and decided to cancel the main course.

Immediately after this disastrous premiere, the production transferred to Milan, where it opened on 17 February 1934, but after one performance it was laid to rest. The Korngolds went back to the Italian Riviera, and from there to Barcelona, where Korngold had been invited by Pablo Casals to conduct his orchestra in a concert of his own works. They stopped off in San Remo to attend a production of Mascagni's opera *Iris* conducted by the composer himself, then aged 71. On the way back to Vienna, they spent a day in Aix-en-Provence, and here Luzi Korngold succeeded in resurrecting the abandoned opera *Die Kathrin*. As she recalled:

> We noticed a large number of students in the streets of the town. Suddenly an idea grabbed me and I had to tell Erich about it. "How would it be," I said, "if we divested *Kathrin* of political overtones and produced it in a small French university town? *Kathrin* would then be no German but a Swiss girl, who meets and falls in love with the soldier François stationed in the local barracks."
>
> "Couldn't we replace the hate of the townsfolk for the military occupation by the usual distaste of students for the soldiers in the garrison?" We started to fantasize and I noted with secret joy the preoccupied expression on Erich's face.
>
> His eyes staring into the void, his lips would open from time to time, seeming to form a word, a sudden affirmative nodding of the head. On our return to Vienna, he got immediately in touch with Dr. Decsey and they set to work at once.[19]

Reinhardt was preparing to leave for England and then America, where he planned to stage his celebrated production of *A Midsummer Night's Dream* at the famous Hollywood Bowl, as well as Franz Werfel's *The Eternal Road* in New York. Warner had been keen to lure Reinhardt to Hollywood for some time. The files at Warner Brothers reveal that tentative negotiations had been in progress as early as 1932.[20]

The Korngolds left for Schloss Höselberg for the summer holiday, and Reinhardt for New York. Korngold planned to devote the summer to his new opera and gradually the structure of the work took form. Ernst Decsey was a frequent visitor. Soon it became apparent to Luzi that this learned man's dramatic proposals were not always completely sound:

> It was difficult to object to the ideas of a man who was so much older, so sensitive, and so ensconced in his work. So much was left in the text of *Kathrin* that, under other circumstances, would doubtless have been improved or cut out altogether.[21]

In spite of the shortcomings of the book, Korngold worked enthusiastically. With the Nazis now in power, requests for Korngold to conduct his own works or his operetta adaptations were no longer forthcoming from Germany. It hardly mattered—by now, he was completely wrapped up in his new work. Reinhardt was far away in the United States, and Luzi noted one evening, not without relief, "It is good that this disturbing ghost has left the country for a while." According to her recollections, that very second the doorbell rang. A messenger delivered a fifty-word telegram from Reinhardt begging Korngold to come immediately to Los Angeles to work with him on a film adaptation of his production of *A Midsummer Night's Dream.* As Luzi pointed out, "Reinhardt had a way with words, even in telegrams, that made it almost impossible to refuse."

Korngold decided to accept the intriguing offer, especially as Reinhardt spoke only of six or eight weeks of work. Furthermore, the project did not involve any original composition but rather an adaptation of Mendelssohn's incidental music for the play. Moreover, it was for a production of Korngold's beloved Shakespeare. He cabled his acceptance.

The proposed visit to America deepened the rift between Korngold and his father and exacerbated the hostility, barely concealed, that Korngold's parents felt for Luzi. Julius Korngold had regarded the seven years since *Heliane* with deep concern. He had watched with mounting distress as his beloved son gradually relinquished his hitherto important position as one of Austria's most promising young composers. He had opposed each new operetta adaptation, and since his retirement in 1932, had tried to reconcile himself to the unhappy realization that his son no longer heeded his advice or his demands. Now, just as it appeared that he was beginning a new and important creative phase, Reinhardt was once again interfering with yet another distraction, one that would take his son out of his reach altogether. He probably laid the ultimate blame for this situation on Luzi von Sonnenthal. If he were not married to her, Julius may have reasoned, Erich would have no need to accept these chores so unworthy of his talent. Erich would have no reason to earn a living, and he would be at home in the bosom of his family.

These conjectures are well founded. The Korngold family recalls many such arguments. Ernst Korngold, Erich's eldest son, particularly remembered the violent rows after his father announced his intention to accept Reinhardt's invitation to America. The situation did not improve over the coming years: as Julius Korngold grew older, the arguments became progressively worse.

The film of *A Midsummer Night's Dream* was scheduled to begin production in autumn of 1934. It was to be the most important film yet made by Warner Brothers. The Korngolds booked passage on the ship *Majestic* and prepared to leave for their American adventure, leaving the two boys with Luzi's mother.

What appeared at the time to be yet another Reinhardt collaboration that would take a few weeks of hard (but enjoyable work) was to be one of the great turning points in Korngold's life. In later years, he would look back on that invitation as the lifeline that saved him and his loved ones from the gas chamber. A new life, a new career, a new world awaited him. It was an adventure that opened up an entirely new creative sphere for his genius; it was also the death-knell of his reputation as a serious composer for the next four decades. His new career would stigmatize him ever after as "just a film music composer"—a fallacy that persisted well into the 1980s. Only recently has the tide begun to turn.

Then, however, Erich Wolfgang Korngold was simply on his way to Hollywood. For the second time in his life, he would come to be regarded as a revolutionary, this time as the pioneer of the symphonic film score. From now on, the film studio and not the opera house would be his artistic home. This was Hollywood's Golden Age, and one of its most illustrious talents was about to make his entrance into the spotlight. One might almost hear the cry: "Lights! Action! Korngold!"

From Vienna to
Hollywood: 1934–1944

CHAPTER SIXTEEN

Lights! Action! Korngold!

By the mid 1930s, the mass exodus to Hollywood by many of the greatest names of the European cultural milieu had gathered momentum with an inexorable tread. Political developments in Germany had already forced Arnold Schoenberg to seek refuge there, and while not every expatriate made the journey to California for reasons of personal safety, the number of those who did was growing.

Of course, Hollywood had long been an international community. During the 1920s, major stars, directors, and writers had flocked from Europe to the movie capital, where huge salaries were to be enjoyed with the benefit of low taxes. Hollywood was like a magnet for anything or anyone it considered a valuable commodity, and it attracted a never-ending stream of the great and near great of that time—Dietrich, Lubitsch, von Sternberg, Garbo, Fritz Lang, Emil Jannings, Billy Wilder, and many more—all were established there by 1934. The drain of talent was not only from the Continent. There had been a considerable English invasion, too, for with the coming of sound to motion pictures, the ability to speak well was almost a prerequisite, and actors such as Clive Brook, Basil Rathbone, Elisabeth Allan, Claude Rains, Diana Wynyard, Henry Daniell, Herbert Marshall, Ronald Colman, and Cary Grant were among the most popular on the screen.

Name value counted for a great deal with the moguls. Well aware of his reputation and status, they inevitably approached Max Reinhardt. Interestingly, it was the unlikely figure of Jack Warner rather than the more refined Irving Thalberg at MGM who managed to get Reinhardt's name on a film contract.

Vollmoeller's play *The Miracle*[1] was planned as Reinhardt's first sound film. A Technicolor production of *The Miracle* was announced by Jack Warner in *The Los Angeles Daily News*, 10 August 1932, listing Reinhardt as producer, Loretta Young as the star, and a famous composer (unnamed) as the writer of the score. Nothing came of this, however, and Reinhardt was not approached again until 1934 when he announced his intention to stage his spectacular production of Shakespeare's *A Midsummer Night's Dream* at the Hollywood Bowl. This announcement had prompted Warner's visit to Salzburg, where he had achieved an agreement with Reinhardt in principle.

The opening night of *A Midsummer Night's Dream* on 17 September 1934 was one of the more extraordinary cultural events held in the film capital during the 1930s. The elite of Hollywood attended the opening, and among them were Jack Warner and his associates Hal B. Wallis and Henry Blanke (the latter a German émigré who had originally been assistant to Ernst Lubitsch on his arrival in Hollywood before moving to Warners in 1932).

Gloria Stuart, the blonde star of many musicals of the 1930s (*Roman Scandals* with Eddie Cantor, *The Goldiggers of 1935* with Dick Powell), was the surprising choice to play Hermia. Perhaps fortuitously, she withdrew at the last moment for other film commitments, and the part went to a young theater student who was the understudy, Olivia de Havilland, who recalled:

> It was the turning point in my career. I was an ambitious and tenacious girl, and I had already taken quite a gamble in joining the company. . . . Someone had seen me in a college production of *A Midsummer Night's Dream* and recommended me to Max Reinhardt.
>
> I never expected to go on stage, as I was only understudying, but, just as if it were a film, I actually went on as Hermia on opening night when Miss Stuart withdrew. She had been cast in a film, as I recall. The production was tremendous—nothing like it had ever been seen before in California—and Professor Reinhardt, in spite of the language barrier, was the most remarkable director I ever worked with. He had such presence, such authority—really, it is very difficult for me to describe his impact—but he was able to manage the huge cast with ease. He had only to raise his hand and there would be silence. I recall it was rather "avant-garde" in theater terms. He made them dismantle the large music shell at the Bowl to give more space and to provide a backdrop of trees and rocks. The audience was

tremendous, and . . . on the strength of it, I landed a contract with Warner Brothers.[2]

Warner Brothers was very keen to project a more cultured image at this time. It had been long associated with gangster films and tough, social dramas laced with brash, witty dialogue. Warners was actually regarded as a sort of "blue-collar" film studio and generally made low-budget films. Their gritty realism make the early Warner sound films hold up today far better than the films of their contemporaries, but at the time, Metro Goldwyn Mayer, with "more stars than there are in heaven" under the cultured aegis of Irving Thalberg, enjoyed a supreme position and led the film world with its elegant screen adaptations of major literary classics such as *David Copperfield, Treasure Island, A Tale of Two Cities,* and *Anna Karenina* and famous plays such as *Grand Hotel, The Barretts of Wimpole Street,* and *Dinner at Eight* with all-star casts.

Korngold with Max Reinhardt at Warner Brothers in 1934 during the filming of *A Midsummer Night's Dream.* The admiring expression on Reinhardt's face sums up their extraordinary relationship. Korngold was Reinhardt's favorite collaborator (courtesy of Jim Silke).

It was well known that Thalberg was preparing a screen version of Shakespeare's *Romeo and Juliet* as a vehicle for his wife, Norma Shearer. Several other film adaptations of Shakespeare were being planned then as well, including two in England: Paul Czinner's film of *As You Like It* (1935) with Elizabeth Bergner and the young Laurence Olivier, and a version of *Hamlet* with John Barrymore by Alexander Korda, which unfortunately was never made. David O. Selznick was also tinkering with the idea of *Hamlet* with Barrymore (in Technicolor), but this too was abandoned.

Shakespeare was suddenly extremely fashionable with film makers, and Jack Warner, who liked to be first in most endeavors, saw in Reinhardt and his epic production of *A Midsummer Night's Dream* an ideal vehicle for elevating Warner Brothers to the status of a major studio.

No expense would be spared in bringing Reinhardt's production to the screen. Reinhardt would have the pick of Warner's stars for the leading roles and would have artistic control of the project. An assistant director, William Dieterle, who (as Wilhelm Dieterle) had worked as an actor with Reinhardt in Germany but had since made his name as a good, workman-like director at Warners, was assigned to assist Reinhardt in transferring his ideas to the screen.

The studio files contain a letter from agent George Volk recommending Franz Waxman (a German émigré composer who was just starting his career in Hollywood) to write the musical scoring of the film, but Reinhardt had already decided to use the famous incidental music by Mendelssohn, realizing that it would have to be tailored to meet the exigencies of the film's requirements. For Reinhardt, there was only one choice for a composer to complete the task—his indispensable collaborator, Korngold.

While Korngold was en route for America, Reinhardt began preparing for the film, assembling his creative team just as if it were one of his own theater productions. The production was assuming a truly international profile: apart from Korngold, Dieterle, Reinhardt, and Henry Blanke (who acted as assistant producer), the Danish costume designer Max Ree[3] (who had worked on the Hollywood Bowl production) joined the company. His costumes were among the major assets of the film, as were the huge sets and overall art direction of the Polish expressionist painter Anton Grot.[4]

Hal Wallis was keen to sign George Balanchine for the choreography, but Balanchine was too ill to undertake the task. Realizing that the film required a "name" for the ballet sequences, he then tried to acquire Leonid Massine (probably on Reinhardt's advice). Production was due to begin, and there followed a series of frantic cables to Jacob Wilk of the New York office to close a deal with him, but his commitments in Paris eventually ruled him out. On 17 October 1934, Wallis cabled Wilk again: "Reinhardt suggests, as alternative, woman who will be of great publicity value; namely Nijinska."[5] Bronislava Nijinska,[6] the sister of Nijinsky, was represented in America by Sol Hurok. After much haggling over her fee, she signed a contract for the picture on 30 October 1934 for six thousand dollars in return for six weeks of work commencing 20 November.[7]

Korngold and his wife left Vienna on 23 October 1934 on the liner *Majestic* and arrived in New York seven days later, besieged by reporters and bemused by their reception. The studio put them up in grand style. Surprisingly (considering that this was 1934), Korngold was repeatedly asked by reporters what he thought of Hitler. He hardly spoke any English at this time, but managed to reply: "I think Mendelssohn will out-live Hitler."[8]

On 31 October, the Korngolds left New York by train for Hollywood via Chicago for their reunion with Reinhardt. Henry Blanke and William Dieterle met them at the station, thus ensuring a warm and friendly welcome in their own language. They booked into the Chateau Marmont Hotel, where a large apartment had been reserved for them.

Casting for the film had already been completed by the end of October. The original tentative cast list reveals that Charles Laughton, Bette Davis, Leslie Howard, and Laurence Olivier had been under consideration for leading roles in the film. The final casting was drastically different. It was headed by James Cagney as Bottom and included Ian Hunter (Theseus), Veree Teasdale (Hypollyta), Victor Jory (Oberon), and Anita Louise (Titania). The only cast members remaining from the stage production were Olivia de Havilland, fourteen-year old Mickey Rooney as Puck, and Otis Harlan as Starveling. The most surprising piece of casting, and also the most successful, was that of Joe E. Brown as Flute the bellows mender.

Most of the cast of *A Midsummer Night's Dream* on the palace set, pictured on the last day of shooting. Left to right: (back row) Olivia de Havilland, Dick Powell, Anita Louise, Victor Jory, Katherine Frey, Ross Alexander, Jean Muir, Hobart Cavanaugh, (seated center) Veree Teasdale, Mickey Rooney, Ian Hunter, Frank McHugh, Hugh Herbert, Otis Harlan, Henry Blanke, Joe E. Brown, Max Reinhardt, James Cagney, Arthur Treacher, (front) Dewey Robinson, Korngold, and William Dieterle. The dog belonged to Reinhardt (Korngold estate).

The first draft of the screenplay was ready by early November, but it clearly did not meet with the approval of Wallis. In spite of embarrassing memories of the very first sound film of Shakespeare—the preposterous 1929 adaptation of *The Taming of the Shrew* by Douglas Fairbanks and Mary Pickford, which bore the immortal credit, "Additional dialogue by Sam Taylor"—Wallis sent the following memorandum to Henry Blanke:

> Can you suggest anyone who could undertake task of making Shakespeare's text more colloquial? Perhaps Thornton Wilder or Paul Green. This is confidential by the way and is not to be used for publicity.[9]

The staff writers Charles Kenyon and Mary McCall were eventually assigned the daunting task of preparing the screenplay, and after a short postponement, shooting finally began on 15 December 1934. From the beginning, the production was hampered by technical problems. The vast forest set by Anton Grot was a dark, Teutonic conception. It extended across two sound stages by means of a huge ramp, and the cinematographer Ernest Haller, one of Hollywood's finest, could not light it properly. After many delays, he was replaced by Hal Mohr, who solved the problem by spraying the dense foliage with aluminum paint. The areas of light and shade were thus painted in, rather in the manner of a German expressionist film. Mohr won an Academy Award for his efforts.

Ballet rehearsal, *A Midsummer Night's Dream*, Warner Brothers, November 1934. From left: William Dieterle, Bronislava Nijinska, Korngold, Max Reinhardt, with unidentified pianist (courtesy of William Dieterle Archive, Ludwigshafen am Rhein Stadtarchiv, Germany).

While the technical problems were being ironed out, Korngold was busy auditioning dozens of prospects for the voice of Titania. Ever the perfectionist, he tried to find the specific type of singing and speaking voice he required. Carol Weiskopf was eventually chosen, and she recalled vividly how she was given the part:

> I was in San Francisco at the time. Mr. Korngold had auditioned nearly 200 sopranos and was still not satisfied, since he had a certain speaking and singing voice in mind to match the personality of Anita Louise.
>
> Someone had heard me sing at the Hollywood First Baptist Church where I was soloist . . . and the studio telephoned me in San Francisco and asked if I cared to audition for Professor Korngold. I did, so I flew down to Burbank on the first plane out. When I arrived on Stage 9 a few hours later, all the singers, sound men, and other personnel were waiting. Korngold sat down at the piano and without letting me catch my breath asked me to read off the manuscript the parts to be sung.
>
> After I had sung a few phrases with Bottom (Mr. Cagney), he said, "Tell the other singers to go home," and we worked diligently on the half spoken–half sung music. Mr. Korngold played with one hand and conducted with the other, with each note, change in volume, pronunciation, inflection indicated precisely. I was a good musician and could read anything at sight, and more important, I could appreciate Mr. Korngold's genius.
>
> He was a hard taskmaster, but was patient and kind. His favorite phrase was: "Do it again, Miss Weiskopf, please!" and when something pleased him he would bounce up and down and shout his appreciation. Then he would repeat "Do it again." The recording sessions went without a hitch, with the exception of a few off-tempo, off-pitch "hee-haws" by James Cagney in the duet which were easily put right.
>
> Mr. Korngold was a great, gentle, Gentleman—quite apt when excited to lapse into his native tongue. He was genuinely complimentary and very encouraging to a young singer.[10]

Music in films had played a significant role even in the silent days. By the mid-1920s, specially commissioned scores for major productions were the norm, and in the larger cinemas there were resident symphony orchestras to play them. With the coming of sound, all this changed. Overnight, hundreds of musicians were out of a job. Although the first real talkie (*The Jazz Singer* with Al Jolson) was arguably a musical, mood music in films was for the time being impossible to utilize. The sheer technical problems created by recording spoken dialogue (so amusingly satirized by the classic 1952 MGM musical *Singin' in the Rain*) precluded any possibility of simultaneously recording a musical score. Early sound films relied on a few bars of introductory music over the opening titles, and for the rest of the film the actors (frequently in a static position) performed unaccompanied.

Multiple tracking was not perfected until 1932. Another Viennese, Max Steiner (1888–1971), was the first to take advantage of the new development. Steiner, a pupil of Mahler, was the grandson of Maximilian Steiner, the famed impresario of the Theater an der Wien. He had made his reputation as a fast and efficient composer who could turn his hand to anything. His work at RKO Radio Pictures for David O. Selznick, especially on the now legendary *King Kong*, in 1933 had opened up the potential of music in sound films. Every studio had its own music department, but after *King Kong* far greater priority was accorded to music in films.

King Kong was a fantasy film that required a rich score to support its extraordinary visual style. Steiner's music was extravagantly scored and it made a tremendous impact, precisely as he intended. His music provided the blueprint for every subsequent film score of this type, just as the film itself paved the way for all other monster movies since.

Happily for Korngold, he arrived when the new technical possibilities were conjoined with a greater awareness of the potential of music in films. Warner Brothers had a thriving music department, under the guidance of Leo Forbstein, who was a first-class administrator but had limited musical ability. To compensate for his lack, he hired the very best musicians available.

The department thrived because Warner Brothers had cornered the market in spectacular musicals beginning with *42nd Street* in 1933, the success of which was almost entirely due to the brilliant, innovative choreographer, Busby Berkeley. The music department also had one of the most gifted arrangers and orchestrators in the industry, Ray Heindorf.[11] Heindorf had started as an assistant to Alfred Newman (another fine composer of film music from this period) at the Samuel Goldwyn studio. He joined the department at Warner Brothers in 1931, and had provided the superb arrangements for *42nd Street* as one of his first major assignments.

One of the longest serving members of the Warner Brothers Orchestra was saxophonist and second clarinetist Teddy Krise, who was 86 years old when I interviewed him in the summer of 1980 at his home in Los Angeles:

> I arrived in Hollywood in 1929, and in those days everyone freelanced. There were very few contract musicians, and it was usually the same musicians playing at all the studios. You see, there was not that much music in the early sound films. We recorded a lot of library music for use in the musicals, and we always played off-camera in those early days. I was with Gus Arnheim's band at the Coconut Grove, and I first went to Warner Brothers in 1931.
>
> In October of 1933, Forbstein issued the first contracts for the Warner orchestra; Heindorf had only recently joined them, and it was a pretty exciting time. The department was expanding quickly to accommodate all the musicals they were making and they not only took on a lot of musicians but also a whole staff of music copyists and arrangers.

The nucleus of the orchestra, which was called the Vitaphone Orchestra after the Warner trademark, consisted of a large brass section, most of whom were from the Jimmy Grier Dance Orchestra, and the rest were either from Gus Arnheim's band (like me) or were pick-up men. These fellows were rough and ready, but believe me, they were all great musicians. They could sight-read anything and were very adaptable. But the real take-off point for the Warner Orchestra came with the arrival of Korngold. He transformed it into a proper symphony orchestra and made Forbstein hire a lot of extra musicians, many from the local symphony orchestras. This was because of the film *A Midsummer Night's Dream*, which used music by Mendelssohn, and clearly you couldn't play classical music using a dance band set-up. He really shook the place up and brought so much class to the department that in a few years, the orchestra was the best there was, in my opinion.[12]

Korngold's approach to film scoring was entirely his own invention. One of the most striking aspects about his achievements in Hollywood is how quickly he adapted to the many technical problems of this new line of work. The first time he was shown around the studio by Henry Blanke, he asked how long one foot of film would last on the screen. Upon being told, he thought for a moment, and remarked: "Ah . . . exactly the same length of time as the first two bars of the Mendelssohn Scherzo!"[13] He had instinctively worked out his own mathematical method of scoring a scene. He solved the exceptional problems of this film—undoubtedly the most complex scoring assignment he ever undertook—with an ease that astonished his American colleagues. From the beginning, he realized that the incidental music by Mendelssohn would be insufficient to "underpaint" the film as Reinhardt intended. A lesser composer would have either duplicated sections or written variations on the existing themes. Korngold, however, was anxious that the musical accompaniment be sequential with the play (as Mendelssohn prescribed in his music) and also stylistically homogeneous. He decided to adapt and integrate music from other Mendelssohn concert works, including the *Scottish Symphony* and several of the *Songs Without Words*.

Although Korngold claimed that every note in the score was pure Mendelssohn, a close examination of the music with the soundtrack reveals that he ingeniously composed short linking passages in the style of Mendelssohn to facilitate a swift bridging from one section to the next. The result is virtually undetectable, although some cues are unmistakably Korngoldian (especially those for Oberon and the sequence in which the forest comes magically to life).

Korngold wrote an article in June 1940 on his approach to scoring films, and he touched on the extraordinary problems he encountered working on this film:

I had to make preliminary recordings, the so-called playbacks, of Mendelssohn's Scherzo and Nocturne, which were relayed over huge loudspeakers during the actual filming [of the ballet episodes]. Further, I conducted the orchestra on stage for complicated simultaneous "takes," and lastly, after the film was cut, I conducted a number of music pieces which were inserted in the completed picture as background music. In addition, however, I had to invent a new method, which was a combination of all three techniques, for the music that accompanied the spoken word.

I wrote out the music in advance, conducted—without orchestra— the actor on the stage in order to make him speak his lines in the required rhythm and then, sometimes weeks later, guided by earphones, I recorded the orchestral part.[14]

This elaborate method ensured that Korngold was more closely involved in the filming than was normal, and it irritated Wallis. He believed that each department should stay within the confines of its work, and he sent a memo to Blanke and Dieterle:

I am concerned about the fact that Korngold is stepping in too much as to how people should speak and how it is going to fit in with his music, and I would rather not have him on the set at all if this is going to be the case.[15]

Nonetheless, Korngold remained on the set, and he extended his influence even to the cutting of the film. In an earlier memo, Wallis notes:

Korngold is notifying Jackman[16] that he has about thirty or forty feet in which to make the shot fit in with the music and Jackman feels it will take about eighty feet.[17]

For a composer to dictate terms in this manner was unheard of then and today. Korngold, however, was so respected that he invariably got his own way in this and every subsequent film.[18]

On 21 November 1934, Nijinska arrived to take charge of the large ensemble scenes. Wallis sent a humorous memo to Henry Blanke:

Nijinska leaves New York today. Will you arrange to have someone meet her? She speaks only Russian, her husband is French, and in as much as you speak only German, you had better take three or four interpreters with you![19]

From the beginning, Nijinska and Korngold did not enjoy cordial relations. The clash of temperaments was perhaps exacerbated by the alien environment in which each was working for the first time.[20] In spite of her legendary reputation, the ballet scenes are the least impressive aspect of the film today. They have a rather journeyman quality, and they singularly lack the imaginative leap that Reinhardt sought.

Yet another Austrian celebrity arrived in America that November, Paul Wittgenstein. On the 22 November 1934 he gave the US premiere of Korngold's Suite for Two Violins, Cello, and Piano for the left hand, Opus 23, in Colorado Springs, and followed it with performances in Denver and Seattle. On 3 December 1934 he arrived in Los Angeles and gave a concert at the Biltmore Hotel featuring the Suite as the main work. Korngold was invited as an honored guest.

The happy event was somewhat clouded by a rift between the two great musicians, however: Wittgenstein was appalled when Korngold told him about the arrangements he was making of the Mendelssohn music for Reinhardt's film. Wittgenstein, a musical purist, highly volatile, and concerned that Korngold was tampering with a masterpiece, showered Korngold with a torrent of abuse. The normally placid Korngold replied in like manner, and they had a violent row, resulting in Wittgenstein's storming off in high dudgeon. A few days later, however, regretting the outburst and anxious to make amends, Wittgenstein sent a letter of apology and a conciliatory gift: an original Mendelssohn letter for Korngold's collection of musical autographs.[21]

Erich and Luzi Korngold in the Green Room at Warner Brothers in the mid-1930s with their dear friend, the producer Henry Blanke. Korngold was always at his wittiest at mealtimes (courtesy of Jim Silke).

By Christmas 1934, it was evident that *A Midsummer Night's Dream* was going to overrun its budget and shooting schedule—unheard of at cost-conscious Warner Brothers. Scenes had frequently to be reshot because of the many difficulties in recording the dialogue clearly on the large forest set. Furious memos from Wallis ordering retakes and emphasizing the need for close shots of the actors speaking to aid understanding of "the more esoteric lines," as he put it, indicate the stress of the production.[22]

The delays were prolonged when Mickey Rooney broke his leg (while tobogganing one weekend) and subsequently had to be wheeled around the stage for a few weeks by stage hands hidden by bushes. He was quickly assigned a stunt-double[23] for all long shots and any athletic work, as his role frequently called for him to swing from trees, and he was one of several actors who were on invisible fly-wires.

Reinhardt, in spite of the assistance of Dieterle, was ill at ease in the medium of film. Furthermore, judging from the memos, Wallis was becoming more irritable as the weeks passed, quite possibly regarding the whole enterprise as a waste of money, and was not impressed with Reinhardt's direction of the actors. In a typical memo to Henry Blanke he states:

> Regarding Jean Muir with her mirror . . . the action and the dialogue [are] too slow . . . if there is any more argument, tell Reinhardt to come up and see me. I know I am right on this regardless of the fact that it has been staged for twenty, thirty, or fifty years. Doing it in the theater is one thing and doing it on the screen is another and *I want the stuff done faster!*[24]

In contrast, Korngold was feeling more at home, especially when he was invited by Otto Klemperer, then the principal conductor of the Los Angeles Philharmonic, to conduct a celebrity concert at the Hollywood Bowl on 17 February 1935. Korngold selected the *Schauspiel Ouvertüre*, two of the *Sechs Einfache Lieder*, the Mariettalied from *Die tote Stadt*, and the *Baby Serenade* (here receiving its US premiere and until the 1990s, its last complete performance anywhere). The soloist was local singer Mariane Mabee, and the concert went extremely well. The "Viennese contingent" was much in evidence, of course; Reinhardt, when Korngold struck up with *Radetzky March* as a salute to Austria, began to sob unashamedly.

The shooting of *A Midsummer Night's Dream* was finally completed on 26 February 1935. For all of March, it was in the hands of film editor Ralph Dawson with extensive notes from Hal Wallis, who was intent on tightening the whole film and increasing the pace wherever possible. Wallis had a superb instinct for cutting a film and contributed more than is often realized to the success of many of the great films of this era.

Because of the delays, Korngold was asked to stay on until 30 April 1935 to ensure that the scoring would be completed. Jack Warner placed his private bungalow at the disposal of the Korngolds. (Even Luzi had worked on the film, rehearsing the children for their dances.) At Korngold's request, a projection room with a piano was made available at night so he could run the reels of film as he sat at the keyboard and matched the music to the running footage—his own method and one that he used in all his subsequent film assignments. As Luzi said, "He fitted his music to the running film just as he would accompany a singer on the opera stage."[25]

The similarity with opera did not end there; in his arrangement of the Mendelssohn music, he employed (with Reinhardt's encouragement) the techniques of operatic leitmotifs for each of the characters wherever possible. This idea of giving characters a musical calling card was highly influential. Other composers quickly grew out of the "one tune" score and began to identify their characters much more strongly in musical terms.

Korngold also conducted all the final post-synchronized music and became deeply involved in the final dubbing in what he called the "doop-room," where he became firm friends with George Groves and his assistant Dave Forrest. He was continually at pains to prevent Mendelssohn's music from being chopped up, and for the most part he succeeded. His judicious editing of the music and his fine conducting of the score meant that musically the film was a joy to the ear. The only major change was the transposition of the Nocturne from E major to E-flat major; as Korngold explained, Mendelssohn envisaged his Nocturne in bright moonlight, whereas Reinhardt's conception was set in darkest night.[26]

Even during post-production after the completion of filming, Warner and Wallis continued to toy with the film. For a time they considered having a long overture before the main titles. Then Reinhardt filmed a new sequence in which the main characters mimed an introduction, but this was cut.[2] The very first-release version, which survives in some rare prints, includes a spoken introduction by Ian Hunter (as Theseus) in front of a theater curtain.

The preview was held in June. An uneasy Jack Warner was unconvinced that it would be a success. He instructed his executives to go all-out in promoting the film, which had already been highly publicized during its making. The Broadway publicist Nathan Zatkin was hired to invent "stunts to put the film over." A huge oversized press book was produced designed to instruct exhibitors in how to sell the film, for in this period the studios still owned the cinemas. The Warner chain of theaters had to be supplied by the studio with a constant supply of films. Not until the late 1940s was the monopoly broken.

Warner decided to give the film a simultaneous premiere in London and New York, the first time this had ever been done. (Korngold must have been reminded of the dual premiere of *Die tote Stadt* in 1920.) Not content with this, Warner suggested to Reinhardt that a private showing before King George V and Queen Mary would be good for publicity. The studios were especially conscious of the foreign market for their films. Often, the overseas box office could mean the difference between profit and loss. Moreover, Shakespeare was an English national treasure, and the film's reception in England was vitally important. Reinhardt promptly wrote to Lady Diana Cooper and Baron von Franckenstein (the Austrian Ambassador in London) to ask them to arrange the royal showing. In spite of their intercession, it never took place.

A special short subject entitled *A Dream Comes True* was put into production. It included footage of the shooting of the film; later, film of the celebrities arriving for the gala premiere in Hollywood was added with a suitably fervent narration. Most important of all, however, it had priceless footage of Korngold playing the piano—the only filmed record of his playing. He was described on the soundtrack as "a gifted composer—a brilliant musician." Warner Brothers clearly realized his worth.

Plans to film him actually conducting the Warner Orchestra for the overture to the film never materialized, although a broadcast was made of the whole score in April 1935 with Korngold conducting. Unfortunately, the original acetates of this historic transmission are lost.[28]

Korngold's commitments to the film were completed by 1 May 1935. Immediately, his thoughts turned to Vienna, his family, and his opera *Die Kathrin*, and he prepared to return home. Before he departed, however, Wallis and Blanke tried to interest him in a one-year contract. Further productions with Reinhardt were being discussed (he had signed a three-picture deal). The next time, original music by Korngold would be required. Korngold offered at least to look at the contract and promised to cable his response from Vienna. Ernst Lubitsch was keen to engage him as well for a musical film at Paramount that he was preparing with Jan Kiepura. He, too, asked Korngold to consider an offer for an original operatic score. This idea was more to Korngold's liking, but once again he refused to commit himself, preferring instead to consider the matter over the summer once he was back in his familiar environment, surrounded by the beautiful scenery of Gmunden.

He booked return passage on the *Majestic* and sailed for Europe on 2 May 1935 with unsigned contracts from both studios in his pocket and Luzi at his side. It was a stimulating voyage; violinist Nathan Milstein and the great Italian maestro Arturo Toscanini were also on board, along with another unexpected guest—Jack Warner.

CHAPTER SEVENTEEN

Operas Without Singing

*T*he winds of change ushered in by *A Midsummer Night's Dream* were long-lasting and represented a serious attempt to establish Warner Brothers as a major producer of films of quality. The entire film industry had been shaken up by the much stricter Production Code of 1934 and by the insistence of the Hays Office (the arbiter of public taste and the administrating censorship body) that Hollywood produce films of decency according to the American ideal.

The upholder of this "tradition of quality" was Metro-Goldwyn-Mayer. Having pre-empted MGM's plans to produce a prestigious screen adaptation of a Shakespeare play, Jack Warner turned his attentions to the burgeoning trend of the costume spectacle. The success of *The Count of Monte Cristo* in 1934 (as well as MGM's new version of *Treasure Island*) pointed the way to this new genre.

The news that MGM was to produce *Mutiny on the Bounty* from the best-selling book by Charles Nordhoff and James Hall led Warner to dust off *Captain Blood* by Rafael Sabatini. It had been filmed in 1923 by Vitagraph, and Warner Brothers had acquired the rights (and the film) in 1928. Originally planned as a vehicle for Robert Donat, it eventually starred the young Errol Flynn in his first major role (opposite Olivia de Havilland), and was the start of a series of swashbuckling costume pictures in which he excelled.

More important still, this new trend in films was tailor-made to the talents of Korngold. The team was perfect. "Flynn, de Havilland, Warners, and Korngold would all set sail together that year ushering in a new age of motion picture romance,"[1] but first Korngold would have to be persuaded. Although he had enjoyed working on Reinhardt's film for the most part, his heart was in Vienna. As soon as his services were no longer required, he returned home, where he planned to remain.

Meanwhile, final post-production work on *A Midsummer Night's Dream* began in earnest. The studio was clearly unsure how to market this extraordinary film, so ill-fitted to the usual cinematic hyperbole. It nearly fell victim to Hollywood's gauche marketing techniques. At one point, the following doggerel penned by a studio publicist was considered for widespread use:

In Elizabethan times,
Though they were well equipped with rimes,
They didn't have the fine art,
Of staging scenes, bizarre, immense,
Of Warners' sheer magnificence,
Directed by a Reinhardt.[2]

Fortunately, a more discreet marketing approach was adopted. The impressive statistics were stressed (for example, a seventy-day shooting schedule, eighty-five miles of film exposed during its making) and the reputations of Reinhardt and his illustrious collaborators were given prominence.

The studio then turned its attention to *Captain Blood*, which was to commence production in June. Blanke and Wallis were both keen to bring Korngold back to Hollywood, so the game of "cat and mouse" began that was to precede all of Korngold's future assignments. Persuasion across so many thousands of miles was difficult but not impossible, especially with the carrot of further projects with Reinhardt. The pleading telegrams and letters began almost as soon as Korngold arrived home on 11 May 1935.

Korngold was back at Schloss Höselberg, where he recommenced work on *Die Kathrin*, but the temptations to return to Hollywood were mounting up. Lubitsch had decided to proceed with the Kiepura film. With the success of Grace Moore in *One Night of Love* (Columbia) in 1934, films featuring opera stars were suddenly all the rage. Grace Moore had made several films in the early days of sound without success, but Victor Schertzinger, the director of *One Night of Love,* had shown that properly showcased (with a variation of the "young unknown becomes a star overnight" theme and the correct musical pacing), opera on screen could be powerful in the box office.

Soon, Hollywood was offering lucrative contracts to major opera stars. Between 1935 and 1938 a series of films featuring the vocal talents of luminaries such as Lily Pons, Lauritz Melchior, Miliza Korjus, Kirsten Flagstad,

James Melton, Helen Jepson, and Gladys Swarthout appeared with considerable success. The most successful of all were the films starring Jeanette McDonald and Nelson Eddy at MGM, beginning with Victor Herbert's *Naughty Marietta* in 1935. Paramount was keen to cash in on the trend, and Jan Kiepura—a magnificent singer, exceptionally handsome, and with a seductive speaking voice—looked to be an ideal choice for a star. He was already a screen veteran, having filmed extensively in Europe since 1931.

The offer of working on a miniature opera for the screen with his old friends Lubitsch and Kiepura greatly tempted Korngold. The advice of the family physician that his young son George, who had just recovered from a tubercular infection, might benefit from a winter in the warm California sun, clinched it. The Korngolds left for America at the beginning of August on the *Ile de France*, this time taking the two children with them over the protests of the elder Korngolds.

Julius Korngold was seriously worried about this new distraction in his son's life and was dismayed that the control he had exercised in the past had gradually diminished to the point that Erich paid little if any attention to his advice. He already had doubts about the dramatic soundness of the libretto for *Die Kathrin*. With the opera still only half completed and no performance even scheduled, he was growing increasingly anxious, especially when it began to be remarked in the press and in the coffee houses that "young Korngold had dried up." Julius Korngold did not relish the thought that his son would now further subjugate his talent and become an arranger and musical illustrator for the movies, a task even more lowly than the time-consuming operetta chores he had endured for more than a decade.

Korngold would not be swayed, however. The combination of factors beckoning toward this endeavor was powerful, and the added attraction of a large fee was not to be overlooked, for the regular income from royalties had all but ceased with the removal of his works from the repertoire in Germany since 1933. New compositions had been few since 1930, and with Clemens Krauss in charge at the Vienna State Opera, conducting assignments were also scarce.

On arrival in New York on the 8 August 1935, Korngold immediately began discussions with Oscar Hammerstein II, who was to write the lyrics and libretto for the Kiepura film, to be called *Give Us This Night*. After four days in New York, the Korngold family arrived in Hollywood and rented a house in Beverly Hills not far from Arnold Schoenberg.

Give Us This Night ranks as one of Hollywood's great missed opportunities. With so much talent behind and in front of the camera, it should have been possible to create a more convincing film for Kiepura's Hollywood debut. The plot must have seemed risible, even to audiences in 1935: a singing fisherman becomes an overnight star when chosen to replace an aging, temperamental, off-key operatic tenor. Kiepura tried very hard to be convincing in the poorly written role, but Michelette Burani (playing his mother) had seemingly little comprehension for the English language. Overall, the film contains few redeeming features. That it has never been shown on television is perhaps an indication of its awfulness. Even after sixty years, this poorly scripted film has failed to acquire a patina of charm or even a degree of quaintness as a compensation, and it is rarely screened.

The cast does its best, given the material. Alan Mowbray, as the prima-donna has-been tenor, and Gladys Swarthout from the New York Metropolitan Opera as the love interest and vocal partner for Kiepura, fare best. Kiepura sings wonderfully and is recorded better here than in any of his European films, but he is clearly unhappy and ill at ease. The constant rewrites hampered his ability to speak his lines convincingly, and English was a difficult language for him. The music was completed by September, despite all the rewrites by other lyricists that infuriated both Hammerstein and Korngold, who remarked at one point, "This thing gets worse, week by week; by the time we start, it will be useless."[3]

The music was recorded partially on the set and partially on the sound stage—a task that held no terrors for Korngold after *A Midsummer Night's Dream*. In one sequence requiring a "rain set," Korngold had to wear a sowester while accompanying at the piano off-camera.

Just as the post-recording commenced, Warner Brothers telephoned that *Captain Blood* was complete and asked Korngold to attend the screening with a view to scoring the film. As extra encouragement, they promised numerous projects with Reinhardt, including a lavish, all-star production of *The Tales of Hoffmann* with Richard Tauber, Grace Moore, Jarmila Novotná, Feodor Chaliapin, and Charles Laughton. Warner Brothers was even considering a follow-up Shakespearean film, *Twelfth Night*, starring, of all people, Marion Davies. Another operetta production of the famed Reinhardt–Korngold version of *Die Fledermaus* with Richard Tauber, Lotte Lehmann, Rosa Ponselle, and Fernando Gravet (who later would play Strauss in *The Great Waltz* for MGM in 1938), was also considered at this time. Regrettably, none of these was made.[4]

Although Korngold had returned to Warner Brothers on different terms, he was expected to score at least one film during his stay. Initially, he had refused, but after the usual series of urgent telephone calls he agreed to look at *Captain Blood*. All these delays in producing *Give Us This Night* juxta-posed with the tight scheduling of *Captain Blood* (the film was already booked to open in New York on Christmas Day) left only a few weeks to complete the scoring, orchestration, and recording. Somehow Korngold managed the task.

For the month of November he spent his days conducting and recording the score for *Give Us This Night* and nights composing the music for *Captain Blood* in the projection room at Warner Brothers. Still more remarkable is that despite being stretched to the limit, he agreed to write the opening march-song for another film musical at Paramount, *Rose of the Rancho,* also starring Gladys Swarthout. Because of the extremely tight schedules, Korngold had to record and conduct this song, "Fight For The

Korngold conducting the Warner Brothers Orchestra, circa 1935. He always conducted his film scores while seated (Korngold estate).

Right," on a Sunday, 3 November.[5] It is scored for full orchestra and chorus and is the only memorable aspect to the entire film, a lamentable affair that can best be described as a sort of "drag" version of *The Mark of Zorro* on a low budget.

The music for *Give Us This Night* also uplifts that film when it has an opportunity to interrupt the plot. The songs were written in a quasi-operatic style, and the best of them, "Sweet Melody of Night" and "I Mean to Say I Love You," were commercially released by Kiepura in one of his finest recordings.[6] The final operatic sequence (loosely based on the story of *Romeo and Juliet* to enable Kiepura, the ideal Romeo, to enact a balcony scene) utilizes much of the earlier score, which Philip Merivale (woefully miscast as the composer) plays on the piano several times. Korngold dubbed the piano track himself—the first of many instances he would do so. By far the most important musical sequence in the film, however, is set in the village church during Mass, entitled "Religioso" in the Paramount cue sheets. Korngold, who loved the ceremony and mystical reverence of the Roman Catholic liturgy, rose to the occasion beautifully.

Somehow Korngold also managed to finish work on *Captain Blood*. He celebrated by taking the technical personnel at Warner Brothers to a hearty breakfast at Gotham's Restaurant, already a particular favorite of his. The score—his first original, symphonic composition for the screen—was written in the grand manner and was the blueprint for all of Korngold's subsequent work for the screen: richly melodic, sumptuously orchestrated, and replete with superbly heraldic passages for the peerless brass section of the Warner Brothers Studio Orchestra. The splendid main title (or overture), with its opening drum roll, announces the film with a heroic theme that sets the tone of this archetypal swashbuckler perfectly. The brass fanfares are a foretaste of similar Korngoldian motifs from the later films such as *The Adventures of Robin Hood* and *The Private Lives of Elizabeth and Essex*, which many subsequent composers have emulated but never surpassed.

The frantic schedule had meant that the orchestral parts of the main title had to be completed in one weekend. They were entrusted to one lone copyist, the 19-year-old Albert Glasser who had just arrived at Warner Brothers looking for work. He recalled that he became so wrapped up in the music that when the main title was to be recorded on the following Monday morning, he hid behind some boxes on the soundstage to hear the finished product:

> And then, here comes the great Korngold. Thick-set, portly, full of humor, making jokes the whole time—a typical Viennese. He walked up to the podium, opened the score, and lifted the baton. As soon as he gave his downbeat, I felt an electric shock run through my body, my hair stood on end, and I knew instantly that here was a truly great, natural-born musician. He had a dynamic something or other, what we later learned to call a "stick hand" that instantly made you sit up straight. I'll never forget it as long as I live.[7]

Even Korngold had his limitations, however, and the rigors of writing the long score coupled with the problems on *Give Us This Night* meant that help would have to be enlisted. Hugo Friedhofer was assigned to Korngold as orchestrator. Having an orchestrator on hand was a necessity for all composers working in films because of the extremely tight schedules and short deadlines. Korngold was not happy about having an orchestrator foisted upon him, but in view of the impossible time factor, he consented. Although he was used to collaborating with orchestrators on most of his operetta arrangements, this was the first time he had to do so with his own music. Unlike the film with Reinhardt, for which he was given nearly half a year to complete the adaptation, every day counted with *Captain Blood* and with all of his subsequent scoring assignments. The lack of time also forced Korngold to resort to music from the standard repertoire for one sequence—the only time he ever did so. The three weeks allotted him to write the score for *Captain Blood* was the shortest period in which he ever had to write a score. As Friedhofer recalled:

> The duel between Flynn and Rathbone is an adaptation and re-orchestration of a fugal episode from Liszt's symphonic poem

Prometheus. I still have the pocket score in my library with Erich's annotations.

It seems that the preview date had been moved up and there simply wasn't time enough left to compose the entire scene. I recall meeting him one evening at 8:30 P.M. to discuss the scene which was scheduled for recording the following morning. He handed me the Liszt score to which he had appended an introduction and a coda and, after a discussion which took about an hour, I set off for home.

I started orchestrating around 11:00 P.M. and worked through the night. At seven the next morning, a messenger from Warners' picked up the completed score for the copyist, and by mid-afternoon the piece was recorded. It was a rough night, as you can well imagine.[8]

Because of this brief interpolation, Korngold insisted that the title card on the screen be amended to read, "Musical Arrangements by Erich Wolfgang Korngold," even though nearly the entire score was his original composition. The scope of the problems he encountered on this film are further born out by Friedhofer himself needing help from Ray Heindorf. In addition, two short cues, "Spanish Soldier" and "Street Scene," were penned by Milan Roder, another staff composer who worked on anything and everything at the studio.

Friedhofer was Korngold's most regular collaborator, however, and was ideally suited to the task, as he had had a thorough schooling in the orchestral idiom of Wagner, Strauss, and Mahler, of which Korngold's style was a natural extension. He later became a composer for the screen himself (his first credited score was for Samuel Goldwyn's *The Adventures of Marco Polo* in 1937, although he had been composing for films since 1929 and had worked on *Rose of the Rancho* at Paramount the previous year) and he seems to have shared a mutually enjoyable collaboration with Korngold. He described their method of working as follows:

We would sit together at the piano with the sequence to be orchestrated and he would play it through, with me filling in the occasional notes that were outside the capacities of ten fingers. He had, incidentally, the most extraordinary way of making the piano sound like an orchestra that I have ever encountered. After the run-through at the keyboard, there would be a detailed discussion of color in the orchestra. This was a give and take affair, with me telling him what I heard and he giving me his conception of what the color should be. Then I would make careful enquiry as to those places in his sketch which were capable of being set as they stood, i.e. without any re-voicing, changes of register, octave doubling, etc.

When I had completed the sections he had given me, he and I would go through the full score together and in detail. As time went on, he came to rely more and more on my discretion in the matter of color and voicing, and in many instances would discuss with me the orchestrations of sections which were to be farmed out to other orchestrators.[9]

The other orchestrators included Simon Bucharoff and Murray Cutter, and later on even composers of the caliber of Ernst Toch. Ray Heindorf's extraordinary facility enabled him to adapt to Korngold's style without reference to Friedhofer.[10] Because of Korngold's meticulously detailed piano sketches and highly personal harmonic and melodic style, these other orchestrations always emerged sounding exactly like a Korngold piece, although he would occasionally make alterations at the recording sessions (clearly obvious now when one examines the original parts, still extant in the special collections at the University of Southern California; they are full of his written emendations).

Korngold's symphonic style did not fundamentally alter when he composed for films. Rather, he invented a new form, the symphonic film score. With this first original score, we can see the prototype of all his subsequent works for the screen, and the formula for these "operas without singing" rarely changed. A dramatic, arresting main title to accompany the credits contained the main themes of the score. Invariably, this overture would segue into a fully scored sequence, often without interruption for the first ten or fifteen minutes of the film, in which major leitmotifs (in the operatic manner) would be stated. As a whole, the scores clearly resemble large symphonic poems rather than operas. The action is musically illustrated, and episodes and adventures punctuate the flow of the music. Unlike any other composer working in films at this time (and with few exceptions since), Korngold composed his scores along symphonic lines, with themes contrapuntally developed throughout. The attention to detail is extraordinary, as is the key scheme; each sequence begins and ends in appropriate keys, so that if played in sequence, the music becomes a continuous whole with rarely any need for bridging.

Hugo Friedhofer knew Korngold better than anyone in the musical sense, and recalled perceptively some of the pleasures of working with him, as well as some of the problems. He was one of the few granted this close relationship, and so I quote his remarks at length:

Korngold's sketches, although quite complete as to detail, pose a pretty problem for the orchestrator, since they are conceived in a highly pianistic fashion, and require re-setting to make effective orchestra sounds. This method of writing was not adopted by Korngold during his "Hollywood" period. I have seen his original manuscripts of several of his "serious" works and the processes were identical. . . . His acquaintance with the vibraphone dates from the time of our association. There was a scene in *Captain Blood* where Errol Flynn was flogged . . . it was in the latter part of the music for this scene that I conceived the notion of doubling certain string and woodwind lines with the vibraphone. In this, I was doubtless influenced by the manner in which Korngold employed the sustaining pedal on the piano while playing the music accompanying this scene for me . . . .

I remember his remarking that this was the sound that [Richard] Strauss had in mind when he wrote a part for the glass-harmonica into the score of his opera *Die Frau ohne Schatten*, and which never quite came off, because of the extremely delicate tone of the instrument.[11]

In orchestrating Korngold's music, I worked for the most part from a three- or four-lined sketch. However, these were not his original manuscripts but copies made therefrom by the one copyist in Southern California who could decipher the originals . . . .[12]

I remember once he spoke of Dukas's unjustly neglected opera *Ariane et Barbe-Bleu* in glowing terms, and saying, at the conclusion of an hour-long eulogy, peppered with excerpts from the score (which he played on the piano from memory) that he "had been living off Ariane for many years." Be that as it may, the fact remains that whatever he borrowed became transmuted in the crucible of his enormous individuality, and the end product was always pure Korngold. . . . tune detecting is, after all, a childish game played by young music students, unimaginative critics, and the second violinist on the next-to-last desk in any orchestra. . . .

Let me say that . . . working . . . with him for so many years was . . . both stimulating and educational, and I can say without fear of overstating the case, that I have undoubtedly benefited as much, if not more, from my contact with him, than from the sum total of all the musicians I have ever known.[13]

Viewed today, *Captain Blood* is rather dated and the restrictions of the budget are clearly evident on screen. Anton Groz achieved a great deal, however, with his effective use of shadow and dramatic lighting, aided by the director Michael Curtiz. Curtiz excelled in pictures of this type. The most famous sequence in *Captain Blood* was the elaborate final sea battle (a forerunner of the definitive version in the later film *The Sea Hawk*). Curtiz characteristically embellished scenes like this and understood the visual poetry of a fluent and mobile camera. (A choice later example is how Curtiz allows the camera to explore Rick's cafe in *Casablanca*, giving viewers the feeling of having really visited that particular establishment.)

For once, the judicious economy of Hal Wallis did not restrain George Amy (the editor on *Captain Blood*): the film originally ran 119 minutes, an extraordinary length for that time.[14] Clearly, the studio had yet to adapt their usual fast pacing to costume drama. When the film was re-issued in 1951, it was trimmed to 95 minutes. Although the cuts helped by removing much of the superfluous footage that had slowed it down, many scenes scored by Korngold were lost in the process. A complete print is rarely seen today.

Although the film has become dated, the music remains fresh. A seductive passage to accompany the scenes in Jamaica was an unusual departure for Korngold but has a parallel in the later Panama sequence in *The Sea Hawk*. The music for the love scenes still makes an indelible impression with its sweepingly heroic lyricism, characterized by arching, repeated rising sevenths that dovetail perfectly with a hypnotic and unforgettable horn call that is redolent of every schoolboy's dream of pirate adventure.

This score, certainly the most complex yet written for an American film, shook the musical establishment in Hollywood. Film music more or less came of age with Korngold, who in this one film showed what could really be achieved with a symphonic score. Not for him an unobtrusive background score that must not compete with the action. For Korngold, music must sweep the action along, a potent counterpoint to the dialogue and the image. His music was designed to elevate the sometimes cardboard events on the screen and to flesh out the romantic dream that he instinctively recognized as underlying the story. His scores taught film composers to write melodies that film audiences would whistle as they left the cinema. With *Captain Blood* he set the pace. Once again, he had entered a new medium, grappled with it, and found his own niche within it—right at the top.

By the year's end Korngold was already generating unprecedented publicity for a composer writing for films. Mention of a composer in a film review was unusual; Korngold's work, together with his reputation, ensured that his name appeared with increasing frequency.

By now *A Midsummer Night's Dream* was finally released. It had received, as planned, a double premiere in New York and London on 9 October 1935 before going on general release on 16 October. At 140 minutes, it was judged to be overlong, however, and the disappointing receipts and reviews underlined its shortcomings. Wallis withdrew the film for further cutting to improve its pace. It was considerably tightened up to a crisp 118 minutes and re-released in February 1936; this version is the one usually available today, although longer prints are extant in private hands. It barely made back its enormous cost of almost two million dollars only after several periodic reissues, but the prestige of the film enhanced the reputation of the studio.

Seen today, it is difficult to appreciate that it represented a major breakthrough in transferring Shakespeare to the screen. The unlikely and rather adventurous casting works in only a few cases. Much of the film seems artificial, set-bound, and in some of the dance sequences almost as though intended for use in one of the lavish Busby Berkeley musicals being made on the adjoining stage (with the same stars; Dick Powell worked on *A Midsummer Night's Dream* simultaneously with *The Goldiggers of 1935*, which may account for his performance). The acting is generally an uneasy mix of broad slapstick and excessively mannered stiltedness. Visually, it must have been stunning (few good prints are available now), and some indication of the spectacle of the stage production survives. As a record of Reinhardt's theatrical genius, however, the film fails to convey the splendor for which he was renowned, with the single exception of the nocturne scene. Here Reinhardt created something of great beauty, and the evidence that it was his conception is still in the files at Warner Brothers, a scenario written in Reinhardt's own hand:

> With the coming of the dawn, as the fairies creep away underneath the great billowing cloak of Oberon, one particular fairy (Nini Theilade) resists the call. She is swept up by one of Oberon's winged messengers and carried off into the receding darkness, until only her white hands can be seen distantly fluttering in the blackness of the forest.

It is a memorable and striking image, haunting and poetic.

Disparate as they are, the elements somehow fuse into an artistic whole held together by Korngold's musical "underpainting," as Reinhardt had specified. His conducting and treatment were inspired, and with only the addition of the harmonium, vibraphone, English horn, and celeste to the orchestra, the adaptation was faithful to Mendelssohn as well as to Shakespeare. The music he devised for the unforgettable sequence in which the forest comes to life is certainly original, but for the most part he created a score that was ninety-eight percent Mendelssohn. The *Songs Without Words* were used extensively and effectively. His orchestration of these in Mendelssohn's style is uncannily accurate.

All of the techniques Korngold would use in his later films are present here. When Oberon says, "I know a bank where the wild thyme grows," Korngold matches the rhythm and pace of the dialogue with a beautiful melody. This theme becomes Titania's lullaby. Until recently it was assumed to be by Mendelssohn, but I have been unable to trace it anywhere in Mendelssohn's *oeuvre,* and it may be by Korngold himself. Two other clues point to this: it is not contained in the musical parts and scores still extant in the Warner Brothers collection at the University of Southern California. More intriguing still, Korngold plays the piece on the piano for the short subject *A Dream Comes True* and the narrator does not specify that it is by Mendelssohn. The narrator's actual words are, "Here he is in his study arranging a beautiful lullaby; let's listen to it." Korngold could have used Mendelssohn's own lullaby for Titania and the fairies, but clearly he did not care for it. The lullaby as set in the film is stylistically correct— and if it is by Korngold, it is one of his loveliest ideas.

After sixty years, *A Midsummer Night's Dream* has become a classic that in its best scenes still stirs the imagination. MGM's *Romeo and Juliet* pales beside it, and is instead a textbook example of an over-reverent approach with uninspired casting. Although it is beautiful to look at (Oliver Messel, another of Reinhardt's collaborators, designed the production), its musical score is woefully inadequate, a mishmash of rearranged

Tchaikovsky supervised by staff composer Herbert Stothart. Reinhardt's film, in contrast, despite its shortcomings, has a vitality that makes it compulsively watchable today. Thalberg's *Romeo and Juliet* seems dead by comparison.

Captain Blood opened to exceptional notices and was nominated for the Academy Award for best film of 1935, along with *A Midsummer Night's Dream*. (Both lost to MGM's *Mutiny On The Bounty*.) Max Steiner won the award for best music with his score for *The Informer*. (Korngold was not nominated because of his insistence on the credit "arranged by"). In spite of all the effort and expense involved in both films, only Hal Mohr won an award—for his superb photography for *A Midsummer Night's Dream*.

Korngold's contribution to *Give Us This Night* was to be recognized, however (the first recognition of Korngold's remarkable talents for film scoring to appear in the American press). In a glowing article by Joseph O'Sullivan in the *Motion Picture Herald*, Korngold was accorded an entire page for his score, complete with musical examples. O'Sullivan concluded: "This . . . distinguished . . . musical writing for the screen . . . reflects the talents of a composer who adds unusual distinction to the new art of fusing music and picture."[15]

Christmas 1935 was a time for reunion for most of the émigrés working in Los Angeles. The Lubitsches, the Klemperers, the Schoenbergs, and all of the other celebrated European figures living there extended a cordial welcome to the Korngolds and others only temporarily away from home. Jan Kiepura and his wife, the Hungarian soprano Marta Eggerth, threw a big party for many of them at the large Hollywood mansion they had rented in Beverly Hills.

Following the Christmas holiday, Korngold waited around, hoping for the promised collaboration with Reinhardt to materialize. The all-star adaptation of *Twelfth Night* was still being considered. A letter agreeing to this in principle, dated 21 October 1935, was sent to Reinhardt, and a copy still exists in the Warner Brothers files. By February 1936, however, the project was obviously still only tentative. Reinhardt returned to Europe, promising to return later in the year to resume discussions, provided that a production date could be agreed upon.

Korngold meanwhile was contracted to score one more film. The studio had just completed filming of *Anthony Adverse* from the best-selling novel by Hervey Allen. It was the most important production for 1936 and, with its epic qualities and prodigious length (running nearly two and a half hours), it was tailor-made for sumptuous musical scoring. Without question, Korngold was the ideal candidate, having demonstrated his abilities in handling historic subjects and, perhaps even more importantly, his tremendous facility in providing almost uninterrupted yet consistently interesting musical scoring to films of two hours and more.

Family party in Hollywood at the home of Jan Kiepura and his wife Marta Eggerth, December 1936. From left: George (seated), the famous bass Adamo Didur, Korngold, unidentified lady, Ernst, Luzi, Tilly Eggerth (Marta Eggerth's mother), and a shirtless Jan Kiepura (courtesy of Marta Eggerth).

The preview was scheduled for early May. Korngold commenced work on the new score on 14 February 1936, following a memo from Wallis to Leo Forbstein reminding him that Korngold "should not still be over at Paramount now that he is on salary at Warners."[16] Korngold was still involved in post-production work on *Give Us This Night* as late as 8 February. A screening of *Anthony Adverse* was arranged on 14 February to enable him to see the size and scope of the picture. As it turned out, this score would be the most complex and lengthy he ever undertook.

Anthony Adverse was another of Warner Brothers' big, prestige productions. It cost over one million dollars and had a shooting schedule of ten weeks. The cast was huge, and the sheer scope of the story demanded a larger-than-life approach. Although the novel covered the French Revolution, the Louisiana Purchase, and adventures in Cuba and Africa, only half of it reached the screen and every location was recreated on the Warner backlot. The story of an orphan boy and his struggles against the adversities of life (hence his name) strongly appealed to Korngold, and he composed an exceptionally fluent score.

The first twenty minutes of screen time are continuously underscored with an outpouring of leitmotifs. A fierce scherzo to accompany the wild carriage ride at the beginning of the story is particularly effective. The score contains countless themes for the many characters and episodes. Of all Korngold's works for the screen, this one most closely assumes the characteristics of an opera. The motif for Faith (the scheming housekeeper, played by Gale Sondergaard, who won the first ever Oscar for Best Supporting Actress in the role) is a striking, dissonant shudder of a theme perfectly evoking her personality, while the lovely, expansive Bonnyfeather theme (for Edmund Gwenn) is yet another distant relation to Korngold's beloved Motto of the Cheerful Heart from his Sinfonietta in B Major. Not surprisingly, it is one of the most memorable in the score.

Korngold was the only sensible choice for creating the score for this picture. The director Mervyn LeRoy, watching Korngold at work, recalled:

> He sat in the projection room with me, while we watched the rough cut of the film, and silently conducted in the dark, totally absorbed in himself. Later, he told me that he was always careful to take note of what pitch or register the actors were speaking in, and then he would score carefully so as not to interfere with it. I was amazed when he told me that. I realized that here was a real genius, because no one else I had ever met was concerned with matters of that sort. He wasn't interested in just turning out musical accompaniment . . . . He was intent on composing music of worth. I was proud to have met and worked with him.[17]

Korngold set to work composing in his usual manner—sitting alone in a projection room improvising freely at the piano until his music matched the reel of film unfolding on the screen. Somehow, each cue, each theme, and each section meshed into a musical whole that was strong enough to survive without the image. This score, along with all his other work for the screen, remains a superb piece of music that is also valid in the concert hall and the recording studio.

Another witness to Korngold's working methods was violinist George Berris, then a member of the Warner Brothers orchestra. He vividly recalled the excitement among the musicians during those early scoring sessions. Berris worked on *Captain Blood* and *Anthony Adverse* before departing for MGM in 1937. Reminiscing in 1975, he was visibly moved as he recalled events of forty years past:

> The Warner orchestra had really only developed with the arrival of Korngold because the music he wrote was really so much more difficult than the usual stuff we played, and it was scored for such a large orchestra. In about two years, the old Vitaphone Orchestra (which had really only been a glorified dance band) was replaced by what amounted to a full-scale symphony orchestra, second to none. Not many people realize or acknowledge Korngold's influence in this happening today, but it's true.
>
> Quite a few of the musicians were real cowboys, who were used to playing in joints, bars, night clubs and that sort, and they were mixing with professionals who had been hired by Forbstein—on Korngold's insistence. On *Anthony Adverse* there were close to sixty musicians on the stage. I remember when we came to one section, and Korngold stopped and explained that the theme was to specifically underscore a line of dialogue on the screen, and he illustrated it by singing the line to use with the words, which were "No Father, No Mother, No · Name," only he sang it "No Fazzer, No Muzzer, No Home," which

broke us all up. I recall, too, that the score was so long that he would often work very late, writing music for scenes to be scored in a few days' time, and the pressure on him was very great.

I remember too, that, because I freelanced at that time, I would go over to Goldwyn or Fox and work on scores by Alfred Newman and I realized that he was obviously very influenced by Korngold, so much of his music was similar especially in duel scenes or action scenes. But Korngold was the originator of the style . . . even though the other fellows would never admit it.[18]

The operatic sequences in the film were neither scored nor conducted by Korngold. Staged by Natale Carrossio, they had been shot in November 1935 before Korngold was actually under contract, while he was still at Paramount working on *Give Us This Night*. By the time Korngold was assigned to *Anthony Adverse*, work on the opera sequences was completed, and Korngold wanted to reshoot them. He was not happy with the choice of music. According to Korngold's son Ernst, Wallis vetoed the extra expense involved in reshooting them. Although the first of these, an excerpt from Monteverdi's *Orfeo*, was historically in keeping with the period of the film, the second, a fifth-rate pseudo-Verdian piece by Aldo Franchetti entitled "The Duchess of Ferrara," was totally inappropriate. The Warner Brothers files reveal that Franchetti was employed at the music department during this period for no specific purpose. This was his only screen assignment. Probably he was engaged in menial tasks and may have inveigled Forbstein into using some of his music, which was unperformed.[19] Olivia de Havilland remembered Franchetti as a friend of the head copyist.[20]

Although Korngold could not alter the opera sequences (typical of his genius for adapting existing music is the marvelous way he segues from the Franchetti aria into his own score), he did put his foot down concerning Angela's Song, which she sings to Anthony in a carriage during the early part of the film. Once again, it seems that a song had already been chosen, recorded, and filmed. Olivia de Havilland recalled that she had to mime to the popular Italian air *Guarda la stella*.

Because Angela's song had become a focal point in Korngold's score, he insisted that his own composition be substituted. As the scene could not be reshot with Frederic March and de Havilland (who had moved on to other films), an inserted shot of two extras in a cart photographed from the rear covers the scene while Angela sings the song on the soundtrack (dubbed by Carol Weiskopf, who had by this time established herself as a regular on the Warner Brothers stages).[21]

The immense scoring job was finally completed on 6 April 1936. The "sneak preview" was held on 8 May in Hollywood. Further adjustments were still being made up to 22 May (mostly at the request of the Hays Office) before it was finally given its premiere on 29 July 1936 at the Cathay Circle in Los Angeles.

Korngold stayed on for a month until the end of May, mostly to benefit his younger son George before the family's return to Vienna for the summer. Before his return, he managed to contribute uncredited sequences to two other Warner features of that year. The first, *Hearts Divided*, was a rather foolish and old-fashioned historical romance starring Marion Davies (noted more as the long-time mistress of William Randolph Hearst than for her acting skills) and the ubiquitous Dick Powell as Jerome Bonaparte.

Heinz Roemheld was assigned to score the film. He was a staff composer at Warner Brothers for much of this period and was friendly with Korngold. Why Korngold agreed to score this short cue (of just over two minutes in screen time) entitled "The Separation" is unclear, but the original piano score bears his name, and there is no doubt that the music is his. The story has an unusual corroboration in the person of Harry Warren, composer of many of the greatest popular songs of the period (including "Lullaby of Broadway," the Academy Award winner of 1936). He recalled meeting Korngold on the backlot, who immediately sang the first two bars of "My Kingdom for a Kiss," the theme song of *Hearts Divided* (by Warren), adding "Good!" before walking on.[22] Korngold uses these two bars as the starting point for the brief musical episode that he composed as a favor to Roemheld. In fact, Roemheld's score is largely based on Korngold's treatment, and one wonders whether Roemheld asked Korngold to score the short scene first to form the blueprint for his own score.

Following this, it so happened that some orchestral passages were needed for another major film, *The Green Pastures*, already in post-production and otherwise dependent on the brilliant arrangement of negro spirituals by Hall Johnson. The film, based on the Broadway stage success by Marc Connelly, was a notable experiment in that the entire cast was black, headed by Rex Ingram as "De Lawd." The film was set in a sort of negro heaven, and the concept could so easily have misfired and degenerated into bad taste (like, for example, the execrable "Goin' to hebben on a mule" number sung by Al Jolson, from the 1934 Warner musical *Wonder Bar*). *The Green Pastures* is rather quaint when viewed today. Korngold provided two short musical sequences, "The Creation" and "The Flood." The latter was later reused in a different orchestration for part of the sea battle in *The Sea Hawk*.

Hall Johnson, an erudite man, quickly became friends with Korngold, helped by the fact that he was fluent in German. Korngold was fairly fluent in English by this time but was never happy or comfortable with it: "In Englitsch I hef no lenguage, only an accent!" he was fond of saying.[23]

Korngold's attitude to the racist conventions of the time highlight his loyal and unprejudiced viewpoint. When he learned that neither Hall Johnson (who was a Doctor of Music) nor Rex Ingram (who played God), both black, were permitted to eat in the Green Room, the executive dining room, but had to be content with the cafeteria, he was both astonished and incensed. When invited to lunch by Wallis, he declined, calling over his shoulder, "I'm going down to the cafeteria to eat with God!" When offered payment for his work on the film, he refused, explaining to an incredulous

Henry Blanke that he had enjoyed doing it, and moreover he did not wish his name to appear on the credits in case it should divert attention away from Hall Johnson and his work. In Hollywood, then as now, it was unheard of for anyone to offer their services without payment. The story became almost legendary in studio circles for this reason.

Korngold by this time had settled into and thoroughly enjoyed the working routine of the music department at Warner Brothers, especially the camaraderie with the orchestra. He liked to feel that he was "one of ze boys," and he became very fond of the musicians. Hal Findlay, another key member of the orchestra in those days, remembered the unusual rapport between Korngold and his colleagues:

> Mr. Korngold on stage was something of a novelty to the musicians, for he never stood behind the conductor's desk. Rather he sat in a very sturdy chair, raised on platforms at least four feet higher than the seated musicians. His conducting was exemplary, yet here again there was a deviation from the norm. He conducted in phrases, and this was something the musicians enjoyed after becoming- accustomed to it.
>
> He would do the greater part of his composing at home, then bring his scores and play them on the piano against the various scenes in the projection room. Very often he would phone the picture editor, ask him to come over, then suggest a shortening or lengthening of a scene to match his music. This was quite unusual, believe me, especially since the picture had been approved in its cutting by the director and producer . . . but it will give you an idea of how highly Erich's talent was appreciated by all, and his desires respected. He was also a greatly loved individual.[24]

At the end of May, the Korngold's left America on the *S. S. Paris* and returned to Vienna. They shared the voyage home with Igor and Vera Stravinsky and Serge Koussevitsky. During the voyage, Luzi expressed an interest in a new form of dieting then in vogue in which the person dieting ate just one type of food each day. A little later, Stravinsky arrived at the door of the Korngold's stateroom with a large box. Handing it to Korngold, he said solemnly, "It's chocolate day Korngold!" Inside was a huge box of candy.[25]

CHAPTER EIGHTEEN

Escape from Hitler — Exile in Hollywood

Back in Vienna, Korngold resumed work on *Die Kathrin*. Publicity about his success in Hollywood had by now reached Austria, where the films were shown with German dubbing, and it was already known that a new opera was in preparation. Korngold justifiably felt confident that his star was again in the ascendant.

The Vienna State Opera had revived *Die tote Stadt* with Vera Schwarz on 6 May 1936. He had missed the performance by a few weeks. This was to be the very last performance of the work in Austria during his lifetime and in fact until the 1960s. A production scheduled for November 1936 that was to have starred Richard Tauber, Jarmila Novotná, and Hilde Konetzni was subsequently canceled for political reasons—the first time the spread of Nazi influence in the arts in Austria had touched Korngold directly.

As usual, the summer was spent at Schloss Höselberg, where a letter arrived in August from Henry Blanke concerning the proposed production of *Danton,* which finally seemed ready. In March, the famous American playwright Maxwell Anderson had been contracted to write the screenplay, but the result did not satisfy the studio, so between March and September S. N. Behrman, Gottfried Reinhardt (the producer's son), Sheridan Gibney, and several others had all worked on the script.

Casting and pre-production were scheduled to begin on Reinhardt's return from the Salzburg Festival. By 9 September 1936, Oliver Messel (another of Reinhardt's favorites, fresh from his success in designing MGM's *Romeo and Juliet*) was assigned to create the costumes. Michael Curtiz was to be Reinhardt's assistant. Paul Muni, Warner Brothers' leading actor, was the first choice to play Danton, and Olivia de Havilland was to portray Marianne. She tested for the role under Reinhardt's direction and has the reel of film to this day, but that is all that survives of this unrealized project.

For the score, Korngold was the only choice. Blanke urged him to return to Hollywood for the winter and to collaborate with Reinhardt in much the same way as he had before. In a general memo, dated 30 September 1936, Blanke wrote: "Wallis estimates picture will start in December, provided whole cast assembled. This is going to be a very important, very big, and very difficult picture to make."[1]

For several months, it seemed that the project would materialize. Anton Grot drew numerous sketches for the sets, and as soon as Reinhardt arrived in Hollywood on 28 September 1936, he began auditions and tests. Korngold was definitely attracted to the idea of working with Reinhardt again, especially as he would create an original score rather than an arrangement. On 4 October, he wrote the following letter to Blanke from Vienna:

Dear Heinz,

A thousand thanks for your frank letter. The critical acclaim for my score for *Anthony* has really been a great pleasure for me. Hopefully, we will be given equal praise next time. As far as my work is concerned, I'm quite pleased—I have orchestrated almost half of the opera. If nothing bad happens, we'll leave from Genoa on the 14th on the *Rex* (I hope without a sea-battle near Gibraltar) and arrive in New York on the 22nd. We will be in Hollywood on the 27th in the morning. I'm already trembling to know whether *Danton* will satisfy all the expectations. I wonder whether you will be able to start shooting before November 1st? I doubt it. Please give my best to Reinhardt, Wallis, Warner (*not* Dieterle).[2]

On arrival, Korngold was given a script for the film and at once began sketching ideas. One of these, a delightful waltz was later transformed into a march for *The Sea Hawk*. The extant file on this projected film ends in mid-November 1936, when the production ceased, never to be revived for reasons unclear. Reinhardt was a difficult man to please, however, and Wallis was probably reluctant to take a huge risk on what would have been an expensive production with an unsatisfactory script and problems with casting. (Paul Muni was one of the most temperamental actors in films and demanded script approval.)

Suddenly, Korngold found himself in Hollywood with a signed contract for two films but without a specific job. The studio placated Reinhardt and

Korngold by offering a steady stream of possibilities while merely "postponing" *Danton*. Among these was a life of Beethoven, also to star Paul Muni, which under Korngold's overall direction and adaptation of the music was to boast a stellar musical triumvirate of Otto Klemperer, Arnold Schoenberg, and Arturo Toscanini. (Just how these volatile musicians would have collaborated is a fascinating subject for speculation.) Reinhardt was also promised a screen version of *Everyman* (again with Korngold and Dieterle, starring Leslie Howard) and Offenbach's *Pariser Leben*. None of these projects came to anything.

To ensure that Korngold would honor his contract, Wallis and Blanke offered him a free choice of the various prestige productions then nearing completion. Korngold (still having difficulties with English) was attracted by a love story directed by Dieterle and starring Errol Flynn, Ian Hunter, and Kay Francis entitled *Another Dawn*. It was shot on the sets left over from *The Charge of the Light Brigade*, Flynn's second major film, and was really just above being a B-grade picture. An appallingly wordy script and the limited abilities of the stars to make its conventional "triangle" situation believable, made the finished film almost unsalvageable. Korngold, unaware of its shortcomings, gave it the full treatment, and the highly romantic score, replete with a rousing Mahlerian desert march and a memorable love theme, lifted the film above the commonplace.

The origin of the main title theme, which later became the first subject of the Violin Concerto in D Major, Opus 35, is fascinating to consider. Did he sketch this for an early version of the concerto, as mentioned in a newspaper interview in May 1937,[3] when he got back to Vienna? Julius Korngold, who did not speak any English and called this film "Anuzzi," always admired the theme and suggested it could be the basis for a Violin Concerto. But which came first? We shall never know.

Another Dawn has a duration of just 73 minutes (most of them underscored) and was the shortest film assignment Korngold ever undertook. It opened in June 1937 to poor reviews and quickly sank without trace. It is rarely shown today. The music Korngold composed is its only memorable feature.

Christmas 1936 was again spent in America. Korngold must have been heartened by the glowing tribute in the *Motion Picture Herald* for *Anthony Adverse*: "The interpretative musical accompaniment by Erich Wolfgang Korngold is an artistic and entertainment treat. One can close one's eyes, unmindful of other sounds, and hear a thrilling symphony."[4] This kind of critical recognition made Warner Brothers even more keen to keep Korngold under contract. A second film assignment was to be completed before he would be allowed to return to Vienna, and Warner Brothers offered him another large-scale historical subject. The lavish production of Mark Twain's *The Prince and the Pauper*, again starring Errol Flynn with two newcomers, Billy and Bobby Mauch, real-life identical twins, was to be one of the most popular films of the year. Wallis recalled in 1975: "By this time, Erich was the number one choice for films of that sort. . . . When I came to make *Anne of the Thousand Days* in 1968, I wished he had been around to do the score."[5]

Early in 1937 the rumor began that Korngold's score for *Anthony Adverse* might win the Oscar for Best Music in the forthcoming Academy Awards. Meanwhile, negotiations with Reinhardt continued. In late January, however, with nothing agreed upon, Reinhardt elected to stay in Salzburg, and Korngold reluctantly viewed *The Prince and the Pauper*. Enchanted with the story, he accepted the assignment and spent most of February and March scoring the long and occasionally slow-paced film.

The music he composed sparkled with wit and charm, with a rousing main title (its jubilant horn call later found its way into the Finale of the Violin Concerto in D Major) and delightful themes for the Mauch twins portraying the "prince and pauper" of Mark Twain's famous story. For a flirtatious scene in a Tudor inn between Flynn and a serving maid, Korngold composed music so intensely and delectably Viennese that he must have been already pining for home. The long end titles allowed him to provide a full development of this nostalgic theme, which resembles a particular phrase in Mahler's Symphony No. 7 in B Minor.[6] It is one of his most affecting melodies.

The most interesting part of this score is the musical setting for Edward VI's coronation, which formed the elaborate climax to the film. The studio was unusually keen to attain a degree of accuracy and authenticity in this sequence, and especially to capitalize on the impending coronation of King George VI in May. Great care was taken to reflect this in the music used. It was recognized that Handel's famous *Zadok the Priest* would be inappropriate, having been composed 180 years later than the period in which the film is set, and Korngold therefore created his own setting with the appropriate archaic harmony. He blended this with excerpts from contemporary psalters and music by Tallis to create a musical background as authentic as possible. The choral music and organ parts were recorded at St. Luke's Episcopal Church in Long Beach, California by its choir and organist. It is interesting to contrast this approach with the far more extravagant treatment by Korngold for the coronation scenes in *The Adventures of Robin Hood* the following year.

The Academy Award ceremony was held on 4 March at the plush Biltmore Hotel. At this time, the award for Best Musical Score was given to the head of the music department, rather than the individual composer, but Korngold was unaware of this. The nominations actually named each of the composers in question. For some reason, which was just as well, Korngold did not attend. As the audience awaited the result, the legendary conductor Leopold Stokowski (then in Hollywood to star opposite Deanna Durbin in the film *100 Men and a Girl*) walked up to the microphone and opened the envelope: "And the winner is, Mr. Leo Forbstein for *Anthony Adverse!*"

Korngold was incensed. He could hardly believe that Forbstein would deliberately take credit for writing the music. Later, news of his reaction reached Forbstein, who already felt uncomfortable about accepting the award, and he sent a conciliatory note to Korngold and published a message of congratulations in the *Hollywood Reporter*. Korngold was not appeased, however, and wrote a letter leaving Forbstein in no doubt as to the damage done, concluding with:

> My original score of *Anthony Adverse*, which contains more than forty original music pieces and which equals a symphony in volume and length, clearly and distinctly bore my name on separate screen credit and, together with four other scores, was nominated for the Academy Award since weeks [sic] . . . .
>
> I cannot believe that Mr. Stokowski, who presented the Academy Award for the score in *Anthony Adverse* and discreetly withheld the name of its composer, did not know that this awarded score was written by that composer whose works surely, he, too, conducted in America. . . .
>
> I am obliged to see a certain intention in the decision of the Academy to give the award to someone other than the composer of the score himself and I am not in a position to accept an award given officially and publicly to you by way of a private gift.[7]

Korngold was good as his word. He refused to take the statuette, even when it was explained to him, and it remained in Leo Forbstein's office for over ten years. After his death in 1949, it was finally returned to Korngold.

This extreme sensitivity was typical of Korngold, who could perceive a slight where none was intended. He was subject to flashes of temperament over trivial matters and could take things very personally, according to his sons. In this particular instance, this trait could have led to him severing his association with Warner Brothers and Hollywood completely, but he was also immensely forgiving and realized that the fault lay not with Forbstein, whom he liked very much, but with the Academy itself. As a result of this embarrassing incident, after 1937 the composer of the best score, not the head of department, would be named and given the Academy Award.

Korngold left Los Angeles at the beginning of May already aware that his next film assignment would be *The Adventures of Robin Hood* (he referred to it in the newspaper interview upon his return; see note 3), and he shared this information with his father. From various letters between them, it seems that Korngold and his father researched the Robin Hood legend in Vienna's public libraries so that work could begin on sketching themes for the main characters. Korngold was also anxious to resume work on *Die Kathrin*, which was scheduled for its premiere at the Vienna State Opera in the 1937–1938 season.

He planned to spend the summer at Schloss Höselberg finishing the orchestration and correcting the parts. As he was leaving, the studio also promised the long-awaited new project with Reinhardt for 1938: Volmoeller's epic drama *The Miracle*, which had been Reinhardt's speciality for almost thirty years. Warner Brothers intended it to be a prestige production starring Bette Davis (who actually did make some costume tests) and to be lavishly made in Technicolor. Enthusiastic, Korngold promised to return to work on both films once *Die Kathrin* was safely premiered.

The summer passed uneventfully, in spite of the deteriorating political situation in Europe. In October, Korngold began rehearsals with Desi Halban for the first performance of his song cycle *Unvergänglichkeit,* postponed since 1934, and the premiere took place in Vienna on the radio on 27 October 1937, in advance of the first public performance announced for 5 November. The radio concert was devoted entirely to Korngold's recent work. Korngold was pianist for the evening. He played two movements of his Piano Sonata No. 3 in C, and accompanied Desi Halban in *Unvergänglichkeit.* Finally, the String Quartet No. 2 in E-flat Major was performed by the Sedlak-Winter Quartet. It was his last premiere in Vienna before the outbreak of war. The review in the *Neues Wiener Tagblatt* was enthusiastic:

> Despite his many years absence from Vienna, Erich Wolfgang Korngold has remained true to himself. The songs are of great melodic power. . . . Among the "younger" composers (how time flies!) Korngold remains now, as then, the most musical and clearly profiled personality.[8]

At the public concert the following week in the Mozart-Saal, he shared the evening with Karl Alwin, who accompanied Desi Halban in Lieder by Mozart, Schubert, Brahms, and Strauss. Korngold's new Lieder cycle was the highlight, however.

Meanwhile, Jarmila Novotná, the fabulous Czech soprano, was the chosen lead for *Die Kathrin.* Korngold had been highly impressed by her in the 1931 Berlin production of *Die schöne Helena* and in the French production of Reinhardt's version of *Die Fledermaus* in 1934. The two had become close friends. By now, Korngold had begun lengthy pre-production meetings with Lothar Wallerstein and had already expressed the wish that his old friend and mentor Dr. Bruno Walter (then co-director at the Vienna State Opera) conduct his new work.

Walter visited Korngold at Schloss Höselberg and listened to him play the entire score on the piano (just as he had heard him play his one-act operas in 1915) and was completely won over. He agreed to conduct, and only the date remained to be fixed. The original lead tenor was to be Jan Kiepura, although Koloman von Pataky had also been approached. When the premiere date was fixed for late January 1938, however, Kiepura reluctantly withdrew. He had already signed a contract with the Metropolitan Opera in New York, and was due to sail for America on 29 January. The search for a new star tenor began. The role of François was crucial to the opera's success, and some of the most ravishing music in the score was his. Korngold had dedicated *Die Kathrin* to "The Vienna State Opera and Its

Artists." With his father now safely retired, this would be the first time that a Korngold opera would receive its premiere in his home city.

Christmas 1937 passed quietly. The possibility of Richard Tauber singing the part of François was now seriously discussed. Tauber, one of Korngold's closest friends and an ideal interpreter, had recently married an English actress (Diana Napier) and was living in London, although he was on his way back from a successful season at Carnegie Hall in New York at this time. He was scheduled to make a film in England, but had agreed to look at the score, and was certainly keen to be reunited with Jarmila Novotná with whom he had enjoyed a triumph in Vienna in Lehár's *Giuditta* four years previously. The date of the premiere was the only question, and this depended on Tauber finishing the film.

Fate stepped in. On 22 January 1938, the young pianist Robert Kohner, the star pupil from Professor Rebay's master class at the Vienna Conservatory, was participating in a concert to be given by Rebay's students and had decided to perform Korngold's Piano Sonata No. 3 in C. This work had scarcely been played since its premiere in 1932, and the Korngolds, who were invited guests, decided to attend. Luzi recalled the dramatic day in her memoirs:

> I was alone in the house when a telegram arrived: "Can you be in Hollywood in ten days time to write the music for *Robin Hood*?" I took the telegram with me to the concert. Erich was late; finally I saw him enter the room and take a seat at the back. I raised the telegram in my hand to show him but he didn't understand—we had to wait for the end of the concert when, in my agitated state, I could share the news.
>
> He looked at me astounded and said, "This is an omen." Then he rang the Director of the Staatsoper right there from the concert hall and told him of the Warner Brothers contract. . . . Dr. Eckmann said word for word on the telephone, "Professor Korngold, take this as an omen and go! I promise you a first-class premiere in October with Bruno Walter conducting and starring Jarmila Novotná and Richard Tauber, who will be free then. I'll make sure we write to you and confirm it."
>
> It was late in the evening. Erich looked at me with uncertainty and suggested we go to the Imperial Hotel to find out what ships there were in the next five days. If it wasn't one of the big liners, he would not travel in winter. The ship due to sail was the *Normandie*. On the spot, Erich reserved two cabins, because we would at least have to take Schurli [George] with us. We had only a day to pack our things, make arrangements for the house, and say our goodbyes to family and friends. We had to leave Ernst with my mother and sister so as not to interrupt his schooling. The last friend I spoke to on the telephone before leaving was Professor Knöpfelmacher, the children's doctor, and the first tragic news we received from Vienna after

Hitler's invasion concerned him: he had fled to a better world with an overdose of sleeping tablets.[9]

Later, the Korngolds learned that one of the first victims of the gas chambers was that brilliant young pianist, Robert Kohner. But for *Robin Hood,* Korngold and his family would have met the same fate, something he would frequently recall in the years that followed. A letter from Henry Blanke arrived the next day announcing that he had already ordered the script to be available in New York and outlining the characters. Blanke compared the love story between Robin Hood and Maid Marian to that in Captain Blood. On 23 January 1938 Korngold sent the following reply to Blanke: "Accept in principle hoping that one further picture possible. Take *Normandie* 29th to Hollywood February 7th. Cable if picture already cut and how many weeks available for scoring. Confirm contract."[10] Wallis replied in an overnight wire on the 23 January: "Satisfactory arrive Hollywood February 7th. Terms OK as wired Friday. Should score picture about four weeks as release date April. Wilk has script for you. Picture cut by 7th. Regards, Wallis."[11]

The die was cast. The dates of the wires indicate the speed with which the decision was taken. The Korngolds left by car for Le Havre on the 25 January 1938. The journey was a tortuous one. Icy roads and a blinding snowstorm made driving through the bitterly cold weather extremely hazardous. At every border, they were stopped and questioned or even sent back for some trivial documentation to be restamped.

Korngold spent the journey contemplating the film. At Le Havre, just before finally boarding the ship, a letter from Julius Korngold arrived containing the telling phrase, "Don't forget my idea to use *Sursum Corda* for the chief theme of the Captain of the Brigands!"[12] In fact, Korngold had already decided to take his father's advice (referred to in earlier letters) and wrote to Schott before he left Vienna asking permission to use portions of the earlier score. Willy Strecker sent a telegram to Le Havre granting Korngold permission.

This idea was a masterstroke and would save Korngold a great deal of time in composing the lengthy score if he accepted the contract. It was also absolutely perfect for the character of the film. This work, dedicated to Richard Strauss, was reminiscent of his tone poems in style. *Robin Hood,* like the heroes of Strauss's works, was ideally suited to the main leitmotif composed eighteen years earlier. As usual, Korngold was anxious about the project (perhaps more anxious than about the growing menace from Germany). He knew that as an Errol Flynn film, it was bound to contain a great many action sequences, and these were the most difficult to score.

The *Normandie* sailed for New York on 29 January 1938. Also on board, ironically, were Jan Kiepura with his wife Marta Eggerth, and Koloman von Pataky—the two original choices for *Die Kathrin.* As the Korngolds stood on deck with their little son wrapped up well against the January cold, they little realized that another eleven years would pass before they would set foot on European soil again. In the intervening years, they would lose their home, their possessions—everything, and their lives would be changed irrevocably.

During the difficult voyage through mountainous seas (apparently the worst crossing ever for this great liner), Korngold paced the decks humming to himself, composing in his head, and making notes, then improvising on the piano in his stateroom, adding to the sketches he had already made in Vienna for the principal themes of the main characters.

The ship arrived in New York on 3 February 1938, and the Korngolds left immediately for the West Coast on the *Santa Fe Chief*. Their adventures were far from over: the train collided with an automobile just before arriving in Pasadena on 7 February, where, much shaken but in reasonable spirits, they were met by Helene Thimig and Iphigenia Castiglioni (by now married to Russian actor Leonid Kinskey, who was to become a valued friend). Together they set off for Hollywood.

They went immediately to Max Reinhardt's home, who welcomed them with the news that he had already found them a house nearby. As Luzi noted, Reinhardt "loved to have his court in easy reach." In fact, they preferred to rent a house near Warner Brothers in the picturesque Toluca Lake district, which was a ten-minute walk from the studio.

The next day, they were driven to the screening of *Robin Hood*. Korngold watched with great attention and became increasingly worried as the fast-paced adventure film unfolded. Each time he looked at Luzi, he shook his head with concern. Back at the house, his desperation exploded. "I can't—I can't do it!" he shouted. Luzi, trying to calm him, said "Then don't." Finally, he left to see Hal Wallis with a carefully constructed letter of rejection, which survives in the Warner Brothers files:

Dear Mr. Wallis,

I am sincerely sorry to have to bother you once more. I do appreciate deeply your kindness and courtesy toward me, and I am aware of the fact that you have made all concessions possible to facilitate my work.

But please believe a desperate man who has to be true to himself and to you, a man who knows what he can do and what he cannot do. *Robin Hood* is no picture for me. I have no relation to it and, therefore, cannot produce any music for it. I am a musician of the heart, of passions and psychology; I am not a musical illustrator for a ninety percent action picture. Being a conscientious person, I cannot take the responsibility for a job which, as I already know, would leave me artistically completely dissatisfied and which, therefore, I would have to drop even after several weeks of work on it, and after several weeks of salary.

Therefore let me say "no" definitely, and let me say it today when no time has been lost for you as yet, since the work print will not be ready until tomorrow.

And please do not try to make me change my mind; my resolve is unshakeable. I implore you not to be angry with me and not to deprive me of your friendship. For it is I who suffers mentally and financially. I ask you to weigh the pictures for which I composed the music, such as *Midsummer Night's Dream*, *Captain Blood*, *Anthony Adverse*, *Prince and the Pauper*, against the one I could not make *Robin Hood*. And if during the next few weeks you should have a job for me to do, you need not cable all the way to Vienna.[13]

Wallis had little option but to accept, and Korngold, delighted at this painless outcome, returned home. The events of the days that followed are almost worthy of a film script in themselves. Luzi recalled:

It was the 12th of February—I got a call from Helene Thimig. I picked up the phone upstairs while Erich, curious as ever, lifted the receiver down below. "Luzi," said Helene with uncertainty, "it's all over. Schuschnigg [Chancellor of Austria] is in Berchtesgaden [meeting with Hitler]."

At that very moment the doorbell rang and Mr. Forbstein, head of music at Warner Brothers, entered the house with the words, "Korngold, you have to do it!" Erich tried to explain that he had already officially declined, and in writing. "That doesn't matter," said Forbstein with a dismissive gesture.

Under the crucifying influence of the news we had just received on the telephone, Erich began to reflect on the matter. Finally he promised Forbstein that he would at least try to write the music for *Robin Hood*. He didn't want a contract. His conditions were "work from week to week, paid from week to week." "If I find that it's not working out, I can give up with a clear conscience; the music I have written up until then will belong to you," he explained. . . .The following evening, he was already at work in the rehearsal room.[14]

Whatever Korngold privately felt about his obligations, an inter-office memo from Walter McEwen, Hal Wallis's executive assistant to the contracts department, dated 14 February 1938 was unequivocal about the result of these discussions: "Korngold is now definitely set to do the music on *Robin Hood*."[15] Korngold, feeling he was under no obligation, worked fluently and at speed.

Luzi, writing years later, was at a loss to explain why they took no steps to rescue their other son and family from the dangerous situation in Vienna. Naive, trusting, they clearly presumed that things would calm down. As she wryly remarked, "And of course we had a high opinion of our countrymen and would never have thought that what had happened in Germany could ever happen in 'our country.'"[16] When it was announced that elections were to be held in Austria on 10 March 1938, Luzi was innocently convinced that Austria would resist the grip of Hitler, but Korngold finally woke up to the reality of the crisis. He knew with terrible certainty what lay ahead. "He must invade! Don't you see? Hitler could never risk an election in Austria."[17]

Indeed, there was no election, and on 13 March Hitler marched in. The Korngolds immediately cabled Luzi's sister asking that Ernst be included on her passport. They received no reply. Transatlantic telephone calls had to be booked in advance in those days, and several anxious hours passed until they could speak to Vienna direct.

Julius Korngold, who had already included the boy on his passport, had in fact shrewdly procured a holiday visa to America some months earlier, having realized the danger long before the rest of his family. They were poised to leave within a few hours. The whole family (with the exception of Hanns, Erich's brother) left Vienna on the last unrestricted train and managed to cross the border into Switzerland on the very last day that this was possible. At Innsbruck, they were taken off the train by the police and allowed to reboard only at the last minute. While the days passed without word, the Korngolds discovered the true warmth and generosity of the American people. Practically everyone they had met in Hollywood wanted to help, and this support was to provide tremendous comfort to them.

Once he was assured that his family was safe, Korngold threw himself into completing the complex score for *The Adventures of Robin Hood*. One of the most written-about films of that era and a genuine classic of the genre, its wonderfully descriptive music undoubtedly contributes a major share of the film's romantic and hypnotic effect. Although Korngold used much of the earlier *Sursum Corda*, most of the score was newly composed for the film. The release date was moved to 12 May 1938, but even so Korngold had only seven weeks to write it, supervise the orchestration (by Hugo Friedhofer, Milan Roder, and Reginald Basset), and then record the finished score. His youngest son George recalled the agony of those weeks:

> My father was on the verge of stopping several times. I shall never forget his anguished protestations of "I just can't do it!" which I overheard in the middle of the night through my bedroom wall. He was suffering, and at the same time producing one of his finest scores.[18]

Filmed in Technicolor with a budget of almost $2 million, *The Adventures of Robin Hood* was one of the major productions of 1938 and one of the most prestigious of all Korngold's film projects. Michael Curtiz, who replaced the leisurely William Keighley as director early in production, distinguished the film with his unique mobile-camera style.

A series of tremendous set-pieces—the Banquet, the Attack on the Treasure Wagon, the Archery Tournament, the Execution and Escape, and the climactic Coronation, Battle, and Finale—underpinned the film and required exceptionally vivid musical accompaniment. Korngold rose magnificently to the occasion with a score that even today is regarded as one of the finest examples of music wedded to the moving image. Each character is clothed in a wonderfully apt theme, from the harsh tones for the villainous Guy of Guisbourne (superbly played by Basil Rathbone) to the melting phrases of Lady Marian's "Heartsong."

Robin's escape from Nottingham Castle early in the film was almost entirely underscored by the development section of *Sursum Corda,* and how well this concert music fitted the action on the screen is fascinating to observe. Korngold had the clout to influence the cutting of his films to fit his scoring, and this must certainly have been the case here.

In the forest sequence, where Robin and Marian begin their romance, Korngold composed a "flirtation" that prompted some members of the orchestra to dub the score "Robin Hood in the Vienna Woods." In this score, Korngold created one of the most thematically complex works ever written for the screen. It is even more remarkable given the duress under which it was composed.

The studio recognized that his score was extraordinary and a unique part of the film's success. In promoting the film, the studio took the unprecedented step of mounting a special radio broadcast of virtually the entire score with Korngold conducting the Warner Brothers Studio Orchestra and Basil Rathbone narrating the story. This took place on 11 May, the week before the film went on general release. Fortunately, this historic performance is preserved on records, for it was Warner Brothers' original intention to issue the recording commercially. Only eight sets were ever made, however (for Korngold and the chief executives at the studio), of which three are known to have survived.[19] The release was abandoned as being uncommercial.[20]

Korngold finished the lengthy recording sessions and post-production work on 14 April 1938. His family had finally arrived in Los Angeles (with the exception of his brother Hanns, who had traveled separately; it is not clear just when he arrived in America), and decisions had to be made about the future. The annexation of Austria clearly meant that there could be no return. Korngold's belongings, his home and property, and his life savings were all confiscated by the Nazis. Of greatest concern was the loss of his entire music library, which included the manuscripts of all his compositions and even his earliest childhood sketches. Among these priceless volumes was the autograph score of his as yet unperformed and unpublished opera *Die Kathrin.*

Korngold decided on a bold plan. He cabled the Josef Weinberger firm in Vienna, which was the publisher of his new opera (Schott was unable to publish Korngold's works by this time because of his "non-Aryan" status) and begged them to rescue his music. To their eternal credit, Weinberger sent two employees to Korngold's house in the Sternwartestrasse to break in during the night. The house was already occupied by German troops, and its contents were awaiting removal either for sale or destruction. Korngold's music was apparently already dumped in the cellar in piles, awaiting incineration. In spite of the risks, almost the entire library was saved, although some volumes had already perished (including half of the second Act of *Die Kathrin*, which fortunately had already been engraved).

Korngold's plan was for Weinberger to conceal his manuscripts in numbered crates of printed music destined for export to America, which would then be sent on to him in California, once they had been separated in New York. Page by page, the manuscripts were carefully placed in newly bound scores of Beethoven, Offenbach, and Johann Strauss. Months later, Korngold would carefully reassemble his music in Hollywood. Thus, it became possible for me to assist the Korngold family in indexing the collection for the Library of Congress in Washington, D.C., where it is now safely preserved for all time.

Though the music manuscripts were saved, it had always been assumed that Korngold's huge correspondence library (and that of his father) had been destroyed by the Nazis. Just before this book was completed, however, virtually the entire collection was discovered in the Austrian National Library. Just when these were deposited is not clear, but apart from the letters of greatest monetary value (from major figures such as Richard Strauss, Mahler, Puccini) the collection is intact. According to the family, Hanns Korngold was entrusted with a suitcase containing the most valuable items, which had been extracted by Julius. These never reached America, but occasionally they turn up for auction on the international market.

Once it became clear that a return to Vienna was impossible, Korngold realized that he must now make his home in Hollywood. In early June 1938, he bought a house in the same district, Toluca Lake, where they had been renting and which they had come to like. This comfortable suburb was built around a natural lake. In those days, before heavy traffic and smog, it was an idyllic place to live, with its uninterrupted view of the mountains and trees. The house was built in the old Spanish style on property that included two willow trees, an old pine tree, and a large plot of land to the side. It was also reasonably priced, and the district was popular with the film community. Nearby, Ann Sheridan had a mock-Tudor "farmhouse," and across the lake, the young Frank Sinatra later had a house. Roy Disney, Walt's brother, lived around the corner, and the "sarong girl" Dorothy Lamour lived almost opposite. Above all, it was just a ten-minute walk from Warner Brothers: for Korngold, the non-driver, it was perfect. Very soon, Korngold found a small house for both his and Luzi's parents, and gradually the entire family settled down to a new life.

For the first time in his life, Korngold had nowhere to go: the traveling, the conducting tours, the performances, the international meetings about new productions of his works, all came to a halt. It was as though he were marooned on a desert island. The ubiquitous palm trees and unremitting sunshine added to the illusion. His only source of income was his work for films. With his concert and operatic works effectively banned in Europe and royalties frozen, he could expect no revenue there; in America, his music was rarely performed. To make matters worse, he now had to support his entire family (together with several friends) from his earnings.

His parents arrived virtually penniless and his father was deeply unhappy in his adopted land. In his memoirs, he wrote of his bitterness:

> I had lost all I had acquired in a long working life—my sparse
> savings, my books, manuscripts, feuilletons, letters, and the material
> about Erich's career which I had carefully assembled for over thirty
> years. Edgar Allan Poe once said that melancholia was the strongest
> of all sentiments. How could I escape this feeling? Can one start a
> new life in old age? Only a new dying.
>
> [This new country] was like a fairy tale, as grotesque as it was
> poetic. The unreality of the people on the screen was matched by the
> unreality of the people around me. The only genuine thing was the
> indefatigable California sun. . . . everything seemed to be growing, but
> nothing had grown naturally, especially art and music. The press
> seemed aware only of composers of "hit tunes."[21]

Indeed, Julius Korngold never really adapted to his new life. He never
mastered the English language and remained within a closed circle of his
old friends and colleagues, all German-speaking, who had also managed to
escape Hitler. These included Franz Werfel and his wife Alma (Mahler's
widow), Leon and Marta Feuchtwanger, Thomas and Heinrich Mann,
Josef Reitler (his old colleague at the *Neue Freie Presse*), and Bruno Walter.

Bruno Walter's arrival in late 1938 sounded the death-knell for the
Vienna premiere of *Die Kathrin*, not that Korngold actually expected it to
proceed under the new regime. Weinberger had managed to secure a production in Sweden even before the annexation of Austria, and so the world
premiere was finally scheduled for October 1939. Incredibly, given the
international situation, Korngold planned to attend. On the reverse of
Weinberger's telegram confirming the premiere date, he actually listed the
available boats and sailing times from New York.

After moving into his new home at 9936 Toluca Lake Avenue, Korngold
took stock of his situation. From now on, his career in Hollywood was to
be his only likely means of support, and so he finally signed a contract with
the studio. This contract was the most generous and flexible ever granted to
a composer in this medium. Warner Brothers, in recognition of his special
gifts, met all of his demands. He would score not more than two films within any twelve-month period. He would be allowed to select his projects and
to reject those he deemed unsuitable. More remarkable still, the music he
composed would remain his property after the film was completed for use
as he saw fit.

Contrast this situation with that of his most famous colleague Max
Steiner, who composed the scores for eleven films during the following
year, including the four-hour epic *Gone With the Wind*. Korngold was
highly paid—$12,500 per assignment—in comparison to other composers
at that time, although it was a modest amount compared to what the stars
of his films were paid.

Korngold's comfortable lakeside home, 9936 Toluca Lake Avenue, North Hollywood, just ten minutes' walk from Warner Brothers, as it looked from the garden in the late 1930s (Korngold estate).

As the situation deteriorated in Europe, so the pleas for assistance increased from relatives and friends anxious to escape. Korngold lodged affidavits for them all until his guarantee of help was finally declined. Among his papers is a draft of a telegram to Richard Strauss begging him to intercede for his aunt, Lori Nossal, who was being sent to a concentration camp. Her beautiful house had been the setting for the card party in Strauss's opera *Intermezzo*. Strauss was unable to help her, and she died in a gas chamber.

Korngold grew increasingly pessimistic. He would sit by the radio and listen to the news, and then speak of his fears, not only for Europe but for the whole world. With nothing much to occupy him except the occasional meeting at the studio for his future film projects, he began to slip into periods of lethargy, brooding for hours at a time. His normal optimism deserted him.

His relationship with his father also deteriorated. Even though they lived only a short distance from each other, Julius wrote to his son on a weekly basis. These letters are often violently abusive and highly critical; collectively through the years, they provide a vivid picture of their volatile relationship. The theme of the correspondence never varied. Julius Korngold begged his son to give up composing for films, to find an agent for his major works in America, and to return to composing absolute music for the

American public. Korngold's response was that if anyone wanted to perform his work, they could contact him—he did not need an agent. He also saw no point in composing new works as long as the Nazis were in power. Luzi often said, "It was almost as if he had made a vow not to write any more until Hitler was defeated."

The secondary theme of these letters was money. The bitter old man felt his son should give far more of his earnings to his now impoverished father. From time to time, these unpleasant exchanges would explode into argument on the occasions when the two men met, resulting in long periods of neither speaking to the other. The situation never improved, and it cast a cloud over Julius Korngold's final years. Significantly, he does not refer to any of this in his memoirs, but the many surviving letters between father and son give a unique insight into what was undoubtedly the most important and influential relationship in Korngold's life. One cannot help but compare it to the equally turbulent relationship between Leopold and Wolfgang Mozart 150 years earlier.

Korngold declined requests to teach, and apart from some isolated concerts, he apparently was not offered any conducting posts in America. Only motion pictures offered him an income and the opportunity to work. *The Adventures of Robin Hood* had now opened across the country and was hailed as one of the best films of the year. The reviews praised its magnificent production values, and Korngold's score was singled out for special commendation. Korngold was invited to conduct some concerts in Oakland and San Francisco with the Bay Region Symphony Orchestra in late June.

He presented his *Schauspiel Ouvertüre*, the Suite from *Much Ado About Nothing,* and a concert suite of four movements from *Robin Hood.* As far as I can tell, this was the first time that a motion picture score was presented in this way, and the critical reaction was enthusiastic. A newspaper article described the scene:

> Jolly and informal in a beer jacket, Korngold was rehearsing the orchestra in the small auditorium at 960 Bush Street, criticizing in an almost incomprehensible mixture of English and German but making himself understood with staccato gestures and eloquent facial expressions. In as hearty and unrestrained a mood, he sat down to talk about Hollywood's lesser known side: "Warner Brothers gave me a piano for my studio, one for my home, and one to use on the lot," he said. "They gave me all the copyists I could possibly need. The only thing they neglected was a composer!" Korngold's favorite kind of fan mail is like the letter sent him by a man who had heard *Robin Hood* seventeen times. He had written down the themes running through the music. "And they were all right," said the composer.[22]

Interestingly, a newspaper article of the time concludes with the comment that his next assignment would be a film of *William Tell,* which was planned for James Cagney but was never made. In fact, Korngold had been promised that his next film would be *The Miracle*, now revived after three years of preparation, which would finally reunite him with Max Reinhardt. The original stage production had been a legendary success in 1912 with a score by Engelbert Humperdinck and starring the legendary Diana Cooper. A silent film of this had been made, and Warner Brothers had owned the property since 1932.

By 1934, Einar Nilson, Reinhardt's musical director for the original stage production, had been approached to compose the score. A memo dated 8 May 1934 indicates that Leo Forbstein had also been sent the original Humperdinck score to study. For some reason, the entire project was shelved until 9 March 1938, when Hal Wallis wrote to Henry Blanke announcing, "We are again thinking of putting *The Miracle* into work. See if Breen will object."[23] This last comment related to Joseph Breen, the chief film censor, and the controversial nature of the plot involving a young nun who gives up her vows and a statue of the Virgin Mary that comes to life.

For much of 1938, the script was revised. Discussions between Reinhardt and Karl Volmoeller (the author, who was still alive and had to be consulted on changes to his text) began in earnest. Ulrich Steindorff was assigned to write the screenplay, and on 15 September 1938 he wrote to Blanke relating that "in my discussions with Mr. Korngold, I suggested to build the story on musical ideas and to use the contrast of church and secular music for a basis. In this event, the lover of the Nun could be a young musician who seduces her by the power of worldly music."[24] Blanke's reply is not recorded. A letter from 7 October 1938 indicates that John Huston was now involved in the screenplay but that creating a realistic script was still a problem. Steindorff improbably suggests combining the story with Schiller's version of *Joan of Arc*.

The film was again placed on hold and at this point Korngold lost interest. Between 1939 and 1944 some of the greatest writers of the day worked on the script, including Franz Werfel, Stephen Vincent Benet, A. J. Cronin, Samson Raphaelson, Wolfgang Reinhardt, Aldous Huxley, and Christopher Isherwood. As late as May 1944, Michael Curtiz was assigned to direct. Finally, on 16 June 1944, Jack L. Warner sent a one-sentence memo to Wolfgang Reinhardt: "I want this to remain dormant for the time being."[25] The film was never made, although Henry Blanke did finally produce a screen version in 1958 starring Carroll Baker and Roger Moore, with a score by Elmer Bernstein.[26]

With the indefinite postponement of this film in 1938, Max Reinhardt's contract quietly lapsed, perhaps as the studio privately intended. With his European career effectively over, Reinhardt's influence and status were rapidly waning. Korngold, however, was becoming increasingly important to the studio. His score for *The Adventures of Robin Hood* was tipped to win the Academy Award for the Best Original Score of 1938.

Hal Wallis had already decided that the next two most important films to be made by the studio would be scored by Korngold. Both were lavishly produced historical subjects, ideally suited to Korngold's sweeping, romantic style. *Juarez* (originally entitled *The Phantom Crown*) was a biography of the Mexican peasant who led the revolution against the Habsburg dictatorship of Mexico in the 1860s; it had an all-star cast led by Paul Muni. *The Private Lives of Elizabeth and Essex*, a stunning historical Tudor pageant to be made in color and starring Bette Davis and Errol Flynn, was based on the successful play *Elizabeth the Queen* by Maxwell Anderson. *Juarez* was in preparation for more than a year before shooting began in November 1938, and Korngold had already spent the late summer researching the music of the period and sketching themes.

With the success of *Robin Hood*, Korngold was in demand at other studios as well. RKO entered into negotiations with him in November to score its lavish production of Rudyard Kipling's *Gunga Din*. For a while, Korngold considered accepting the commission. According to his son George, he sketched a theme for Gunga Din himself, which was not subsequently used anywhere else. Finally, however, he declined when the preview date was moved up, thus leaving very little time for composing the score. A deciding factor was the considerable distance he would have to travel to RKO Studios compared to Warner Brothers, just minutes from his front door, and the less congenial conditions under which he would have to work. At least at Paramount, he had been on cordial terms with Kiepura and Lubitsch from happier days in Europe; at RKO, he knew no one. In the end, Alfred Newman, a confessed admirer of Korngold, composed the score for *Gunga Din*.

Christmas 1938 saw the Korngold family united and safe from war-torn Europe. Korngold himself now began the painful process of adapting to a sedentary lifestyle and to his new country. Unlike many of his friends and former colleagues who also found themselves in Los Angeles, he was extraordinarily successful in this new milieu. The musical giants of Europe—Schoenberg, Stravinsky, Bartók, Hindemith—were barely able to establish themselves in their new homeland, or did so with difficulty. Yet Korngold was to find a new beginning—a new period of creativity in which he would write not only a series of major motion picture scores but also one of the last, significant romantic symphonies of the twentieth century.

CHAPTER NINETEEN

The Golden Age of Film Music

Juarez was a difficult subject, not the least for political reasons, and the production was beset with problems from the beginning.[1] The script by John Huston, Aeneas MacKenzie, and Wolfgang Reinhardt went through numerous rewrites to accommodate the dual sensibilities of the strict censorship code and the contemporary administration in Mexico. It was still being revised as late as January 1939, just a month before shooting was completed in early February.

The structure of the film was based in part on a 1926 play, *Juarez and Maximilian*, by Franz Werfel, and a 1934 book, *The Phantom Crown*, by Bertita Harding, a close friend of the film's director William Dieterle. The studio undertook an enormous amount of research, including a visit to Mexico in September 1938 by Dieterle, Henry Blanke, Hal Wallis, and Paul Muni to research the scene of the actual events. A budget of $1.75 million was set, the highest in the studio's history to date, and Anton Grot began creating the fifty-four sets for the production; the largest was an eleven-acre, miniature version of Mexico City on the Warner ranch at Calabasas.

Korngold composed one of his most idiomatic scores for this film, incorporating the accented rhythms of the Mexican style, as well as the necessary pomp for the court sequences featuring the Habsburgs, including a most effective grand march for the scene in which childless Maximilian and Carlotta (Brian Aherne and Bette Davis) adopt a young Mexican boy as crown prince. The love theme for the doomed couple, an ardent melody built on a rising seventh, may already have been sketched for the abandoned Violin Concerto in D Major. Certainly, it features strongly as the second subject of the first movement in the revised version of 1945, and it strikes just the right degree of poignancy here.

This was Korngold's first opportunity to compose for Davis, an actress whom he found particularly inspiring, especially in the next film he was to score, *The Private Lives of Elizabeth and Essex*. He often remarked that the sound of her voice, particularly her nervous inflections and rhythmic delivery, inspired his music. In the scene in which Carlotta kneels before a statue of the Madonna to pray for a child, Korngold's underscoring is operatic. A choir sings an *Ave Maria* as the camera pans in to Davis, whose words are inaudible. As she begins to speak in close-up, the orchestra follows the rhythm of her speech after each phrase before actually supporting the words, almost as though she had sung them. One wonders whether Korngold was actually present on the set to achieve this (as he was in *A Midsummer Night's Dream*), so closely knit are words and music.

Later, when Davis eventually slips into insanity, Korngold's music slips into eerie dissonance with a chain of consecutive minor seconds, reminiscent of the scene after Marietta's murder in the third act of *Die tote Stadt*. In the orchestration, he specified additional instruments (including castanets) to achieve the correct Mexican coloring, particularly in a seguidilla that is no longer in the finished film.

In a rare interview for *Film Guide*, Korngold revealed some surprising findings from his own research:

> In writing the score, I discovered that the music composed in Mexico during the period from 1864 to 1870 was not Mexican music at all! But unmistakably Viennese. Some of the castanets also tapped out the rhythms of Chopin and Schubert. The European influence was so strong at the time that the composers abandoned their native music. Fandangos and native polkas of the period are actually Strauss waltzes and marches. Only the instrumentation was changed. Instead of violins and cellos, the Mexican players undoubtedly used their native guitars and mandolins; thus the people of the country failed to note the really subtle change.[2]

He did use one very famous piece of source music in this score, the popular song *La Paloma* by de Yradier, which was reputedly Empress Carlotta's favorite melody. Korngold's use of this—and more importantly, his elaboration and adaptation of it—is one of the outstanding features of the score. In particular, the crucial addition of a rising scale in the whole orchestra that builds to an altered plagal cadence with a leading diminished seventh chord before resolving to the tonic D major of the song, is remarkably similar to a phrase in the Vorspiel to the opera *Violanta*. It becomes a *leitmotif* in the film to create tension, just as in the earlier opera. Korngold absorbs the melodic contours of this song so completely into his own style that one might almost believe that he actually composed it.

Korngold completed his score in late February and spent the whole of March marrying the music to the finished film. Its original length ran to some 150 minutes but was cut to 132 minutes. (According to Korngold's eldest son Ernst, who was present on set, much of Davis's mad scene was trimmed because of her excessive hamming). With such a major film, Warner Brothers decided on a "prestige" simultaneous premiere at the Hollywood Theater in New York and the Beverly Hills Theater in Hollywood on 25 April 1939.

The New York premiere was as much a political as a cinematic event. Diplomatic representatives from a dozen Latin American countries arrived aboard a special train from Washington, D. C. Korngold was asked to assemble a special concert overture from his score for the Hollywood premiere, and he conducted the studio orchestra in this eight-minute work before the film actually began—an indication of the studio's opinion of how importantly his music contributed to the finished picture. This was the first of several concert overtures he would be asked to prepare for the premieres of his films.

Reviews of *Juarez* were mixed. *The New York Times* stated that the film was unbalanced and "while Juarez is clearly the hero of history, Maximilian is the hero of the picture."[3] The political reception was even more complex. A separate Mexican version of the film was released (entitled *Carlotta, the Mad Empress*) with certain sequences deleted (and the final words of Juarez as he stands over Maximilian's coffin, "Forgive me," removed), but even so, it did not fare well. Disappointing box office returns caused its swift disappearance in the early 1940s.

In 1954, Warner Brothers reissued the film, heavily cut to 100 minutes—the version that is generally available today (although a print running 118 minutes is held by the BBC). Only one print of the original 132-minute film survives—and that on the highly unstable nitrate stock and kept at the Warner Brothers studio in Burbank, California—so an evaluation of Korngold's complete score for this film has not been possible.

With the collapse of any further film projects, Max Reinhardt was facing an uncertain future. As with Korngold, the artistic merry-go-round between Berlin, Vienna, London, and Salzburg was now over. His property, including the magnificent Schloss Leopoldskron, had been confiscated. Nonetheless, Reinhardt was not a man to sit and brood. In early 1938, he decided to establish the Max Reinhardt Studio for Stage, Film, and Radio (which became known as the Max Reinhardt Workshop, or "The Workshop") in the middle of Hollywood on Sunset Boulevard. It was created to mount innovative productions with the help of the huge influx of talented émigrés to assist in the schooling of young American actors, directors, and musicians.

Reinhardt threw himself into the project with enthusiasm and gathered around him as many of his former colleagues as possible. Leading the school were the writer and Goethe authority, Gert von Gontard, singer Nina Koshetz, cameraman Rudolph Mate, writers John Huston and Samson Raphaelson, actors Paul Muni and Basil Rathbone—and Korngold. In the prospectus, the philosophy was clearly stated:

> To Hollywood, a cosmopolis and climate uniquely adapted to a theatrical workshop, which can unite every dramatic form of expression, both spectacular and intimate, Max Reinhardt brings a rich heritage of traditions gleaned from the cultural centers of the world, sympathetically tempered with true understanding of present day requirements.[4]

In fact, most of these "names" seldom appeared. According to Luzi Korngold, most of the real work was carried out by Reinhardt, his wife Helene Thimig, and the "old staff" comprising the dancer Lisa Sokoloff, Iphigenia Castiglioni (who had scored a success in her youth as Shaw's Cleopatra in the Vienna Burgtheater), and Luzi herself, who deputized for her husband when he was busy at the studio.

Korngold genuinely enjoyed working at the Workshop. It was his only opportunity to recapture something of the theatrical world he had lost in Europe, and he worked with gusto in helping Reinhardt and his young students. Everyone worked without pay. Young hopefuls flocked to join the experimental theater school; among them were Robert Ryan and Nanette Fabray, both of whom later found fame in films. The first production was to be Reinhardt's adaptation of Goldoni's farce *Servant of Two Masters*, which became *At Your Service*, for which Korngold arranged and adapted themes by Rossini to complement the eighteenth-century setting of the play.

The premiere took place on 31 May 1939 at the Max Reinhardt Workshop, later transferring to the Assistance League Playhouse, where it ran until 5 June. Korngold and concert pianist Max Rabinowitz (another émigré, formerly an accompanist to Chaliapin) played the two pianos with a small ensemble. The production was mounted on a shoestring, and the cost of hiring the theater depleted most of the available budget. The premiere (in aid of the European Film Fund) was attended by many Hollywood celebrities, including Miriam Hopkins, Mrs. Ira Gershwin, Salka Viertel, and many former colleagues of Reinhardt who were newly arrived from Europe.

It was only a limited success. The American audience did not understand the delicate comedy or the balletic style of the piece, for the *commedia dell'arte* was unknown to most of them. The reviews were mixed. All praised Korngold's contribution while denigrating the play and inexperience of the actors. Philip K. Scheuer summed up the problem in the *Los Angeles Times*: "Performances were, to put it mildly, uninhibited, and the youthful actors supplied in ebullience what they lacked in finesse. The play must be regarded as a curiosity in the theater of today."[5] In spite of the lukewarm success, the production was revived in November 1939 at Occidental College in Pasadena, and again in January 1940 in San Francisco. Reinhardt was undaunted by failure. He continued with the Workshop, moving to larger premises where a small theater was at his disposal.

If Reinhardt was trying to create a useful existence in exile, Korngold's father found adjusting to life in Hollywood not so easy and felt increasingly isolated, thus placing an additional burden on Korngold, who, as well as supporting his aged parents, also supported Luzi's mother and younger sister. These genteel, gracious women were never able to adapt to American life, and they certainly were unable to earn a living. They spent their days trying to cope with simple domestic chores (like changing the bedlinen) or working on tapestry, which Korngold, under the pretense of having found a rich American buyer, would purchase from them for large sums to ensure they had an income.

In 1939, his brother Hanns finally arrived in Los Angeles, having made a detour to Monte Carlo *en route*. Korngold settled a small allowance on his troublesome brother (by now married for the third time) and told him to earn his own living.

His father was not satisfied with these arrangements and—incredibly, given that Erich Korngold was now 42 years of age—wanted greater control over his son's finances. The elder Korngold began a long series of highly critical letters beseeching his son to make a new will to provide for his parents and to increase his financial support for his brother. The composer's estate is full of this acrimonious correspondence. It is all the more astounding in that it dates from a period in which Korngold's father still attended the scoring sessions at Warner Brothers and for the most part remained on speaking terms with his son.

During the intensive period of composing the score for *Juarez*, Korngold received a twenty-page assault that repeated the usual demands and accused Luzi of trying to turn his son against him. Korngold's reply was eloquent:

> Dear Papa,
>
> If you do not wish to see my respect for you as a father and as a human being battered to pieces, if, furthermore, you have any desire for me to perform the labor which for fourteen hours a day for the next six weeks will require the utmost concentration, a head free from distractions, and more or less calm nerves without being paralyzed and broken by tumultuous agitation, then let me beseech you one last time: curb your unholy demons, and silence—in utterances to me, at least—the ugly, nocturnal abortions of your fantasies. After three more or less peaceful weeks, your renewed, insane suspicions, which are of the basest sort, insult my wife and me in a manner which it will not be possible to remedy and which fill us with shame for you.[6]

Across the bottom of this letter, Julius Korngold wrote: "Incredible accusations by an ungrateful child, alienated by prolonged baiting. J K" (The "baiting" refers to Luzi.) Why did he write this and for whom?—a future biographer?

Ten days after this exchange of letters, Korngold won the Academy Award for Best Original Score of 1938 (for *Robin Hood*) at the Academy Award banquet held at the Biltmore Hotel, one of the most memorable evenings in the Academy's history. The proceedings began with Miliza Korjus (who had starred in MGM's lavish film version of *The Great Waltz,* which did not use Korngold's adaptation) singing "The Star-Spangled Banner." The occasion was especially star-studded. Walt Disney received seven little "Oscars" from the equally small hands of Shirley Temple in recognition of *Snow White and the Seven Dwarfs.* Bob Hope was master of ceremonies for the first time, a role he would undertake on many future occasions.

Korngold wins the Oscar for Best Original Score of 1938 for *The Adventures of Robin Hood,* 24 February 1939. Standing to Korngold's left is Jerome Kern, who presented the award and whom Korngold much admired (Korngold estate).

The Award for Best Original Score was presented to Korngold by Jerome Kern, one of the few American composers he admired. This happy occasion made up for the previous disappointment over his award for *Anthony Adverse* and was something of a consolation for the interruption of his European career. It also gave him encouragement that his work for the screen was of genuine value.

In this frame of mind—encouraged by his peers, disparaged by his father—Korngold began work in late June on *The Private Lives of Elizabeth and Essex,* which was the most important film of the year for Warner Brothers.

Bette Davis had wanted Laurence Olivier to play Essex, but Jack Warner (his eye firmly on the box office) insisted on Errol Flynn. Anton Grot designed some impressive sets, and Orry-Kelly created the stunning costumes. A marvelous supporting cast included Henry Daniell at his icy best as Robert Cecil, Donald Crisp as Sir Francis Bacon, a young Vincent Price as Sir Walter Raleigh, Olivia de Havilland in the small role of Lady Penelope Grey (for marquee value; her name paired with Flynn's would guarantee that their legion of fans would flock to see it in expectation of a further on-screen romance; in the film they share only one brief scene), and young Nanette Fabray fresh from the Reinhardt Workshop for her film debut.

The entire film was to be made in color, and director Michael Curtiz used the medium with a flair that was based on his knowledge of black and white film. In fact, he directs the film as though it were in black and white, using shadow and lighting in his usual expressionistic manner.

Though the portions of Maxwell Anderson's play (written in blank verse) that remained in the final screenplay were at odds with the remainder of the script, in general the film emerged as a lavish, improbable, colorful history book that was hugely entertaining. Sweeping it along is one of Korngold's most resplendent scores, embellished with heroic fanfares and some of his most expressive melodic writing.

The opening titles are superb, accompanied by a full, rich statement of Elizabeth's theme, the only time it is heard complete. This title music is conceived exactly like an overture, or operatic prelude, and eight bars of it are lifted entirely from the *Kaiserin Zita-Hymne* written twenty-three years earlier. No doubt when considering his music for an English queen, Korngold recalled the music he had written for an Austrian queen in his youth. No other explanation for this unexpected interpolation seems likely.

The title segues (complete with cannon fire) to the triumphal march of Essex through the streets of London. Then the camera cuts to Elizabeth dressing behind a screen and we hear a poignant theme to symbolize her doomed love for the younger man, although we only see Davis and Donald Crisp in silhouette. The climax of the march blends into the heraldic Elizabeth's theme once more. The music only stops when we finally see Elizabeth as Flynn kneels before her, the camera traveling from her footstool up her body to the chalk-white face above: "Do you kneel in homage, my Lord Essex, or in shame?"

This long opening sequence is magnificent, virtuosic film making, thrillingly scored throughout and directed with rare skill. The expectancy and excitement created are not sustained, however. Flynn's inept reply, delivered so weakly, "Shame, your Majesty?" completely shatters the mood. Nevertheless, the remainder of the film contains many fine moments. A superb mini–horn concerto accompanies Essex's hawking party, while the scene in which Elizabeth smashes her mirrors is riveting.

De Havilland (whose fictitious character is secretly in love with Essex and jealous of the Queen) sings a duet with Fabray of Marlowe's "Come

Live with Me and Be My Love," with answering couplets supposedly by Walter Raleigh that poke fun at an aging lover. Korngold used a song he had already written for the Max Reinhardt Workshop but to a text by Shakespeare ("O Mistress Mine" from *Twelfth Night,* later published as part of the Opus 29 *Narrenlieder).* It is deliberately couched in a simple style, not exactly Elizabethan but not incongruous either. Korngold actually plays the spinet on the soundtrack—except that it is not a spinet but a "thumbtack" piano (thumbtacks are driven into the soundboard where the hammers strike the strings), the sound of which is usually associated with honky-tonk bars. A real spinet would not have recorded properly, but the thumbtack piano achieved the brittle, metallic effect.

The jibes at Elizabeth's age prove too much and she erupts. Nobody could erupt like Bette Davis, and her display of temperament as she hurls candlesticks and goblets at every mirror in sight is equally matched by Korngold's scoring.

Later in the film, after Davis has had Flynn arrested, she turns and, accompanied by great swirls of harp and string glissandi, walks back to her throne (in shadow) and slowly sits down, alone once more as thunder and lightening flash outside. This is superb cinema and shows what this film might have been with a more distinguished screenplay and a great actor to match Davis.

The Irish sequence, though unconvincing on screen (the echoes of the sound stage detract from any sense of realism), also contains some highly complex scoring, complete with a trumpet obbligato (for an on-screen trumpeter) that is in a different key than the rest of the music. Is this the first truly bitonal music cue in a film? It seems to have been added to the score at the recording sessions, as the instrumental part is now missing.[7]

A great musician joined the Warner orchestra in 1939 and worked with Korngold for the first time on *The Private Lives of Elizabeth and Essex*: Eleanor Aller Slatkin, daughter of Victor Aller and wife of Felix Slatkin (later of the superb Hollywood Quartet) became principal cellist. She had vivid memories of these sessions:

I had come from a very strict classical training, and when the position became available at Warner Brothers, I jumped at it. The studios in those days were a magical place for musicians. No one thought that it was slumming when Jascha Heifetz was down the street at Goldwyn making a film, or Stokowski and Stravinsky were over at Disney making *Fantasia!*

I knew Korngold by reputation, and was excited that my first assignment was to be *Elizabeth and Essex.* When I opened the score, it was just black with notes—a tremendous instrumentation. I thought to myself, I can't possibly play it, it's an effect that he wants. Well, the sessions were pure joy, unforgettable hours of music making. Korngold was not a conventional conductor by any means, and sometimes it was hard to follow his beat. In fact, he didn't conduct the orchestra, he *hypnotized* them. I recall that he always had his father present at the sessions. I never met him, but I observed; when he walked in the room, the air of Vienna walked in with him. And you know, after each take, Korngold would look round to his father, to get a nod of approval—as all children do with their parents.[8]

The soundtrack recordings of Korngold conducting his scores are a valuable record of the performance tradition of his work and of his own interpretation. In spite of his untraditional approach, no one conducted his music as magnificently as he did. Fortunately, these performances have been preserved for posterity.[9]

Korngold gave a rare interview to Bruno David Ussher for the *Hollywood Spectator* about *The Private Lives of Elizabeth and Essex*. The writer was unusually percipient in estimating Korngold's contribution to the film:

When I asked Korngold why he had not used traditional Tudor music or imitated it, he gave me a good explanation. "The loves and hates of Elizabeth and Essex, the ideas expressed by the playwright generally, while taken from history are symbolical. It is a play of eternally true principles and motives of love and ambition, as recurrent today as three hundred years ago. The characters speak the English spoken today. Why then should the composer use 'thou' and 'thee' and 'thine' if the dialogue does not?"

Sometimes it seemed to me as if Korngold had written music, not according to what he read in the script . . . but on what he heard in the marvelously articulate inflections of Bette Davis' voice, or what he perceived in the motions of her hands, in the wonderfully mobile and again passive, subtly guarded mimicry of her features. "We have changed," the Queen reflects to Essex, and the harmony changes minutely (F-sharp major to G major according to Korngold).

Elizabeth's self-killing, regally stubborn and murderous determination is drilled through her very heart fiber by the terrific drum crescendo, the end of which brings the curtain down on everything. Korngold told me he wrote this finale first of all.

All in all, Korngold has written eight film scores. This one, running 65 minutes, almost as long as *Salome* by Strauss, strikes me as singular.[10]

The Private Lives of Elizabeth and Essex premiered on 27 September 1939 at the Beverly Hills Theater. Once again Korngold compiled a short overture to be performed by the Warner Brothers Studio Orchestra before the film began. He conducted on stage before the screen was lowered for the film. *The Private Lives of Elizabeth and Essex* was successful but not the "smash hit" that the studio had hoped. Korngold's score, however, was acclaimed and nominated for an Academy Award. (It lost, inexplicably, to *Stage Coach* and *The Wizard of Oz*.)

By now, the Korngolds had settled down to the Hollywood life. So many old friends from Europe now lived in Los Angeles that the promise of a "New Weimar" that Thomas Mann once predicted almost seemed real. But the flood of artists and intellectuals was not to flourish in the California soil.

Richard Neutra, the architect who had been so impressed by Korngold's piano playing in Vienna, had arrived in Los Angeles in the late 1920s, and was more acclimatized than most. He had created some of the most distinctive houses in the area. His widow Dione still lived in the magnificent all-glass house that her husband designed in the mid-1930s on Silverlake Boulevard when I met her in 1981. Her shrewd perspective on the "émigré situation" gives a unique insight into how this amazing group of people coped in their new habitat and of the great opportunity that was lost at the time:

The first thing to be understood is that cultural life in Los Angeles was still fairly limited at that time, in spite of—or maybe even because of—the motion picture industry. Of course there was the Los Angeles Philharmonic and Klemperer, but there was no established operatic or instrumental concert life, and the same was true of theater. Everyone went to the films and that was that.

For us, and our friends, this meant almost intellectual starvation. Is it any wonder then that we turned to each other for stimulus and support? I know that Korngold—and especially his father, the old critic—found it very difficult in the beginning to get used to this environment. We all shared a common fate; we were expatriates with no homeland anymore. We clung together, for that gave us security and a feeling of continuity. At that time, there was concentrated within a few square miles, the greatest community of artistic talent ever assembled in one place.

And yet, we were largely ignored by the Americans who did not know who we were, still less what we stood for. Great actors like Albert Basserman were reduced to playing supporting roles in films, which kept them from starving. But it was harder still for writers and musicians, who did not understand the American way. Looking back, we clearly retreated into our own little world, expecting everything to return to normal once the war was over. How naïve we were.[11]

An amusing example of American naïveté occurred at a party given by Ira Gershwin, attended by Oscar Levant, Salka Viertel, Basil Rathbone and his wife Ouida, and Schoenberg, among others. The famous and somewhat garrulous society hostess Elsa Maxwell, noticing that Schoenberg seemed to be rather aloof, and anxious to involve him in the entertainment, enquired of Levant who he was and what he did. On being told that he was a musician, she marched over and took him by the arm, led him to the piano and cooed, "Come along Arnold, give us a tune." This would have held no terrors for Korngold, who was always the star of any party, if a piano was available.[12]

Although Korngold may have found his new life difficult in the beginning, he did make a niche for himself in the Hollywood community and, with his loveable personality and sparkling wit, made many new friends. Among these was Edward G. Robinson, who off-screen was nothing like his "Little Caesar" screen characterization. He spoke eight languages fluently and was a connoisseur of painting and literature. Akim Tamiroff, the Russian character actor was another, and S. Z. "Cuddles" Sakall, of the chubby cheeks and astonished expression, became a confidante and "chocolate partner," especially when Korngold discovered that he employed a magnificent Viennese cook. Paul Henreid was close, as was Paul Muni. Muni's brother Joe Weisenfreud (Muni's real last name), ran a fashionable cocktail bar in Hollywood where many of the émigrés congregated. Korngold was understandably a regular.

More surprising was Korngold's friendship with the Chinese cinematographer James Wong Howe, given that neither spoke English terribly well. Ernst Korngold remembers that "Jimmy Wong Howe ran his own Chinese restaurant at this time and my father often went. He liked the taste of Chinese food because, as he put it, it was so close to Viennese!"[13]

Other composers were always good company for Korngold. He knew and respected Franz Waxman, enjoyed a friendly rivalry with Max Steiner, and was on cordial speaking terms with Miklos Rósza, who wrote in his memoirs that when he first came to Hollywood, Korngold was the only composer he respected.[14]

Bronislaw Kaper was another friend. This Polish émigré had arrived in 1935. The very first music he composed was the popular, very American song "San Francisco" (for the famous film of the same name starring Clark Gable and Jeanette McDonald). Working mostly at MGM (he composed the lovely waltz in *Waterloo Bridge* without screen credit), he often socialized with Korngold. He recalled one memorable encounter, a choice example of how Korngold's wit crossed the language barrier with ease:

> Sigmund Romberg threw a party at his beautiful hilltop home, in the fall of 1939 and I was invited. Siggy asked me to bring Korngold along (whom he admired) as he wanted to get Erich to play the piano.
>
> Well, to understand the point of this story, it's important to realize that Romberg was renowned for his "borrowings" from other composers. The most famous example is the Serenade from *The Student Prince*, which is a steal of Massenet's Meditation from *Thaïs*.
>
> Anyway, we get to the party, and it's all terribly smart but slightly dull. A young, very inexperienced composer was with us who today is very famous indeed—I'll spare his blushes by not revealing his name—and at one point, Romberg asks us if we'd like to see around the house. So Korngold, myself, and this young man set off with

Romberg, and when we reach the library, the young composer is awe-struck at the walls lined from floor to ceiling with bound scores in fabulous tooled leather volumes. Romberg goes to answer the telephone and the young guy says out loud, "My god, is all this music his?" Quick as a flash Korngold says, "Not *yet!*" He was one of the wittiest men I have ever known.[15]

Schoenberg was another unlikely friend in Hollywood. Although the two had known each other in Europe, Korngold's father had prevented any possibility of a close relationship. Now united by the incongruity of their situation, the two men became friends, helped initially by the closeness of Schoenberg's wife (Trude Kolisch) and Luzi, who had known each other since childhood. Trude's sister Mitzi had, of course, been one of Korngold's first girlfriends. To complete the cozy domestic situation, Schoenberg's little daughter Nuria became the inseparable friend of Korngold's youngest son Georg (now called George in America). Ernst Korngold recalled his father's relationship to Schoenberg well:

My father was always glad to see Schoenberg because, although he didn't agree with his principles, he enjoyed the stimulus of discussion and respected him. I remember once when Schoenberg, my father, and Otto Klemperer were all in deep conversation about serial music. My father would not accept Schoenberg's theory that if you wrote a series of notes and then reversed the series, the theme remained the same. Finally, Schoenberg took out a pencil and held it up and said, "Erich, what is this in my hand?" and my father said, "It's obvious, it's a pencil." Schoenberg turned it upside down with the eraser at the bottom and said, "Now what is it?" and my father replied, "It's still a pencil—but now you can't write with it !" With that, Schoenberg gave up. I remember another occasion Schoenberg saying to my father, "Erich, do you like *any* of my music?" and being astonished when my father went over to the piano and played the little piano pieces—you know, from around 1910—from memory. I doubt if he'd seen the music for thirty years, and I don't think Schoenberg could have played them.
  Another time, Schoenberg came by to see my father and I was in the garden. My father was at the studio, so Schoenberg sat at the piano to wait, and began to doodle on a piece of music paper. After about twenty minutes, he stood up and said he couldn't wait any longer, and handing me the paper said, "This is for you." I showed it to my father, who looked at it and grunted. It was actually a double canon which could be played no matter which end of the page you started from. I wish I could find it today.[16]

Schoenberg also encountered Korngold's father for the first time in Hollywood and tried hard to persuade his former adversary of the validity of his beliefs—to no avail. Julius devotes many pages in his memoirs to the excesses of the moderns, and Schoenberg is not spared. While admiring him as a teacher, the critic could not accept him as a composer. Julius's attitude seems to have mellowed in Hollywood. It was inevitable that their paths would cross in such a limited circle of émigrés and expatriates. Dr. Korngold wrote:

> In Europe I never exchanged a single word with Schoenberg: we avoided each other. It was different with my son; the Pope of the Atonal Church showed benevolent tolerance for Erich, even though Erich did not pray at those altars. But then in Hollywood, the scene of dream-like adventures, I found myself one day in Schoenberg's beautiful country home. He displayed respect and indulgence, and the critic guarded his words so that old frictions could be forgotten. Schoenberg behaved more like a bourgeois husband and tender father than a musical revolutionary.
>
> He could be very amiable; when he played a recording which explained his theories, he did so in the most tactful manner. He admitted to slow progress with his opera *Moses und Aron*; his asthma and his teaching schedule hindered his work on a major project. . . . [T]he innovator Schoenberg did not appear to me like someone who had lost the inner longing for the effects and beauty of the old style. He seemed to have grown tolerant, very tolerant, and tolerance is not one of the characteristics of a real revolutionary.[17]

In October 1944, Schoenberg wrote a letter of thanks to Julius Korngold for birthday greetings received (Schoenberg turned 70 that September) and urged a final reconciliation on musical principles. He wrote:

> Honored Dr. Korngold,
>
> Many sincere thanks for your so kind letter. In truth, you eighty, I seventy, and both of us still young enough to engage in music theory polemics! I won't have it taken from me: I *must* try to convince you. It is unfortunate that I didn't try this twenty years ago when we were both younger. Unfortunately, the atmosphere between critic and composer—through fault of certain elements—was always bitter. If I can try again, I'll do it better.[18]

The reconciliation was not achieved, however, and Julius Korngold died the following September. Schoenberg wrote a touching letter of condolence to Korngold, unusually (given that they always conversed in German) in English, saying in part:

> I had the opportunity unfortunately only late in our lives—of having contact with your father and I must say that I regret it has not happened earlier. A man like he, whos [sic] knowledge and judgment

of music was based on a profound love for this art, such a man should have lived earlier and longer in this country.[19]

By late 1939, the Hollywood community had grown to include almost every major European figure in art and literature. The Los Angeles telephone directory for that year provides amazing reading. Among the many who had escaped Europe were Alma Mahler and her third husband, the novelist, playwright, and poet Franz Werfel, and their home became a meeting point for the émigrés. They became very close to the Korngolds. Luzi recalled this special friendship in her book:

> The best of times were when there were just the four of us together— Werfel, Alma, Erich, and I. After dinner we made music. Spurred on by Alma's enchantedness, Erich played either something from his own works or from one of Verdi's operas, which Werfel so loved . . . . Werfel had something of the bohemian about him, even though Alma took great care that he was always carefully dressed.
>
> In this respect, Werfel resembled Erich with whom I had to fight all my life about his personal appearance which he did not value at all. This . . . was all the more astonishing as he was a perfectionist . . . in every other respect. He would never go to an orchestral rehearsal without first convincing himself that the orchestral parts were entirely without mistakes, even if it cost him an entire night's rest . . . . On the other hand, I had to rush out after him into the street sometimes to prevent him from wearing a soiled garment in which he intended to face the world!
>
> Only for his public appearances did he show even a fleeting interest in his clothing. He also had the unusual peculiarity of having his hair cut just prior to an opening performance, so that only short bristles covered his head . . . . It may be that subconsciously, he was protesting against the typical lion's mane of an artist.[20]

The announcement in September that Britain had declared war on Germany finally closed the door on any possibility of an early return to Europe. It also made plans to attend the world premiere of *Die Kathrin*, which took place in Stockholm on 7 October 1939, out of the question. By all accounts, it was a successful novelty with the public, but the reviews of the opera were uniformly bad. In one, a nascent anti-Semitism was revealed:

> The emigrant Jew Korngold's disgusting opera *Kathrin* is performed while Swedish composers are forced to have their works performed abroad. . . . the libretto is a typically Jewish mishmash . . . a typical example of what Jewish cultural Bolshevism can achieve. And this Jewish filth is allowed to desecrate our foremost national stage![21]

The world premiere of *Die Kathrin* in Stockholm, 7 October 1939. Act II, the nightclub scene: Gertrude Palson-Wettergren as Monique (on stage, right) sings her cabaret song. This was the last music by Korngold to be performed in Europe before World War II (courtesy of Archives of the Royal Opera House, Stockholm).

After only seven performances, *Die Kathrin* disappeared. News of this failure probably reached Korngold at the same time he heard of the death of his close friend Julius Bittner, who had finally succumbed to the thrombosis which had left him crippled in a wheelchair.

He had little time to be depressed, however. The next film assignment was already demanding his attention: *The Sea Hawk*, a lavish historical swashbuckler, again set in Elizabethan England and starring Errol Flynn, scheduled to begin filming in February 1940 (although it had been planned since 1936 as a follow-up to *Captain Blood*).

Warner Brothers delayed production until a new "maritime sound stage" was built. Stage 21 (at that time, the largest and most modern in the world) was capable of being filled with water. On it two complete sailing ships were built: a full-scale British man-of-war and a Spanish galleass. A huge painted cyclorama was erected to serve as both sea and sky. To complete the illusion, Anton Grot developed a unique ripple machine to create the illusion of moving sea water. This meant that the usual unrealistic "back projections" could be dispensed with, and Grot was given a special Academy Award for his work. A special launch party with most of the studio's stars and supporting players opened the new stage in February 1940, including "Admiral" Errol Flynn as master of ceremonies.

Korngold with his two great colleagues at Warner Brothers, Max Steiner (center) and Leo Forbstein, 13 October 1939, the only extant photograph of them together. Korngold's concentration has already wandered, probably to a new musical idea (courtesy of Ted Krise).

The Sea Hawk would be the last swashbuckler to be scored by Korngold—and the best. Even though it was filmed in black and white, the final cost was close to $2 million, and the high production values show in every frame. Many of the palace sets from *The Private Lives of Elizabeth and Essex* were reused, and, incredibly, all of the many exterior locations were created on the studio backlot. The elaborate shooting schedule of some sixty-seven days (unusually long for that time) produced a finished film of two hours and seven minutes, 96 minutes of which is underscored by Korngold in what many consider to be his finest film score.

The film was wonderfully cast, with the exception of its leading lady, the disappointing and lackluster Brenda Marshall. Flynn's usual co-star Olivia de Havilland was announced for the part of Dona Maria, daughter of the Spanish Ambassador (another superb performance by Claude Rains), but she refused. Having been promised better parts after her success in *Gone with the Wind*, she chose to go on suspension rather than be in yet another Flynn epic.[22]

The film finished shooting on 18 April, and was turned over to George Amy for final editing. Amy had already cut a great deal of the first half of the film, and scoring began on Stage 9 just two days later. Korngold had been sketching themes for many months. Even so, and despite the length of the film, he was still given only seven weeks to develop the complete score.

Once again, Korngold was called upon to create a theme for Queen Elizabeth I (to be played by Flora Robson, reprising her performance from the earlier British film *Fire Over England*). Cleverly, he adapted his original theme from *The Private Lives of Elizabeth and Essex*. The rhythm of the first four notes is identical, but the notation is altered from the third beat and develops quite differently. He created a thrilling march based on this theme for the major court scene in which the queen and her acolytes progress through Anton Grot's cavernous palace corridors to the throne room. Other highlights of the score include the extraordinary music for Flynn's pet monkey to match his curious limping gait, and of course the exquisite love music. The conductor Charles Gerhardt has compared this ravishing theme with its shifting and totally unrelated harmonies to *the* waltz in *Der Rosenkavalier*. Korngold "interrupts" the melody by leaping to a distant key at each strategic phrase, just as Richard Strauss uses a series of outlandish modulations during the course of his waltz.

As in *The Private Lives of Elizabeth and Essex*, a song was required for one of the court scenes, to be sung by Brenda Marshall (dubbed by Sally Sweetland on the soundtrack). Howard Koch, coauthor of the screenplay with Seton Miller (and later, to write the screenplay for *Casablanca*), provided lyrics for the song, which Korngold later published in his Opus 38 collection *Fünf Lieder* under the title of "Alt Spanisch." What has not been revealed until now, however, is that Korngold actually composed this song thirty years earlier, intending it to be part of his Opus 9, *Sechs Einfache Lieder*. It was rejected from the final six and remained forgotten. Clearly, on seeing the need for a song in the script, Korngold went to his music cabinet to see whether there was an existing song he could use. Perhaps he hoped to see whether another of the Shakespearean songs Opus 29 would suffice, and then turned back to his juvenilia. The text of the original song, entitled "Das Mädchen," was a poem by Eichendorff. Unlike the Marlowe song in *The Private Lives of Elizabeth and Essex*, Korngold used the principal melody of this early composition as the basis for Dona Maria's leitmotif throughout the score, and it forms an important part of the love music.

The scoring sessions were completed on 18 June 1940, and George Korngold attended them:

> As a boy I was fortunate to attend all the scoring sessions for *The Sea Hawk* and was allowed to sit with Dave Forrest, Warners' wonderful music mixer. A total of 58 hours was spent over a period of weeks to record the music with the Warner orchestra, which in this case numbered 54 men. During the Panama sequence scoring, additional percussionists were called in to play tambourine, timbales, marimba, temple blocks, and other exotic instruments unusual to Korngold.
>
> When there was one percussionist short, Ray Heindorf, who had orchestrated the sequence, ran round the studio filling in on one instrument and then another. I recall he was wearing beltless trousers and almost dropped them twice while dashing about the stage.[23]

In a moment that is purely operatic, a full male chorus sing a spirited sea song "Strike for the Shores of Dover" to the melody of the main title music, as Flynn and his crew escape from a Spanish galley. The Warner Brothers music department employed its own choir, drawn from choirs in the Los Angeles area, under the direction of Dudley Chambers. Carol Weiskopf, who had sung Titania in *A Midsummer Night's Dream* was now married to John Ellis, a baritone in the male chorus. He remembered Korngold and the scoring of this sequence clearly:

> Korngold was a very amiable, loveable man who felt no reluctance at being with a member of the chorus. In other words he had absolutely no "greater than thou" attitude about him, which did endear him to many—including me. With regards to his conducting, he would often forget the conductor's pattern and use other gestures to get his ideas, nuances, rubatos et. al. over to the musicians . . . .
>
> For example, I remember him creeping down among the first violins and bowing with them with his baton, in an excited manner during a take—I think it was the main title of *The Sea Hawk*. He wanted to be sure that the waves splashing against the bow of the boat had the effect he wanted. It was great and he got what he wanted.[24]

The score for *The Sea Hawk* was nominated for an Academy Award. This time, Korngold's masterly composition lost to a Walt Disney cartoon *Pinocchio* and its composer Leigh Harline—a perverse result, notwithstanding the charm of this delightful animated fairytale.

Beginning with *Captain Blood* and climaxing with *The Sea Hawk*, his music for this series of magnificent swashbucklers has been the yardstick by which other scores are measured. Listen to the scores by Alfred Newman for *Son of Fury* and *The Black Swan* made a few years later: Korngold's influence is much in evidence. This influence can still be felt today in the music of John Williams, James Horner, and many others, all of whom make no secret of the homage they pay to Korngold in their music. Only with the benefit of hindsight can we now evaluate his contribution. For many years, Korngold's concert music was criticized for being too reminiscent of film music, but this was simply his dramatic style. He brought it to motion picture scoring, where it found a natural home.

He was a true pioneer in this new art form. For these few years, from *The Adventures of Robin Hood* in 1938 until *Kings Row* in 1941, his work was the high watermark of motion picture scoring, reaching a standard that would never be surpassed. No composer, before or since, has ever invested a motion picture score with such symphonic complexity as Korngold. Eleanor Aller Slatkin puts it best:

With Erich, everything was "composed through." There were no held chords or repeated melodies marking time until the scene changed. Everything was organic; themes grew from one to the other, and there were so many subtle effects, so many counter-melodies, some of which would never be heard on the soundtrack, that we used to marvel at the skill and the sheer detail of the scores.[25]

The Sea Hawk previewed at Warner Brothers' Hollywood Theater for the press and industry on 17 July 1940, one month after Korngold finished marrying his epic score to the finished film.[32] Acclaimed upon general release, and in spite of its preview length, it was not cut until its 1947 reissue, when almost twenty minutes were removed. Prints vary today, and the English version also includes a crucial scene with Donald Crisp warning Flynn about treachery at court. After the Hollywood preview, Max Reinhardt sent a congratulatory telegram to Henry Blanke saying: "It is a marvelous realization of our boyhood dreams."

Korngold wrote an article at this time about his experiences and approach to film music in which he fully described his methods. Korngold so rarely expressed himself on the subject that I quote this article at length:

I consider the task of composing and recording music for the completed picture the most interesting and, for the composer, the most stimulating. When, in the projection room or through the operator's little window, I am watching the picture unroll, when I am sitting at the piano improvising or inventing themes and tunes, when I am facing the orchestra conducting my music, I have the feeling that I am giving my own and my best: symphonically dramatic music which fits the picture, its action, and its psychology, and which nevertheless will be able to hold its own in the concert hall.

However I am fully aware of the fact that I seem to be working under much more favorable conditions than my Hollywood colleagues.[27] . . . So far I have successfully resisted the temptations of an all-year contract because, in my opinion, that would force me into factory-like mass production.

Further, I am told that my method of composing is entirely different from that employed by other Hollywood composers. I am not composing at a desk writing music mechanically, so to speak . . . but I do my composing in the projection room, while the picture is unrolling before my eyes. And I have it run off for me again and again, reel by reel, as often as I need to see it.

It is entirely up to me to decide where in the picture to put music. But I always consult with the music-chief whose judgment, based on years of experience, I consider highly important. I also keep the producer well informed and always secure his consent for my musical intentions first. But in none of my assignments have I ever "played" my music first to either the music-chief, the producer, or the director. The executive producer always calls me in for the running of the picture's final cut and I am invited to voice my opinion for or against proposed changes, and I may make suggestions myself.

I have often been asked whether, in composing film music, I have to consider the public's taste and present understanding of music. I can answer that question calmly in the negative.

Never have I differentiated between my music for the films and that for the operas and concert pieces. Just as I do for the operatic stage, I try to invent for the motion picture dramatically melodious music with symphonic development and variation of the themes.

The toughest problem in film music production is and remains the dupe system, i.e. the combining of dialogue, sound, and music. It is difficult from the beginning to strike the right balance. . . . I am convinced that in time better solutions will be found. Motion pictures are young and neither the public nor those who are making them have a right to be impatient or ungrateful for what has already been achieved.[28]

With *The Sea Hawk* completed, Korngold turned his attention to Reinhardt's next Workshop production, an evening of Shakespearean excerpts, and his next film assignment: another maritime adventure—not from a boyhood dream, but Jack London's dark-toned psychological thriller, *The Sea Wolf*.

CHAPTER TWENTY

New Triumphs — Hollywood and Broadway

The Sea Wolf, Jack London's grim novel about survivors of a ferry crash who are picked up by a psychopathic freighter captain, kept prisoner, and brutalized on his ship *The Ghost*, is one of the most filmed stories in movie history. It first appeared on celluloid in 1913. Warner Brothers decided to make the second sound version (an early talkie with Milton Sills was made in 1929) with the new maritime stage and one of the ships built for *The Sea Hawk* entirely redressed. This striking film, now regarded as the classic version of the novel, starred Edward G. Robinson as the sadistic Wolf Larsen, British actor Alexander Knox as the intellectual van Weyden whom Larsen treats brutally, and Ida Lupino as the escaped convict (in the novel the character is a prim Victorian). Robert Rossen was commissioned to write the screenplay, for which he created a new character not in the novel, another escaped convict, Leach, played by John Garfield, in one of his finest characterizations. Once again, the great Michael Curtiz directed. What emerged was an unusually somber and intelligent film, highly atmospheric and beautifully photographed.

Korngold was inspired to compose a sinister, brooding score, quite unlike anything he had done before, reflecting the cruel personality of Larsen. Apart from an exquisite love theme of bare rising fourths scored unusually but appropriately for harmonica, the music is unrelenting in its harshness and is spiced with brutish, dissonant harmonies. Korngold was much more sparing in his use of music in the film, and this is one of his shortest scores. Perhaps he realized that the performances on screen were sufficiently strong to stand alone without musical support. The menacing silences with just the creaking of the ship created an unreal atmosphere, helped considerably by Warner Brothers' new "fog machine" developed by the ingenious art director Anton Grot especially for this film.

According to the manuscript, Korngold completed his unusual score on 12 February 1941, and recorded the music in March just prior to the film's release at the end of that month. The reviews were uniformly praiseworthy. Korngold won a special award for his music from the National Federation of Music Clubs of America. This was some compensation to him when, at the Academy Awards two weeks later, his magnificent score for *The Sea Hawk* lost to Walt Disney's *Pinocchio*. Korngold was not to be nominated again for any of his subsequent work in film.

On 15 March, as a special treat, Luzi and others arranged for the Warner Brothers orchestra to perform extracts from the opera *Die Kathrin* at one of the Sunday rehearsal sessions at the Hollywood High School. These had become a regular feature when some of the musicians in the orchestra, wanting a break from film work, got together for several weeks during the summer to rehearse concert music. Korngold conducted segments of his opera and Vera Schwarz (newly arrived from Europe) and Jan Kiepura were available to sing.

Around this time, he was approached by the chief rabbi in Los Angeles, Dr. Jacob Sonderling, to compose music for liturgical use. Although Korngold was not a practicing Jew, he agreed to consider some Hebrew texts. The result was *A Passover Psalm* and *Prayer*, accorded Opus 30 and 32, respectively. *A Passover Psalm* was later dedicated "To the Society of the Friends of Music, Vienna" for a concert in 1951. These two works are the only nonsecular compositions written by Korngold, who did not profess any strong religious beliefs. He presented both works together with his Shakespearean Lieder in a box marked "My *last* four—or more *optimistically*—my latest four works. For my dear parents on their Golden Wedding Anniversary, Hollywood, 27 September 1941."

By this time, Julius Korngold had become a virtual recluse in Los Angeles and worked daily on his memoirs quietly at home. He spent the rest of his time in relentless correspondence with former colleagues and with his famous son. Many of the letters to his son were unsent, or else placed in an envelope marked, "To be opened after my death." Those that were sent continued to rail against the recurring themes of alleged neglect by his son, the squandering of his talent on films, and accusations of Luzi's treachery. Curiously, the same letters contain many terms of endearment.

The letters that remained unsent are more direct in their abuse. In one especially violent letter written in March 1941, Julius reminds his son that because he refused his guidance and advice, the career he had helped so much to create was at a standstill:

And another thing, in defense of a rumor I heard! In the piano score of *Kathrin*, I allowed myself, in the text of the last third of the second act, to cross out some terrible, repulsive sentences, riddled with greasy defamatory words and gloomy pictures of the childish "stage-villain" Malignac, which also contains superfluous details completely adverse to opera.

This piano score, of which no one has had inspection, not even you, is entirely special and shall remain after my death as a warning—as will an envelope with explanatory remarks. In parentheses, I admit that I only introduced you to that undisciplined, often incomprehensibly tasteless scribbler Decsey in order to lead you from the operetta period to that of opera composition appropriate to your great and specific talent, dignity, and name. Unfortunately, I was then eliminated.

You can of course, in my lifetime or after my death—after which, admittedly, this opposing attitude against the father would cease!—do what you like. You cannot refuse me—and not only because I am the pest who supplied you with the text for *Die tote Stadt,* was active during the reorganization of *Der Ring des Polykrates,* and also advised and took interest in the shaping of *Violanta* and *Heliane.*[1]

Are these the ravings of an old man, unable to cope with exile in a foreign culture, increasingly isolated and neglected, or is there a cunning motive for such an outpouring (hundreds of pages written from 1939 to 1944)? Julius Korngold's handwriting was notoriously indecipherable, yet here, he has written in a deliberately clear and legible hand—almost as though he were writing for a future biographer.

Korngold was not particularly astute about libretti or matters literary, and the works for the stage with which his father (who was an exceptional writer) was not closely involved were based on weak books; consequently, *Das Wunder der Heliane, Die Kathrin*, and the comedy *Die stumme Serenade* (The Silent Serenade, composed 1946–1950) suffer from poor libretti or unrealistic plots. Korngold's poor judgment can also be seen in some of the later films he chose to accept. The guiding hand of his father was clearly an important influence that should not be underestimated in Korngold's work.

The relationship between father and son never improved and in fact got progressively worse, especially when Korngold resumed arranging and conducting operettas in 1942. Korngold for the most part tactfully rebuked his father for his unreasonable behavior, and in spite of the constant friction and abusive criticism he tried to maintain a normal relationship with his parents. Still, the months of complete impasse were punctuated by a few weeks of rapprochement at best.

Otherwise, work went on as normal. In the summer of 1941, another call had come from Reinhardt. This was for a tribute to *Shakespeare's Women, Clowns, and Songs,* which had been in preparation at the Max Reinhardt Workshop since 1937. It was the last Workshop production in which Korngold participated and the only one for which he composed original music. For the excerpts from *Twelfth Night* he wrote a set of fine Lieder, *Narrenlieder* (Songs of the Clown), Opus 29. Nanette Fabray sang them at the first performance on 28 June 1941. He also composed incidental music and four other songs, Opus 31, for scenes from *Othello* and *As You Like It.* For some scenes, Korngold reused parts of his incidental score to *Much Ado About Nothing.*

Around this time, he made one of his rare visits to the recording studios, where he made the definitive version of the suite from *Much Ado About Nothing* in his arrangement for violin and piano with the great Russian violinist Toscha Seidel.[2] Seidel, an exact contemporary of Jascha Heifetz (with whom he used to give recitals when they were both boy prodigies) and another illustrious pupil from the class of Leopold Auer, brought an intense, rhapsodic style to the music. The composer provided one of his finest performances on piano, even adding the chordal introduction from the Hornpipe (otherwise not recorded). This was music making of a very high order, indeed. The discs were never issued owing to wartime restrictions, but fortunately the original masters are preserved in the vaults of RCA.

Almost as soon as Reinhardt's production was over, Korngold was offered another film. The best-selling novel of 1940 was Henry Bellamann's sensational story of life in a small American town at the turn of the century, *Kings Row.* In spite of its more lurid plot twists involving incest, nymphomania, and homosexuality, Warner Brothers bought the screen rights after writer Casey Robinson persuaded Jack Warner that he could develop an effective screenplay that would avoid problems of censorship.

After many rewrites and difficulties with casting, shooting was completed in October. Directed by Sam Wood, designed by William Cameron Menzies, and photographed by James Wong Howe (all of whom were nominated for Academy Awards, as was the film) and with a fine cast, *Kings Row* is now regarded as a screen classic. It is also noted as the only film of substance to feature Ronald Reagan, whose character has both legs amputated by a sadistic doctor, thus leading him to utter the famous line, "Where's the rest of me?" which he used as the title of his autobiography many years later.

From the title of the film, Korngold assumed that this was another "royal" story, and his very first idea was the celebrated fanfare-like main theme. Once he read the script, however, he realized his mistake but decided to retain this strong main theme and to develop and vary it throughout the story. This theme connects the entire score, accompanying the action spanning some twenty-five years on screen.

Exploiting every possible variation, Korngold skillfully uses a key phrase in another of the major themes, that for the Grandmother (Maria Ouspenskaya), who symbolizes the old world that is slowly disappearing and who is so important to the hero, Parris (Robert Cummings). A wonderful moment comes as Parris (as a little boy) walks out of view and returns, grown up, to the powerful strain of this main theme.

Korngold was particularly attracted by the psychological elements in the story, especially the heroine Cassandra's gradual descent into madness, and wrote some of his most erotically charged music for her illicit meetings with Parris. The scene of their (supposed) first sexual encounter during a violent thunderstorm, only partly lit by lightning, is outstanding for its blend of sound effects and music that matches the action.

When Parris plays the piano (Beethoven's Sonata *Pathétique* and Chopin's *Fantaisie Impromptu*), Korngold declined to dub the music and asked Norma Boleslawski, a fine pianist and wife of the noted film director Richard Boleslawski, to perform instead. Korngold felt unusually insecure about interpreting music by other composers, believing his style and technique to be incompatible. He may also have found it difficult to subdue his own personality and performing style in playing classical works. The only exception to this was his inimitable playing of Strauss (both Richard and Johann) and the operas of Verdi and Puccini, which he knew by heart.

Kings Row contains a lovely theme for Randy Monaghan, the girl from the "other side of the tracks" (played by Ann Sheridan in her best screen performance), which resembles the main theme from Sibelius's *Finlandia* (except that it is entirely different in harmonization and development). According to George Korngold, when Hugo Friedhofer pointed out the similarity, Korngold immediately wanted to change it, for it had been entirely unconscious and, according to Friedhofer, Korngold was not especially fond of Sibelius anyway. By then, however, it was too late to change the score, which as usual had to be composed and orchestrated fully in just six weeks. Ernst Korngold added an interesting aside to this:

> My father was aware that his next film after *Kings Row* would be *The Constant Nymph* based on the book by Margaret Kennedy, and although there was no script available, he had started to read the novel to get a feel for the characters. The climax of the film was to be a performance of a symphonic poem, for which Miss Kennedy had especially written a new text. "When I Am dead, another love will cheer thee" were the opening lines.
>
> One day, I was sitting in the music room in our house and my father was working at the piano. It must have been in the summer of 1941. He was developing his ideas for this text which had just arrived, and played the opening bars of what became the tone poem "Tomorrow" as used in the film and asked me what I thought. I told him I liked it. Then, he suddenly said, "Of course, a fifth-rate

composer would set the words to a tune like this," and promptly played what became Randy's theme in *Kings Row*! I remember telling him that, actually, that sounded pretty good too. He must have taken me at my word, because as you know, he used it in the film.[3]

Korngold composed his superbly atmospheric music between September and December 1941. Out of the film's 127 minute running time, Korngold scored sixty-seven. It is one of the most thematically complex scores he composed, with major themes for all the many characters.

Kings Row was previewed one week before the Japanese attack on Pearl Harbor. Believing that the public would not respond to a period film after the attack, the studio held up its general release even though Wallis and Warner realized that the film was outstanding. Following Pearl Harbor, a special all-star benefit concert organized by the Deutsch-Jüdischer Club in Los Angeles on 24 January 1942 brought together a distinguished roster of performers and musicians, including Siegfried Arno, Albert and Elsie Basserman, Elisabeth Bergner, Felix Bressart, Bronislaw and Jacob Gimpel, Friedrich Hollaender, Paul Henreid, Fritz Kortner, Fritzi Massary, Vera Schwarz, Helene Thimig, Ludwig Stössel, Fritz Zweig, and many others. All wanted to make their contribution to the war effort. Korngold accompanied Vera Schwarz in the "Mariettalied" from *Die tote Stadt*.

Kings Row was finally released in the spring. Korngold's exceptional musical score struck a chord with the public and stimulated a stream of letters to the studio. George Korngold remembered:

Letters about the music literally poured into Warner Bros. Studio in Burbank. Unable to cope with the sheer numbers, my father, who tried to answer every one personally, finally resorted to using me in addition to his secretary (Jaro Churain) for answering the most interesting of these letters. And so it became my duty after school, and sometimes on Saturdays and Sundays, to type the replies to his "fans," which he dictated to me. And what letters had come! Contrary to the belief of the studios and producers of "the golden era" that music was only good if it wasn't noticeable, the response from the thousands of admirers who wrote to express their feelings showed exactly the opposite was true: the "viewer" had matured into a "listener."

Requests for a recording of the score were contained in almost every letter, but of course, at that time a soundtrack album was almost unheard of. A piano copy of the *Kings Row* theme was sent to all those that had asked for it, but that was the extent to which these calls for a recording could be satisfied.[4]

The studio issued a form letter to all those who wrote to the music department, rather than to Korngold personally. This went out in August

1942. In England, a young 28-year-old composer and teacher named Harold Truscott[5] was one of the many who wrote to Korngold about his score. He told me in 1975 that he saw *Kings Row* on more than thirty occasions just to hear the score, once with his eyes completely closed, and was able to memorize and write down the major portions of it.

The Constant Nymph was one of the best-selling novels of the 1920s, so successful in fact that it was quickly turned into a play by Basil Dean, which provided the young Noël Coward with one of his best roles. John Gielgud also scored a triumph in the part of the young composer Lewis Dodd, who is idolized by a young teenage girl Tessa, but marries an older, more sophisticated woman instead of waiting for Tessa to grow up. Tessa, who inspires Dodd's greatest work, a symphony, dies of heart failure while Dodd conducts the first performance.

The play was filmed twice, first in 1928 starring Ivor Novello in a silent version, and again in 1933 with Brian Aherne and music by Eugene Goosens (who had earlier written music for the play) and John Greenwood. Warner Brothers purchased it in 1940, and negotiations with Margaret Kennedy began for a new treatment by Kathryn Scola to be based on Basil Dean's original.[6] The new film was to star Charles Boyer (as Dodd), Joan Fontaine (as Tessa), Alexis Smith, Peter Lorre, Charles Coburn, Dame May Whitty, and Montagu Love as Sanger, the composer-father of Tessa.

Preparation and production of the film occupied much of the first half of 1942. Because of the film's musical content, Korngold was much more involved than usual. It was presumably Korngold's idea to change Lewis Dodd's symphony, the performance of which provides the climax of the story, into a symphonic poem for contralto, women's chorus, and orchestra. Margaret Kennedy clearly approved, because she willingly provided a vocal text for the work. Korngold's involvement in the film even extended to the dialogue, and I am sure he collaborated with Kathryn Scola on the script. Perhaps he even suggested the central idea that *Tomorrow*, as the symphonic poem was now called, be developed and presented in different ways throughout the film. We first hear it near the beginning of the film in a simple chamber arrangement (violin, viola, cello and piano with vocal).[7] Later, at a musical soiree in London, Lewis Dodd plays a dissonant, modern version for two pianos (Korngold and Max Rabinowitz on the soundtrack). Finally, the full symphonic version is heard at the climax of the film.

The background score was written throughout March and April 1942 and it fairly glows with melody—in particular, a typically heroic main title, the warm, expansive theme for Florence, and an exquisite elegy for strings entitled "Tessa's Farewell." This story clearly inspired the romantic Korngold to new heights of expression.

A memorable moment comes early in the film when Dodd is talking with old Sanger in his music room. Through the door, the strains of the chamber version of *Tomorrow*, which Dodd has brought as a present for

Sanger's musical children, can be heard from the other room. "What is that music?" asks the old man. "It's nothing, just a trifle for the children," replies Dodd. Sanger listens intently: "It is very nice." Dodd grimaces, "Nice? Sugar candy!" Sanger looks at him gravely, saying, "You're afraid of melody, aren't you." Then Sanger goes to the piano and begins to play the simple tune in a rich, fully harmonized and sweepingly romantic way. It is the unmistakable sound of Korngold playing on the soundtrack that we hear, and it makes the spine tingle. I am sure this scene was partly scripted by Korngold. Perhaps he was making a direct rebuke to the atonal revolutionaries.[8]

The climactic concert performance[9] is a rare example in film of a substantial piece of music performed in its entirety without interruption. Lasting some six minutes, *Tomorrow* opens with a purely orchestral introduction, which seems to look back to the music of *Violanta* and *Die tote Stadt*. The deep bells are particularly reminiscent of the peculiar sound world of these operas. The main vocal section is an effective setting of the poem and reaches a fulsome climax with the wordless women's chorus continuing the final phrases, climbing upward through the whole tone scale. Korngold was evidently proud of it, for he decided to give it Opus Number 33. Following the success of the film on its release in the summer of 1943, a commercial recording was made for Decca, with the Warner Brothers Studio Orchestra under the composer's baton. Unfortunately, this was not issued, again due to the wartime shortage of shellac, and the original materials appear to have been lost. For the premiere in July 1943, Korngold also prepared another concert overture based on the main sequences of the score, as well as a purely instrumental version of *Tomorrow*.

The Constant Nymph is the least known of Korngold's films because the literary copyright, which is still controlled by the estate of Margaret Kennedy, prohibits it from being shown, and it has not yet been released for either television or video. Few prints of the film are known to exist. The master negative (on highly combustible nitrate film) is stored at Warner Brothers Studios in Burbank, California. An inferior copy is held in the National Film Archive in London, but it is in such bad condition that it cannot be screened.

Yolanda Mero was an extraordinary Hungarian musician, who in the early years of the century had been one of the greatest pianists of her generation. By 1942, she had settled in New York as the wife of Herbert Irion, a wealthy industrialist. With his financial help, she was a founder sponsor of the New Opera Company,[10] which was established to provide popular opera and operetta performances for Broadway in contrast to the loftier traditions of the Metropolitan Opera. Perhaps her greatest success in this endeavor was the 1944 revival of *The Merry Widow* starring Marta Eggerth and her husband Jan Kiepura. In 1942, she asked Korngold to conduct his famous version of *Die Fledermaus* in a new production to be directed by Felix Brentano. *Die Fledermaus* had never enjoyed success in America. To attract American audiences (and, given the wartime situation, to avoid a German title), it was to be called *Rosalinda* after the main soprano role, with English translation by Gottfried Reinhardt and John Meehan, Jr.

On 26 September, Korngold left Los Angeles for New York. According to Luzi, Korngold went with the express intention of persuading Yolanda Mero Irion to invite Max Reinhardt to produce *Die Fledermaus*, and he threatened to walk out on the show unless it was agreed. He was successful. It was to be their final collaboration and one of their happiest.

Oskar Karlweis reprised his performance as Orlofsky from the original 1929 Berlin production; otherwise, the cast, including a very young Shelley Winters, was largely unknown. The choreography was in the hands of George Balanchine, and Korngold conducted from the piano, as he had always done in Europe. By all accounts, he was the star.

The production opened at the 44th Street Theater on 28 October 1942 (and later transferred to the Imperial Theater and the 42nd Street Theater) and was an unprecedented success, running to some 520 performances. Olin Downes (writing in *The New York Times*) particularly appreciated the cadenza played by Korngold on the piano in waltz rhythm to accentuate the spoken text of Orlofsky's toast. The critic Winthrop Sargent also attended the production and wrote an insightful letter to me about it:

> I always admired Korngold as a composer and conductor, and I especially remember him for his remarkable services to Johann Strauss' *Fledermaus* on Broadway under the title *Rosalinda*.
>
> I learned the traditional rubatos for this work as an orchestra player under Walter Damrosch, who heard Strauss himself conduct when he visited this country . . . . Damrosch knew and used all the proper rubatos. Since then, I have been disappointed in the interpretation of this work by most conductors. Eugene Ormandy knew nothing of the tradition when he conducted it at the Metropolitan and Erich Leinsdorf was equally ignorant. Korngold, however, knew every one of the proper rubatos and conducted a brilliant performance.[11]

Luzi had traveled to New York to attend final rehearsals, and Reinhardt showed her around New York for the first time. She recalled one evening in particular when for the first time he called her husband by his first name, adding, "Yes Lucia, he's a splendid man, and I'm happy that our paths have crossed so often."[12]

Perhaps Reinhardt, who was approaching his seventieth birthday, realized that time was running out. Certainly, with the reduced circumstances and collapse of his international career, he felt keenly the value of his close friends—and no one was closer to this often remote genius than his indispensable collaborator Korngold. Reinhardt, used to making the grand gesture of giving projects to others, must have been touched by Korngold's loyal stand to involve him in *Rosalinda*. Korngold felt sincerely, and often stated, that he owed his life and the lives of his entire family to Max Reinhardt, who had been instrumental in bringing him to America and offering him the lifeline of film work. Now he was able to repay his old friend with this last, triumphant production.

Dress rehearsal for *Rosalinda*, New York, 26 October 1942: Korngold, center, Shelley Winters, seated right, hand under chin (Korngold estate).

Korngold conducted only the first four weeks of *Rosalinda*. Before leaving New York, he took part in a charity concert devoted entirely to his own works at the Waldorf Astoria, arranged by the New Opera Company. Excerpts from *Die Kathrin* were performed (with soloists from the company), and Jarmila Novotná made a guest appearance. Korngold performed at the piano throughout.

New York's classical radio station WQXR invited him to give a recital of Lieder with Desi Halban on 9 November 1942, and two days later he conducted a broadcast of his own works with the Columbia Concert Orchestra, with Eileen Farrell and Robert Nicholson as soloists.

The Irions hoped to produce *Die Kathrin* in 1943, and plans to star Jarmila Novotná in the production were announced. As a follow-up to *Rosalinda*, Korngold and Reinhardt were asked to adapt *Die schöne Helena*, and Mme. Novotná was contracted to reprise the title role. For the first time since his enforced exile, Korngold felt that his career was beginning to take off in America, and future plans looked promising.

Back in Los Angeles for Christmas 1942, he signed a new contract to write the music for the film *Devotion*, a biography of the Brontë family starring Ida Lupino, Olivia de Havilland, and Arthur Kennedy, then in production. The period and subject were to his taste. He intended to complete the score by early spring and then return to New York in time for Max Reinhardt's seventieth birthday and to prepare *Die schöne Helena* for production in the autumn. On Christmas Eve, however, he received a telegram from the Irions:

> Am talking to Reinhardt next week but *Helena* hit a snag because Grace Moore is contemplating production with Darius Milhaud revising score. Will find out more after January first.[13]

Devotion marked the beginning of the decline in the quality of films offered to Korngold. He had enjoyed a remarkable run of classic productions, all of them memorable in cast, script, and direction. Although there is a very good film to be made about the Brontë family, *Devotion* was definitely not the one. Apart from its highly fictionalized plot, the principal stars were miscast—especially Paul Henreid, who played the curate Nichols with an Austrian accent. One of the screen's most risible exchanges occurs when Sidney Greenstreet (as Thackeray) greets a bearded man on the street with "Morning Dickens." The best scenes were Emily's dreams, or rather

Julius Korngold in Hollywood, 1942 (Korngold estate).

nightmares, of a hooded figure, the Angel of Death, who swoops down and envelopes her with his cape.

Korngold's score is considerably better than the film, in particular the sweeping main title. For some reason, *Devotion* required the largest number of orchestrators of any of Korngold's films. In addition to the faithful Friedhofer, Milan Roder, Simon Bucharoff, Leonid Raab, Bernhard Kaun, and even Ernst Toch all worked on it.

By the time scoring was complete in April, America was heavily involved in World War II, and studio production was almost entirely turned over to films with a war theme. *Action in the North Atlantic, Casablanca, Edge of Darkness, Air Force,* and *Northern Pursuit* were all released in 1943. Warner Brothers decided that, given the dramatic weakness of *Devotion* and its period setting, it would do better at the box office in peacetime. Release was held up until April 1946, but it still did relatively poor business and quickly disappeared.

Korngold attended the trade show of *The Constant Nymph* at the Warner Studio on 25 June 1943. With the release of *Devotion* postponed and no further project in sight, he was pleased to hear of the possibility of another production of *Rosalinda* in Chicago. He left for meetings in Chicago en route to New York for further meetings about *Die schöne Helena* and to prepare for Reinhardt's birthday.

Die schöne Helena was a troubled production. First was the problem of casting. A major star was clearly needed, but the availability of Jarmila Novotná had become questionable. Gertrude Lawrence, Lenore Corbett, Jeanette McDonald, Lucille Ball, and even Joan Crawford had all been considered.

From the extant correspondence between Korngold and Lilli Darvas (the wife of Ferenc Molnar, who was Reinhardt's assistant on this production), it appears that the relationship between the author Gottfried Reinhardt and Yolanda Mero Irion was, to say the least, hostile. He refused to grant her the credit "Presented by . . ." and she threatened to pull out of the contract over agreed percentages. Korngold went back to Los Angeles in mid-August until the differences could be settled. As a result of the prevailing bad feeling (especially toward Gottfried Reinhardt), Korngold decided not to attend Max Reinhardt's seventieth birthday celebration in September, although as a gift he did pay Helene Thimig's expenses (Reinhardt's wife) from Los Angeles to New York.[14]

The gathering was perhaps the greatest assembly of European literary and theatrical celebrities yet seen in New York and included Elisabeth Bergner, Hans Jaray, Thomas and Heinrich Mann, Grete Mosheim, Ernst Lubitsch, Tilly Losch, Erich von Stroheim, Berthold and Salka Viertel, Bruno Walter, Kurt Weill, Carl Zuckmayer, Ferenc Molnar, and scores of others. As a gift, Franz Werfel wrote a special congratulatory epistle that was incorporated in an original lithograph drawing by Victor Tischler and surrounded by the signatures of all who attended plus many others.

Within a month Reinhardt was dead, following complications arising from a dog bite. Korngold in Hollywood was devastated by the news. Immediately, preparations for memorial events in New York and Los Angeles got underway, and Korngold took charge of the latter, held at the Wilshire Ebell Theater on 14 December 1943. For the Carnegie Hall concert Bruno Walter had succeeded in persuading the New York Philharmonic to give its services free, but the labor union in California had refused to allow its members to perform in Hollywood on the same terms. Korngold quickly had to arrange his own musical program comprising a version for piano of the "Urlicht" from Mahler's Symphony No. 2 in C Minor followed by three of his own *Four Shakespearean Lieder* with mezzo soprano Belva Kibler, and the Adagio from Mozart's Fifth Violin Concerto, in which he accompanied Joseph Szigeti. The extant manuscript (in Korngold's hand) of the "Urlicht" contains the words and melody line only—Korngold played Mahler's music entirely from memory, needing only the English text as a guide. Thomas Mann, Edward G. Robinson, Olivia de Havilland, and William Dieterle were among the speakers, and the nocturne scene from the film of *A Midsummer Night's Dream* was shown. Among the audience were Stravinsky, Vicki Baum, Otto Klemperer, Alma Mahler, and many others.

Despite Korngold's best efforts, there was an unpleasant postcript, as George Korngold remembered:

> Upon Reinhardt's death, it was my father who was named executor of the estate. Shortly thereafter, he ceded even the European royalties [of their joint productions] back to Helene Thimig. If you read Gusti Adler's book . . . you know that my father financed Thimig's last trip from Hollywood to New York, so that she could be at her husband's side during his last days.
>
> What you cannot know is that my father also bought Helene Thimig the rented house in which she and Reinhardt lived in California and from which she was about to be evicted.
>
> Their simple agreement was that, if ever the house were sold, my father would be entitled to half the profits. In due course, Helene did sell the property but without notifying my father.
>
> Nevertheless, upon discovering the facts of the sale, he never once mentioned the matter again. I will also mention in passing that Wolfgang Reinhardt was fired from his job at Warner Brothers shortly before Reinhardt's death because of chronic absenteeism and failure to report to work on time. When Helene told my parents how worried Max Reinhardt was about his son, my father went to Jack Warner and managed to have Wolfgang reinstated.[15]

Erich and Luzi Korngold remained friendly with Helene Thimig, who eked out a living playing tiny roles in films, including what amounted to a bit part (a waitress in a Tyrolean inn) in one of Korngold's last film assignments, *Escape Me Never*. He may even have been responsible for her getting these little jobs. When she was not acting in films, she was a regular visitor at Toluca Lake.

Following these sad events, another film was offered, appropriately with death as a central theme. *Between Two Worlds* actually seems a better film now than it did at the time. A remake of the early talkie *Outward Bound* from the play of the same name by Sutton Vane (which gave Leslie Howard his screen debut), it was entirely rewritten and updated by Daniel Fuchs to a wartime setting. It tells of a motley group of characters en route from London to America who are all killed in an air raid and find themselves on a fog-bound liner taking them to the next world.

In a newspaper interview Korngold revealed how much Reinhardt's death had affected him and the comfort he derived from working on this film:

I was in no mood for writing a film score . . . .The thing which haunted me for weeks after the death of Max Reinhardt was the realization that this unique, prodigious artist was alive no more, and that still things were going ahead as before, life proceeding just as it always had. It was horrible.

I found it quite impossible to adjust myself to any of the films which came along for me to write. Then I was offered *Outward Bound*, a story about life after death. It was the very subject I had been living with ever since I heard the shocking news. I accepted immediately, and the picture proved to be as gratifying artistically as it was spiritually.[16]

The film was not to be as uplifting as Korngold believed, however. An interesting cast—Edmund Gwenn, Eleanor Parker, Sydney Greenstreet, George Colouris, Paul Henreid, and John Garfield—was completely let down by the leaden direction of Edward A. Blatt. The film lacked any sense of fantasy, a quality that clashed badly with the somewhat delicate and philosophical theme.

Korngold was immensely attracted to the story. Regardless of the short-comings of what happened on screen, he composed a moody, atmospheric score that was highly reminiscent of his opera *Das Wunder der Heliane*, especially in the music for the final love scene. This music underscores the return to life and a second chance for the two central characters, who have committed suicide (Henreid and Parker). The ecstatic melody is clearly influenced by the aria "Ich ging zu Ihm" from *Das Wunder der Heliane*. Even more telling is the moment when the parson is told by "The Examiner" (Greenstreet) that his pastoral work is not over—he will be able to carry on in the afterlife, as before. Here, Korngold quotes directly from *Heliane*; it is the moving theme of the Porter from Act III.

The character played by Henreid is supposedly a concert pianist, and Korngold composed a short rhapsody, dubbing the piano solos himself throughout the film. The original scoring for the main title (which bears the description, "Hymn—with beauty") included a wordless chorus to be used as orchestral color as in *Das Wunder der Heliane*, but for some reason it was not used in the final take. Each character is given a memorable theme. The scoring is unusually detailed, incorporating harmonium, organ, vibraphone, and celeste to add to the otherworldly effect.

The music was composed and recorded during the first quarter of 1944 and proceeded smoothly until final dubbing and mixing. Regrettably, a decision was taken to reduce the sound level of the music recording in several key scenes to create a "ghostly effect," and, according to his son George, for the first time Korngold was not consulted. Korngold disputed this with Nathan Levinson, head of the sound department, and as a result some sequences were reinstated at the correct level.

It was an unhappy experience for Korngold, who was becoming increasingly disenchanted with films, though *Between Two Worlds* was his favorite among all the films he scored. It opened on 20 May 1944, and in spite of its shortcomings, it did reasonably well. *Variety* welcomed the film with an unusually enthusiastic review: "Brilliant dialogue and excellent performances, as well as thoughtful imaginative direction . . . sustain the interest."[17]

In spite of Reinhardt's death, plans for *Die schöne Helena* had been revived. Casting problems were overcome, Jarmila Novotná became available, and Herbert Graf (no relation to Max) directed. Melville Cooper, who had been such a memorably comic Sheriff of Nottingham in *The Adventures of Robin Hood*, was hired as dialogue director, and Leonid Massine revised his original choreography.

Korngold returned to New York on 25 March 1944 and completely revised his original adaptation, working closely with Herbert Baker, who had written entirely new English lyrics, including a new setting of the famous Barcarolle to the words "Love at Last." *Die schöne Helena* also underwent a title change to make it more "accessible." It was now called *Helen Goes to Troy*, and it opened at the Alvin Theater on 24 April 1944 to mixed reviews.

Offenbach's comedy did not translate effectively in the new book by Gottfried Reinhardt. Lewis Nichols, writing in *The New York Times*, observed:

> While the singing and music come right up to spell out the Broadway form of perfection, let the honeymoon suspend here for a moment to consider the book. *Helen Goes to Troy* is not the wittiest piece of literature just off Times Square.[18]

Korngold conducted for the first three weeks, but audiences were disappointing and the show closed after just fourteen weeks. By then, Korngold had returned to Hollywood. A new film project had come up—yet another remake, this time of Somerset Maugham's tragic novella *Of Human Bondage*. It was to mark the lowest point of Korngold's career in films.

The Return to Absolute Music: 1944–1955

CHAPTER TWENTY-ONE

Farewell to Films

Of Human Bondage was filmed in 1934 by RKO. It had provided Bette Davis with her first opportunity to demonstrate her acting range. Leslie Howard co-starred, and Max Steiner wrote an effective score. Warner Brothers' decision to remake the story as a vehicle for Eleanor Parker (then being groomed for stardom) probably stemmed from the English director Edmund Goulding's enthusiasm for it and his personal friendship with Somerset Maugham. A shortage of leading actors because of the war resulted in Paul Henreid again being miscast in the role of the English medical student who becomes obsessed with a promiscuous waitress. There were major problems during shooting, a severe clash of temperaments between Henreid and Goulding, and considerable rewriting. The film looked good, but in spite of a very strong supporting cast of Edmund Gwenn, Patric Knowles, Alexis Smith, and Henry Stephenson, fine period detail and excellent photography, the result was unconvincing and unmoving.

George Korngold remembered that his father was not at all happy to be offered the assignment:

> Henry Blanke invited my father to a screening of the rough cut, even though some scenes were still being reshot. After it was over, he asked

my father to compose the biggest score he had ever done, to sweep the film along, and give it the drama and emotion it so obviously lacked.

The orchestration is much larger than usual, with lots of extra brass, but even with Korngold's music, the film sank. In fact it was held up for release until 1946. My father actually composed much more music than ended up in the film, which was cut and re-edited several times. One of the most delightful pieces was for a Christmas scene, which was actually photographed and recorded, but later cut. When I produced the "Classic Film Scores" series for RCA in the 1970s, I included it in the suite from this score, but it isn't in the film.[1]

Korngold worked on the film from November 1944 until the spring of 1945. He produced an overwhelming score, which completely swamps the shallow portrayal on screen. For once, his music is out of place, at odds with the film it is meant to support. Although the score contains much that is beautiful, with one stunning melody following another, this rich outpouring never seems to connect with the film. (One scene required a lullaby for Mildred's baby,[2] and the result was an affecting, darkly scored miniature for viola and oboe d'amore.) It succeeds wonderfully as concert music but fails in its primary role as film music. Tony Thomas aptly describes it as a "rich symphony hanging on a scarecrow."[3] In spite of Korngold's best efforts, *Of Human Bondage* was unsalvageable. It is rarely shown today because of another copyright problem resulting from the third remake in 1964.

At some point during the scoring, Korngold, despairing over the dismal way the film was developing, and perhaps seeking inspiration, asked to see the earlier version with Bette Davis. By chance, he bumped into her on the backlot shortly afterward, when the following, often quoted exchange took place:

> Hullo Betty, vot do you think? Ve just screened your wersion of *Of 'Uman Bondaage* and you verr just marrrrvelous! (Miss Davis blushed modestly.) Of course, after ten years, some scenes ver a little bit ridiculous. (Miss Davis looked askance.) But we wiz our new wersion are ten years ahead of time, because ve are ridiculous already!

Around the same time, Korngold, in the music department one afternoon when perhaps the word was out that Korngold's latest offering was not one of his best, delivered his other most-quoted quip. He bumped into his colleague and friendly rival Max Steiner, who never missed an opportunity to rib other composers. They greeted each other, and Steiner said:

> "Erich, we've both been working at Warners for ten years now" (Korngold nodded and winced) "and during that time, it seems to me, your music has gotten worse and worse whereas mine has gotten better and better—now why do you suppose that is?"

Without pausing for breath, Korngold replied, "That's easy Steiner; it's because you have been stealing from me and I have been stealing from you!" And with that, he walked off with a flourish.[4]

Disenchanted with films, Korngold had secretly turned to composing absolute music once again. His ailing father, now aged 84, never ceased exhorting his son to return to his true calling. Luzi also raised the subject whenever she could, but this usually resulted in bleak moods and silences. For Christmas 1944, however, she got a surprise: the final sketch of a new string quartet. "Erich was his old self again. The desire to write had returned. I had known nothing of the quartet; he had carefully avoided playing even a note of it on the piano."[5]

This String Quartet No. 3 in D Major, which became Opus 34, was his third and last essay in the medium. It is a much more introspective work than one might expect, containing some of his most eloquent music, some of it derived from his film scores. After ten years of composing an extraordinary amount of music for motion pictures—perhaps the equivalent of twenty symphonies in length—he made the deliberate decision to utilize material and themes from these scores in his future concert works. After all, long before, he had ensured that his contract with Warner Brothers permitted him to do so. For him, there was no difference between what he created for the screen and what he wrote for the concert hall and opera stage, except that, understandably, he felt that the music he composed for films would be buried and forgotten along with the films themselves. By using his best ideas in his future concert works, he could at least salvage something of value from his Hollywood years. Although Korngold has been severely criticized for incorporating themes from his film scores in his post-war concert works (the oft-used sobriquet "film composer" dates from this time), he was only emulating his illustrious forebears—Mahler, Schubert, Handel, and even Beethoven—who never wasted a good idea and thought nothing of re-using material in different works.

The String Quartet No. 3 in D Major is a finely crafted work in four movements. As the first work of his late period, it is interesting to observe a refinement of style and technique. The highly chromatic opening movement, with its sinuous main theme and serenely beautiful second subject, marks a new development: a greater restraint. Only in the development does the tempestuous character so typical of Korngold reappear. The opening movement is followed by an extraordinary Scherzo, a string of dissonant sevenths providing a grotesque dance-like accompaniment to the shrill melody that would have delighted Prokofiev. The Trio—a warm, singing melody borrowed from the recently completed score for *Between Two Worlds*—could not provide a greater contrast.

The slow movement (marked "Sostenuto, like a folk tune") is based entirely on the love music from *The Sea Wolf* (originally written for harmonica, it works even better when scored for string quartet). The Finale is a typical boisterous romp, with a vigorous opening of rugged octaves followed by a second idea taken from the score for *Devotion* (which was still unreleased). This theme, in turn, owes much to the Hornpipe from the score to *Much Ado About Nothing* written in 1918. I draw attention to this merely to highlight the continuum of Korngold's musical style.

On 22 June, Korngold conducted the world *concert* premiere of his *A Passover Psalm* at a special event in the Hollywood Bowl. He shared the podium with his old friend Bruno Walter. The concert was given by the Los Angeles Philharmonic in aid of the Russian War Relief Fund.

The optimism engendered by the end of the war in Europe was diminished by another sad loss, however. Korngold's father died in September 1945 after a long illness. The illness and subsequent loss of his father stimulated Korngold's return to major composition. It must have been an emotionally wrenching experience for him. Within twelve months, Korngold had lost the two most important and influential figures in his life, and this spurred him on to re-establish his music and his reputation.

The quartet was completed shortly before his father's death. Earlier that year, he returned again to the violin concerto he had begun to sketch in the late 1930s—the Violin Concerto in D Major—this time largely at the behest of Bronislaw Huberman, an old friend of the family since Korngold's teenage years. It had become a running family joke that every time Huberman met Korngold he would ask, "Erich! Where's my violin concerto?"

Huberman was invited to dinner at Toluca Lake after giving a concert in Los Angeles. After dinner, he asked *the* question as usual, whereupon Korngold went to the piano and played the opening phrases of the concerto, in fact, a melody originally from *Another Dawn*. Huberman cried, "That's it! That will be my concerto—promise me that you'll write it."

Events are somewhat confusing following this. At one point, the young Bronislaw Gimpel (then leader of the Los Angeles Philharmonic) expressed an interest in the work, now completely revised and ready for its first performance. Huberman was on tour, and Korngold felt obliged to inform him of Gimpel's interest. Back came an indignant telegram: "I absolutely forbid you to even show it to another violinist!" Yet on being pressed for a date when he might give the first performance, Huberman demurred, saying he had not even read it yet and could hardly set a date for performance. Korngold was angry at this vague response. When the great Jascha Heifetz learned of the concerto (Rudi Polk, his business manager, was a friend of the Korngolds) and asked to hear it, Korngold met Heifetz and played through the entire work. Heifetz listened with an expressionless face, then asked if he could take the score away with him to study some passages. A few weeks later, Korngold was invited again, and this time Heifetz played the work through with the composer in a flawless performance. Luzi remembered:

Shortly afterwards, Huberman came to Los Angeles and despite the tension, paid us a visit. As we sat at lunch, Erich said: "Huberman, I haven't been unfaithful yet, I'm not engaged . . . but I have flirted." Huberman's reaction upon finding out who Erich had flirted with was typical of his pleasantness and astute character.

The main thing was to clear up the misunderstanding. Brahms had been happy to take Joachim's advice, he said, and in the same way he envisaged working with Korngold. When Erich played the concerto through, he said, "Even if Heifetz does play the world premiere, I'll play it anyway."[6]

This was to be their last meeting, for Huberman died in 1947. Jascha Heifetz, meanwhile, became good friends with Korngold and was a frequent visitor at Toluca Lake, especially when Korngold acquired a television set. At that time, virtually the only programs to be seen were of wrestling tournaments. The two former prodigies would sit glued to the set— Heifetz convinced that the men involved would suffer serious injury.

The premiere of the Violin Concerto in D Major was finally settled for February 1947 in St. Louis, with further dates in Chicago and New York. In the meantime, Korngold, who had been searching for a comic subject for an opera since the early 1930s, began work on a light musical comedy, one of his father's last suggestions, which became *Die stumme Serenade* (The Silent Serenade), Opus 36. The origins of this work are complex. In 1939, Julius Korngold began a correspondence with Raoul Auernheimer, an Austrian writer (recently arrived in America) who had succeeded Moritz Benedikt as editor of the *Neue Freie Presse* (after Julius had retired). Auernheimer had been a friend of the Korngolds since 1906 or even earlier, and they often visited him in Alt-Aussee during holidays, where he and his beautiful wife Irene Leopoldine lived. Auernheimer had written a short amusing story which Julius Korngold thought would make an interesting libretto. As late as 24 June 1944, he was writing:

An especially clever librettist could enliven this story with scenes and dialogue. Anyway, I will give the piece to my son, who . . . does not like costume-novels and kings. But he will have to praise Auernheimer as his father did! I am deeply convinced that your piece will have a future, though perhaps it is too fine and too good for America![7]

Korngold handed the story to another Hollywood exile, Rudolf Lothar, the librettist of d'Albert's opera *Tiefland,* who revised the story, modernized it, and developed the characters. This version was then revised substantially by the Hungarian author Victor Clement, who prepared an English version. For the English lyrics for the main songs, Korngold approached William Okie, who had worked with him at the Reinhardt Workshop, and for the German, he asked Bert Reisfeld. Then Auernheimer retranslated the entire book and lyrics back into German!

The final convoluted plot can be summarized thus: It is 1820 in Naples. Silvia Lombardi, fiancee of Lugarini, the prime minister of Naples, is disturbed by a nocturnal intruder, who escapes after one passionate kiss. The trail leads to her lovelorn couturier, Andrea, who was in her garden but only to serenade her silently (i.e. in thought). A bomb attempt on Lugarini's life that same night means that two criminals must be discovered, and Andrea consents to admit to both crimes after the police chief promises a pardon to commemorate the king's eightieth birthday. Unfortunately, the king dies before signing the reprieve, and by ill-luck Lugarini becomes regent. After much confusion and incident, Andrea overcomes these obstacles and is united with Silvia, who has realized that he is the man she loves.

Korngold set this comedy of mistaken identity for a small ensemble of two pianos, celeste, two violins, cello, trumpet, flute, clarinet (doubling tenor saxophone), timpani, and varied percussion. It was completed in late 1946, whereupon Paul Gordon (Victor Clement's brother) attempted to place it for a first performance, initially in the United States. After much haggling and delay involving the impresario J. J. Shubert, the singer Deanna Durbin heard the score and wanted to perform it. Before her husband Felix Jackson, the executive producer at Universal Studios, could present his offer for film rights to the board of directors, J. Arthur Rank took over Universal Studios, so the offer was never approved.[8]

Die stumme Serenade was finally performed on 26 March 1951 in a production for Vienna Radio with Korngold conducting from one of the two pianos. It received its stage premiere in Dortmund on 20 December 1954, after which it disappeared for good. The inept and rather forced comedy of the weak book, and its confused development by so many hands, made for very heavy going, in spite of the witty and melodious music provided by Korngold. The song "Ohne Dich" (Without You) might have been very popular had it been widely performed, although it is almost operatic. This song may give a clue as to the main problem with the piece overall: it sits uncomfortably between the genres of operetta, musical comedy, and in places, even opera. Nevertheless, Korngold doggedly tried to promote it, but with little success.

While he was composing *Die stumme Serenade,* there were also two more film projects to be completed. The first was another remake of a British film based on Margaret Kennedy's novel *The Fool of the Family.* The earlier film made in 1935, which seems to be lost, was entitled *Escape Me Never* (after Kennedy's play based on her book) and starred Elisabeth Bergner (who was nominated for an Academy Award) with music by William Walton. Warner Brothers retained the title and commissioned a new screenplay.

The new version starred an improbable Errol Flynn as a ballet composer, with Ida Lupino as his "lodger" who has a baby son. Eleanor Parker and Gig Young costarred in this muddled melodrama that cannot decide whether it is comic or tragic. The central theme of the story is the ballet *Primavera* that Flynn is writing, encouraged by Parker. Lupino's baby dies from neglect thanks to Flynn, but they end up together nevertheless in one of the most unconvincing plot twists in movies. Flynn is miscast, and the entire production is studio-bound, with poor back projections standing in for the Dolomites. Exterior scenes in Venice were made by flooding the Warner backlot and splicing in stock footage of the real thing.

Korngold provided a voluptuous, intensely Viennese score throughout the film, and the ballet sequence was especially outstanding, choreographed by LeRoy Prinz and danced by Milada Mladova and George Zoritch. Korngold was considerably involved in the musical sequences. For the scene where Flynn plays his ballet score on the piano, Korngold once again dubbed the playing on the soundtrack in his inimitable way.

The studio decided the film needed a hit song to attract audiences. This marketing technique had become popular ever since the main theme from the 1942 Bette Davis classic *Now Voyager* by Max Steiner had been turned into a popular song called "It Can't Be Wrong" with lyrics by Kim Gannon, which reached number two in the "hit parade" that year. George Korngold relates that Ray Heindorf, who was the assistant orchestrator on *Escape Me Never,* was discussing the film one day in the music department at Warner Brothers:

> Heindorf was talking with Leo Forbstein and saying, "We need a hit song to put this film over; who should we get to write it?" and my father said "What do you mean who? I'll do it," and went off to his studio. Thirty minutes later, to their amazement, he returned with "Love for Love," which indeed was a hit, with lyrics by Ted Koehler.[9]

Even a hit song could not save *Escape Me Never,* however. Finally released 22 November 1947, it quickly sank without trace. The reviews were generally disparaging, especially about Flynn's performance.

On the set of *Escape Me Never*, early 1946: playback of the ballet *Primavera* during shooting. From left: George Zoritsch, Milada Mladova, Korngold, choreographer LeRoy Prinz (courtesy of LeRoy Prinz).

The second film offered to Korngold in early 1946 was more to his taste, a story entirely about musicians and classical music: *Deception*, yet another remake, of a film called *Jealousy* made in 1929 that had starred Jeanne Eagels and Frederic March. It was based on the play *Monsieur Lamberthier* by Louis Verneuil, which, retitled *Obsession* on Broadway, had starred Basil Rathbone and Eugenie Leontovitch.

For the remake, considerable rewriting was done, and Korngold was much involved in the story conferences—a highly unusual departure from normal procedure. Paul Henreid played a cellist recently released from a concentration camp, Bette Davis the concert pianist who was his former lover in Europe, and Claude Rains the egomaniac composer Hollenius, who has been Davis's lover since and who has decided to allow Henreid to play his new cello concerto. Davis is desperate to keep her affair secret, and to avoid causing Henreid, who is close to a breakdown, any stress. The film was one of the most enjoyable of its period, chiefly because of Rains, who steals every scene in which he appears.

The film was part of the vogue for stories about classical music initiated by two major films the previous year about Gershwin and Chopin *(Rhapsody in Blue* and *A Song to Remember)*. The cycle continued for several years, during which lavish, fictionalized biographies of Schumann and Brahms *(Song of Love)* and Paganini *(The Magic Bow)* were made, as well as films with a classical music background (the superbly ridiculous Joan Crawford movie *Humoresque* in 1947, also at Warners).

Deception, however, was a film apart. It has been described as one of the few films about classical music that makes sense. When the characters talk about music, they speak knowledgeably. The dialogue is clearly influenced by Korngold in several key scenes. Near the opening, a student asks Henreid which composers he most admires. Henreid replies: "Richard Strauss when I think of the past, Stravinsky when I think of the present—and of course, Hollenius, who combines the rhythm of today with the melody of yesterday." (For Hollenius—read Korngold perhaps?) When Davis expresses surprise that Rains has turned off the radio (Beethoven is being performed), he looks at her, with his famous querulous eyebrow, and says: "Compose a piece yourself my dear, and then try listening to Beethoven." Contrast this with some of the lines in *Humoresque*: "Martinis are an acquired taste—like Ravel" or, worse still, "Bad manners—the infallible sign of genius." *Deception* was at least musically credible.

Deception occupied Korngold from May until August, an unusually long time. The film went over budget and over schedule, partly because of technical difficulties in trick photography and partly because Davis was involved in a serious car accident half way through filming. Korngold was more involved in the actual filming than in any of his previous pictures. He coached Rains in conducting, taught Davis (who was an amateur pianist) how to play the opening page of Beethoven's *Appassionata* sonata, and supervised the orchestral rehearsals, offering suggestions on realistic touches. The dialogue in the rehearsal scene and the moment when the solo flutist cannot keep time with Rains's baton, was entirely Korngold's invention, and the flutist's repeated mistake is written into the score.

Although Korngold dubbed Rains's playing the piano, he asked the young Shura Cherkassky to dub the Beethoven sonata for Bette Davis, having already auditioned (and rejected) Witold Malcuzynski for the job. The solo cello for Henreid was dubbed entirely by Eleanor Aller Slatkin, who gave a superb performance. She had vivid memories of the production:

> We . . . made several recordings, including a test of the Haydn concerto with Erich at the piano, that I still have. I admired Erich as a composer and as a musician. Every scoring session was an event, and he radiated music in such a way that it was unforgettable. But it was in the area of mathematics that he really astonished me. He made one cut in one portion of the concerto that I felt contained some of my very best playing. He didn't want this particular take because of something that happened in the orchestra. Well, one doesn't argue with the composer beyond a certain point but he said . . . "Ve have no problem—I will put it in." . . . This, remember was before the days of editing on tape. And I thought, *on film* he's going to do this! I said, "Professor, please don't bother." And he said, "No, if you feel that this makes the sun shine, ve vill have it." And mathematically, he figured out how to make the cut on film—and I defy anyone to know. He was a genius.[10]

The score for *Deception* is unusual for Korngold in the general sparseness of thematic material. Apart from the passionate main title and the "Hollenius" Cello Concerto, the music is entirely classical, and Korngold carefully chose the repertoire. For the scene in which Rains is listening to Henreid's recent recordings, Korngold made a beautiful arrangement of Schubert's Impromptu No. 4 in A-flat. Korngold also composed a short piece for cello and piano entitled "Romance Impromptu" that he recorded with Eleanor Slatkin, but it was cut from the finished film.[11] For the opening sequence, a performance of the finale from Haydn's Cello Concerto in D Major, he added his own modernistic cadenza. During the filming, Korngold stated in an interview on the set:

> It is not true that the cinema places a restraint on musical expression. Form may change, the manner of writing may vary, but the composer needs to make no concession whatever in what he conceives to be his own musical ideology. Fine symphonic scores for motion pictures cannot help but influence mass acceptance of finer music. The cinema is a direct avenue to the ears and hearts of the great public, and we should see it as a musical opportunity.
>
> Even actors . . . will sometimes prove to be an inspiration. This was the case in *Deception*, and my greatest inspiration came from the expressive voice and movements of its star, Bette Davis.[12]

Whether any composer for films has subscribed to this philosophy since is doubtful. Music in modern-day cinema has become a means to a commercial end—a marketing tool to help sell the product on screen. In 1946, however, before television had taken a hold of popular culture and communication, Korngold still naively believed that one day the musical tastes of the world would be influenced by what they saw and heard on the motion picture screen.

The Cello Concerto in C Major in *Deception* is a singular work. Portions of it are used throughout the film, both in straight performance and as underscoring. In the complete performance at the climax of the film, it lasts barely six minutes and uses material from several previous film scores, notably *The Private Lives of Elizabeth and Essex* for the central Adagio. The aggressive opening subject is entirely new and is one of Korngold's most rhythmically exciting ideas. It is deliberately cast in a modern vein (although written in the key of C major, perhaps in defiance that modernity should equal atonality) and contains some brilliant instrumental effects. The climax of the concerto is reached with a bravura flourish on the solo cello of an ascending twelve-note scale.[13]

Korngold subsequently expanded the concerto into an eleven-minute, one-movement work, published as Opus 37. One might question why he did not expand it much further to a regular length of, say, thirty minutes? Its brevity has limited its life in the concert hall: the expense of hiring a soloist for such a short piece is prohibitive. I believe that Korngold could not extend the work further because he had already condensed enough material for three movements into one, and found it impossible to improve on his original. Even at eleven minutes, it is a very satisfying piece. Clearly, he decided to leave well enough alone.

Filming the concerto was extremely difficult. Henreid did not play the cello. Irving Rapper solved this problem in much the same way as he had done for *Rhapsody in Blue* when Robert Alda (as Gershwin) appeared to play the piano. Henreid wore a special jacket in which holes were cut in both shoulders (for the arms of others to reach through). Two cellists sat behind him out of range, helped by the acute angle of the camera, with their arms and hands visible to the camera; Henreid's were tied behind his back under the jacket. The two cellists bowed and fingered the piece to a "playback" of the music on loudspeakers, accurately matching what is heard, watched carefully by Korngold. Rapper recalled:

> To make the cadenza sound even more difficult, he had the cello play a passage that was actually impossible to realize in real life. This was done by recording it on a double track. He was most amused by this, especially when, after the film was released, real cellists would apparently ask Henreid how he did it.[14]

Bette Davis, reminiscing about this film in 1975, said:

Although I knew Max [Steiner] more, Erich was a genius, and everyone at Warners was aware of it. The music department at Warners was the absolute best in those days and the work he did on *Deception* was actually better than the film itself, in my opinion. . . . For his contribution, and my gorgeous Claude Rains as the composer, the film was worthwhile.[15]

Deception was premiered on 18 October 1946 at the Hollywood Theater in New York and went on general release on 19 November to mixed reviews. ("It's like grand opera—only the people are thinner. . . . I wouldn't have missed it for the world," wrote Cecelia Ager.) On 29 December, Eleanor Aller Slatkin, who was by now very heavily pregnant (with her first son, the future conductor, Leonard Slatkin), gave the world concert premiere with the Los Angeles Philharmonic conducted by Henry Svedrofsky before an audience of around 2000 people at one of the popular Standard Oil Sunday concerts broadcast coast to coast at that time. Korngold listened at home with Luzi and George. Afterwards, George asked, "Poppa, what did you think of the performance?" Quick as a flash, Korngold replied: "Allegro con *em*brio!"[16]

Korngold at fifty, in 1947—his own favorite portrait (Korngold estate).

Deception was the last film to be scored by Korngold at Warner Brothers. After it was completed, only a few months before his fiftieth birthday, he decided not to renew his contract, particularly as he was hoping finally to return to Vienna in 1947. In an interview he gave at the time, he said:

> I feel that my fiftieth year is a turning point. I look back to my life and I see three periods. First, I was a prodigy, then a successful opera composer in Europe until Hitler, and then a movie composer. Fifty is very old for a child prodigy. I feel I have to make a decision now if I don't want to be a Hollywood composer the rest of my life.[17]

But further film assignments were still offered to him, even from other studios. David O. Selznick approached him to score his epic western *Duel in the Sun*, having decided to ask all the leading composers in Hollywood to "compete" for the job by scoring one scene as a kind of audition. When Korngold declined, Selznick, puzzled, asked why. "I might win!" said Korngold. In August, he turned down *Arch of Triumph* (Charles Boyer, Ingrid Bergman), a troubled, independently made film eventually scored by Louis Gruenberg, preferring to work on *Die stumme Serenade* instead.

The changing tastes of movie audiences as the war ended demanded a new realism on the screen. Romantic melodramas and historical subjects, at which Korngold excelled, were eschewed in favor of strong political dramas and *film noir*. In many respects, this development paralleled the arrival of *Neue Sachlichkeit*, or new objectivity, in the opera and drama of the 1920s, which had made Korngold's operas so unfashionable. Now, his film scores were suffering a similar fate.

With the war in Europe at an end a number of charitable events and benefits were organized for the impoverished war victims in Europe, and Korngold contributed to a number of them, either as performer or as a financial sponsor, or both. One such, a fascinating gala in aid of the Palestine Emergency Fund, took place just before Christmas 1946. This was *That We May Live*, a dramatic spectacle starring Jan Kiepura, Marta Eggerth, Jacob Gimpel, Howard da Silva, Bela Lugosi, "and a cast of five hundred." Eric Zeisl, Hugo Strelitzer, and Korngold presided over the music, and Korngold conducted an overture based on material from *Die tote Stadt*.

The Korngolds finally decided to return to Europe in the autumn of 1947. In the meantime, the most important event of the new year was to be the world premiere of the Violin Concerto in D Major in St. Louis, scheduled for 15 February. Vladimir Golschmann was to conduct, and Korngold traveled to St. Louis for the rehearsals.

Anxious that his idiomatic English might not convey his opinions and feelings accurately to the media, he wrote an interesting article to give to the press (it was not used) in which he said, in part:

I want a confirmation, an answer to a question of decisive importance for me: is there still a place and a chance for music with expression and feeling, with long melodic themes, formed and developed on the principles of the classic masters—music conceived in the heart and not constructed on paper? Please don't get me wrong. I was never and I am not today, a reactionary or an old-fashioned composer. On the contrary; brought up with the sound of Richard Strauss's *Elektra* and the symphonies of Gustav Mahler (which by the way, still today—after forty and fifty years—are progressive, more daring, and newer than most of certain symphonies written in the last ten years!), I was one of the first ardent admirers of Stravinsky.

I remember well the time when I, as a musical child prodigy of eleven and twelve years, baffled and scared the music authorities with my own harmonically ultra-modern compositions. But ever since I started . . . I always remained true to my own beliefs; that music should be melodic, and as an old Viennese master used to preach and teach to me— "wohllautend" (well-sounding). The world premiere of my concerto this coming Saturday will be a most important and exciting event in my life.[18]

In the program, Korngold wrote the following:

In spite of its demand for virtuosity in the finale, the work with its many melodic and lyric episodes was contemplated rather for a Caruso of the violin than for a Paganini. It is needless to say how delighted I am to have my concerto performed by Caruso and Paganini in one person: Jascha Heifetz.[19]

Jascha Heifetz, Vladimir Golschmann, and Korngold during the rehearsals for the world premiere of the Violin Concerto in D Major, Opus 35, in St. Louis, February 1947 (Korngold estate).

To his immense satisfaction, the first performance was completely sold out and was a tremendous success. One local critic wrote: "Whether the concerto is great music, one, after only a first hearing, would hate to say. . . . Only Time will assess its authentic values. This enthusiastic admirer believes Time will find true values there."[20]

Korngold was not so naive as to expect a warm welcome for his concerto in New York, however. Sounding desperate, he wrote to Josef Reitler, his father's old colleague from the *Neue Freie Presse,* now a professor at Hunter College in New York with Lothar Wallerstein and Fritz Stiedry, on 20 February 1947:

> My violin concerto was triumphantly received in St. Louis. A success like in the best times in Vienna. My father often sprang to mind. . . . Heifetz put his heart and soul into the work—and played with intense ardor. I enclose a copy of the only morning paper in St. Louis which mentions two inestimable things: the most enthusiastic ovation in the history of the hall and the prophecy of a lifespan like that of Mendelssohn's concerto (I need no more than that!).
>
> I now have five weeks until the New York critics tear it apart (it is even possible that I shall conduct it myself in New York). I must use this time to the full. I would be most grateful for your help in this. Is there any chance you could get a small report of its success into the New York music press or even a daily paper . . . ? I seem to be helpless and neglected here, I have no manager, no agent, not even a publisher in America. (All I can do is to send a copy to Schott in London who will print the work. But they obviously have no influence in New York.) Please do what you can. If the knowledge of this success reaches the music world (violinists, directors, and audience) before the New York critics vent their snobbish, atonal anger on it, the violin concerto may be a decisive turning point for me, a comeback![21]

His worries were well founded. When the concerto reached New York in April it found little favor. Olin Downes, writing in *The New York Times,* called it a "Hollywood Concerto," while Irving Kolodin, writing in *The Sun,* earned his only claim to immortality with the obvious quip, "More corn than gold." This stuck to the work, and Korngold's music in general, for forty years.

Yet in the 1990s, this is the concerto—then so disparaged for its yearning romanticism, lyrical sweetness, and heady atmosphere—that is now the most performed of all Korngold's works, especially in America.

The concerto received a more favorable response in Chicago, a consolation to Korngold. Later, in June 1947, it was to receive its European premiere by Bronislaw Gimpel in the closing concert of the Vienna International Music Festival under Otto Klemperer, another old friend who conducted a bravura performance. The reviews, apart from that of Joseph Marx, were condescending and made much of Korngold's Hollywood connections.

In spite of the mixed critical reception to this new work, Luzi was pleased that he had returned to his own world again, but she was also increasingly worried about his health. Always overweight since his childhood, he had become much heavier and had begun to suffer with angiospasms, which he dismissed as unimportant. On return from Chicago, Luzi insisted on a medical examination, which revealed "a slight inadequacy of the heart muscles." Korngold laughed it off and told his wife not to worry.

In May, he celebrated his fiftieth birthday during the run of a new production of *Rosalinda* for the Los Angeles Civic Light Opera. Edwin Lester, its founder, who had first met Korngold during the production of *A Midsummer Night's Dream* when he had supplied singers for the choral sequences from the company, became a close friend. He had been keen for Korngold to conduct for his productions, and this finally happened when *Rosalinda* was produced. Lester remembers that Korngold's

> musical gifts were miraculous. For instance, his memory. On one occasion, he visited my house to discuss a new arrangement and asked me for some music paper so that he could sketch it out for me. I said, "There's some in the music bench." Lying on top of the pile was a song I had written at the age of sixteen and which my Mother had paid to have published. "Vot is zis, Edvin?" he says, "I never knew you verr a composer too!" I blushed and told him to ignore it, it was just a youthful attempt. He looked it over and put it away, and we carried on discussing *Rosalinda*. About three weeks later, it was my birthday and Erich was invited. Naturally, and inevitably, he was implored to play the piano. He sat down and played *my* song—but in the most fantastic way, making it sound like a masterpiece. "How did you do that?" I asked him, for he had barely glanced at it. "Oh, it vos just a little surprise I had for you." I loved him for that.[22]

Although Korngold was pleased to be working in operetta again, Luzi was alarmed by this new distraction, especially as she had tried to get him to promise not to take on any more stressful rehearsals or conducting—in vain, of course. When Korngold's doctor raised no objections, he pressed ahead. Even though the pains returned, he ignored them and threw himself into his work.

The premiere took place in San Francisco on 19 May 1947 with Korngold conducting a bravura performance, as usual. At the end of the first act he collapsed in his dressing room with serious pains and heart spasms. According to his wife, even though he was barely recovered, he insisted on conducting the rest of the performance "with energy of steel," and indeed carried on with the rest of the engagement, which was sold out every night for the next two weeks before transferring to the Los Angeles Philharmonic Auditorium.

Korngold promised Luzi that as soon as his commitments were complete, he would take a short vacation. He had never been to Canada and planned a holiday there. Luzi was not sure about this, but, as she admitted, "since on the one hand it was impossible to overcome his stubbornness and on the other hand, I didn't want to worry him unduly, we set off on our journey."

Korngold loved Canada, and its breathtaking scenery clearly inspired him. He wrote to his mother, telling her in passing: "I have begun to write a symphony."[23] This is the earliest mention of his Symphony in F-sharp, not to be completed until 1952. The mountains and forests of Canada provided the creative spark for what many consider his greatest postwar work. The holiday was to prove only a temporary respite, however. Within a few weeks of his return, Erich Wolfgang Korngold would be hospitalized for the first time in his life.

CHAPTER TWENTY-TWO

Return to Europe

On 9 September 1947 during a visit to his old friend, the violinist Robert Pollak, Korngold suffered a serious heart attack. Luzi managed to get him to the hospital by ambulance, where he remained for two weeks. In those days, treatment was rather limited and heart bypass surgery as yet unknown. He was required to lie absolutely motionless for his entire stay. When he was allowed to go home, he was confined to bed for a further month.

All plans for the return trip to Europe were indefinitely postponed. He was forbidden to conduct and was advised by his doctors to forego activities that would involve stress of any kind. If he had seriously made the decision to retire from motion pictures for artistic considerations, he now had an equally important reason—his health. For this reason, he turned down the offer to score *Forever Amber*[1] at Twentieth Century Fox and *The Adventures of Don Juan* at Warner Brothers, which he had begun to sketch in 1945. This latter film, which marked Errol Flynn's return to swashbuckling, had begun shooting in 1945 but was interrupted by Flynn's bouts of drinking. Max Steiner, his old rival, composed one of his best scores for it, very much in the Korngold manner. It is interesting to ponder what might have been; among Korngold's manuscripts is a sketch for a poignant love theme he composed for *Don Juan*, and which is not used anywhere else.

If he could not conduct, he could at least still compose and play the piano. One day, he began to play a charming melody that Luzi had not heard before. It was the opening movement of the *Symphonic Serenade* in B-flat Major for string orchestra, Opus 39, which he had composed entirely in his head while lying in the hospital.

For most of 1948, he worked quietly at home. Occasional social and musical events were sparingly allowed by Luzi. One of the most memorable (in June) was a dinner honoring Alma Mahler, given by Eugene Ormandy prior to his conducting Mahler's Eighth Symphony at the Hollywood Bowl. Among the distinguished guests were eleven noted composers: George Antheil, Eugene Zádor, Arthur Bergh, Italo Montemezzi, Miklos Rósza, Richard Hageman, William Grant Still, Igor Stravinsky, Ernst Toch, Louis Gruenberg, and Korngold.

As a hobby, Luzi had begun to write a biography of Chopin, whose music she played extremely well. One of Korngold's favorite means of relaxation was to ask his wife to play the works of Chopin for him, but on learning that she was writing about another composer, he actually showed signs of jealousy, which greatly amused the family. Then, realizing his foolishness, he presented the biographer with a manuscript as a gift for their silver wedding anniversary in April 1949. It was a waltz marked "Frederic Chopin—Opus posthumous," with the inscription "From the beyond." In this unpublished "Waltz for Luzi," Korngold uncannily captures the style of Chopin, and yet the music stands completely on its own merits.

Otherwise, Korngold pressed on with the *Symphonic Serenade* and a collection of Lieder eventually published as Opus 38. He appears to have set aside the symphony begun in Canada. For the songs, he once again rescued material from the film scores. The first song, "Glückwunsch," is based on the glorious main title from *Devotion*, "Der Kranke" uses a motif from *Juarez*, "Alt Englisch" is a song written for (but not used in) *The Private Lives of Elizabeth and Essex*, and "Alt Spanisch" is Dona Maria's song from *The Sea Hawk*. The last in the set, to Shakespeare's sonnet *My Mistress' Eyes*, was newly composed as a gift to his eldest son Ernst, who shared his father's passion for Shakespeare and, recently married and having returned from serving in the US Marines, was now embarking on a teaching career. This final Lieder collection is dedicated to "Maria Jeritza, my unforgettable Violanta and Marietta in Friendship and Admiration."

The *Symphonic Serenade* in B-flat major for string orchestra is an important work and another example of Korngold's talent for taking an existing model and breathing new life into it. Its title gives a clue to the composer's intention. Korngold wanted to write a work for strings alone that would be symphonically constructed yet, by its use of string texture, give the impression of the full orchestra by extracting every nuance and tone color. He certainly succeeded. At no time does one miss the other sections of the orchestra in this richly scored work, which deserves a place alongside the Tchaikovsky and Dvořák serenades of the previous century.

Symphonische Serenade in B–Dur

I.

Erich Wolfgang Korngold
1897 - 1957

Symphonic Serenade, Opus 39, the opening of the first movement. The first bar begins on the flat mediant before swinging to the tonic major in bar two. (Reproduced by permission of the publishers Schott Musik International, Mainz, Germany.)

There are a number of surprising aspects of this work from a technical point of view. Here again Korngold's original harmonic thinking is completely spontaneous. The written key is B-flat major, but the music actually begins in the flat mediant of D-flat major with appropriate harmony, although this opening melody, which so charmed his wife, is entirely in the key of B-flat major. So assured is Korngold's handling, it is analogous with the subdominant opening of Beethoven's Concerto No. 4 in G or even the submediant opening of the finale of his *Rasoumovsky Quartet* No. 2. As with Beethoven, I feel sure that this is how the melody occurred to him and is not a contrived or premeditated device, for it sounds so utterly natural. He saw at once its possibilities, and the whole progress of the movement is governed by this ingenious opening. As in the Piano Concerto in C-sharp of 1923, in which the tonality is "split" between two keys, Korngold expands the borders of his chosen key and finds new ways to move within a traditional key scheme.

This first movement is followed by a delicate Scherzo played entirely pizzicato. Once again, we see an extraordinary economy at work—a spartan theme, a simple triplet used so resourcefully—swinging widely from its nominal key of F major, demanding great articulation. The Trio is played *con sordini* (on the bridge, with a mute)—an eerie contrast, like a ghostly shiver.

The slow movement marked *Lento religioso* is one of Korngold's finest, extracting an amazing depth of expression and color from a purely string texture. Here we are in two sharps, the mediant key of D major, and enter a profound world reminiscent of Korngold's boyhood idol— Gustav Mahler.

The main theme, a noble, deeply felt, and long-spanned elegy extending for thirty-three bars, is concluded with a short, secretive chorale taken from the score for the film *Anthony Adverse*. The impassioned development section is striking, with its anguished octave leaps like piercing cries of despair. Was this an attempt to reflect the tragedy of war? Certainly, it sounds a new note of tragedy in Korngold's style. The recapitulation is in the favorite key of F-sharp major, where the main theme is now decorated with a variation in 12/8 time for the middle voices before the chorale returns in the divided cellos to a transfigured close.

The Finale, an exultant allegro con fuoco, brings us back to B-flat major with a rushing, agitato figure in sixteenth-notes that recalls the opening of the finale to the Suite for Two Violins, Cello, and Piano for the left hand, Opus 23, except that here it develops into a moto perpetuo. Korngold adopts a concertante technique by throwing a subsidiary motif in bare fifths from the lower strings to a quartet of soloists and back to the full orchestra, thus creating an effective antiphonal dialogue. The soaring second subject is a rapturous, seemingly endless, songlike melody in E major, rather like the cantabile theme in the finale to Rachmaninov's Symphony No. 2 in E Minor. It comes from the score to *Captain Blood*, where it was somewhat buried—here it is allowed to blossom. The ingenious coda, in which the opening theme from the first movement suddenly returns before growing imperceptibly into the moto perpetuo, is a masterstroke. Korngold loved such cyclical devices to demonstrate the interrelation and organic growth of his thematic plan.

This exceptional work was completed on 13 October 1948 (according to the manuscript), and it bears a touching dedication: "For Luzi, my beloved wife, my best friend." Korngold felt that it was a significant work and was anxious to arrange a first performance as soon as possible, preferably in Europe. The delayed return to Vienna was now planned for the summer of 1949.

Korngold turned to a former colleague at Warner Brothers, the German composer Franz Waxman, who at that time was director of his own Los Angeles Festival Orchestra, which was dedicated to performing modern works, often as world premieres. Korngold admired and respected Waxman, who was well known in Hollywood for his scholarship. Waxman suggested that the work could be included in a concert that he and his orchestra were to give in Paris in June of the following year.

Korngold agreed, and set about organizing the orchestral parts in Hollywood. Schott was still recovering from the effects of war, and the first materials for Opus 39 were copies of hand-written parts probably produced by former colleagues at Warner Brothers paid privately by Korngold.

On 20 March 1949, Waxman rehearsed the first two movements with the composer present, and the date of 10 June was confirmed for the premiere. It was not to be, however. Waxman and his orchestra were literally standing on the quayside waiting to board ship when a telegram arrived advising them that the financial backer for their planned European tour had withdrawn. There was nothing else to do but return to Los Angeles.

This setback did not deter Korngold. He asked Luzi to write to Helene Thimig in Salzburg to ask her to suggest the work to Wilhelm Furtwängler for the Vienna Philharmonic. One may ask why he did not write to Furtwängler directly. A close examination of the draft of Luzi's letter, with Korngold's additions, reveals the answer. Furtwängler was under attack for his supposed Nazi sympathies (he had remained director of the Berlin Philharmonic throughout the war). Korngold wanted Thimig to suggest that it might be politically expedient for him to conduct a new composition "by a Jew," a suggestion he could hardly make personally. This slightly devious tactic worked perfectly. Furtwängler wrote back at once, adding that he had long appreciated Korngold's gifts and would be delighted to give the performance, perhaps at a concert during the Salzburg Festival, and urgently requested a score.

Before he left America, Korngold had begun to prepare a sixth opera. Encouraged by Bruno Walter, it was to be based on the eighteenth-century gothic novel *Das Kloster bei Sendomir* (The Monastery at Sendomir) by Franz Grillparzer, which had later been turned into a play entitled *Elga* by Gerhart Hauptmann. It was an ideal basis for an opera libretto, just as the

Siegfried Trebitsch adaptation of Rodenbach's *Das Trugbild* had been for *Die tote Stadt.*

An opera had already been written in 1914 by Erwin Lendval based on Hauptmann's play. Korngold, in collaboration with Bruno Walter, decided to dramatize Hauptmann's text from a different angle: the story would be told in flash-back by the main character. This approach was actually more in keeping with the novel, in which the main character, as an old man, tells of the romantic and passionate events of years past to the young couple who take shelter from the storm in the forbidding monastery.

Korngold also wanted to revert to the original title of Grillparzer's novel to avoid copyright difficulties. The theme of this book was ideal for a composer of Korngold's predilections, as it held the brooding passion and mystical elements of *Die tote Stadt* and *Das Wunder der Heliane.* It was to remain an unrealized project, however. Despite the assurance from Hauptmann's widow that the rights to the play had lapsed, Korngold set the opera aside until his return from Europe. His son Ernst recalls many discussions about how the opera would be staged. Korngold was unconvinced until Ernst actually built a miniature set to show how it could be done, but Korngold lost interest and did not return to the subject again.

In late May 1949, the Korngolds finally left Hollywood for Europe via New York, where they were able to visit old friends, including Rudolf Kolisch and the Duschnitzes. George was now his father's secretary and chauffeur. Once in Europe, they traveled by car along the same roads through Switzerland that they had driven eleven years earlier in the opposite direction. They arrived in Paris on 9 June and received a special invitation to dinner with the Duke and Duchess of Windsor (the former King Edward VIII and Mrs. Simpson). Korngold was invited to perform a short recital with cellist Jean Reculard (the Cello Concerto in C Major) and soprano Lotte Schöne (Lieder and excerpts from Johann Strauss II). Elsa Maxwell and Lord and Lady Mendel were among the guests. The Duchess, resplendent in a magnificent gown and her fabulous jewelry, asked Korngold for a special request, *The Blue Danube*; he obliged with a virtuoso performance. Later, Korngold remarked on the Duke's perfect command of German.

After the heady atmosphere of this command performance, they went on to Basel, where they met Manzi Ganz, Korngold's first girlfriend. Luzi thought her unchanged except for her eyes, "so adventurous and sarcastic in her youth, now betrayed a certain melancholy." They also visited Hans Müller, the writer who had provided the librettos of *Violanta* and *Heliane.* He had retired to Switzerland (where he died the following year).

They crossed the border to Austria with considerable trepidation, not knowing what awaited them. A stop for gasoline at Vorarlberg reassured Korngold that at least he was not forgotten. As he was signing various documents (gas was still rationed), he was surprised when the pump attendant asked, "Korngold? Any relation to the composer?"

Austria looked much the same as they drove through Salzburg and on to Gmunden and their former home, Schloss Höselberg. Gmunden had not changed. Even the waiter they had known in the local coffee shop was still there. Schloss Höselberg, however, was now a home for refugees, so the Korngolds stayed in a local hotel. None of their furniture or belongings remained, and the house was very run down.

From there, they drove through St. Florian, arriving in Vienna on the 22 June. Vienna was like a dead city. Almost all of Korngold's relatives and friends had either left or been killed. Their former house on Sternwartestrasse, too, was occupied by others, and they had to fight to get it back. For the first few weeks, they lived in the Pension Opernring, opposite the burned-out shell of the State Opera House, the sight of which brought tears to Korngold's eyes.

The premiere of the _Symphonic Serenade_ had now been postponed again. Furtwängler could not fit it into his concerts, and the date seemed to get pushed further and further into the future. There was another Korngold premiere to welcome them, however: the European premiere of the String Quartet No. 3 in D Major and _Narrenlieder_, Opus 29, on 26 June at the concert hall of RAVAG (Austrian Radio) by the Swoboda Quartet and Julius Patzak.

In Venice, late summer 1949, where Korngold encountered Joan Fontaine (pictured), one of his favorite actresses (Korngold estate).

Three days later, there was another happy occasion. The critic Heinrich Kralik, an old friend, had arranged a radio performance of *Violanta* two years previously in 1947 in honor of Korngold's homecoming. He managed to arrange a repeat performance once Korngold finally arrived, and although Korngold was forbidden to conduct it for health reasons, he was able to express his wishes about tempi and dynamics. For this performance (which still exists in the Austrian Radio archives), Korngold's 1931 revised scoring was used, including the superb, altered version of the great duet, otherwise not recorded.[2]

The most pressing matter, however, was the long-delayed premiere of the opera *Die Kathrin*. The Austrian State Theaters were now under one administration, whose director, Dr. Egon Hilbert (a former police official with an all-consuming passion for opera) promised Korngold that the original 1938 contract would be honored.

For these first months then, all seemed to go well. After a court case, they won their house back, and were encouraged when Franz Salmhofer, director of the Theater an der Wien (now the home of the State Opera) wrote to confirm that *Die tote Stadt* would be revived there next season.

Content that prospects for his future career were good, Korngold set off on a holiday to the happy place of his youth, Alt-Aussee. It was a nostalgic holiday, visiting the places of his childhood: Innsbruck, Salzburg (where he had a reunion with the Streckers), Maria-Wörth, and on eventually toward Garmisch where he hoped to visit his old mentor Richard Strauss. After enquiring when such a visit might be convenient, Korngold was advised to postpone it on account of Strauss's illness. The Korngold party took a detour to Italy instead for the last week of August, before spending a week in the south of France with Lilly Duschnitz at her country estate "La Lirodou," which somehow had survived the war. While there, they received the news of Strauss's death. Lilly Duschnitz remembered the event:

> We heard the news of Strauss's passing on the radio. Erich sat motionless for several minutes, unable to speak. Then, he walked over to the piano, slowly and with a look of great sadness on his face, and sitting down, began to play *Elektra*. It was a magnificent performance—no one could play the piano like Erich—with all of the orchestral details in his tempestuous playing.
>
> He played almost the whole opera from memory, without stopping—completely carried away by the fantasy of the music. No one spoke or moved during the extraordinary performance. It was an unforgettable tribute from a great composer to a dead master.[3]

The death of Strauss perhaps symbolized more than any other event the death of the golden age of Korngold's youth. It underlined how irrevocably the world had changed through war and the destruction of the Europe he had known. This painful realization was to be hammered home to him over the coming years.

Before he left "La Lirodou" he confided to Lilly Duschnitz that a sparkling tune he had written at the end of the First World War and set to a word-play on the name of this beautiful villa was now to be a prominent theme in his new symphony, especially in the jaunty, optimistic finale. Clearly, he had already sketched out a considerable part of the work by this date.

The Korngolds returned to Italy, to Florence, and then on to Torre di Lago, where Korngold visited the grave of the other musical god of his youth, Puccini. Perhaps he had a growing sense of his own mortality. While in Florence, he received yet another request to score a film from William Dieterle, who was making *Vulcano* with Anna Magnani on location in Italy. In spite of his determination to retire from motion pictures, Korngold was intrigued enough to watch the rough cut of the film twice and even to begin composing. He actually completed an overture for the main title, but he later sent it to his friend Eric Zeisl in Hollywood, having already recommended Zeisl to Dieterle. He stressed to Zeisl that he no longer wanted anything to do with films.[4]

After visits to Rome and Venice (where they enjoyed a reunion with Joan Fontaine, also on vacation), the Korngolds returned to Austria for the preparation of the Furtwängler premiere at last. Although most of their time was taken up with endless cables and calls about *Die stumme Serenade*, the sale of Schloss Höselberg, and attempts to speak with Furtwängler about the *Symphonic Serenade*, now scheduled for January 1950, they were able to attend a performance in Vienna of the Cello Concerto in C Major by cellist Karl Maria Schwamberger, who had already given the European premiere the previous February. Korngold wrote to his mother the same day (13 November) with a report, concluding with the important announcement: "I have started to compose a larger symphonic composition; the first movement is already sketched, the Scherzo and slow movement are in my head."[5]

Even Korngold's operetta arrangements were enjoying a mini-revival. At the end of November, the operetta *Das Lied der Liebe* was exhumed in Salzburg, followed by a revival of *Rosen aus Florida* on New Year's Eve at St. Gallen. Still, the important date for the premiere of *Die Kathrin* remained elusive. Korngold was frustrated at how bureaucratic Vienna had become. So many petty officials had to be involved in negotiations, and the old days seemed to have gone forever when the autocratic will of the intendant or conductor to perform a work of choice would be obeyed.

The premiere of the *Symphonic Serenade* was a traumatic occasion for all concerned. Set for 15 January 1950, it was to be one of the major concerts of the Vienna Philharmonic in the winter season. On the way to the rehearsal, Furtwängler's car became stuck in a snow drift, and against all advice and pleas from Luzi and George, Korngold decided to rehearse the orchestra himself in the difficult work. Furtwängler did arrive in time for the concert, but with no time for a run-through. The performance was somehow successfully realized (although not without mishaps) because of the musicianship of the magnificent string section and Furtwängler's ability to conduct virtually at sight. The audience and the reviews generally approved, but for Korngold it had been a nightmare experience. Luzi wrote to his mother:

> Erich was repeatedly applauded by the audience. People went wild in the interval, and told me how miraculous they had found it; in the corridors they talked excitedly about how happy they were that "once again" a new piece had been played. . . . Furtwängler . . . never stopped repeating how much joy he had derived from conducting this charming and masterly piece.

Korngold wrote a postscript to his wife's letter:

> All in all, a worthy event. It is a miracle that the performance succeeded at all, and could only have been due to the virtuosity and marvelous improvisation of the Philharmonic. The reviews have been superb. For the past five days a big question mark has hung over our opera plans. The technicians are on strike and all theaters are closed. . . . We must just wait patiently.[6]

His luck, so newly returned, seemed to evaporate. The planned revival of *Die tote Stadt* had to be canceled owing to a typical Viennese intrigue. A leaked announcement of the cast resulted in two tenors being promised the lead role. Both were aggrieved and refused to be mollified. Neither would sing the role.

With no prospect for a spring premiere for *Die Kathrin,* the Korngolds left Vienna for another country trip at the end of May, traveling first to Stuttgart for a meeting with the Streckers, on to Munich to meet with the intendant of the opera house there, and then to the Dolomites and the Austrian Tyrol. At Garmisch, Korngold paid his respects to the Strauss family. He had not attended Richard Strauss's funeral, but had sent a telegram of condolence. Now, he felt strong enough to visit Strauss's beautiful villa, where thirty-five years earlier he had accompanied his father for an unforgettable afternoon. George Korngold recalled that over coffee, Franz Strauss asked Korngold if he would like an original manuscript as a keepsake:

> Dr. Strauss got up and went over to a large chest, pulling open the top drawer. Inside were dozens of pages of music, sketches, printed scores, all kinds of things. Before his father's death, his son had got him to sign and date everything. It was from this large bundle of material that he invited my father to select something.
>
> After several minutes of going through the drawer, my father picked up a four-page manuscript and asked if he could have it. Dr. Strauss looked at it and said, "Oh, of course," dismissing it as

unimportant. Later, when we got back to our hotel, my mother and I both knew that my father would not have picked just anything, and could hardly wait to find out what it was.

My father slowly opened up the pages and showed what appeared to be a very old manuscript, yet dated March 1949. He explained that it was *the* famous waltz melody from *Der Rosenkavalier* but harmonized very simply, without the extraordinary modulations that we know from the opera. He believed that this was Strauss's first sketch of this melody with just an indication of harmony, and from the age of the paper and the style of notation, it must have been written about 1908. He was tremendously excited about his find, which he treasured.[7]

The premiere of *Die Kathrin* was finally rescheduled for October with the best cast that Vienna could assemble at this difficult time. Maria Reining, the preeminent Strauss soprano of the post-war era, led the cast as Kathrin, and the tenor Karl Friedrich was François. Otto Edelmann as the villainous Malignac and Hilda Ceska as the soubrette completed the main cast.

The story of this opera, which underwent so many changes, dilutions, and adaptations from earlier versions of the original, is the kind of melodrama that went out of fashion fifty years earlier. Act I is set in a small French town near the Swiss border in 1930. Kathrin, a Swiss serving girl is in love with a French soldier, François, who is actually a wandering minstrel. Advised that her nobleman employer will fire her if he learns of the affair, she writes François a letter in which she explains that they must not meet again. Undeterred, François climbs through her window one night and tells her that he is only a soldier temporarily, he is really a singer. Kathrin responds, and the two spend the night together. As François marches off to Algiers, unable to tell her of his departure, the act ends with Kathrin, now pregnant, praying for the future of her lover and child.

In Act II, she meets Malignac who owns a night-club in Marseilles. He takes her there and attempts to seduce her. At the same time, François has been employed at the night-club as a singer and is desired by Chou-Chou, one of the singers. Malignac declares his love for Kathrin and tries to force himself upon her, and he later dies from a gunshot wound from his jilted lover Monique. Assuming Kathrin to be the killer, François takes the blame and goes to jail.

The last act shows François wandering the Swiss countryside years later. He comes to an inn, managed by Kathrin. The first person he meets is a young boy, to whom he sings the "Wanderlied" (Wanderer's Song), explaining that he is simply a homeless wandering minstrel. The appearance of Kathrin reveals that the boy is their son and the years of longing end in happy fulfillment for both of them.[8]

Korngold's last opera, originally composed as a reaction to the complexity of *Das Wunder der Heliane,* is almost schizophrenic in style, unable to settle into either opera or operetta, comparable to Puccini's *La Rondine* in this respect. Although the music, a constant outpouring of melody, is consistently effective, the libretto is tawdry, convoluted, and clichéd, full of commonplace devices and coincidences. In his desperate attempt to please an audience of the 1930s infatuated with modern effects on stage (Křenek's *Jonny spielt auf* succeeded as a novelty by incorporating such twentieth-century inventions as a radio into its plot), Korngold embellished his orchestration with modern jazz instruments, including a trio of saxophones and a banjo.

As to what this opera's critical fate would have been in Vienna in 1938 is interesting to speculate. As it was, a jaded post-war audience was completely uninterested in its simple lyricism or its implausible story. In the severe climate of the 1950s, when the prevailing tendency was to repair links with the twelve-tone revolution that was disrupted by the war, its musical style was indeed dated, and the "sensationalist" jazz effects were passé.

Only the famous "Brief-Szene" recalls Korngold's earlier operas, yet here again one finds a deliberate attempt to repeat the effect of Marietta's "Lautenlied" in *Die tote Stadt.* The accompaniment is almost identical, even if the lovely melody is entirely new. The nightclub sequence has an extraordinary cabaret song, to be sung by a voice more suited to Zerbinetta (in Richard Strauss's opera *Ariadne auf Naxos*), a sound unique in Korngold's output. The other standouts in the score include a highly effective march, the taxingly difficult "Prayer" at the end of Act I, an atmospheric prelude to Act II (which had so impressed Bruno Walter in 1937), and the beautiful tenor aria, the "Wanderlied," which with just a simple rising scale, achieves a potent, dreamily nostalgic mood.

If *Die Kathrin* were revived today, it would be regarded very much as a child of its time (that is, 1938)—a particular moment in musical history when the strands of popular and classical culture intermingled, when there was a deliberate attempt by composers to integrate the disparate elements of jazz, *Zeitoper,* film, and musical comedy into a new form. Musically, at least, *Die Kathrin* would offer an extraordinary snapshot of this era, so soon to be branded *entartet* or degenerate by the Nazis. In 1950, however, it did not stand a chance.

The opera was to be staged in the Volksoper, a house larger than the Theater an der Wien. Dr. Herman Juch, an old friend, was the director in charge. The production was directed by Heinz Arnold, who had the idea to frame each set like an open book; the chapter headlines appeared at the top, "like motion picture titles," as Marcel Prawy noted at the time. Rudolf Moralt was to conduct. From the beginning, however, there were serious disagreements between Korngold and the production team. The orchestral rehearsals in particular were extremely painful for Korngold. The atmosphere was icy. Korngold did not see eye to eye with the stage-set designer either:

He absolutely couldn't get used to the new trend of implied scenery. The stage designer Walter von Hoesslin had designed a room for Kathrin, naturally without a ceiling. "Where's the ceiling?" asked Korngold. Hoesslin explained that a modern, intellectual visitor to the theater who saw this room would imagine the ceiling for himself. Korngold couldn't get the thing out of his mind, and a few weeks later, he wrote to Hoesslin (who had a property at Waidring in the Tyrol), "I am coming to spend the day with you to have another talk about the scenery. Please book me a hotel room. If possible, with ceiling."[10]

With or without ceilings, the production was a resounding flop, lasting only eight performances. At opening night, the theater was half empty, the people looked poor and dispirited. In his box, he turned to Marcel Prawy saying, "This is no Korngold house; I am forgotten."[11] Later he hoped against hope for applause for the "Letter Song." When none was forthcoming, he was heard to murmur sadly, "They're all Nazis." Yet the audience began to thaw, and by the end of the evening they were applauding as in the old days. Korngold was able to count forty curtain calls.

The reviews next day offered no consolation, however, apart from an effusive report from faithful Heinrich Kralik, who tried hard to justify the libretto and simplistic sentiment of the story by maintaining that Ernst Descey had attempted to create a new form fusing revue, radio, film, opera, operetta, and popular musical, thereby "making banal reality suitable for musical illustration."[12] Dwindling box office receipts and a mysterious, anonymous threat of violence to Maria Reining if she continued in the role led to its withdrawal. A radio performance of excerpts from the opera took place in April 1950 with Ilona Steingruber, Anton Dermota, Rosl Schwaiger, and others, which has survived and has been recently issued on compact disc. Apart from this, however, *Die Kathrin* sank without trace.

The failure of *Die Kathrin* to secure a place in the repertoire (it has never been performed since) also ensured that plans to revive *Die tote Stadt* were permanently shelved. Radio Vienna (thanks to Kralik) continued to be supportive, however, and mounted the first performance of *Die stumme Serenade* on 26 March 1951 with Korngold himself conducting from one of the two pianos.

Marcel Prawy, who had known Korngold since the late 1920s, was one of his most devoted admirers and remains so today. In early 1951, he produced a long-playing record of Korngold's music performed and conducted by the composer, thus ensuring that Korngold's unique style of playing the piano would be preserved for posterity. The historic album, entitled *Korngold by Korngold*, includes performances of the Passacaglia from the first piano sonata of 1908, two of the *Sieben Märchenbilder*, the Largo from the Piano Sonata No. 2 in E Major, and improvisations on *Die tote Stadt*, *Violanta*, and *Die Kathrin*. Korngold played from memory.[13] His extraordinary performances are full of embellishments not in the printed music: octave doubling, spread chords, additional glissandi, and doubled bass notes, which gives an almost overpowering orchestral effect. I am sure he always played the music in this manner, even as a child. In his published piano sonatas, he put on paper as much as he possibly could, but in performance, he was able to restore the additional details he no doubt heard in his head when composing. Dr. Fritz Zweig, the noted conductor, observed, "Unlike any other composer-interpreter I can recall, his works are recreated a second time under his hands, because the urge to create is alive in his interpretation."[14]

The Korngold album quickly became a collector's item; original copies changed hands for over $250 in the late 1980s. A brief reissue in 1978 ensured wider circulation of these unique recordings, which still await release on compact disc.

With no further projects in view, Korngold resigned himself to the knowledge that a comeback in Europe was not to be easily managed. After much soul-searching, Korngold decided to return to America for the time being. He had arranged for the sale of the house in Sternwartestrasse, and had already decided to dispose of Schloss Höselberg. After one last concert of entirely his own works on 14 March 1951, organized by the *Gesellschaft der Musikfreunde*, including the European concert premiere of both the String Quartet No. 3 and *A Passover Psalm*, in which he was a participating soloist, and following the broadcast of *Die stumme Serenade*, he prepared to go home. He now truly felt that America was home. The concert had been a success and had even received enthusiastic reviews, but Korngold was depressed. The Brahms-Saal had been only half full, although he had been able to spot Otto Klemperer, incognito, at the very back.[15]

In Mainz, a reunion with the Strecker brothers at Schott was pleasant enough, but, as Luzi noted, it was perhaps a sign of the times that Korngold, once the pet composer of the ancient publishing house, now found no backing even from them for a relaunch of his works. Feeling out of step with the prevailing mood, the Korngolds journeyed on to Paris and on 16 April 1951 they sailed on the *S. S. De Grasse* back to New York.

Back in Hollywood, Korngold threw himself into new activities to dispel his depression. He had decided to remodel his house, and plans were duly drawn up under his watchful supervision. In addition to these purely domestic pleasures, he decided to concentrate once more on the symphony he had been trying to finish since 1947. Work progressed rapidly once he was free of the distractions of trying to adjust to an alien environment, which is what Vienna had now become for him.

By September 1952, he had completed the entire score of the Symphony in F-sharp and felt proud of what he had achieved. It is certainly his most significant composition from this time, and seems far removed from such works as *Die stumme Serenade*. One of the most remarkable aspects of Korngold's musical personality is that he could write music of such a high order, both in intensity and depth, yet also compose a score of superficial, lightweight charm, as in his intimate stage comedy *Die stumme Serenade*.

The Symphony in F-sharp, although constructed entirely in this period, does have its origins far earlier in his career. While assisting in the preparation of his musical manuscripts for deposit in the Library of Congress in 1980, I came across a four-page sketch of the main theme of the first movement, harmonized differently but in the correct key. The original title had been rubbed out, and the words "Sinfonie—Hauptthema" (Symphony—Main Theme) written over it. These words are clearly in Korngold's handwriting as it was circa 1950. The score is dated by Julius Korngold as Christmas 1919, however, and the notation and paper are clearly from this time. So, we can infer that this highly original theme was first intended for another composition and then rescued thirty years later for his Symphony in F-sharp. I believe that Korngold began to compose the horn call from the Scherzo while in Canada, stimulated by the spectacular rocky landscape and mountainous scenery, although I have no actual proof.

Once again, as in his Piano Concerto in C-sharp, Korngold does not specify major or minor. The tonality of the first movement swings between the two, although the written key signature is F-sharp major. A symphony in F-sharp major is rare: Mahler's incomplete Symphony No. 10 and Messiaen's *Turangalîla-symphonie* are the only important examples of which I am aware, but in Korngold's *oeuvre* it was clearly a favorite key.

The scoring is for a large orchestra, including an expanded percussion group (including marimba), four horns, three trumpets, four trombones, celeste, and piano. The early theme from 1919 gives the first movement its driving force, accompanied by a dissonant three-note motif, which is rhythmically interchanged and scored for two bassoons, marimba, piano, and pizzicato strings. The theme, intoned by the B-flat clarinet, receives its impetus from a rising seventh.

Its complex structure unravels for some fifty bars before giving way to a lyrical second subject, a tranquil song built on rising fourths and fifths. This is actually the merry jingle "La Lirodou" composed for Lilly Duschnitz. Korngold described this (in an unpublished note on the work) as a "bucolic episode."[16]

The Scherzo is a swift tarantella demanding articulate virtuosity, with a heroic secondary idea for horns. The Trio is sparse, ethereal, eerily chromatic, based on a simple, descending theme that passes through a seemingly endless series of modulations. Korngold was especially proud of this Trio and its economy of material.

Once again, Korngold borrows material from his film scores, but only in the third and fourth movements. For the Adagio, a solemn elegy in D minor pervaded by an air of great tragedy and penetrated by three ecstatic climaxes, he turned to three of them: the main idea is the theme for the Earl of Essex from *The Private Lives of Elizabeth and Essex*, the secondary theme is a fragment from the main title to *Captain Blood*, and the development is the atmospheric jungle theme from *Anthony Adverse*. Korngold's use of these themes is entirely different, however, and they are transformed into a cohesive symphonic whole. This is his finest slow movement, and many recent commentators have described it as the greatest since Bruckner and Mahler. Korngold described the conclusion of the Adagio as an "ecstatic Abgesang."

In the Finale Korngold takes the dreamy second subject of the first movement (the early jingle on "La Lirodou") and transforms it into a jaunty dance. One of the subsidiary ideas is another film melody; the noble Grandmother theme from *Kings Row,* now syncopated and almost unrecognizable. The movement is in expanded rondo form with cyclic references to the preceding movements before it returns to the solemn coda of the first movement, which then hurtles on to its triumphant finale in the key of F-sharp major. The orchestration of the symphony, while still recognizably Korngold, has taken on a much harder profile. The shifting perspectives and instrumental clusters act almost like a prism of kaleidoscopic color in which each instrumental group is intermittently revealed.

Korngold, writing in the third person, declared in his commentary on this symphony:

> The composer characterizes his new symphony as a work of pure, absolute music with no program whatsoever, in spite of his experience that many people—after the first hearing—read into the first movement the terror and horrors of the years 1933–1945, and into the Adagio the sorrows and sufferings of the victims of that time.[17]

The symphony is dedicated to the memory of Franklin Delano Roosevelt. Korngold had become an American citizen in 1943 and felt grateful to the country that had offered him a safe haven and employment. Roosevelt's death affected him deeply. Because of the dedication, many believe that there is a deliberate quotation of the patriotic song "Over There" by George M. Cohan in the last movement. There is no evidence to support this, however.

A letter written to a German admirer, Dr. Herman Lewandowsky, on 21 August 1952 as the work was nearing completion, gives some insight into his feelings concerning modern music and the impact he hoped the symphony might have:

> No—I have *not* become atonal and I also think that my new Symphony will prove to the World that monotony and "modernism" at the cost of abandoning invention, form, expression, beauty, melody—in short, all things connected with the despised "romanticism"—which after all has produced some not so negligible masterpieces!—will ultimately result in disaster for the art of music.[18]

With the Symphony in F-sharp completed and orchestrated, he again had to organize the materials and attempt to find a first performance, this time in America. He had formed a close friendship with the conductor Vladimir Golschmann, who had impressed him with his sympathetic interpretation of the Violin Concerto in D Major, but Golschmann was unable to schedule the work immediately. So began the tortuous process of trying to place the symphony for performance. Luzi was again appointed secretary, writing letters on behalf of the composer, trying her best to stimulate interest, and arranging the supply of scores to anyone who requested one.

In the meantime, in January 1953, Heifetz finally recorded the Violin Concerto in D Major with the Los Angeles Philharmonic under Alfred Wallenstein for RCA Victor, with the composer present. It is the definitive account of this work and has been re-issued many times. Many consider it to be the finest recording ever made by Heifetz, and it was the first major Korngold work to be issued on long playing records.

At this moment, operetta called again. Edwin Lester announced that the Los Angeles Civic Light Opera Company had decided to revive *The Great Waltz*. He asked Korngold to revise the entire score, which in America had become increasingly overblown and rather unwieldy. This adaptation was closer to the original *Walzer aus Wien* and included new songs and ballet pieces. It opened on 8 June 1953, although Korngold was not on the podium. Arthur Kay conducted, while Korngold sat in his box beating time. Later, as a special treat by his doctor, he was allowed to conduct the *Radetzky March* at the performances in San Francisco. This was the last time he would ever conduct in the theater.

He also composed what was to be his last song, an impassioned hymn in praise of the Vienna of his youth, set to an unpublished text by Hans Kaltneker. This poem, part of a set of sonnets, was given to him by a Dr. Margaret Steger, who paid him a visit on his return from Europe. Her mother had been a close friend of Kaltneker, who had given her these manuscripts as a gift. Korngold set the words to a completely revised version of his lyrical overture to the film *Escape Me Never* and the song, entitled "Sonett für Wien," was published as Opus 41.

At the same time, he had received a commission to write two works for American school orchestras. He obliged with *Theme and Variations for Orchestra*, Opus 42, which was to be his last published composition to an original theme and demonstrated that he had lost none of his powers of thematic extemporization.

The second was *Straussiana for Orchestra*, an arrangement of three little known pieces by his beloved Waltz King, which bears no opus number: "Fürstin Ninetta," a new pizzicato polka; the "Bitte-Schön-Polka" from *Cagliostro in Wien*; and a waltz from *Ritter Pazman*. The orchestral works and the "Sonett für Wien" were completed by August 1953. The former were given their first performance at a concert in Inglewood that November.

According to his wife, Korngold became highly superstitious, and said, "Opus 42. Ever since I was a boy I have known that I would never write more than Opus 42." Of course, she rightly protested that with his film scores and other unpublished work, he had far exceeded this figure, but the uneasy feeling remained.

Although he was supposedly retired from motion pictures, film offers continued to come in. Errol Flynn suggested that Korngold be approached for his abortive version of *William Tell* to be made on location in Italy (Korngold rejected this),[19] and Henry Blanke at Warner Brothers offered an epic romantic saga, the remake of Edna Ferber's sprawling drama about the depression, *So Big*. Korngold did sketch some themes for this, but only half-heartedly. After a few weeks, he turned it down; Max Steiner again stepped in to fill the assignment.

He had no sooner refused than another film project arose, of a much more substantial nature. William Dieterle approached him with a proposal to make a film about the life of Richard Wagner, to be made in Germany in the original locations. Korngold was to arrange and edit Wagner's music, not compose an original score.

Korngold hesitated to return again to Europe so soon, and for such a strenuous production, but the world premiere of the Symphony in F-sharp was finally announced by Austrian Radio, to be given in October 1954, conducted by Harold Byrns. Korngold wanted to be on hand for this event, which could prove decisive.

The persuasive Dieterle got his way, and Korngold finally agreed to do the film, on condition that not a single note of Wagner's music be changed. On 28 July 1954, the Korngolds set off from Los Angeles once again for what would prove to be their final trip to Europe together.

Return to Europe, 1954. The Korngolds en route to Munich for *Magic Fire* (Korngold estate).

CHAPTER TWENTY-THREE

Faith in Music

M*agic Fire*, as Dieterle's film was to be called (after the book by Bertita Harding, a friend of his, who also wrote the screenplay), was another great missed opportunity. Dieterle had persuaded Republic Pictures in Hollywood to back the project with money frozen in German banks after World War II that could not be transferred to the United States. Republic Pictures enjoyed a reputation for producing westerns and lurid melodramas although they had more recently made some prestige productions with John Ford, including the Oscar-winning *The Quiet Man*. Even so, the studio seemed an odd choice for such a serious artistic project. Before shooting even began the president of Republic Pictures, Herbert J. Yates, visited Germany, where he announced in an interview that the studio planned to make a film there about "the life of George [sic] Wagner, a love story with some music." This did not augur well for the film and caused great disquiet among the German music-loving public, which considered Wagner to be nothing less than holy.

According to George Korngold, the primary reason for his father taking on the difficult task was to protect the music of Wagner, which he revered. He felt that in less capable hands, Wagner would suffer the same hatchet job that so many other great composers had in earlier "Hollywood" biographies. Yates's remarks merely reinforced his concerns.

Korngold stipulated that he would have absolute control over chosen repertoire, artists, orchestra, chorus, and even the recording venue. His wishes in musical/dramatic matters were to be obeyed no matter what. In a statement he prepared in English for the press for the film's American release, he said, in part:

> When I accepted William Dieterle's invitation to supervise the musical shaping of his Richard Wagner film *Magic Fire*, I did it with the understanding that it would be my artistic intention to use Wagner's music in its original form, without adding a single bar to satisfy the demands of the "background music" or changing the orchestration of the opera excerpts actually performed.
>
> I need not explain or apologize for the obvious: namely that there was much music to be cut—the fifteen hours of the *Ring* are flashed on the screen in less than three minutes!—that I had to insist on livelier tempos throughout . . . and that I was forced to transpose some passages into different keys in order to avoid adding "bridges" or modulations.[1]

Because he was no longer allowed to conduct, a conductor had to be found in Germany. The composer-conductor Alois Melichar (who had worked in films and had been in correspondence with him about his own works) seemed ideal to Korngold, and indeed there was never a disagreement between them. Together they assembled a wonderful cast of singers: Leonie Rysanek, Hans Hopf, Otto Edelmann, and Annelies Kupper. Professor Rudolf Hartmann, Director of the Munich Opera, was to direct all of the opera sequences.

The film was to be photographed in something called Trucolor, but at least it would be supervised by award-winning cameraman Ernest Haller, who had photographed *Gone With the Wind*, as well as *Devotion* and *Deception*. For the scenes in which Wagner or Hans von Bülow played the piano, Korngold dubbed the track himself. When Liszt and Wagner played together in a scene, Korngold dubbed both tracks, and created an overwhelming effect.

George Korngold, who was music editor on the film, vividly recalled the elaborate production:

> Shooting began in late August 1954 in Schwetzingen, Germany, a small town . . . that boasted one of the few remaining undamaged baroque Court Theaters. The *Lohengrin* sequence was filmed there with over 1000 dress-extras in the audience. I was in charge of "playbacks," entire musical sequences previously recorded in Munich to which the actor-singers mouthed the singing and an orchestra "played." Suddenly, it was discovered that Dieterle had forgotten his white gloves, without which he absolutely refused to begin shooting

any film. He was quite superstitious and also firmly believed in astrology, having signed his contract for *Magic Fire* at exactly 5:22 A.M. on the day prescribed by his astrologer, thus apparently ensuring the picture's success!

A messenger was dispatched to Heidelberg to find white gloves, and when he finally returned after four hours, shooting could begin. In the meantime, the entire crew, the stars and the extras had all waited patiently, and the production manager, Lee Lukather, a veteran of Republic westerns, who hated this film and in particular the music which "cost a bundle" ranted at the loss of time—and money. (Ironically, this rough and tough man, who only came into his own when real horses were used during the shooting of the "Ride of the Valkyries," developed an almost touching attachment to my father.)

This had not been an auspicious beginning, but nevertheless, things began to improve immediately, with Dieterle pushing ever forward with the complicated schedule which included locations in Bayreuth and Munich.

While shooting in the Bayreuth Festspielhaus, it was discovered that the actor who was to portray the conductor Hans Richter had not shown up . . . and Dieterle appealed to my father to take his place so that filming of the difficult *Ring* sequence could commence. Dressed in tails and made up with a beard and wig, my father thus made his acting film debut.

Magic Fire, 1954. A dynamic Korngold gives Alan Badel, who portrayed Richard Wagner in the film, lessons in how to conduct (Korngold estate).

Throughout the making of *Magic Fire* my father labored to preserve the essence and character of Wagner's music, and in the first-cut version, which lasted over two and a half hours, fifty minutes of music was presented uninterrupted by dialogue.

He strove to structure the "background score," in such a way that no piece would be played in depicting any particular time in Wagner's life that Wagner would not already have written. He felt that even though he had to substantially prune and shorten some of the music due to its inherent length, he could maintain its integrity and musical value. Little did he know what lay in store. . . .

Half way through shooting, a reel of magnetic film arrived from Hollywood marked "Main Title Song." I played it when my father was not present and found that it contained a pop arrangement of the "Siegfried Idyll" complete with a crooned vocal and disrespectful reharmonization of Wagner's chord structures. The lyrics were something on the line of "Magic Fire, you're my heart's desire . . . ." When Dieterle heard of this outrage, he made everyone who knew swear that my father would never find out about it because he knew that he would resign on the spot.

He then cabled Republic that if they really insisted this "song" be used, he would immediately stop production. Not another word was heard . . . ! Later, when the film was completely finished, I played this travesty for my father who was amused but not really shocked because he knew that anything was possible in Hollywood and that at least he had protected Wagner to the best of his abilities.[2]

Korngold worked long hours on this difficult film. In spite of Luzi's protests, he even contrived to conduct a long eight-hour rehearsal himself, with, he assured her, "slow, unstressful" pieces. He was in his element, fully involved in all aspects of the production, in the recording studio, on the platform, on the set, attending script conferences—even coaching the actors—especially Alan Badel as Wagner, who had to learn how to conduct properly. Korngold would not brook an attempt at "pantomime," but, just as he had done with Claude Rains in *Deception*, ensured that when Badel conducted, his baton strokes were correct and in time with the music.

Luzi tried hard not to be worried, even when the heart spasms returned. In October, the premiere of the Symphony in F-sharp was to take place at the studios of Austrian Radio in Vienna, where Korngold also was to accompany Hildegard Rössel-Majdan in some of his new Lieder, including the first performance of "Sonett für Wien."

The performance of the symphony depressed him deeply.[3] There were far too few rehearsals, and, in fact, after the final rehearsal, Korngold begged for the performance to be canceled. This was impossible, however, and the performance went ahead. In spite of reasonable reviews—contemporary critics compared him to Mahler and Bruckner—Korngold

Magic Fire, 1954. A mischievous Korngold surrounded by the leading ladies in the cast, Rita Gam (left) and Valentina Cortese (right) (Korngold estate).

asked for the tapes to be erased, particularly because of the quality of the tape recording: "the sound of the tape was louder than the trumpets," he complained to Kralik.[4]

A comeback and success for the symphony now depended on a good performance in America. Golschmann wrote asking that the parts be sent as a matter of urgency, so that a premiere could be scheduled for the spring of 1955. When they failed to arrive, the performance was postponed, only to be canceled again because Golschmann broke his arm. Apart from broadcast performances in Graz by faithful Alois Melichar and by Jan Koetsier[5] with the Munich Philharmonic in 1955, it was not performed again during Korngold's lifetime.

Korngold took another break from filming in November for the stage premiere of _Die stumme Serenade_. This received a volley of bad reviews, which effectively buried it, and like _Die Kathrin,_ it has never been performed since.

Disheartened, he returned to Munich for the completion of _Magic Fire_. Post-production proceeded smoothly. The final cut version ran 150 minutes, and was, if not the greatest film ever made, at least a fair representation of Wagner's art, largely because of the considerable amount of his music that was heard rather than the pedestrian script. When this version was screened for the executives of Republic Pictures, however, they immediately ordered it to be cut to two hours. This was the version shown at the Royal Command Performance in London in 1955. The distributors then insisted on further cuts, until the final version ran at only 93 minutes. George Korngold remembered his father's despair at these events:

Throughout the filming, my father began to see more and more of his "dreams" fading, and when we watched the first screening . . . he turned to me with a twinkle in his eye and whispered ". . . perhaps Dieterle should have signed his contract at 6:30 in the morning!"

Later, as the film was being shortened more and more, he nevertheless kept his undaunted good humor and once remarked that "when I had to compress sixteen hours of the *Ring* into five minutes, that was already drastic, but now that they have cut it down to four minutes—that's too much."[6]

Magic Fire was released (or as one of the production team quipped, "it escaped") on 15 July 1955, and quickly disappeared as a second feature at cheap movie theaters or "grind houses," as they are known. It occasionally appears now on late-night television in an even shorter version.

Korngold had planned to return to America in April 1955 as soon as post-production on *Magic Fire* was complete. But Professor Hartmann asked him to postpone his trip by a few weeks, since there was a premiere at the Prinzregententheater which might interest him. "Really?" asked Korngold, "What of?" "*Die tote Stadt,*" replied Hartmann.

This was to be the last great musical joy of Korngold's life. A fine cast led by Marianne Schech and Hans Hopf, exquisite designs, and, on the podium, another friend from happier days, Robert Heger, contributed to a wonderful production. The atmosphere was a happy one, and the rehearsals went without a hitch. The premiere was a genuine success, dispelling Korngold's fears that his most famous work would mean nothing to a modern audience. After Marietta's "Lautenlied," spontaneous applause and stamping of feet erupted for a full three minutes—something that had never happened before. At the end of the first act, the audience gave a standing ovation—it was unbelievable, just like the early days of Korngold's youth.

Richard Strauss's son Franz, who came especially from Garmisch for the premiere, was not so convinced by this outpouring, however. He took Luzi aside in the interval and said, "They are cheering him now—but tomorrow they will tear him to shreds, you'll see." The following day, the critics indeed tore the opera to shreds, without even mentioning the triumphant success of the evening. Nevertheless, the remaining seven performances were sold out and, in spite of the critical reaction, Korngold had seen the indestructible effect of his opera on an audience. Although any thought of a comeback was now inconceivable, he was content with the knowledge that his music could still move people, and he resigned himself to return to America for good.

As he prepared to leave, he was visited by the music critic Karl Schumann, who requested an interview. Schumann's article provides a depressing picture of Korngold at this time:

Korngold looked like the less familiar photographs of himself; small, plump, and pale. He had an anachronistic effect with his obligatory bow tie, old-fashioned courtesy, and broad Viennese German. His years in the United States did not seem to have left a mark on him.

Speaking with him was like being taken back thirty years in time. He seemed to be appallingly weary, this man who had been through emigration and the mill of the film studio. That he was suffering from heart disease was obvious; so was his heartsickness.[8]

Korngold had much cause for "heartsickness." Before he left, there was the sale of Schloss Höselberg to be completed, and he insisted on making one last trip to say farewell. Just as when he had first seen it nearly thirty years earlier, it was magical, covered in snow, on a clear, bright, starry night. The years between had brought unbelievable upheaval, and, reflecting this, the beautiful carved ceiling of the dining room was virtually destroyed. Only one carving was unscathed, Luzi noted: "God Punishes."

The return journey by car once more took them through Belgium, as the return passage was booked on the *S. S. Ryndam* from Rotterdam. Korngold decided to visit Bruges, the "dead city," for the first time. Luzi remembered:

We arrived there in the pouring rain and first took shelter in a bar at the market place. At the next table sat a man who recognized Erich. He hailed from Vienna but now lived in Bruges, and offered not only to give us a guided tour but insisted on introducing Erich to the Bürgermeister, where he was ceremoniously received. This unexpected honor cost us much precious time, but like Erich's Paul [in *Die tote Stadt*], we were still able to stand by the "minnewater" "staring into the dark depths," to listen to the bells of the countless churches, to see the Beguine whisk through the narrow alleyways; on this overcast and comfortless day, Erich's "dead city" came alive for us.[9]

On May 18 1955, the Korngolds left Europe for the last time.

In Hollywood once more, Korngold resolved to try to arrange the US premiere for his Symphony in F-sharp and began the depressing task of writing what amounted to begging letters to the directors of America's major orchestras. He also asked his old friend Bruno Walter to write on his behalf to major conductors with whom he was not acquainted personally and give his personal endorsement to the new symphony.

Walter had already declined to conduct the work because of his advancing years. He was no longer able to learn new, difficult scores and confined his repertoire mostly to Mozart and Mahler, but he did admire Korngold's new work and wrote a glowing testimonial to many conductors, including Fritz Reiner in Chicago, Charles Munch in Boston, and the Greek maestro Dimitri Mitropoulos, saying:

Yesterday I had the opportunity to hear a recording of a symphony by Erich Wolfgang Korngold. It was a profound impression for here was an important work of original thematic substance, of a rare emotional power in a masterly symphonic form. The instrumentation is also that of a master.[10]

With the exception of Mitropoulos, not one of them showed the slightest interest in it, and the most depressing collection of letters in Korngold's estate are the terse notes of rejection, often not even written by the conductors themselves but by a secretary or other minion.

Luzi wrote to Alma Mahler:

Dimitri Mitropoulous wrote to Erich saying, "For a long time I was searching for a work that would please me entirely, and believe me, I found it in your symphony."[11]

Even so, Korngold was writing to the Greek maestro as late as April 1957 to ask what plans he had concerning the work and offering him the score. In any event, Mitropoulos did not conduct it for reasons impossible to determine.

Korngold wrote his final published essay in October 1955 in a foreword to a book by a young friend and admirer, Ulric De Vaere, entitled *Faith in Music*, a collection of essays about the influence of religious belief on the composition of great musical works. It provides further insight into his pessimistic view of the modernistic trends prevailing at the time, yet could almost serve as his final testament. Here he comes closest to ever affirming a belief in any deity. Korngold typically saw two meanings in the title.

Could not one rightfully assume that the creative musician, who must surely believe in his own creativity in order to be able to transmit it convincingly to his audience, is bound to believe in the highest creator of all being, all life, all the mysterious forces of nature? . . .

As we bring to mind the immeasurable wealth of beauty which the prodigious, creative masters have left to us through their great works as their legacy, it is difficult to suppress serious regrets that in the musical arts, indeed in all arts, there exists a tendency away from beauty towards ugliness, away from the noble towards the revolting, ill-sounding, and chilling.

I, myself, do not believe in the mistaken thesis that art should mirror its time. The horrors of the Napoleonic war years are hardly recognizable in the compositions of Schubert or Beethoven; the beginning of the industrial-mechanical age, which surely had its roots in the invention of the steam-driven locomotive, is mirrored in no way in the poetic works of Chopin, and still less in the music dramas of Richard Wagner, derived as they are from German legend.

No, I am much more inclined to believe the opposite: the genuine artist creates at a distance from his own time, even for a time beyond. The true creative artist does not wish to recreate for his fellow man the headlines screaming of atom bombs, murder, and sensationalism found in the daily paper. Rather, for his fellow man, he will know how to take and uplift him into the purer realm of phantasy.

May I be permitted then to offer a slight variation, another meaning to the title of this book. I have "Faith in Music." I have faith and I have confidence that the classic and romantic masterworks of Bach, Haydn, Mozart and Beethoven, Schubert, Schumann and Mendelssohn, the symphonies of Brahms, Tchaikovsky, Bruckner and Mahler, as well as the charming French and Italian operas, and last, but not least, the operas of the German masters, Mozart, Wagner, and Richard Strauss will continue to maintain their unbroken vigor and impact, and will bring to mankind today and in the future, pleasure and exaltation, dedication and happiness.

That this book may contribute to a genuine comprehension and enjoyment of the purest of all the arts, "holy music" as it is called so beautifully in Strauss's *Ariadne,* is my sincere wish.[12]

The American premiere of the *Symphonic Serenade* in B-flat Major was finally given in Pittsburgh on 30 December 1955, by William Steinberg, another old friend from before the war and Zemlinsky's former assistant in Prague. Korngold did not attend, preferring to listen to the broadcast. He trusted Steinberg completely, and made a tape recording of himself playing the work on the piano as a guide for tempi. Steinberg followed the composer's instructions to the letter.[13]

With no hope of a performance of his symphony, Korngold had begun to plan a house for his eldest son Ernst and his wife Helen on the large plot of land beside his own. They had presented Korngold with a grandaughter Kathrin, named after the opera, or "Katy" as she quickly became known, who was to be one of the joys of Korngold's last years. The new house was completed in 1955, having been built on the foundation of the original music room of the main house. George and his wife Monika (and by now their two sons) had already moved into a house nearby. Korngold had his family close by him at last.

Any composing Korngold might have done was again interrupted by yet another invitation to adapt the music of Johann Strauss, in this case a further revision of *Rosalinda.* Edwin Lester wanted to alter the earlier version to include Cyril Ritchard in the prologue. Ritchard could not sing, and so, against his wishes, Korngold had to provide him with "musical accompaniment," which somewhat detracted from the overture. The manuscript score for this is marked in bold "under protest." It was the last Strauss revision he undertook, and it opened in Los Angeles on 30 April 1956, transferring to San Francisco sometime later. It was televised by NBC.

Although he was still not allowed to conduct, he threw himself into the production, working long hours, attending every rehearsal, demonstrating tempi at the piano, and correcting the orchestral parts himself, often long into the night. His health began to deteriorate, and he frequently complained of dizzy spells as well as occasional angina, but as usual he laughed them away.

After the *Rosalinda* production was over, Luzi tried to convince him to rest, and she was not pleased when Henry Blanke sent him the script of the film *John Paul Jones* that he was then planning, but she need not have worried. Korngold was tired of films, tired of the "treadmill" that motion picture composition had become. He instantly rejected it, without even sketching a single theme. His interest in films had completely evaporated after *Magic Fire*.

His energy seemed to evaporate, too. As long as his new compositions languished without performance, he was unable to muster enthusiasm for anything. He was also deeply depressed about the complete indifference to his work in Austria. On 15 October 1956 he laid bare all his emotions to Joseph Marx in what would appear to be his last letter before his final illness:

> Your lovely, heartfelt letter almost created in me a genuine desire to once more give Vienna a go—a Vienna that doesn't want to hear anything from me—not at the opera, not in the concert hall. If the powers that be would allow it, I would let myself be tempted to try and have my *Tote Stadt* heard at the Vienna Opera on the occasion of my "60th"(!!) . . . . But it is as if I had been obliterated, yes; in three or four books about the Vienna Opera, I am totally ignored (including the sensational Jeritza premieres!) and also, my Father into the bargain, who for over thirty years as Hanslick's successor, had the last word on all musical matters. . . .
>
> What dreadfulness in Art has taken over the world, and not only in Music alone, also sculptors and painters surpass themselves in monstrosities. The Atomic age has produced atomic painters and atomic musicians (unfortunately, it's not a laughing matter).
>
> Since Graz, my wife is not so good. It is thank God, not heart trouble, but rather an extremely painful facial nerve. I myself cannot complain about my health.[14]

These last words seem to tempt fate. Only two days later, on 17 October 1956 after a visit with Ernst and his wife, where as usual, he had tried to speak English for Helen's sake, he complained of having trouble finding certain words and expressions. He also noticed that there was something wrong with his voice.

Luzi secretly telephoned the doctor. Within a day or two, the speech impediment had become noticeable, and he could no longer read the paper properly. The next day, Luzi called a neurologist who diagnosed a slight brain thrombosis, but was nevertheless extremely optimistic, suggesting a short hospital stay "as a preventive measure." By 22 October, his condition was substantially worse. He was becoming rapidly more incoherent as he tried to explain financial matters to his wife (of which she was blissfully ignorant), and when she observed that he could no longer write properly, she summoned George from the nearby Disney Studio, where he worked. Within a few days, paralysis set in. Korngold had suffered a major stroke, and for three weeks was unable to move the right side of his body. He was also unable to speak. His doctors reassured Luzi that recovery was possible, depending on the will of the patient. He returned home and a nurse was hired to help with his convalescence. Thus his last depressing year began, a tragic end to an active life.

From the beginning, he resigned himself to his fate. A completely defeatist air descended on him, and he refused to carry out any of the exercises prescribed for him to stimulate his nervous system. Although he could not remember the names of his closest friends, the names of composers and their works remained deeply implanted in his memory, and though he could not read a newspaper, he could follow ascore with no difficulty whatsoever —an indication, as Luzi remarked, of how exclusively he lived within the realm of music. The part of his brain that controlled his musical ability was clearly intact, but he declined to attempt any further composition. Sketches for a second symphony lay untouched in his desk drawer at his death.

The first page of some sixty pages of manuscript for Korngold's second symphony (composed 1955–1956), which remained uncompleted in his desk drawer at the time of his death and is now preserved in the Korngold collection at the Library of Congress. No indication of scoring is given anywhere in the manuscript, although the page numbering indicates three separate movements. The music is written out in three staves, without any revision throughout (Korngold estate/ Library of Congress).

Dissatisfied with the somewhat passive medical advice she was receiving, Luzi secretly began to write to specialists in New York, Munich, and Vienna in the hope that more effective treatment could be found. In particular, she had been recommended to Dr. Lawrence S. Kubie in New York, an eminent psychiatrist. Her letter to him reveals the desperation she felt and the tragic circumstances she faced:

> Dear Doctor Kubie,
>
> Last September [sic, really October], my husband, composer Erich Wolfgang Korngold, suffered a thrombosis of the brain. His right arm and leg were paralyzed temporarily and his power of speech was almost totally impaired. By now, my husband has almost completely regained the use of his leg and, to a lesser extent, of his arm and hand.
>
> His speech is better too, but still far from normal and he often uses the wrong words to designate objects; then, when one is unable to guess immediately what he wants to say, he becomes very impatient. At times he associates and speaks fairly correctly while at other times he will become almost incoherent, frequently substituting one word for another of quite unrelated meaning.
>
> My husband is frequently very depressed and probably because of this despondency, he refuses even to try doing the therapeutic speech exercises recommended by his physician.
>
> Knowing you to be an eminent psychiatrist and that you have great experience in the field of hypnotism as well, I wondered whether it might be possible, by means of hypnotism, to eliminate my husband's reluctance to apply himself to speech exercises and also perhaps to improve his self-confidence in using his speech faculties. At present, one has the impression that he doesn't care very much whether or not he uses inapt words, yet I feel that deep down, he is exceedingly discouraged about his plight.
>
> Of course I am well aware dear Dr. Kubie, that any diagnosis in absentis is impossible; however, a journey to New York would be quite an onerous undertaking for my husband now.
>
> Before I consider subjecting him to the strain and effort, I would therefore be most grateful if you could answer my questions.[15]

Dr. Kubie wrote a very kind and polite letter of refusal, asking her to be patient and to anticipate a long period of recovery. Her reply gives further insight into Korngold's state of mind and, most remarkably, his unimpaired musical gifts:

> Your advice is most valuable to me, all the more that I felt intuitively that I must not force my husband, who himself assures me repeatedly: "All this is nonsense. If it comes back, then nature will take care of it." Musically everything seems to be "intact" with him. He listens to

interesting musical broadcasts, score in hand, otherwise he does not care to read. He knows every piece of music, in what key it is written, the composer—but even though he started just prior to his illness on a composition, he is reluctant to try out his capacity of writing music. In spite of his assurance that he doesn't care at all, I know that this is the source of most of his depressions.

There is another question in my mind: how to prevent another attack? My husband also suffered a heart attack nine and a half years ago and I am living in constant fear.

Please excuse this long letter which was intended to bear no more than heartfelt thanks. But when I tell you that my husband and I have never been separated since [sic] forty years (when he was 19 and I was 16!) you will understand my anxiousness.[16]

In 1956, there was very little, medically speaking, that could be done for Korngold, and one by one, the eminent physicians consulted all declined to treat him.

By Christmas, he was able to walk without a stick, if a little unsteadily. He could even write his name with his left hand. The greatest tragedy for him, however, was that he was unable to play the piano as he had formerly.

The last photograph taken of Korngold in the late summer of 1957. He maintained his dignity in the face of increasing infirmity (Korngold estate).

One morning, Luzi was upstairs and George was in the garden, when suddenly, they heard the unmistakable sound of Korngold playing, cascades of chords and notes. Both rushed to the music room expecting a miracle. "I just wanted to see if I could still do it," he said, closing the lid. He had been playing with his left hand alone, making a greater sound than most pianists could make with two. He never touched the piano again.

Nevertheless, on 29 May 1957, his sixtieth birthday was the cause of much celebration. Luzi had ensured that everyone was told well in advance, and he was showered with cards and telegrams, including greetings from Alma Mahler, Bruno Walter, Lotte Lehmann, Maria Jeritza, Ray Heindorf, Margit Ganz, Walter Slezak, and, of course, his publishers. One that particularly pleased him was signed "Your Vienna Philharmonic." There were also radio tributes and some celebratory articles, and many letters from ordinary music lovers from throughout America, Europe, and England. All this was a great comfort to him, especially as he had been convinced that he was forgotten.

In the summer of 1957, he decided to make the journey to hear *Elektra* being performed in San Diego, about two hours drive away, by the Salzburg Festival Orchestra. He took his score with him, and spent many hours lying on the beach, reading it. He seemed to move more easily and was more his old self, or so Luzi thought. Friday 29 November 1957 began like any other day. Luzi wrote in her memoirs:

> Erich finished his breakfast and read the paper. Then he reminded me of an important phone call regarding his *Symphonic Serenade*. I picked up the phone, but before I could speak two words, I heard his heavy breathing behind me. I threw down the receiver—he had lost consciousness. A further seven hours of torment, of fruitless attempts to save his life. At 4:30 in the afternoon, he left us.[17]

Although Luzi declared in her memoirs that news of his death caused "reverberations around the world," the truth is less comforting. Korngold's passing merited only small mention in the obituary columns; most described him as a famous film composer, a label he would have hated. Telegrams of condolence were plentiful, however, many from the musical "greats" he had known, including Igor Stravinsky, Bruno Walter, Lotte Lehmann, and Maria Jeritza, who characteristically advised Luzi that she was free to use her telegram for "publicity purposes" if she chose. Although the Vienna Opera House flew the black flag of mourning as a mark of respect, when George told his mother this, she murmured quietly, "It's a little late."

Luzi Korngold was, of course, deeply affected by his passing. Encouraged by her sons, she kept busy and began to write a book about their life together, as well as maintaining a relentless campaign to arrange performances of his music.

After the well-attended funeral, Korngold was buried in the Hollywood Cemetery, where so many of the great stars and artists of the golden age of

Hollywood found their final resting place. Within a few feet of his grave are those of Douglas Fairbanks Sr., D. W. Griffith, and, in a marble mausoleum, Rudolf Valentino. Korngold's simple gravestone included a facsimile of his musical autograph of "Glück das mir verblieb" from *Die tote Stadt*.

With the funeral over, the first task to which Luzi applied herself was a memorial concert. She had hoped that a suitable event might be held in Vienna and even entertained hopes of a revival of *Die tote Stadt*, but the Vienna Opera (now re-established in the fully restored opera house) put her off with vague promises of trying to assemble a first-rate cast. Finally, she conceded that the only place where a memorial tribute was likely was in Los Angeles, where she could at least direct matters with the help of her sons and the remaining friends from the old days.

A concert committee was established under the aegis of Mrs. Erich Lachmann with help from the redoubtable Dorothy Huttenback, a wealthy friend and patron of the Los Angeles Philharmonic, and soon an impressive list of patrons and honorary sponsors was secured. This included Rudi Bing, Mario Castelnuovo-Tedesco, Bronislaw Kaper, Fritz Kreisler, Josef Krips, Lotte Lehmann, Edwin Lester, Darius Milhaud, Miklos Rósza, William Steinberg, Ernst Toch, Bruno Walter, Roy Harris, Hal Wallis, Ellen Reichert, Dr. Jacob Sonderling, Eugene Zádor, Fritz Zweig, and Tilly de Garmo—all devoted friends and admirers who contributed enough to pay for the evening, which was scheduled for 7 June 1959 in Schoenberg Hall at the University of California, Los Angeles. How ironic that Korngold's memorial should take place in a hall named after his chief musical rival.

The evening was well attended. Performed were the Piano Sonata No. 3 in C Major played by John Crown, who had given the US premiere in 1935; a selection of Lieder given by Eva Gustavson accompanied by Dr. Gerhard Albersheim; the Suite from *Much Ado About Nothing* performed by Louis Kaufman with his wife Annette; and finally the String Quartet No. 3 in D major performed by Kaufman's Quartet. An address was to have been given by Bruno Walter, but illness prevented him from attending, so this was read to the audience by actor Robert Ryan, who added some personal reminiscences of his own. Luzi wrote a short program note in which she concluded:

> Korngold in his youth was a Sunday child. He was happy in his art going from success to success, and happy in his human relationships. His crystal clear intellect, his overwhelming sense of humor, modesty, and his generous heart won as friends everyone he encountered.[18]

Regrettably, the memorial concert did not win him a new audience, however, and it was to be viewed as an isolated event over the coming decades. Apart from occasional performances, Korngold's music was almost to disappear from the repertory until the mid 1970s. In 1961, Warner Brothers finally consented to a long playing album of excerpts from the film scores in performances conducted by Lionel Newman and Kurt Graunke. This sold remarkably well but was quickly deleted from the catalog.

Luzi Korngold was a highly gifted caricaturist, as this delightful example shows. *Der elegante Herr* was an album of sketches presented as a Christmas gift for her husband that gently poked fun at his often untidy appearance. He was incapable of tying his bow tie neatly, and she invariably did it for him (Korngold estate).

Luzi was ever hopeful of a revival and continued to write letters advocating performances of his major works. Otherwise, she lived quietly. Korngold's aged mother died in August 1958, and his brother Hanns died of cancer and heart disease in Vienna in 1964. Luzi herself died on 29 January 1962 of heart failure. She was just sixty-one, her condition worsened by years of heavy smoking. Ellen Reichert, her regular card partner for over thirty years, said:

> She really died of a broken heart, not heart failure. Without him she could not live. He was everything to her and she to him. It was a marriage made in heaven, and she pined for him so much that I really believe she wanted to die so that she could be with him once more.[19]

Her last will and testament seems to concur with this. In it she wrote:

> I beg my sons to do their very best to keep alive their father through his works, and not to grow weak in the struggle. I shall leave this world without regret because, since my husband has predeceased me, life has lost for me its meaning and purpose.

With her passing, the story of Erich Wolfgang Korngold seemed finally to have come to an end. There seemed little chance in 1962 of a revival of his work. Modern trends completely eschewed anything that was remotely tonal or, worse, romantic. Yet it was to be Gustav Mahler—the first to recognize Korngold's extraordinary gifts—who would also, indirectly, be responsible for the revival of interest in his work, a revival that, at the time of this writing, shows no sign of abatement.

CHAPTER TWENTY-FOUR

Afterword —
The Korngold Renaissance

*I*f this book had been completed ten years ago, it would have been a biography with a depressing conclusion, telling a story of tremendous early success followed by a sad decline into failure. As late as 1984, Korngold and his music still suffered from a general antipathy based on prejudice engendered by his involvement with Hollywood.

The constant harping on Korngold's connection with Hollywood, as though this somehow disqualified him from ever being taken seriously again as a musician, tended to obfuscate his achievements in other fields and particularly his earlier works. His last compositions were especially disparaged, because it was subsequently learned that in them he had utilized some of his finest thematic material from his film scores.

Then, something unexpected happened. Toward the end of the 1980s, a movement to re-examine the trends and composers suppressed by Hitler (other than Schoenberg and his followers) coincided with a critical *volte face* concerning composers such as Zemlinsky, Schreker, and especially Erich Wolfgang Korngold. This re-awakening of interest in Korngold and his milieu can, I believe, be traced to an earlier trend in the 1960s with the rediscovery of Gustav Mahler and his symphonies.

It is easily forgotten that until the pioneering work of Bruno Walter in the late 1950s and early 1960s, Mahler's works were considered hopelessly long-winded statements of late-romantic rhetoric—a last, overblown gasp of the romantic symphonic tradition. There were no complete recordings, and performances were few. In the British Isles, the symphonies were not performed as a cycle until the late 1960s, when Sir Charles Groves performed them with the Royal Liverpool Philharmonic.

Mahler was of course eventually, and rightly, recognized as one of the greatest symphonists who ever lived, not a sterile reactionary, but a composer who paved the way for radical harmonic change. He now has become arguably the most frequently performed twentieth-century composer. Embraced by a younger generation throughout the 1970s and championed by Bernstein, von Karajan, and Haitink, this revival of interest in Mahler—and late romantic music in general—also led to a reappraisal of Richard Strauss. Once again, it is easy to forget that in the 1950s, apart from in Germany, Strauss was perhaps known for comparatively few works in spite of his huge output. Of his fifteen operas, only *Salome*, *Elektra*, *Der Rosenkavalier*, and *Arabella* were regularly performed or recorded at this time.

It was only natural, therefore, that the artistic followers of these two giants of the first half of the century would also eventually become the focus of attention. The cause of the forgotten was undoubtedly helped by a desire in Germany to come to terms with the tragic events of the Nazi period. This need to expiate the sins of that time led to a major exhibition in 1983 to mark the fiftieth anniversary of the burning of the Reichstag. Performances of music not heard in Berlin for five decades accompanied major art exhibitions and theater retrospectives. This continued well into the 1990s, especially with the re-examination of the infamous *Entartete Kunst* and *Entartete Musik* exhibitions of 1937 and 1938, when the Nazis ridiculed what they considered to be degenerate art and music. A recreation of the *Entartete Musik* Festival held in 1988 in Düsseldorf was enormously successful, and traveled to many other cities in Germany, Austria, and Switzerland before coming to Los Angeles in 1991 and New York the following year.

A major recording project was commenced by Decca Records to enable works banned or unfairly neglected as a result of Nazi persecution at last to be heard. The inaugural issue in this series was ironically, Křenek's *Jonny spielt auf* and Korngold's *Das Wunder der Heliane*, almost sixty years after these operas had polarized musical opinion in Vienna and Berlin.

In Korngold's case, this revival had also been helped in no small measure by the increasingly passionate interest in his work for the cinema—again, a supreme irony given that it was this same work that had so damned him in the eyes of the critics. A major new recording for RCA, produced by his son George, with the National Philharmonic Orchestra under the inspired direction of Charles Gerhardt of orchestral suites from *The Sea Hawk* and other films, became a best seller in 1972, leading to a whole series of "Classic Film Score" albums. It also inspired the writing of this book.

Of course, this recording did not counter the usual criticism that Korngold had prostituted his talent in writing film music, according to musical opinion in the 1970s. It is fascinating to compare the reviews of the first recording of *Die tote Stadt* in 1976 with those of its compact disc reissue almost sixteen years later. Critics of 1976 talked of "pre-echoes" of his film music in this 1920 score, and derided its unashamed emotional outpouring, its unrestrained and extravagant language. In 1991, the reviews spoke of the incredible virtuosity of the writing and the exultant lyricism. Most importantly, whereas before the fashion was to describe Korngold as "derivative" or "eclectic," now, suddenly, he spoke with a voice that was "individual," "personal," even "original."

More recently, the constant stream of new recordings of Korngold's works, which at the time of this writing is approaching some seventy-five compact discs, is greeted with rapturous praise. Indeed, Korngold is now revered by many as a master, a youthful genius, an important bridge between the extreme radical movements of the 1920s and the conservative older traditions.

This revival is not confined to recordings. Performances of his Symphony in F-sharp, Violin Concerto in D Major, Sinfonietta in B Major, and the major operas are steadily increasing in number, and this is also true of his Lieder and chamber works, which a younger generation of performers is gratefully rediscovering. Korngold now takes his rightful place on recital programs alongside Mahler, Berg, Strauss, Schoenberg, and Wolf—not because of his novelty value, but because he sprang from the same tradition and contributed valuably to it.

Bust of Korngold by Anna Mahler (Korngold estate, photo by Len Engel).

The modern revival of Korngold's works was given tremendous impetus by the new production of *Die tote Stadt* by Götz Friedrich at the Deutsche Oper Berlin in 1983 (aptly coinciding with the fiftieth anniversary retrospective of the burning of the Reichstag, mentioned above). This important, controversial, and highly successful staging refocused attention on Korngold as a serious composer perhaps more than any other single event, and traveled to Vienna and Los Angeles, the two main centers of his creative life. At the time of writing, it is about to be revived by the Flanders Opera in Antwerp and Ghent.

In 1982, I decided to found a Korngold Society with my friend and colleague Konrad Hopkins, which has subsequently provided a focus for much needed research and a repository for archival materials, much of it lost or misplaced since the war. A European office organized by Bernd Rachold in Hamburg has contributed the major part of this work in the German-speaking world.

The growth of interest has been constant, even spreading to the British Isles, where the BBC Philharmonic has undertaken what amounts to a single-handed revival by one orchestra, giving no fewer than five UK premieres since 1983. Modern interpreters are championing his work. Artists of the caliber of Gil Shaham, Anne Sofie von Otter, Thomas Hampson, Dagmar Schellenberger, André Previn, Franz Welser-Möst, John Mauceri, Gary Graffmann, Sir Edward Downes, Carl Davis, Libor Pešek, Zubin Mehta, Mathias Bamert, and many others perform the music of Korngold regularly and with devotion. This will undoubtedly continue, especially during his centenary year, when this book is published.

At the anniversary of his birth, a return to the kind of wholesale endorsement and admiration that first greeted Korngold can be seen, accompanied by the growing realization and understanding, at last, that here is a composer who speaks with one of the most individual and personal voices of the past century.

How best, then, to sum up his achievements and his contribution to twentieth-century music? I believe Korngold is important for a number of reasons, not the least is his unswerving belief that to abandon tonality is mistaken. That he has been proved right, that there is still much to be created tonally, can be seen by the number of younger composers now turning away from serial procedures and other abstract devices and returning to conventional key structures, albeit in an advanced form.

Korngold was convinced that the possibilities of tonality could never be exhausted, and according to his wife, he often compared the process of artistic creation with the eternal cycle of exhaustion and renewal in nature. "You cannot make an apple tree produce apricots," he would declare, meaning one could and should not produce artificially or alter natural processes. He could not accept the regimen of note rows or the strict absolutism of rejecting all that had gone before in favor of the Schoenbergian dictum. What he would have made of such developments as Milton Babbitt's "hexachordal combinatorialities" I would rather not speculate.

He also considered himself one of the last of a "dying breed of composers," and his later music, especially his Symphony in F-sharp, can be viewed as a lone, defiant scream in the austere, anti-romantic, post-war era of the 1950s, when he was, in the words of Nicolas Slonimsky "the very last breath of the romantic spirit of Vienna."

Certain critics have derided Korngold for a lack of development from his early to his late works. Although this is not strictly true—for example, the orchestration and form of his Symphony in F-sharp compared with the earlier Sinfonietta in B Major shows a marked development—it is quite remarkable that Korngold remained so consistent stylistically, and that the profile was fixed from the very beginning. Above all, his original use of traditional forms and highly personal harmonic thinking is not fully recognized, even now.

Influences are present, as they are in every composer, but like his great contemporaries, he sublimates them, fusing them to serve his own creativity. Having lived with and studied this music for a quarter of a century, I can recognize the voice of Korngold in a single chord, so extraordinarily personal is his style. This intense stylistic synthesis perhaps occurs only in a handful of other composers; for example, Brahms, particularly in the way he writes chords for woodwind, or Berlioz, whose orchestral "voice" is still completely original after over 150 years.

There are others: Richard Strauss (the opening of *Rosenkavalier* could be by none other) and Rachmaninov. Korngold has this instantly recognizable stamp and can therefore be classed with these highly individual masters and not, as some would have it, dismissed as derivative or second rate. Does this make him a great composer? I think, in considering his best work, that it does.

There has perhaps been no other composer this century who possessed such an unquenchable source of original melody as Korngold. But if I have to single out his paramount gift, it is the truly elemental force in his major scores to move, to excite, and to overwhelm with the sheer power of his spontaneous inspiration. Korngold is quite addictive in this respect.

Every artist is shaped and conditioned by his environment and circumstances. From each experience Korngold took much and produced some extraordinary music as a result. I would not be without one note of his film music, which admired as it undoubtedly is, still deserves wider recognition in the concert hall and still awaits comprehensive publication.

A quarter of a century has passed since I first began this project, and I feel sure that my book is only the beginning of the real study of Korngold and his achievements. A detailed musical analysis of his major scores and new editions of his operas and symphonic works are urgently needed. There is a good deal of material that is still missing—letters, certain original manuscripts and photographs—and perhaps this book will stimulate the rediscovery of some of it. I am also hopeful that as a result of my work, which has been a labor of love, the study of his art will continue and that as a result, the number of Korngold's friends will increase all the more rapidly.

Erich Wolfgang Korngold was indeed the last prodigy. He sprang from the glorious decade that saw the end of imperial Vienna, and lived through the most astonishing century of the millennium, seeing his music proclaimed and dismissed within his own short life. He considered himself to be the last of a dying breed—yet he may prove to be the leader of a new age in musical expression. I hope that this book will play its part in his rediscovery, so that, at last, he can take his rightful, prominent place, in the history of this century's musical development.

Notes to Chapters One Through Twenty-three

Notes to Chapter One

1. Georges Enescu (1881–1955) is perhaps the only prodigy in recent history comparable to Korngold, with whom he is almost contemporary. He was an accomplished pianist, conductor, violinist, and composer. He possessed a phenomenal memory, and was a formidable teacher (Menuhin is his most famous pupil). After entering the Vienna Conservatory at age seven to study violin, he progressed to the Paris Conservatoire, where as a pupil of Massenet he developed into a highly regarded composer. At the age of 16 he produced his first works of note: four study symphonies that are delightful in their melodic vivacity and orchestration. He is best known today for his *Romanian Rhapsodies.*

2. Two other composing prodigies who were contemporary with Korngold deserve mention: Julian Grigorievich Krein, born in Moscow 5 March 1913, was the son of Russian composer Grigory Krein (1879–1955). Julian began composing at the age of four but had to wait until 1926 before his first sonata, written in the manner of late Scriabin, was published. In 1927, Paul Bechert, the Vienna correspondent of the *London Musical Times,* wrote, "There is a feature about his music which inspires keen interest—i.e. Krein's compositions are already conceived atonally . . . . his 'inner ear' is unspoilt by diatonic associations and tradition . . . . and what makes him still more appealing is the dubiety of his pianistic feats, which are mediocre and bespeak his aversion to technical display and brilliance of execution" (1 February 1927). None of Krein's works has survived in the repertory, however, and apart from a symphonic movement once performed by the Philadelphia Orchestra under Stokowski, he was not endorsed by musicians of stature.
The second prodigy, Heikki Theodor Suolahti, was born in Finland 1920. At his death at the age of 16 (1936), he left a violin concerto, a complete Agnus Dei (1936), *Sinfonia Piccola* (1935), and, in unfinished form, a piano concerto, an opera, a ballet, and various symphonic poems. Professor Andrwj Rudnev described these works in Grove (fifth edition) as "amazingly mature works of romantic style."

3. Max Mareczek (or Maretzek) was born in Brünn in 1821, and died in New York in 1897. First a violinist, then a composer and conductor, he emigrated to New York in 1848. He became an impresario and presented many great artists in the United States for the first time, including Adelina Patti. None of his music seems to have survived.

4. Eduard Korngold (Kornau), 1863–1939.

5. The letter, no longer extant, was quoted in J. Korngold 1991.

6. This phrase was first used by George Steiner in a television lecture on Austrian cultural influences for *The Southbank Show,* London Weekend Television, 1985.

7. The streets of Brno (Brünn) have been renamed and renumbered several times under the Nazi occupation and the subsequent Communist regime since Korngold's time. Nonetheless, the district in which this house stood has scarcely altered in 200 years,

so it may be assumed that the house where Korngold was born is still there. Perhaps one day a plaque will stand at the site.

8. A favorite trick of Hanns Korngold's was to order a grand piano in his brother's name, have it delivered to a semifurnished rented apartment, and then sell it and pocket the cash. His brother Erich always settled the bill to avoid an embarrassing story in the newspapers.

9. Letter to the author, 6 September 1975. Paul Elbogen (1894–1986), a writer, was editor of the journal *Blau Rot* in Berlin. He later worked in Hollywood at MGM and other studios.

10. See Geza Revesz, *Erwin Nyiregyhazy*, 1916, Leipzig: Verlag Veit, an extremely thorough account of the early career of this extraordinary child pianist, who emerged from retirement in 1977 to record for CBS. Nyiregyhazy was examined by Professor Erich von Hornbostel, who also observed the young Korngold, and was submitted to the same intelligence tests.

11. Max Graf (1873–1958) was a musicologist, historian, music critic, and a professor at the Vienna Conservatory and the State Academy of Music and Dramatic Arts. The author of many books, he had been a pupil of Anton Bruckner. He emigrated to the United States in 1938, where he continued his writing and lecturing career. He was the father of Herbert Graf, also a writer on music and an opera stage director.

12. Ernst Decsey (1879–1941) was an Austrian musicologist, music critic, and a biographer of Bruckner (his teacher), Hugo Wolf, Franz Lehár, Franz Schreker, and, as mentioned, Johann Strauss. Later he was the librettist of Korngold's last opera, *Die Kathrin* (1932–1937).

13. J. Korngold 1991.

14. L. Korngold 1967.

15. Written by Dr. Böhm for the liner notes for the CBS recording (MK 79229) of *Violanta* (Korngold's second opera) in 1977.

16. J. Korngold 1991.

17. See complete list of works.

18. Quoted in Prawy 1969.

19. J. Korngold 1991.

Notes to Chapter Two

1. A. Mahler 1960.

2. "And so with Zemlinsky," he wrote, "it was always 'Once Upon a Time,'" a reference to Zemlinsky's opera *Es war einmal* (Once Upon a Time) (J. Korngold 1991).

3. J. Korngold 1991.

4. Interview with the author, Los Angeles, 7 September 1975.

5. Recalled by Elisabeth Duschnitz, a friend of the composer, in a letter to the author, 26 September 1976.

6. Printed in the journal *Auftakt* in Prague, January 1921. Korngold actually went on to orchestrate all seven of the *Seven Fairy Tale Pictures*. They were performed only once in Karlsbad (see complete list of works). The manuscript scores of six have survived and are in the Library of Congress.

7. In her memoirs (1960), Alma Mahler recalled how young Erich used to play with their daughter Anna, who was considerably younger than he. Once she invited Erich indoors to have tea with the adults, but he declined. When asked why, he replied sheepishly, "Because I don't eat nicely."

8. Statement taken from the privately printed scores of the Piano Sonata No. 1 in D Minor, *Der Schneemann*, and *Don Quixote, Six Character Studies* for piano. Library of Congress, Washington, D.C.

9. Hermann Kretzschmar (1848–1924), Joachim's successor at the Berlin Hochschule, also taught music history at Berlin University and directed the Institute for Church Music. He was perhaps the most respected pedagogue in Germany at the time.

10. Arthur Nikisch (1855–1922) was one of the most renowned conductors of the

twentieth century. He held posts at the Leipzig Opera (1882) and the Boston Symphony Orchestra (1889–1893) and, most significantly, had a long association with the Berlin Philharmonic Orchestra and the Leipzig Gewandhaus until his death. From the beginning, he was a loyal, enthusiastic advocate of the young Korngold and he conducted all of his early orchestral music.

11. Engelbert Humperdinck (1854–1921), composer of the operas *Hänsel und Gretel* and *Königskinder*, was a pupil of Ferdinand Hiller, assistant to Wagner at Bayreuth, and a prolific composer of incidental music, choral works, and songs. His son Wolfram Humperdinck was also a childhood friend of Erich Korngold.

12. Dr. Arthur Seidl (1863–1928) was formerly dramaturg at Dessau Court Theater.

13. This paper has not been located, and only Dr. Korngold's recollection of the conclusion is noted.

14. Max von Schillings (1868–1933) was director of the Berlin State Opera (1919 –1925) and later the Prussian Academy of Arts (1932) and intendant of the Berlin Städtische Oper (1933). His opera *Mona Lisa* (1915) was one of the most successful of its time and has recently been revived. His reputation suffered because of supposed anti-Semitic views and his later allegiance to Nazi principles.

15. Otto Lessmann (1844–1918) was editor of the *Allgemeine Musikzeitung* from 1882 to 1907 and a minor composer.

16. Hugo Leichtentritt (1874–1951) was a composer, critic, and musicologist.

17. Ferdinand Pfohl (1862–1949) was chief music critic of the *Hamburger Nachrichten* and later director of the Hamburg Conservatory of Music.

18. Viktor von Herzfeld (1856–1920), violinist and composer, was born in Pressburg. He studied at the Vienna Conservatory, where he probably met Julius Korngold. He was professor of theory at the National Academy of Music in Budapest, and a member of the Hubay Quartet.

19. Erich von Hornbostel (1877–1935) was the son of singer Hélène Magnus. His parental home was the focus of Viennese musical life. A pupil of Mandyczewski, he was an accomplished pianist and composer by his late teens. He frequently played four-hand piano with Artur Schnabel at his mother's famous soirees in the late 1890s. A very prolific writer, among his most important studies is "The Psychology of Musical Perception" (reproduced in *Beiträge zur Akustik and Musikwissenschaft*, 1910–1911). He examined Korngold in 1908–1909 and submitted him to the same tests as Erwin Nyiregyhazy; it is reported that Korngold achieved far superior results, but the files and documents on this study have not been located.

20. Károly Goldmark (1830–1915) was an Austro-Hungarian composer, whose first opera, *The Queen of Sheba*, was his greatest success. His violin concerto is still performed.

21. Letter quoted in Julius Korngold's memoirs (1991), lost in 1938.

22. Letter dated 3 January 1909 (actually it was 1910: Strauss had forgotten that a new year had dawned), lost in 1938, subsequently rediscovered and purchased at auction in 1983 and now in the Bavarian State Library, Munich.

23. Ernst Korngold (1925–1996), the composer's eldest son, recalled his father flinging the music stand from the piano at his grandfather in the early 1930s after he had remarked unfavorably about the modernity of a particular improvisation.

24. Berg actually attended the rehearsals in Vienna for *Die tote Stadt* and in a letter to his wife wrote how amazed he was at the music (see Berg's published letters, *Briefe an seine Frau*, ed. A. Langen, G. Müller, 1965. Ed. and trans. B. Grun 1971. New York: Faber and Faber/London: St. Martin's Press).

25. Interview with the author, Paris, 16 April 1976.

26. Related to the author by Ernst Korngold, Hollywood, California, 4 September 1975.

27. Paul Bekker, "Sounds of the Future," 1910.

28. The article has not been located. Dr. Korngold mentions the publication in his memoirs (J. Korngold 1991).

29. J. Korngold 1991.

Notes to Chapter Three

1. It was surely no coincidence that Zemlinsky's own early trio (Opus 3) composed in 1893 employs a cyclic recapitulation in the finale of the themes from the preceding movements, exactly as Korngold does in his, composed during 1910.
2. Whether the Emperor Franz Josef actually attended a performance of *Der Schneemann* is not recorded. The guest of honor on 4 October 1910, however, was Albert, King of Belgium.
3. Korngold's orchestral version was not published because Julius Korngold felt that these pieces were not important enough. In a letter to Ludwig Strecker (Schott) he writes, "We must have something more fitting and important after the *Sinfonietta*" (Korngold's second major orchestral work). Thus, these delightful works, superbly orchestrated, were completely forgotten except in their original piano version.
4. *Auftakt,* Prague, Zemlinsky Festschrift Issue, April 1921.
5. These were "real" German Marks, and this would have been a huge sum in those days, perhaps equal to as much as $50,000 today.
6. Although Schott remained Korngold's principal publisher until his death, the appointment of Hitler as Chancellor of Germany in 1933 and the control exerted by National Socialism over every aspect of German commercial and artistic life, meant that an alternative publishing agreement was necessary for his fifth opera, *Die Kathrin,* completed in 1937. By then, Korngold had already entered into an agreement with Josef Weinberger in Vienna for his adaptations of operettas in collaboration with the Marischka brothers and the *Theater an der Wien.* Thus, Weinberger published *Die Kathrin* and also one of the first post-war compositions, the musical comedy *Die stumme Serenade.*
7. Grädener wrote an opera called *Die heilige Zita,* which was given at the Vienna Court Opera in 1918 before the Empress Zita, a year after his pupil Korngold had conducted his own *Zitahymne* at Schloss Schönbrunn, in her presence. Professor Grädener was above all a thorough musician. He played the violin, piano, and organ professionally and in 1886 he was elected director of the Gesangsverein in Vienna.
8. J. Korngold 1991.
9. Related in Dr. Korngold's memoirs (1991).
10. Review by Rudolf Stefan Hoffmann from *Neues Wiener Tagblatt,* 5 October 1910.
11. Richard Specht (1870–1932) was by far the most important of young Korngold's advocates, and one of the most lucid commentators on musical events of his time. He later became addicted to morphine and died prematurely at the age of 62. Specht was not only a critic but a highly respected author who had written numerous biographies, including the first of Johann Strauss and Richard Strauss, and an excellent thematic analysis of Mahler's music, which is still important today because Specht was a close friend of Mahler and discussed his works with him while writing his book. From the beginning, he was an adamant supporter of Erich Wolfgang Korngold and was later commissioned by Schott to write thematic analyses of Korngold's operas and orchestral works.
12. *Neue Freie Presse,* 5 October 1910.

Notes to Chapter Four

1. Adele Margulies was a friend of Dr. Korngold, and it was no coincidence that the New York premiere took place so quickly. She may have visited Vienna earlier in 1910 and acquired a score at that time.
2. *The New York Sun,* 18 November 1910.
3. It was a great sorrow to Korngold that Buxbaum eventually became a tragic victim of the concentration camps and endured considerable torture before his death.
4. Related in Prawy 1969 and numerous other published sources; confirmed by the Korngold family.

5. *Wiener Sonn- und Montagszeitung,* 11 May 1914, pp. 1, 5.

6. Letter quoted in J. Korngold 1991, subsequently lost in 1938.

7. Letter quoted in J. Korngold 1991, subsequently lost in 1938.

8. In his memoirs, Dr. Korngold (1991) recalls that when the Berlin Philharmonic scheduled the *Schauspiel Ouvertüre,* the critic Paul Bekker asked him for some information on the work, because he had been asked to prepare the program notes. Bekker and Dr. Korngold were rarely on congenial terms, so the composer's father decided "to invent point-blank that Erich had had Shakespeare's *A Winter's Tale* in mind. Bekker started from there and found a way of interpreting this piece of music, which was completely free from poetic associations." Oddly, in a letter to Toscanini many years later, Dr. Korngold referred again to the overture, this time attributing *The Tempest* as the source of inspiration. The enigma of the *Schauspiel Ouvertüre* must therefore remain unsolved.

9. Related by Eva Maria Wiesner née Loewenfeld (1905?–1953), daughter of Dr. Hans Loewenfeld, intendant of the Hamburg State Opera.

10. Saerchinger 1957.

11. "Korngold, Strauss and Others," *The Musical Times,* London, May 1922.

Notes to Chapter Five

1. *Die Musikalische Welt,* Leipzig, 15 December 1911.

2. J. Korngold 1991.

3. *Neue Freie Presse,* Vienna, 15 December 1911.

4. Hoffmann 1922.

5. Interview with the author, Glasgow, 6 April 1977.

6. L. Korngold 1967.

7. L. Korngold 1967.

8. Gustinus Ambrosi (1893–1975).

9. Feuilleton, *Neue Freie Presse,* Vienna, 21 May 1911. An interesting footnote to Mahler's Vienna period concerns the Korngold family. When Mahler pinned his famous letter of resignation to the noticeboard of the Vienna Opera House in 1907, his friends took it down and kept it safe. After his death, it was mounted in a solid silver casket, with the signatures of Mahler's illustrious colleagues impressed into the silver lid, and presented to Mahler's widow, Alma. In 1952, she gave this unique artifact (minus the letter, alas, which had been given to Walter Slezak) to George Korngold, Erich's younger son (1928–1987), as a christening gift for his first son, Gary, who still owns it today.

10. While the critic certainly made his tenure difficult, the root of Weingartner's failure was his refusal to acknowledge his debt to Mahler, who had left a superb roster of singers and a very comprehensive repertoire, both of which Weingartner proceeded to dismantle.

11. L. Korngold 1967.

12. The Motto of the Cheerful Heart, comprising five notes of rising intervals of the perfect fourth, is a significant idea in Korngold's work. It can be detected in the early sketches, and is used by him in nearly all of his major works, from *Der Schneemann* to the *Sieben Märchenbilder,* where it makes its first major appearance in "Der Ball beim Märchenkönig" (The Fairy King's Ball). Later it appears in various guises, both hidden and obvious, in the operas, chamber works, and even film scores.

13. Ernest Newman (1868–1959), born William Roberts in Liverpool, was a distinguished British musicologist noted for many fine books on the music of Wagner, Bach, and Hugo Wolf. He was music critic of the *Sunday Times* from 1920 to 1958.

14. *The Nation,* 24 August 1912.

15. Edward Dent, *The Musical Standard,* 31 January 1914.

16. Richard Specht, 22 October 1913.

Notes to Chapter Six

1. After the premiere of the *Schauspiel Ouvertüre*, the Vienna Philharmonic gave a silver pocket watch to young Korngold with the inscription: "To the young master in his first hour of triumph," which he wore for the rest of his life.
2. Extract from Erik Tawaststjerna, 1976, *Sibelius*, Vol. 1, London: Faber & Faber, which includes extracts from Sibelius's diary when he was in Berlin in 1914 listening to all the "New Music." The following day, Korngold's Piano Trio in D Major was performed along with Schoenberg's String Quartet in F-sharp Minor.
3. One composer who did not rejoice in Korngold's success was Anton Webern, who wrote bitterly to Arnold Schoenberg after the Vienna premiere of the Sinfonietta: "Those dogs—who never play a note by you" (30 November 1913). Earlier in a letter dated 13 November 1910 he had complained to Schoenberg: "Publishers, performances—the boy has everything. I will become old before *that*."
4. *The London Daily Telegraph*, 11 January 1914.
5. *The Musical Courier*, 17 December 1914.
6. Leo Feld (1869–1924), today remembered as Zemlinsky's librettist *(Kleider machen Leute)*, also wrote the libretto for the opera *Die Stunde* by Karl Lafite, which was produced after his death in 1932, as well as many operas.
7. No librettist is credited in the published score.
8. Isidor Cohn (born in Hamburg 1856, died in Manchester 29 October 1928), a student of Hans von Bülow and Scharwenka, came to England in 1879, where he lived first in Bradford. After a successful London debut in 1892, he took up residence in London, frequently giving recitals with the Joachim Quartet. He moved to Manchester in 1898, where he was a prominent figure in the city's musical life. He performed most of Korngold's early works and was doubtless instrumental in bringing them to the attention of the Hallé Orchestra and Sir Henry J. Wood.
9. J. Korngold 1991.
10. Hans Müller-Einigen (1882–1950) was later co-librettist for the operetta *Im weissen Rössl*, which became *White Horse Inn*. After a lengthy career as a playwright and novelist and also chief dramatist at UFA (then Germany's leading film company), he went to Hollywood, where he became a scriptwriter for MGM until 1931, when he semiretired to Einigen in Switzerland. There he remained until his death in 1950. (His brother Ernst Lothar was an equally interesting character, who, as well as being a poet of some renown, also worked in the theater, especially with Max Reinhardt. He was married to the great actress Adrienne Gessner, who sacrificed her career for her ideals once Hitler came to power.)
11. The chord can be analyzed in various ways. According to Dr. David Kram, it could be described as a modified dominant thirteenth on E natural with a flattened fifth, omitting the eleventh (see his thesis on the opera). Like the "Tristan" chord, however, it is ambiguous and open to several interpretations. For a full thematic analysis of both one-act operas, see Specht 1916b.
12. J. Korngold 1991.
13. Letter from Paul Elbogen to the author, 12 December 1975.
14. J. Korngold 1991.

Notes to Chapter Seven

1. Hans Gregor (1866–1945) was a former actor at the Deutsches Theater, Berlin, and founder of the Komische Oper in Berlin. He was director of the Vienna Court Opera from 1911 to 1918.
2. Dr. Carl Ritter von Wiener was also extremely helpful in arranging for Korngold to be stationed in Vienna during his military service during World War I—another good reason for the composer's gratitude (J. Korngold 1991).
3. J. Korngold 1991.
4. J. Korngold 1991.
5. Franz Gruber, who also sang in *Der Ring des Polykrates*.

6. Review from the *Dresdener Neuste Nachrichten*, 30 March 1916.
7. Review from the *Berliner Tagblatt*, 30 March 1916.
8. Walter 1946.
9. Wilhelm von Wymetal left Germany for New York, where in the 1920s he became the chief set designer for the Metropolitan Opera. His son (also Wilhelm) later went to Hollywood, where he staged most of the opera sequences for the popular films of Jeanette McDonald and Nelson Eddy at MGM in the 1930s.
10. *Violanta* was first performed at the Metropolitan Opera on 5 November 1927. The US premiere of *Der Ring des Polykrates* was given by the Philadelphia Opera Company on 10 February 1927. *Die tote Stadt* was first performed at the Metropolitan on 19 November 1921 and was the first opera in German to be performed in the United States after World War I.
11. The celebrated affair between Elisabeth Schumann and Otto Klemperer was one of the greatest scandals of the time, especially after Schumann's husband Walther Puritz attacked Klemperer with a riding crop during a performance of *Lohengrin*, which Klemperer was conducting at the Hamburg Stadttheater (1912). Although by the time of this performance *of Der Ring des Polykrates* the affair was practically forgotten, Klemperer and Elisabeth Schumann remained close.
12. According to the military records for this period, the official reason for Korngold's exemption was his poor physical condition (especially his weight). He was deemed unfit for strenuous military activity (Austrian War Achives, Nottendorfer Gasse, 1030 Vienna).
13. This grand work, scored for large orchestra, organ, baritone solo, and mixed choir (including children), is one of the rarest of Korngold's works, and copies of the piano score are extremely scarce. Set to a text by Baroness Hedda von Skoda, it was premiered in a number of versions in 1917 (9 May 1917 on Empress Zita's twenty-fifth birthday, and with orchestra later). The orchestral *partitur* appears to be lost.

Notes to Chapter Eight

1. *Fremdenblatt*, 25 March 1916, signed "J. St." (= Julian Sternberg).
2. Michael Curtiz later went to Hollywood and became famous as a great action director. He directed many of Errol Flynn's finest films, among them *Captain Blood, The Adventures of Robin Hood, The Private Lives of Elizabeth and Essex,* and *The Sea Hawk*, all of which were scored by Korngold.
3. L. Korngold 1967.
4. Siegfried Trebitsch is best known today as the German translator of the plays of George Bernard Shaw.
5. Unpublished memoir by Siegfried Trebitsch, Korngold Society Archive.
6. J. Korngold 1991.
7. Paul Schott's identity was a closely guarded family secret until 1975, when *Die tote Stadt* was revived in New York.
8. J. Korngold 1991.
9. J. Korngold 1991.
10. From an article written by Korngold for the *Wiener Blätter des Opentheaters* 1921.
11. Both Puccini and Leo Fall are known to have considered Rodenbach's story as a possible libretto, though what Fall would have done with it is impossible to imagine.
12. Julius Korngold states in his memoirs that he and his son visited Bruges circa 1913, whereas Luzi's memoirs describe a visit in the 1950s as Korngold's first. This seems more likely. If Korngold had been there before, he would surely have wished to show his wife the places he had visited with his father. She makes no mention of this, nor is there any record in the local newspapers of an earlier visit, which, given Korngold's celebrity at that earlier time, would be expected. Dr. Korngold's error is therefore inexplicable.
13. *Neue Freie Presse*, 6 May 1917.
14. J. Korngold 1991.

15. The revised version of 1913 was never published, but the score is preserved in the archives of Universal Edition, Vienna.
16. L. Korngold, 1967.

Notes to Chapter Nine

1. Korngold also composed a delightful "Dance in the Old Style" for small orchestra (unpublished), and he orchestrated the Piano Scherzo in B Minor by Mendelssohn in a highly original manner, which was first performed in 1922 by Rudolf Nilius (the score appears to be lost), and several military marches, one of which was later performed in 1930 and published in 1932 without opus number. It has just received its first recording (see discography).
2. 6 May 1920.
3. Only four of the orchestral versions were published in settings for baritone and mezzo soprano.
4. L. Korngold 1967. Luzi auditioned for the role as the pageboy Balthazaar in *Much Ado About Nothing* so that she and Korngold could be together "officially" but failed to get the part.
5. The Schalk/Strauss appointment commenced officially on 1 January 1920, although it had been approved by the new State authority on 1 March 1919. Strauss conducted several performances of his own works during the festival.
6. Undated review quoted in Schmidt 1916. Max Kalbeck (1850–1921), an opera librettist as well as a noted critic, was best known for his four-volume biography of Brahms.
7. *Neuen Tag*, 2 June 1919.
8. Korngold later used this principal motif as the theme for Robin Hood for the film score he composed in 1938 for the film *The Adventures of Robin Hood*.
9. Hans Duhan (1890–1971) was a close friend of the composer. He sang at Vienna from 1914 until he retired in 1940. His roles covered a wide range, from Don Giovanni and Papageno to Rigoletto and Amfortas. He sang the part of Pierrot in Korngold's opera *Die tote Stadt* and the Blind Judge in Korngold's opera *Das Wunder der Heliane*. Also a noted Lieder singer, he was the first to record all three Schubert cycles.
10. *Sursum Corda* was subsequently performed in the United States, London (it is believed), and throughout Germany, and was given by both Nikisch and Furtwängler. It never achieved success.
11. A witty reference to Mozart's serenade *Eine kleine Nachtmusik*.
12. Rudolf Kolisch (1896–1978), noted Austrian violinist, was founder of the Kolisch Quartet (1922–1939), which was famous for performing modern music, moreover, without scores. Kolisch was a pupil of Sevcik, Schreker, and Schoenberg. He championed Korngold's String Quartet No. 1 in A Major (composed in 1922). In 1942 he became leader of the Pro Arte Quartet.
13. Dr. Hans Loewenfeld (1874–1921) had been a *répétiteur* at the Vienna Court Opera during the early years of Mahler's directorship. He had been director of the Leipzig Opera from 1908, and was a close friend of Richard Strauss and other noted composers of the period. He was not merely an administrator, but a gifted musician and producer. He also encouraged the young Otto Klemperer in his early career.
14. Egon Pollak (1879–1933), a Czech conductor, had directed the Hamburg premiere of *Der Schneemann* as well as the early operas. Later, in 1927, he conducted the world premiere of Korngold's *Das Wunder der Heliane*, also in Hamburg.
15. Fritz Rémond (1864–1931) was an actor, singer, and theater director, and was formerly a singer at the Cologne Opera.
16. Richard Schubert (1885–1959), a noted Heldentenor, was famous as *Tristan* opposite Frieda Leider. He lived in Hamburg from 1918 to 1935, where he sang in Korngold's adaptation of *Eine Nacht in Venedig*; he later sang as a guest in Vienna for the fiftieth performance of *Die tote Stadt* on 30 May 1929.
17. Anny Münchow and Josef Degler were leading lights in Hamburg at the time.

18. 30 October 1920.
19. J. Korngold 1991.
20. Luzi's mother Adele (Lillie) had two famous sisters: Stephanie, who married Adolf Matthias, and Lori, who married Robert Nossal. Magda Loewenfeld was Adolf Matthias' sister.
21. Interview with the author on 3 June 1978 in Liverpool. Frau Wiesner was married to the Czech architect Ernst Wiesner, who was the first to hold the Chair of Architecture at Liverpool University.
22. *Signale*, 29 December 1920.
23. *Kölnische Zeitung*, 6 December 1920.
24. Letter given to the author by Frau Dione Neutra, the architect's widow.
25. L. Korngold 1967.

Notes to Chapter Ten

1. L. Korngold 1967.
2. Strauss also personally congratulated him backstage during each intermission.
3. *Neues Wiener Journal*, 11 January 1921.
4. Franz Schalk described *Die tote Stadt* as the "sum of Austrian Opera." Even before the premiere Korngold received an unequivocal accolade that gave him confidence in the work. He confided in Luzi that after the "Lautenlied" had been performed at the dress rehearsal, the fire officer at the Vienna Opera House had come up to him and said, "Herr Korngold that was something splendid!" On many occasions afterwards, Korngold would be seen in deep conversation with his new friend, and they would walk together in animated conversation, their arms around each other's shoulders.
5. Musically, however, the production was so sloppy that Korngold was apparently reduced to tears in his box.
6. J. Korngold 1991. A surviving letter from Puccini to Korngold gives some indication of the warmth of their friendship. Dated 1 November 1922, it reads:

   Dear esteemed Maestro,
   I received your welcome letter at Viareggio—be warned that my scores are very incorrect and also incomplete—particularly *Manon*, which will come out in a second impression. It is very flattering to me that you should be interested in my music. I would like to live in Vienna where one breathes in the true essence of art—I believe now, and I have always done so, that it is and has been the only country where the art of music finds spirits passionately devoted to and with an eclectic feeling for this, our art—how often I think of that dear monument to Mozart!
   Greetings to you and to your country—you, however, are strong and young; write, write as your heart dictates and you will overcome every obstacle—clarity and simplicity!
   Affectionately yours,
   Giacomo Puccini

   Rudolph Duschnitz, who acted as the interpreter in these meetings, recounted years later how Erich would sit at the piano and, to the melody of "Mein Sehnen, mein Wähnen" (the "Pierrotlied" from *Die tote Stadt*), would sing "Puccini, Puccini," laughing uproariously the whole time.
7. Jeritza 1924.
8. Similarly, Mandryka's aria in Strauss's opera *Arabella* (composed 1932–1933) resembles the "Mariettalied," especially in its instrumentation.
9. Letter dated 29 March 1922. Earlier, Korngold had been moved to write one of his rare defensive articles against a scurrilous critique by Dr. Karl Höll following the production in Frankfurt. Höll assumed that the poor musical performance (particularly by the orchestra, which was under-rehearsed) was due to the "sloppiness" of Korngold's workmanship in orchestration. This reproach could not be allowed to pass. Höll's review appeared in the *Frankfurter Zeitung*. Korngold replied in the

Frankfurter Nachrichten (8 March 1922) and quoted the opinions of five noted conductors who had already conducted the opera: Franz Schalk, Karl Alwin, Egon Pollak, Hermann Kutzschbach, and Eugen Szenkar. They concurred unanimously on the fabulous precision of the scoring:

> I constantly marvel at the meticulous care that has been lavished on the smallest detail . . . this is a score that has been worked on with a precision that is elsewhere only to be found in Mahler (Eugen Szenkar).
>
> In particular I must call attention to the unusually careful markings of dynamics and phrasing, rarely found in modern scores (Hermann Kutzschbach).
>
> Höll cannot have studied the score. I know of no score in the entire opera canon of today that is more worked out in thematic processes, and of the lovingly executed art of dynamics and phrasing evinced by every bar of this masterly score (Egon Pollak).
>
> He who calls this wonderful score "sloppy" can only be pitied for his lack of professional experience (Karl Alwin).
>
> This is sloppy criticism indeed . . . . There are few modern works, and even classical works, in which such stupendous care has been taken over the construction, vocal line, declamation, thematic and motivic development . . . as in this score (Franz Schalk).

Despite Korngold's valiant attempt to redress the balance of opinion, the leave of absence by the leading singer interrupted the performances in Frankfurt. Naturally, this was attributed to Höll's denigration of the work, not the failure to find a replacement. It was a sad end to an unfortunate episode.

10. L. Korngold 1967. This was not the first encounter with the music of Korngold for Richard Tauber. In November 1916, he had sung the role of Wilhelm Arndt in the Dresden production of *Der Ring des Polykrates* opposite Elisabeth Rethberg as Laura.

11. Reported in correspondence and documents in the Hamburg State Library, copies of which are held in the Korngold Society Archive in Hamburg.

12. Jeritza 1924.

13. Later in the same letter, he also comments that on the very last day of the old year, "I have found my new opera theme." This probably refers to *Messalina*. Korngold had received a libretto based on the story, and considered it but subsequently abandoned the idea. Meanwhile, work on both the String Quartet No. 1 in A Major (originally planned in five movements, according to this letter) and the Piano Quintet in E Major preoccupied him for much of the year.

Notes to Chapter Eleven

1. Josef Mathias Hauer (1883–1959), Austrian composer and theorist, developed and expounded a technique of composing by use of twelve notes, which differed from Schoenberg's in that it relied on diatonic harmony rather than on total serial methods. Hauer's technique may have influenced Schoenberg in the development of his own theories.

2. Julius Korngold saw a direct parallel between Hanslick's fight against Wagner and his own campaign against the New Viennese School. In his memoirs (1991), he writes:

> This battle against Neue und Zeitmusik—New Music for Our Time, brought my life's work as a critic to a peak, resulting in what may have been its most fruitful achievements. My situation was more favorable than Hanslick's had been in his fight against Wagner. He had faced a tide of real progress. I was facing a movement of regression: music, as it were, wanted to crawl again on all fours. Where Hanslick faced innovation within traditional styles and forms, . . . I faced complete abnegation of the natural fundament of music, of its linguistic elements . . . . Hanslick dealt with a genius who was bound to achieve overwhelming success: I dealt with a dozen little pseudo-Wagners, misdirected talents, and an even greater number of semi- and untalented hangers-on.

3. Interview with the author, Edinburgh, 5 August 1985. Hans Gál (1890–1987), a distinguished Austrian composer, author, and teacher, composed over 100 works, including several operas and large-scale symphonic works.

4. The Piano Quintet in E Major had received its world premiere in Hamburg on 16 February 1923 and had been given its Vienna premiere in June by the Mairecker-Buxbaum Quartet. Korngold played the solo piano part on both occasions.

5. Interview published in the *Neue Freie Presse* 12 September 1921.

6. From the New York Philharmonic Program, dated 26 October 1922.

7. L. Korngold 1967.

8. It has been impossible to trace any of Luise von Sonnenthal's film appearances.

9. J. Korngold 1991.

10. Letter donated to the New York Public Library by Zemlinsky's widow.

11. Hubert Marischka (1882–1970) was an actor, tenor, manager, director, and operetta idol. Like Korngold, he was born in Brünn. Together with his brother Ernst and his wife Lilian Karczag (daughter of the music publisher William Karczag, who controlled the Theater an der Wien), he dominated the operetta scene in Vienna from the early 1900s onward. His relationship with Korngold was not entirely harmonious, as recently discovered correspondence shows. Korngold justifiably felt that Marischka was exploiting him at a time when he knew the composer needed money, by committing him to conduct dozens of lowly afternoon matinee concerts.

12. The original libretto by Friedrich Zell and Richard Genée was completely overhauled by Korngold with the assistance of Ernst Marischka (1893–1963). The production was a tremendous success, not only in Germany but also in England. It was presented at the Cambridge Theater in London on 25 May 1944 with Dennis Noble and Henry Wendon, where it enjoyed a successful run.

13. L. Korngold 1967.

14. Emmy Wohanka, *Hans Kaltneker*, Ph.D. thesis, 1931. In her (unpublished) thesis, Wohanka describes the play and its origins as follows:

> Kaltneker wrote *Die Heilige* between 23 May and 14 June 1917, calling it "a mysterium for music." The time is legendary gothic, the costumes are based on the figures of the great cathedral dome at Nürnberg. A youth languishes in the jail of a cruel King. . . .
>
> On the evening before his execution, the Queen visits him, roguishly charming like Grillparzer's hero . . . . blonde as Melisande, effecting the miracle of a cure like Isolde. Her beauty, the last breath of life tempts him to ask her to be his. The first act ends very tenderly, when the two come close together and she offers him her hair and her feet . . . and her dream of paradise:
>
>> "It is morning. Creation is still young.
>> On a meadow in Paradise we sit
>> From distant gates angels call each other.
>> We are waiting still. Will God pass by?
>> At this hour he comes through the garden
>> And plays with animals and trees. We are waiting still.
>> The hands gently intertwined.
>> You turn your head. You look at me.
>> And my glances are sinking into you.
>> Listen: does not music rain from the stars?
>> We look at each other. God has passed by."
>
> The Queen shows herself to him in her purity. The King's captain orders the prisoner to be strangled, and the Queen is placed in chains. The King puts his wife before the judges. To prove her innocence, she is to bring back to life a plague victim before the town gates. She already feels that it had not been pity but earthly love—therefore sin—which had moved her to grant the prisoner's last wish. She admits her guilt and is ready to face death when suddenly the dead man rises from the bier, and as a radiant archangel who resembles the young prisoner, he receives

the soul of the saintly Queen to conduct her from the stake to the place before the throne of God.

15. The play was a modest success. In a review in the *Neue Freie Presse,* Korngold was praised for his "fine, incidental score which holds the many scenes together like a mystical ribbon of sound." The play had only nine performances and the music was never performed again or published. The manuscript, which is incomplete, is preserved in the Library of Congress.

16. Paul Wittgenstein (1887–1961) was one of the richest musicians in Austria. He had lost his right arm in World War I, and subsequently devoted himself to playing music written for the left hand. Because there was little contemporary music written for the left hand, he commissioned works from a great number of twentieth-century composers, including Ravel, Prokofiev, Franz Schmidt, Benjamin Britten, Hans Gál, and Richard Strauss.

17. In a postcard to the conductor Egon Pollak written by Korngold from Alt-Aussee and dated 21 July 1923, he writes: "I work very pleasantly on a new concerto for piano (the string quartet, thank God, is finally finished) and I start a grand opera."

18. Interview by letter with the author, 12 September 1985.

19. Letter to the author, 15 March 1977.

Notes to Chapter Twelve

1. *The Musical Times,* London, 1 March 1924.

2. This variation is quoted (exactly as it appears in the Quartet) in Korngold's fifth opera *Die Kathrin.*

3. Ella Flesch (born in Budapest 1902, died in New York 1957), a Hungarian soprano, made her debut at the Vienna State Opera at age eighteen in *Aida.* She sang in Vienna and Munich, and emigrated to the United States in 1940, where she made her debut at the Metropolitan Opera in New York in 1944 as *Salome.* She was the daughter of violinist Carl Flesch.

4. L. Korngold 1967.

5. In her memoirs, Luzi Korngold (1967) mistakenly notes this visit as taking place during their honeymoon. The last performance of *Die tote Stadt* with Tauber and Lehmann took place on 29 April 1924, however, one day before the wedding. The "chaperone" Pollak was undoubtedly necessary therefore.

6. Franz Ludwig Hörth produced the celebrated Berlin production of Berg's opera *Wozzeck* in 1925.

7. Emil Pirchan (born in Brünn 1884, died in Vienna 1957) was a fascinating figure who was extremely important in the Expressionist movement. He was the leading stage designer at the Munich State Theater before joining producer Leopold Jessner at Berlin. His style embodied an absolute rejection of naturalism, which was the perfect approach for a dream opera such as *Die tote Stadt.* Pirchan was a fabulous painter and a prolific author, not only of works on art but also of novels, opera and ballet libretti, and major works on his methods and the history of the theater. His production designs for *Richard III* at the Berlin Playhouse in 1920 are legendary.

8. L. Korngold 1967.

9. L. Korngold 1967.

10. The Korngolds had only a civil ceremony because, according to their son George Korngold, neither could face the epic length of a Jewish wedding ceremony and the attendant strain of entertaining the whole family of both.

11. L. Korngold 1967.

12. L. Korngold 1967.

13. Paul Géraldy (1885–1983) was a French poet and dramatist.

14. Germaine Lubin (1890–1979) was the chief dramatic soprano at the Paris Opera from 1914 to 1945. Her career ended after the war as a result of her collaboration with the Nazis.

15. Paul Clemenceau was the brother of the French prime minister.

16. Berta Szeps-Zuckerkandl (1864–1945), wife of the famous anatomist Emil Zuckerkandl, introduced Mahler to Alma Schindler.

17. Letter quoted in E. Fred Flindell, "Einige Dokumente der Sammlung P. Wittgenstein," in *Die Musikforschung*, No. 22, Kassel, 1969. Dr. Flindell provided a copy of the original letter, and I was able to clarify that the date (from Korngold's notoriously difficult handwriting) was 1924 rather than 1919 as was quoted in the article.

18. This festival was notable also for the first performance of music from Mahler's unfinished Symphony No. 10 in F-sharp Major by the Vienna Philharmonic, conducted by Franz Schalk in the Vienna State Opera.

19. L. Korngold 1967.

20. Joseph Haas (1879–1960) was one of Reger's most important pupils.

21. Lothar Windsperger (1885–1935) was a composer of choral music. From 1913 he was a reader and adviser on new music for Schott.

22. J. Korngold 1938 (unpublished, privately printed).

23. Willi Reich, critic, September 1923.

24. *Neue Freie Presse*, undated clipping, 1922.

25. The "Jew" referred to was Bruno Walter.

26. The original of this letter is lost, but it is quoted verbatim in J Korngold 1991.

27. Ernst Benedikt (died in Vienna, 1973) was the son of Moritz Benedikt and succeeded his father as editor of the *Neue Freie Presse* in 1920. He retired in 1932 to devote himself to writing. (He wrote a significant biography of the Emperor Franz Josef.) He emigrated to the United States in 1938 but returned to Vienna after the war.

28. Carl Alwin (1891–1945) was a pianist, composer, and conductor. Despite some personal differences, he remained a loyal ally and faithful interpreter of Korngold's music.

29. This canary imitation became very popular on a gramophone record, and it delighted Richard Strauss. Schumann tried unsuccessfully to persuade Strauss to compose a song for her that would take the form of a conversation between a child and her pet canary.

30. Lotte Schöne (1891–1977), soprano, had an exquisite, delicate voice with a superbly controlled coloratura. She later sang Laura in *Der Ring des Polykrates* in Vienna and Annina in the lavish production of Korngold's version of Johann Strauss II's *Eine Nacht in Venedig*, conducted by Erich Kleiber in Berlin in 1931, as well as starring in the French production of *Die Fledermaus* at the Théâtre Pigale in Paris, 1933.

31. Refers to Lotte Lehmann's appearance at the world premiere of Strauss's opera *Intermezzo* at the Dresden State Opera, 4 November 1924, under Fritz Busch. At the composer's wish, she created the leading part of Christine.

32. Refers to Strauss's ballet *Schlagobers* (Whipped Cream), which had received its lavish world premiere earlier that year at the Vienna State Opera on 9 May 1924 with Strauss himself conducting. It had been poorly received, and its astronomic cost at a time of high inflation had been much criticized.

33. *Neue Freie Presse*, 7 November 1924.

34. Josef Turnau was an insignificant stage director but efficient "yes man" for Strauss. Later he was the manager of the Municipal Theater at Breslau, where he produced the world premiere of Weinberger's *Schwanda the Bagpiper*.

35. Prior to this incident, Schalk went on a mysterious trip to Germany. Anxious to parry Strauss's intrigue, he visited his protégé Clemens Krauss in Frankfurt to seek advice. Krauss had the gifted Dr. Lothar Wallerstein at his disposal, a distinguished operatic producer, then chief producer at Frankfurt with Krauss. Krauss proposed that Wallerstein become "guest producer" at Vienna and promised to release him when required. This suited both Krauss's future plans and Schalk's in that it pleased the Austrian authorities and seemed to be far more satisfactory than Strauss's appointment.

36. L. Korngold 1967.

37. Recalled by Marcel Prawy (Prawy 1969).

38. Hans Knappertsbusch (1888–1965) was one of the great German conductors of the pre-war period. A renowned interpreter of Wagner, he was director of the Munich Opera from 1922 to 1936 and of the Vienna State Opera from 1938 to 1945.

Notes to Chapter Thirteen

1. Pierre Monteux (1875–1964), the famous French conductor, became conductor of Diaghilev's Ballet Russe in 1912, with which he gave the premieres of Stravinsky's *Petrushka* and *Rite of Spring,* among others. From 1917 to 1919 he conducted at the Metropolitan Opera in New York. Later he conducted in Boston, Paris, San Francisco (1936–1954), and was principal guest conductor with the London Symphony Orchestra until his death.
2. L. Korngold 1967.
3. The songs (Opus 18) were premiered on 11 March 1926 in Vienna by Rosette Anday, with the composer at the piano. The songs are operatic, densely chromatic, and almost impressionistic (the first song, for instance, bears the instruction, "*mysteriously like a breath, always color*")
4. *Neues Wiener Journal,* 14 April 1927.
5. Oskar Strnad (1879–1935), architect and stage designer, often worked with Reinhardt. He later designed the brilliant production of Korngold's fourth opera *Das Wunder der Heliane* in Berlin for Bruno Walter in April 1928.
6. Paumgartner (1887–1971) was really a conductor. A unidentified critic wrote after the premiere: "The score consists of first-hand Paumgartner with a lot of second-hand Puccini." One of Paumgartner's pupils was Herbert von Karajan.
7. Published in the journal *Musikleben,* November 1931.
8. L. Korngold 1967.
9. Korngold may be referring here to the effect he created of having a small stage band interact in antiphonal response with the main orchestra during "Marietta's Dance" at the end of Act 1 in *Die tote Stadt.*
10. Letter dated 11 August 1926. Reproduced by kind permission of Karl Pollak, the conductor's son.
11. Hindemith was Schott's other main composer. His opera *Cardillac* was eventually given its world premiere on 9 November 1926 in Dresden, with Fritz Busch conducting.
12. Original letter preserved in the Austrian National Library.
13. J. Korngold 1991.
14. *Neues Wiener Tagblatt,* 23 May 1926.
15. Letter to the author dated 9 September 1975.
16. Jan Kiepura (1902–1966) and his wife, the Hungarian soprano Marta Eggerth (born 1912), became two of Korngold's close friends. Eggerth recalled that the two men were addicted to practical jokes, like little boys. In the 1930s, Kiepura combined his career in opera with spectacular success in films, and appeared in *Give Us This Night* (his only American film), which was also scored by Korngold.
17. J. Korngold 1991.
18. *Hamburger Nachrichten,* 9 October 1927.

Notes to Chapter Fourteen

1. New productions of *Die tote Stadt* were staged at Duisburg and Rostock in the 1930–1931 season, the latter under the direction of Hans Schmidt-Isserstedt. Many other theaters were either still playing the original production or mounting a new staging.
2. Hans Liebestöckl, *Neues Wiener Tagblatt,* 30 October 1927.
3. Grete Stückgold (1895–1977) was born in London. Her father was German. She was a pupil of Jacques Stückgold, whom she subsequently married. She sang many concerts with Nikisch and the Gewandhaus before signing a contract with the Berlin

State Opera in 1928. She sang *Aida* at Covent Garden before ending her career at the Metropolitan Opera in New York circa 1945.

4. Emil Schipper (1882–1957) created the role of Borromeo in Pfitzner's *Palestrina*.

5. Hans Fidesser (1889–1982) spent most of his career in Germany. He is forgotten today because he made no recordings.

6. Alexander Kipnis (1891–1978), the legendary Russian bass, also settled in the United States after Hitler came to power. The role of the Blind Judge is written for tenor, so it must have been altered for this production.

7. L. Korngold 1967.

8. Quoted in Prawy 1969.

9. See "Elisabeth Schumann and the Vienna Opera," in *Opera*, January 1961.

10. J. Korngold 1991.

11. 12 November 1927.

12. 5 November 1927, when it was paired with *Hänsel und Gretel*.

13. 31 March 1928, when it was paired with *Gianni Schicchi*. A few days earlier, on 28 February, *Die tote Stadt* received its premiere in Lemberg (in Poland) in Polish translation. New productions were presented in Coburg and Hagen.

14. The song was "Was du mir bist?"

15. L. Korngold 1967.

16. Interview, Los Angeles, 2 September 1975.

17. Interview, Los Angeles, 30 August 1981.

18. L. Korngold 1967.

19. L. Korngold 1967.

20. This was a similar biographical operetta on the life of Schubert, in which his great melodies were used with added lyrics.

21. The concert took place on the 25 January 1930.

22. Poll in *Neues Wiener Tagblatt*, 15 August 1930.

23. L. Korngold 1967.

24. *Daily Telegraph*, London, 4 January 1932.

Notes to Chapter Fifteen

1. Letter dated 5 May 1931 (Korngold estate).

2. It may have been the operetta *Ronny* with music by Emmerich Kálmán.

3. Claude Anet's (1868–1931) most famous work is *Mayerling*, the story of the doomed Habsburg love affair that ended in the suicide of the son of the Emperor Franz Josef.

4. Heinrich Eduard Jacob (1889–1967).

5. Ernst Descey (1870–1941), critic on the *Grazer Tagespost*, later wrote biographies of Bruckner, Hugo Wolf, Franz Léhar, and Debussy.

6. It opened as *Sissy* at Christmas 1932 at the Theater an der Wien. After a tremendous success it was later filmed in 1936 in Hollywood as *The King Steps Out* by Josef von Sternberg, starring Grace Moore, and after the war was performed with Romy Schneider.

7. Peruter was a high-ranking Austrian official in the Ministry of Education.

8. 4 October 1933 (Vienna State Opera Archives).

9. Only one other tenor, Jan Kiepura, performed this aria as a solo.

10. The interview was given during the rehearsal for his Hollywood Bowl concert in February 1935, when the *Baby Serenade* received its US premiere, and was published in the program.

11. Korngold left the manuscript in the office of his lawyer in Berlin. It has not been seen since.

12. This was Harold von Oppenheim's only stage appearance. He ended his days in South America singing in cheap bars. A tragic figure, he died from drug addiction.

13. Korngold shared this skill at billiards with another prodigy—Mozart!

14. L. Korngold 1967.
15. Eleanore van der Straten (1873–?).
16. L. Korngold 1967.
17. Letter to the author 4 June 1978
18. L. Korngold 1967.
19. L. Korngold 1967.
20. Reinhardt had flirted with the cinema since the silent days. In 1912 he produced a film of *The Miracle* in Vienna along with several others. Later in 1920, he collaborated with Ernst Lubitsch on an Arabian Nights fantasy entitled *One Arabian Night* starring Pola Negri and Paul Wegener. In 1921, he entered into an agreement with Paramount Pictures to make several major films, including *Ben Hur* and Milton's *Paradise Lost*. But nothing came of it and the films, sadly, were not made. Similarly, in 1924, he tried to remake *The Miracle* without success, and in 1927 he planned a film with Lillian Gish, whom he greatly admired (and who, some said, he secretly loved). A script by Hugo von Hofmannsthal was prepared, but the project was eventually abandoned in 1929. With the coming of sound to motion pictures, however, his interest was reawakened. At last, cinema offered him unlimited possibilities ideally suited to his extravagant imagination, so of course he embraced the offer from Jack Warner.
21. L. Korngold 1967.

Notes to Chapter Sixteen

1. *The Miracle* was a spectacular mystery play first produced by Reinhardt in 1912. It had a highly controversial religious text and would have undoubtedly incurred serious objections from the Roman Catholic Church if it had been made before the relaxation of the censorship code.
2. Interview with the author, Paris, 8 May 1980.
3. Max Ree is unjustly forgotten as a designer. Born in Copenhagen, he worked with Reinhardt in Berlin as early as 1921 for his productions of *A Midsummer Night's Dream* and *Orpheus in the Underworld* (Offenbach). In 1925, he left Europe and came to Hollywood to work for MGM, probably at the behest of the director Mauritz Stiller, for whom he worked on Greta Garbo's first two American films, *The Torrent* and *The Temptress*. He also worked for Erich von Stroheim on *The Wedding March* and the unfinished, ill-fated *Queen Kelly*. He joined Radio Pictures in 1929 as art director, and worked on *Cimarron* (which won the Academy Award for Best Picture in 1931) and *The Lost Squadron* (1932). Reinhardt asked him to design the costumes for the Hollywood Bowl production of *A Midsummer Night's Dream*, and he was contracted for the film production on the strength of his work. His striking concepts contributed much to the bizarre look of the film (note the winged bat-men who carry the errant fairy away in the nocturne scene), but this was to be his only Warner Brothers credit. His last film seems to have been *Carnegie Hall* in 1947.
4. Anton Grot (1884–1974) was a Polish artist and interior designer. He emigrated to the United States in 1909. In films since 1913, his first major film was the silent version of *The Thief of Bagdad* with Douglas Fairbanks in 1924. He was highly influential, and worked for De Mille before moving to Warner Brothers in 1927, where he remained until his retirement in 1948.
5. Warner Brothers files (telegram copy).
6. Bronislava Nijinska (1891–1979) created roles for Diaghilev in *Carnaval* and *Petrushka*. She worked with Reinhardt previously on his Berlin production of Offenbach's *The Tales of Hofmann*. Like Reinhardt, she settled in Los Angeles after 1938 and opened her own studio.
7. She actually worked nine weeks and received $9000.
8. *New York Times*, 31 October 1934.
9. Undated memo (draft), Warner Brothers files, probably October 1936.
10. Letter to the Author dated 8 May 1981.

11. Heindorf was also a composer, a brilliant pianist, and an inspired practical joker. He once scored a "stag movie" for a Christmas party for the largely male studio orchestra with the music for a duel from Korngold's *The Adventures of Robin Hood* intercut with shots of Leo Forbstein taking off his jacket. He loved Korngold and his music, so much so that he borrowed a theme from *Anthony Adverse* for a song he composed for the Errol Flynn western *San Antonio* in 1946; Korngold ribbed him about it ever afterward.

12. Interview, Los Angeles, 5 September 1980.

13. Quoted many times, especially in Thomas 1973.

14. E. W. Korngold 1940.

15. Memo dated 31 December 1934 (Warner Brothers files).

16. Fred Jackman was in charge (with Byron Haskin and H. F. Koenekamp) of the special photographic effects unit for the picture.

17. Memo dated 31 December 1934 (Warner Brothers files). It is clear Korngold set his own precedent from the beginning in determining how the film would be cut to fit his music.

18. The job was so complex that thirty-five metal disk recordings were made during the shooting as a guide to assist him in scoring.

19. Memo dated 19 November 1934 (Warner Brothers files).

20. George Korngold often remarked that his father could not stand the temperamental Mme. Nijinska.

21. Wittgenstein gave the New York premiere of the Suite on 23 January 1935 as a further demonstration of his affection and loyalty, and the rift was healed.

22. From various memos in the Warner Brothers files.

23. Georgie Breekstone.

24. Memo dated 12 February 1935 (Warner Brothers files).

25. L. Korngold 1967.

26. E. W. Korngold 1940.

27. The result was farcical and unbelievably hammy, an indication of Reinhardt's problem in evaluating what would work on film. Korngold alleviated a delicate situation by playing Dieterle off against Reinhardt: he told Reinhardt that while it was a brilliant conception, Dieterle's handling of it was ruinous, and then he told Dieterle that while his direction was inspired, Reinhardt's idea was shabby and out of keeping with the film. The sequence was subsequently cut and destroyed.

28. The radio script survives in the Korngold estate.

Notes to Chapter Seventeen

1. Thomas 1973.

2. Warner Brothers file, *A Midsummer Night's Dream*, on permanent loan to Professor Leonard Fiedler, University of Frankfurt.

3. Verbal communication by George Korngold.

4. All these projects are noted in the private papers of Max Reinhardt and William Dieterle and referred to in various recent biographies, including Mierendorff (1993).

5. Paramount Pictures Music Department, cue sheets, November 1935.

6. Kiepura actually recorded several versions of these popular songs.

7. Interview with Albert Glasser, 29 August 1975.

8. Letter dated 22 December 1956 from Hugo Friedhofer to Lawrence J. Burton, reproduced by kind permission of Mr. Burton.

9. Letter to Rudy Behlmer dated 24 March 1967, reproduced by kind permission.

10. Korngold often remarked that Heindorf was the fastest and most expert orchestrator he had ever encountered.

11. The vibraphone was to become an integral part of Korngold's orchestration from this point on, and added to the already rich spectrum of Korngold's "sound."

12. Probably Jaro Churain.

13. Remarks combined from letters to Behlmer and Burton as cited in notes 8 and 9.
14. The average running time for an "A" feature film circa 1935 was between 90 and 100 minutes. Korngold's early films were all prodigiously long: *A Midsummer Night's Dream,* 140 minutes; *Captain Blood,* 119 minutes; *Anthony Adverse,* 136 minutes; *The Prince and the Pauper,* 117 minutes; *Juarez,* 132 minutes; *The Sea Hawk,* 127 minutes.
15. Joseph O'Sullivan, *Motion Picture Herald,* 14 March 1936.
16. Warner Brothers files, 12 February 1936.
17. Interview, Los Angeles, 6 September 1975.
18. Interview, Los Angeles, 30 August 1975.
19. This Aldo Franchetti is not the same as Alberto Franchetti (1860–1942), the composer of the operas *Cristoforo Columbo, Germania,* and *La figlia di Jorio.* Aldo Franchetti's relationship with this composer has not been proven and his origins are obscure.
20. Interview, Paris, 8 May 1980.
21. Weiskopf did not, however, provide the voice for the operatic sequences; these were sung by Yvonne Galen.
22. Interview, Beverly Hills, 13 September 1975.
23. Interview, Toluca Lake, Los Angeles, 4 September 1975.
24. Letter to the author, 15 September 1977.
25. Mentioned in an interview with George Korngold, London, 19 September 1974. Korngold met Stravinsky for the first time at the end of December 1930, when Stravinsky visited him in Vienna. Willy Strecker (from Schott, also Stravinsky's publisher then) wrote to Korngold's father on 2 January 1931, saying that Stravinsky told him in confidence that Erich Korngold was the only thoroughbred musician he met in Vienna. Apparently, Korngold helped an unnamed conductor who was to perform a work by Stravinsky, and through his advice, this concert was a success, for which Stravinsky was extremely grateful.

Notes to Chapter Eighteen

1. Warner Brothers files on *Danton,* on loan to Professor Leonard Fiedler, University of Frankfurt.
2. Warner Brothers files. Korngold did not get along with Dieterle in the beginning. Later they became good friends, and the Korngolds were frequent house guests at Dieterle's palatial ranch. It is not widely known that Dieterle initially planned both *Anthony Adverse* and *The Adventures of Robin Hood* but that both films were given to other directors by Jack Warner. In 1951, Dieterle was investigated by the House Committee for Un-American Activities because of his support for the Russian War Relief Fund. As Korngold also supported this during the mid-1940s, we may assume that the FBI holds a file on him also.
3. *Das Echo,* Vienna, 18 May 1937.
4. *Motion Picture Herald,* December 1936.
5. Interview, Universal Studios, Hollywood, 4 September 1975.
6. Actually the opening phrase of the fourth "Nachtmusik" movement of Mahler's Symphony No. 7 in B Minor.
7. From a copy of the letter (Korngold estate). The original is no longer extant.
8. Review in *Neues Wiener Tagblatt,* 7 November 1937.
9. L. Korngold 1967.
10. Warner Brothers files, *The Adventures of Robin Hood,* archived at the University of Southern California.
11. Warner Brothers files, *The Adventures of Robin Hood,* University of Southern California.
12. Letter to Korngold from his father, dated 21 January 1938 (Korngold estate).
13. Letter dated 11 February 1938, Warner Brothers files, University of Southern California.

14. L. Korngold 1967.
15. Warner Brothers files, University of Southern California.
16. L. Korngold 1967.
17. L. Korngold 1967.
18. Liner notes for the Varese Sarabande recording *The Adventures of Robin Hood* number VCDM 704.180, June 1983.
19. One is in the Korngold estate; one in the possession of Albert Glasser, the copyist who attended the radio broadcast to be on hand for last-minute adjustment to the parts; and one is in the author's private collection. This last copy was a gift from Teddy Krise, who had purchased the set of discs in 1938 for $10 from Tenny Wright, the Warner Brothers studio production manager.
20. It was issued on LP by Delos Records in 1976, subsequently on CD.
21. J. Korngold 1991.
22. Undated clipping *The San Francisco Chronicle* (Korngold estate).
23. Warner Brothers files, *The Miracle*, on loan to Professor Leonard Fiedler, University of Frankfurt.
24. Warner Brothers files, *The Miracle*, on loan to Professor Leonard Fiedler, University of Frankfurt.
25. Warner Brothers files, The Miracle, on loan to Professor Leonard Fiedler, University of Frankfurt.
26. When I asked Henry Blanke (interview, Hollywood, California, 27 August 1975) why, after so much effort, Warner had abandoned the project, he paused for a moment, leaned forward in his chair as though imparting some secret information, and replied:

> It was a very difficult and expensive project, and Reinhardt was almost impossible to deal with, but we would have gone ahead except for the war. With the coming of the war, the making of films with a German subject or by German authors became impossible. I think Jack Warner kept it alive for so long in the hope that the war would end and we could recoup our investment. But after the war, nobody wanted to see a huge allegorical pageant on the screen. They wanted realism, not fantasy. It was a great pity. I believe it would have been one of the greatest pictures ever made—especially if Bette Davis had starred and Erich had written the music as I planned. It was an ideal subject for him.

> Mr. Blanke's recollection is not entirely correct. Hollywood did not cease to make films with German subject matter until well into the 1940s. A more likely explanation would be the difficulties with the script combined with the anticipated cost and Reinhardt's insistence on having his own way.

Notes to Chapter Nineteen

1. For a detailed account of its troubled history, see Vanderwood 1983.
2. Quoted in Styne 1975.
3. *The New York Times*, 28 April 1939.
4. Max Reinhardt School for Stage, Film, and Radio. 1938. Prospectus (Korngold estate).
5. *The Los Angeles Times*, 2 June 1939.
6. Hollywood, 14 February 1939 (Korngold estate).
7. Korngold reused part of the music for this Irish battle for the Panama scenes in *The Sea Hawk* the following year, changing the rhythm and scoring, and slightly altering the melodic line.
8. Interview, Los Angeles, 30 August 1975.
9. Although the entire library of separate nitrate film tracks of the musical scores to all of Warner Brothers' films of 1929–1954 was destroyed by the studio in 1980, George Korngold requested 15 ips magnetic tape copies of his father's recordings. These are now preserved in the Korngold estate, and excerpts have just been issued on CD (see discography).

10. *Hollywood Spectator*, September 1939.
11. Interview with the author, Los Angeles, 26 August 1981.
12. Anecdote related by the actor Fritz Feld, interviewed in Los Angeles, 8 September 1981.
13. Interview, Los Angeles, 7 September 1981.
14. Rósza 1982.
15. Interview, Los Angeles, 9 September 1975.
16. Interview, Toluca Lake, Hollywood, 4 September 1975.
17. J. Korngold 1991.
18. Letter dated 3 October 1944 preserved in the Korngold estate.
19. Letter preserved in the Korngold estate.
20. L. Korngold 1967.
21. Review in *Operan*, 9 October 1939, Stockholm.
22. Interview, Paris, 8 May 1980.
23. Liner notes for the recording *The Sea Hawk* (symphonic suite), Varese Sarabande 704.380.
24. Letter to the author dated 7 July 1977.
25. Interview, Los Angeles, 30 August 1975.
26. A separate ending was added for the release prints in England in which Flora Robson as Elizabeth delivers a stirring speech, thus drawing a deliberate parallel between Philip of Spain and Hitler.
27. No composer before or since has enjoyed such luxurious conditions in which to create music for the screen.
28. *Music and Dance in California*, June 1940.

Notes to Chapter Twenty

1. Letter dated 29 March 1941 (Korngold estate).
2. Toscha Seidel (1900–1962) first came to Hollywood in the autumn of 1937 to dub the violin solos for Fernand Gravet (as Johann Strauss) in MGM's lavish version of *The Great Waltz*, which did not use Korngold's adaptation, but a newly commissioned score from Dmitri Tiomkin, an old friend of Seidel's. The violinist stayed on to perform the same task in 1939 for Leslie Howard in the romantic classic *Intermezzo—A Love Story* for David O. Selznick.
3. Interview with Ernst Korngold, Portland, Oregon, 8 September 1992.
4. Liner notes for recording *Kings Row—Symphonic Suite*, Chalfont SDG 305 (rel. 1979).
5. Harold Truscott (1914–1992) was a composer, pianist, teacher, historian, author, and expert on music of all kinds, especially Korngold's. In the early stages of this book, he was of inestimable help to me.
6. The contract with Margaret Kennedy also included the rights to remake her follow-up to *The Constant Nymph*, *Escape Me Never*.
7. Joan Fontaine was dubbed by Sally Sweetland.
8. Korngold's many friends in the music department persuaded director Edmund Goulding to allow them to place a framed poster of *Die tote Stadt* on the wall of Sanger's music room, which is clearly visible in this scene. This was to surprise Korngold, but he never noticed it. When it was pointed out to him, he had to see the film a second time before he actually saw the poster.
9. The soloist was Clemence Groves, wife of George Groves, one of the key executives in the sound department at Warner Brothers, and a trained singer.
10. The New Opera Company was actually founded by Mrs. Lytle Hull in 1941 with Fritz Busch as its musical director. Initial performances of *Così Fan Tutte* and *Macbeth*, based on the Glyndebourne productions which Busch had directed in the 1930s, were followed by a varied repertoire. Yolanda Mero Irion and her husband were indispensable to the fledgling company, not only financially but also because of their exceptional European contacts with talented émigrés in America at that time.

11. From a letter to the author dated 25 October 1975, Salisbury, Connecticut.
12. L. Korngold 1967.
13. 24 December 1942, Korngold estate.
14. Information supplied by George Korngold.
15. Undated letter from George Korngold to Bernd O. Rachold (The Korngold Society, Hamburg Office), received spring 1987.
18. Interview in *The Cincinnati Inquirer* 26 March 1944.
19. *Variety*, 25 May 1944.
20. *The New York Times*, 25 April 1944.

Notes to Chapter Twenty-one

1. Interview, 17 June 1978, London.
2. Around this time, the young Frank Sinatra had bought a house across the lake from Korngold's and would often swim across at breakfast time, attracted by the sound of Korngold playing the piano. Sinatra's wife Nancy had just given birth to their first child, and Korngold presented the young father with a manuscript of the lullaby from the film, dedicated to the new arrival.
3. Thomas 1973.
4. Both stories recounted by Ernst Korngold (who apparently did an uncanny impersonation of his late father) August 1980, Toluca Lake, Hollywood.
5. L. Korngold 1967.
6. L. Korngold 1967.
7. Draft of letter to Raoul Auernheimer (Korngold estate).
8. George Korngold explained in a letter to the author, 14 June 1976:

   J. J. Shubert, the noted impresario, came to our house and asked to hear the music. Victor Clement's brother was a man named Paul Gordon (originally Kelemen)—an agent and manager—who was entrusted to find a stage for the show. I think he had contacted Shubert in the beginning. Anyway, Shubert asked to hear the music, fell in love with it, and immediately wanted the show for Broadway.

   When the contract arrived, it contained clauses that gave Shubert full control over the orchestration, libretto, and so on. My father refused to sign, and Shubert, not used to being rejected, went to Victor Clement and offered to option the libretto on its own if he would split it from the music. Being a Hungarian, he agreed, and thus for two years, book and music were separated, while Shubert had one score after another written for it. He finally gave up and gave the book back to Clement. Just after this, Deanna Durbin, the famous singing star and her husband Felix Jackson, the executive producer at Universal Studios, heard about it (through Gordon I guess) and asked to hear the score. She fell in love with the music, wanted all the numbers for herself, and Jackson made an offer for film rights in the amount of $250,000 (not bad for an unperformed, untried work). The day he was to propose it to the Board of Directors, J. Arthur Rank took over Universal, Jackson was out and so was Durbin. C'est la vie!

9. Interview, Los Angeles, 2 September 1980.
10. Interview, Los Angeles, 30 August 1975.
11. This came near the beginning of the film, when Davis takes Henreid back to her palatial apartment. At the words "Do you still play?" she originally walked over to the piano and began to play Chopin's Nocturne in E-flat Major. Henreid then took his cello out and also started to play. Korngold, who had made the arrangement of the piece (as directed by the script) complained that it was unidiomatic for a cellist to play a Chopin Nocturne. He then composed his own short piece, but even though it was recorded, the scene was filmed differently, probably because of the technical problems of accomplishing trick shots of both Davis and Henreid appearing to play.
12. Published in *The Musician* and *Overture*, Los Angeles, November 1946.
13. Bartók made a similar gesture at the end of his *Concerto for Orchestra*. Whether Korngold had ever heard this work at the time is unknown, but is unlikely.

14. Interview, London 6 May 1976.
15. Interview, Southport, England, during Bette Davis's UK tour of her celebrated "One Woman Show," June 1975.
16. Letter to the author, 12 January 1979.
17. Published in *The Hollywood Musician*, November 1946.
18. Preserved in the Korngold estate.
19. St. Louis Symphony Orchestra program, 15 February 1947.
20. Review, 16 February 1947.
21. Letter quoted in L. Korngold 1967. The letter is no longer extant, but Mr. Reitler's sympathetic reply of a few days later is preserved.
22. Interview, Los Angeles, 7 September 1975.
23. Letter dated August 1947 (Korngold estate).

Notes to Chapter Twenty-two

1. *Forever Amber* was eventually scored by David Raksin. Around the same time, Korngold was also asked to compose the score for *The Adventures of Casanova* (for Eagle Lion starring Arturo de Cordoba, Lucille Bremer, and Turhan Bey). Although he turned this down as well, he did compose a main title, which is preserved as a sketch in his estate.
2. The revisions in the duet mostly concern the tenor line, which at the climactic phrase doubles the horns, thus creating a thrilling effect. These revised parts are preserved (with Korngold's written emendations) in the archives of the Vienna State Opera.
3. Letter to the author, 26 September 1976.
4. Eric Zeisl (1905–1959) did not score this film (it was scored by Enzo Masetti), and the overture written by Korngold has not yet been traced.
5. Letter dated 13 November 1949 (Korngold estate).
6. Letter dated 16 January 1950 (Korngold estate).
7. Interview 16 July 1979, London.
8. Synopsis provided by Josef Weinberger Verlag, London.
9. *Opera News*, 11 December 1950.
10. Prawy 1967.
11. Prawy 1967.
12. Review in *Die Presse*, 21 October 1950.
13. Released on Masterseal MW 46, re-released Varese Sarabande LP VC81040, now deleted. It is interesting that Korngold added a concluding four bars to the Passacaglia that are not in the score.
14. Interview with the author, Hollywood, 16 August 1980.
15. Verbal communication by George Korngold, August 1980.
16. Notes written by the composer for the aborted American premiere of the Symphony in 1955 (Korngold estate).
17. Notes written by the composer for the aborted American premiere of the Symphony in 1955 (Korngold estate).
18. Reproduced by kind permission of Dr. Lewandowsky. Copy preserved in the Korngold Society Archive.
19. Mario Nascimbene was actually contracted for the score but the film was never completed and brought Flynn to the brink of financial ruin.

Notes to Chapter Twenty-three

1. Preserved in the Korngold estate.
2. Liner notes to *Magic Fire* soundtrack LP issued on Varese Sarabande STV 81179 (nla).
3. The concert took place on 17 October 1954.
4. Undated draft of letter sent shortly after the broadcast (Korngold estate).

5. To ensure accurate tempi, Korngold made a tape of himself playing the entire symphony on the piano, and sent it to Koetsier. This tape is preserved in the Korngold estate.

6. Liner notes to *Magic Fire* soundtrack LP issued on Varese Sarabande STV 81179 (nla).

7. L. Korngold 1967.

8. Article published in *Neue Zeitschrift für Musik*, May 1987. Mainz: Schott.

9. L. Korngold 1967.

10. Letter preserved in the Korngold estate.

11. Letter to Alma Mahler, preserved in the Alma Mahler Collection, University of Pennsylvania.

12. Devaré 1956. De Vaere (as he now spells his name) later delivered the eulogy at Korngold's funeral.

13. The US premiere took place on 30 December 1955.

14. Letter preserved in the Korngold estate.

15. Undated carbon copy of letter preserved in the Korngold estate, probably written 15–20 May 1957.

16. Undated draft of letter preserved in the Korngold estate sent in reply to a letter from Dr. Kubie dated 23 May 1957.

17. L. Korngold 1967.

18. Program of Korngold Memorial Concert preserved in the Korngold estate.

19. Interview, Los Angeles, 29 August 1975.

The Complete Works of Erich Wolfgang Korngold

In preparing this work list, I have divided Korngold's compositions into four categories: (1) published works with opus numbers, (2) unpublished works and arrangements together with published works without opus numbers, (3) operetta arrangements, and (4) film scores and arrangements. The list of unpublished material comprises all the works and short pieces preserved in the Korngold manuscript collection in the Library of Congress. All manuscripts of the published concert works and other works are at the Library of Congress unless otherwise noted. The film scores are mostly intact and preserved in the Special Collections at the University of Southern California, Los Angeles. Korngold's publisher is Schott unless otherwise noted. Comprehensive first-performance details are included wherever possible.

Part 1. Works with Opus Numbers

Opus 1. Piano Trio in D Major for violin, cello, and piano. Composed December 1909–May 1910. Dedicated "To My Beloved Father." First performance 4 November 1910, Munich: Schwartz Trio. Published by Universal Edition, Vienna.

Opus 2. Piano Sonata No. 2 in E Major. Composed July–December 1910. Dedicated to Alexander von Zemlinsky. First performance 13 October 1911, Berlin: Artur Schnabel.

Opus 3. *Sieben Märchenbilder* for piano (Seven Fairy Tale Pictures). Composed June–December 1910. Dedicated to Archduke Eugen. Text by Hans Müller. First complete performance 30 March 1912, Berlin: Marta Malatesta. (Individual movements performed 20 March 1912, Hamburg: Erich W. Korngold and other artists.) Orchestral version (completed March–May 1911; not published) first performance 27 June 1911, Karlsbad.

Opus 4. *Schauspiel Ouvertüre* in B Major for large orchestra (Overture to a Play). Composed July–August 1911; orchestrated August–17 September 1911. Dedicated to Arthur Nikisch. First performance 14 December 1911, Leipzig: Gewandhaus Orchestra, conducted by Arthur Nikisch.

Opus 5. Sinfonietta in B Major for large orchestra. Composed April 1911–August 1912 (chief themes and sketches); orchestrated by 14 September 1913. Dedicated to Felix von Weingartner. First performance 30 November 1913, Vienna: Vienna Philharmonic Orchestra, conducted by Felix von Weingartner.

Opus 6. Sonata in G Major for violin and piano. Composed 1912–19 August 1913. Dedicated to Artur Schnabel and Carl Flesch. First performance 21 October 1913, Berlin: Artur Schnabel and Carl Flesch.

Opus 7. *Der Ring des Polykrates,* opera buffa in one act. Composed 1913–1914. Libretto by Julius Korngold and Leo Feld (uncredited) to a text by Heinrich Teweles. Revised, shorter version 1919 (not published). First performance 28 March 1916, Munich Court Theater: conducted by Bruno Walter.

Opus 8. *Violanta,* tragic opera in one act. Composed 1914–1915; orchestrated 1 September 1915–16 February 1916. Libretto by Hans Müller. First performance 28 March 1916, Munich Court Theater: conducted by Bruno Walter.

Opus 9. *Sechs Einfache Lieder* (Six Simple Songs). Composed 1911–1913. Dedicated to Luise von Fraenkel-Ehrenstein. 1. "Schneeglöckchen" (text: Eichendorff); 2. "Nachtwanderer" (text: Eichendorff); 3. "Ständchen" (text: Eichendorff); 4. "Liebesbriefchen (text: Edith Honold); 5. "Das Heldengrab am Pruth" (text: Heinrich Kipper); 6. "Sommer" (text: Siegfried Trebitsch). First performance (Nos. 1–3) 15 February 1912, Frankfurt: Hans Vaterhauss, accompanied by Erich W. Korngold.

Opus 10. Sextet for Strings in D Major. Composed summer 1914–December 1916. Dedicated to Dr. Carl Ritter von Wiener. First performance 2 May 1917, Vienna: Rosé Quartet.

Opus 11. *Much Ado About Nothing*, incidental music for chamber orchestra, to the play by William Shakespeare. Composed summer 1918–1919. Dedicated to Egon Pollak. First performance 6 May 1920, Schönbrunn Palace, Vienna: Vienna Philharmonic Orchestra, conducted by Erich W. Korngold. Orchestral suite, first performance 24 January 1920, Vienna: Vienna Symphony Orchestra, conducted by Erich W. Korngold. Suite for Duo or Trio, first performance 21 May 1920, Vienna: Rudolf Kolisch, Paul Breisach, and Erich W. Korngold.

Opus 12. *Die tote Stadt* (The Dead City), opera in three acts. Composed 1916–1920. Dedicated to Dr. Ludwig Strecker. Libretto by Julius and Erich W. Korngold (under the pseudonym Paul Schott), with contributions by Hans Müller. After George Rodenbach's novel *Bruges la Morte*, his play *Le mirage*, and its German translations *Die stille Stadt* (1903) and *Das Trugbild* (1913) by Siegfried Trebitsch. First performance 4 December 1920, Hamburg and Cologne: conducted by Egon Pollak (Hamburg), Otto Klemperer (Cologne).

Opus 13. *Sursum Corda*, symphonic overture for large orchestra. Composed summer 1919. Dedicated to Richard Strauss. First performance 24 January 1920: Vienna Symphony Orchestra, conducted by Erich W. Korngold.

Opus 14. *Vier Lieder des Abschieds* (Four Songs of Farewell). Composed 1920–1921 except "Gefasster Abschied" composed summer 1915 (early version: "The Austrian Soldier's Song of Farewell"). Dedicated to Franz Schalk. 1. "Sterbelied" (text: Rosetti/Alfred Kerr); 2. "Dies eine kann mein Sehren nimmer fassen" (text: Edith Ronsperger); 3. "Mond, so gehst du wieder auf" (text: Ernst Lothar); 4. "Gefasster Abschied" (text: Ernst Lothar). First performance 5 November 1921, Vienna: Maria Olszewska (mezzo soprano), accompanied by Erich W. Korngold. Orchestral version, first performance 14 January 1923: Rosette Anday, Chamber Orchestra of the Vienna State Opera, conducted by Erich W. Korngold.

Opus 15. Piano Quintet in E Major. Composed 1921–1922. Dedicated "To the Sculptor Gustinus Ambrosi." First performance 16 February 1923, Hamburg: Bandler Quartet with Erich W. Korngold.

Opus 16. String Quartet No. 1 in A Major. Composed December 1920–spring 1923. Dedicated to the Rosé Quartet. First performance 8 January 1924, Vienna: Rosé Quartet.

Opus 17. Piano Concerto in C-sharp for the left hand alone, with orchestra. Composed by summer 1923. Commissioned by and dedicated to Paul Wittgenstein. First performance 22 September 1924, Vienna: Paul Wittgenstein with the Vienna Symphony Orchestra, conducted by Erich W. Korngold.

Opus 18. *Drei Lieder* (Three Songs). Composed 1924. Dedicated "To My Beloved Father." Texts by Hans Kaltneker. "In meine innige Nacht," "Tu ab den Schmerz," "Du reine Frau." First performance 11 March 1926, Vienna: Rosette Anday, accompanied by Erich W. Korngold.

Opus 19. *Vier kleine Karikaturen für Kinder* (Four Little Caricatures for Children), four satirical pieces for piano solo after the composers Schoenberg, Stravinsky, Bartók, and Hindemith. Composed end of 1926. "Kuckuck" (Cuckoo), "Zum Einschlummern" (Going to Sleep), "Frisch gewagt ist halb gewonnen" (Nothing Ventured, Nothing Gained), "Ernste Zeiten" (Serious Times). First performance 31 May 1978, Liverpool, England: Michael Young, pianist. Published in *Musikleben* November 1931. Published by Schott in 1993.

Opus 20. *Das Wunder der Heliane* (The Miracle of Heliane), opera in three acts. Composed 1923–1927. Dedicated "To My Wife." Libretto by Hans Müller, after a mystery play by Hans Kaltneker, *Die Heilige* (The Saint). First performed 7 October 1927, Hamburg: conducted by Egon Pollak.

Opus 21. *Geschichten von Strauss* (Tales from Strauss) for solo piano. Fantasy on themes of Johann Strauss (Sr. & Jr.) and Eduard Strauss in the tradition of Rosenthal, Schulz-Eweler, Lehvinne, Moscheles, and Godowsky. Adapted and arranged 1927. Dedicated to Hubert Marischka. Orchestral version prepared 1931 by Franz Kopriva and performed by several orchestras.

Opus 22. *Drei Lieder*. Composed 1928–1929. Dedicated "To My Mother." 1. "Was du mir bist?" (text: Eleonore van der Straten); 2. "Mit dir zu schweigen" (text: Karl Kobald); 3. "Welt ist stille eingeschlafen" (text : Karl Kobald). First performance of No. 1, 9 December 1928, Vienna: Margit Angerer, accompanied by Erich W. Korngold. First performance of No. 3, 1 January 1930, Vienna: Hanna Schwarz, accompanied by Erich W. Korngold.

Opus 23. Suite for Two Violins, Cello, and Piano for the left hand alone. Composed 1930. Commissioned by and dedicated to Paul Wittgenstein. First performance 21 October 1930, Vienna: Paul Wittgenstein and members of the Rosé Quartet.

Opus 24. *Baby Serenade* for 14 wind instruments, banjo, piano, harp, percussion, and string orchestra. Composed 1928–1929. Overture: "Baby tritt in die Welt" (allegro vivace). Lied: "Es ist ein braves Baby" (molto moderato). Scherzino: "Es hat auch die schönsten Spielsachen" (molto allegro). Jazz: "Baby erzählt eine Geschichte" (molto comodo). Epilogue: "Und nun singt es sich in den Schlaf" (tempo di minuetto molto moderato). First performance 5 December 1932, Vienna: Vienna Symphony Orchestra, conducted by Erich W. Korngold.

Opus 25. Piano Sonata No. 3 in C Major. Composed summer 1931. Dedicated "To Julius Bittner, in friendship." First performance 3 March 1932, Vienna: Paul Weingarten.

Opus 26. String Quartet No. 2 in E-flat Major. Composed 1933. First performance 16 March 1934, Vienna: Rosé Quartet.

Opus 27. *Unvergänglichkeit* (The Eternal). Composed 1933. Song cycle to texts by Eleonore van der Straten, English translation by Erna McArthur (1942). "Release," "The River Flows," "The Child Asleep," "Stronger than Death," "Release." First performance 27 October 1937, Vienna: Desi Halban, accompanied by Erich W. Korngold.

Opus 28. *Die Kathrin*, opera in three acts. Composed 1932–1937. Dedicated "To the Vienna State Opera and Its Artists." Text by Ernst Decsey after the novel *Die Magd von Aachen* by Heinrich Eduard Jacob and other sources. First performance 7 October 1939, Stockholm: Royal Opera, conducted by Nils Grevillius. Published by Josef Weinberger.

Opus 29. *Narrenlieder* (Songs of the Clown) from *Twelfth Night* by William Shakespeare. Composed for the Max Reinhardt Workshop 1937. "Come Away Death," "Hey Robin!," "Adieu, Good Man Devil," "O Mistress Mine," "The Rain It Raineth Every Day." First performance 28 June 1941, Los Angeles: Nanette Fabray. Published 1995.

Opus 30. *A Passover Psalm,* hymn for solo voice, chorus, and orchestra to Hebrew texts. Composed 1941. Dedicated in 1951 "To the Society of the Friends of Music, Vienna" on the occasion of its first performance there. First performance 12 April 1941, Los Angeles: Elks Temple, conducted by Erich W. Korngold. Published 1995.

Opus 31. *Four Shakespearean Lieder,* from *Othello* and *As You Like It.* Composed 1937–1941 for the Max Reinhardt Workshop. "Desdemona's Song," "When Birds Do Sing," "Blow, Blow Thou Winter Wind," "Under the Greenwood Tree." First performance 28 June 1941, Los Angeles: Nanette Fabray and others, accompanied by Erich W. Korngold. Published 1995.

Opus 32. *Prayer* for tenor, women's chorus, harp, and organ. Composed by September 1941. Text by Franz Werfel. First performance 1 October 1941, Los Angeles: conducted by Erich W. Korngold. Published 1995.

Opus 33. *Tomorrow*, tone poem for mezzo soprano, women's chorus, and orchestra. Composed 1941–1942 for the film *The Constant Nymph*, 1942. Text by Margaret Kennedy. First performance 10 May 1944, New York: Eileen Farrell, Columbia Symphony Orchestra, conducted by Erich W. Korngold. Published by Warner Brothers Music.

Opus 34. String Quartet No. 3 in D Major. Composed 1944–1945. Dedicated "To Bruno Walter in Admiration and Friendship." First performance 1946, Los Angeles: Roth Quartet.

Opus 35. Violin Concerto in D Major. Partly composed 1937–1939; revised July–October 1945. Dedicated to Alma Mahler-Werfel. First performance 15 February 1947, St. Louis, Missouri: Jascha Heifetz, St. Louis Symphony Orchestra, conducted by Vladimir Golschmann.

Opus 36. *Die stumme Serenade* (The Silent Serenade), comedy with music in two acts with a scenic overture. Composed 1946–1950. Based on an idea by Raoul Auernheimer, revised by Rudolph Lothar. English book by Victor Clement. Lyrics by Bert Reisfeld and William Okie. German version by Raoul Auernheimer. First performance 26 March 1951: Radio Vienna. First staged performance 10 November 1954, Dortmund. Published by Josef Weinberger.

Opus 37. Cello Concerto in C Major in one movement. Composed April–August 1946 for the film *Deception*. First performance 29 December 1946, Los Angeles: Eleanor Aller Slatkin, Los Angeles Philharmonic Orchestra, conducted by Henry Svedrofsky.

Opus 38. *Fünf Lieder* (Five Songs) for middle voice and piano. Composed 1948; melodic material written earlier. Dedicated "To Maria Jeritza, My Unforgettable Violanta and Marietta in Friendship and Admiration." "Glückwunsch" (text: Richard Dehmel), "Der Kranke" (text: Eichendorff), "Alt Spanisch" (text: Howard Koch), "Alt Englisch" (anon.), "Kein Sonnenglanz im Auge" (text: William Shakespeare). First performance 19 February 1950, Vienna: Rosette Anday, accompanied by Erich W. Korngold.

Opus 39. *Symphonic Serenade* in B-flat major for string orchestra. Composed 1947–1948. Dedicated "To Luzi Korngold, my wife, my best friend." First performance 15 January 1950, Vienna: Vienna Philharmonic Orchestra, conducted by Wilhelm Furtwängler.

Opus 40. Symphony in F-sharp for large orchestra. Composed August 1947–September 13 1952. Dedicated to Franklin Delano Roosevelt. First performance 17 October 1954, Vienna: Vienna Symphony Orchestra, conducted by Harold Byrns.

Opus 41. "Sonett für Wien" (Sonnet for Vienna) for mezzo soprano and piano. Composed 1953. Dedicated "To Frau Gretel Kralik in admiration." Text by Hans Kaltneker. First performance 17 October 1954, Vienna: Hildegard Rössel-Majdan, accompanied by Erich W. Korngold.

Opus 42. *Theme and Variations for Orchestra*. Composed summer 1953. Dedicated "To the School Orchestras of America." First performance 22 November 1953: Inglewood Symphony Orchestra, conducted by Ernst Gebert. Published 1996.

Part 2. Works Without Opus Number

Works are unpublished, unless otherwise indicated. They are listed in chronological order, and performances are noted. The manuscripts of these works are in the Library of Congress.

1905

Melodie Opus 1 (sic)

Melodie Opus 2 (sic)

"Knabe" for voice and piano. First performance 29 April 1995, Munich: David Ian Kram.

1906

Theme with Three Variations for Piano

1907

Waltz No. 3 for piano
Waltz No. 4 for piano
Waltz No. 5 for piano
Waltz No. 7 for piano
Waltz No. 8 (Waltzes 1–2, 6 are no longer extant) for piano
"Kleiner Wunsch" for soprano and piano. Lyrics by Erich W. Korngold.
"Rondando" for piano
"Valse Charmante" Nos. 3 and 6 for piano
Scherzando for piano
Der Tod for piano. Lyrics by Wilhelm Fabri. Later adapted for "Don Quixote's Conversion and Death" as part of *Don Quixote: Six Characteristic Pieces*, see below.

1908

"Beim Grossmütterchen," waltz for piano. First performance 29 April 1995, Munich: David Ian Kram.
Der Schneemann, ballet pantomime for piano in two acts. Composed Christmas 1908–Easter 1909. Orchestrated March 1910 by Alexander von Zemlinsky. Revised by Erich W. Korngold January 1913. Libretto by Erich W. Korngold. First performance 14 April 1910, Vienna. Orchestrated version, first performance 4 October 1910: Vienna Court Opera. Published by Universal Edition.
Piano Sonata No. 1 in D Minor. Composed 1908–October 1909. First performance (incomplete) 3 August 1910, Salzburg: Erich W. Korngold. Published by Universal Edition.
"Valse Pensive" for piano
"Trauer Marsch" for piano
"Die Nixe." Fragment of one-act play. Text by Wilhelm Fabri.
"Im Zauberwald" for piano solo
"In der Klavierstunde" for piano solo
"Konzertwalzer" for piano
Impromptu for Piano. Dedicated to Miss Sophie de Bauer.
"Lustspiel Ouvertüre" for piano

1909

"Valse Lente" for piano
"Valse Tardadine" for piano
Andantino for piano
Don Quixote: Six Characteristic Pieces for piano. Composed July–August 1909 (except first: 1907). "Don Quixote's Dreams of Heroic Deeds," "Sancho Panza and His Gray Donkey," "Don Quixote Goes Forth," "Dulcinea von Toboso," "Adventure," "Don Quixote's Conversion and Death." Published privately in 1909. Published by Schott in 1996.
Was der Wald erzählt, suite for piano. Dated 27 December 1909. "Erwachen der Vögel am Morgen," "Der verliebte Jägerbursch," "Heinzelmännchen."

1911

Vespers for voice and piano. Composed 28 March 1911 (possibly intended for Opus 9). Lyrics by Eichendorff.
Twelve Songs. Dated 24 December 1911 (originally intended for Opus 9). "Schneeglöckchen," "Das Ständchen," "Nachtwanderer," "Waldeinsamkeit," "Sangesmut," "Winternacht," "Das Mädchen," "Die Sperlinge," "Der Friedensbote," "Aussicht," "Abendlandschaft," "Vom Berge." Texts by Eichendorff. First performance of "Waldeinsamkeit" and "Sangesmut" 15 February 1912, Frankfurt: Hans Vaterhauss, accompanied by Erich W. Korngold. The first three songs were published as Opus 9.

"Andenken" for voice and piano. Composed 25 September 1911. Text by Eichendorff.

Character Study for Large Orchestra. Dedicated to Empress Maria Josefa.

"Reiselied" for voice and piano. Composed 6 September 1911. Text by Eichendorff. First performance 15 May 1994, Kiel.

"Abendgebet" for voice and piano. Composed 28 March 1911. Dedicated "To Miss Daisy Thalberg—In Remembrance." Text by Eichendorff.

"Nachklänge" for voice and piano. Text by Eichendorff.

"Die Geniale" for voice and piano. Composed 1911(?). Text by Eichendorff. First performance 23 August 1995, New Brunswick Music Festival, Canada: Marcia Swanston accompanied by Robert Kortgaard.

1912

Vier kleine fröhliche Walzer (Four Little Happy Waltzes), Opus 5 (sic), for piano solo. "Gretl" (Margarethe Heller), "Margit" (Margit "Manzi" Ganz), "Gisi," "Mitzi" (Mitzi Kolisch). Published 1997.

Fugue for String Quartet. Composed 20 December 1912.

1913

Der Sturm (The Storm) for chorus and orchestra. Composed by 18 December 1913. Lyrics by Heinrich Heine.

"Nachts" for voice and piano. Composed December 1913. Text by Siegfried Trebitsch. First performance 15 May 1994, Kiel: Robert Klopper, accompanied by Thorsten Schmid-Kapfenburg.

1914

"Der innere Scharm" for voice and piano. Dedicated "For My Mother's 42nd Birthday (she says)."

1915

"For Mother's Birthday," a parody on contemporary composers for piano.

"Austrian Soldier's Song of Farewell" for voice and piano. Composed by December 1915 for his father's birthday. First performance 11 March 1917, Vienna: Rudolf Hofbauer. Published privately for charity sale, 1917.

1916

Kaiserin Zita-Hymne for solo voice, choir, and piano. Text by Baronin Hedda von Skoda. Published privately for charity sale, 1917. First performances 9 May 1917, Schloss Schönbrunn, Vienna, in the presence of Empress Zita: morning concert of 250-member children's choir, conducted by Ms. von Manussi; evening concert with Leo Slezak, accompanied by Erich W. Korngold. First performance orchestral version 12 October 1917: Vienna Symphony Orchestra, organ, and chorus, Hans Duhan, conducted by Erich W. Korngold.

1917

"Dance in Old Style" for small orchestra. Composed May 1917.

B Minor Scherzo by Felix Mendelssohn-Bartholdy. Orchestrated August 1917. First performance 1 February 1922: Vienna Symphony Orchestra, conducted by Erich W. Korngold.

"Kindermarsch" by Franz Schubert. Orchestrated August 1917.

Military March in B Major for Orchestra. Published by Schott & Co., 1932.

"Oberst Hirsch" March for Orchestra.

"Etwas ganz Persönliches," love song. Composed Christmas 1917. Dedicated "seiner lieben Mitzi [Kolisch]."

1919

"Die Gansleber im Hause Duschnitz, eine festliche Würdigung für Solostimme und Klavier." Composed 6 April 1919. Text by Erich W. Korngold.

1922

Der Vampir: eine discrete Bühnenmusik für ein Drama von Hans Müller for chamber orchestra and organ. First performance 3 February 1923, Vienna: Deutsches Volkstheater.

1939

At Your Service. Arrangements of Rossini for the Max Reinhardt Workshop production of Goldoni's "Servant with Two Masters." Text by William Okie. First performance 31 May 1939, Los Angeles: Erich W. Korngold.

1946

Romance-Impromptu for Cello and Piano. Composed but not used for the film *Deception.* Published by Sunbury Music, 1975.

1949

"Waltz for Luzi" for piano (in the style of Frédéric Chopin). Composed for Luzi and Erich W. Korngolds' Silver Wedding Anniversary. First performance 15 May 1995, Kiel: Thorsten Schmid-Kapfenburg.

1953

Straussiana for Orchestra. Arranged and orchestrated summer 1953. Based on works by Johann Strauss. Dedicated "To the School Orchestras of America." First performance 22 November 1953: Inglewood Symphony Orchestra, conducted by Ernst Gebert.

Part 3. Operetta Arrangements

Eine Nacht in Venedig by Johann Strauss II. Arranged with variations spring/summer 1923. Original libretto by Friedrich Zell and Richard Genée. New text by Ernst Marischka. First performance 25 October 1923: Theater an der Wien, conducted by Erich W. Korngold. Revised for the Vienna State Opera, first performance 23 June 1929. Published by Josef Weinberger.

Cagliostro in Wien by Johann Strauss II. Arranged autumn 1926–spring 1927. Original libretto by Friedrich Zell and Richard Genée. Revised version by Dr. Ludwig Herzer. First performance 13 April 1927, Vienna: Wiener Burgertheater, conducted by Erich W. Korngold. Published by Josef Weinberger.

Rosen aus Florida by Leo Fall. Arranged with new compositions summer 1928. Dedicated "To Hubert Marischka, the Master of the Vienna Operetta." Libretto by Dr. Alfred Maria Willner and Heinz Reichert. Musical score based on sketches by Fall and new compositions in the style of Fall by Erich W. Korngold. Orchestrated by Erich W. Korngold and Franz Kopriva. First performance 22 February 1929, Vienna: Theater an der Wien, conducted by Korngold.

Die Fledermaus by Johann Strauss II. Arranged spring 1929 for the Max Reinhardt production. Libretto by Henri Meilhac, Ludovic Halévy, revised by Carl Haffner and Marcellus Schiffer. First performance 8 June 1929, Berlin: Deutsches Theater, conducted by Erich W. Korngold. Published by Josef Weinberger.

Walzer aus Wien, based on life of Johann Strauss II. Arranged spring–summer 1930. Singspiel in three acts by Dr. Alfred Maria Willner, Heinz Reichert, and Ernst Marischka. Musical score (after Strauss) by Erich W. Korngold, with orchestrations by Julius Bittner and Bruno Granichstaedten. First performance 30 October 1930: Vienna Stadttheater, conducted by Erich W. Korngold. Published by Josef Weinberger.

Die schöne Helena (La Belle Hélène) by Jacques Offenbach. Arranged spring 1931 for the Max Reinhardt production. Opera-buffa by Henri Meilhac and Ludovic Halévy, based on the Paris version by Egon Friedell and Hanns Sassmann. First performance 15 June 1931, Berlin: Theater am Kurfürstendamm, conducted by Erich W. Korngold. Published by Bote und Bock.

Das Lied der Liebe, based on Johann Strauss II. Arranged and composed summer 1931. Original operetta by Dr. Ludwig Herzer. Music by Strauss with original interpolations by Erich W. Korngold. First performance 23 December 1931, Berlin: Metropol Theater, conducted by Erich W. Korngold.

Die geschiedene Frau by Leo Fall. Arranged and composed summer 1932. Based on a book by Victor Leon; new version by Victor Leon and Heinz Reichert. Couplets by Max Colpet. Music based on Fall's operetta with "enrichments" by Erich W. Korngold. First performance 1 February 1933, Berlin: Theater am Nollendorfplatz, conducted by Erich W. Korngold. Unpublished (manuscript lost).

Rosalinda. US Version of the Korngold/Reinhardt version of *Die Fledermaus* by Johann Strauss II. Arranged summer 1942. Text by Gottfried Reinhardt and John Meehan, Jr. Lyrics by Paul Kerby. First performance 28 October 1942, New York: 44th Street Theater, conducted by Erich W. Korngold. Published by Witmark and Son.

Helen Goes to Troy. US Version of the Korngold-Reinhardt version of Jacques Offenbach's *La Belle Hélène (Die schöne Helena).* Arranged spring 1944. Text by Gottfried Reinhardt. First performance 24 April 1944, New York: Alvin Theater, conducted by Erich W. Korngold. Published by Chappell and Co.

The Great Waltz. US Version of *Walzer aus Wien.* Adapted and supervised for the Los Angeles Civic Light Opera Company by Erich W. Korngold. Productions in Los Angeles and San Francisco 1947, 1949, 1953, 1956.

Part 4. Film Scores

All films were produced by Warner Brothers unless otherwise stated. All scores were conducted by Korngold on the soundtrack, except Magic Fire. None of the scores is commercially published in its entirety, but suites from some of the more famous films are available from Warner Bros. Music, Chappell & Co., and Bote und Bock. The durations of the films are those of the original release version: beware of edited television and video prints.

1934–1935

A Midsummer Night's Dream by William Shakespeare. Arrangements of music by Felix Mendelssohn-Bartholdy with original interpolations by Erich W. Korngold. Directed by Max Reinhardt and William Dieterle. Produced by Hal Wallis and Henry Blanke. Screenplay by Charles Kenyon and Mary McCall. Choreography: Bronislava Nijinska. Art direction: Anton Grot. Costumes: Max Ree. Photography: Ernest Haller, Hal Mohr. Cast: Ian Hunter, Mickey Rooney, Olivia de Havilland, Dick Powell, et al. Anita Louise dubbed by Carol Weiskopf. Premiere 9 October 1935, New York and London. Academy Award nomination for Best Film of the Year. Academy Award for Best Photography. Duration 140 minutes (1936 version, 132 minutes).

1935

A Dream Comes True. Short subject about the making of *A Midsummer Night's Dream.* Music by Mendelssohn, conducted by Erich W. Korngold. Written by George R. Bilson. Edited by Norman A. Cerf. Narrated by Addison Richards. Features the only footage of Korngold playing the piano; includes film of the Hollywood premiere of *A Midsummer Night's Dream.* Duration 8 minutes.

Rose of the Rancho (Paramount Pictures). Opening sequence: "Fight for the Right" and "Without Freedom." Text by David Ormont. Cast: Gladys Swarthout, et al. Duration 82 minutes.

Captain Blood. Based on the novel by Rafael Sabatini. Directed by Michael Curtiz. Cues "Street Scene" and "Spanish Soldier" by Milan Roder. Duel sequence based on *Prometheus* by Franz Liszt. Orchestration by Hugo Friedhofer and Ray Heindorf. Photography: Ernest Haller, Hal Mohr. Cast: Errol Flynn, Olivia de Havilland, Basil Rathbone, Lionel Atwill. Academy Award nomination for Best Picture of the Year. Duration 119 minutes.

1935–1936

Give Us This Night (Paramount Pictures). Piano solos by Erich W. Korngold; "Di Quella Pira" from *Il Trovatore* by Verdi arranged by Erich W. Korngold. Lyrics by Oscar

Hammerstein II. Directed by Alexander Hall. Screenplay by Edwin Justus Meyer. Photography: Victor Millner. Art direction: Hans Dreier. Cast: Jan Kiepura, Gladys Swarthout, Alan Mowbray. Alan Mowbray dubbed by Allen Rogers. Premiere April 1936, New York. Duration 93 minutes.

1936

Anthony Adverse. Based on the novel by Hervey Allen. Directed by Mervyn LeRoy. Screenplay by Sheridan Gibney. Opera sequence "The Duchess of Ferrara" by Aldo Franchetti and "Orfeo" by Monteverdi. Orchestration by Hugo Friedhofer and Milan Roder. Photography: Tony Gaudio. Art direction: Anton Grot. Cast: Frederic March, Claude Rains, Olivia de Havilland, Gail Sondergaard. Olivia de Havilland dubbed by Carol Weiskopf, Yvonne Galen. Premiere 29 July 1936, Los Angeles. Academy Award nomination for Best Picture of the Year. Academy Awards for Best Score, Best Photography, Best Supporting Actress (Sondergaard). Duration 136 minutes.

Hearts Divided. One scene: "The Separation" based on opening bar of the song "My Kingdom for a Kiss" by Harry Warren. Directed by Frank Borzage. Screenplay by Laird Doyle and Casey Robinson, based on *The Glorious Betsy* by Rida Johnson Young. Score by Heinz Roemheld (mostly based on Korngold's sequence). Cast: Marion Davies, Claude Rains, Dick Powell. Duration 87 minutes.

The Green Pastures. Two sequences: "The Creation" and "The Flood" (reused in *The Sea Hawk*). Directed by William Keighley and Marc Connelly. Written by Marc Connelly from his play of the same name. Main score by Dr. Hall Johnson. Orchestration by Hugo Friedhofer. Photography: Hal Mohr. Cast: Rex Ingram, Oscar Polk, Eddie Anderson. Duration 93 minutes.

1936–1937

Another Dawn. Directed by William Dieterle. Screenplay by Laird Doyle. Orchestration by Hugo Friedhofer and Milan Roder. Photography: Tony Gaudio. Cast: Errol Flynn, Kay Francis, Ian Hunter. Premiere June 1937. Duration 73 minutes.

1937

The Prince and the Pauper. Directed by William Keighley. Screenplay by Laird Doyle based on the novel by Mark Twain. Orchestration by Hugo Friedhofer and Milan Roder. Photography: Sol Polito. Cast: Errol Flynn, Claude Rains, the Mauch Twins, Henry Stephenson. Duration 118 minutes.

1938

The Adventures of Robin Hood. Directed by Michael Curtiz and William Keighley. Orchestration by Hugo Friedhofer, Milan Roder, Reginald Basset. Photography (Technicolor): Tony Gaudio, Sol Polito, Howard Green. Cast: Errol Flynn, Olivia de Havilland, Claude Rains, Basil Rathbone. Premiere 12 May 1938. First performance of orchestral suite 24 June 1938, Oakland, California: the Bay Region Symphony Orchestra, conducted by Erich W. Korngold. Academy Award nomination for Best Film of the Year. Academy Award for Best Original Score, Art Direction, and Film Editing. Duration 102 minutes.

1938–1939

Juarez. Directed by William Dieterle. Screenplay by John Huston, Aeneas MacKenzie, Wolfgang Reinhardt, based on texts by Franz Werfel and Bertita Harding. Orchestration by Hugo Friedhofer and Milan Roder. Photography: Tony Gaudio. Cast: Paul Muni, Bette Davis, Claude Rains, Brian Aherne, John Garfield. Premiere 25 April 1939. Academy Award nomination for Best Supporting Actor (Aherne). Duration 132 minutes.

1939

The Private Lives of Elizabeth and Essex. Directed by Michael Curtiz. Screenplay by Norman Reilly Raine, Aeneas Mackenzie from the play *Elizabeth the Queen* by Maxwell Anderson. Orchestration by Hugo Friedhofer and Milan Roder. Spinet solo by Erich W. Korngold. Photography (Technicolor): Sol Polito. Cast: Bette Davis, Errol

Flynn, Vincent Price, Henry Daniell. Premiere 27 September 1939. Academy Award nominations for Best Film, Best Photography, Best Original Score. Duration 106 minutes.

1940

The Sea Hawk. Directed by Michael Curtiz. Screenplay by Seton I. Miller and Howard Koch, based loosely on the novel by Rafael Sabatini. Orchestration by Hugo Friedhofer, Ray Heindorf, Simon Bucharoff, Milan Roder. "Spanish Song" lyrics by Howard Koch. Brenda Marshall dubbed by Sally Sweetland. Photography: Sol Polito. Art direction: Anton Grot. Cast: Errol Flynn, Flora Robson, Claude Rains, Henry Daniell. Premiere July 1940. Academy Award Nomination for Best Picture, Original Score. Duration 127 minutes.

1941

The Sea Wolf. Directed by Michael Curtiz. Screenplay by Robert Rossen after the novel by Jack London. Orchestration by Hugo Friedhofer and Ray Heindorf. Photography: Sol Polito. Cast: Edward G. Robinson, Ida Lupino, John Garfield. Premiere March 1941. Duration 100 minutes.

Kings Row. Directed by Sam Wood. Production design by William Cameron Menzies. Screenplay by Casey Robinson after the novel by Henry Bellamann. Orchestration by Hugo Friedhofer and Ray Heindorf. Piano solos by Max Rabinowitz and Norma Boleslawski. Photography: James Wong Howe. Cast: Robert Cummings, Ronald Reagan, Anne Sheridan, Claude Rains. Premiere 2 February 1942. Academy Award nominations for Best Picture, Best Direction, and Best Photography. Duration 127 minutes.

1942

The Constant Nymph. Directed by Edmund Goulding. Screenplay by Kathryn Scola after the book and play by Margaret Kennedy. Contains the tone poem *Tomorrow*, Opus 33, sung by Clemence Groves, mezzo soprano, with the Warner Brothers Studio Orchestra, conducted by Erich W. Korngold. Piano solos by Erich W. Korngold. Piano duet by Erich W. Korngold and Max Rabinowitz. Joan Fontaine dubbed by Sally Sweetland. Orchestration by Hugo Friedhofer. Photography: Tony Gaudio. Cast: Charles Boyer, Joan Fontaine, Peter Lorre, Montagu Love. Premiere 23 July 1942. Academy Award nomination for Best Actress (Joan Fontaine). Duration 112 minutes.

1943

Devotion. Directed by Curtis Bernhardt. Screenplay by Keith Winter after a biography of the Brontë sisters by Theodore Reeves. Orchestration by Hugo Friedhofer, Ernst Toch, Leonid Raab, Bernhard Kaun, Simon Bucharoff, Milan Roder. Photography: Ernest Haller. Montages: Don Siegel (uncredited). Cast: Olivia de Havilland, Ida Lupino, Paul Henreid, Sydney Greenstreet. Premiere 5 April 1946, New York. Duration 107 minutes.

1944

Between Two Worlds. Directed by Edward A. Blatt. Screenplay by Daniel Fuchs after the play *Outward Bound* by Sutton Vane. Piano solos by Erich W. Korngold. Orchestration by Hugo Friedhofer, Simon Bucharoff, Leonid Raab. Photography: Carl Guthrie. Cast: Paul Henreid, Eleanor Parker, Sydney Greenstreet, John Garfield. Premiere 20 May 1944. Duration 112 minutes.

1944–1945

Of Human Bondage. Directed by Edmund Goulding. Screenplay by Catherine Turney after the novel by Somerset Maugham. Orchestration by Hugo Friedhofer. Photography: Peverell Marley. Cast: Paul Henreid, Eleanor Parker, Edmund Gwenn, Patric Knowles. Premiere July 1946, Los Angeles. Duration 105 minutes

1946

Escape Me Never. Directed by Peter Godfrey. Screenplay by Thames Williamson after the novel *The Fool of the Family* and the play *Escape Me Never* by Margaret Kennedy.

Piano solo (for Flynn) by Erich W. Korngold. Song "Love for Love" music by Erich W. Korngold, lyrics by Ted Koehler. Song "O Nene" music by Erich W. Korngold, lyrics by Koehler and Aldo Franchetti. Orchestration by Hugo Friedhofer and Ray Heindorf. Choreography: LeRoy Prinz. Ballet sequence "Primavera" danced by George Zoritch and Milada Mladova. Photography: Sol Polito. Cast: Errol Flynn, Ida Lupino, Eleanor Parker, Gig Young. Premiere 22 November 1947, Los Angeles. Duration 104 minutes.

Deception. Directed by Irving Rapper. Screenplay by John Collier and Joseph Than after the play *Monsieur Lamberthier* by Louis Verneuill (titled *Obsession* in US). Orchestration by Murray Cutter. Orchestration of the cello concerto by Cutter revised by Erich W. Korngold. Jazz arrangement of Mendelssohn's Wedding March by Ray Heindorf. Cadenza in Haydn concerto by Erich W. Korngold. Cello solos by Eleanor Aller Slatkin. Piano solos by Erich W. Korngold (for Rains) and Shura Cherkassky (for Davis). Bach prelude and Schubert impromptu arranged by Erich W. Korngold, performed by Eleanor Aller Slatkin and Norma Boleslawski. Radio commercial by Milan Roder. Photography: Ernest Haller. Cast: Bette Davis, Paul Henreid, Claude Rains. Premiere 18 October 1946, Los Angeles. Duration 112 minutes.

1954–1955

Magic Fire (Republic Pictures). Directed by William Dieterle. Music by Richard Wagner arranged and edited by Erich W. Korngold. Screenplay by Bertita Harding, E. A. Dupont, David Chantler. The Bavarian State Opera Orchestra conducted by Alois Melichar. Piano solos (Liszt and Wagner) by Erich W. Korngold. Choreography: Tatjana Gsovsky. Singers: Leonie Rysanek, Otto Edelmann, Hans Hopf, Anneliese Kupper. Photography: Ernest Haller. Cast: Alan Badel, Yvonne de Carlo, Rita Gam, Peter Cushing; featuring Erich W. Korngold as Hans Richter. Premiere 15 July 1955. Duration 120 minutes (no longer available at this length).

Selected Bibliography

The publications and sources consulted for this book are diverse, and reflect the complexity of Korngold's life and his several careers. The following bibliography aims to present the most important published sources on the period and the composer, and to provide future scholars with an accessible reference list from which to delve deeper.

Adler, Gusti. 1980. *. . . aber vergessen Sie nicht die chinesischen Nachtigallen. Erinnerungen an Max Reinhardt.* Munich: Langen Müller.

Axelrod, Herbert R. 1990. *Heifetz—An Unauthorized Pictorial Biography.* Neptune City, New Jersey: Paganiniana Publications, Inc.

Batka, Richard. 1909. "Kind und Kunst—Ein Gespräch." *Der Merker,* 25 October. Vienna.

———. 1911. "Zum Wunderkind Problem." *Der Merker,* No. 8. Vienna.

———. 1916. "Erich Korngolds Opern." *Fremdenblatt,* 11 April. Vienna.

Baxter, John. 1976. *The Hollywood Exiles.* London: McDonald & Jane's.

Bechert, Paul. 1922. "Korngold, Strauss, and Others." *The Musical Times,* 13 January. London.

———. 1923. "The Supplementary Festival at Salzburg." *The Musical Times,* 1 October. London.

———. 1929. "Korngold and Modern Operetta." *Christian Science Monitor,* 20 July. Boston.

Behlmer, Rudy. 1967. "Erich Wolfgang Korngold—Established Some of the Filmmusic Basics Film Composers Now Ignore." *Films in Review* 182:86–100.

———. 1973. *A Day on Stage 9.* Commemorative booklet with Warner Brothers 50th Anniversary triple LP set. Warner Bros. Records, 3XX 2736.

———. 1979. *The Adventures of Robin Hood.* Complete script and annotations. Madison: University of Wisconsin Press.

———. 1982. *The Sea Hawk.* Complete script and annotations. Madison: University of Wisconsin Press.

———. 1985. *Inside Warner Brothers (1935–1951).* New York: Viking Penguin, Inc.

———. 1987. "George Korngold Interviewed." Liner notes, LP recording of the Symphonic Suite to *The Sea Hawk.* Hollywood: Varese Sarabande. 704.380.

Bekker, Paul. 1909. "Zukunftsklänge." *Die Musik,* No. 9.

———. 1922. *Klang und Eros.* Berlin: Deutsche Verlags-Anstalt.

Bienenfeld, Elsa. 1921. "*Die tote Stadt.*" *Neues Wiener Tagblatt,* 11 January. Vienna.

———. 1927. "*Das Wunder der Heliane.*" *Neues Wiener Tagblatt,* 30 October. Vienna.

Blickensdorfer, Sonia. 1993. *Erich Wolfgang Korngold—Opern und Filmmusik.* Doctoral Thesis, University of Vienna.

Bonneure, Ferdinand. 1992. "'George Rodenbach en zijn Brugse romans' Van Houtryve, Marcel 'Hoc het gedenkteken Georges Rodenbach niet te Brugge kwam' Puype Karel 'Bruges-la-Morte, de controverse vourbij.'" In *Ht Stille Brugge—100 jaar Bruges-la-Morte.* Vitgeverij Stichting Kunstboek bvba.

Brand, Juliane, Christopher Hailey, and Donald Harris, eds. 1987. *The Berg-Schoenberg Correspondence.* London: Macmillan.

Brockhoven, J. van. 1919. "A Precocious Musical Genius." *The Musical Observer* 9:402–409.

Brosche, Günter. 1983. *Strauss-Schalk Korrespondenz.* Tutzing: Verlag Hans Schneider.

Cargnelli, Omasta. 1993. *Aufbruch ins Ungewisse, Österreichische Filmschaffende in der Emigration vor 1945.* Wien: Wespennest.

Carroll, Brendan G. 1977. "Erich Wolfgang Korngold." In *The New Grove Dictionary of Music and Musicians,* vol. 6. London: Macmillan.

———. 1980. "Korngold's *Violanta.*" *The Musical Times* (November): 695–698.

———. 1983. "Erich Wolfgang Korngold—A Re-Appraisal." *Austria Today,* March.

———. 1983. *Erich Wolfgang Korngold—His Life and Works. The Music Makers.* Paisley, Scotland: Wilfion Books.

———. 1983. "Korngold's *Die tote Stadt.*" Premiere booklet, 5 February, Götz Friedrich Revival, Deutsche Oper Berlin.

———. 1986. "Korngold's Piano Sonatas." Liner notes. Amsterdam: Etcetera Recording. ETC 1042.

———. 1986. "Korngold's Trio and Sextet." Liner notes, Amsterdam: Etcetera Recording. ETC1043.

———. 1990. "Korngold and Schoenberg—An Uneasy Friendship." Liner notes, Hyperion recording of Korngold's Sextet for Strings in D Major, Opus 10, and Schoenberg's *Verklärte Nacht.* CDA 66425.

———. 1992. "The Background to Korngold's *Das Wunder der Heliane*: *Das Wunder der Heliane*—An Appraisal." *A Musical Guide to the Opera* (booklet accompanying the first recording). Decca. 436-636-2.

———. 1993. "Korngold's Symphony and *Abschiedslieder.*" Liner notes, BBC Philharmonic recording. Chandos Records. CHAN 9171.

———. 1994. "Korngold and His Sinfonietta." Program, The Royal Ballet production of *La Ronde* (which used Korngold's Opus 5 score).

———. 1995. "Korngold's Sinfonietta and *Sursum Corda.*" Liner notes, BBC Philharmonic recording. Chandos Records, CHAN 9317.

———. 1995. "Korngold's Trio and Violin Sonata." Liner notes, EMI recording.

———. 1995. "Erich Korngold: Piano Sonatas." In booklet accompanying Chandos recording CHAN 9389.

Chevalley, Heinrich. 1920. "Erich Wolfgang Korngold: Holla auf den hab acht. " *Der Merker,* 11 January. Vienna.

———. 1927. "Das Wunder der Heliane." *Musikwelt* 7:3-5. Hamburg.

Cohn, Isidor. 1914. "Korngold's New Sonata." *The Musical Standard* 3(57):109.

Crawford, Dorothy Lamb. 1995. *Evenings On and Off the Roof: Pioneering Concerts in Los Angeles, 1939–1971.* Berkeley, Los Angeles: University of California Press. 46, 90.

Dachs, Robert. 1992. *Sag beim Abschied—Wiener Publikumslieblinge in Bild & Ton.* Exhibition Catalog, Jewish Museum, Vienna.

Darby, William, and Jack De Bois. 1990. *American Film Music—Major Composers, Techniques, Trends, 1915–1990.* London: McFarland/Jefferson.

Duchen, Jessica. 1987. *Musical and Dramatic Structure in E. W. Korngold's* Die tote Stadt. Thesis, Jesus College, Cambridge.

———. 1996. *Erich Wolfgang Korngold.* London: Phaidon Press.

Dümling, Albrecht, and Peter Girth. 1988. Entartete Musik: Dokumentation und Kommentar. Düsseldorf: dkv—der Kleine Verlag (zur Düsseldorfer Ausstellung von 1938).

Ewen, David. 1927. "The Futuristic Music of Honegger and Korngold." *The Jewish Tribune,* 2 December. New York.

———. 1934. *Composers of Today.* New York: The H. W. Wilson Co.

Fuhrich-Leisler, Edda, and Gisela Prossnitz. 1976. *Max Reinhardt in Amerika*. Salzburg: Otto Mueller Verlag.

Gänzl, Kurt, and Andrew Lamb. 1988. *Gänzl's Book of the Musical Theater*. London:Bodley Head.

———. 1995. *The Encyclopedia of the Musical Theatre*. London: Blackwell.

Gayda, Thomas. 1993. "And the Banned Played On." *The Gramophone,* April. London.

Gerhardt, Charles. 1976. "Recording Die tote Stadt." In booklet accompanying the RCA complete recording, RCA 3-1199.

Gerlach, Hans Jürgen. 1994. *Heinrich Eduard Jacob: Zwischen Zwei Welten*. Berlin: Published privately.

Gilliam, Bryan. 1992. *Richard Strauss and His World*. Princeton, NJ: Princeton University Press (collection of essays, including some by Julius Korngold).

Glass, Beaumont. 1988. *Lotte Lehmann: A Life in Opera and Song*. Santa Barbara, California: Capra Press.

Goldberg, Albert. 1958. "The Sounding Board: Late Erich Korngold's Theater Sense and Sharp Wit Paid Tribute by Edwin Lester." *The Los Angeles Times*, 23 March.

Gould, Glenn. 1974. "Korngold and the Crisis of the Piano Sonata." Liner notes, Genesis Recording (Antonin Kubalek). GS 1055.

Graffman, Gary. 1985. "Korngold Was More Than A Movie Composer." *New York Times*, 15 September.

Hailey, Christopher. 1993. *Franz Schreker—A Cultural Biography*. London: Cambridge University Press.

Halliwell, Leslie. 1977. *Halliwell's Film Guide—A Survey of 8000 English Language Movies*. London: Granada Publishing (and subsequent editions).

Halperson, Maurice. 1921. "Korngold's Gifts Flower in The Dead City." *Musical America* 35(3):3, 35.

Himmel, Helmuth. 1951. *Die Problematik im Werke Hans Kaltnekers und ihr Ort in der Österreichischen Literatur des XX. Jahrhunderts*. Thesis, University of Graz.

Hirschorn, Clive. 1979. *The Warner Brothers Story*. London: Octopus Books.

Hoffmann, Rudolf Stefan. 1922. *Erich Wolfgang Korngold*. Vienna: Carl Stephenson Verlag.

Humperdinck, Engelbert. 1912. In *Sang und Klang im 19. und 20. Jahrhundert*. Berlin: Verlag von Neufeld und Henius.

Jefferson, Alan 1988. *Lotte Lehmann*. London: Macrae Books.

Jeritza, Maria. 1924. *Sunlight and Song—A Singer's Life*. New York, London: Appleton & Company.

———. 1975. "The Challenge of Korngold's Marietta-Marie." In booklet accompanying the complete RCA recording RCA ARL 3-1199 (LP version only).

Jezic, Diane Peacock. 1989. *The Musical Migration and Ernst Toch*. Ames: Iowa State University Press.

Kalbeck, Max. 1916. "Erich W. Korngold's *Violanta* und *Der Ring des Polykrates*." *Neues Wiener Tagblatt*, 11 April. Vienna.

Kalinak, Kathryn. 1992. *Settling the Score: Music and the Classical Hollywood Film*. Madison: University of Wisconsin Press. (Contains analysis of Korngold's score for *Captain Blood*.)

Kaltneker, Hans,1925. *Dichtung und Drama*. Berlin, Vienna, Leipzig: Edition Zsolnay.

Kapp, Julius. 1922. *Die Oper der Gegenwart*. Berlin: Max Hesses Verlag.

Karlin, Fred. 1994. *Listening to the Movies: The Film Lovers' Guide to Film Music*. New York: Schirmer.

Karpath, Ludwig. 1916. "Verehrer des jungen Korngold." *Der Merker*, 1 April. Vienna.

———. 1916. "Besucher der Korngold-Premiere." *Der Merker*, 15 May. Vienna.

Keegan, Susanne. 1991. *The Bride of the Wind: The Life and Times of Alma Mahler-Werfel*. London: Secker and Warburg; New York: Viking Penguin.

Kim Park, So Young. 1996. *Untersuchungenen zu den für Paul Wittgenstein (1887–1961) geschrieben Klavierwerken.* Dissertation, Institut für Musikwissenschaft der Universität Karlsruhe.

Kirsch, Winfried. 1994. *Die Fledermaus von Johann Strauss. Operettenbearbeitungen von Erich Wolfgang Korngold.* Thesis, Johann-Wolfgang Goethe-Universität, Frankfurt am Main.

Konta, Robert. 1921. "*Die tote Stadt.*" *Wiener Mittags-Zeitung,* 11 January. Vienna.

Korb, Willi. 1966. *Richard Tauber.* Vienna: Europäischer Verlag.

Korngold, Erich Wolfgang. 1920. "*Die tote Stadt.*" *Musikwelt,* 3 December.

———. 1920. "Der Fall Mauke und andere Fälle." *Komödie—Wochenrevue für Bühne und Film.* Jahrgang 1, No. 6, 6 November. Vienna

———. 1921. "Erinnerungen an Zemlinsky aus meiner Lehrzeit" (Zemlinsky, the Exemplar of My Youth). *Auftakt,* January. Prague.

———. 1922. "Die Partitur der toten Stadt." *Der Merker.* Vienna.

———. 1937. "Composing for the Pictures." *Etude Music Magazine,* January.

———. 1940. "Some Experiences of Film Music." *Music and Dance in California,* June.

———. 1956. Foreword: "Faith in Music?" In *Faith in Music,* Ulric Devaré. New York: Philosophical Library.

Korngold, George. 1983. "Erich Wolfgang Korngold and *The Adventures of Robin Hood.*" Liner notes, LP recording of the score. Varese Sarabande, Hollywood, 704.180.

———. 1983. *Making Magic Fire.* Liner notes, soundtrack album Varese Sarabande, Hollywood STV 81179.

Korngold, Julius. 1921. *Deutsches Opernschaffen der Gegenwart* Leonhardt, Vienna.

———. 1922. *Die romanische Oper der Gegenwart.* Vienna: Rikola Verlag.

———. 1938. *Atonale Götzendämmerung.* Vienna: Doblinger.

———. 1945. *Child Prodigy: Erich Wolfgang's Years of Childhood.* New York: Willard Press.

———. 1991. *Die Korngolds in Wien: Der Musikkritiker und das Wunderkind.* (Memoirs: original 1944 title *Postludes in Major and Minor).* Zürich: M&T Verlag, Edition Musik & Theater.

Korngold, Luzi. 1967. *Erich Wolfgang Korngold—Ein Lebensbild.* Vienna: Verlag Elisabeth Lafite und Österreichischer Bundesverlag.

Kram, David. 1990. *Violanta—an opera by Erich Wolfgang Korngold.* Thesis, University of Adelaide, Elder Conservatorium.

Kralik, Heinrich. 1927. "*Das Wunder der Heliane.*" *Neues Wiener Tagblatt,* 30 October. Vienna.

———. 1950. "Korngolds *Die Kathrin.*" *Die Presse,* 21 October. Vienna.

Kraus, Karl. 1910. "Der kleine Korngold." *Die Fackel,* No. 313–314, December 31.

———. 1932. "Korngold und Reinhardt." *Die Fackel* No. 868–872, March.

Krogel, Meta. 1987. *Gesammelte Erinnerungen von und an Richard Tauber.* Düsseldorf: H. Sieben-Eigenverlag.

Krones, Hartmut. 1995. *Alexander Zemlinsky: Äesthetik, Stil und Umfeld.* Vienna/Cologne: Böhlau Verlag.

Kuhlo, Alexander. 1995. *Analytische Untersuchungen zur Sinfonie in Fis Opus 40 von Erich Wolfgang Korngold unter besonderer Berücksichtigung der Form, der Harmonik und der Instrumentation.* Thesis, Hochschule für Musik und Theater, Hanover.

Lebrecht, Norman. 1987. *Mahler Remembered.* London: Faber & Faber.

Lek, Robert van der.1991. *Diegetic Music in Opera and Film: A Similarity Between Two Genres of Drama Analysed in Works by Erich Wolfgang Korngold.* Amsterdam: Rodopi.

Liebestöckl, Hans. 1912. "Erich Korngold." *Die Zukunft.* Berlin.

———. 1920. "Korngold." *Komödie—Wochenrevue für Bühne und Film.* Vienna.

⎯⎯⎯⎯⎯. 1927. "Oper." *Wiener Sonn- und Montagszeitung*, 31 October. Vienna.

Lubin, Alma. 1944. "Mainly About Musical Manhattan." (Contains interview with Korngold about *Between Two Worlds*). *The Cincinnati Enquirer*, 26 March.

Maeder, Edward. 1987. *Hollywood and History: Costume Design in Film.* New York/ Los Angeles: Thames and Hudson/ Los Angeles County Museum of Art.

Mahler, Alma. 1940. *Erinnerungen an Gustav Mahler.* Rpt. Berlin, Frankfurt, Vienna: Ullstein, 1968, 1978.

⎯⎯⎯⎯⎯. 1960. *Mein Leben.* Frankfurt-am-Main:Fischer-Verlag.

Mathis, Alfred. 1961. "Elisabeth Schumann and the Vienna Opera." *London Opera* (January):968-979.

Merrill-Mirsky, Carol. 1991. *Exiles in Paradise.* Catalogue of the Hollywood Bowl Exhibition (including interviews and essays). Hollywood, California: Hollywood Bowl Museum.

Mierendorff, Marta. 1993. *William Dieterle. Der Plutarch von Hollywood.* Berlin: Henschel Verlag.

Moderwell, Hiram. K. 1913. "Erich Korngold—Prodigy and Artist." *The Harvard Musical Review* 1(10):7.

Moldenhauer, Hans. 1979. *Anton von Webern: A Chronicle of His Life and Work.* New York: Alfred A. Knopf.

Mosley, Philip. 1986. *Bruges la Morte.* (Rodenbach) Transl. from the French, with a chronology of editions and analytical introduction. Paisley, Scotland: Wilfion Books.

Newman, Ernest. 1912. "The Problem of Erich Korngold." *The Nation*, 24 August.

Nieminski, Simon. 1990. *Compositional Techniques in Early Hollywood Talking Pictures with an Examination of Certain Film Scores of Erich Wolfgang Korngold.* Thesis, University of Cambridge.

Noelte, A. Albert. 1916. "*Violanta* und *Der Ring des Polykrates*—Uraufführung am Hoftheater München." *Allgemeine Musikzeitung, Berlin*: 43:182–183, 205–207.

Oppenheimer, John F., ed. 1967. *Lexikon des Judentums.* Gütersloh: C. Bertelsmann Verlag.

O'Sullivan, Joseph. 1935. "Current of Song Moves Story in *Give Us This Night.* Korngold Shows How Screen Operetta Can Be Done." *Motion Picture Herald*, 17 April 1936. Los Angeles.

⎯⎯⎯⎯⎯. 1936. "Motif Music Adds Strength to Screen in *Anthony Adverse.*" *Motion Picture Herald* , 22 August, p. 15. Los Angeles.

⎯⎯⎯⎯⎯. 1938. "Korngold Raises Film Music To True Function in *Robin Hood.*" *Motion Picture Herald*, 7 May. Los Angeles.

Palmer, Christopher. 1990. *The Composer in Hollywood.* London: M.Boyars Publ.

⎯⎯⎯⎯⎯. 1975. *Korngold and Die tote Stadt.* Booklet for RCA Recording ARL 3-1199 (only LP version).

⎯⎯⎯⎯⎯. 1980. *Korngold's Violanta.* Booklet for CBS recording. MK 79229.

Pass, Walter, Gerhard Scheit, and Wilhelm Svoboda. 1995. *Orpheus im Exil. Die Vertreibung der österreichischen Musik von 1938 bis 1945.* Wien: Verlag für Gesellschaftskritik.

Pfohl, Ferdinand. 1927. "Erich W. Korngolds *Das Wunder der Heliane.*" *Neue Freie Presse*, 8 October. Vienna.

Pöllmann, Helmut. 1993. *Erich Wolfgang Korngold—Untersuchungen zur Psychologie, Aesthetik und Kompositionstechnik seines Schaffens.* Thesis, J. Gutenberg-Universität, Mainz.

Pottmeier, Sebastian J. 1995. *Traditionelle und fortschrittliche Stil- und Gattungselemente im Violinkonzert von E. W. Korngold.* Thesis, Universität Hanover.

Prawy, Marcel. 1950. "Erich Wolfgang Korngold's *Die Kathrin.*" *Opera News*, 11 December. New York.

⎯⎯⎯⎯⎯. 1969. *The Vienna Opera.* Vienna, Munich, Zürich: Verlag Fritz Molden.

Rachold, Bernd O. 1986. "Vom Genie zum Talent." *Stimmen die um die Welt gingen*, Heft 14, Münster, Germany.

————. 1991. "Epilog." In *Die Korngolds in Wien: Der Musikkritiker und das Wunderkind*, Julius Korngold. Zürich/St. Gallen: Edition Musik & Theater.

————. 1993. "Wiedersehen mit Europa." *Oper, Jahrbuch der Zeitschrift Opernwelt*, Seelze.

Reich, Willi. 1932. "Ein Fall Korngold." *23: Eine Wiener Musikzeitschrift.*

Reinhardt, Gottfried. 1975. *Der Liebhaber—Erinnerungen an Max Reinhardt*. Munich, Zürich: Knaur.

Reitler, Josef. 1917. "Erich Wolfgang Korngolds Sextet." *Neue Freie Presse*, 18 May. Vienna.

————. 1921. "Erich Wolfgang Korngolds *Die tote Stadt.*" *Neue Freie Presse*, 11 January. Vienna.

————. 1927. "*Das Wunder der Heliane.*" *Neue Freie Presse*, 30 October. Vienna.

Renisch, Franz. 1990. *Gustinus Ambrosi*. Vienna: Eigenverlag (self-published).

Reynolds, Naomi. 1955. "From the Reviewing Stand: An Important Musical Picture." (about *Magic Fire*) *Music Clubs Magazine*, November.

Richards, Jeffrey. 1977. *Swordsmen of the Screen*. London: Routledge & Kegan Paul Ltd.

Robert, Richard. 1914. "Der Fall Korngold." *Wiener Sonn- und Montagszeitung* 11 May. Vienna.

————. 1916. "E. W. Korngolds *Violanta—Der Ring des Polykrates.*" *Wiener Sonn- und Montagszeitung*, 17 April. Vienna.

Rode-Breymann, Susanne. 1994. *Die Wiener Staatsoper in den Zwischenkriegsjahren*. Tutzing: Hans Schneider.

————. 1995. "Erich W. Korngold." In *Komponisten des Gegenwart*. Tutzing: Hans Schneider.

Rosenzweig, Sidney. 1982. *Casablanca and Other Major Films of Michael Curtiz*. Ann Arbor, Michigan: UMI Research Press.

Rózsa, Miklos. 1982. *A Double Life*. London, New York: Midas Books/Hippocrene Books.

Saerchinger, Cesar. 1957. *Artur Schnabel: A Biography*. Westport, Connecticut: Greenwood Press.

Schmidt, Leopold. 1916. "Erich W. Korngolds *Violanta* und *Der Ring des Polykrates.*" *Berliner Tageblatt*, 30 March. Berlin.

————. 1922. *Musikleben der Gegenwart*. Berlin: Max Hesses Verlag.

Schott & Söhne, B. 1913. *Kritiken-Sammlung zur Schauspiel Ouvertüre Opus 4*. Mainz: B. Schott & Söhne.

————. 1915. *Kritiken-Sammlung zur Sinfonietta Opus 5*. Mainz: B. Schott & Söhne.

————. 1919. *Kritiken-Sammlung zu Violanta und Der Ring des Polykrates (May)*. Mainz: B. Schott & Söhne.

————. 1921. *Kritiken-Sammlung zur Toten Stadt Opus 12*. Mainz: B. Schott & Söhne.

————. 1927. *Kritiken-Sammlung zum Wunder der Heliane Opus 20*. Mainz: B. Schott & Söhne.

Schneiderheit, Otto. 1976. *Richard Tauber—Ein Leben—Eine Stimme*. Berlin: VEB Lied der Zeit.

Schumann, Karl. 1987. "Naivität und Gebrochenheit des Gefühls—Erich Wolfgang Korngold zum 90. Geburtstag." *Das Orchester*, May. Mainz: Verlag B. Schott & Söhne.

Seidl, Arthur. 1926. "Erich Wolfgang Korngold." *Neuzeitliche Tondichter und zeitgenössische Tonkünstler: gesammelte Aufsätze und Skizzen*. Deutsche Musikbücherei, Bd. 18–19. Regensburg: Gustav Bosse Verlag.

Specht, Richard. 1910. "Korngolds *Schneemann.*" *Neue Freie Presse*, 5 October.

————. 1913. "Sonatenabend von Schnabel und Flesch." *Neue Freie Presse*, 14 November.

————. 1916a. "Korngold als Opernkomponist." *Der Merker* 7(8):295–299.

————. 1916b. *Thematische Führer zu Erich W. Korngolds Opern-Einaktern* Violanta *und* Der Ring des Polykrates. Mainz: B. Schott & Söhne.

————. 1916c. "A Young Master of the Opera [orig. in German]." *Dresdner Neueste Nachrichten*, 30 March.

————. 1925. "Von Wiener Musik und Wiener Lärm." *Musikwelt*, vol. 3 (1 February). Hamburg.

————. 1926. "Erich Wolfgang Korngold." *Die Musik* No. 19. Vienna.

Springer, Max. 1916. "Zwei Erstaufführungen in der Hofoper." *Reichspost*, 11 April.

————. 1927. "Das Wunder der Heliane." *Reichspost*, 30 October. Vienna

Stang, Karl. 1918. "Erich Wolfgang Korngold." *Neue Musik Zeitung*, July. Leipzig.

Stefan,Paul. 1910. "Wiener Musikbrief." *Neue Musik Zeitung*, vol. 14, October.

————. 1921. *Neue Musik und Wien*. Vienna: E. P. Tal Verlag.

Stewart, Donald Ogden, with Meyer Levin. 1939. "*Juarez* in Hollywood and New York." *The Hollywood Spectator*, April 28, pp. 2, 19.

Stollberg, Arne 1994/1995. *Erich Wolfgang Korngolds Sinfonietta Opus 5. Eine analytische Betrachtung unter Bezugnahme auf das biographische Umfeld sowie die musikhistorischen und kompositionsästhetischen Voraussetzungen.* Thesis. Johann Wolfgang Goethe Universität, Frankfurt am Main.

Strauss, Franz, and Alice Strauss. 1967. *Die Welt um Richard Strauss in Briefen*. Tutzing: Hans Schneider.

Styne, Whitney, with Bette Davis. 1975. *Mother Goddam*. London: W. H.Allen.

Taylor, John Russell. 1984. *Strangers in Paradise: The Hollywood Emigres*. London: Faber & Faber.

Teweles, Heinrich. 1927. *Theater und Publikum: Erinnerungen und Erfahrungen*. Prag: Gesellschaft Deutscher Bücherfreunde in Böhmen.

Thomas, Tony. 1964. *The Films of Errol Flynn*. New York: Citadel Press.

————. 1973. *Music for the Movies*. London: Tantivy Press; New York: A. S. Barnes & Co.

————. 1979. *Film Score: The View from the Podium*. New York: A. S. Barnes & Co.

————. 1991. *Film Score: The Art and Craft of Movie Music*. Burbank, CA: Riverwood Press.

Törnblom, Folke. 1939. "Erich Wolfgang Korngold—Kompositör till Operans första varldspremiär." *Theater Magazine*, October. Stockholm.

Traubner, Richard. 1984. *Operetta—A Theatrical History*. London: Victor Gollancz Ltd.

Trebitsch, Siegfried. 1920. "Georges Rodenbach." *Blätter des Operntheaters*, No. 1. Vienna.

————. 1951. "Chronik eines Lebens." Unpublished. Korngold Society Archive.

Truscott, Harold. 1985. *Erich Wolfgang Korngold's Concerto for Piano (Left Hand) in C Sharp Opus 17 (1924)*. Paisley, Scotland: Wilfion Books.

Ussher, Bruno David. 1939. "Music in the Films." *Hollywood Spectator*, May.

————. 1939. "Film Music and Its Makers." *Hollywood Spectator*, September.

————. 1939. "*The Private Lives of Elizabeth and Essex.*" In booklet accompanying September issue of *Photoplay Magazine*: *Cinemusic and Its Meaning*. Hollywood, California: Photoplay Magazine.

Vaget, Hans Rudolf, ed. 1992. *Briefwechsel 1937–1955*, Thomas Mann. Frankfurt am Main: Fischer Verlag.

Vanderwood, Paul J. 1983. Juarez *Script, Annotations and Introduction*. Madison: University of Wisconsin Press.

Viertel, Salka. 1970. *The Kindness of Strangers*. New York: Holt Rinehart Winston.

Wagner, Randel R. 1993. *Wunderkinder Lieder—A Study of the Songs of Erich Wolfgang Korngold*. Ph.D. Thesis, University of Nebraska.

Walter, Bruno. 1946. *Theme and Variations*. New York: Alfred A. Knopf.

Weber, Horst. 1995. *Alexander Zemlinsky: Briefwechsel mit Arnold Schoenberg, Anton Webern, Alban Berg, und Franz Schreker*. Darmstadt, Germany: Wissenschaftliche Buchgesellschaft. (A collection of very important letters.)

Wegner, Dirk. 1995. *Studien zu Erich Wolfgang Korngolds Oper* Das Wunder der Heliane. Thesis, Ruprecht-Karls Universität Heidelberg.

Weingartner, Felix von. 1922/1928. *Lebenserinnerungen.* Zürich: Orell Füssli Verlag.

Weissmann, Adolf. 1922. *Die Musik in der Weltkrise.* Stuttgart/Berlin: Deutsche Verlagsanstalt.

Wohanka, Emmy. 1933. *Hans Kaltneker.* Thesis, University of Vienna.

Wojnarowicz, Gernot. 1987. "Traditionelles und Fortschrittliches in Erich Wolfgang Korngolds Oper *Die tote Stadt.*" *Fakultät für Geschichtswissenschaft an der Ruhr-Universität Bochum,* July.

Sources Without Credited Author (Listed by Year)

1912. "Urteile Hamburger Meister über Erich Wolfgang Korngold." *Die Hamburger Woche,* No.16, 20 March.

1922. "A Protest from Korngold." *The Musical Times,* 22 January. London.

1926. "Der Kunstpreis der Stadt Wien." *Neue Freie Presse,* June 1. Vienna.

1932. "E. W. Korngold: Der musikalische Bearbeiter der Schönen Helena." *Die Theaterstunde* No.10, 15 May. Berlin.

1937. "Erstes Wiener Gespräch mit Korngold." *Das Echo,* May 18, Vienna. (Interview with Korngold about new plans and current work, including *Die Kathrin, The Adventures of Robin Hood,* and Violin Concerto in D Major.)

1937. "Eindrücke eines Wieners in Hollywood—Aus einem Gespräch mit Erich Wolfgang Korngold." *Mein Film,* 26 November. Vienna. (Interview about *The Adventures of Robin Hood.*)

1938. "Music by the Yard," by "The Cinemaid." *San Francisco Chronicle,* 24 June.

1939. "Operan." *Social-Demokraten,* October 6. Stockholm.

1946. "Film Music Raised To Artistic Stature." *The Musician,* November. Los Angeles.

1946. "It's On The Soundtrack." *Overture,* November. Los Angeles. (Profile of Korngold and the Warner Music Dept., concerning the film *Deception.*)

1950. "Erich Wolfgang Korngold's *Kathrin.*" *Die Presse,* 21 October. Vienna.

Discography: 1914–1996

The discography contains all the known commercial recordings of the music of Erich Wolfgang Korngold from 1914 to 1972. The number of recordings since 1972 has increased to such an extent that I cannot claim confidently that it is absolutely complete through 1996. For discophiles and admirers of Korngold's work, however, it will provide an invaluable checklist and should also encourage collectors to seek more.

Listed are all issued recordings known of Korngold's works and his performances as conductor and pianist on 78 rpm and LP, certain important unissued discs, and the most recent compact disc issues. The date of recording is given where possible. Several interpretations are now on record of Korngold's major works, and this trend promises to continue. That the majority of his compositions are now very well served on gramophone records indicates his increasing popularity.

To enable the reader to find recordings of a particular work with ease, the discography is arranged first according to Opus number, followed by supplementary categories that cover Korngold's other music and recordings:

Works Listed by Opus Number
Works Without Opus Number
Korngold's Film Music
Korngold as Performer (of music other than his own)
Piano Roll Recordings

For recordings of Korngold playing or conducting his own music, see Opus 2, 3, 8, 9, 11, 12, 14, 33 in Works Listed by Opus Number; Piano Sonata No. 1, Passacaglia, in Works Without Opus Number; and (c–h) and (16, 40) in Korngold's Film Music.

Long playing records and 78 rpm discs are generally no longer available but can be traced via specialized shops and collector magazines. Some compact discs may also be unavailable, as record companies now withdraw products after a much shorter time in circulation. In the interests of space, I have omitted details of recordings issued on musicassette, 8-track cassette, or other tape systems, as these are either no longer available or are extremely hard to obtain. I have also omitted recordings of Korngold's operetta arrangements, except where he himself is the conductor.

At the time of this writing, several important new CDs have been announced, including two major recordings of the Symphony in F-sharp (Franz Welser-Möst and the Philadelphia Orchestra, André Previn and the London Symphony Orchestra), a new recording of *Die tote Stadt*, the first and much needed complete recordings of the operas *Der Ring des Polykrates* and *Die Kathrin,* and numerous film score and chamber music recordings. The flow of new discs shows no sign of abating and provides a further indication of the continued rehabilitation of Korngold as a composer.

I am delighted to be able to include a unique appendix to this discography: a complete list of all Korngold's known piano roll recordings, as well as rolls made by others of his music. Korngold made a number of piano rolls even in childhood, yet he ventured into the recording studios rarely. This compilation by Hans W. Schmitz of Stuttgart, the world's leading authority on mechanical and reproducing pianos, has been certified as correct up to the time of publication. I am grateful to him for providing additional information on this little-known aspect of Korngold's activity, published here for the first time anywhere.

I am also indebted to my colleagues Roger Wilmut and Dr. Dr. Peter Aistleitner (Hamburg) for assisting with the research and compilation of this discography, and to Bernd Rachold and Colin Oxenforth for checking the final draft.

Works Listed by Opus Number

Opus 1. Piano Trio in D Major
  Pacific Art Trio
  USA Stereo LP Delos DEL 25402
  (rec. 1975)
  USA CD Delos CD1009

  Göbel Trio
  Netherlands Stereo LP Etcetera ETC
  1043 (rec. 1983)
  Netherlands CD Etcetera KTC 1043

  Röhn Trio
  Germany CD Calig 50 905 (rec.
  1990)

  Beaux Arts Trio
  Germany CD Philips 434 072-2
  (prod. 1992)

  Soloists of the New York
  Philharmonic
  UK CD EMI CDC 5 55401 2 (rec.
  1994)

Opus 2. Piano Sonata No. 2 in E Major
  Antonin Kubalek
  USA Stereo LP Genesis GS 1055 (rec.
  1974)
  USA CD Citadel CTD 88109

  Mathijs Verschoor
  Netherlands Stereo LP Etcetera ETC
  1042 (rec. 1983)
  Netherlands CD Etcetera ETC 1043

  Rudolph Ganz
  USA Stereo LP "The Welte Legacy of
  Piano Treasures" RT 671(from a
  Welte-Mignon piano roll (see list of
  rolls); reissue of a special edition by
  Book-of-the-Month Club

  E. W. Korngold (third movement
  only)
  USA LP Masterseal MW46 (rec.
  1951)
  USA LP Varése Sarabande VC
  81040
  Ilona Prunyi
  Germany CD Marco Polo 8.223384
  (prod. 1990)

  Geoffrey Tozer
  UK CD Chandos CHAN 9389
  (prod. 1995)

Opus 3. *Sieben Märchenbilder* (Seven
  Fairy Tale Pictures) for piano
  Antonin Kubalek
  USA Stereo LP Genesis GS 1055 (rec.
  1974)
  reissued on USA CD Bay Cities BCD
  1032, Citadel CTD 88109
  No. 4: Alfred Grünfeld
  Germany Gramophone Co. GC
  45594 (rec. 15 May 1914) mat.
  16726L.
  UKCD Opal CD9850

  Nos. 2, 7: E. W. Korngold
  USA LP Masterseal MW46 (rec.
  1951)
  USA LP Varése Sarabande VC
  81040

  4. Ilona Prunyi
  Germany CD Marco Polo 8.223384
  (prod. 1990)

Opus 4. *Schauspiel Ouvertüre* in B
  Major for large orchestra
  MIT Symphony Orchestra, cond.
  David Epstein
  USA and UK Stereo LP Turnabout
  TV 34760 (rec. 7 Nov. 1978)
  Germany Stereo LP FSM 334760

  Nordwestdeutsche Philharmonie,
  cond. Werner Andreas Albert
  Germany CD cpo 999 037-2 (rec.
  Jan. 1985)

Opus 5. Sinfonietta in B Major for large
  orchestra
  Radio Symphony Orchestra Berlin,
  cond. Gerd Albrecht
  USA Stereo LP Varése Sarabande
  704.200 (rec. 27–28 Sept. 1983)
  USA CD Varése Sarabande VCD
  47214

  Nordwestdeutsche Philharmonie,
  cond. Werner Andreas Albert
  Germany CD cpo 999 037-2 (rec.
  July 1986)

BBC Philharmonic Orchestra, cond. Mathias Bamert
UK CD Chandos 9317 (rec. 1995)

Dallas Symphony Orchestra, cond. Andrew Litton
USA CD Dorian DOR 90216 (rec. Nov. 1994)

Opus 6. Sonata in G Major for violin and piano
Endre Granat, violin, Harold Gray, piano
USA Stereo LP ORION ORS 74166 (rec. 1974)

Stacey Woolley, violin, Scot Woolley, piano
USA CD Bay Cities BCD 1027 (rec. 1991)

Andras Kiss, violin, Ilona Prunyi, piano
Germany CD Marco Polo 8. 223385 (rec. 1991)

Andreas Röhn, violin, Kerstin Hindart, piano
Germany CD CALIG 50 905 (rec. 30 Sept. 1992)

Glenn Dichterow, violin, Israela Margalit, piano
UK CD EMI CDC 5 55401 2 (rec. July 1994)

Opus 7. *Der Ring des Polykrates*, opera buffa in one act
Slightly edited performance: Waldemar Kmentt, Ruthilde Boesch, Erich Majkut, et al., Vienna State Opera in the Volksoper, cond. Hans Swarowsky
USA LP The Golden Age of Opera EJS 363 (rec. 28 Nov. 1952)

"Tagesbuch der Laura"
Gundula Janowitz, soprano, Austrian State Radio Orchestra, cond. Wilhelm Loibner
USA CD Cambria CD1032 (rec. circa 1961, not 1949 as stated on box)
"Tagesbuch der Laura"
Polly Jo Baker, soprano, George Calusdian, piano
USA Stereo LP Entr'acte ERS 6502 (prod. 1975)
USA CD Entr'acte ESCD 6502

Potpourri of themes (for piano solo)
Scot Woolley

USA KOCH CD 3-7277 2 41 (rec. 4 Nov. 1994)

First complete recording: Endrik Wottrich, Beata Bilondzija, Jürgen Sucher, Kirsten Blanck, Dietrich Henschel, Deutsches Symphonie-Orchester Berlin, cond. Klauspeter Seibel
Germany CD cop 999 402-2 (rec. 1995)

Opus 8. *Violanta*, tragic opera in one act
Abridged recording based on the 1931 revised score: Leopold Winklhofer, Ilona Steingruber, Willy Friedrich, et al., mixed chorus and Grand Orchestra of RAVAG, Vienna, cond. Gottfried Kassowitz (rec. 29 June 1949, under the supervision of the composer with sanctioned cuts and revised final duet)
USA LP The Golden Age of Opera EJS 362

Complete recording, cuts restored, original 1916 score: Walter Berry, Eva Marton, Siegfried Jerusalem, et al., Bavarian Radio Chorus, Munich Radio Orchestra, cond. Marek Janowski
USA Stereo LP Columbia M2-35909 (CX) (rec. summer 1976, June–July 1977)
UK Stereo LP CBS 79229
UK CD reissue MK 79229
USA and Canada CD MK 35909

Prelude and Carnival
The Royal Philharmonic Orchestra, cond. Jascha Horenstein.
USA Stereo LP Quintessence PMC 7047 (rec. 1976)

The Austrian Radio Orchestra, Vienna, cond. Max Schönherr (supervised by the composer)
USA CD Cambria CD 1066 (rec. 1949)

Improvisation on Themes from *Violanta*
E. W. Korngold, piano
USA LP Masterseal MW46 (rec. 1951)
USA LP Varése Sarabande VC 81040

Excerpt, "Wie schön seid ihr"
Heinz Hoppe, tenor, Hildegard Hillebrecht, soprano, Munich

[Opus 8]
Philharmonic Orchestra (not
Austrian State Radio Orchestra, as
stated on box), cond. Joseph Strobl
USA CD Cambria CD 1032 (rec. 28
June 1962, not 1949 as stated on
box)

Opus 9. *Sechs Einfache Lieder* (Six
Simple Songs)
Steven Kimbrough, baritone, Dalton
Baldwin, piano
Germany Stereo LP Acanta
40.23539 (rec. 1984)
German CD Acanta 43 539

Nos. 1, 2, 3, "Schneeglöckchen,"
"Nachtwanderer," "Ständchen"
Boje Skovhus, baritone, Helmut
Deutsch, piano
Germany SONY SK57969 (rec. May
1993)

No. 4, "Liebesbriefchen"
Rosette Anday, mezzo, E. W.
Korngold, piano
Germany Vox 02174 (rec. 1924)
Austria LP Preisser LV 32
Canada LP Rococo 5350

Polly Jo Baker, soprano, George
Calusdian, piano
USA Stereo LP Entr'acte ERS 6502
(rec. 1975)
USA CD Entr'acte ESCD 6502

Anne Sofie von Otter, mezzo soprano, Bengt Forsberg, piano
Germany CD Deutsche
Grammophon 437 515-2
(prod.1994)

Nos. 1, 3, 4, and 6 for soprano with
orchestra
Barbara Hendricks, soprano, the
Philadelphia Orchestra, cond.
Franz Welser-Möst
Worldwide CD EMI 7243 5 56169 -
2 0 (rec. Nov. 1995)

Opus 10. Sextet for Strings in D Major
Berlin String Sextet
Netherlands Stereo LP Etcetera ETC
1043 and CD Etcetera KTC 1043
(rec. 1983)

The Raphael Ensemble
UK Compact Disc Hyperion CDA
66425 (rec. April 1990)

Opus 11. *Much Ado About Nothing*,
incidental music for orchestra

Suite for Orchestra (five movements):
Graz Chamber Orchestra, cond.
Anton Bauzer (fictitious names)
USA LP Phorion 9002 (bootleg label
under fictitious names of the
Boston Chamber Artists recording;
see below)

Niederösterreichisches Tonkünstler-
Orchester, cond. E. W. Korngold
USA LP Masterseal, MW46
(prod.1951)
USA LP Varése Sarabande VC
81040
Austria 78 rpm Harmona 15002
(Movements 1, 3, 5 only)
Austria 78 rpm Harmona 15012
(Movement 1 only)

Westphalian State Symphony
Orchestra, cond. Siegfried Landau
USA Quadraphonic LP Candide
31091 (rec. July 1974)
UK Stereo LP Turnabout TVS 37124
Germany Stereo LP FSM 31091

South German Radio Symphony
Orchestra, Stuttgart, cond. Willy
Mattes
UK Stereo LP EMI EMD 5515 (rec.
13 July 1973)
USA Stereo LP Angel S-36999
Germany Stereo LP Electrola 1C
065-02460

Boston Chamber Artists, cond. Eric
Simon (rec. 1959)
USA LP Boston 411, Stereo 1012
UK LP Argo RG 187, Stereo ZRG
5187

The Austrian Radio Orchestra, cond.
Max Schönherr (rec. 1949)
USA CD Cambria CD-1066

Nordwestdeutsche Philharmonie,
cond. Werner Andreas Albert
Germany CD—cpo 999 046-2 (rec.
June 1989)

Individual Movements:
Movement 1, The Vienna Symphony
Orchestra, cond. Paul Kerby
UK Edison Bell F 3022 (rec. 22 July
1930)

Movement 4, Josef Sakanov, violin,
London Festival Orchestra
UK Stereo LP Decca PFS 4256 (rec.
1973)
France Stereo LP Decca 390.190

UK CD Decca London Phase 4 444 786 2LPF

Movement 5, Victor Symphony Orchestra
USA 45 single 45-5015

Movements 2, 3, and 5, arranged for piano
Richard Corbett, piano
USA LP Music Library MLR 7017

Ilona Prunyi, piano
German CD Marco Polo 8.223384 (rec. Aug.—Sept. 1990)

Movements 2–5, arranged for violin and piano
Mischa Elman, violin, Josef Seiger, piano
USA LP London LL1467 (rec. April 1959, New York)
UK LP Decca LXT 5231 (unissued)

Endre Granat, violin, Harold Gray, piano
USA Stereo LP Orion ORS 74166 (rec. 1974)

Max Rostal, violin, with piano accompaniment.
Germany Vox 06172/3 (rec. March 1924)

Toscha Seidel, violin, E. W. Korngold, piano
USA RCA Victor (rec. 31 July 1941, unissued)

Gil Shaham, violin, André Previn, piano
Germany CD Deutsche Grammophon 439 886-2 (rec. 1994)

Movements 3, 4, and 5 arranged for violin and piano
Robert Pollack, violin, E. W. Korngold, piano
UK Homochord HB 2097, 2112 (rec. 1924)

Movement 3 arranged for violin and piano
Jascha Heifetz, violin, Arpád Sándor, piano
USA Victor 1864 (rec. Feb. 1934)
UK HMV DA 1378
USA LP (box set) RCA ARM-4 0943
Germany LP (box set) RCA 00943 FK

Jascha Heifetz, violin, Emanuel Bay, piano
USA Victor 10-1314 (rec. 18 Oct.1946)
USA LP (box set) RCA ARM - 4 0946
USA LP MJA 5003

Jascha Heifetz, violin, Emanuel Bay, piano
USA Victor 12-0430, 18-1086 (rec. 18 Dec. 1947)
USA 45 rpm Victor 49-0626
UK HMV D3 6878
USA LP (box set) RCA ARM-40946
Canada LP Rococo ROC 2071
USA LP MJA 5003

Jascha Heifetz, violin, Brooks Smith, piano
USA Stereo LP RCA SPS 33-565 (rec. 15 Sept. 1970, excerpt only)
USA Stereo LP RCA LSC 3256
USA CD GD 60928

Movement 4 arranged for violin and piano
Derek Collier, violin, Daphne Ibott, piano
UK Stereo LP Decca SPA 405 (rec. 1975)

Movements 4, 5 arranged for violin and piano
Grete Eweler, violin with unidentified piano accompaniment
German Homochord 4-2598 (rec. circa 1927–1928)

Lied des Pagen (Page Boy's Song)
Rosette Anday, mezzo soprano, E. W. Korngold, piano
Germany Vox 02174 (rec. 1924)
Austria LP Preisser LV 32
Canada LP Rococo 5350

Polly Jo Baker, soprano, George Calusdian, piano
USA Stereo LP Entr'acte ERS 6502 (rec. 1975)
USA CD Entr'acte ESCD 6502
Lionel Tertis made and recorded an arrangement for viola and piano in England before 1939, but it has not been traced.

Opus 12. *Die tote Stadt,* opera in three acts
  Abridged version: Maud Cunitz, Karl Friedrich, Benno Kusche, et al., with the Choir and Symphony

[Opus 12]
Orchestra of Bavarian Radio, cond.
Fritz Lehmann (broadcast)
USA LP "The Golden Age of Opera"
EJS 263 (2 records) (rec. 8–15 Sept.
1952)

Complete recording: Carol Neblett,
René Kollo, Benjamin Luxon,
Hermann Prey et al., with the
Munich Radio Orchestra, Bavarian
Radio Chorus, Tölzer Knabenchor,
cond. Erich Leinsdorf
USA Quadraphonic LP RCA ARD 3-
1199 (3 records) (rec. June 1975)
USA and UK Stereo LP RCA ARL 3-
1199 (3 records)
Germany Stereo LP RCA RL 01199
(3 records)
Worldwide CD Reissue RCA GD
87767 (2)

"Pierrot's Dance Song"
Hermann Prey, Munich Radio
Orchestra, cond. Erich Leinsdorf
(from complete recording, above)
Germany Stereo LP RCA 40.23515
DX

"Der Erste, der Lieb' mich gelehrt"
(Act 3)
Lotte Lehmann, soprano, cond.
Georg Szell
Germany Odeon Lxx 80945 (rec. 17
April 1924)
Austria LP LV94
Germany LP EMI 137-30704/05 M
Canada LP Rococo 5356
UK CD EMI CDH 7 61042 2
Germany Odeon O-9502 (reissued
with orchestral accompaniment
added electronically in 1933)

"Die Tote—wo- lag sie nicht hier"
(final scene, Act 3)
Richard Tauber, tenor
USA LP Eterna 494 (rec. 1924 ?)

"Glück, das mir verblieb"
(Marietta's Lute Song, Duet, Act 1)
Lotte Lehmann, soprano, Richard
Tauber, tenor, cond. Georg Szell
Germany Odeon Lxx 80944
Odeon 0-9507, 0-8613
(Matrix xxB 6993, Takes 1, 2, 4 rec.
17 April 1924).
This most famous of all the early
recordings has been reissued many
times in all formats. The acoustic
original of the Tauber/Lehmann

version is preferred to the electron-
ic reissue by collectors; however, it
is not always clear which version
has been used. The main reissues
are as follows (incomplete for reasons of space):
USA Decca 29012
Germany 45rpm Odeon 0-20479
Germany LP EMI 1C 147-
29116/7M
UK LP (box set) HMV RLS 7700
UK CD EMI CDH 7640292
UK CD Nimbus NI 7830

Reissue with electronically added
orchestral accompaniment, cond.
Frieder Weissmann (rec. 13 May
1933):
Germany Odeon R 20258
Odeon O BL 1073
UK Parlophone E 20258
Australia Parlophone AR 1081
UK LP Pearl GEMM 214
Austria CD Preisser 89219

Annelies Kupper, Lorenz
Fehenberger, tenor, Bamberg
Symphony Orchestra, cond. Victor
Reinshagen
Germany Polydor 6296, 32014 (rec.
15 Dec. 1953)
Germany 45 rpm DGG 32014 NL
Germany LP DGG 19015 LPEM
UK LP DGG DGM 19105

Ilona Steingruber, soprano, Anton
Dermota, tenor, Austrian State
Radio Orchestra, cond. E. W.
Korngold
USA CD Cambria CD 1032 (rec.
1949)

Melitta Muszely, soprano, Rudolf
Schock, tenor, Berlin Symphony
Orchestra, cond. Berislav Klobucar
Germany 45 rpm Electrola E41099
(rec. 17 April 1959)
Germany Stereo 45 rpm Electrola
ETE 41099
UK CD EMI CZS 7671832

Hilde Zadek, soprano, Anton
Dermota, tenor, Austrian State
Symphony Orchestra, cond.
Wilhelm Loibner
USA LP Masterseal MW 46 (rec. 11
June 1951)
Austria Harmonia 14004, 15012 ·
USA LP Remington R-199-123

USA LP Varése Sarabande VC 81040

"Glück, das mir verblieb" (arranged as a solo for soprano unless otherwise stated)
Lucine Amara, with Richard Woitach, piano
USA Stereo LP Advent 5023 (rec. 1976)

Rosette Anday, mezzo soprano, transposed down a fourth, E. W. Korngold, piano
Germany VOX 02174 (rec. 1924)
Canadia LP Rococo 5350
Austria LP Preisser LV 32

Polly Jo Baker with George Calusdian, piano
USA Stereo LP Entr'acte ERS 6502 (rec. 1975)
USA CD Entr'acte ESCD 6502

Dorothy Coulter, Orchestra Sinfonica of Rome, cond. Dean Ryan
USA LP Phoenix 435

Helen-Ray Eberley with Donald Isaak, piano
USA Stereo LP Eb-Sko Productions 1009 (rec. 1983)

Eileen Farrell with orchestra
USA CD IRCC CD 807 (rec. 11 Nov. 1942)

Hilde Gueden, Vienna Philharmonic Orchestra, cond. Horst Stein
UK Stereo LP Eclipse ECS 2122

Joan Hammond, Philharmonia Orchestra, cond. Walter Süsskind
UK HMV DB 21625 (rec. 1955)
UK CD EMI CHS 7 697412

Mary Henderson with orchestral accompaniment
USA LP Allegro Royale 1637 (rec. 1955)

Maria Jeritza with Orchestra of J. Pasternak, cond. F. Lapitino.
USA Victrola 66057 (single-sided) (recorded Camden, New Jersey, 8 March 1922)
USA Victrola 688 (double-sided)
UK HMV 7-43041 (reissued in the 1930s on DA 524)
USA LP (box set) MET 403
also issued in Czechoslovakia (details unknown)

UK and Germany LP (8 record set) RCA RL 85177 GX
USA CD RCA 09026 61580 2
UK CD Nimbus NI 7864

Maria Jeritza with orchestral accompaniment (electric recording)
USA Victrola 1273 (rec. 1927)
Austria LP Preisser LV 122
UK (box set) EMI EX 290131-3
Austria CD Preisser LV 89079

Siegfried Jerusalem, tenor, Munich Radio Orchestra, cond. Heinz Wallberg
Germany Stereo LP Ariola-Eurodisc 200 089-366 (rec. 6 Nov. 1979)
Germany CD Eurodisc GD 69109

Irene Jessner. Victor Symphony Orchestra, cond. Bruno Reibold
Austria HMV ED64
USA Victor 17256

Selma Kurz with E. W. Korngold, piano
German Gramophone Co. Matrix CJ 156-1,-2,-3 (rec. Vienna, 26 Jan. 1926; not issued: original masters appear to be lost)

Pilar Lorengar, Vienna State Opera Orchestra, cond. Walter Weller
USA Stereo LP London 26246 (rec. 1971)
UK Stereo LP Decca SXL 6525
USA Stereo LP OS-26381
UK CD Decca 443931-2

Melitta Muszely, Grand Orchestra of Berlin Radio, cond. Horst Stein
DDR (former) 45 rpm Eterna 520307 (rec. 31 May 1960)
DDR (former) LP Eterna 720115

Maria Nemeth with orchestral accompaniment
Germany Polydor 66623 (rec. 1927)
UK Decca-Polydor CA 8190
USA LP "Club 99" CLKM 007
Austria LP Preisser LV214
USA CD CL 99 07
UK CD Pearl GEMM CD 9197

Rosa Ponselle accompanying herself at the piano
USA LP Garrison Recording Co. RPX 101 (rec. 1953)
USA LP The Golden Age of Opera EJS 243
USA LP MDP 36

[Opus 12]
USA LP Anna 1037 (wrongly gives year of rec. as 1957)
USA CD Cantabile BIM-701-2

Leontyne Price, New Philharmonia Orchestra, cond. Nello Santi
Germany and USA Stereo LP RCA ARL 1-2529 (rec. 1977)
USA Stereo LP RCA ARL 1-4884
USA CD RCA 09026 612362 (set, disc 1)

Stella Roman with orchestral accompaniment
USA LP The Golden Age of Opera EJS 426 (rec. 1948)
USA CD Legato LCD-139-1
USA CD Eclipse EKR CD 42 (rec. 1950)

Joseph Schmidt, orchestra cond. Otto Dobrindt
Germany Odeon O-25991 (rec. 24 April 1933)
Germany Parlophon 48813
UK Parlophone R 1604
Germany LP Odeon O 60796
Germany LP EMI 1M 145-30087/88
Germany LP EMI 1C 047-28558M
USA LP Top Artists Platters TAP T-330
UK LP (double album) EMI EX 290 169-3
UK CD EMI CDM 7 69478 2

Vera Schwarz, orchestra cond. Felix Günther
Germany Homochord 4-8921 (rec. 1928)
Austria LP Preisser LV24
Germany LP, box set: "300 Years of the Hamburg Opera," ST 1005/6

Elisabeth Schwarzkopf, Hamburg Radio Orchestra, cond. Wilhelm Schüchter
Italy LP Melodram 14 (rec. 6 Dec. 1952)

Beverly Sills, London Philharmonic Orchestra, cond. Julius Rudel
USA Stereo LP Audio Treasury ATS 20009 (rec. 1971)
Germany Stereo LP EMI/Angel AV-34037
UK CD EMI Angel CD-7 47524 2

M. Sterkens
Belgium HMV 78 rpm AU21

Polyna Stoska, Metropolitan Opera Orchestra, cond. Max Rudolf
USA Columbia 72512 D & MX 294 (box set)

Ingeborg Wenglor, Staatskapelle Berlin, cond. Rudolf Neuhaus
DDR LP Eterna 820493 (rec. 23 May 1964)

Dame Kiri te Kanawa, London Symphony Orchestra, cond. Steven Barlow
UK and USA CD Decca 443 600-2 (rec. 10 March 1994)

Barbara Hendricks, the Philadelphia Orchestra, cond. Franz Welser-Möst
Worldwide CD EMI 7243 5 56169-2 0 (rec. Nov. 1995)

"Ich werde sie nicht wiedersehn" (final scene, Paul, Act 3)
Siegfried Jerusalem, Munich Radio Orchestra, cond. Heinz Wallberg
Germany Stereo LP Ariola Eurodisc 200 089 (rec. 6 Nov. 1979)
Germany CD Eurodisc GD 69109

Rudolf Schock, Berlin Symphony Orchestra, cond. Berislav Klobucar
Germany LP Electrola E 41099 (rec. May 1959)
Germany Stereo LP Electrola STE 41099
Germany LP Electrola-Columbia C 80612
Germany LP box set EMI 1C 147-29140/41M
Germany LP Acanta 40.23553
Germany CD Acanta 43 553
Germany CD Gala GL 313 (earlier rec. 19–20 Oct. 1951, cond. Heinrich Hollreiser)

Richard Tauber, orchestra cond. Georg Szell
Germany Odeon Lxx 80946, 0-9507, 0-8613 (rec. 17 April 1924)
USA Decca 29012
Germany 45 rpm Odeon 0-20479
UK LP (box set) HMV RLS 7700
UK CD Nimbus NI 7830
UK CD EMI CDH 7640292
UK CD Testament SBT 1005
Austria CD Preisser 89219

Richard Tauber, with electronically recorded orchestral accompaniment, cond. Frieder Weissmann

(whether this version or the preceding one was used in some of the LP reissues is not absolutely certain)
Germany Odeon R 20258 (rec. 13 May 1933)
Germany Odeon O BL 1073
UK Parlophone R 20258
Australia Parlophone AR1081
Germany LP EMI 1C 137-178130/3M
UK LP Pearl Gemm 214

"Mein Sehnen, mein Wähnen" (Pierrot's dance song, Act 2) (all soloists are baritones)
Richard Bonelli
USA LP The Golden Age of Opera EJS 445

Carl Drago-Hrzic with orchestral accompaniment
Germany Polydor 95105 (rec. circa 1927)

Hans Duhan with orchestral accompaniment
Germany Odeon Rxx 80129 (rec. 1922)
Germany Odeon 0-8042 Rxx
UK LP (box set) HMV RLS 743 ("The Record of Singing" side 23 HLM 7192)
UK LP (reissue of above) HMV RLS 7705
UK LP (box set) EMI EX 290131-3

Arnold Gábor
Germany Odeon 0-6153
Italy (?) Odeon AA 79347

Karl Hammes, Choir and Orchestra of the Vienna State Opera, cond. Karl Alwin
Austria HMV BB 207 (rec. 1930)
Czechoslovakia HMV AN 618
UK LP Belcantodisc BC 232
Austria LP Preisser LV 33
USA LP (box set) Seraphim IM 6143 ("The Record of Singing," Vol. 3)
UK LP (box set) EMI EX 290 169-3

Thomas Hampson, Munich Radio Orchestra, cond. Fabio Luisi
USA/UK CD EMI 7243 5 55233 2 (rec. March 1994)

Stefan Kaposi (the aria is identified on the label as "Da ihr befehlet, Königin," which is two lines before the beginning of the aria proper)

Germany Polydor 19270 (rec. circa 1922)

Hermann Prey, Hamburg Radio Orchestra, cond. Wilhelm Schüchter
Germany LP Electrola WBPL 543 (rec. circa 1952)
Germany LP Columbia C 60140
Germany 45 rpm Electrola-Columbia C 40267
Germany 45 rpm Electrola E 60095

Hermann Prey, Berlin Symphony Orchestra, cond. Horst Stein
Germany LP Electrola E 80675 (rec. Feb. 1957)
Germany Stereo LP Electrola E 80675
Germany LP Electrola 1C 063-28424
UK LP Columbia 33 CX 1846
UK Stereo LP Columbia SAX 2489
UK CD EMI CDM 7 695072

Paul Schwarz, cond. Egon Pollak
Germany Grammophon 20748 (rec. 1926)
Germany LP "300 Years of the Hamburg Opera" ST 1005/6 (2 LP set) issued by Günther Stoeck, Hamburg
Germany LP "Paul Schwarz" ST 1004 issued by Günther Stoeck, Hamburg

Heinrich Tiemer
Germany Vox 3110

Alfred Poell, baritone, with Rosl Schwaiger, soprano, Austrian State Radio Orchestra, cond. E. W. Korngold
USA CD Cambria CD 1032 (rec. April 1950)

Pierrot's dance song, arranged for violin and piano
Fritz Kreisler with Carl Lamson, piano
USA Victor 1062 (rec. 28 March 1924)
UK CD Biddulph LAB 069 (box set)

Robert Pollack with E. W. Korngold, piano
UK Homochord HB 2097 (rec. 1924)

[Opus 12]
"Walzerlied" (Pierrot's song for
orchestra)
Bamberg Symphony Orchestra,
cond. Fritz Lehmann
Germany 45 rpm single DGG 32127
NL (rec. Sept. 1955; probably a
broadcast)
Germany EP DGG 30472 EPL

I Salonisti
Germany Stereo LP EMI 1 C 067-16
9585 1 (rec. 26–28 May 1986)
Germany Stereo CD EMI C 7 47572

"Improvisation on Themes from *Die
tote Stadt*"
E. W. Korngold, piano
USA LP Masterseal MW 46 (rec.
1951)
USA LP Varése-Sarabande VC
81040

Opus 13. *Sursum Corda,* symphonic
overture for large orchestra
Nordwestdeutsche Philharmonie,
cond. Werner Andreas Albert
Germany CD cpo 999 046-2 (rec.
Nov. 1989)

BBC Philharmonic Orchestra, cond.
Mathias Bamert
UK CD Chandos CHAN 9317 (rec.
15–16 Nov. 1994)

Opus 14. *Vier Lieder des Abschieds*
(Four Songs of Farewell)
Rosette Anday, mezzo-soprano, E.
W. Korngold, piano
Germany Vox 02176/7 (rec. 1924)
Austria LP Preisser LV 32

Steven Kimbrough, baritone, Dalton
Baldwin, piano
Germany Stereo LP Acanta
40.23539 (rec. 1984)
Germany CD Acanta 43 539

Nos. 1 and 4: Anne Sofie von Otter,
mezzo soprano, Bengt Forsberg,
piano
German CD Deutsche Grammophon
437 515-2 (rec. 1994)

Orchestral version: Linda Finnie,
mezzo-soprano, The BBC
Philharmonic Orchestra, cond. Sir
Edward Downes
UK Stereo CD Chandos
9171(rec.14–15 Dec. 1992)

Opus 15. Piano Quintet in E Major
Harold Gray, piano, Granat Quartet

USA Stereo LP Genesis GS 1063 (rec.
1975; version is heavily cut)

Ilona Prunyi, piano, Danubius
Quartet
Germany CD Marco Polo 8.223385
(rec. March 1991)

Scot Woolley, piano, The Korngold
Quartet
USA CD Bay Cities BCD 1037
(prod. 1992)

Opus 16. String Quartet No. 1 in A
Major
Chilingirian String Quartet
UK Stereo LP RCA RL 25097 (rec.
1977)
UK Stereo CD RCA GD 87889

The Franz Schubert Quartet of
Vienna
UK CD Nimbus NI 5506 (rec. 18–21
Jan. 1996)

Opus 17. Piano Concerto in C-sharp for
the left hand alone
Steven de Groote, piano,
Nordwestdeutsche Philharmonie,
cond. Werner Andreas Albert
Germany CD cpo 999 046-2 (rec.
June 1988)

Howard Shelley, piano, BBC
Philharmonic Orchestra, cond.
Mathias Bamert
UK CD Chandos 9508 (rec. May
1996)

Opus 18. *Drei Lieder* (Three Songs)
Steven Kimbrough, baritone, Dalton
Baldwin, piano
Germany Stereo LP Acanta
40.23539 (rec. 1984)
Germany CD Acanta 43 539

Anne Sofie von Otter, mezzo soprano, Bengt Forsberg, piano
Germany CD Deutsche
Grammophon 437 515-2 (prod.
1994)

Opus 20. *Das Wunder der Heliane* (The
Miracle of Heliane), opera in three
acts
Complete Recording: Anna
Tomowa-Sintow, Hartmut Welker,
John David de Haan, et al.,
Rundfunk Chor, Berlin, RSO
Berlin, cond. John Mauceri.
UK CD Decca 436 636-2 (rec.
Berlin, 20–29 Feb. 1992)

"Zwischenspiel," Act 3, Grand Symphony Orchestra, cond. Frieder Weissmann
Germany Odeon 0-6571 (rec. 1928)
USA Odeon 5167
USA LP Ritornello R-1002

Aria "Ich ging zu ihm," Act 2
Lotte Lehmann, soprano, members of the Staatskapelle Berlin, cond. Manfred Gurlitt.
Germany Odeon 0-8722 (rec. 13 March 1928)
USA Decca 25805
Germany LP (box set) EMI 1C 147-29116/17 M
UK LP Belcantodisc BC 243
UK LP Parlophone PMA 1057
USA LP Angel COLO 112
Japan LP Toshiba GR 2046
UK CD EMI CDH 7 61042 2

Dagmar Schellenberger, soprano, Munich Radio Orchestra, cond. Ralf Weikert
Germany CD EMI 7243-55283-2-2 (rec. April 1994)

Opus 24. *Baby Serenade*
Nordwestdeutsche Philharmonie, cond. Werner Andreas Albert
Germany CD cpo 999 077-2 (rec. June 1989)

Opus 25. Piano Sonata No. 3 in C Major
Harold Gray, piano
USA Stereo LP Genesis GS 1063 (rec. 1975)

Matthijs Verschoor, piano
Netherlands Stereo LP Etcetera ETC 1042 (rec. 1986)
Netherlands Stereo CD Etcetera KTC 1042

Geoffrey Tozer, piano
UK Stereo CD Chandos CHAN 9389 (rec. 1995)

Opus 26. String Quartet No. 2 in E-flat Major
New World Quartet
USA Stereo LP (box set, "New World Composers from the Old World") VOX SVBX 5109 (rec. 1978)
USA CD "Unknown String Quartets," vol. 2 VOX1157752
Lyric Art String Quartet
USA CD Bay Cities BCD 1014 (rec. April 5–8 1990)

Opus 27. *Unvergänglichkeit* (The Eternal)
No. 4: Steven Kimbrough, baritone, Dalton Baldwin, piano
Germany Stereo LP Acanta 40.23539 (prod. 1984)
Germany CD Acanta 43 539

Nos. 1–5: Steven Kimbrough, baritone, Dalton Baldwin, piano
Germany CD KOCH 3-1094-2-41 (prod. 1990)

Opus 28. *Die Kathrin,* opera in three acts
"Wanderlied" and "Ständchen" (The Wanderer's Song and Serenade)
Walter Anton Dotzer, tenor, E. W. Korngold, piano
Austrian HMV GA 5049 (rec. circa 1950–1951)

"Briefszene" (Kathrin's Letter Song) and "Gebet" (Prayer)
Polly Jo Baker, soprano, George Calusdian, piano
USA Stereo LP Entr'acte ERS 6502 (rec. 1975)
USA CD ESCD 6502

"Improvisation on the Letter Song"
E. W. Korngold, piano
USA LP Masterseal MW 46 (rec. 1951)
USA LP Varése-Sarabande VC 81040

Excerpts
"Briefszene": Ilona Steingruber, soprano, Austrian State Radio Orchestra, cond. Gottfried Kassowitz (rec. April 1950)
"Ich bin ein Liedersänger": Gundula Janowitz, soprano, Rudolf Christ, tenor, Austrian Radio Orchestra, cond. Wilhelm Loibner (rec. 1960)
"Soldaten Marsch und Gebet": Ilona Steingruber, soprano, Austrian Radio Orchestra, cond. Gottfried Kassowitz (rec. April 1950)
"Szene im Nachtlokal": Rosl Schwaiger, soprano, Anton Dermota, tenor, Austrian Radio Orchestra, cond. Gottfried Kassowitz (rec. April 1950)
"Arie des Malignac": Alfred Poell, baritone, Austrian Radio Orchestra, cond. Gottfried Kassowitz (rec. April 1950)

[Opus 28]
"Wanderlied": Anton Dermota, tenor, Austrian Radio Orchestra, cond. E. W. Korngold (rec. April 1950)
USA CD Cambria CD 1032

Opus 29. *Narrenlieder* (Songs of the Clown) from *Twelfth Night* by Shakespeare (in English)
Paul Wade, tenor, Geoffrey Hamilton, piano
UK Stereo LP Look Records LK/LP 7-6125 (rec. 1977)

No. 2. (with words by Christopher Marlowe, as in the film *The Private Lives of Elizabeth and Essex*)
Polly Jo Baker, soprano, George Calusdian, piano, (rec. 1975)
USA Stereo LP Entr'acte ERS 6502
USA CD ESCD 6502

Opus 33. *Tomorrow*, tone poem for mezzo soprano, women's chorus, and orchestra (From the film *The Constant Nymph*)
Clemence Groves, solo, and the Warner Brothers Studio Orchestra and Chorus, cond. E. W. Korngold
USA Decca (rec. 1943 or 1944; not issued)

Norma Procter, contralto, The Ambrosian Singers, The National Philharmonic Orchestra, cond. Charles Gerhardt
USA Stereo LP RCA LSC 3330 & AGL 1-3707 (rec. 1977)

UK Stereo LP RCA SER 5664
Uk and USA CD RCA GD87890

Orchestral version only
Austrian Radio Orchestra, cond. Max Schönherr
USA CD Cambria CD 1066 (rec. 1949)

Thomas Hampson, baritone, Armen Guzelimian, piano
USA and UK CD EMI CDC 7540512 (rec. London Nov. 1989)

Opus 34. String Quartet No. 3 in D Major
Chilingirian String Quartet
UK Stereo LP RCA RL 25097 (rec. 1977)
UK CD RCA GD87889

Angeles Quartet

USA CD KOCH 3-7325-2H1 (rec. 8–13 Aug. 1993)

Opus 35. Violin Concerto in D Major
Eckhard Fischer, violin, Orchestral Society of Stuttgart, cond. Fritz Roth
German LP (Orchestral Society Stuttgart) 65255 (rec. 18 Oct. 1984)

Jascha Heifetz, violin, New York Philharmonic Orchestra, cond. Efrem Kurtz
Canadian LP Rococo 2047 (radio broadcast rec. live at the third New York performance 30 March 1947)
USA CD Music & Arts CD 766 (double CD set)
Japan CD King KICC 2184

Jascha Heifetz, violin, Los Angeles Philharmonic Orchestra, cond. Alfred Wallenstein
USA LP RCA LM 1782 (rec. 10 Jan. 1953)
USA LP RCA AGM 1-4902
UK LP HMV ALP 1288
UK LP RCA LSB 4105
Germany LP RCA 26.41236 AW
UK and USA CD RCA Gold Seal GD87963

Ulf Hoelscher, violin, Stuttgart Radio Orchestra, cond. Willy Mattes
Germany Stereo LP Electrola 1C 065-02460 (rec. 22 March 1973)
UK Stereo LP EMI EMD 5515
USA Stereo LP Angel S-36999

Itzhak Perlman, violin, Pittsburgh Symphony Orchestra, cond. André Previn
Germany Stereo LP EMI 067-03976 T (rec. May 1980)
UK Stereo LP HMV ASD 4206
USA Stereo LP Angel OS 37770
UK and USA CD EMI CDC-747846-2
UK and USA CD EMI CMS-7-64617-2 (1992 reissue for Mr. Perlman's birthday)

Gil Shaham, violin, London Symphony Orchestra, cond. André Previn
Germany CD Deutsche Grammophon 439 886-2 (rec. June 1993)

Ulrike-Anima Mathé, violin, Dallas
Symphony Orchestra, cond.
Andrew Litton
USA CD Dorian DOR 90216 (rec.
Nov. 1994)

Chantal Juillet, violin, RSO Berlin,
cond. John Mauceri
Germany DC Decca 779 09 44 (rec.
1995)

Opus 36. *Die stumme Serenade* (The
Silent Serenade)
"Freund, du lebst vorbei am Glück"
and "Die Nacht ist einsam"
Polly Jo Baker, soprano, George
Calusdian, piano
USA Stereo LP Entr'acte ERS 6502
(rec. 1975)
USA Stereo CD ESCD 6502

Opus 37. Cello Concerto in C Major
Francisco Gabarro, violoncello, The
National Philharmonic Orchestra,
cond. Charles Gerhardt
USA and UK Stereo LP RCA ARL1-
0185 (rec. 1971)
UK Stereo LP RCA GL 43438
UK and USA CD RCA GD 80185

Gabor Rejto, violoncello, orchestra
and conductor not named. (Rejto
never played this concerto; the preceding Gabarro/Gerhardt recording
was issued on the bootleg label
Phorion under Rejto's name.)
USA LP Phorion LP 9002

Julius Berger, violoncello,
Nordwestdeutsche Philharmonie,
cond. Werner Andreas Albert
Germany CD cpo 999 077-2 (rec.
Feb. 1991)

Peter Dixon, violoncello, BBC
Philharmonic Orchestra, cond.
Mathias Bamert
UK CD Chandos CHAN9508 (rec.
May 1996)

Opus 38. *Fünf Lieder* (Five Songs) for
middle voice and piano
Nos. 1, 3: Georg Jelden, baritone,
Hans-Dieter Wagner, piano
Germany Stereo LP Calig CAL
30842 (rec. 3 Oct. 1985)

Nos. 1, 2: Steven Kimbrough, baritone, Helmut Deutsch, piano
Germany CD KOCH 3-1094-2-41
(prod. 1990)

Anne Sofie von Otter, soprano,
Bengt Forsberg, piano
Germany CD Deutsche
Grammophon 437 515-2 (prod.
1994)

No. 2: Boje Skovus, baritone,
Helmut Deutsch, piano
Germany CD Sony SK 57969 (rec.
May 1993)

No. 3: Polly Jo Baker, soprano,
George Calusdian, piano
USA Stereo LP Entr'acte ERS 6502
(rec. 1975)
USA CD ESCD 6502

Hermann Prey, baritone, Günther
Weissenhorn, piano
Germany Stereo LP (box set) Philips
6747 061

Opus 39. *Symphonic Serenade* in B-flat
major for string orchestra
Pittsburgh Symphony Orchestra,
cond. William Steinberg
USA LP Phorion LP-9002 (live radio
broadcast of the US premiere, rec.
30 Dec. 1955)

Nordwestdeutsche Philharmonie,
cond. Werner Andreas Albert
Germany CD cpo 999 077-2 (rec.
March 1990)

Deutsches Symphonie Orchester
Berlin, cond. John Mauceri
USA and UK CD London/Decca 444
170-2 (rec. April 1994)

BBC Philharmonic Orchestra, cond.
Mathias Bamert
UK CD Chandos CHAN 9508 (rec.
May 1996)

Opus 40. Symphony in F-sharp for large
orchestra
Munich Philharmonic Orchestra,
cond. Rudolf Kempe
Germany Stereo LP RCA ARL
1-0443 (rec. 27 Nov. 1972)
USA and UK (number identical to
above)
UK Stereo LP RCA GL 42919
Reissued on USA Stereo CD Varése-
Sarabande VSD 53446

Nordwestdeutsche Philharmonie,
cond. Werner Andreas Albert
Germany CD cpo 999 146-2
(rec. Nov. 1988)

[Opus 40]
McGill Symphony Orchestra, cond.
Timothy Vernon
McGill University CD 750043-2
(rec. 1992)

BBC Philharmonic Orchestra, cond.
Sir Edward Downes
UK CD Chandos CHAN 9171
(rec. 14–15 Dec. 1992)

The Philadelphia Orchestra, cond.
Franz Welser-Möst
Worldwide CD EMI 7243 5 56169-
2 0 (rec. Nov. 1995)

Opus 41. "Sonett für Wien" (Sonnet for
Vienna) for mezzo soprano and
piano
Steven Kimbrough, baritone, Dalton
Baldwin, piano
Germany Stereo LP Acanta
40.23539 (rec. 1984)
Germany CD Acanta 43 539

Anne Sofie von Otter, soprano,
Bengt Forsberg, piano
Germany CD Deutsche
Grammophon 437 515-2

Opus 42. *Theme and Variations for
Orchestra*
Inglewood Symphony Orchestra,
cond. Ernst Gebert
USA Acetate recording without number (rec. at world premiere
22 Nov. 1953)

Radio Orchestra of Stuttgart, cond.
Willy Mattes
Germany Stereo LP Electrola 1C
065-02460 (rec. 17 July 1973)
UK Stereo LP EMI EMD 5515
USA Stereo LP Angel S-36999

Austrian Radio Orchestra, cond.
Max Schönherr
USA CD Cambria CD 1066
(rec. 1949)

Nordwestdeutsche Philharmonie,
cond. Werner Andreas Albert
Germany CD cpo 999 146-2
(rec. June 1990)

Deutsches Symphonie-Orchester
Berlin, cond. John Mauceri
USA and UK CD London/Decca 444
170-2 (rec. April 1994)

Works Without Opus Number

Der Schneemann (The Snowman)
Vorspiel and Serenade
Dol Dauber's Salon Orchester
Austrian HMV AM 2038
(rec. late 1920s)

Vorspiel and Serenade
Austrian Radio Orchestra, cond.
Max Schönherr
USA CD Cambria CD 1066
(rec. 1949)

Vorspiel, Serenade, and Entr'acte
Nordwestdeutsche Philharmonie,
cond. Werner Andreas Albert
Germany CD cpo 999 037-2
(rec. June 1990)

Vorspiel, Walzer, Serenade, and
Entr'acte
Antonin Kubalek, piano
USA Stereo LP Citadel CT-6009
(rec.1977)

Complete score for piano solo
Scot Woolley
USA Stereo CD KOCH 3-7277 2 41
(rec. 1995)

Piano Sonata No. 1 in D Minor
Passacaglia (Finale)
E. W. Korngold, piano
USA LP Masterseal MW 46
(rec. 1951)
USA LP Varése-Sarabande VC
81040

Antonin Kubalek, piano
USA Stereo LP Citadel CT 6009
(rec. 1977)
USA Stereo CD Citadel CTD 88109

Matthijs Verschoor, piano
Netherlands Stereo LP Etcetera ETC
1042 (rec. 1986)
Netherlands Stereo CD Etcetera
KTC 1042

Ilona Prunyi, piano
Germany CD Marco Polo 8.223384
(rec. Aug.–Sept. 1990)

Geoffrey Tozer, piano
UK Stereo CD Chandos CHAN
9389 (rec. 12 May 1995)

*Don Quixote: Six Characteristic Pieces
for Piano*
Antonin Kubalek, piano
USA Stereo LP Citadel CT-6009
(rec.1977)

USA Stereo CD Citadel CTD 88109

Military March in B Major for Large
Orchestra
BBC Philharmonic Orchestra, cond.
Mathias Bamert
UK CD Chandos 9508
(rec. May 1996)

Romance-Impromptu for Cello and Piano
Francisco Gabarro, cello, John
Curtis (pseudonym for Charles
Gerhardt), piano
USA LP (box set) Readers Digest
"Fountain of Melody" RD-4-62

Straussiana for Orchestra
Inglewood Symphony Orchestra,
cond. Ernst Gebert
USA Acetate recording Electro Vox,
no number (rec. at world premiere,
22 Nov. 1953)

Nordwestdeutsche Philharmonie,
cond. Werner Andreas Albert
Germany CD cpo 999 146-2
(rec. Feb. 1987)

Korngold's Film Music

The Films

Korngold conducted all soundtrack
recordings himself. The following list
includes CD reissues and 78 rpm discs
(including some not issued at the time).

Because the many compilation discs
and numerous CD reissues include individual selections on different discs, films
are grouped here by a key code of letters
and numbers in brackets. These refer to
the records in the following two subsec-
tions and enable the reader to identify
records of music from individual films
easily. The *letters* refer to the subsection
devoted to film soundtracks; the *numbers*
refer to the varied list of recordings of
complete film scores and excerpts that
follows immediately after it.

Key

1935. *A Midsummer Night's Dream*
(d, f)
1935. *Captain Blood* (a, d, e, f, h, 7, 11,
13, 29)
1936. *Give Us This Night* (b, 1, 2, 19)
1936. *The Green Pastures* (h)
1936. *Anthony Adverse* (h, 5, 7, 9, 25)
1937. *The Prince and the Pauper* (h, 5, 9,
27, 28)

1937. *Another Dawn* (3, 9)
1938. *The Adventures of Robin Hood*
(c–f, h, 5, 7, 13, 16, 22, 23, 31, 40)
1939. *Juarez* (h, 7, 10, 30)
1939. *The Private Lives of Elizabeth and
Essex* (h, 3, 9–11, 15, 26)
1940. *The Sea Hawk* (c, d, f, h, 5, 7, 12,
13 14, 15, 22, 24, 39)
1941. *The Sea Wolf* (d, f, h, 9)
1941. *Kings Row* (c, d, f, h, 4, 5–7,
17, 20)
1942. *The Constant Nymph* (h, 5, 7,
18, 36)
1943. *Devotion* (h, 7, 30, 35, 37)
1944. *Between Two Worlds* (h, 7, 21,
33, 34)
1945. *Of Human Bondage* (h, 7, 9)
1946. *Escape Me Never* (h, 6, 7, 22, 34,
35, 41)
1946. *Deception* (h, 6, 7, 9, 15, 35, 38)
1954. *Magic Fire* (g)

Korngold also scored one brief sequence for two 1936 films (see Complete
List of Works), *Hearts Divided* and *Rose
of the Rancho*, but music from these
films is unavailable on records. Parts of
the score for *Between Two Worlds* were
reused by Warner Brothers for the films
Home Before Dark and *Up Periscope*
(1957 and 1953); similarly, his score for
Juarez was used extensively by Warners
Brothers for the Mexican version of the
film entitled *The Mad Empress* (1939).
None of these can truly be classed as
Korngold films as he had nothing whatever to do with their production.

Film Soundtrack Excerpts on Gramophone Records

a.   *Captain Blood*: brief excerpt from
the soundtrack, 23 seconds with
Flynn and de Havilland.
UK 78 rpm "Voice of the Stars No.
3" VS3 (charity record sold in UK
cinemas to aid the Cinematograph
Trade Benevolent Fund; four
issued, 1934–1937)

b.   *Give Us This Night*
"Processional," Gladys Swarthout
and Jan Kiepura
USA LP EJS 223 "The Golden Age
of Opera"
UK CD Pearl GEMM CD 9976

[Film Excerpts]
  "Di quella pira" (Verdi, *Rigoletto*, arr. E. W. Korngold), Jan Kiepura and male chorus.
  UK CD Pearl GEMM CD 9976

c. *50 Years of Film Music*: includes excerpts from the original optical music tracks (i.e. without dialogue, sound effects) of *The Sea Hawk* (suite), *Kings Row* (suite, includes excerpt of Korngold playing the main title theme on the piano, rec. 1951 during a party given by Ray Heindorf), *The Adventures of Robin Hood* (suite).
  Warner Brothers Studio Orchestra, cond. E. W. Korngold.
  USA three-LP boxed set Warner Brothers 3XX 2736 (prod. 1973). Includes many excerpts of other music. Part of this set is in artificial stereo, not mentioned in the accompanying material.

d. *50 Years of Film*: brief excerpts from the soundtracks (with dialogue) from *The Adventures of Robin Hood*, *Kings Row*, *The Sea Wolf*, *The Sea Hawk*, *Captain Blood*, *A Midsummer Night's Dream*
  USA three-LP boxed set (includes many other excerpts) Warner Brothers 3XX2737

e. *Requiem for a Cavalier*: radio documentary on the life of Errol Flynn, produced and narrated by Tony Thomas. Includes brief excerpts from the soundtracks of *Captain Blood* and *The Adventures of Robin Hood*, other clips, and many interviews.
  USA LP Delos DEL/F 25409 (prod. 1976)
  USA CD Facet (Bellaphon) 8104

f. *The Golden Age of Hollywood Stars*: a remix of c and d, above, issued in 1977. Includes shortened excerpts from original music tracks from *The Adventures of Robin Hood*, *The Sea Hawk*, and *Kings Row*, and sound-track clips from *Captain Blood*, *A Midsummer Night's Dream*, *The Adventures of Robin Hood*, *Kings Row*, and *The Sea Wolf*.
  USA and UK LP (double album) United Artists USD 311

g. *Magic Fire*: original motion picture soundtrack featuring operatic excerpts from various Wagner operas sung by Leonie Rysanek, Anneliese Kupper, Hans Hopf, Otto Edelmann with the Chorus and Orchestra of the Bavarian State Opera, cond. Alois Melichar (and E. W. Korngold, uncredited), and five extracts performed by Korngold on the piano.
  USA LP Varése Sarabande STV 81179 (rec. 1954; rel. 1983)

h. *Erich Wolfgang Korngold—The Warner Brothers Years (1935–1946)*: original optical music tracks from all Korngold's films for Warner Brothers except *Another Dawn* and *Hearts Divided*, rescued by George Korngold in 1975 before Warners destroyed its entire sound library. Suites from each film.
  Warner Brothers Studio Orchestra, cond. E. W. Korngold
  USA CD (Box Set) RHINO R2 72243 (rel. April 1996)

Film Music on Gramophone Records

1. *Give Us This Night*
    Songs "Sweet Melody of Night" and "I Mean to Say I Love You": Jan Kiepura, tenor
    UK Parlophone-Odeon RO 21310 (rec.1936)
    Germany Odeon 281.061
    France Odeon (no. not traced)
    UK Decca 23008
    Canada LP Ariel OSH 14
    UK CD Pearl GEMM CD 9079

2. *Give Us This Night*
    Song "I Mean to Say I Love You": Gladys Swarthout, orchestra cond. Alexander Smallens
    USA: Victor (rec. 3 April 1936; never issued)

3. *Hollywood Rhapsodies*: includes *Another Dawn*, "Theme Romantique" (i.e. night scene, also the main theme of the Violin Concerto in D Major), *The Private Lives of Elizabeth and Essex*, love theme
    Victor Young and His Singing Strings, and Anatole Kaminsky, violin

USA LP Decca 8060 (prod. 1954)
UK LP Brunswick LAT 8041

4. *Love Music from Hollywood*:
includes *Kings Row* main title and
love theme, arr. by Paul Weston.
Paul Weston and his Orchestra
USA LP Columbia CL 794
(prod. 1956)
UK LP Philips BBL 7085
USA LP Corinthian Records
COR-107

5. *Film Music by Korngold*: includes
Kings Row (main title, the children,
Randy and Drake, Grandmother),
Anthony Adverse (Anthony is born,
love scene, Anthony comes home),
The Sea Hawk (main title; the
reunion), *The Prince and the Pauper*
(the boys go to play), *The Constant
Nymph* (main title; farewell), *The
Adventures of Robin Hood* (march
of the merry men, battle in
Sherwood Forest, Robin and
Marian, Epilog).
Symphony Orchestra Graunke, cond.
Lionel Newman and Kurt Graunke
USA and Australia LP Warner
Brothers 1438
USA and Australia Stereo LP Warner
Brother S-1438 (rec. Aug. 1961)
USA LP Warner Brothers K26120,
K26121, and K26122 (excerpts)
USA CD Stanyan STZ 117

6. *Great Music from the Movies*:
includes *Kings Row* suite(RCA
Symphony Orchestra, cond. Charles
Gerhardt), *Escape Me Never*, "Love
for Love," *Deception* main title
(orchestra cond. Harry Rabinowitz)
USA and UK LP (box set) Readers
Digest RD-3-39 (rec. 1964) and
RD 4-39

7. *The Sea Hawk: The Classic Film
Scores of Erich Wolfgang Korngold*.
Includes selections from *The Sea
Hawk*, main title, love scene,
reunion, finale; *Of Human Bondage*,
Nora's theme; *The Adventures of
Robin Hood*, march of the merry
men; *Juarez*, love theme; *Kings Row*,
main title; *The Constant Nymph*;
Tomorrow, Opus 33 (Norma
Procter, mezzo soprano, with the
Ambrosian Singers); *Captain Blood*,
main title; *Anthony Adverse*, Maria's

death, "No Father, No Mother, No
Name"; *Between Two Worlds*, main
title, mother and son; *Deception*,
main title, *Devotion*, Emily Brontë's
death; *Escape Me Never*, suite, main
title, Venice, march, love scene and
finale (Sidney Sax, violin solo).
The National Philharmonic
Orchestra. cond. Charles Gerhardt
USA Stereo LP RCA LSC 3330
(rec. 1971)
UK Stereo LP RCA SER 5664, GL
43446, GK 43446
UK and USA Compact Disc RCA
GD 87890
Two versions have been reissued on
CD with slightly different selections
re-edited by Charles Gerhardt.

8. Excerpt from No. 7 above
UK Stereo 45 rpm RCA 2311

9. *Elizabeth and Essex: The Classic
Film Scores of Erich Wolfgang
Korngold*: includes *The Private Lives
of Elizabeth and Essex*, concert over-
ture; *The Prince and the Pauper*,
main title, the boys go out to play,
epilogue; *The Sea Wolf*, main title,
escape in the fog, love scene, finale;
Deception, Cello Concerto in C
Major, Opus 37; *Another Dawn*,
night scene; *Anthony Adverse*, in the
forest; *Of Human Bondage*, suite,
main title, Christmas (not in released
film); Sally, lullaby, finale.
The National Philharmonic
Orchestra conducted by Charles
Gerhardt (rec. 1971–1973)
UK and USA Stereo LP RCA
ARL1-0185
UK Stereo LP RCA GL 43438
UK and USA CD RCA GD80185
Some items were included on a CD
reissue in extended versions
re-edited by Charles Gerhardt.

10. *Classic Film Scores for Bette Davis*:
includes *Elizabeth & Essex*,
Elizabeth; *Juarez*, love theme for
Carlotta
The National Philharmonic
Orchestra, cond. Charles Gerhardt
USA and UK Stereo LP RCA ARL1-
0183 (rec. 1973)
USA Stereo LP RCA AGL1-3706 UK
Stereo LP RCA GL43436
UK Stereo LP RCA PL 43764
UK and USA CD RCA GD 80183

[Film Music]

11. *The Spectacular World of Classic Film Scores:* includes *Captain Blood,* main title from No. 7, above; *The Private Lives of Elizabeth and Essex,* Elizabeth's theme from No. 9, above
The National Philharmonic Orchestra, cond. Charles Gerhardt
UK Stereo LP RCA RL 42005

12. Excerpt from *The Sea Hawk*
Stanley Black and his orchestra
UK Stereo LP Decca PFS 4242, STBA 1-3 (set)
USA Stereo LP London SP 44173
USA and UK Stereo LP (box set), Readers Digest "Lights! Camera! Action!"

13. *Captain Blood—Classic Film Scores for Errol Flynn:* includes *The Sea Hawk,* the albatross, the throne room, entrance of the sea hawks, the orchid, Panama march, the duel, strike for the shores of Dover (with the Ambrosian Singers); *Captain Blood,* ship in the night; *The Adventures of Robin Hood,* archery tournament, escape from the gallows, love scene, coronation procession.
The National Philharmonic Orchestra, cond. Charles Gerhardt.
USA & UK Stereo LP RCA ARL1-0192; rec. 1975
UK Stereo LP RCA GL 43444
UK & USACD RCA GD80912
Selections from this recording are included on the CD reissue of No. 7, above.

14. *Musik Aktuell 4—Film Music:* includes *The Sea Hawk,* the duel (from No. 13, above)
Germany LP Bärenreiter Musicaphon BM 5103

15. *Songs and Arias of Erich Wolfgang Korngold* includes: *The Private Lives of Elizabeth and Essex,* "Come Live With Me," lyrics by Christopher Marlowe; *The Sea Hawk,* "Old Spanish Song," lyrics by Howard Koch (see Opus 38)
Polly Jo Baker, soprano, George Calusdian, piano
USA Stereo LP Entr'acte ERS 6502 (prod. 1975)
USA CD Entr'acte ESCD 6502

16. *The Adventures of Robin Hood— Symphonic Suite*
Prologue(main title), banquet, Robin's entrance, Little John, Friar Tuck, battle in Sherwood Forest, feast and flirtation, Robin's escape from the gallows, "Lady Marian's Heartsong," victory.
Narrated by Basil Rathbone, Warner Brothers Studio Orchestra, cond. E. W. Korngold
Edited, shortened transfer from original acetates from the historic radio broadcast on 11 May 1938 Radio KFWB
USA LP Delos DEL/F25409 (prod. 1976)
USA CD Facet (Bellaphon) 8104

17. *Classic Film Themes for Organ* includes: *Kings Row,* main theme.
Gaylord Carter, on the Simonton Grande Wurlitzer Organ
USA Stereo LP Delos DEL/F25419 (prod. 1976)

18. *Castaway's Choice* includes: *The Constant Nymph,* suite
The Philharmonic Pops Orchestra, cond. Charles Gerhardt
USA and UK (box set) LP Readers Digest RD 4-26 (rec. 1965) reissued on USA CD Varèse Sarabande VSD 5207

19. *Film Songs by Erich Wolfgang Korngold and Max Steiner* includes: *Escape Me Never,* "Love for Love," lyrics by Ted Koehler; *Give Us This Night,* "Sweet Melody of Night," "I Mean To Say I Love You," "My Love and I," "Music in the Night," lyrics by Oscar Hammerstein II
Maria Martino, soprano, William Teaford, pianist and arranger
USA Stereo LP Citadel CT 7005 (prod. 1979)

20. *Kings Row,* symphonic suite of the main portions of the score.
National Philharmonic Orchestra, cond. Charles Gerhardt
USA Stereo LP Chalfont 5DG 305 (digital rec. 25 July 1979)
USA Stereo LP DBX PS-1030
Germany Stereo LP Colosseum 1 066
UK CD That's Entertainment CDACD - 85707
USA CD Varése Sarabande VCD-47203

Germany D Colosseum 34 85 707
excerpt "Finale," USA CD Tandy
Realistic 51 5003

21. *Film Music for Piano*: includes
"Between Two Worlds," piano rhap-
sody, arr. Albert Dominguez
Albert Dominguez, piano
USA Sereo LP Citadel CT 7010 (rec.
May 1979)

22. *The Berlin Philharmonic Concerts*
includes: *The Sea Hawk*, suite; *The
Adventures of Robin Hood*, suite in
three movements
RIAS Jugendorchester, cond. Mark
Fitgerald
France Stereo LP Kilan A 037/38 CD
Milan A CH 037/38 (rec. 21 Feb.
1984, 16 Feb. 1985)

23. *The Adventures of Robin Hood*,
symphonic suite
Utah Symphony Orchestra, cond.
Varujan Kojian
USA Stereo LP Varése Sarabande
704.180 (rec. 31 May, 1 June
1983)
USA CD Varése Sarabande VCD
47202

24. *The Sea Hawk*, symphonic suite
The Utah Symphony Orchestra and
Chorus, cond. Varujan Kojian
USA Stereo LP Varése Sarabande
704 380 (rec. 29, 30 July 1987)
USA CD Varése Sarabande VCD
47304
UK CD TER 1164

25. *Anthony Adverse*, symphonic suite
The Berlin Radio Symphony
Orchestra, cond. John Scott
USA CD Varése Sarabande VSD
5285 (rec. 1990)

26. *The Private Lives of Elizabeth and
Essex*, complete score
The Munich Symphony Orchestra,
cond. Carl Davis
USA CD Bay Cities BCD 3026
(rec. Dec. 1991)

27. *The Prince and the Pauper*, sym-
phonic suite
The Brandenburg Philharmonic
Orchestra, cond. William T.
Stromberg
USA CD RCA Victor Red Seal
09026 62660 2 (rec. Feb. 1995)

28. *The Prince and the Pauper*
"Flirtation" (waltz)

The National Philharmonic
Orchestra, cond. Charles Gerhardt
USA CD Varése Sarabande VSD
5207 (rec. 1973)

The Hollywood Bowl Orchestra,
cond. John Mauceri
USA CD Philips 438 685-2
(rec. 1995)

29. *Captain Blood*, suite
Brandenburg Philharmonic
Orchestra, Potsdam, cond. Richard
Kaufman
German CD Marco Polo 8.223607
(rec. April–June 1994)

30. *Juarez*, Overture (arr. E. W.
Korngold for the premiere of the
film, 1939): disc also includes brief
sequence from *Devotion*
Brandenburg Philharmonic
Orchestra, Potsdam, cond. Richard
Kaufman
Germany CD Marco Polo 8.223608
(rec. April–June 1994)

31. *Hollywood Dreams*, includes *The
Adventures of Robin Hood* (suite,
three movements)
Hollywood Bowl Orchestra, cond.
John Mauceri
USA CD Philips 432 109-2
(rec. Feb. 1991)
USA CD Philips 446 499-2 (different
compilation)

32. *The Adventures of Robin Hood*,
suite
East of England Orchestra, cond.
Malcolm Nabarro
UK CD ASV CD WHL 2069

33. *Between Two Worlds*, symphonic
suite
Rundfunk-Sinfonieorchester Berlin,
cond. John Mauceri
USA/UK CD Decca/London 444
170-2 (rec. April 1995)

34. *Between Two Worlds*
"Mother and Son" and Piano
Rhapsody; disc also includes "Love
for Love" from *Escape Me Never*
National Philharmonic Orchestra,
cond. Charles Gerhardt
USA CD Varése Sarabande VSD
5207 (rec. 1965)

35. Themes from *Devotion*, *Escape Me
Never*, and *Deception* and Romance-
Impromptu from *Deception*
arranged for Cello and Piano; also

[Film Music]
includes *Sieben Märchenbilder* (Seven Fairy Pictures), Opus 3 (perf. Antonin Kubalek)
Gayle Davis, cello, Thomas G. Groth, piano
USA CD Bay Cities BCD 1032

36. *The Constant Nymph*, extended overture
National Philharmonic Orchestra, cond. Charles Gerhardt
USA CD Verése Sarabande VSD 5207 (rec. 1965)

37. *Devotion*, excerpt
The Brandenburg Philharmonic Orchestra, Potsdam, cond. Richard Kaufman
Germany CD Marco Polo 8.223608 (rec. April–June 1994)

38. *Deception*, Cello Concerto in C Major, Opus 37
Julius Berger, violoncello
Nordwestdeutsche Philharmonie, cond. Werner Andreas Albert
Germany CD cpo 999 077-2 (rec. February 1991)

Peter Dixon, violoncello
BBC Philharmonic, cond. Mathias Bamert
UK CD Chandos CHAN 9508 (rec. May 1996)

Francisco Gabarro, violoncello, The National Philharmonic Orchestra, cond. Charles Gerhardt
USA and UK Stereo LP RCA ARL1-0185 (rec. 1971)
UK Stereo LP RCA GL 43438
UK and USA CD RCA GD 80185

39. *The Sea Hawk*, suite
The BBC Film Orchestra
UK CD The Collection OP0040

40. *The Adventures of Robin Hood*, suite
Royal Philharmonic Pops Orchestra, cond. John Scott
UK CD Denon CD 75470

41. *Escape Me Never*, "Love for Love"
The Hollywood Bowl Orchestra, cond. John Mauceri, E. W. Korngold, piano solo, from private rec. made in 1951
USA CD Philips 446 681-2 "'Always and Forever': Movies' Greatest Love Songs" (prod. Aug.–Sept. 1995)

Korngold as Performer (music other than his own)

Ludwig van Beethoven, Sonata No. 1 for Violin and Piano in D Major, Opus 12, No. 1, "Tema con Variazioni" (second movement)
Robert Pollack, violin, E. W. Korngold, piano
UK 78rpm Homochord HB 2091 (rec. 1924)

Leo Fall, *Die Geschiedene Frau*, arr. E. W. Korngold
"Eine Frau von meinem Rang," "Filmchanson der Gonda," "Man steigt nach," (duet)
Lucie Mannheim with Adolf Wohlbrück (Anton Walbrook), Orchester des Nollendorf-Theaters, Berlin, cond. E. W. Korngold
Germany Electrola EG 2767, 2745 (rec. Feb. 1933, Berlin)

Bruno Granichstaedten, *Die Bacchusnacht*
"Pflück die Blumen"
Richard Tauber, tenor, Orchester des Theaters an der Wien, cond. E. W. Korngold
Germany 78 rpm Odeon RXX 80860 (rec. 23 Jan. 1924)

Franz Lehár, *Frasquita*
"Hab' ein blaues Himmelbett"
Richard Tauber, tenor, Orchester des Theaters an der Wien, cond. E. W. Korngold
Germany Odeon RXX 80859 (rec. 23 Jan. 1924); on matrix xxB 6912, takes 1, 2 are used
USA Odeon 1012
UK LP HMV HLM 7172 (includes unpublished take)

Franz Lehár, *Die Lustige Witwe*
"Ballsirenen-Walzer, Lippen schweigen"
Richard Tauber, tenor, Odeon-Künstler Orchester, cond. E. W. Korngold
Germany Odeon 4501 (rec. 5 Jan. 1932)
UK Parlophone-Odeon RO 20175
USA Decca 20393, 196196, 236832
Australian Odeon 165
Japan Nippon Columbia 2087, 530102
and innumerable LP re-issues.
UK CD CDH 7 69787 2

Johann Strauss I and II and E. W. Korngold
Das Lied der Liebe, operetta in two acts

Fantasia (Grosses Potpourri)
Odeon-Künstler Orchester, cond. E. W. Korngold
Germany Odeon 0-11582
(rec. 5 Jan. 1932)

"G'schichten aus dem Wienerwald"
Richard Tauber, tenor, Odeon Künstler Orchester, cond. E. W. Korngold
Germany Odeon 4501, 4668
(rec. 5 Jan. 1932)
UK Parlophone-Odeon RO 20190, RO 20432
Australia Odeon 185
USA Decca 20261, 196196, 236832
USA Columbia G 4076M
and innumerable LP reissues
Portugal CD Gala GL 314

"Man glaubte so gerne an Frauenlieb' und Glück" and "Du bist mein Traum"
Richard Tauber, tenor, Odeon Künstler Orchester, cond. E. W. Korngold
Germany Odeon 4500 (rec. 17 Dec. 1931)
UK Parlophone-Odeon RO 20216
USA Decca P-G-20259,20219, 27059, 196261
USA LP Eterna 727

Johann Strauss II, *Eine Nacht in Venedig,* arr. E. W. Korngold
"Sei mir gegrüsst, du holdes Venezia"
Richard Tauber, tenor
Orchester des Theaters an der Wien, cond. E. W. Korngold
German Odeon RXX 80862, O-80869, 217824 (rec. 23 Jan. 1924)
USA LP Scala 837
USA LP Eterna 459 727
Germany LP EMI Da Capo 1C 147-29137 (also includes "Treu sein, das liegt mir nicht")

Piano Roll Recordings*

Frankfurt/Main, Philipps A.G. (Duca, Ducartist and Philag, Ducanola)

1084-1087, Piano Sonata No. 2, Opus 2, Artur Schnabel, 13 Jan. 1912
1117-1123, *Sieben Märchenbilder,* Opus 3, E. W. Korngold, 14 Feb. 1912

Freiburg/Breisgau, M. Welte & Söhne (Welte-Migron, red and green system)
2985, *Sieben Märchenbilder,* Opus 3, No. 5, Eugen D'Albert, 1913
3055/3056, Piano Sonata No. 2 in E Major, Opus 2, Rudolf Ganz, 1915
3829, 3901, Piano Sonata No. 2 in E Major, Opus 2, Rudolf Ganz, 1915
3841, 3842, *Sieben Märchenbilder,* Opus 3, Kaethe Heinemann, 1923
3991, *Die tote Stadt,* "Pierrotlied," Hans Haass, 1925
4196, *Die tote Stadt,* "Mariettalied," Willy Peterka, 1928

Leipzig, Ludwig Hupfeld A.G. (1. Animatic; 2. Phonola ; 3. T = Triphonola)
50588, 16720, *Der Schneemann,* Waltz, Oswin Keller, 1921
54419,18721, *Der Schneemann,* Entr'acte, Oswin Keller, 1921
58740, 18198, T 58740, *Die tote Stadt,* "Pierrotlied," E. W. Korngold, 1921
58741, 18199, T 58741, *Die tote Stadt,* "Mariettalied," E. W. Korngold, 1921
58742, 18200, T 58742, *Much Ado About Nothing,* Opus 11, "Maiden in Bridal Chamber," E. W. Korngold 1921
58743, 18201, T 58743, *Much Ado About Nothing,*Opus 11, March, E. W. Korngold, 1921 (A further roll, numbered 58744, was probably made by Korngold from Opus 11: details are as yet unknown.)
58745, 18203, T 58745, *Much Ado About Nothing,* Opus 11, Garden Scene/Intermezzo, E. W. Korngold 1921
T 58746, *Violanta,* Prelude and duet, E. W. Korngold, 1921
T 58794, *Violanta,* love duet, E. W. Korngold, 1921
58795, 18246, T58795, *Sieben Märchenbilder,* Opus 3, No. 5, E. W. Korngold, 1921

*Compiled by Hans W. Schmitz, Stuttgart, October 1995, reproduced with his permission. Korngold probably made more rolls during his subsequent visit to London in 1924, but details have not yet been discovered. This list is almost certainly incomplete; further information would be appreciated. Please note that Philag, Ducanola, Animatic and Phonola are player piano rolls, while all others listed are "reproducing" piano rolls.

[Piano Roll]
  58796, 18247, *Sieben Märchenbilder*, Opus 3, No. 7, E. W. Korngold, 1921
  59011, 18412, T59011, *Violanta*, Alfonso's aria, Julius Prüwer, 1923
  59015, 18416, T59015, *Violanta*, love duet, Julius Prüwer, 1923
  T 59670, *Die tote Stadt*, selections, Alfred Szendrei, 1928

New York, M. Welte & Sons, Inc. (red system only)
  3829, 3901, *Sieben Märchenbilder*, Opus 3, Nos. 4, 7, Rudolf Ganz, 1915

New York, The Aeolian Corporation (Duo-Art)
  65290, *Die tote Stadt*, selections, Lawrence Schauffler, 1922

68796, *Sieben Märchenbilder*, Opus 3, No. 4, Frances Hall, 1925
70407, *Sieben Märchenbilder*, Opus 3, No. 7, Daisy Hoffmann, 1928
105064 = br 01317 = Ampico 3091, "I Mean to Say I Love You," from the film *Give Us This Night*, Robert Farquhar (alias Frank Milne) 1936

New York, The Ampico Co. (Ampico)
  62031 G (3091= Aeolian 105064 = br 01317), "Pierrotlied," *Die tote Stadt*, Frances Nash, 1923

London The Aeolian Company, Limited (Duo-Art)
  br 080 (br. 01317 = Aeolian 105064 = Ampico 3091), *Der Schneemann*, Entr'act, E. W. Korngold 1922

Index

Erich Wolfgang, Julius, Josephine (Witrofsky), and Luise "Luzi" (von Sonnenthal) Korngold are not included as main index entries. All of Erich Wolfgang Korngold's works, however, including his film scores, are cited under "Korngold's works." References to Erich Wolfgang Korngold in other entries are abbreviated to "K." References to his father are shortened to "Julius." Page numbers that refer to illustrations or music examples are in italics.

Aargard-Oestvig, Karl, 143–145, 183
Abbazia, Yugoslavia, 32
Action in the North Atlantic (1943 film), 311
Adelphi Theater, London, 215
Ader, Rose, 132, 152
Adler, Guido, 31
Adler, Gusti, 312
Adolf Rebner Quartet, 76
The Adventures of Casanova (1946 film), 394
The Adventures of Don Juan (1948 film), 333
Aeolian Hall, London, 98
Agate, James, 214
Ager, Cecelia, 327
Aherne, Brian, 280, 306
Ahlers, Anny, 214
Aigen-Vogelhub, near Salzburg, 187
Air Force (1943 film), 311
Aix-en-Provence, 226
Albersheim, Dr. Gerhard, 365
Albert, Eugen d', 138
  Tiefland, 32, 44, 205, 321
Albert, King of Belgium, 376
Alda, Robert, 326
Alexander, Ross, *235*
Alfano, Franco, 189
Alhambra Theater, London, 211
Alice of Athlone, Princess, 214
Allan, Elisabeth, 231
Allen, Hervey, 256
Aller, Victor, 406

The Almanac for the Musical World 1914–1915, 68
Alpar, Gitta, 215
Alt-Aussee, Austrian Salzkammergut, 110, 111, 165, 177, 222
  Korngold family takes a villa, 106
  K's nostalgic holiday (1949), 340
  K's playing attracts nearby residents, 111
  Raoul Auernheimer's home in, 321
Altenberg, Peter, 82
Alvin Theater, New York, 314
Alwin, Carl, 182–184, 217, 267, 382, 385
Ambrosi, Gustinus, 80, 82, *83*, *119*, 377
Amsterdam Concertgebouw, 187, 188, 195
Amy, George, 253, 295
Anday, Rosette, 166–167, 183, 186, 386
  Julius on, 183
  premiere of *Drei Lieder*, Opus 18, 386
  premiere of *Vier Lieder des Abschieds*, Opus 14, 153, 166–167, 186
Anderson, Maxwell, 262, 279, 286
Anet, Claude, 218
Angerer, Margit, 197
Anne of the Thousand Days (1968 film), 265
Antheil, George, 334
Anti-Semitism, 71–72, 174, *293*
Arch of Triumph (1948 film), 328
Ariane (1931 film), 218–219

437

Arnheim, Gus, 238, 239
Arno, Siegfried, 305
Arnold, Heinz, 344
Arriaga, Juan, 21
As You Like It (1935 film), 233
As You Like It (Shakespeare play), 172, 303
Aschau, near Ischl, 213
Assistance League Playhouse, 283
Association of Vienna Music Critics, 65, 74, 150
Atonality/atonalism, 23, 156, 180, 292, 326
Auer, Leopold, 303
Auernheimer, Irene Leopoldine, 321
Auernheimer, Raoul, 321
Auftakt (Prague journal), 48
Augusteo, Rome, 167
Austrian Composers' Society, 223
Austrian National Library, 274
Austrian Radio, 339–340, 350, 354
Austrian State Theaters, 198, 340
Austrian Tobacco Company, 199

Babbitt, Milton, 371
Bach, Johann Sebastian, 36, 39, 51, 87, 187, 359
Badel, Alan, *353*, 354
Bahr, Hermann, 31, 112
Baker, Carroll, 278
Baker, Herbert, 314
Balanchine, George, 234, 308
Ball, Lucille, 311
Ballet Russe, 386
Balzac, Honoré de, 175
Bamert, Mathias, 370
Bankhead, Tallulah, 215
Barrymore, John, 233
Bartók, Béla, 44, 180, 190, 279
    Concerto for Orchestra, 393
Bartsch, Rudolf, 80
Basserman, Albert, 289, 305
Basserman, Elsie, 305
Basset, Reginald, 272
Bath, Hubert, 211
Batka, Richard, 63
Baum, Vicki, 312
Bayliss, Lillian, 71
Bay Region Symphony Orchestra, 277
Bayreuth Festspielhaus, 353
BBC (British Broadcasting Corporation), 282
BBC Philharmonic Orchestra, 370
Beatrice's Veil (Schnitzler), 102
Bechert, Paul, 171–172, 373
Bechstein Hall, London, 52
Beer, Dr. August, 46

Beethoven, Ludwig van, 43, 63, 87, 264, 319, 324, 358, 359
    early music of, 28
    and Arthur Nikisch, 138
    and Strauss's *The Ruins of Athens*, 178
    WORKS: *Egmont* Overture, 134; *Fidelio*, 34; Piano Concerto No. 4 in G, 336; Piano Sonata in C Minor ("Pathétique"), 304; Piano Sonata in F Minor ("Appassionata"), 324, 325; piano sonatas, 39, 50, 61, 74; String Quartet No. 2 ("Rasoumovsky"), 336
Behrman, S. N., 262
Bekker, Paul, 145
    and Julius, 377
    and K's first opera, 45
    one of K's most venomous opponents, 45
    "Sounds of the Future," article by, 45
Bellamann, Henry, 303
Benedikt, Ernst, 74, 182
Benedikt, Moritz, 385
    Auernheimer succeeds, 321
    commissions Decsey to write about K, 46
    death, 74
    as the editor of the *Neue Freie Presse*, 26
    engages Julius, 26
    and Graf-Korngold libel suit, 66
    and Gregor, 111
    and Rosenthal's complaint, 74
Benet, Stephen Vincent, 278
Berg, Alban, 44–45, 51, 138, 180, 369
    Piano Sonata, 38
    Wozzeck, 157, 197, 384
Berg, Helene, 138
Bergh, Arthur, 334
Bergman, Ingrid, 328
Bergner, Elisabeth, 218, 233, 305, 311, 322
Berkeley, Busby, 238, 254
Berlin
    Sonata in G Major for violin, premiered, 92
    Das Wunder der Heliane receives stormy critical response in, 262, 264–267
Berliner Theater, 187
Berlin Hochschule, 42
Berlin Kroll Opera, 51, 214
Berlin Lessing Theater, 121
Berlin Metropol Theater, 214

Berlin Philharmonic Orchestra, 167, 214, 217, 337, 377
Berlin State Opera, 173, 191, 386–387
Berlioz, Hector, 371
Bernassi, Memo, 225–226
Bernstein, Elmer, 278
Bernstein, Leonard, 368
Berris, George, 258
Berry, W. H., 214
Best, Edna, 214
Beverly Hills Theater, Hollywood, 282, 288
Bey, Turhan, 394
Bie, Oscar, 71
Bienenfeld, Dr. Elsa, 145
Bienerth, Baroness von, 46
Biltmore Hotel, Los Angeles, 241, 265, 285
Bing, Rudolf, 365
Bittner, Emilie, 158, 174–175, 210
Bittner, Julius, 158, 174–175, *210*, 210, 223, 294
    Das Rosengärtlein, 197
Bizet, Georges, 21
The Black Swan (1942 film), 297
Blanca, Archduchess, 46
Blanke, Henry ("Heinz"), *235*, *241*, 244, 246, 261, 263
    and *The Adventures of Robin Hood*, 269
    and *Danton* (unproduced 1936 Reinhardt film), 262, 263
    and *John Paul Jones* (1956 film), 360
    and *Juarez*, 280
    K shown round Warner's Studio by, 246
    keen to bring K back to Hollywood, 246
    as Lubitsch's assistant, 232
    and *A Midsummer Night's Dream*, 232
    and *The Miracle* (unproduced 1938 Reinhardt film), 278, 391
    and *Of Human Bondage*, 317–318
    and *The Sea Hawk*, 298
    and *So Big* (1953 film), 350
Blatt, Edward A., 313
Blech, Leo
    as conductor of the Royal Opera, Berlin, 70
    and K's Piano Trio in D Major, 70–71
    and the Nazis, 72
    and performances of *Der Ring des Polykrates* and *Violanta*, 113–114, 125
    resignation, 173, 174

Bockelmann, Rudolf, 199
Bodanzky, Artur, 154
Bohemian String Quartet, 72
Böhm, Karl, 32, 204
Boleslawski, Norma, 304
Boleslawski, Richard, 304
Bonn, 93
Bösendorfer, Ludwig, 73
Boyer, Charles, 306, 328
Brahms, Johannes, 63, 79, 324, 359
    Hanslick champions, 24–25
    Julius and, 24–25
    personal style, 371
    WORKS: Fourth Symphony, 24–25; Lieder, 267; *Zigeunerlieder* (Gypsy Songs), 80
Brahms-Saal, Vienna, 346
Breekstone, Georgie, 389
Breen, Joseph, 278
Breisach, Paul, 134
Bremer, Lucille, 394
Brentano, Felix, 307
Bressart, Felix, 305
British Broadcasting Corporation. *See* BBC
Britten, Benjamin, 45, 85, 384
Brno. *See* Brünn
Brontë family, 310
Brook, Clive, 231
Brosig, Paula, 211
Brown, Joe E., *235*, *235*
Bruch, Max, 21
Bruckner, Anton, 54, 348, 359, 374
    centenary of his birth, 178
    Julius advocates the music of, 30
    Julius attends his classes, 24
    K compared to, 354
Bruges, 122, 123, 357
Bruges la Morte (Rodenbach), 120–123
Brünn (now Brno), 23–24
    Julius born in, 23
    Julius moves to Vienna, 26
    K born in, 27
Brunner, Fritz, 46
Brünner Montags-Zeitung, 24–25
Brünner Morgenpost, 24
Bucharoff, Simon, 252, 311
Budapest, 72
Buhlig, Richard, 77
Bülow, Hans von, 71, 83, 352, 378
Burani, Michelette, 247–248
Bürgertheater, Vienna, 189
Burgtheater, Vienna, 119, 130, 134, 283
Busch, Adolf, 93
Busch, Fritz, 98, 385, 386, 392
Busoni, Ferruccio, 174
Buxbaum, Friedrich, 63, 71, 80, 279

Buxbaum Quartet, 383
Byrns, Harold, 350

Café Museum, Vienna, 34, 181
Café Rumpelmayer, Berlin, 99
Cagney, James, 235, *235*, 237, 277
Calabasas (Warner ranch), 280
Cambridge Theater, London, 383
Canada, 332, 347
Cantor, Eddie, 232
Carlotta, Empress, 281
Carnegie Hall, New York, 98, 268, 312
Carrossio, Natale, 259
Caruso, Enrico, 329
Casablanca (1942 film), 253, 296, 311
Casals, Pablo, 226
Casella, Alfredo, 55, 168
Casino Theater, San Remo, 225
Casson, Lewis, 215
Castelnuovo-Tedesco, Mario, 365
Castiglioni, Iphigenia, 270, 283
Cathay Circle, Los Angeles, 259
Catholicism, ritual and mysticism of, 72,
    249
Cavanaugh, Hobart, *235*
Cervantes, Miguel, 36
Ceska, Hilda, 343
Chaliapin, Feodor, 248, 283
Chambers, Dudley, 297
Charpentier, Gustave (*Louise*), 26
Cherkassky, Shura, 325
The Chinese Hat (Franc-Nohain), 218
Chopin, Frédéric François, 65, 281, 324,
    358
    Luzi's biography of, 334
    WORKS: Fantaisie Impromptu, 304;
    Nocturne in E-flat Major, 393
Churain, Jaro, 305, 389
Churchill, Sir Winston, 36
Claire, Ina, 214
Claridge's Hotel, London, 214
Clausetti, Carlo, 148
Clemenceau, Georges, 82
Clemenceau, Paul, 175, 384
Clemenceau, Sophie, 175
Clement, Victor, 321, 322, 393
Clutsam, G. H. (*Lilac Time*), 211
Coburn, Charles, 306
Cochran, Charles B., 213, 214
Cohan, George M., 348
Cohn, Isidor, 378
Colman, Ronald, 231
Cologne, 79, 98, 139–140
    world premiere of *Die tote Stadt*, 136
Cologne Opera, 136
Colouris, George, 313
Colpet, Max, 222

Columbia Concert Orchestra, 309
Comedie-Française, Paris, 121
Commedia dell'arte, 39, 283
Connelly, Marc, 260
Conrat, Hugo, 79, 80
Conrat, Ida, 79
The Constant Nymph
    book by Kennedy, 304, 306
    films (1928, 1933), 306
    play, 306
Constructivism, 23
Contes Drolatiques (Balzac), 175
Cooper, Lady Diana, 214, 244, 278
Cooper, Melville, 314
Corbett, Lenore, 311
Cortese, Valentina, *355*
Court Theater, Vienna, 118
Coward, Noël, 214, 306
Crawford, Joan, 311, 324
Crisp, Donald, 286, 298
Cronin, A. J., 278
Crown, John, 365
Cummings, Robert, 304
Curtiz, Michael, 379
    and *The Adventures of Robin Hood*,
        272
    and *Captain Blood*, 253
    and *Danton* (unproduced 1936
        Reinhardt film), 263
    directs silent films featuring Luzi von
        Sonnenthal, 120
    and *The Miracle* (unproduced 1938
        Reinhardt film), 278
    and *The Private Lives of Elizabeth
        and Essex*, 286
    and *The Sea Wolf*, 300
Cutter, Murray, 252
Czinner, Paul, 218, 233

Daily News (London), 65
Daily Telegraph (London), 98, 214
Damrosch, Walter, 308
Daniel, Heinz, 199
Daniell, Henry, 231, 286
Danton (unproduced 1936 Reinhardt
    film), 262–264
Darvas, Lilli, 189, 311
da Silva, Howard, 328
Davies, Fanny, 82
Davies, Marion, 248, 260
Davis, Bette, 323
    and *Deception*, 324–327, 393
    and *Juarez*, 280–282
    and *A Midsummer Night's Dream*,
        235
    and *The Miracle* (unproduced 1938
        Reinhardt film), 267, 391

and *Of Human Bondage*, 317, 318
and *The Private Lives of Elizabeth
    and Essex*, 279, 281, 286–288
Davis, Carl, 370
Dawson, Ralph, 242
Dean, Basil, 306
Debussy, Claude, 22, 26, 43, 89
Decca Records, 307, 368
de Cordoba, Arturo, 394
Decsey, Dr. Ernst, 220, 374
    article on K when a child prodigy, 46
    and biography of J. Strauss, 31
    Julius on, 302
    and *Die Kathrin*, 226–227
    and *The Maid from Aachen*, 219,
        220
de Garmo, Tilly, 224
Degler, Josef, 136
de Havilland, Olivia
    and *Anthony Adverse*, 259
    and *Captain Blood*, 245
    and *Danton* (unproduced 1936
        Reinhardt film), 263
    and *Devotion*, 310
    and *A Midsummer Night's Dream*,
        232–233, 235, 235
    and *The Private Lives of Elizabeth
        and Essex*, 286–287
    and Reinhardt's memorial concert,
        312
    and *The Sea Hawk*, 295
Dehmel, Ilse (later von Sonnenthal), 120
Dehmel, Richard, 120
De Mille, Cecil B., 388
Dent, Edward J., 90–91, 157, 180, 188
Dermota, Anton, 345
The Desert Song (1930 film), 218
Deutsche Oper Berlin, 370
Deutsches Theater, Berlin, 207, 208
Deutsches Volkstheater, 164
Deutsche Zeitung (Berlin), 184
Deutsch-Jüdischer Club, Los Angeles,
    305
Deutsch-österreichische Tageszeitung
    (Dötz), 198
De Vaere (previously Devaré), Ulric,
    358, 395
Diaghilev, Sergei, 45, 386, 388
Dickens, Charles, 219
Didur, Adamo, 257
Dieterle, William (Wilhelm), 235, 264,
    341, 390
    and *Another Dawn*, 264
    and *Juarez*, 280
    K plays him off against Reinhardt,
        389
    and *Magic Fire*, 350–353, 356

and *A Midsummer Night's Dream*,
    234, 235, 236, 242
and Reinhardt's memorial concert,
    312
Dietrich, Marlene, 231
Disney, Roy, 274
Disney, Walt, 274, 285, 297, 301
Disney Studios, 287, 361
Domgraf-Fassbaender, Willi, 215
Donat, Robert, 245
Donaueschingen Festivals, 180
Don Quixote (Cervantes), 36
Dovsky, Beatrice, 137
Downes, Sir Edward, 370
Downes, Olin, 308, 330
Das Dreimäderlhaus, 211, 222
Dresden, 69, 151
Duel in the Sun (1946 film), 328
Duhan, Hans, 134, 158, 179, 183, 207,
    211, 380
Dukas, Paul, 51, 54, 55
    Ariane et Barbe-Bleue, 51, 253
Durbin, Deanna, 265, 322, 393
Duschnitz, ("Lilly") Elisabeth, 82, 340,
    341, 347, 374
Duschnitz, Rudi, 82, 120, 131, 133, 381
Duschnitz family, 125, 131, 141, 174,
    338
Dvořák, Antonin (Serenade for String
    Orchestra), 334

Eagels, Jeanne, 324
Eagle Lion Film Corporation, 394
Eckmann, Dr. (Director, Vienna State
    Opera), 268
Écorcheville, Jules, 54, 55
Eddy, Nelson, 247, 379
Edelmann, Otto, 343, 352
Edge of Darkness (1943 film), 311
Eggerth, Marta, 256, 257, 269, 307,
    328, 386
Eggerth, Tilly, 257
Eichendorff, Joseph von, 84, 107, 296
Eisler, Edwin, 44–45
Eisler, Hanns, 44
Eisner-Eisenhof, Angelo Franz von, 158
Elbogen, Paul, 27, 106, 374
Electrola Record Company, 222
Elga (Hauptmann), 337
Elizabeth the Queen (Anderson), 279
Ellis, John, 297
Elman, Mischa, 135
Elsie, Lily, 214
Emperor Franz Josef's Home for
    Widows and Orphans, 46
Enescu, Georges, 21, 373
Engelmann, Dr. Guido, 81, 82

Engelmann, "Poldi," 82
Engelmann family, 82
Entartete Kunst (degenerate art), 368
Entartete Musik (degenerate music), 23,
    344, 368
Entartete Musik (recreation of Nazi festi-
    val, 1988), 368
Epstein, Richard, 98
Erb, Karl, 112
Erwin Nyiregyhazy (Revesz), 374
Escape Me Never
    1935 British film, 322
    play (Kennedy), 322, 392
The Eternal Road (Werfel), 226
Eugen, Archduke, 54, 55
European Film Fund, 283
Everyman (proposed 1936 Reinhardt
    film), 264
"The Exemplar of My Youth"
    (Korngold), 48–51
Expressionism, 22

Fabray (Fabares), Nanette, 283, 286,
    303
Fabri, Wilhelm, 32, 36, 37
Fairbanks, Douglas Sr., 236, 365, 388
Faith in Music (Devaré; now De Vaere),
    358, 359
Fall, Leo, 205, 206, 379
    Brüderlein Fein, 211
    Die geschiedene Frau, 222
Fantasia (1940 Disney cartoon film), 287
Farrell, Eileen, 309
FBI (Federal Bureau of Investigation),
    390
Feld, Fritz, 392
Feld, Leo, 99, 378
Feldhammer, Jacob, 81, 189
Ferber, Edna, 350
Feuchtwanger, Leon, 275
Fidesser, Hans, 202–203, 387
Fiedler, Prof. Leonard, 389, 390
Film Guide (US magazine), 281
Film noir, 328
Findlay, Hal, 261
First World War
    cessation of hostilities, 129
    K's health records, 379
    K's military service, 114, 122, 124,
        129, *130*, 378
    outbreak of, 106
Fischer, Betty, 162, 211
Flagstad, Kirsten, 247
Flanders Opera, 370
Die Fledermaus (projected 1937
    Reinhardt film), 248
Flesch, Carl, 73, 91, 92, 384

Flesch, Ella, 172, 384
Flindell, Dr. E. Fred, 385
Flynn, Errol, 246, 379, 389
    and *The Adventures of Don Juan*,
        333
    and *The Adventures of Robin Hood*,
        269
    and *Another Dawn*, 264
    and *Captain Blood*, 245, 250, 252
    and *Escape Me Never*, 322, 323
    and *The Prince and the Pauper*, 264,
        265
    and *The Private Lives of Elizabeth
        and Essex*, 279, 286, 287
    and *The Sea Hawk*, 294–298
    and *William Tell* (unfinished 1953
        film), 349–350, 394
Fontaine, Joan, 306, *339*, 341
The Fool of the Family (Kennedy), 322
Forbstein, Leo, 257, 259, *295*, 389
    and *The Adventures of Robin Hood*,
        271
    and *Anthony Adverse* (incident over
        Academy Award), 265–266
    and *Escape Me Never*, 323
    as a first-class administrator, 238
    and *The Miracle* (unproduced 1938
        Reinhardt film), 278
    and the Warner orchestra, 238, 258
Ford, John, 351
Forever Amber (1947 film), 333, 394
Forrest, Dave, 243, 296
42nd Street (1933 film), 238
42nd Street Theater, New York, 308
44th Street Theater, New York, 308
Fraenkel, Alfred von, 107
Fraenkel-Ehrenstein, Luise von, 107
Fraenkel-Ehrenstein salon, 107, 108, 110
Franchetti, Alberto, 390
Franchetti, Aldo, 259
Francis, Kay, 264
Franckenstein, Baron Clemens von, 111,
    244
Frankfurter Allgemeine Zeitung, 79, 381
Frankfurter Nachrichten, 382
Frankfurt Opera, 187
Franz Ferdinand, Archduke, 99
Franz Josef, Emperor, *Der Schneemann*
    premiered on his name day, 47,
    50, 57
Fremdenblatt, 118
Freud, Sigmund, 26
Frey, Katherine, *235*
Fried, Oskar, 55
Friedell, Egon, 212
Friedhofer, Hugo, 250–253, 272, 304,
    311

Friedländer, Max, 71
Friedrich, Elizabeth, 187
Friedrich, Götz, 370
Friedrich, Karl, 343
Frind, Anni, 209
Fuchs, Anton, 111
Fuchs, Daniel, 313
Fuchs, Robert, 33
    teaches K, 33, 36, 48
    at the University of Vienna, 24
Fuehrer, Hansi (Eduard Korngold's
    wife), 24
Fürstner (music publisher), 187
Furtwängler, Wilhelm, 113, 172, 173,
    380
    American tour, 150
    and the Berlin Philharmonic, 217,
        337
    premieres the *Symphonic Serenade*,
        337, 341–342
    under attack for his supposed Nazi
        sympathies, 337

Gable, Clark, 290
Gade, Niels W., 21
Gál, Hans, 22, 157, 190, 383, 384
    incidental music to Levetzhof's *Ruth*,
        158
    Das Lied der Nacht, 197
Galen, Yvonne, 390
Gam, Rita, 355
Gannon, Kim, 323
Ganz, Dr. Hugo, 79
Ganz, Margit "Manzi," 80–82, 90, 338,
    364
Ganz, Rudolph, 77
Ganz family, 80, 82
Ganz salon, 79, 80, 82
Garbo, Greta, 231, 388
Garfield, John, 300, 313
Garmisch-Partenkirchen, Bavaria, 110,
    111, 340, 342, 356
Garmo, Tilly de, 224, 365
Gartner, Prof. Eduard, 125
Gaumont-British Film Corporation, 211
Genée, Richard, 383
Georg, Rita, 206, 211
George, Stefan, 40
George V, King, 243
George VI, King, 265
Géraldy, Paul, 175, 384
Géraldy family, 176
Gerhardt, Charles, 296, 368
German Landestheater, Prague, 48, 98
Gershwin, George, 324
Gershwin, Ira, 289
Gershwin, Mrs. Ira, 283

Gesangsverein (Vienna), 376
Gesellschaft der Musikfreunde, 97, 346
Gessner, Adrienne, 378
Geyersbach, Gertrude, 158, 206
Gibney, Sheridan, 262
Gielgud, (Sir) John, 306
Gimpel, Bronislaw, 305, 320, 330
Gimpel, Jacob, 305, 328
Gish, Lillian, 338
Glasser, Albert, 250, 391
Glazunov, Alexander, 21
Gluck, Christoph Willibald, 204
Glyndebourne Opera House, 392
Gmunden, 133, 223, 244, 339
Godlewsky, Karl, 46, 57, 58, 125
Godowsky, Leopold, 74
Goldberger, Richard (*Mondweibchen*),
    58
The Golddiggers of 1935 (film), 254
Goldmark, Karl, 31, 41–44, 375
Goldoni, Carlo, 283
Goldschmidt, Berthold, 22
Goldwyn, Samuel, 238, 251
Golschmann, Vladimir, 328, 329,
    348–349, 355
Gone With the Wind (1939 film), 275,
    295, 352
Gontard, Gert von, 283
Goossens, Eugene, 85, 306
Gordon, Paul, 322, 393
Gotham's Restaurant, Hollywood, 249
Goulding, Edmund, 392
Gozzi, Carlo, 189
Grädener, Prof. Hermann, 54, 376
Graf, Herbert, 314, 374
Graf, Max, 374
    and illegal copy of Association of
        Vienna Music Critics' letter,
        65–66, 74
    as Julius's enemy, 30, 133
    and *Der Schneemann*, 61
    takes the Korngolds to court, 65
Graffman, Gary, 166, 370
Grainger, Percy, 111
Gramophone Company, 79
Grant, Cary, 231
Graunke, Kurt, 365
Gravet, Fernand, 248, 392
Graz, anti-Semitic demonstration against
    K in, 71
The Great Depression, 214
The Great Waltz (1938 film), 248, 285,
    392
Green, Paul, 236
Greenstreet, Sydney, 310, 313
Greenwood, John, 306
Gregor, Hans, 108–113, 132, 143, 378

Griffith, D. W., 365
Griffiths, Herbert, 211
Grillparzer, Franz, 337, 338
Gropius, Manon, 138
Gropius, Walter, 138
Grosser Konzerthaus-Saal, Vienna, 186
Grosses Schauspielhaus, Berlin, 215
Grosz, Wilhelm, 22, 158, 223
Grot, Anton, 388
    and *Captain Blood*, 253
    and *Danton* (unproduced 1936
        Reinhardt film), 263
    and *Juarez*, 280
    and *A Midsummer Night's Dream*,
        234, 236
    and *The Private Lives of Elizabeth
        and Essex*, 286
    and *The Sea Hawk*, 294, 296
    and *The Sea Wolf*, 301
Groves, Sir Charles, 368
Groves, Clemence, 392
Groves, George, 243, 392
Gruber, Franz, 378
Gruenberg, Louis, 328, 334
Grünfeld, Alfred, 46, 79
Grüters, Hugo, 98
Gunga Din (1939 film of Kipling novel),
    279
Günther, Carl, 199
Gustavson, Eva, 365
Gutheil-Schoder, Marie, 58, 60
Guttmann, Arthur, 222
Gwenn, Edmund, 257, 313, 317

Haas, Joseph, 179, 385
Hafgren, Lilly, 114
Hageman, Richard, 334
Haitink, Bernard, 368
Halban, Desi, 267, 309
Hall, James, 245
Hallé Orchestra, 378
Haller, Ernest, 236, 352
Halliday, Robert, 211
Hamburg
    K's decision to leave, 152
    K's special relationship with, 113,
        136
    remains true to K, 200
    world premiere of *Die tote Stadt*,
        136, 139
Hamburg Stadt-Theater (Hamburg
    Opera), 84, 139, 146, 151, 161,
    190, 379
Hamlet (abandoned 1936 film), 233
Hamme, von (dancer at the Vienna
    Imperial Ballet), 46
Hammerstein, Oscar, 247, 248

Hampson, Thomas, 370
Handel, George Frideric, 21, 42, 215,
    319
    Zadok the Priest, 265
Hansen, Max, 215
Hanslick, Eduard
    champions Brahms, 24–25
    fight against Wagner, 382
    hears the young K perform, 29
    Julius attends his classes, 24
    Julius meets Brahms through, 24
    Julius succeeds at the *Neue Freie
        Presse*, 23, 27, 30, 360
    Julius's ally, 24–26
Harding, Bertita, 280, 351
Harlan, Otis, 235, *235*
Harline, Leigh, 297
Harris, Roy, 365
Harrold, Orville, 154, *155*
Hartmann, Georg, 151
Hartmann, Prof. Rudolf, 352, 356
Harvey, Lilian, 218
Haskin, Byron, 389
Hauer, Josef Mathias, 156, 223, 382
Hauptmann, Gerhart, 82, 337, 338
Haydn, Franz Joseph, 63, 188, 325, 359
    Cello Concerto in D Major (in the
        film *Deception*), 325, 326
    development as a young boy, 43
    re-use of musical ideas, 65
Hays Office, 245, 259
Hearst, William Randolph, 260
Heger, Robert, 198, 206, 217, 356
Heifetz, Jascha, 287, 320
    and *Much Ado About Nothing*, 135
    records the Violin Concerto in D
        Major, 349
    and Toscha Seidel, 303
    visits K at Toluca Lake, 321
    and the world premiere of the Violin
        Concerto in D Major, 329, *329*,
        330
Die Heilige (The Saint, play by
    Kaltneker), 163–164
Heindorf, Ray, 238, 251, 252, 296, 323,
    364, 389
Heine, Heinrich, 70
Henderson, W. J., 62
Henreid, Paul, 290, 305
    and *Between Two Worlds*, 313
    and *Deception*, 324–326, 393
    and *Devotion*, 310
    and *Of Human Bondage*, 317
Herbert, A. P., 213
Herbert, Evelyn, 211
Herbert, Hugh, *235*
Herbert, Victor, 247

Herrmann, Rudolf, 66
Hertzka, Alfred, 57, 58
Hertzka, Dr., 125
Herzer, Dr. Ludwig, 189, 214, 219
Herzfeld, Prof. Viktor von, 42, 375
Heuberger, Richard (*Der Opernball*), 26
Heymann, Werner Richard, 218
Hilbert, Dr. Egon, 340
Hiller, Ferdinand, 375
Hindemith, Paul, 44, 179, 190, 192, 279
    Cardillac, 197, 386
Hirschfeld, Robert, 30, 56, 65
Hitchcock, Alfred, 211
Hitler, Adolf, 271, 275, 277, 328, 367,
    392
    annexation of Austria, 212
    comes to power, 200, 222, 376, 378,
      387
    invades Austria (1938), 269, 272
    K on, 234, 271–272
Hoesslin, Walter von, 345
Hoffmann, Dr. Rudolf Stefan (K's first
    biographer), 58–59, 71–72, 78,
    154–155
Hofmannsthal, Hugo von, 69, 70, 82,
    178, 388
Holl, Dr. Karl, 381–382
Hollaender, Friedrich, 305
Hollywood
    as an international community, 231,
      293
    K's home in (Toluca Lake), 270, 274,
      275, 276
    lucrative contracts to major opera
      stars in, 246
Hollywood Bowl, 334
    K conducts a celebrity concert in
      (1935), 242
    K conducts premiere of *A Passover
      Psalm* in, 320
    K conducts US premiere of *Baby
      Serenade* in, 242, 387
    A Midsummer Night's Dream and,
      226, 232, 234
Hollywood Cemetery, 364–365
Hollywood First Baptist Church, 237
Hollywood High School, 301
Hollywood Quartet, 287
Hollywood Reporter, 266
Hollywood Spectator, 288
Hollywood Theater, New York, 282,
    298, 327
Homochord gramophone company, 176
Homolka, Oskar, 189
Honegger, Arthur, 188
Hope, Bob, 285
Hopf, Hans, 352, 356

Hopkins, Konrad, 370
Hopkins, Miriam, 283
Hornbostel, Prof. Erich von, 42, 374,
    375
Horner, James, 297
Hörth, Franz Ludwig, 174, 384
Hotel Österreichischer Hof, Salzburg, 54
Hotel Regina, Munich, 56
House Committee for Un-American
    Activities, 390
Howard, Leslie 235, 264, 313, 317, 392
Howe, James Wong, 290, 303
Hubay Quartet, 375
Huberman, Bronislaw, 215, 320–321
Hull, Mrs. Lytle, 392
Hülsen, Georg von (Intendant of Berlin
    Court Opera), 113
Humoresque (1946 film), 324
Humperdinck, Engelbert, 71, 88, 375
    Blech a pupil of, 113
    draws Loewenfeld's attention to K,
      113, 139
    on K, 42, 72
    WORKS: *Hänsel and Gretel*, 42; *The
      Miracle* (incidental music to the
      play), 278
Humperdinck, Wolfram (son of
    Engelbert), 375
Hunter, Ian, 235, 235, 243, 264
Hurok, Sol, 254
Hussa, Maria, 145, 199
Huston, John, 278, 280, 283
Huttenback, Dorothy, 365
Huxley, Aldous, 278

Ibert, Jacques, 188
IGNM (Internationale Gesellschaft für
    Neue Musik). *See* International
    Society for New Music
Im weissen Rössl. See White Horse Inn
Imhoff, Fritz, 162, 206, 211
Imperial Ballet, 46, 125
Imperial Theater, New York, 308
Impressionists, 26
Incorporated Society of Contemporary
    Music, 188
Indy, Vincent d', 56
The Informer (1935 film), 256
Ingram, Rex, 260
Internationale Gesellschaft für Neue
    Musik (IGNM). *See* International
    Society for New Music
International Society for New Music,
    179, 201
    dominates the 1923 Salzburg Festival,
      157
    makes overtures to K, 157

[International Society for New Music]
Nazis remove works from the
repertoire, 185
promotes Schoenberg and his pupils,
90
Vienna Festival (1924), 180
Irion, Herbert, 307, 309, 310
Irion, Yolanda Mero, 307–311
Isherwood, Christopher, 278
Ivogün, Maria, 112

Jackman, Fred, 240, 389
Jackson, Felix, 322, 393
Jacob, Heinrich Eduard, 219
Janáček, Leoš, 85, 195
Jannings, Emil, 231
Jaray, Hans, 311
The Jazz Singer (1927 film), 200, 237
Jealousy (1929 film), 324
Jellinek, Franz, 124
Jellinek, Hans, 81
Jellinek, Paul, 119–120
Jepson, Helen, 247
Jerger, Alfred, 162
Jeritza, Maria, 334, 360, 364
   in *La Belle Hélène*, 72
   in *Die Frau ohne Schatten*, 143
   in *Eine Nacht in Venedig*, 162, 207
   and telegram of condolence on K's
      death, 364
   in *Die tote Stadt*, 137, 144, 145, 149,
      154, *155*, 197
   in *Violanta*, 113, 124, 132, 196, 204
   and *Das Wunder der Heliane*, 192,
      193, 195, 196
Jessner, Leopold, 384
Jimmy Grier Dance Orchestra, 239
Joachim, Joseph, 42, 321
Joachim Quartet, 378
Joan of Arc (Schiller), 278
John Paul Jones (1956 film), 360
Johnson, Hall, 260, 261
Jolson, Al, 200, 237, 260
Jory, Victor, 235, *235*
Juarez and Maximilian (play by Franz
   Werfel), 280
Juch, Dr. Herman, 344

Kabasta, Oswald, 220
Kainz, Josef, 79
Kalbeck, Max, 58, 132
Kálmán, Emmerich, 174, 218, 387
Kálmán, Vera, 174
Kalter, Sabine, 199
Kaltneker, Hans, 163–164, 194, 349
   Bergwerk (The Mines), 164
   dissertation by E. Wohanka on, 383

Die Heilige (The Saint, play),
   163–164, 383–384
Die Opferung (The Sacrifice), 164
Die Schwester (The Sister), 164
Kaper, Bronislaw, 290–291
Karajan, Herbert von, 368, 386
Karczag, Lilian, 383
Karczag, William, 383
Karlsbad, 72
Karlweis, Oskar, 209, 308
Kassel Staats-Theater (Kassel Opera), 45
Kaufman, Annette, 365
Kaufman, Louis, 365
Kaufman Quartet, 365
Kaun, Bernhard, 311
Kay, Arthur, 349
Keighley, William, 272
Kennedy, Arthur, 310
Kennedy, Margaret, 304, 306, 307, 322
Kenyon, Charles, 236
Kern, Adele, 162, 187, 207, 209
Kern, Jerome, 285, *285*
Kibler, Belva, 312
Kienzl, Wilhelm, 158, 180
Kiepura, Jan, *196*, 256, *257*, 279, 301,
   386
   in *Give Us This Night*, 244, 246–249
   and *Die Kathrin*, 267, 269, 301
   in *The Merry Widow*, 307
   in *That We May Live*, 328
   in *Das Wunder der Heliane*, *196*,
      197, 201
Kierkegaard-Rothe, Amelie, 188
King Kong (1933 film), 238
The King Steps Out (1936 film), 387
Kings Row (novel by Henry Bellamann),
   303
Kinskey, Leonid, 36, 270
Kipling, Rudyard, 279
Kipnis, Alexander, 202, 387
Kittel, Hermine, 113, 145
Klamm am Semmering, 190
Kleiber, Erich, 173–174, 224, 385
Klein, Franz, 124
Kleiner Musikvereinsaal, Vienna, 223
Klemperer, Johanna, 136
Klemperer, Otto, 51, 55, 82, 136,
   139–140, 256, 264, 380
   and Berlin State Opera, 173
   and Brahms-Saal concert (1951), 346
   and Elisabeth Schumann, 113, 379
   and the Los Angeles Philharmonic,
      242, 289
   and Reinhardt's memorial concert,
      312
   and serial music, 291
   and *Die tote Stadt*, 136

and the Violin Concerto in D Major, 330–331
Eva Maria Wiesner on, 138
Klimt, Gustav, 26
Das Kloster bei Sendomir (The Monastery at Sendomir, Grillparzer), 337
Knappertsbusch, Hans, 185, 386
Knöpfelmacher, Professor, 268–269
Knorr, Thomas, 44
Knowles, Patric, 317
Knox, Alexander, 300
Koch, Howard, 296
Koehler, Ted, 323
Koenekamp, H. F., 389
Koetsier, Jan, 355
Kohner, Robert, 268, 269
Kokoschka, Oskar, 80
Kolisch, Maria ("Mitzi"), 81, *90*, 120, 291
Kolisch, Dr. Rudolf, 81
Kolisch, Rudolf (son of the above), 72, 81, *90*, 134, 338, 380
Kolisch, Gertrud ("Trudi") (later Schoenberg's second wife), 81, 120, 291
Kolisch Quartet, 81, 188, 380
Kölnische Zeitung, 140
Kolodin, Irving, 330
Komische Oper, Berlin, 110
Komperz-Bettelheim, Karoline von, 32
Konetzni, Hilde, 262
Der Kongress tanzt (The Congress Dances, 1931 film), 218
Korda, Sir Alexander, 233
Korjus, Miliza, 247, 285
Kornauth, Eduard (Egon), 158, 223
Korngold, Eduard (Kornau; Julius's half-brother), 24, 211, 373
Korngold, Ernst Werner (K's elder son, 1925–1996), 7, 190, 227, 257, 259, 359–360, 375, 393
birth, 187
and *The Constant Nymph*, 304–305
and *Juarez*, 282
and *Das Kloster bei Sendomir*, 338
on K's friendship with James Wong Howe, 290
on K's friendship with Schoenberg, 291
passion for Shakespeare, 334
stays in Austria with grandmother, 268, 271
taken to America (1935), 247
teaching career, 334
Korngold, Gary (K's grandson), 377

Korngold, Georg (later George; K's younger son, 1928–1987), *257*, 359, 364
and the *Baby Serenade*, 205
and *Between Two Worlds*, 314
birth, 205
and copies of his father's recordings, 391
and *Deception*, 327
employed at the Disney Studio, 361
and *Escape Me Never*, 323
friendship with Schoenberg's daughter, 291
and his parents' wedding, 384
Intermezzo (Piano Sonata No. 3) written for, 213
on K being given a Richard Strauss manuscript, 342–343
and *Kings Row*, 304–305
as K's secretary and chauffeur, 338
and K's work on *Gunga Din*, 279
and K's writing of score to *The Adventures of Robin Hood*, 272
and *Magic Fire*, 351–356
and Mahler resignation letter silver casket, 377
and Bronislawa Nijinska, 389
and *Of Human Bondage*, 317–318
produces a major new recording of K's music (1972), 368
and *The Sea Hawk*, 296
taken to America, 247, 260, 268–269
Helen Thimig episode, 312
Korngold, Hanns Robert (K's brother), 28, 272, 274, 374
birth, 27
as the "black sheep" of the family, 27
death (1964), 366
K appears on the same bill with, 211
leads own jazz band, 211
relationship with K, 27
travels to America (1938), 269, 273, 284
Korngold, Helen (K's daughter-in-law), 359, 360
Korngold, Kathrin ("Katy"; K's granddaughter), 359
Korngold, Monika (K's daughter-in-law), 359
Korngold, Simon (K's paternal grandfather), 24
Korngold's musical language and style
altered diminished sevenths, 77
augmented triads, 85, 104
character delineation in stage and film works, 36, 39, 40
chromaticism, 32, 78, 104, 165, 319

[Korngold's musical language and style]
  color, sense of instrumental, 45, 78,
    85, 134, 140, 281, 314, 336
  "delayed resolution" in harmonic
    progressions, 49, 51
  form, 43, 45, 69
  harmony, 21, 23, 28, 29, 31, 33, 36,
    38, 43–45, 49–51, 55, 63–65, 76,
    88–92, 102–104, 106–108, 122,
    140, 153, 154, 157, 165,
    194–195, 300, 329, 336
  jazz influence, 220, 344
  Korngold "sweep," 85
  leitmotifs for characters in films, 243
  melody and melodic style, 21, 23, 28,
    45, 102, 122, 157, 371
  "Motto of the Cheerful Heart" (K's
    motto theme), 85, 86, 102, 124,
    134, 172, 257, 377
  orchestral style, 78, 122, 123,
    148–149, 194
  pioneers the symphonic film score,
    228, 252, 254
  rhythm, 21, 23, 60, 63, 102, 103,
    117, 134, 194, 326
  rising fourths, 51, 85, 300
  skill for variation in early music, 39
  tonality, 23, 50–51, 123, 165, 194,
    195, 326, 336, 347
  use of the vibraphone, 252, 253, 389
  "Violanta chord," 104, 378
Korngold Society, 370
Korngold's works
  CHAMBER AND INSTRUMENTAL
  Andantino in A Major (unpub.), 33
  *Don Quixote: Six Characteristic
    Pieces* for Piano, 36, 38, 41, 42,
    54, 55
  Fugue for String Quartet (unpub.), 54
  Geschichten von Strauss (Tales from
    Strauss), 163
  Melodie, Opus 1 (sic., unpub.), 31
  Melodie, Opus 2 (sic., unpub.), 31
  "Moderne Sonata" for piano (1907,
    unpub.), 33
  Much Ado About Nothing, Opus 11
    (chamber version), 134, 135, 146,
    158, 303, 365
  Piano Quintet in E Major, 92, 152,
    158, 167, 179, 188, 383
  Piano Sonata No. 1 in D Minor,
    38–41, 43, 49, 54, 89, 345
  Piano Sonata No. 2 in E Major, 38,
    51–53, 56, 69, 72–74, 76, 77, 88,
    89, 91, 131, 132, 188

Piano Sonata No. 3 in C Major, 24,
    163, 213, 220, 267, 268, 345,
    365
  Piano Trio in D Major, 51, 52, 54,
    62–65, 64, 68–71, 76, 77, 79, 89,
    132, 378
  Romance-Impromptu for Cello and
    Piano, 325
  "Rondando" for piano (unpub.), 33
  Scherzando for piano (unpub.), 33
  Sextet for Strings in D Major, 106,
    110, 124, 132, 153, 159, 171,
    172
  Sieben Märchenbilder (Seven Fairy
    Tale Pictures), 39, 50, 52, 53, 55,
    69, 77, 79, 89, 99, 102, 125, 345,
    377
  Sonata in G Major for violin and
    piano, 73, 91–93, 98, 107
  String Quartet No. 1 in A Major,
    141, *147,* 152, 165, 171–172,
    188, 380
  String Quartet No. 2 in E-flat Major,
    267
  String Quartet No. 3 in D Major,
    319–320, 339, 346, 365
  Suite for Two Violins, Cello and
    Piano, 163, 205, 211, 241, 336
  Theme with Three Variations for
    Piano, 33
  "Valse Charmante" for piano Nos. 3
    and 6 (unpub.), 33
  Vier kleine fröhliche Walzer (Four
    Little Happy Waltzes), 81
  Vier kleine Karikaturen für Kinder
    (Four Little Caricatures for
    Children), 190
  "Waltz for Luzi" for piano in the
    style of Chopin (unpub.), 334
  Waltzes for piano (1907, unpub.), 33
  FILM SCORES
  The Adventures of Robin Hood, 250,
    265, 266, 268–273, 277, 278,
    279, 285, *285,* 297, 314, 379,
    380, 389, 390
  Another Dawn, 264, 320
  Anthony Adverse, 256–259, 263,
    265–266, 271, 285, 336, 347,
    389, 390
  Between Two Worlds, 313–314, 319
  Captain Blood, 245, 246, 248–250,
    252–254, 256, 258, 271, 294,
    297, 336, 347, 379, 390
  The Constant Nymph, 304–307, 311
  Deception, 324–328, 352, 354
  Devotion, 310–311, 320, 334, 352

A Dream Comes True (short subject), 244, 255
Escape Me Never, 312, 322–323, 323, 349
Give Us This Night, 247–250, 256, 257, 259, 386
The Green Pastures, 260
Hearts Divided, 260
Juarez, 279–282, 284, 334, 390
Kings Row, 297, 303–306, 348
Magic Fire, 350–356, 350, 353, 355, 360
A Midsummer Night's Dream, 227, 228, 234–237, 233, 235, 236, 239–243, 245, 246, 248, 250, 254–256, 271, 281, 297, 312, 331, 390
Of Human Bondage, 314, 317–318
The Prince and the Pauper, 264–265, 271, 390
The Private Lives of Elizabeth and Essex, 250, 279, 281, 285–288, 295, 296, 326, 334, 347, 379
Rose of the Rancho, 249–251
The Sea Hawk, 253, 254, 260, 263, 294–299, 301, 334, 368, 379, 390–392
The Sea Wolf, 165, 299–301, 319
OPERAS
Die Kathrin, 221, 226, 227, 244, 246, 247, 262, 266–269, 273–275, 293–294, 294, 302, 309, 340–345, 355, 374, 376, 384
Der Ring des Polykrates, 45, 63, 84, 98–102, 109–114, 125, 130, 132–133, 206, 224, 302, 379, 382, 385
Die tote Stadt, 44, 113, 120–124, 129–131, 133–139, 135, 142, 144–154, 144, 155, 158–161, 164, 165, 172–174, 178, 181–182, 185, 191–193, 196, 197, 199–202, 206, 206, 242, 243, 262, 281, 302, 305, 307, 328, 338, 340, 342, 344, 345, 356, 357, 360, 365, 369, 370, 379, 380, 387, 392
Violanta, 51, 85, 101, 102–105, 106, 109–114, 118, 119,   123–125, 130–134, 145, 148, 154, 168, 184, 188, 193, 204, 206, 217, 281, 302, 307, 338, 340, 345, 374
Das Wunder der Heliane, 23, 50–51, 123, 145, 163–164, 172, 179, 187, 189–200, 194, 196, 201–203, 204, 216, 218, 302,

313, 314, 338, 344, 368, 380, 386
OPERETTA ARRANGEMENTS
Cagliostro in Wien, 189, 349
Die Fledermaus, 207–209, 212, 215, 219, 224–226, 267, 307–308
Die geschiedene Frau, 222, 223
The Great Waltz (US version of *Walzer aus Wien*), 211, 349
Helen Goes to Troy (US version of *La Belle Hélène*), 314
Das Lied der Liebe, 214, 219, 223, 341
Eine Nacht in Venedig, 162, 165, 172, 187, 189, 207, 209, 224, 380, 383, 385
Rosalinda (US version of *Die Fledermaus*), 307–309, 309, 311, 331–332, 359–360
Rosen aus Florida, 205–206, 209, 341
Die schöne Helena (*La Belle Hélène*; *Helen* in the London production), 212–215, 212, 218, 224, 267, 309–311, 314
Walzer aus Wien (*Waltzes from Vienna* in London; *Valses de Vienne* in Paris; *The Great Waltz* in New York), 209–210, 211, 222, 349
ORCHESTRAL
Baby Serenade, 163, 205, 220–221, 242
Cello Concerto in C Major, 326, 338, 341
"Dance in Old Style" for small orchestra (unpub.), 380
Military March in B, 114
Much Ado About Nothing (orchestral suite from incidental music for the play), 134–135, 154, 159, 167–163, 172, 188, 220, 277, 303
A Passover Psalm, 301, 320, 346
Piano Concerto in C-sharp, 165–165, 172, 177–178, 204, 336, 347
Schauspiel Ouvertüre (Overture to a Play), 53–54, 58, 70–72, 76–79, 84, 87, 130, 188, 242, 277, 378
Scherzo in B Minor (arrangement of Mendelssohn piano work, unpub.), 380
Sieben Märchenbilder (Seven Fairy Picture Tales, orchestral version, unpub.), 50, 72, 374, 376

[Korngold's orchestral works]
Sinfonietta in B Major, 72, 79,
84–85, *86,* 91, 93, 97–99, 101,
103, 119, 124, 133, 134,
167–168, 172, 257, 369, 371, 376
Straussiana for Orchestra, 349
Der Sturm (unpub.), 70
Sursum Corda, 133–134, 146, 151,
159, 168, 269, 272, 273, 380
Symphonic Serenade in B-flat major
for string orchestra, 84, *335–337,*
339, 341–342, 359, 364
Symphony in F-sharp, 332, 334,
346–348, 350, 354–355,
357–359, 369, 371
Symphony No. 2 (incomplete and
unpub.), 361, *361*
Theme and Variations for Orchestra,
349
Tomorrow, tone poem for mezzo
soprano, women's chorus and
orchestra, 304, 306–307
Violin Concerto in D Major, 84, 92,
264–265, 281, 320–321, 328,
329–331, 349, 369
OTHER DRAMATIC
At Your Service, 283
Der Vampyr (incidental music for the
play by Müller, unpub.), 164, 384
Gold (cantata, ms. lost), 32, 33, 44
Much Ado About Nothing (incidental
music for the play), 125,
129–130, 150, 213, 303, 320
"Die Nixe" (fragment of a one-act
cantata, unpub.), 32
Der Schneemann (The Snowman,
ballet-pantomime), 32, 39–51,
53–62, *57,* 59, 68, 72, 77, 79,
87–88, 93, 98, 110, 113, 119,
125, 139–140, 189, 217–218,
377, 380
Die stumme Serenade (The Silent
Serenade), 302, 321–322, 328,
341, 345–347, 355, 376
Der Tod (cantata, unpub.), 36, *37*
OTHER WORKS
Kaiserin Zita-Hymne, 115, 116, 286,
376
Prayer, 301
SONGS
Drei Lieder, Opus 18, 189, 386
Drei Lieder, Opus 22, 223, 224
Four Shakespearean Lieder, 301, 312
Fünf Lieder, Opus 38, 296, 334
"Die Gansleber im Hause Duschnitz"
(The Gooseliver in the Duschnitz
House, unpub.), 133

"Kleiner Wunsch" (A Little Wish,
unpub.), 33
Narrenlieder (Songs of the Clown,
from "Twelfth Night"), 287, 296,
303, 339
Sechs Einfache Lieder (Six Simple
Songs), 81, 84, 92, 107–108, 130,
141, 172, 242, 296
"Sonett für Wien," 349, 354
Twelve Songs (1911, unpub.), 84
Unvergänglichkeit (The Eternal),
223–224, 267
Vier Lieder des Abschieds (Four
Songs of Farewell), 51, 129,
140–141, 152–153, 158,
166–167, 186, 188, 224
Kortner, Fritz, 305
Koshetz, Nina, 283
Koussevitsky, Serge, 261
Kralik, Heinrich, 145, 202, 340, 345
Kram, Dr. David, 378
Kraus, Karl, 150
Krauss, Clemens, 187, 219, 247, 385
Julius on Krauss regime at the Vienna
State Opera, 217
values K's work, 217
Krein, Grigory, 373
Krein, Julian Grigorievich, 373
Kreisler, Fritz, 135, 219, 365
Křenek, Ernst, 180, 201, 204
antipathy toward K, 44
Jonny spielt auf, 196–199,
203–204, 216, 344, 368
Krenn, Franz, 24
Kretzschmar, Hermann, 42
Krips, Josef, 365
Krise, Teddy, 238–239, 391
Krüger, Emmy, 112
Kubie, Dr. Lawrence S. (correspondence
with Luzi), 362–363
Künneke, Eduard, 219
Kunstpreis der Stadt Wien (Arts Prize of
the City of Vienna), 190
Kupper, Annelies, 352
Kurkapelle, Karlsbad, 72
Kurz, Selma, 108, 113
Kutzschbach, Hermann, 98, 382

La Jana, 213
Lachmann, Mrs. Erich, 365
Lafite, Karl (*Die Stunde*), 378
Lamm, Emil, 29
Lamour, Dorothy, 274
Landro (Korngold family's summer resi-
dence), 33, 70
Lang, Fritz, 231
Langer, Otto, 162, 206

Laughton, Charles, 235, 248
Lawrence, Gertrude, 215, 311
Laye, Evelyn, 214
Le Havre, 269
Lederer, Fritz, 98
Legrand, Maurice, 218
Lehár, Franz, 214, 218, 374
    Giuditta, 268
    The Merry Widow, 307
Lehmann, Lotte, 108, 130, 132, 174,
    182–183, 186–196, 197,
    201–202, 217, 248, 364–365, 384
Leichtentritt, Hugo, 42, 375
Leider, Frieda, 380
Leigh, Vivien, 214
Leinsdorf, Erich, 308
Leipzig Conservatory, 42
Leipzig Gewandhaus Orchestra, 172,
    386
    world premiere of the *Schauspiel*
      Ouvertüre, 77, 78
Lempicka, Tamara di, 82
Lendval, Erwin, 338
Léon, Victor, 222
Leontovitch, Eugenie, 324
Leopold of Prussia, Prince, 113
LeRoy, Mervyn, 258
Leschetizky, Theodor, 54, 74
Lessing Theater, Berlin, 121
Lessmann, Otto, 42, 375
Lester, Edwin, 331, 349, 359, 365
Leux, Leo, 219
Levant, Oscar, 289
Levetzhof (*Ruth*), 158
Levinson, Nathan, 314
Lewandowsky, Dr. Herman, 348
Library of Congress, Washington, D.C.,
    31, 274, 347
Liebstöckl, Hans, 180, 202
Lion, Karl, 150, 182, 184
"La Lirodou," 340–341
Liszt, Ferencz, 21, 166, 352
    Prometheus, 250–251
Little Dorrit (Dickens), 219
Loewenfeld, Dr. Hans, 113, 135–139,
    145–146, 151–152, 377, 380
Loewenfeld, Magda, 381
London, Jack, 299–300
London Daily News, 65
London Daily Telegraph, 98, 214
London Musical Times, 171, 373, 377
London Promenade Concerts, 87
Lorre, Peter, 306
Los Angeles Civic Light Opera
    Company, 331
Los Angeles Daily News, 232
Los Angeles Festival Orchestra, 337

Los Angeles Philharmonic Auditorium,
    332
Los Angeles Philharmonic Orchestra,
    289, 320, 327, 349, 365
Los Angeles Times, 283
Losch, Tilly, 312
Lothar, Ernst (née Ernst Lothar Müller,
    brother of Hans Müller), 30, 378
Lothar, Rudolf, 321
Louise, Anita, 235, 235, 237
Love, Montagu. 306
Löwe, Ferdinand, 54, 98
Löwy, Gertrud, 79–82
Lubin, Germaine, 175, 384
Lubitsch, Ernst. 231–232, 244,
    246–247, 256, 279, 311, 388
Ludwig, Prince of Bavaria, 56
Lugosi, Bela, 328
Lukather, Lee, 353
Lupino, Ida, 300, 310, 322

Mabee, Mariane, 242
MacKenzie, Aeneas, 280
Maeterlinck, Maurice, 102
The Magic Box (1947 film), 324
Magnani, Anna, 341
Magnus, Hélène, 375
Mahler, Alma (née Schindler; Mahler's
    wife; later Werfel), 35, 80, 138,
    175, 275, 293, 334, 364, 369,
    374, 377
Mahler, Anna, 374
    bust of K, 374
Mahler, Gustav, 49, 80, 98, 108, 123,
    139, 141, 153, 238, 251, 274,
    319, 348, 357, 359, 382
    anti-Semitism against, 71–72
    death, 82–83
    first public figure to recognize K's
      gifts, 34, 83
    as a pupil of Fuchs, 33
    and Marie Gutheil-Schoder, 80
    influences K, 22, 55, 65, 336
    and Julius, 26, 33–34, 56, 82–83
    on K, 41
    K compared to, 354
    and the late romantic tradition,
      367–368
    and rediscovery of K, 366, 368
    revival, 367–368
    and serialism, 157
    Specht's book, 376
    supports K, 35, 39, 63
    suppression of his music, 23
    symphonies, K on, 329
    use of his Lieder, 92

[Mahler, Gustav]
and Vienna Court Opera, 26, 33–35,
41, 56, 377
WORKS: *Kindertotenlieder*, 97, 134;
Das Lied von der Erde, 141, 154;
Symphony No. 2 in C Minor,
312; Symphony No. 4 in G
Major, 153; Symphony No. 5,
108; Symphony No. 7 in B Minor,
265, 390; Symphony No. 8 in E-
flat Major, 44, 55, 334;
Symphony No. 10 in F-sharp
Major, 347, 385
and Zemlinsky, 34–36, 48, 51
The Maid from Aachen (Heinrich
Eduard Jacob), 219
Maikl, Georg, 145
Mairecker-Buxbaum Quartet, 383
Malatesta, Marta, 77
Malcuzynski, Witold, 325
Manchester, regional preview of *Helen*,
214
Mandyczewski, Eusebius, 375
Mann, Heinrich, 275, 311
Mann, Thomas, 55, 275, 289, 311–312
Mannheim, Lucie, 222
Mannheim school, 28
Manzer, Robert, 72
Marcel, Lucille, 56
March, Frederic, 259, 324
Mareczek (also spelt Maretzek), Max
(*Hamlet* - opera), 24
Margulies, Adele, 376
Margulies Trio, 62
Marischka, Ernst, 209, *210*, 383
Marischka, Hubert, 162, 172, 205–207,
209, 211, 383
Marischka brothers, 219, 376
Marlowe, Christopher, 286–287, 296
Marshall, Brenda, 295–296
Marshall, Herbert, 214, 231
Marx, Joseph, 158, 180, 331, 360
Mary, Queen, 243
Mascagni, Pietro
Cavalleria Rusticana, 184
Iris, 226
Masetti, Enzo, 394
Massary, Fritzi, 000
Massenet, Jules, 54
Thaïs, 290
Massine, Leonid, 213, 234, 314
Maté, Rudolph, 283
Matthias, Adolf, Dr., 381
Matthews, Jessie, 211
Mauceri, John, 370
Mauch, Billy, 264–265
Mauch, Bobby, 264–265

Maugham, W. Somerset, 314, 317
Mauke, Wilhelm, 137
Mautner, Jenny, 79
Max Reinhardt Studio for Stage, Film,
and Radio (Hollywood), aka The
Max Reinhardt Workshop,
282–284, 286–287, 299, 303, 321
Maxwell, Elsa, 289, 338
Mayerling (Anet), 387
Mayr, Richard, 145
McCall, Mary, 236
McDonald, Jeanette, 247, 290, 311, 379
McEwen, Walter, 271
McHugh, Frank, *235*
Meehan, John Jr., 308
Mehta, Zubin, 370
Meihuizen, J., *206*
Melchior, Lauritz, 246
Melichar, Alois, 352, 355
Melton, James, 247
Mendel, Charles (later Lord), 214, 338
Mendel, Elsie (later Lady), 214, 338
Mendelssohn-Bartholdy, Felix, 21, 28,
63, 234, 359
incidental music to *A Midsummer
Night's Dream*, 28, 87, 227, 234,
239–241, 243, 255
Scherzo in B Minor (orchestral
arrangement by K, unpub.), 380
Songs Without Words, 239, 255
Symphony No. 3 ("Scottish"), 239
Violin Concerto in E Minor, 330
Menjou, Adolphe, 214
Menuhin, Yehudi, 373
Menzies, William Cameron, 303
Merivale, Philip, 249
Der Merker (musical magazine), 62–64,
65
Messalina (planned opera by Korngold),
382
Messel, Oliver, 213–214, 255,
262–263
Messiaen, Olivier, *Turangalîla-
Symphonie*, 347
Metro-Goldwyn-Mayer (MGM),
232–233, 237, 245, 247, 255,
258–259, 285, 287, 290
screen adaptations of major literary
classics, 233–234
Metropolitan Opera, New York, 161,
192, 248, 267, 307, 379, 387
Metzger-Lattermann, Ottilie, 199
Meyerbeer, Giacomo
The Huguenots, 181
Robert le Diable, 122
A Midsummer Night's Dream
(Shakespeare), 28

See also under Korngold's works;
  Mendelssohn-Bartholdy, Felix;
  Reinhardt, Max
Milhaud, Darius, 310, 365
Miller, Seton, 296
Millöcker, Karl, 214
Milstein, Nathan, 244
The Miracle
  1912 film, 388, 278
  1912 stage production, 278
  1938 film (unproduced), 266–267,
    277–278, 388
  play by Karl Vollmoeller, 187, 232,
    266
Le Mirage (stage version of *Bruges la
  Mort* by Rodenbach), 121
Mitropoulos, Dimitri, 357–358
Mladova, Milada, 323, *323*
Mohr, Hal, 236, 256
Molinari, Bernardino, 167
Molnar, Ferenc, 311
Mona Vanna (Maeterlinck), 102
Monsieur Lamberthier (Verneuil), 324
Montemezzi, Italo, 334
Montenuovo, Prince, 56–57
Monteux, Pierre, 188, 386
Monteverdi, Claudio, *Orfeo*, 259
Moore, Grace, 246, 248, 310, 387
Moore, Roger, 278
Moralt, Rudolf, 344
Moser, Hans, 189, 206, 213
Mosheim, Grete, 215, 311
Motion Picture Herald, 256, 264
Mowbray, Alan, 248
Mozart, Leopold, 27, 31, 69, 134, 277
Mozart, Wolfgang Amadeus, 27, 43,
    120, 160, 214, 267, 277, 357,
    359, 387
  as a child prodigy, 21–22, 28, 69, 87,
    89
  WORKS: *Don Giovanni*, 22, 29; *La
    Finta Giardiniera*, 22; *Eine Kleine
    Nachtmusik*, 380; *The Marriage
    of Figaro*, 51, 55, 69; Violin
    Concerto No. 5, 51, 55, 69
Mozarteum, Salzburg, 189
Mozart-Saal, Vienna, 267
Muck, Karl, 72, 98
Muir, Jean, *235*, 242
Müller-Einigen, Hans (known as Hans
  Müller, brother of Ernst Lothar),
    194, 378
  contributes to *Brünner Montags-
    Zeitung*, 24
  contributes to the libretto of *Die tote
    Stadt*, 121, 164

  contributes to the *Neue Freie Presse*,
    30, 102
  encourages K to get away from
    one-act operas, 121
  and K's first invitation to work in
    films, 213
  K's last meeting with (1949), 338
  libretto for *Violanta*, 102
  libretto for *Das Wunder der Heliane*,
    164
  text for *Sieben Märchenbilder*, 69,
    102
  and *Der Vampyr*, 164
Multiple tracking (motion picture
  soundtracks), 238
Munch, Charles, 357
Münchow, Anny, 136
Muni, Paul, 263–264, 279–280, 283,
    290
Munich, premieres of K's first two
  operas, 111–113
Munich Court Opera, 111
Munich Philharmonic Orchestra, 355
Municipal Music and Theater Festival,
  Vienna 177, 182, 211
Munsch, Hermann, 179
The Musical Courier, 98
The Musical Times, 171, 373, 377
Mussolini, Benito, 82
Mussorgsky, Modest Petrovich, 32
Mutiny on the Bounty (1935 film), 245,
    256
My Mistress' Eyes (Shakespeare sonnet,
  set by K), 334

Napier, Diana (later Mrs. Richard
  Tauber), 268
Nascimbene, Mario, 394
The Nation (magazine), 87
National Federation of Music Clubs of
  America, 301
National Film Archive, London, 307
National Philharmonic Orchestra, 368
National Socialism (Nazism)
  Blech and, 72
  confiscation of K 's property,
    273–274
  congress in Nürnberg (1926), 191
  controls every aspect of German
    commercial and artistic life, 376
  demonstration at *Die tote Stadt*
    production, 238
  and *Entartete Musik/Kunst* exhibi-
    tions (1937–1938), 23, 368
  invasion of Austria (1938), *83*
  and *Jonny spielt auf*, 198–199, 203

[National Socialism]
  K ceases conducting his own works in
    Germany because of, 227
  K first touched by the spread of Nazi
    influence in the arts, 262
  and K's composing absolute music,
    277
  K's home broken into (1938), 82
  post-war need to expiate the sins of
    the Nazi period, 368
  removal of K's works from the reper-
    toire, 185, 247
National Theater of Prague, 72
Naughty Marietta (1935 film), 247
Nazism. *See* National Socialism
Nedbal, Oskar, 54, 72
Negri, Pola, 388
Nemeth, Maria, 153, 211
Neue Freie Presse, 41, 46, 69, 74, 111,
    118, 133, 140–141, 150
  anti-Křenek articles, 198
  anti-Richard Strauss feeling in, 167
  Auernheimer succeeds Benedikt, 321
  Decsey article on K, 46
  Ganz writes for, 79
  Hanslick as chief music critic, 23, 26
  and *Jonny spielt auf*, 198, 204
  Julius becomes chief music critic,
    23–24, 27, 30
  Julius revolutionizes the musical out-
    look of, 30
  Julius's obituary on Mahler, 82–83
  Julius supports Mahler in, 33
  Hans Müller contributes to, 30, 102
  Puccini on K, 158
  reviews premiere of *Der Schneemann*,
    59–60
  Rosenthal's case settled out of court,
    74
  and *Die tote Stadt*, 181–182
  vain attempt to defuse Korngold-
    Křenek wrangle, 204
  as Vienna's leading newspaper, 26
Neue Musikfesthalle, Munich, 55
Neue Sachlichkeit (New Realism), 149,
    328
Neues Deutsche Theater, Prague, 113
Neues Wiener Journal, 145, 189
Neues Wiener Tagblatt, 30, 163, 193,
    202, 211, 267
Neue und Zeit Musik (Music for Our
    Time), 180, 382
Neue Wiener Schule (New Viennese
    School), 44, 91, 382
Neutra, Dione, 289, 381
Neutra, Richard, 82, 140–141, 289

New Opera Company (New York), 307,
    309, 392
New Viennese School. *See* Neue Wiener
    Schule
New York, *Die tote Stadt* premiered in,
    153–154, 161
New York Philharmonic Orchestra, 98,
    159, 312
The New York Sun, 62, 330
The New York Times, 282, 308, 314,
    330
Newman, Alfred, 238, 259, 279, 297
Newman, Ernest, 87–91, 377
Newman, Lionel, 365
Nichols, Lewis, 314
Nicholson, Robert, 309
Nijinska, Bronislava, 234, *236*, 240, 388
Nikisch, Arthur, 42, 71, 97–99,
    138–139, 374–375, 380, 386
  American tour, 150
  as a close friend of K, 78, 146
  death, 147, 172
  and Louise Wolff, 71
  world premiere of the *Schauspiel
    Ouvertüre*, 77–78
Nikisch, Micha, 77
Nilius, Rudolf, 158, 186, 380
Nilson, Einar, 278
Noble, Dennis, 383
Nohain-Franc, 218
Nordhoff, Charles, 245
Northern Pursuit (1943 film), 311
Nossal, Lenore ("Lori"), 276
Nossal, Robert, 381
Novello, Ivor, 214, 306
Novotná, Jarmila, 213, 215, 224–225,
    248, 262, 267–268, 309, 311, 314
Now Voyager (1942 film), 323
Nürnberg, 191
Nyiregyhazy, Erwin, 28, 374

Obolensky, Prince, 214
Obsession (play by Verneuil), 324
Occidental College, Pasadena, 283
Ochs, Siegfried, 71
Oestvig-Aargard, Karl, 143–145, 183
Offenbach, Jacques
  La Belle Hélène, 72, 187, 212–215,
    218, 224, 267, 309–11, 314
  La Vie parisienne, 207, 264
Of Human Bondage (story by
    Maugham), 314
Okie, William, 321
Olczewska, Maria, 153, 183
Olivier, Laurence (later Lord), 215, 233,
    235, 286
One Arabian Night (1920 film), 388

100 Men and a Girl (1937 film), 265
One Night of Love (1934 film), 246
Oppenheim, Harold von, 222, 387
ORF (Österreichischer Rundfunk:
    Austrian Radio), 339–340, 350,
    354
Ormandy, Eugene, 308, 334
Orry-Kelly, 286
O'Sullivan, Joseph, 256
Othello (Shakespeare), 303
Otter, Anne Sofie von, 370
Ouspenskaya, Maria, 304
Outward Bound (1930 film), 313
Outward Bound (play, Vane), 313

Paalen, Bella, 175
Paganini, Niccolò, 324, 329
Pahlen, Richard, 46
Palestine Emergency Fund, 328
Pallenberg, Max, 189, 215
Palson-Wettergren, Gertrude, *294*
Paramount Pictures, 244, 247–248, 251,
    257, 259, 279, 388
Parker, Eleanor, 313, 317, 322
Pataky, Koloman von, 162, 198, 211,
    267, 269
Patti, Adelina, 373
Patzak, Julius, 339
Paumgartner, Bernhard, 158, 190, 386
Pearl Harbor, 305
Peltenburg, Mia, 188
Penn, Heinrich, 24
Peruter (official at Ministry of
    Education), 220
Pešek, Libor, 370
Pester Lloyd (Budapest journal), 46
Petrie, Hay, 214
Pfitzner, Hans, 137, 174
    Christelflein, 146
    Palestrina, 387
Pfohl, Ferdinand, 42, 145, 199–200,
    202, 375
The Phantom Crown (Harding), 280
Philadelphia Opera Company, 379
Philadelphia Orchestra, 373
Philipps-Duca piano roll company, 77
Piccaver, Alfred, 80, 113, 132, 202
Piccini, Niccolò, 204
Pickford, Mary, 236
Pinocchio (1940 Disney cartoon film),
    297, 301
Pirchan, Emil, 174, 384
Poe, Edgar Allan, 275
Polk, Rudi, 320
Pollak, Annie, 138

Pollak, Egon, 71, 77, 110, 136,
    138–139, 153, 176, 190, *194*,
    199, 380. 382
Pollak, Karl (son of Egon), 386
Pollak, Robert, 158, 172, 175–176, 333
Pommer, Erich, 218
Pons, Lily, 246
Ponselle, Rosa, 248
Poulenc, Francis, 85
Powell, Dick, 232, *235*, 254, 260
Prague
    K reunites with Zemlinsky in, 72
    Zemlinsky moves to, 48, 50
Prawy, Dr. Marcel, 344, 345, 385, 387
Preger, Dr. Mixsa, 222
Previn, André, 370
Price, Vincent, 286
Priestley, J. B.. 214
The Prince and the Pauper (novel by
    Mark Twain), 264, 265
Prinz, LeRoy, 323, *323*
Prinzregententheater (Munich), 356
Pro Arte Quartet, 380
Production Code for film censorship
    (1934), 245
Prokofiev, Sergei, 166, 319, 384
Puccini, Giacomo, 39, 40, 274, 304, 379
    and K, 148–149, 158, 168, 341, 381
    WORKS; *La Fanciulla del West*, 158;
        Gianni Schicci, 387; *Madam
        Butterfly*, 158; *Manon Lescaut*,
        381; *La Rondine*, 148, 222, 344;
        Tosca, 148; *Turandot*, 149,
        189–190, 197
Puritz, Walther, 379

Raab, Leond, 311
Rabinowitz, Max, 283, 306
Rachmaninov, Sergei Vassilievich, 166,
    371
    Symphony No. 2 in E Minor, 336
Rachold, Bernd O., 370
Radio Vierna, 345
Radio WQXR (New York), 309
Rainer, Luise, 189
Rains, Claude, 231, 295, 324–325, 327,
    354
Rajdl, Maria, 145, 207, 209, 222, 224
Raksin, David, 394
Rank, (Lord) J. Arthur, 322, 393
Raphaelson, Samson, 278, 283
Rapper, Irving, 326
Rathbone, Basil, 231, 250, 273, 283,
    289, 324
Ravel, Maurice, 166, 175, 188, 218,
    324, 384

RCA Victor Recording Co., 303, 318, 349, 368
Reagan, Ronald, 303
Rebay, Prof. Ferdinand, 268
Rebner-Quartet, 76
Reculard, Jean, 338
Ree, Max, 234, 388
Regeniter, Arthur, 140
Reger, Max, 31, 91, 385
Reich, Willi, 180–181
Reichert, Ellen, 208, 365–366
Reichert, Heinz, 208–209, *210*, 222
Reichstag fire (1933), fiftieth anniversary exhibition, 368, 370
Reichwein, Leopold, 113
Reiner, Fritz, 357
Reinhardt, Gottfried, 262, 308, 311, 314
Reinhardt, Max, 79, 119, 246, 248, 255–256, 265, 270, 298, 303, 378
  and *La Belle Hélène*, 72, *212*, 212–215, 218, 309–310
  and *Danton* (unproduced 1936 film), 262–263
  death, 312, 314
  and William Dieterle, 234, 389
  establishes his Workshop (Studio) in Hollywood, 282–284
  Die Fledermaus collaboration with K, 207–209, 215, 219, 224–226, 267
  influence wanes, 278
  and Jack Warner, 226, 232, 234
  K in conflict with, 224
  K meets, 56
  K turns down *Turandot* offer, 189–190
  and Eduard Kornau's forty years on stage celebration, 211
  and *A Midsummer Night's Dream* (play), 226, 232
  and *A Midsummer Night's Dream* (film), 227, 232, 234, *233*, *235*, *236*, 240, 242–244, 246, 250, 254, 256, 312
  and *The Miracle* (unproduced 1938 film), 232, 266–267, 278, 391
  persuasive charm, 207, 227
  promised projects fail to come to fruition, 263–264
  property confiscated, 282
  and *Rosalinda*, 308–309
  seventieth birthday, 310–311
  silent film career, 388
  and *The Tales of Hoffmann*, 388
  undaunted by failure, 283–284
  and *La Vie parisienne*, 207
Reinhardt, Wolfgang, 278, 280, 312
Reining, Maria, 343, 345

Reisfeld, Bert, 321
Reitler, Josef, 124, 145, 165, 180, 202, 275, 330, 394
Rémond, Hofrat Fritz, 136, 380
Renner, Karl, 136, 183
Republic Pictures (American film company), 351, 354, 355
Respighi, Ottorino, 168
Rethberg, Elizabeth, 382
Revesz, Geza, 374
Rhapsody in Blue (1945 film), 324, 326
Richter, Hans, 353
Ricordi (publisher), 148, 158
Der Ring des Polykrates (Teweles), 98–99
Rio Rita (1929 film), 218
Ritchard, Cyril, 359
Ritter Pazman (by Johann Strauss II, used by K in *Straussiana*), 349
RKO (Radio Keith Orpheum) Radio Pictures, 238, 279, 317
Robert, Richard, 67
Robey, George, 214
Robinson, Casey, 303
Robinson, Dewey, *235*
Robinson, Edward G., 290, 300, 312
Robson, (Dame) Flora, 295, 392
Rodenbach, Constantine, 175
Rodenbach, Georges, 120–123, 175, 338
Roder, Milan, 251, 272, 311
Roemheld, Heinz, 260
Rolland, Romain, 82
Romanticism, 22, 348
Romberg, Sigmund, 290–291
  The Student Prince, 290
Romeo and Juliet (1936 film), 233, 255–256, 263
Ronsperger, Edith, 153
Rooney, Mickey, 235, *235*, 242
Roos-Reuter, Beate, 175
Roosevelt, Franklin Delano, 348
Rosé, Arnold, 55, 58, 63, 71–72, 118, 124
Rosé Quartet, 58, 124, 132, 159, 171, 179, 211
Rosenthal, Moriz, 73–75, 150
Rössel-Majdan, Hildegard, 354
Rossen, Robert, 300
Rossini, Gioacchino, 283
Roswaenge, Helge, 224
Rósza, Miklos, 290, 334, 365
Rotter, Alfred, 214
Roussel, Albert, 188
Royal Command Film Performance (London, 1955), 355
Royal Liverpool Philharmonic Orchestra, 368

Royal Opera House, Berlin, 70, 97
Rudnev, Prof. Andrwj, 373
Rufer, Josef, 156
Rundt (director of the Vienna
    Volksbuhne), 129
Russian War Relief Fund, 320, 390
Russka, Ida, 189
Ryan, Robert, 283, 365
Rysanek, Leonie, 352

Sabatini, Rafael, 245
Sachs, Leon, 56
Sachse, Leopold (Intendant, Hamburg
    Stadt-Theater, 1921–1933), 152,
    191–192, *194*, 199, *206*
Sadlers Wells Theater, London, 71
Saerchinger, Cesar, 73
St. Luke's Episcopal Church, Long
    Beach, 265
Saint-Saëns, Camille, 56
Sakall, S. Z. "Cuddles," 290
Salmhofer, Franz, 190, 340
Saltenburg, Heinz, 222
Salzburg Festival, 54–55, 157–158, 167,
    180, 189, 262, 337
Salzburg Festival Orchestra, 364
San Antonio (1946 film), 389
San Remo, 225–226
Sargent, Winthrop, 308
Sassmann, Hanns, 212
Savonarola, Girolamo, 102
Scale Theater, Copenhagen, 187–188
Schalk, Franz, 54, 58, 132, 135–137,
    144, 148, 381–382, 385
    death, 217
    as director of the Vienna State Opera,
        132–133, 143, 150
    and *Jonny spielt auf*, 198, 203, 216
    machinations to unseat as director,
        216
    resigns from Vienna State Opera,
        216–217
    turns against Richard Strauss,
        183–184
    at the University of Vienna, 24
    and *Das Wunder der Heliane*, 190,
        192, 196, 201
Scharwenka, Franz Xaver, 378
Schattenstein, Nicholas, 82
Schaumburg-Lippe, Prince of, 31
Schech, Marianne, 356
Schellenberger, Dagmar, 370
Schenck, Richard von, 187
Schertzinger, Victor, 246
Scheuer, Philip K., 283
Schiele, Egon, 26
Schiller, Friedrich von, 100, 278

Schillings, Max von, 22, 42, 173, 174,
    375
    Mona Lisa, 102, 106
Schipper, Emil, 202, 387
Schlesinger, Mimi, 82
Schloss Höselberg (K's country home in
    Austria), 223, 226, 246, 262,
    266–267, 339, 341, 346, 357
Schloss Leopoldskron, Salzburg, 282
Schloss Schönbrunn, 116, 130, 134, 376
Schmidt, Franz, 33, 180, 205, 384
    Fredigundis, 197
Schmidt, Joseph, 220
Schmidt, Leopold, 112, 145
Schmidt-Isserstedt, Hans, 386
Schnabel, Artur, 72–74, 76, 79,
    91–92, 174
Schnabel-Rossi, Riccardo, 148
Schneider, Louis, 54
Schneider, Romy, 387
Schneiderhan, Franz, 198, 216
Schnitzler, Arthur, 26, 102, 120
Schoder, Gustav, 80
Schoenberg, Arnold, 23, 44–45, 55, 72,
    81, 120, 149, 158, 180, 193, 247,
    256, 264, 279, 289, 367, 369,
    380
    fiftieth birthday, 178
    friendship with K in Hollywood, 44
    harmonic writing, 88
    influenced by Wagner, 157
    and International Society for New
        Music, 90
    introduces his new method with three
        works, 157
    and Julius in Hollywood, 291–293
    K satirizes, 190
    musical revolution, 155–156, 197
    and newspaper poll linking him with
        K, 211–212
    and Romanticism, 22
    seeks refuge in America, 231
    WORKS: *Five Little Piano Pieces*, 157;
        Die glückliche Hand, 178; *Moses
        und Aron*, 292; Piano Suite, Opus
        25, 157; *Pierrot Lunaire*, 156;
        Serenade, Opus 24, 157; String
        Quartet No. 2 in F-sharp Minor,
        40, 378
    Zemlinsky and, 35, 40, 49, 51
Schoenberg Hall, University of
    California, Los Angeles, 365
Schoenberg, Mathilde (née Zemlinsky;
    Schoenberg's first wife), 35
Schoenberg, Nuria, 291
Schönbrunn Palace, 130, 134
Schöne, Lotte, 183, 215, 224, 338

Schott (B. Schott's Söhne; now Schott
    Musik International), 114, 121,
    179, 187, 189–190, 219, 222,
    269, 330, 337
  commissions Specht, 376
  competition held by, 179
  K commissioned to write some new
    piano music, 190
  K's contract arranged, 52–53
  as K's principal publisher, 52
  K's suggestions for opera libretti
    rejected by, 273, 376
  unable to publish K because of "non-
    Aryan" status, 273, 376
"Schott, Paul" (pseudonym of Julius and
    K), 121
Schramm, Hermann, 187
Schreker, Franz, 123, 174, 180, 209,
    367, 374, 380
  and Robert Fuchs, 33
  and Julius, 58
  suppression of his music, 22–23
  WORKS: chamber symphony, 158; *Die
    Gezeichneten*, 102, 144; *Irrelohe*,
    197; *Die Rote Tod* (unproduced
    play), 102; *Der Schatzgräber*, 146,
    154
Schreker, Maria, 209
Schröder, Karl, 136
Schubert, Franz, 50, 63, 87, 108, 160,
    176, 198, 211, 267, 281, 319,
    358–359
  as a child prodigy, 21–22
  Impromptu No. 4 in A-flat, 325
Schubert, Richard, 136, 380
Schulhof, Otto, *Paraphrase on Themes
    by Josef Strauss*, 220
Schumann, Clara, 82
Schumann, Elisabeth, 108, 113,
    182–184, 198, 217, 379
Schumann, Karl, 356–357
Schumann, Robert, 27, 51, 65, 324, 359
  Kinderszenen, 69
Schuschnigg, Kurt von, 271
Schuster, Friedel, 213
Schwaiger, Rosl, 345
Schwamberger, Karl Maria, 341
Schwartz, Heinrich, 62
Schwartz Trio, 62
Schwarz, Vera, 113, 183, 198, 262, 301,
    305
Schwetzingen, 352
Scola, Kathryn, 306
Scott, Cyril, 111
Scriabin, Alexander Nikolaievich, 373
The Sea Wolf (novel by Jack London),
    299–300

Second World War
  Britain declares war on Germany,
    293
  the end of the war in Europe, 320
Sedlak-Winter Quartet, 267
Seguidilla (cut from score for *Juarez*),
    281
Seidel, Toscha, 303, 392
Seidl, Dr. Arthur, 375
  seminar on K, 42
Seitz, Mayor Karl, 178, 180, 186
Seligmann, Dr. Ludwig, 199
Seligmann, Otto, 120
Selznick, David O., 233, 238, 328, 392
Serialism
  acclaimed as the music of the future,
    23
  K and, 23, 45, 157–158, 291,
    370–371
  repressed in totalitarian Europe, 23
  Schoenberg discovers, 156
Servant of Two Masters (Goldoni), 283
Ševčik, Otakar, 380
Shaham, Gil, 370
Shakespeare, William, 28, 70, 129, 172,
    227, 232–234, 236, 243, 245,
    248, 254–255, 287, 296, 303, 334
"Shakespeare's Women, Clowns, and
    Songs" (Max Reinhardt
    Workshop production, 1941), 303
Shaw, George Bernard, 283, 379
Shearer, Norma, 233
Sheridan, Ann, 274, 304
Show Boat (1928 film), 218
Shubert, J. J., 322, 393
Sibelius, Jean, 97
  diaries, ed. Tawaststjerna, 378
  Finlandia, 304
Sievert, Ludwig, 146, 187
Signale (journal), 140
Sills, Milton, 300
Sinatra, Frank, 274, 393
Sinatra, Nancy, 393
Singin' in the Rain (1952 film), 237
Sirota, Leo, 77
Sissys Brautfahrt (Sissy's Bridal Journey;
    later *Sissy*, operetta by Fritz
    Kreisler), 219
Skoda, Baroness Hedda von, 379
Slatkin, Eleanor Aller, 287–288,
    297–298, 325, 327
Slatkin, Felix, 287
Slatkin, Leonard, 327
Slezak, Leo, 132
Slezak, Walter, 364, 377
Slonimsky, Nicolas, 371
Smith, Alexis, 306, 317

Snow White and the Seven Dwarfs (1937 Disney cartoon film), 285
So Big (1953 film), 350
Société des auteurs, 218
Société Française des Amis de la Musique, 54
Society for Esthetic Culture, 76
Society of Dramatic Authors, 137
Society of the Friends of Music, Vienna, 301
Sokoloff, Lisa, 283
Sondergaard, Gale, 257
Sonderling, Dr. Jacob, 301, 365
Song of Love (1947 film), 324
A Song to Remember (1945 film), 324
Sonn und Montagszeitung (Brünn newspaper), 74
Sonnenthal, Adele von ("Lillie"; Luzi's mother), 139, 172, 284
Sonnenthal, Adolf Ritter von (Luzi's grandfather), 119
Sonnenthal, Helene von (Luzi's sister), 119, 211
Sonnenthal, Lori von (later Nossal), 381
Sonnenthal, Paul von (Luzi's brother), 120
Sonnenthal, Stephanie von (later Matthias), 381
Sonnenthal, Susanne von (Luzi's sister; later Jellinek), 119
Son of Fury (1941 film), 297
"Sounds of the Future" (Bekker), 45
Specht, Richard, 59–60, 62–63, 65, 66, 78, 85, 92, 104, 112, 132, 145, 180
    on the demonstration at the Vienna Opera involving K, 184
    supports K, 72, 201–202, 376
    writes thematic analyses of K's work, 376, 378
Spiegelfeld, Countess, 141
Springer, Max, 145
Springer, Richard, 77
Staatsakademie, Vienna, 109
Staatskapelle, Berlin, 173
Stage Coach (1939 film), 288
Standard Oil Sunday concerts, 327
Steger, Dr. Margaret, 349
Steinbach, Fritz, 79, 98
Steinberg, William, 359, 365
Steindorff, Ulrich, 278
Steiner, George, 373
Steiner, Max, 238, 256, 275, 290, 295, 317–319, 323, 327, 333, 350
Steiner, Maximilian, 238
Steingruber, Ilona, 345
Stephenson, Henry, 317

Sternberg, Josef von, 231, 387
Sternberg, Julian, 117–119
Stiedry, Fritz, 330
Stiegler, Karl Anton, 134
Still, William Grant, 334
Die stille Stadt (The Silent City, Rodenbach; German trans. Trebitsch), 121
Stiller, Maurice, 388
Stokowski, Leopold, 265–266, 287, 373
Stoll, Oswald, 211
Stolz, Robert, 218
Stössel, Ludwig, 305
Stothart, Herbert, 256
Stransky, Josef, 98, 159
Straus, Oscar. 218
Strauss, Adele, 30–31, 59, 79, 162, 209
Strauss, Dr. Franz, 342–343, 356
Strauss, Johann I, 163
    Radetzky March, 221, 242, 349
Strauss, Johann II, 30, 79, 131, 146, 163, 209, 214, 304, 338, 359, 374, 376
    Julius's loyalty to, 69, 162
    K admires his music, 162
    reawakening of interest in, 162
    rhythms of, 23
    WORKS: *Blue Danube*, 146, 338; *Die Fledermaus*, 162, 182–183, 187–188, 207–209, 212; *Eine Nacht in Venedig*, 162; *Ritter Pazman*, 349; *Das Spitzentuch der Königin* (The Queen's Lace Handkerchief), 214; *Wiener Blut*, 239; *Der Zigeunerbaron*, 162
Strauss, Richard, 28, 43, 55, 72, 79, 82, 91, 108, 112, 118–119, 123–124, 137, 139, 145–146, 153, 166, 182, 187, 201, 251, 267, 269, 274, 304, 324, 359, 369, 376, 384
    death. 340, 342
    as director of the Vienna State Opera, 70, 74, 132–133, 143–144, 150, 167, 183–184
    first meets K, 44
    harmonic writing, 88–89
    and Julius, 69–70, 74, 110–111, 132–133, 143, 150, 154, 178, 181–183, 195
    K begs him to intercede for his aunt, 276
    K influenced by, 22
    the Korngolds visit him at Garmisch, 110–111
    and Krauss's Vienna State Opera appointment, 217

[Strauss, Richard]
  letter proclaiming K a genius, 43
  at the Loewenfeld house, 138
  and newspaper poll, 211–212
  offers K a permanent engagement at
    the Vienna State Opera, 133
  orchestral style, 88
  reappraisal of, 368
  relationship with K, 111, 143,
    150–151
  and serialism, 45, 157
  supports K, 43–44, 59, 70, 97–98,
    154
  Sursum Corda dedicated to, 133
  WORKS: *Die ägyptische Helena*, 197;
    Eine Alpensinfonie, 111; *Arabella*,
    368, 381; *Ariadne auf Naxos*,
    344, 359; *Le Bourgeois
    Gentilhomme*, 158, 178; *Elektra*,
    37, 69–70, 97, 131, 329, 340,
    364, 368; *Fanfare* (1924), 178;
    "Festmarsch," 87; *Die Frau ohne
    Schatten*, 110, 143, 154, 184,
    253; *Intermezzo*, 197, 276, 385;
    Die Josephslegende, 111, 151,
    174; *Parergon zur Sinfonia
    Domestica* (for piano, left hand),
    188; *Der Rosenkavalier*, 38, 69,
    88, 146, 296, 342–343, 368, 371;
    The Ruins of Athens, 178;
    Salome, 69, 166, 288, 368;
    Schlagobers (Whipped Cream,
    ballet), 183, 385
Strauss—Father and Son (Marischka and
    Reichert, early version of *Walzer
    aus Wien*), 209–210
Stravinsky, Igor, 261, 279, 312, 324,
    329, 334, 364
  and *Fantasia* (1940 Disney cartoon),
    287
  K first meets, 390
  K influenced by, 22
  K satirizes, 190
  WORKS: *Petrushka*, 45, 386; *The Rite
    of Spring*, 386
  Zemlinsky and, 51
Stravinsky, Vera, 261
Strecker, Dr. Ludwig, 121, 179, 187,
    346
  memoir of K in Luzi's biography,
    52–53
  offers Julius an attractive contract, 52
Strecker, Willy, 346, 390
  and *The Maid from Aachen*, 219
  and *Sursum Corda*, 269
  and *Vier kleine Karikaturen für
    Kinder*, 190

Strecker family, 52, 191, 340, 342, 346
Strelitzer, Hugo, 328
Strindberg, August, 43, 82
Strnad, Oskar, 189, 198, 202, 386
Strobl, 133
Stroheim, Erich von, 311, 388
Stuart, Gloria, 232
Stückgold, Grete, 202, 386–387
Stückgold, Jacques, 386
Stukart, Clarissa, 223
Stumpf, Karl, 42
Der Sturm (poem by Heinrich Heine), 70
Sulkowski, Count, 223
Suolahti, Heikki Theodor, 373
Svedrofsky, Henry, 327
Swarthout, Gladys, 247, 248
Sweetland, Sally (née Mueller), 296, 392
Swoboda Quartet, 339
Szell, George, 174
Szenkar, Eugen, 382
Szeps-Zuckerkandl, Berta, 175
Szigeti, Joseph, 312

Tagesbote (Brünn newspaper), 24
The Tales of Hoffmann (unproduced
    1936 Reinhardt film), 248
Tallis, Thomas, 265
The Taming of the Shrew (1929 film),
    236
Tamiroff, Akim, 290
Tauber, Richard, 151, 154, 162, 174,
    183, 187, 214–215, 248, 262,
    268, 382, 384
Taussig family, 81
Tawaststjerna, Erik, 378
Taylor, Sam, 236
Tchaikovsky, Pyotr Ilyich, 21, 166, 256,
    359
    Serenade for String Orchestra, 334
Tcherepnin, Alexander, 179
Teasdale, Veree, 235, *235*
The Tempest (play by Shakespeare), 70
Temple, Shirley, 285
Terriss, Ellaline, 214
Teweles, Heinrich, 98, 99
Thalberg, Irving, 232, 233, 256
Thaller, Willy, 211
That We May Live (dramatic stage
    spectacle), 328
Theater am Kurfürstendamm, Berlin,
    213
Theater am Nollendorfplatz, Berlin, 209,
    222
Theater in der Josefstadt, Vienna, 207,
    211
Theater an der Wien, Vienna, 162, 187,
    205, 209, 238, 340, 344, 376

Théâtre Pigalle, Paris, 224, 385
Theilade, Nini, 344
Thimig, Helene, 189, 209, 214,
    270–271, 283, 305, 311–313, 337
Thomas, Tony, 318
Thorndyke, (Dame) Sybil, 215
Thumbtack piano, 287
Tiomkin, Dmitri, 392
Tischler, Victor, 311
Toblach, 33
Toch, Ernst, 179, 252, 311, 365
Toluca Lake, Hollywood (K's residence),
    270, 274–276, 313, 320
Toscanini, Arturo, 148, 189, 244, 264
Treacher, Arthur, *235*
Trebitsch, Siegfried, 82, 121, 338, 379
The Triumph of Life (Dovsky), 137
Das Trugbild (Rodenbach; 1913 trans.
    by Trebitsch), 121, 338
Truscott, Harold, 165–166, 306, 392
Turnau, Josef, 183, 385
Twain, Mark, 264–265
Twelfth Night (Shakespeare), 287, 303
Twelfth Night (unproduced 1936
    Reinhardt film), 248, 256
Twentieth Century Fox Film
    Corporation, 259, 333

UFA (German film studio), 218, 378
United States of America
    artists accept offers to conduct and
        perform in, 150
    K's music reaches the US for the first
        time, 62
    K's operas performed in, 379
    K's Sinfonietta in B Major well
        received in, 98
Universal Edition, 380
    Julius allows publication by, 46
    and Křenek's *Jonny spielt auf*,
        203–204
    as Křenek's publishers, 203
    last K composition to be published
        by, 51–52
    offers *Der Schneemann* to the Vienna
        Court Opera, 50–51, 57
Universal Studios (American film
    company), 322, 393
University of Salzburg, 55
University of Southern California, 252,
    255
University of Vienna, Julius Korngold at,
    187
Ursuleac, Viorica, 187, 217
Ussher, Bruno David, 288

Valentino, Rudolf, 365

Vanbrugh, Irene, 215
Van den Berg, Henk, *206*
Van den Laan, Miss, *206*
Van der Straten, Eleanore, 223, 388
Vanderwood, Paul J., 391
Vane, Sutton, 313
Variety, 314
Velden am Wörthersee, 32
Venice Music Festival, 188
Verdi, Giuseppe, 104, 111, 214, 293,
    304
    Aida, 141, 387
    Il Trovatore, 141
Verneuil, Louis, 324
Vienna
    cognoscenti flock to Julius's
        Theobaldgasse apartment, 30
    as a cultural "melting pot," 26
    embraces K, 21–22
    influence on K, 33, 63
    Julius moves to, 26
    K's home broken into by the Nazis
        (1938), 82
    K's last premiere in Vienna before the
        outbreak of war, 267
    Music Week, 76
    world premiere of the Sinfonietta in
        B Major, 84, 97
    Das Wunder der Heliane, Austrian
        premiere of, 200
Vienna Brahms-Saal, 346
Vienna Bürgertheater, 189
Vienna Conservatory, 24, 268
Vienna Court Opera, 107, 114, 158, 220
    Gregor succeeds Weingartner, 108,
        109
    K makes his debut as conductor, 124
    Mahler effects major changes, 26
    Mahler's resignation, 33–34, 41, 56,
        377
    Mahler's stormy and controversial
        tenure as director, 33
    Der Schneemann premiered at
        (1910), 47–48, 50, 57, 58–60, 68
    Universal Edition offers *Der
        Schneemann* to, 50–51, 57
    Weingartner's directorship, 57, 68,
        84
    Zemlinsky's *Es war einmal*
        performed at, 35
Vienna Grosser Konzerthaus-Saal, 186
Vienna International Music Festival
    (1947), 330
Vienna *Jugendstil*, 51
Vienna Kleiner Musikvereins-Saal, 223
Vienna Municipal Music and Theater
    Festival (1924), 177–278

Vienna Philharmonic Chorus, 58, 205
Vienna Philharmonic Orchestra, 58, 84,
    134, 144, 146, 150, 154, 167,
    364
    Furtwängler's major triumph with,
        217
    gift to K, 377
    plays at first K opera premiere to be
        broadcast, 201
    premieres the Sinfonietta in B Major,
        97
    premieres the *Symphonic Serenade*,
        337, 341
    Richard Strauss as a freelance guest
        conductor, 184
Vienna Radio (aka ORF and RAVAG),
    322, 339–40, 350, 354
Vienna State Opera, 146–147,
    150–151, 162, 166, 172, 182,
    198, 266, 360
    as a burned-out shell, 339
    fiftieth anniversary, 132
    and K's death, 364
    Krauss regime, 217, 247
    long run with *Eine Nacht in Venedig*,
        207, 209
    machinations to unseat Schalk, 216
    refuses to withdraw K's operas from
        the repertoire, 150
    revival of *Der Ring des Polykrates*,
        206, 224
    revival of *Die tote Stadt*, 262
    Schalk resigns from, 216–217
    Richard Strauss as director, 70, 74,
        132–133, 143–144, 150, 167, 181
    Theater an der Wien becomes home
        of, 340
    Bruno Walter as co-director, 267
Vienna Symphony Orchestra, 130, 134,
    172
Vienna Volksbühne, 129, 130
Viertel, Berthold, 311
Viertel, Salka, 283, 289, 311
Vinton, John, 85
Vitagraph Film Co., 245
Vitaphone Orchestra, 239, 258
La Voile (Der Schleier, German trans. of
    play by Rodenbach), 121
Volk, George, 234
Volksoper, Vienna, 148, 198, 205, 215,
    344
Vollmoeller, Karl, 187, 189, 232, 267,
    278
Vorarlberg, 338
Vulcano (1949 Italian film), 341

Wagner, Richard, 87, 110, 122, 164,
    184, 251, 358–359
    Hanslick's fight against, 382
    Humperdinck assists at Bayreuth,
        375
    Julius advocates the music of, 30
    music adapted by K in *Magic Fire*
        (film), 350, 351–356
    Schoenberg influenced by, 157
    WORKS: *Lohengrin*, 352, 379; *Das
        Rheingold*, 32, 44, 217; "Ride of
        the Valkyries," 353; *Der Ring des
        Nibelungen*, 352, 353, 356;
        Siegfried Idyll, 354; *Tristan und
        Isolde*, 195, 217
Wagner, Siegfried, 55–56
Walbrook, Anton (Adolf Wohlbrück),
    222
Waldorf Astoria, New York, 309
Wallenstein, Alfred, 349
Wallerstein, Dr. Lothar, *196*, 198, 202,
    220, 267, 330, 385
Wallis, Hal B., 244, 253, 257, 260, 264,
    365
    and *The Adventures of Robin Hood*,
        269–271
    and *Anthony Adverse*, 259
    complains about K's approach to film
        scoring, 240
    and *Danton* (unproduced 1936
        Reinhardt film), 263
    eager to bring K back to Hollywood,
        246
    and *Juarez*, 278–280
    on K, 264–265
    and *Kings Row*, 305
    and *A Midsummer Night's Dream*,
        232, 234, 236, 240, 242–243, 254
    and *The Miracle* (unproduced 1938
        Reinhardt film), 266–267, 278
    and *The Private Lives of Elizabeth
        and Essex*, 278–279
Walter, Bruno, 55, 63, 71–72,
    111–112, 118, 173, 190–191,
    202–203, *203*, 214–215,
    267–268, 275, 311–312, 320,
    337–338, 344, 357–358,
    364–365, 367, 385–386
Walton, (Sir) William, 322
Waltzes from Vienna (1933 British film),
    211
Warner, Jack L., 234, 242, 244, 390
    K intercedes with, for Wolfgang
        Reinhardt, 312
    and *Kings Row*, 303, 305
    and *A Midsummer Night's Dream*,
        232, 243

and *The Miracle* (unproduced 1938 Reinhardt film), 232, 278
and *The Private Lives of Elizabeth and Essex*, 286
and Max Reinhardt, 226, 232, 234
Warner Brothers Studio, 200, 245, 264, 274, 277, 319, 333, 365
and *The Adventures of Robin Hood*, 273, 391
and *Anthony Adverse*, 257
and *Captain Blood*, 245–246, 248–249, 251
cinemas owned by, 243
collection at the University of Southern California, 252, 255
and concert overtures for premieres of K's films, 282
and *The Constant Nymph*, 306–307
eager to project a more cultured image, 233, 245
and *Escape Me Never*, 322–323
Franchetti employed by, 259
and *The Jazz Singer* (1927 film), 200
and *Juarez*, 282
K decides not to renew his contract, 328
K starts to work for, 200
and *Kings Row*, 303, 305
K's demands met in his contract, 275
lures Reinhardt to Hollywood, 226
and *A Midsummer Night's Dream*, 228, 233, 234, 242
and *The Miracle* (unproduced 1938 Reinhardt film), 278
music department, 238–239, 261, 297, 318, 323, 327
and *Of Human Bondage*, 317
and *The Private Lives of Elizabeth and Essex*, 285
and *The Sea Hawk*, 294
and *The Sea Wolf*, 300–301
Warner Brothers Studio Orchestra, 238–239, 244, 249, 250, 258–259, 261, 273, 287–288, 296, 301, 307
Warren, Harry, 260
Waterloo Bridge (1940), 290
Waxman, Franz (formerly Wachsmann), 234, 290, 337
Webern, Anton, 44, 55, 180, 378
The Wedding of Ariane (projected opera), 219–220
Weel, Liva, 188
Wegener, Paul, 388
Weigl, Karl, 54, 158, 223
Weill, Kurt, 311

Weinberger, Jaromir (*Schwanda the Bagpiper*), 385
Weinberger, Josef (publisher), 273–275, 376
Weingarten, Josef, 24
Weingarten, Paul, 24, 220
Weingartner, Felix von, 108, 119
conducts K's first orchestral works, 69
directs the Vienna Court Opera, 56, 68, 143
at the Hamburg Opera, 84
and Julius, 56–58, 68, 84, 110
premieres *Der Schneemann*, 56–58, 61, 68
premieres the Sinfonietta in B Major, 84, 97
resigns from the Vienna Court Opera, 84
supports K, 68–69, 84
Swiss premiere of K's Piano Concerto in C-sharp, 204
Weisenfreud, Joe, 290
Weiskopf, Carol, 237, 259, 297
Wellesz, Egon, 132–133
Welser-Möst, Franz, 370
Wendon, Henry, 383
Werfel, Franz, 226, 275, 280, 293, 311
Werfel-Mahler, Anna. *See* Mahler, Anna
White Horse Inn (English version of *Im weissen Rössl*, Ralph Benatzky), 209, 378
Whitty, Dame May, 306
Whole-tone scale, 91
Widor, Charles, 56
Wiedemann, Hermann, 145
Wiener Bürgertheater (Theatre of Vienna's Citizens), 189
Wiener, Dr. Carl Ritter von, 109–110, 378
Wiener Konzert-Verein, 186
Wiener Sonn- und Montags Zeitung, 67
Wiesbaden Music Festival, 146
Wiesenthal, Grete, 225
Wiesner, Ernst, 381
Wiesner, Eva Maria (née Loewenfeld), 137–139, 377
Wilde, Oscar, 91
Wilder, Billy, 231
Wilder, Thornton, 236
Wilk, Jacob, 234, 269
William Tell (unproduced 1938 film), 277
William Tell (unfinished 1953 film), 349–350
Williams, John, 297
Wilshire Ebell Theater, 312

Windsor, Duchess of (formerly
  Mrs. Wallis Simpson), 338
Windsor, Duke of (formerly King
  Edward VIII), 338
Windsperger, Lothar, 179, 385
Winter, Dr. Ludwig, 46
Winters, Shelley, 308, *309*
A Winter's Tale (Shakespeare), 70
Witrofsky, Hermann (K's maternal
  grandfather), 24
Wittgenstein, Paul, 165, 172, 177–178,
  188, 204–205, 211, 241, 384
The Wizard of Oz (1939 film), 288
Wohanka, Emmy, 164, 383
Wolf, Hugo, 33, 87, 108, 369, 374
  String Quartet, 87
Wolff, Louise, 71–72, 113
Wolf-Ferrari, Ermanno, *Susanna's
  Secret*, 58
Wonder Bar (1934 film), 260
Wood, Sir Henry, 68, 87, 378
Wood, Sam, 303
Wopalensky Louise, 46, *57*, 58
Wright, Tenny, 391
Wymetal, Wilhelm von, 113, 137, 145,
  151–152, 379
Wymetal, Wilhelm von (son), 379
Wynyard, Diana, 231

Yates, Herbert J., 351
Young, Gig, 322
Young, Loretta, 232
Yradier, Sebastian de, *La Paloma*, 281

Zádor, Eugene, 334, 365
Zatkin, Nathan, 243
Zeisl, Eric, 328, 341, 394
Zell, Friedrich, 383
Zemlinsky, Alexander von, 41, 44,
  53–54, 72, 85, 113, 173, 359, 367
  article on K, 39

  conducts the Berlin Kroll Opera, 51
  conducts *Die tote Stadt* in Prague,
    160–161
  flees to America (1938), 51
  his style rendered obsolete, 51
  influence on K, 38, 48–51
  and Julius, 374
  K begins lessons with, 35–36
  K's relationship with, 36, 39, 48–51,
    160–161
  leaves Vienna for Prague, 48, 50
  Mahler and, 34–36, 48, 51
  music of, 22
  orchestrates *Der Schneemann*, 39, 50,
    58, 61
  as a pupil of Fuchs, 33
  and Schoenberg, 35, 40, 49, 51
  and serialism, 157
  WORKS: *Es war einmal* (Once Upon A
    Time), 35, 374; *Eine
    Florentinische Tragödie* (A
    Florentine Tragedy), 102; *Kleider
    machen Leute* (Clothes Make the
    Man), 49–51, 161, 378; String
    Quartet No. 1, 158; Trio, Opus 3,
    376
Zesewitz, Hans, 154
Ziegler (director of the Vienna
    Volksbühne), 129
Zita, Empress, 116, 376, 379
Zoritsch, George, 323, *323*
Zscherneck, Georg, 77
Zsolnay, Paul (publisher), 163
Zsolt, Nandor, 98
Zuckerkandl, Emil, 385
Zuckmayer, Carl, 311
Zweig, Dr. Fritz, 51, 208–209, 305, 346,
    365
Zweig, Stefan, 55, 82
Zwerenz, Mizzi, 211